THE HANDBOO
AND ANTHROPOLOGY

THE HANDBOOK OF FOOD AND ANTHROPOLOGY

Edited by
Jakob A. Klein and James L. Watson

BLOOMSBURY ACADEMIC
LONDON · NEW YORK · OXFORD · NEW DELHI · SYDNEY

BLOOMSBURY ACADEMIC
Bloomsbury Publishing Plc
50 Bedford Square, London, WC1B 3DP, UK
1385 Broadway, New York, NY 10018, USA
29 Earlsfort Terrace, Dublin 2, Ireland

BLOOMSBURY, BLOOMSBURY ACADEMIC and the Diana logo are trademarks
of Bloomsbury Publishing Plc

First published 2016
This edition published 2019
Reprinted 2019 (twice), 2021

Bloomsbury Publishing Plc does not have any control over, or responsibility for, any
third-party websites referred to or in this book. All internet addresses given in this
book were correct at the time of going to press. The author and publisher regret any
inconvenience caused if addresses have changed or sites have ceased to exist, but
can accept no responsibility for any such changes.

A catalogue record for this book is available from the British Library.

A catalog record for this book is available from the Library of Congress.

ISBN: HB: 978-0-8578-5594-7
PB: 978-1-3500-8333-2
ePDF: 978-1-3500-0113-8
ePub: 978-1-3500-0114-5

Typeset by Deanta Global Publishing Services, Chennai, India
Printed and bound in Great Britain

To find out more about our authors and books visit www.bloomsbury.com
and sign up for our newsletters.

To the memory of Sidney W. Mintz (1922–2015) and Jack Goody (1919–2015),
two pioneers in the field

CONTENTS

LIST OF FIGURES

LIST OF TABLES

LIST OF CONTRIBUTORS

Emma-Jayne Abbots is Senior Lecturer in Anthropology at the University of Wales Trinity Saint David. Her research addresses the cultural politics of food and drink and the visceral practices of their production, preparation and consumption. She is broadly concerned with material engagements with food, the (re)production and mediation of food knowledges, particularly through the body and the ecologies in which knowledge-making takes place. Abbots is the author of *The Agency of Eating* (Bloomsbury, 201), and the coeditor of *Why We Eat, How We Eat* (Ashgate, 2013) and *Careful Eating* (Ashgate, 2015).

Nir Avieli is an associate professor of anthropology in the Department of Sociology and Anthropology, Ben Gurion University, Israel. As a cultural anthropologist, Avieli is mainly interested in food and tourism. He has been conducting ethnographic research in the central Vietnamese town of Hoi An since 1998. His book, *Rice Talks: Food and Community in a Vietnamese Town* (Indiana University Press, 2012), is a culinary ethnography of Hoi An. Avieli has conducted ethnographic research in Thailand, India, Singapore, and Israel. His most recent book, *Food and Power: A Culinary Ethnography of Israel*, was published by The University of California Press in 2017.

Joëlle Bahloul is a professor emerita of Anthropology and Jewish Studies at Indiana University in Bloomington, Indiana. She has conducted ethnography among Sephardic Jews of France, Israel, Italy and the United States for over forty years. She is the author of *The Architecture of Memory* (Cambridge University Press, 1996), *Le culte de la Table Dressée* (Editions A.M. Métailié, 1983), *Lectures Précaires* (B.P.I., 1987), and of a number of articles presenting her long-time ethnographic research on food and collective memory, Sephardic identity and kinship practices, and urban Jewish places.

Francesca Bray, Professor Emerita of Social Anthropology at the University of Edinburgh, is an anthropologist and historian of technology and gender in China and Asia, with a special interest in agriculture and food. Fieldwork in Kelantan, a rice bowl region of Malaysia, during the Green Revolution led her to publish *The Rice Economies: Technology and Development in Asian Societies* (Blackwell, 1986; University of California Press, 1994). Her most recent publications on rice and society include 'Rice as Self: Food, History and Nation-Building in Japan and Malaysia' (Max Planck Institute for Social Anthropology, Halle, 2014) and a co-edited volume, *Rice: Global Networks and New Histories* (Cambridge University Press, 2015).

Melissa L. Caldwell is Professor of Anthropology at the University of California, Santa Cruz, and Editor of *Gastronomica: The Journal of Critical Food Studies*. Her ethnographic research in Russia focuses on the entanglement of political systems in the most ordinary spaces and dimensions of people's lives, with particular attention to food cultures. She has written on fast food and globalization, food nationalism, culinary tourism, gardening and natural foods, food insecurity and food relief programmes. Her publications include *Dacha Idylls: Living Organically in Russia's Countryside* (University of California Press, 2011), *Not by Bread Alone: Social Support in the New Russia* (University of California Press, 2011), and the edited volume *Food & Everyday Life in the Postsocialist World* (Indiana University Press, 2009).

Maris Boyd Gillette, Professor of Social Anthropology, School of Global Studies, the University of Gothenburg, is a sociocultural anthropologist and filmmaker who has studied urban Chinese Muslims in Xi'an (northwest China) and porcelain workers and entrepreneurs in Jingdezhen (southeast China). Her recent publications include 'Gender in the Xi'an Muslim District' in *Contesting Feminisms: Gender and Islam in Asia*, edited by Huma Ghosh (State University of New York Press, 2015) and *China's Porcelain Capital: The Rise, Fall, and Reinvention of Ceramics in Jingdezhen* (Bloomsbury, 2016). In addition to her academic research, Gillette has participated in numerous community engagement initiatives, including the community history and digital media project *Muslim Voices of Philadelphia*, for which she received a Courage in Media Award from the Council on American Islamic Relations in 2012.

Cristina Grasseni is Professor of Anthropology at the University of Leiden and Principal Investigator of the Project 'Food Citizens? Collective Food Procurement in European Cities: Solidarity and Diversity, Skill and Scale' (2017–2022), funded by the European Research Council. Her main research interests in the field of food and anthropology concern the politics of heritage foods, innovation for sustainability in grassroots economic networks, as well as the transformation of skills and the cultural ecology of food production, notably dairy farming. She is the author of *The Heritage Arena: Reinventing Cheese in the Italian Alps* (Berghahn, 2017), *Beyond Alternative Food Networks: Italy's Solidarity Purchase Groups* (Bloomsbury, 2013), and *Developing Skill, Developing Vision: Practices of Locality at the Foot of the Alps* (Berghahn, 2009).

Michael Herzfeld is Ernest E. Monrad Professor of Social Sciences in the Department of Anthropology, Harvard University; IIAS Visiting Professor of Critical Heritage Studies at the University of Leiden; Professorial Fellow, University of Melbourne; and Chang Jiang Scholar, Shanghai International Studies University. He has authored eleven books – including *Siege of the Spirits: Community and Polity in Bangkok* (2016) – and is the producer of two films (including *Roman Restaurant Rhythms* [2011]), and has served as editor of *American Ethnologist* (1995–98). His research in Greece, Italy, and Thailand addresses historic conservation and gentrification, nationalism, bureaucracy, crypto-colonialism, commensality, and knowledge production among artisans and intellectuals.

Elizabeth Hull is a senior lecturer in Anthropology at SOAS University of London and Deputy Chair of the SOAS Food Studies Centre. She is author of *Contingent Citizens: Professional Aspiration in a South African Hospital* (Bloomsbury, 2017), published as part of the LSE Monographs on Social Anthropology series. Other publications include 'The Social Dynamics of Labor Shortage in South African Small-Scale Agriculture' (*World Development*, 2014) and a volume coedited with Deborah James on 'Popular Economies in South Africa' (Special Issue of *Africa*, 2012). Her research interests include agriculture, food systems, livelihoods and health in South Africa.

Yuson Jung is Associate Professor of Anthropology at Wayne State University (Detroit, Michigan). Her research explores issues of consumption, food politics, globalization, and postsocialism. She is the author of *Balkan Blues: Consumer Politics after State Socialism* (Indiana University Press, 2019), which examines everyday consumer experience in postsocialist Bulgaria. Her work has also appeared in peer-reviewed journals and edited volumes, and she is the coeditor (with Jakob Klein and Melissa Caldwell) of *Ethical Eating in the Postsocialist and Socialist World* (University of California Press, 2014). Currently, she is working on a book project about the cultural politics and transformation of the Bulgarian wine industry, and a collaborative research project (with Andrew Newman) regarding food politics and urban governance in Detroit.

Jakob A. Klein is Senior Lecturer in Social Anthropology at SOAS University of London and Chair of the SOAS Food Studies Centre. He has carried out ethnographic research in south China and has written on regional cuisine, food movements and food safety. Klein's publications include several coedited collections: *Consuming China: Approaches to Cultural Change in Contemporary China* (Routledge, 2006), *Ethical Eating in the Postsocialist and Socialist World* (University of California Press, 2014), *Food Consumption in Global Perspective: Essays in the Anthropology of Food in Honour of Jack Goody* (Palgrave Macmillan, 2014), and *Consumer and Consumed: Humans and Animals in Globalising Food Systems* (Special Issue of *Ethnos*, 2017).

Eriberto P. Lozada, Jr., is Associate Dean of Faculty and Professor of Anthropology and Environmental Studies at Davidson College, North Carolina, and Adjunct Professor of Anthropology at Fudan University, Shanghai. He has written on issues in Chinese society ranging from: religion and politics; food, the environment and globalization; sports and society; and the cultural impact of science and technology. His current research examines the growth of sustainable aquaculture in the rural areas around Shanghai. More can be found at https://lozada.davidson.edu.

Peter Luetchford is Senior Lecturer in Anthropology at the University of Sussex, where he teaches political and economic anthropology and on the Development

Studies program. In his fieldwork in Costa Rica and Southern Spain he has pursued his interests in moral economies, ethical consumption, and the political cultures of food provision. He is the author and coeditor of several volumes on these themes including a study on coffee and cooperatives in Costa Rica published as *Fair Trade and a Global Commodity* (Pluto, 2008), *Ethical Consumption: Social Value and Economic Practice* (Berghahn, 2012) and *Food for Change: The Politics and Values of Social Movements* (Pluto, 2014).

Jennifer Patico received her PhD in sociocultural anthropology from New York University and is an associate professor of anthropology at Georgia State University. She is the author of *Consumption and Social Change in a Post-Soviet Middle Class* (Stanford University Press and Woodrow Wilson Center Press, 2008), an ethnography of consumerism, shifting class identities and moral discourses in post-Soviet St Petersburg. Her current project, a book tentatively titled *Sugar and Selfhood: Children's Food and Middle Class Ways of Being* (NYU Press), examines parenting practices, children's food, and underlying concerns about self in urban Atlanta. Her work has been published in journals including *American Ethnologist*, *Slavic Review*, *Ethnos*, *Critique of Anthropology*, and *Gastronomica*.

Heather Paxson is William R. Kenan, Jr. Professor of Anthropology at the Massachusetts Institute of Technology, where she teaches courses on food, craft practice, and family. She is the author of *The Life of Cheese: Crafting Food and Value in America*, published by University of California Press in 2013, and winner of the 2014 Diana Forsythe Prize. She was an area editor for *The Oxford Companion to Cheese* (2016) and is now serving a four-year term as coeditor of the journal *Cultural Anthropology*.

Johan Pottier is Emeritus Professor of Anthropology with reference to Africa at SOAS University of London. He specializes in the social dynamics of food security. He has researched in Central, East, and Southern Africa, and has published on local-level perceptions of food security; food policy and land reform; post-drought and post-famine recovery; humanitarian aid; and most recently, on urban food security in Kampala and Lilongwe. He has also researched dimensions of the global food trade in relation to the consumption of Bangladeshi foods in East London (UK). His publications include *Anthropology of Food: The Social Dynamics of Food Security* (Polity Press, 1999) and *Re-Imagining Rwanda: Conflict, Survival and Disinformation in the Late 20th Century* (Cambridge University Press, 2002).

Alan Smart (PhD, University of Toronto, 1986) is a professor at the Department of Anthropology and Archaeology, University of Calgary. His research has focused on urban issues, housing, foreign investment, social change, food safety, zoonotic diseases and agriculture in Hong Kong, China, and Canada. He is author of *Making Room: Squatter Clearance in Hong Kong* (Hong Kong University Press, 1992), *Petty Capitalists and Globalization* (coedited with Josephine Smart, SUNY Press, 2005), *The Shek Kip Mei Myth: Squatters, Fires and Colonial Rule in Hong Kong,*

1950–1963 (Hong Kong University Press, 2006), and numerous articles in journals and edited volumes.

Josephine Smart (PhD, University of Toronto, 1987) is Professor of Anthropology at the Department of Anthropology and Archaeology, University of Calgary. Her research and teaching interests include economic anthropology, food production and zoonotic diseases, social and economic development in post-1978 China, Chinese international migration, immigrant entrepreneurs and the international mobility of capital and labour. She conducts fieldwork in Hong Kong, South China, Canada, and, most recently, Central America. She is a coeditor of *Petty Capitalists and Globalization: Flexibility, Entrepreneurship and Economic Development* (SUNY, 2005), coeditor of *Plural Globalities in Multiple Localities and New World Borders* (University Press of America, 2001), and sole author of *The Political Economy of Street Hawkers in Hong Kong* (University of Hong Kong Press, 1989), and has published numerous articles in journals and chapters in edited volumes.

James Staples is Reader in Anthropology at Brunel University London. He is author of *Holy Cows and Chicken Manchurian* (Washington University Press, forthcoming), *Peculiar People, Amazing Lives* (Orient Longman, 2007), and *Leprosy and a Life in South India* (Lexington Books, 2014), as well as editor of *Livelihoods at the Margins* (Left Coast Press, 2007), *Extraordinary Encounters: Authenticity and the Interview* (with Katherine Smith and Nigel Rapport, Berghahn, 2015), and several special issues of journals, including *Consumer and Consumed* (Ethnos, 2017, coedited with Jakob A. Klein). He has also published numerous journal articles and chapters on his work in South India.

David Sutton is Professor of Anthropology at Southern Illinois University Carbondale. Since the early 1990s he has been conducting research on the island of Kalymnos and has published two books on the food culture of the island: *Remembrance of Repasts: An Anthropology of Food and Memory* (Berg, 2001) and *Secrets from the Greek Kitchen: Cooking, Skill and Everyday Life on an Aegean Island* (University of California Press, 2014). These explore food practices in relation to questions of memory, the senses, gender, technology, and social change. He is also coeditor of *The Restaurants Book: Ethnographies of Where We Eat* (Berg, 2007).

James L. Watson is Fairbank Professor of Chinese Society and Professor of Anthropology Emeritus at Harvard University. Watson's research has focused on Chinese emigration, ancestor worship, popular religion, family life, village organization, food systems and the emergence of a post-socialist culture in China. He has worked with graduate students in Harvard's Department of Anthropology to investigate foodways in China, Russia, Eastern Europe, South Asia, and North America. Among other publications Professor Watson is coeditor (with Melissa Caldwell) of *The Cultural Politics of Food and Eating* (Blackwell) and editor of *Golden Arches East: McDonald's in East Asia* (Stanford University Press).

Rubie Watson received her PhD from the London School of Economics and has taught anthropology at the University of Pittsburgh and Harvard University. From 1997 to 2004, she was Director of the Peabody Museum of Archaeology and Ethnology at Harvard University. She retired from Harvard in 2008 and now lives on a farm in Western Illinois.

Harry G. West is Professor of Anthropology at the University of Exeter. He is author of numerous books, book chapters and journal articles based upon his extended study of the culture, history, and political economy of agrarian northern Mozambique. His current research focuses on artisan cheese, discourses of 'terroir' and 'authenticity', and the regulatory and marketing regimes giving shape to a growing global niche in 'heritage foods'.

Andrea S. Wiley is Professor of Anthropology and Director of the Human Biology Program at Indiana University, Bloomington. She is the author of four books: *Cultures of Milk: The Biology and Culture of Dairy Consumption in India and the United States* (Harvard University Press, 2014); *Re-imagining Milk* (Routledge, second edition, 2016); *Medical Anthropology: A Biocultural Perspective* (with John S. Allen, Oxford University Press, third edition, 2016); and *An Ecology of High-Altitude Infancy* (Cambridge University Press, 2004). Her current research focuses on the relationship between milk consumption and child health in the United States and in India.

Introduction: Anthropology, Food and Modern Life

JAMES L. WATSON AND JAKOB A. KLEIN

The study of food and foodways has emerged as a core feature of twenty-first-century anthropology. Anthropologists play leading roles in degree programmes devoted to food and in food-related research institutes in North America, Europe and Asia. The *Handbook of Food and Anthropology* is designed to serve the needs of this growing academic enterprise, one that incorporates environmental studies, demography, science and technology studies, journalism, information/computer sciences, transnational business and global studies.

Anthropology's strengths lie in the study of everyday life. By focusing on the ordinary, seemingly unproblematic aspects of human interaction, anthropologists inevitably focus on food. Dining and provisioning reveal underlying, otherwise hidden, aspects of social stratification, hierarchy, gender divides, class differences, political divisions, ethnic and racial discrimination and economic inequalities. Food also reflects the warmth of human bonding and the strength of kinship; the celebration of marriage is, with very few exceptions, marked by a feast.

Until recently, family life in many societies revolved around shared food, at regular intervals (meal time) in domestic kitchens. Is this true in 'advanced' capitalist societies today? Depending upon how one defines it, the family meal in parts of North America, Europe and Asia has on many accounts become a fragmented, feed-yourself enterprise that would shock earlier generations.[1] Simultaneously, wealthy urbanites who themselves do not have time for family meals, spend large sums in heritage restaurants that offer commercialized versions of nostalgia cuisine that represent what they imagine to be the simpler, rustic past of their predecessors. No serious social scientist or investment analyst can safely ignore changing food customs if she or he hopes to understand the structure of modern life.

The contributors to this handbook are active researchers who have conducted original, on-the-ground, person-to-person studies in a wide range of societies. There are no armchair analysts among their number. The majority of our contributors are senior, internationally recognized scholars; the editors have also recruited several 'rising stars' in the field of food studies. Some of the best anthropological work on food is being done by younger anthropologists who are not afraid to go beyond received paradigms. The editors have also made a special effort to recruit several authors who work closely with colleagues from the 'real world' of business, consulting, health care, food provisioning, food policy and international development. As will become evident in the pages that follow, the anthropology of food has become a postdisciplinary field of study that cuts across the traditional boundaries of academe. This volume demonstrates that food anthropology is best done as a cooperative enterprise among researchers, practitioners and students who are eager to explore big issues in a turbulent and challenging new century.

The Handbook of Food and Anthropology is divided into three sections, each reflecting a set of closely related research themes (see the overview at the end of this introductory chapter). Our goal is to give readers a brief introduction to earlier work in a specific domain of research and – equally important – to focus on future developments: Why is the production and marketing of children's food so lucrative and yet so difficult to predict? What is the next phase in the development of transnational food industries? Are fast food and supermarkets destined to conquer the planet? What future is there for peasant and artisan food producers? Who will ensure the safety of the food supply? Why have school lunches become such a hot-button issue in rural America? Will kitchens shrink and eventually disappear in the homes of Asian, North American and European elites? What's in your refrigerator, and what does this say about you?[2]

HISTORY OF FOOD STUDIES IN ANTHROPOLOGY

According to some accounts, food has 'been central to the discipline of anthropology from its earliest days' (Tierney and Ohnuki-Tierney 2012: 118).[3] A fundamental necessity of human life, food has long been recognized by anthropologists to be a cornerstone of culture and social organization. The classic ethnographic literature abounds with descriptions of food provisioning, production and exchange; of hosting, eating and drinking (but less often cooking, as Sutton observes in Chapter 16, this volume); and of the use of food and drink in ritual and symbolism. Food figures, more or less prominently, in anthropological theorizing of the nineteenth and twentieth centuries, for example in William Robertson Smith's (1889) discussion of the role in 'Semitic' religions of 'commensality' in creating bonds between worshippers and between the worshippers and God; in Mauss's (1990) mid-1920s essay on gift exchange; in Malinowksi's (1935) deliberations on Trobriand gardening, magic and language; in the Boasians' development of the 'culture area' concept (e.g., Wissler 1926); in Evans-Pritchard's (1940) study of the social structure and cosmology of the Nuer; and, most famously, in Lévi-Strauss's (e.g., 1966, 1969, 1978) mythological explorations in search of the underlying structures of human cultures and thought.

Nevertheless, the anthropology of food is in many ways a new field of study. Biological and nutritional anthropologists have of course long researched diet as a key dimension of human health, adaptation and evolution, and recent decades have also seen a rapprochement between biological and cultural approaches in these fields – a development reflecting and contributing to food studies in anthropology and beyond (Messer 1984; Ulijaszek 2007; Wiley 2015, and Chapter 10, this volume). Yet for much of the history of social and cultural anthropology, food and 'foodways' – the latter term used to denote the range of material and non-material cultural practices in which food is embedded (Camp 1989) – were only exceptionally (notably, Richards 1932, 1939) the main focus of research. Indeed, given the extensive coverage of food in contemporary academic circles, younger scholars might be surprised to learn that the topic was overlooked, ignored and (sometimes) dismissed as a serious pursuit until the late twentieth century. College and university courses that included the term 'food' in their titles were rare in anthropology departments until the late 1990s.[4] Marvin Harris, who played a key part in the rise of anthropological food studies, mentions 'food' only once in the index to his monumental survey, *The Rise of Anthropological Theory*, first published in 1968 (the reference is to 'food taboos' among East African pastoralists). The pioneers in this field were innovators of the first order; all had established their academic credentials in other fields before paying specific attention to the study of food: Mary Douglas (1966, 1971, 1984), Jack Goody (1982), K. C. Chang (1977), R. S. Khare (1976, 1992), Sidney Mintz (1985), Marvin Harris (1985a) and Arjun Appadurai (1981, 1988).

As suggested by this list of pioneers, the period around 1980 saw the publication of a number of studies, which helped bring food to the centre stage of anthropology – a trend encouraged by the growing attention to 'consumption', including of food and drink, across the social sciences (e.g., Bourdieu 1984; Campbell 1987; Douglas and Isherwood 1979; Mennell 1985; Miller 1987). Two of the most important monographs, in terms of establishing an anthropology of food, were Mintz's (1985) historical anthropology of sugar, which linked the political economy of sugar production in the Caribbean to its transformation in Europe (England, in particular) from an elite luxury to an everyday good, and Goody's (1982) 'comparative sociology' of the culinary cultures of Eurasia and sub-Saharan Africa, which sets out to explain why only some societies develop 'high cuisines', and subsequently moves beyond this question to explore the development and diffusion of industrial foods through the 'world system'. Characteristic of both these works was their attempt to move beyond entrenched debates between proponents of 'symbolic' and 'materialist' theories, advocating historically and ethnographically grounded studies that explored the relationship between material practices, power and meaning. Further, by using patterns of food and drink production, distribution, consumption, communication and taste to explore the increasingly transnational connections shaping social relations and everyday experiences, Mintz and Goody demonstrated that the study of food was in fact a key way into the study of modern life.[5]

The decades following the 1980s saw a wealth of ethnographies of food in the modern world. These explore how tastes and food practices, including cooking, eating, growing and exchanging, are profoundly shaped by and come to mediate experiences of the social and economic impact of structural adjustment, market expansion, industrialization, postsocialist reforms, development programmes and other projects and processes associated with recent global modernity (e.g., Weismantel 1988; Sutton 2001; Jing 2000; Farquhar 2002; Counihan 2004; Holtzman 2009). Several of these studies – notably Sutton (2001) and Farquhar (2002) – theorize the role of food in connecting the political-economic and experiential dimensions through a focus on food and the senses, memory and the body. More recent ethnographies have built on this work to show how attention to the material dimensions of food may be crucial to understanding its significance in contemporary societies, be it in the everyday life of South Asian cities (Janeja 2010) or among craftspeople and aficionados involved in North America's artisanal food movement (Paxson 2012).

Others have investigated the development and workings of the 'global food system' itself (see Phillips 2006). In a volume first published in 1997, Watson (2006a) and his colleagues examine localized cultural responses to the spread of McDonald's in East Asia. Wilk's (2006) historical anthropology of Belizean cuisine demonstrates that much of what is understood to be 'local' culinary culture is itself a product of a history of transnational connections. A number of studies investigate a single food commodity, following its movements through one or more phases from production, processing and packing, distribution and consumption, to shed light on the significance of transnational food trade for farmers, workers, traders, consumers, and for wider social and political relations in the countries of production and consumption (e.g., Barndt 2002; Gewertz and Errington 2010; Moberg and Striffler 2003). Others focus specifically on revealing the often highly exploitative conditions in the food industries of labourers and non-human animals (Striffler 2005; Pachirat 2011). A seminal work by Pottier (1999) – one of the two books to first use 'anthropology of food' in the title, both published in the same year (the other being Counihan 1999) – synthesizes and develops ethnographic approaches to food security and famine relief.

These studies build upon and move beyond the foundations laid by the likes of Sidney Mintz, Jack Goody, Audrey Richards, Lévi-Strauss, Mary Douglas and Marvin Harris. The large – and growing! – number of studies investigating the role of food in the modern world, and the breadth of their discussions and theoretical specializations, reflect the growing maturity of the anthropology of food and food studies, apparent also in dedicated readers (e.g. Counihan and Van Esterik 2013; Watson and Caldwell 2005), journals (including *Gastronomica*, *Food and Foodways* and *Food, Culture & Society*), and degree programmes (e.g. Indiana University's PhD programme in the anthropology of food, New York University's master of arts in food studies, and the MA programme in the anthropology of food at London's School of Oriental and African Studies (SOAS)).

THE FUTURE OF FOOD ETHNOGRAPHY

Anthropological research on food is on the threshold of a transdisciplinary revolution, a movement that migrates freely across (and often against) the academic boundaries established in the early- to mid-twentieth century. Guardians of disciplinary purity still exist in many universities, but most scholars have long since abandoned any pretence that anthropology is an academic subject grounded on notions of 'fieldwork' (usually in a foreign society) conducted by 'participant-observers' who worked alone to gather information from 'informants' who lived in 'foreign' (usually 'non-Western') 'cultures', preferably far from the anthropologist's home (where he or she wrote about the experience, often in the 'ethnographic present' – as if the experience was locked in history, never to change).

Anthropologists today are best described as omnivorous *ethnographers* who do not hesitate to cooperate (and often co-author published works) with local people and scholars, while they borrow freely from other researchers who describe themselves as sociologists, economists, psychologists, geographers, historians and environmental scientists. Ethnography is a *style* of research that places the analyst *in the midst of* the social issues under investigation – talking to people, living in their midst, digging into local archives, eating and drinking locally, interviewing leaders, attending meetings, listening to people complain/boast/worry, watching football matches, singing at weddings and sitting quietly at wakes. Ethnography is an all-consuming enterprise focused on the unremarkable, mundane, often boring lives of ordinary people: everything is important and nothing is irrelevant. Research among elites (in the business world, for instance) presents an additional, and usually far more challenging, set of restraints (see Caldwell, Chapter 20, this volume), but the fundamentals of ethnography remain essentially the same: focusing on what people, irrespective of income or education level, consider to be important.

Everyone eats and, fortunately for anthropologists, most people like to talk about food. Over nearly five decades of ethnographic encounters in south China, James Watson has learned that the surest way to break the ice in unfamiliar settings is to broach the topic of food: 'Last year I was in the mountains of western Jiangxi and I had steamed bean curd with catfish.' Or, another sure-fire conversation starter: 'Two years ago I was just in time for the harvest of first-crop rice, served with pop-eyed shrimp in the Pearl River Delta, just south of Guangzhou.' After a few minutes of this, even the most hard-bitten, suspicious Communist Party official will be waxing lyrically about the noodles he ate as a youth in Shandong Province – and there will be tears in his eyes.[6]

Jakob Klein has similarly found it methodologically fruitful to investigate Chinese society through its food and foodways, something he has been doing since the late 1990s. Not only may food practices reflect and channel wider social changes, but people also creatively use food as a medium for reflecting upon these changes in all their complexities, be it through material practices of cooking and sharing food or through 'food talk' (Mintz 1996; Klein 2007; Herzfeld, Chapter 1, this volume). Teahouse goers Klein met in Guangzhou (Canton) in the 1990s celebrated the diversity and innovative nature of the city's dim sum and contrasted this to the austerity of the 1950s–70s, when the city's few remaining establishments were all run by the state and offered only a small number of familiar snacks. On other occasions, however, the same informants would lament what they perceived to be a loss of local culinary traditions brought about by the closure or privatization of the state-run teahouses and the growing influence of Hong Kong-style Cantonese cuisine (Klein 2007, 2009). Similarly, people in the city pointed proudly to the variety of tasty mooncakes now offered by competing bakeries and companies in the run-up to the Mid-Autumn festival, yet commented that 'the people who like them don't buy them, and the people who buy them don't like them', a sardonic reflection on the expansion of the gift economy that had accompanied the growth of the market, and on the tendency of gifts to flow upwards through the social hierarchy, particularly to high-level cadres (see also Yan 2002).

As suggested by the teahouse example above, the ethnography of food often usefully includes investigation of the sites where food is prepared, served and consumed. As more food consumption takes place outside the home, the ethnography of restaurant spaces – from the kitchen to the dining table – offers unique vantage points into changing social relations, labour patterns, forms of sociality and taste, while a consideration of the relationship between restaurants and their surrounding environments provides a way into (often contested) constructions of localities at a variety of scales, from the neighbourhood to the city to the nation-state (Beriss and Sutton 2007; Sutton and Beriss 2015).

Increasingly, restaurants and other sites of food consumption reflect the transnational movements of foodways, capital, and people, and are at the same time signs of the distinctiveness of places within a global cultural economy (e.g., Bak 2015; Farrer 2010). As such, they provide settings for studying negotiations of self and other, not least in contexts of culinary tourism (Long 2004; Caldwell 2006; Herzfeld, Chapter 1, this volume; Avieli 2012, and Chapter 6, this volume), and of the cultural impact of global capitalism. As James Watson and his collaborators argued in *Golden Arches East*, ethnographic accounts of actual restaurant practices may complicate pronouncements of 'cultural homogenization' through globalization; instead what we often see are new diversities emerging through processes of 'localization', as consumers fit globalized foodways into their own changing patterns of consumption, and as transnational corporations themselves adapt to local tastes, culinary categories and styles of interaction (Watson 2006a; Yan 2005; Caldwell 2005).

Yet ethnography also shows us that the *fear* of homogenization at the hands of transnational capital, especially in the guise of food corporations, is a widespread condition of global modernity, which itself informs the actions of persons, social movements and institutions keen to protect local culinary distinctiveness (Wilk 1999; Watson 2006b; Avieli, Chapter 6, in this volume; West, Chapter 19, in this volume). Indeed, given the conquest of global capitalism (see, e.g., Piketty 2014), it is not surprising that consumers everywhere are preoccupied with a shared set of concerns around issues including food safety, food costs and provisioning, nutritional content and, as mentioned, local culinary identity. This is not to say that all concerns are shared or that all shared concerns are uniformly experienced: while problems of over- and undernutrition now coexist in many places, the 'moral panic' surrounding the childhood obesity 'crisis' in the United States (Patico and Lozada, Chapter 9, this volume) is, nevertheless, not likely to make much sense to the urban poor of Kinshasa or Kampala (Pottier, Chapter 7, this volume). With regard to 'overweight' and 'obesity', anthropologists have an important role to play not only in pointing to the culturally specific understandings of body weight and size and their significance for health (e.g. Popenoe 2005; Sobo 1997), but also in exploring the processes by which 'obesity' becomes defined as a social problem and in tracing the effects of such diagnoses (Yates-Doerr 2015). In short, the future of food ethnography – carried out in restaurants, homes, boardrooms, marketplaces, farms, government bureaus, clinics, cheese rooms or elsewhere – lies in its ability to provide multiple, grounded perspectives on contemporary food systems, on the numerous issues these raise for people's lives, and the convergent and divergent ways in which these issues are experienced and addressed. The contributors to this volume cover many of these issues in detail and point to a set of problems that will preoccupy the next generation of anthropologists. In this introduction, we begin to address a few of them: genetic modification, meat eating, industrial farming and food safety.

Genetic Modification and the Future of Food

The rapid emergence of genetically modified organisms (GMOs) presents the most dramatic challenge to traditional methods of food production. GMO maize and soybeans dominate the international trade in feed grain and now account for approximately 90 per cent of American grain production (ERS 2015). High-oleic soybeans – some of which reproduce omega-3 fatty acids – will soon be on the market, and drought-resistant maize is poised to transform agriculture in sub-Saharan Africa (Gilbert 2010; Pollack 2013).

These and similar developments have been challenged by international consortia of anti-GMO movements that warn of unintended health consequences, thereby encouraging African, Asian and European governments to halt grain imports and field trials (Chen 2010; Shannon 2013). To date, no conclusive evidence has emerged to prove that GMO foods cause human health problems, but the protest movements have gained strength rather than subsided in recent years. Biotech corporations that specialize in GMO research and development are under constant attack by critics (see e.g., Bennett 2014), and the Internet discourse on this issue is dominated by anti-GMO sites that reproduce spurious news reports that never die (e.g. the claim that GMO maize pollen kills Monarch butterflies).

Yet while opponents to GMOs are often accused of being 'anti-science', the extent to which concerns surrounding GMOs in North America and elsewhere tend to be articulated in the language of science and risk may itself be a reflection of the power of industry and regulatory regimes to set the terms of the debate, with the effect of sidelining other issues (Kinchy 2012; Heller 2004). Yet the alleged hegemony of this 'scientism' is far from unchallenged. For example, Heller (2004) has argued that in France the radical farmers' movement, the Confédération Paysanne, contributed to a broadening of the national GM debate from the frame of science and risk to human health and the environment, to include issues around food quality, cultural homogenization and farmers' welfare. In India, where wild varieties of brinjal (aubergine) are used in Ayurvedic medicine, the controversy over, and the eventual government moratorium on, Bt brinjal was driven by opposition from the Ayurvedic medical establishment (Kudlu and Stone 2013).

Many food companies have responded to consumers' unease by withdrawing GMO products from their standard offerings. The latest was Chipotle, a restaurant chain that has gained market share over older companies such as McDonald's and KFC (Strom 2015). In 2013 Whole Foods Market – a high-end grocery store chain that pioneered the mainstreaming of organic produce – jolted the industry when it announced that it would soon require suppliers to label all foods containing GMO ingredients (Strom 2013a). For ordinary American shoppers, however, it was General Mills' decision to produce GMO-free Cheerios that brought the controversy home, in a quite literal sense (Horovitz 2014).

In the United Kingdom, where EU regulations since 2004 have required the labelling of foods containing GM ingredients – but not of meat, eggs or dairy made from animals fed on GM feed – the large supermarket chains were much earlier than their counterparts in the United States to respond to consumer concerns about GMOs, particularly in regard to animal feed. However, recent years have seen a shift towards a more GMO-friendly approach among both retailers and policy makers in the United Kingdom. In 2013, for example, all but one of the major British supermarkets (the exception being the high-end retailer, Waitrose) announced that they would reverse policies that had prohibited suppliers from feeding GM soy to chickens used for their own-brand eggs and poultry (Doward 2013; Montague-Jones 2013). Meanwhile, it is expected that some GM crops, including Dupont Pioneer's 'Supercorn' GM maize 1507, will soon be grown by farmers in the United Kingdom and in some other EU member states – probably not including France! – following the recent loosening of EU regulations restricting the commercial cultivation of genetically modified crops (Neslen 2015).

Anthropologists are beginning to work on both sides of this controversy, although the biggest challenge remains access to the corporate and scientific communities that produce and develop GMO crops (see e.g., Barrows 2014 and Stone 2002 for excellent guides). Research on the environmental and social consequences of the GMO revolution is a particularly promising development for anthropologists (Brunk and Coward 2009; Fitting 2006, 2011; Grandia 2014; Pottier, Chapter 7, this volume). New GMO crops, such as apples, oranges and potatoes, will soon be available in supermarkets in many parts of the world (Harmon 2013; Pollack 2015a). One of the most serious problems confronting farmers in the developing world is the inability to save and plant GMO seeds for future crops. Distributors and developers of GMO maize are particularly vigilant against any form of seed reuse, a process they equate with piracy and theft (Monsanto Newsroom 2014). In Latin America and elsewhere in the Global South, opposition to GMOs is often articulated in terms of the perceived threats often posed by US-based biotech corporations to the livelihoods and rights of small-scale farmers, to indigenous cultures and to regional and national self-determination (Fitting 2014). Disputes of this nature are not restricted to the twenty-first century or to the Global South, however. An earlier generation of North American farmers faced similar restrictions in the 1920s and 1930s when seed companies began to develop hybrid maize (protected by patents) that made replanting impossible (Fitzgerald 1990).

Supporters claim that at its beginning in the twenty-first century, the GMO revolution had one important salutary effect on the environment, namely the reduction of insecticides and herbicides used to suppress crop pests. In recent years, however, 'super weeds', which are resistant to gyphosate (Roundup®) – the primary protector of GMO maize, soybeans, sugar beets and alfalfa – have migrated from southern states to northern prairies (Wines 2014). Many soy farmers have reverted to an old practice called 'walking the beans' with hoe in hand, hunting for rogue weeds (Palmer amaranth, waterhelp, horseweed, among others) that threaten to engulf their fields. Biotech corporations are pushing hard to develop a new generation of herbicides that will kill these invaders and not harm basic crops.

The reappearance of hand labour in American soybean and maize fields is particularly interesting, given the trend towards automation and specialized robots in the American farm sector. Recent innovations include grape-picking machines (Dembosky 2014), automated strawberry harvesters (Brat 2015), automatic milking machines (McKinley 2014) and John Deere's driverless tractor (Kopytoff 2014). Future developments in industrial agriculture present irresistible challenges for the next generation of environmental anthropologists.

Meat Futures

At the close of the twentieth century, 'futurologists', as they were then called, predicted that vegetarianism would sweep the developed world and that meat – as a dietary foundation – would soon lose its centrality and slowly fade from the scene (see, e.g. Vegan Future 2007). Pork and poultry producers declared that they were now purveyors of 'white meat', in counter distinction to unhealthy forms of 'red' meat (primarily beef). Fish and other marine products were privileged over all forms of mammalian flesh. By the second decade of the twenty-first century the demand for fish and poultry has indeed risen, but, paradoxically, premium cuts of meat – beef in particular – have found new markets and a new consumer frontier in emerging economies.

China, in particular, is in the midst of what can only be called a meat revolution driven by ever-increasing demand (Schneider 2014a, b; Watson 2014). The world meat industry was jolted in 2013 when Smithfield Foods, a leading pork producer in the United States, announced that the company had been sold to a Shuanghui International in China (De La Merced and Barboza 2013). Brazilian beef production has expanded dramatically in recent decades at the expense of rubber-tapping ecosystems that sustained earlier generations of frontier peoples (Hoelle 2014, 2015). In India, too, the availability of affordable, industrially reared chicken is transforming the eating habits of millions in the cities and villages, for whom animal flesh was until recently a rare treat (Staples, forthcoming).

In the 1980s, Marvin Harris published a path-breaking analysis of the North American preoccupation with beef, outlining the historical and cultural origins of the 'taste' for this expensive and ultimately impractical form of protein (1985b). His argument is that commercial interests, rather than inherent dietary preferences, drove this market to its current supremacy, first in the United States and now (by extension) to other parts of the world. The recent work of Jeffrey Hoelle (2015) and Mindi Schneider (2014b) supports Harris's original argument.

Anthropologists and historians are now seriously exploring the cultural implications of industrial meat production, including in regions previously designated as 'meat poor' or 'culturally vegetarian' (Staples and Klein, forthcoming). Rather than viewing 'meat' as a stable category and demand for it as 'natural', scholars are investigating how demand is produced and how some types of animal flesh or certain types of meat become accepted as 'meat', while others may be rejected as 'food' altogether (Horowitz 2006; Yates-Doerr 2012; Yates-Doerr and Mol 2012). Similarly, rather than making grand predictions about wholesale 'cultural shifts' to vegetarianism, ethnographers are investigating emerging ethical practices and debates surrounding the raising, slaughtering and eating of animals (e.g., Heath and Meneley 2010).

In this vein, restaurant ethnographies in market-socialist China and Vietnam have discussed how the boom in meat eating in urban areas has been followed by a growing popularity of vegetarian dining (Avieli 2014; Klein, forthcoming). In both cases, vegetarianism has been fuelled by a resurgence of Buddhism, by concerns over industrial meat production and animal-borne illnesses, and by the emergence of a health- and status-conscious middle class. And in both countries – or at least in Hoi An (Vietnam) and Kunming (China) – there is also a great deal of ambivalence surrounding vegetarian practices. This ambivalence has to do (perhaps especially in China) with vegetarianism's challenges to the importance of meat in family meals and other forms of commensality; with accusations (reported particularly in Vietnam) that eating vegetarian meals is simply a way for the new rich of compensating for their immoral business practices; and (at least in Vietnam) with the perceived links between vegetarian eating and anti-state religious movements.

In China, the eating practices and meanings surrounding different kinds of animal flesh are also shifting. Despite the boom in pig farming and pork consumption and the centrality of pig flesh to Han Chinese foodways (Watson 2014), several Han households in Kunming interviewed by Klein were claiming to have begun to eat more beef and goat meat instead, in the belief that goats and cattle were being raised on grass rather than on the industrial feed fed to pigs (Klein, forthcoming). Game, once a high-status food in China, is now typically avoided by the country's urban middle class, a consequence not only of government regulations but also of the perception – in the aftermath of the 2003 outbreak of Severe Acute Respiratory Syndrome (SARS), a zoonosis publically linked to the farming of 'wild' civet cats – that game eating marked the Chinese as 'uncivilized', 'wild' consumers in the eyes of Western observers (Zhan 2008). Similar notions of civility and a concern with outsiders' perceptions of oneself, as well as government hygiene regulations and a growing animal protection movement, may be at play in the falling popularity of dog-meat eating reported in urban China (e.g. Sun 2015).

In America, the livestock industry has responded to consumer demand for healthier forms of meat by introducing premium products bearing complex labels: for example 'Locally Produced', 'Hormone and Antibiotic Free', 'Organic', 'Non-GMO', 'Grass-fed' and 'Free-Range'. In the absence of clear, state-regulated guidelines, consumers are left to judge the real meaning behind many of these labels. Perhaps the most serious health challenge presented by industrial meat production is the increasing use of antimicrobial and hormone additives in animal feeds (see, e.g. Silbergeld, Graham and Price 2008). In 2013, the US Department of Agriculture collected samples of ground turkey, pork chops and beef hamburger from supermarkets; more than half contained bacteria resistant to antibiotics (Strom 2013b).

Today, antibacterial agents are routinely added to livestock feed in many parts of the world. Reproduced below is a typical label attached to a bag of calf feed produced by a local company in rural Illinois in 2014:

> 15% Optimizer, A Complete Feed for Beef Cattle. Active Drug Ingredients: Chlortetraycline, Lasalocid, Methoprene.[7] Do not use in calves to be processed for veal. Do not allow horses or other equines access to feeds containing Lasalocid: may be fatal.

The rapid expansion of livestock 'confinements' (sealed, environmentally restricted buildings) presents a new set of challenges for producers and consumers (see Thu and Durrenberger 1998 for background discussion). Animal breeding no longer involves even the possibility of chance. Modern methods of 'artificial' insemination (as opposed to 'natural mating') and embryo implantation make it possible to engineer select offspring that bear the desired genes for low-fat pork (aimed at the North American market) or high-fat beef (for elite steakhouses and certain Asian markets). Designer piglets, born to sows in confinements, are often farmed out to 'finishers' who raise them to market weight.

To date, these biological manipulations have not involved cloning and bioengineering of mammalian genomes. There is little doubt that such procedures are already underway and will soon hit the market. A strain of bioengineered salmon was presented for regulatory approval in 1996, but the US Food and Drug Administration did not declare the fish suitable for human consumption until November 2015. The new fish is 'genetically modified so that it grows to market size faster than conventionally farmed salmon' (Pollack 2015b; see also Smith et al. 2010). Cloning as a method of controlling livestock reproduction has spread rapidly; the first cloned mammal, Dolly the Sheep, was born in 1996 (Williams 2003). In 2010, cloned beef and milk were declared safe for human consumption, and the practice has now become common in many parts of the world (Batty 2010; Kanter 2010).

The final frontier (to borrow from science fiction lore) is the creation of 'cultured meat' grown from the stem cells of animal muscle. The world's first cultured hamburger was produced – and consumed – on 5 August 2013 by Dr Mark Post, a Dutch biologist who refers to himself as a 'Tissue Engineer' (Fountain 2013a, b). The 'hamburger' consisted of 20,000 thin strips of muscle tissue grown from foetal calf serum; it cost (in research development terms) 250,000 Euros. The first meal, essentially a publicity stunt featured in a London webcast,[8] is almost certainly not the last of its kind, but it is unlikely to challenge the global livestock industry during the lifetimes of those reading this text. Nonetheless, it is important for anthropologists to watch – and study – developments of this nature because they represent what may well be the evolutionary drivers of the human diet.

Industrial Food Production

During the past two decades, anthropologists have documented the widespread reaction against industrial farming and the turn towards local food production in many parts of the world (see e.g.; Caldwell 2007, 2011; Janssen 2010; Klein

2014; Pratt 2007; Counihan and Sinscalchi 2014; in this volume, see especially Luetchford, Chapter 18; West, Chapter 19; Avieli, Chapter 6; Jung, Chapter 13). Some of the best research has been carried out by researchers who are themselves personally committed to the goals of these movements. More research needs to be done on the other side of the issue, namely the social systems that sustain industrial agriculture as a core feature of global capitalism.

The 'family farm', run by independent, small-scale operators, was a core element of North America's political mythology (see e.g., Vogeler 1982), and, in any case, it has long since disappeared. European societies also have strong ideologies of family farming that survive, and serve as charter myths, as agriculture rapidly disappears as a mainstay of post-industrial economy (Hill 1993). The ongoing power of these charter myths is evident in the anti-GMO movement in France, mentioned above, and in the attempts to protect 'artisan producers', including through the EU-backed use of geographic indication regimes and protected designations of origin (West 2013; West, Chapter 19, this volume). Such charter myths, and the often contradiction-riddled co-existence of family farming and industrial agriculture, can be seen also in East and Southeast Asia. Both Japan (Ohnuki-Tierney 1993) and, as Bray discusses in Chapter 8 of this volume, Malaysia have long been using state subsidies to protect a class of farmers growing rice for the nation on small-scale family farms. In China, the market-socialist state promotes the expansion of agribusiness, the scaling up of agriculture and the increased role of science and technology in farming, while at the same time maintaining a land regime, introduced during the dismantling of the rural people's communes in the late 1970s and early 1980s, built around collective ownership and long-term private land usage rights for household-based farmers (Zhang and Donaldson 2008).

Today, in the American 'corn belt', kinship-based corporations (not all of which are defined by the nuclear or stem family) operate as small-scale capital-intensive businesses that survived the 'sort out' of small-scale farms during the 1980s and 1990s. These corporations have expanded their landholdings and rent land owned by former neighbours who have either retired or retreated from farming (a process summarized by Sumner 2014). Future ethnographers will also need to consider ancillary developments underlying modern industrial farming, such as rural depopulation and labour 'rationalization' caused by rapid mechanization. Thousands of acres can now be farmed by two or three people operating high-tech machinery guided by GPS and on-board computer technology. Technical knowledge – sustained by daily, online updating – is more important than physical strength or stamina for successful farming in the American heartland. Increasingly this is true (or soon will be) in other parts of the world, including China, Russia, South America and parts of Southeast Asia (see e.g., Schneider 2014a, b; Visser, Mamonova and Spoor 2012; Santos 2011), raising serious questions about the future of 'peasantries' (Bray, Chapter 8, this volume; West, Chapter 19, this volume).

The future may entail even more radical departures from twentieth-century modes of agricultural production. Bioengineers are working to recombine the natural building blocks of DNA in novel ways to create new forms of 'artificial life'. Craig Venter, a pioneer in the human genomics field, promises new industrial products that will help clean toxic and radioactive wastes. He also promises a rev-olution in the way humans feed themselves: 'Agriculture as we know it', Venter claims, 'needs to disappear. We can design better and healthier proteins than we can get from nature.'

Food Safety

Food safety has emerged as a global preoccupation among consumers in the early twenty-first century. Food-related health concerns take many forms, from a preoccupation with glutens, allergens and GMO ingredients to industrial poisons and dangerous levels of insecticide in fruit or vegetables. Nothing evades the vigilant: the US Food and Drug Administration reported that twelve per cent of spices imported into the United States in 2013 were contaminated with insect parts, rodent hair and other extraneous materials (Harris 2013). A Google search under the category 'food threats' reveals an impressive roster of recent episodes, including the following, selected at random: 'six thousand hidden dangers of processed foods', 'threat of food irradiation', 'dirty secrets of the food processing industry'.

The United States has a long history of real (as opposed to imaginary) food crises, including industrial excesses associated with the industrial boom and urbanization movements of the early twentieth century – a period of economic upheaval and social realignment (see, e.g., Levenstein 2012). It should be no surprise that China is experiencing a similar outburst of food scares during its own economic boom. Consumers in every part of the country are affected, irrespective of social class or level of wealth. In 2014, for instance, the Chinese Ministry of Environmental Protection reported that one-fifth of China's arable land was contaminated – some beyond redemption – by pollutants such as cadmium, nickel, arsenic and various by-products of the coal industry (Wong 2014). In 2013, high levels of cadmium, a particularly dangerous pollutant that can cause kidney and liver problems, was found in rice samples drawn from markets and restaurants all over south China in 2013; it also appeared in meat samples originating from animals fed on rice husks (Wong 2013).

But perhaps the most dramatic food scare in China's recent history was the widespread contamination of infant formula and milk powder that killed at least six children and sickened thousands in 2008 and 2009 (Tracy 2010; Xiu and Klein 2010). Melamine, a chemical additive used in the manufacture of plastics, was added to milk that had been diluted with water in order to raise the liquid's protein content level and thereby giving it the appearance of being 100 per cent milk. Several of China's leading milk producers and processors, including Sanlu, Mengniu and Yili, were implicated in a scandal that riveted the nation. Consumers are still wary of domestic milk powder and infant formula (Gong and Jackson 2012). Soon after the problem was publicized an informal network of Chinese citizens travelling abroad started importing vast quantities of foreign-made milk products (in 2013 shops in London restricted customer purchases to one container of powdered milk per day). The disappearance of milk powder and infant formula in Hong Kong grocery stores – swept up by tourists from China – was cited by many local residents as one among many reasons to support the 2014 pro-democracy Umbrella Movement (Sheehan and Mao 2014).

Yunxiang Yan has studied the rise of food crises in contemporary China and concluded that ordinary citizens now find themselves operating uneasily in a postmodern 'risk society', essentially unprotected by a state that has withdrawn from the micro-surveillance of all commercial activity – a hallmark of the Maoist state. In their haste to modernize, Chinese authorities have supported capitalist ventures that do not prioritize safety procedures, paralleling American developments in the early twentieth century. Yan (2012, following Beck 1992) argues that China is making a rapid transition into a modern 'risk society' in which consumers enjoy the benefits of an open, unregulated market but can no longer expect to be protected from manufacturing and commercial dangers.

Ethnographers have been exploring the social practices and moral discourse shaping Chinese farmers' perceptions and usage of pesticides and other agrichemicals (Lora-Wainwright 2009; Santos 2011). Others have documented consumers' widespread distrust of the food supply, the wider social issues this distrust raises for people and the everyday social practices and skills developed by urban food shoppers in their attempts to supply their households with tasty, healthy, affordable, safe foods (Veeck, Yu and Burns 2010; Gong and Jackson 2012; Klein 2013). Such skills include those needed to competently navigate the brave new world of packaging, branding, nutritional information and food safety labelling (cf. Jung 2009). Indeed, in China, as in other places going through 'neoliberal' reforms, the growing emphasis on individual responsibility and apparent 'retreat' of the state has gone hand in hand with the proliferation of new regulatory bodies and forms of management governing the food supply. In addition to their significance for consumers, food ethnographers have also shown that these new forms of food safety governance are profoundly challenging to producers and retailers, shaping the production practices and social identities of people, including Puer tea processors in southwest China (Zhang 2014: 55–77), American artisan cheese makers (Paxson 2012, and Chapter 12, this volume) and Lithuanian women vendors of raw milk (Mincyte 2014). In the area of food safety, as in other aspects of food, ethnography has a crucial role to play in revealing the complexities and challenges of modern life.

THIS HANDBOOK

Each of the authors contributing to the *Handbook of Food and Anthropology* has been invited to provide a critical overview of a key topic or theme in the anthropology of food. Some of the topics, such as food security (Pottier, Chapter 7), nutrition and health (Wiley, Chapter 10; Paxson, Chapter 12) and commensality and food prohibitions (Staples, Chapter 3; Bahloul, Chapter 4; Gillette, Chapter 2; J. L. Watson, Chapter 14), have long been core staples of anthropology. Others, such as supermarket expansion (Hull, Chapter 17; see also R. Watson, Chapter 15), heritage and tourism (West, Chapter 19; Avieli, Chapter 6), ethical consumption (Luetchford, Chapter 18; Jung, Chapter 13) and – surprisingly – cooking (Sutton,

Chapter 16), have emerged more recently as areas of ethnographic enquiry. Whether addressing novel topics or more familiar ones, the authors build on long-standing anthropological debates and modes of enquiry, while developing new approaches and questions, critically interrogating fundamental categories and assumptions of anthropology and food studies – including even the concept of 'food' itself (Paxson, Chapter 12; Caldwell, Chapter 20). In so doing, the chapters provide a unique set of insights into the social significance of food in the contemporary world and offer models for further research in the anthropology of food.

Authors have been asked to include examples from their own empirical research, in order to ground their arguments in everyday-life perspectives and to convey to readers the distinctiveness of anthropological approaches to food, even as authors necessarily move beyond the disciplinary boundaries of anthropology itself. Some writers have chosen to build their discussions around a single, extended example, in some cases drawing on years or even decades of research with a particular group of people or place (e.g., Avieli, Chapter 6; Bahloul, Chapter 4; Bray, Chapter 8; Staples, Chapter 3). Others (e.g., Patico and Lozada, Chapter 9; Pottier, Chapter 7; West, Chapter 19) illustrate their discussions with briefer ethnographic examples, often drawn from a number of sites and contexts.

Part One, 'Food, Self and Other', addresses a cluster of classic questions in anthropology: Why does food play such a central role in the construction of identities and hierarchies? How is food used to construct and negotiate boundaries between selves and others through likes and dislikes, avoidances and prohibitions, commensality and hospitality, and gift exchange? What is the role of religion in shaping food habits? The authors here do not seek to unearth unchanging structures and classificatory systems, but to shed light on dynamic processes. They demonstrate that food is a major medium for the redefinition of identities, hierarchies and localities in a world increasingly defined by *mobilities* – of capital and economic resources (Staples, Chapter 3); of people – for example as migrants (Abbots, Chapter 5; Bahloul, Chapter 4; Herzfeld, Chapter 1) and tourists (Avieli, Chapter 6; Herzfeld, Chapter 1); and of foods and ideas about food, travelling not only with migrants but also through trade and media (Gillette, Chapter 2; Bahloul, Chapter 4; Staples, Chapter 3).

Part Two is centrally concerned with the problem of provisioning in a world beset by problems of hunger and food insecurity, overweight and obesity, and by deep-seated concerns about the safety and healthiness of the food supply. While the industrialization and scientization of food production, processing and distribution have raised hopes of solving some of these issues, the 'technical fixes', as the chapters show, often raise new issues and are inseparable from the political and cultural contexts in which they operate. Anthropologists are often uniquely positioned to disentangle the complexities of these questions 'from the ground up', and the authors here offer subtle, ethnographically and historically grounded analyses that, to return to debates raised earlier in this introduction, neither reject science and technology out of hand nor offer simple, one-sided solutions to multifaceted problems. Instead, they invite readers to question received wisdom and influential rhetoric. To what extent do policies and technologies that encourage impoverished farmers to leave the land help ensure the right to food, and how do we address food insecurity, long understood primarily as a rural problem, as farmers increasingly move to the cities (Pottier, Chapter 7)? What has been the role of science in shaping our understandings of what is 'good' and 'safe' to eat (Patico and Lozada, Chapter 9; Paxson, Chapter 12) – not least for our children – and how does this compare cross-culturally (Wiley, Chapter 10)?

The different sections of the *Handbook of Food and Anthropology* are not hermetically sealed, but are meant to speak to one another. Thus, the role of food as a marker of 'ethnic' or 'national' identity, a theme introduced in Section One, may be highly relevant to understanding attempts to resolve problems of food security, as discussed in Section Two by Bray (Chapter 8) and Pottier (Chapter 7). And an investigation of food safety and nutrition may destabilize accepted boundaries such as those between food and non-food and food and eaters, raising new questions about the role of food substances in mediating between selves and others (Paxson, Chapter 12; see also Abbots, Chapter 5).

Issues relating to food safety and animal-borne illnesses may also compel us to reexamine our understanding of transnational mobility: as Smart and Smart (Chapter 11) discuss, the 'global food system' is as much about policing the movement of people, animals and foods across borders as it is about generating movement (see also Paxson, Chapter 12; Watson 2006c). And despite the alleged triumph of global capitalism and the 'neoliberal food regime' (McMichael 2009), nation-states may continue to play a central role in providing affordable food for its citizens while simultaneously preserving an indigenous peasantry on the land (Bray, Chapter 8). Indeed, citizens in a variety of countries continue to make moral demands on the state for ensuring citizens' basic nourishment and a food supply that is safe and nutritious and tasty. These moral demands may take on particular complexities in post-socialist contexts, where people may be less prone either to assume 'the market' as the natural state of affairs or to harbour illusions about the benevolence of the state (Jung, Chapter 13). Indeed, while many look to the state to provide alternatives to the power of corporations over the food supply, in Chinese contexts such thoughts may be tempered by memories of the disastrous consequences of the communist party state's attempts during the Great Leap Forward to use its control over food resources to forge new collectivities through 'forced commensality' (J. L. Watson, Chapter 14).

Despite the ongoing role of the state and the various limitations on the transnational circulation of foods, it is difficult to deny the power of agribusiness, supermarkets and other corporations to shape what we eat and grow, or to refute the significance of transnational food trade and the dependence on biotechnologies, fossil fuels, processing, additives and packaging, and the attendant gap that has emerged between processes of production and consumption. Increasingly, across the globe, eaters, a majority of whom now live in cities, are also consumers. Developing on the themes introduced in Part One (e.g., Gillette, Chapter 2; Avieli, Chapter 6) and Part Two (e.g., Pottier, Chapter 7; Paxson, Chapter 12; Jung, Chapter 13), contributors in Part Three explore the cultural, economic and ethical dimensions of this state of affairs, from the perspectives of consumers, preparers, producers and providers of food, be they households, small-scale farmers and artisans or major corporate players.

R. Watson (Chapter 15) sets the stage for Part Three through a meticulous investigation of the transformation of cooking and eating in the twentieth century in a rural county in the Upper Midwest of the United States. As is evident from this account, the 'distance' between production and consumption is apparent even among many rural populations, who may focus on a small number of crops for agribusinesses, but produce little or none of their own food. And while this may appear to be an extreme case, the processes are familiar from a variety of settings. Still, even as the knowledges of cooking, crafting and eating food are transformed through industrialization, such knowledges do not simply disappear without a trace (Sutton, Chapter 16; R. Watson, Chapter 15; West, Chapter 19). Nor do such transformations necessarily lead to the 'liberation' of women from the drudgery of 'feeding the family' (R Watson, Chapter 15). Instead, as Sutton (Chapter 16) discusses, we need to investigate ethnographically and theoretically the ways in which cooking skills are performed, developed and transmitted, often in highly gendered ways.

Moreover, experiences of distance between processes of production and consumption have informed the emergence of movements promising 'alternative', allegedly more 'ethical' forms of food consumption, as Luetchford (Chapter 18) discusses in his critical examination of food as an 'ethical' problem in Western societies (cf. Jung, Chapter 13, who addresses food and morality in postsocialist contexts). Such desires for 'reconnection' – with the land, with food producers, with 'traditional' flavours – have, as West (Chapter 19) discusses, also created new opportunities for producers of 'artisanal', 'craft' and 'local' foods, even as such producers must constantly reinvent themselves to accommodate changing consumer demands; new technologies; the requirements of food safety and other regulatory bodies; and the social movements, tourism providers and state bodies keen to derive value in the cultural marketplace from these producers of culinary 'heritage' (see also Avieli, Chapter 6; Paxson, Chapter 12).

Clearly, the expansion of industrialized food chains needs to be understood in conjunction with the persistence, emergence and reinvention of a number of other modes of production, distribution and consumption. Moreover, it would be quite wrong to assume that industrialized, globalized food chains and food corporations are themselves all much the same, knowable without the need for ethnographic research (see Bestor 2001; Pritchard 2013; Watson 2006a). Rather, the expansion of, for example, supermarkets may take on very different forms in different national and regional contexts – in some cases, such as rural South Africa, even providing new opportunities for producers and traders in the 'informal' food sector and facilitating food acquisition strategies among the poor (Hull, Chapter 13; cf. Jung and Newman 2014). Indeed, while anthropologists have studied the dissemination and localization of global foods from the perspective primarily of consumers, the growing collaborations between anthropologists and the food industries increase possibilities for understanding such processes from within food corporations (Caldwell, Chapter 20). This kind of 'studying up', as Caldwell demonstrates in her chapter, presents anthropologists with particular challenges, not least to do with access and confidentiality. But it also provides opportunities for anthropologists to move beyond both sweeping critiques and unfettered celebrations of the food industries, to provide more nuanced analyses of the cultures of the food institutions that are so profoundly shaping the modern world.

Many anthropologists are deeply uneasy with corporate research and collaboration. How to do this without becoming beholden to power? At the same time, food is fundamental to human life, and any engagement with food practitioners outside the world of academia, be it businesses, farmers, development organizations, nutrition programmes, food safety regulators or household cooks, raises difficult ethical responsibilities and dilemmas. We should not ignore these (see Pottier, Chapter 7; Caldwell, Chapter 20). But we should also not use them as an excuse not to carry out the kind of on-the-ground ethnographic research that is so sorely needed to comprehend a complex and constantly changing world of food.

NOTES

1. Writing in our companion volume, *The Handbook of Food Research* (Murcott, Belasco and Jackson 2013), Julier (2013: esp. 343–6) provides an overview of the sociology of the 'family meal'. For a critical analysis of fears of the alleged decline of the family meal in the United Kingdom, see Murcott (1997). In *The Handbook of Food and Anthropology*, food and the family or household is discussed across a variety of regional and other contexts. See, especially, Abbots, Chapter 5; Bahloul, Chapter 4; Hull, Chapter 17; Patico and Lozada, Chapter 9; Pottier, Chapter 7; Staples, Chapter 3; J. L. Watson, Chapter 14; R. Watson, Chapter 15; Wiley, Chapter 10; and Sutton, Chapter 16.
2. See Shove and Southerton (2000); and Hand and Shove (2007).
3. Discussions of food studies in anthropology include, in addition to Tierney and Ohnuki-Tierney (2012), also Messer (1984); Mintz and Du Bois (2002); and Klein, Pottier and West (2012). Murcott (2013) usefully situates anthropological approaches within the wider social sciences of food.
4. When James Watson first offered a course on food at the University of Pittsburgh in 1984, eight (enthusiastic) undergraduates enrolled. By 2002, essentially the same course was drawing 400+ students as a core curriculum course at Harvard. Several of the contributors to this handbook 'cut their teeth' in this field by serving as teaching assistants for the Harvard course.
5. Mintz's contributions to the field are widely recognized, Goody's perhaps less so – but see Klein (2014a) for a discussion of Jack Goody's enduring influence on the anthropology of food.
6. Borrowed from the original published version of Chapter 14 in this volume (Watson 2011).
7. Chlortetracycline is a tetracycline antibiotic; lasalocid is an antibacterial agent, toxic to horses and dogs; methroprene is a juvenile hormone that disrupts the growth of larvae, preventing fly breeding in dung.
8. YouTube, 2013, 'World's First Lab-Grown Hamburger Taste Tested.'

REFERENCES

Appadurai, A. (1981), 'Gastro-politics in Hindu South Asia', *American Ethnologist*, 8(3): 494–511.

Appadurai, A. (1988), 'How to Make a National Cuisine: Cookbooks in Contemporary India', *Comparative Studies in Society and History*, 30(1): 3–24.

Avieli, N. (2012), *Rice Talks: Food and Community in a Vietnamese Town*, Bloomington: Indiana University Press.

Avieli, N. (2014), 'Vegetarian Ethics and Politics in Late-Socialist Vietnam', in Y. Jung, J. A. Klein and M. L. Caldwell (eds), *Ethical Eating in the Postsocialist and Socialist World*, 144–66, Berkeley: University of California Press.

Bak, S. (2015), 'Exoticizing the Familiar, Domesticating the Foreign: Ethnic Food Restaurants in Korea', in K. O. Kim (ed.), *Re-Orienting Cuisine: East Asian Foodways in the Twenty-First Century*, 170–85, New York: Berghahn.

Barndt, D. (2002), *Tangled Routes: Women, Work, and Globalization on the Tomato Trail*, Lanham, MD: Rowman and Littlefield.

Barrows, G., Sexton, S. and Zilberman, D. (2014), 'Agricultural Biotechnology: The Promise and Prospects of Genetically Modified Crops', *Journal of Economic Perspectives*, 28(1): 99–120.

Batty, D. (2010), 'Scientists Give All Clear for Meat and Milk from Cloned Cattle', *The Guardian*, 25 November 2010.

Beck, U. (1992), *Risk Society: Towards a New Modernity*, London: Sage Publications.

Bennett, D. (2014), 'Inside Monsanto, America's Third-Most-Hated Company', *Bloomsberg Businessweek*, 3 July 2014.

Beriss, D. and Sutton, D. (eds) (2007), *The Restaurants Book: Ethnographies of Where We Eat*, Oxford: Berg.

Bestor, T. C. (2001), 'Supply-side Sushi: Commodity, Market, and the Global City', *American Anthropologist*, 103(1): 76–95.

Bourdieu, P. (1984), *Distinction: A Social Critique of the Judgement of Taste*, translated by R. Nice, London: Routledge.

Brat, I. (2015), 'Robots Step into New Planting, Harvesting Roles', *Wall Street Journal*, 23 April 2015.

Brunk, C. and Coward, H. (eds) (2009), *Acceptable Genes? Religious Traditions and Genetically Modified Foods*, Albany: State University of New York Press.

Caldwell, M. L. (2005), 'Domesticating the French Fry: McDonald's and Consumerism in Moscow', in J. L. Watson and M. L. Caldwell (eds), *The Cultural Politics of Food and Eating*, 180–96, Malden, MA: Blackwell Publishing.

Caldwell, M. L. (2006), 'Tasting the Worlds of Yesterday and Today: Culinary Tourism and Nostalgia Foods in Post-Soviet Russia', in R. Wilk (ed.), *Fast Food/Slow Food: The Cultural Economy of the Global Food System*, 97–112, Lanham, MD: Altamira Press.

Caldwell, M. L. (2007), 'Feeding the Body and Nourishing the Soul: Natural Foods in Postsocialist Russia', *Food, Culture and Society*, 10(1): 43–71.

Caldwell, M. L. (2011), *Dacha Idylls: Living Organically in Russia's Countryside*, Berkeley: University of California Press.

Camp, C. (1989), *American Foodways: What, When, Why and How We Eat in America*, Little Rock, AS: August House.

Campbell, C. (1987), *The Romantic Ethic and the Spirit of Modern Consumerism*, Oxford: Blackwell.

Chang, K. C. (ed.) (1977), *Food in Chinese Culture: Anthropological and Historical Perspectives*, New Haven, CT: Yale University Press.

Chen, N. (2010), 'Feeding the Nation: Chinese Biotechnology and Genetically Modified Foods', in A. Ong and N. Chen (eds), *Asian Biotech*, 81–93, Durham, NC: Duke University Press.

Counihan, C. (1999), *The Anthropology of Food and Body: Gender, Meaning, and Power*, New York: Routledge.

Counihan, C. (2004), *Around the Tuscan Table: Food, Family, and Gender in Twentieth-Century Florence*, New York: Routledge.

Counihan, C. and Siniscalchi, V. (eds) (2014), *Food Activism: Agency, Democracy and Economy*, London: Bloomsbury Academic.

Counihan, C. and Van Esterik, P. (eds) (2013), *Food and Culture: A Reader*, 3rd edn, New York: Routledge.

De La Merced, M. and Barboza, D. (2013), 'Smithfield To Be Sold To Chinese Meat Processor', *New York Times*, 29 May 2013.

Dembosky, A. (2013), 'Robots Rising in "Salad Bowl of the World"', *Financial Times*, 29 June 2013.

Douglas, M. (1966), *Purity and Danger: An Analysis of the Concepts of Pollution and Taboo*, London: Routledge & Kegan Paul.

Douglas, M. (1971), 'Deciphering a Meal', in C. Geertz (ed.), *Myth, Symbol, and Culture*, 61–81, New York: W. W. Norton.

Douglas, M. (ed.) (1984), *Food in the Social Order: Studies of Food and Festivities in Three American Communities*, New York: Russell Sage Foundation.

Douglas, M. and Isherwood, B. (1979), *The World of Goods*, New York: Basic Books.

Doward, J. (2013), 'M&S, Co-op and Sainsbury's say chickens will be fed on GM soya', *The Guardian*, 11 May 2013.

ERS (2015), 'Adoption of Genetically Modified Crops in the U.S.', Economic Research Service, United States Department of Agriculture.

Evans-Pritchard, E. E. (1940), *The Nuer*, Oxford: Clarendon Press.

Farquhar, J. (2002), *Appetites: Food and Sex in Postsocialist China*, Durham, NC: Duke University Press.

Farrer, J. (2010), 'Eating the West and Beating the Rest: Culinary Occidentalism and Urban Soft Power in Asia's Global Food Cities', in J. Farrer (ed.), *Globalization, Food and Social Identities in the Asia Pacific Region*, Tokyo: Sophia University Institute of Comparative Culture. http://icc.fla.sophia.ac.jp/global%20food%20papers/html/farrer.html

Fitting, E. (2006), 'Importing Corn, Exporting Labor: The Neoliberal Corn Regime, GMOs, and the Erosion of Mexican Biodiversity', *Agriculture and Human Values*, 23: 15–26.

Fitting, E. (2011), *The Struggle for Maize: Campesinos, Workers and Transgenic Corn in the Mexican Countryside*, Durham, NC: Duke University Press.

Fitting, E. (2014), 'Cultures of Corn and Anti-GMO Activism in Mexico and Columbia', in C. Counihan and V. Siniscalchi (eds), *Food Activism: Agency, Democracy and Economy*, 175–92, London: Bloomsbury Academic.

Fitzgerald, D. (2009), *The Business of Breeding: Hybrid Corn in Illinois, 1910-1940*, Ithaca, NY: Cornell University Press.

Fountain, H. (2013a), 'Building a $325,000 Burger', *New York Times*, 12 May 2013.

Fountain, H. (2013b), 'A Lab-Grown Burger Gets A Taste Test', *New York Times*, 5 August 2013.

Gewertz, D. and Errington, F. (2010), *Cheap Meat: Flap Food Nations in the Pacific Islands*, Berkeley: University of California Press.

Gilbert, N. (2010), 'Inside the Hothouses of Industry', *Nature*, 466: 548–51.

Gong, Q. and Jackson, P. (2012), 'Consuming Anxiety? Parenting Practices in China after the Infant Formula Scandal', *Food, Culture & Society*, 15(4): 557–78.

Grandia, Liza (2014), 'Modified Landscapes: Vulnerabilities to Genetically Modified Corn in Northern Guatemala', *Journal of Peasant Studies*, 41(1): 79–105.

Hand, M. and Shove, E. (2007), 'Condensing Practices: Ways of Living with a Freezer', *Journal of Consumer Culture* 7(1): 79–104.

Harmon, A. (2013), 'A Race to Save the Orange by Altering Its DNA', *New York Times*, 27 July 2013.

Harris, G. (2013), 'F.D.S. Finds 12% of U.S. Spice Imports Contaminated', *New York Times*, 30 December 2013.

Harris, M. (1968), *The Rise of Anthropological Theory: A History of Theories of Culture*, New York: Thomas Y. Crowell.

Harris, M. (1985a), *Good To Eat: Riddles of Food and Culture*, New York: Simon and Shuster.

Harris, M. (1985b), 'Holy Beef, U.S.A.', in his *Good To Eat: Riddles of Food and Culture*, 109–29, New York: Simon and Shuster.

Heath, D. and Meneley, A. (2010), 'The Naturecultures of Foie Gras: Techniques of the Body and a Contested Ethics of Care', *Food, Culture & Society*, 13(3): 421–52.

Heller, C. (2004), 'Risky Science and Savoir-faire: Peasant Expertise in the French Debate over Genetically Modified Crops', in M. E. Lien and B. Nerlich (eds), *The Politics of Food*, 81–99, Oxford: Berg.

Hill, B. (1993), 'The "Myth" of the Family Farm: Defining the Family Farm and Assessing Its Importance in the European Community', *Journal of Peasant Studies*, 9(4): 359–70.

Hoelle, J. (2014), 'Cattle Culture in the Brazilian Amazon', *Human Organization*, 73(4): 363–74.

Hoelle, J. (2015), *Rainforest Cowboys: The Rise of Ranching and Cattle Culture in Western Amazonia*, Austin: University of Texas Press.

Holtzman, J. (2009), *Uncertain Tastes: Memory, Ambivalence, and the Politics of Eating in Samburu, Northern Kenya*, Berkeley: University of California Press.

Horovitz, B. (2014), 'Cheerios Drops Genetically Modified Ingredients', *USA Today*, 2 January 2014.

Horowitz, R. (2006), *Putting Meat on the American Table: Taste, Technology, Transformation*, Baltimore, MD: The Johns Hopkins University Press.

Hylton, W. S. (2012), 'Craig Venter's Bugs Might Save the World', *New York Times Sunday Magazine*, 30 May 2012.

Janeja, M. K. (2010), *Transactions in Taste: The Collaborative Lives of Everyday Bengali Food*, New Delhi: Routledge.

Janssen, B. (2010), 'Local Food, Local Engagement: Community Supported Agriculture in Eastern Iowa', *Culture and Agriculture*, 32(1): 4–16.

Jing, J. (ed.) (2000), *Feeding China's Little Emperors: Food, Children, and Social Change*, Stanford, CA: Stanford University Press.

Julier, A. (2013), 'Meals: "Eating in" and "Eating out"', in A. Murcott, W. Belasco and P. Jackson (eds), *The Handbook of Food Research*, 338–51, London: Bloomsbury Academic.

Jung, Y. (2009), 'From Canned Food to Canny Consumers: Cultural Competence in the Age of Mechanical Production', in M. L. Caldwell (ed.), *Food and Everyday Life in the Postsocialist World*, 29–56, Bloomington: Indiana University Press.

Jung, Y. and Newman, A. (2014), 'An Edible Moral Economy in the Motor City: Food Politics and Urban Governance in Detroit', *Gastronomica: The Journal of Critical Food Studies*, 14(1): 23–32.

Kanter, J. (2010), 'Cloned Livestock Gain A Foothold in Europe', *New York Times*, 29 July 2010.

Khare, R. S. (1976), *The Hindu Hearth and Home*, New Delhi: Vikas Publishing House.

Khare, R. S. (ed.) (1992), *The Eternal Food: Gastronomic Ideas and Experiences of Hindus and Buddhists*, Albany: State University of New York Press.

Kinchy, A. (2012), *Seeds, Science, and Struggle: The Global Politics of Transgenic Crops*, Cambridge, MA: The MIT Press.

Klein, J. A. (2007), 'Redefining Cantonese Cuisine in Post-Mao Guangzhou', *Bulletin of the School of Oriental and African Studies*, 70(3): 511–37.

Klein, J. A. (2009), '"For Eating, It's Guangzhou": Regional Culinary Traditions and Chinese Socialism', in H. G. West and P. Raman (eds), *Enduring Socialism: Explorations of Revolution and Transformation, Restoration and Continuation*, 44–76, New York: Oxford Books.

Klein, J. A. (2013), 'Everyday Approaches to Food Safety in Kunming', *The China Quarterly*, 214: 376–93.

Klein, J. A. (2014a), 'Introduction: *Cooking, Cuisine and Class* and the Anthropology of Food', in J. A. Klein and A. Murcott (eds), *Food Consumption in Global Perspective: Essays in the Anthropology of Food in Honour of Jack Goody*, 1–24, Basingstoke: Palgrave Macmillan.

Klein, J. A. (2014b), 'Connecting with the Countryside? "Alternative" Food Movements with Chinese Characteristics', in Y. Jung, J. A. Klein and M. L. Caldwell (eds), *Ethical Eating in the Postsocialist and Socialist World*, 116–43, Berkeley: University of California Press.

Klein, J. A. (forthcoming), 'Buddhist Vegetarianism and the Changing Meanings of Meat in Urban China', *Ethnos*.

Klein, J. A., Pottier, J. and West, H. G. (2012), 'New Directions in the Anthropology of Food', in R. Fardon, O. Harris, T. H. J. Marchand, M. Nuttall, C. Shore, V. Strang and R. A. Wilson (eds), *The SAGE Handbook of Social Anthropology*, vol. 2, 299–311, Los Angeles, CA: SAGE.

Kopytoff, V. (2014), 'Driverless Tractors on the Farm', *Fortune*, 29 December 2014.

Kudlu, C. and Stone, G. D. (2013), 'The Trials of Genetically Modified Food: Bt Eggplant and Ayurvedic Medicine in India', *Food, Culture & Society*, 16(1): 21–42.

Levenstein, H. (2012), *Fear of Food: A History of Why We Worry About What We Eat*, Chicago: University of Chicago Press.

Lévi-Strauss, C. (1966), 'The Culinary Triangle', *Partisan Review*, 33(4): 586–95.

Lévi-Strauss, C. (1969), *The Raw and the Cooked*, London: Jonathan Cape.

Lévi-Strauss, C. (1978), *The Origin of Table Manners*, London: Jonathan Cape.

Long, L. (ed.) (2004), *Culinary Tourism*, Lexington: The University Press of Kentucky.

Lopez, R. (2012), 'As Drought Hits Corn, Biotech Firms See Lush Field in GMO Crops', *Los Angeles Times*, 17 September 2012.

Lora-Wainwright, A. (2009), 'Of Farming Chemicals and Cancer Deaths: The Politics of Health in Contemporary Rural China', *Social Anthropology/Anthropologie Sociale*, 17(1): 56–73.

Malinowski, B. (1935), *Coral Gardens and Their Magic*, 2 vols, London: George Allen and Unwin Ltd.

Mauss, M. (1990), *The Gift*, translated by W. D. Halls, London: Routledge.

McKinley, J. (2014), 'With Farm Robots, The Cows Decide When It's Milking Time', *New York Times*, 22 April 2014.

McMichael, P. (2009), 'A Food Regime Genealogy', *Journal of Peasant Studies*, 36(1): 139–69.

Mennell, S. (1985), *All Manners of Food: Eating and Taste in England and France from the Middle Ages to the Present*, Oxford: Basil Blackwell.

Messer, E. (1984), 'Anthropological Perspectives on Diet', *Annual Review of Anthropology*, 13: 205–49.

Miller, D. (1987), *Material Culture and Mass Consumption*, Oxford: Blackwell.

Mincyte, D. (2014), 'Homogenizing Europe: Raw Milk, Risk Politics, and Moral Economies in Europeanizing Lithuania', in Y. Jung, J. A. Klein and M. L. Caldwell (eds), *Ethical Eating in the Postsocialist and Socialist World*, 25–43, Berkeley: University of California Press.

Mintz, S. W. (1985), *Sweetness and Power: The Place of Sugar in Modern History*, New York: Viking Penguin Inc.

Mintz, S. W. (1996), 'Cuisine: High, Low, and Not at All', in his *Tasting Food, Tasting Freedom: Excursions into Eating, Culture, and the Past*, Boston, 92–105, MA: Beacon Press.

Mintz, S. W. and Du Bois, C. M. (2002), 'The Anthropology of Food and Eating', *Annual Review of Anthropology*, 31: 99–119.

Montague-Jones, G. (2013), 'Waitrose Boss Mark Price: "GM is Tech Looking for a Problem to Solve"', *The Grocer*, 20 June 2013.

Monsanto (2014), 'Why Does Monsanto Sue Farmers Who Save Seeds?' MonsantoNewsroom.com.

Murcott, A. (1997), 'Family Meals: A Thing of the Past?', in P. Caplan (ed.), *Food, Health and Identity*, 32–49, London: Routledge.

Murcott, A. (2013), 'A Burgeoning Field: Introduction to *The Handbook of Food Research*', in A. Murcott, W. Belasco and P. Jackson (eds), *The Handbook of Food Research*, 1–25, London: Bloomsbury Academic.

Murcott, A., Belasco, W. and Jackson, P. (eds) (2013), *The Handbook of Food Research*, London: Bloomsbury Academic.

Neslen, A. (2015), 'GM Crop Vote was Just the Beginning of Europe's Biotech Battle', *The Guardian*, 19 January 2015.

Ohnuki-Tierney, E. (1993), *Rice as Self: Japanese Identities through Time*, Princeton, NJ: Princeton University Press.

Pachirat, T. (2011), *Every Twelve Seconds: Industrialized Slaughter and the Politics of Sight*, New Haven, CT: Yale University Press.

Paxson, H. (2012), *The Life of Cheese: Crafting Food and Value in America*, Berkeley: University of California Press.

Phillips, L. (2006), 'Food and Globalization', *Annual Review of Anthropology*, 35: 37–57.

Piketty, T. (2014), *Capital in the Twenty-First Century*, Cambridge, MA: Harvard University Press.

Pollack, A. (2013), 'In a Bean, a Boon to Biotech', *New York Times*, 15 November 2013.

Pollack, A. (2015a), 'Gene-Altered Apples and Potatoes Are Safe, F.D.A Says', *New York Times*, 20 March 2015.

Pollack, A. (2015b), 'Genetically Modified Salmon Approved For Consumption', *New York Times*, 19 November 2015.

Popenoe, R. (2005), 'Ideal', in D. Kulick and A. Meneley (eds), *Fat: The Anthropology of an Obsession*, 9–28, New York: Tarcher/Penguin.

Pottier, J. (1999), *Anthropology of Food: The Social Dynamics of Food Security*, Cambridge, UK: Polity Press.

Pratt, J. (2007), 'Food Values: The Local and the Authentic', *Critique of Anthropology*, 27(3): 285–300.

Pritchard, B. (2013), 'Food Chains', in A. Murcott, W. Belasco and P. Jackson (eds), *The Handbook of Food Research*, 167–91, London: Bloomsbury Academic.

Richards, A. I. (1932), *Hunger and Work in a Savage Tribe: A Functional Study of Nutrition among the Southern Bantu*, London: Routledge.

Richards, A. I. (1939), *Land, Labour and Diet in Northern Rhodesia*, Oxford: Oxford University Press.

Santos, G. (2011), 'Rethinking the Green Revolution in South China', *East Asian Science, Technology and Society*, 5: 479–504.

Schneider, M. (2014a), 'Developing the Meat Grab', *Journal of Peasant Studies*, 41(4): 613–33.

Schneider, M. (2014b), *China's Pork Miracle? Agribusiness and Development in China's Pork Industry*, Minneapolis, MN: Institute for Agriculture and Trade Policy.

Shannon, V. (2013), 'Japan and South Korea Bar Imports of U.S. Wheat', *New York Times*, 31 May 2013.

Sheehan, M. and Mao, J. (2014), 'How Chinese Milk Smugglers Are Fueling Hong Kong Protests', *Huffington Post*, 1 October 2014.

Shove, E. and Southerton, D. (2000), 'Defrosting the Freezer: From Novelty to Convenience', *Journal of Material Culture*, 5(3): 301–19.

Silbergeld, E., Graham, J. and Price, L. (2008), 'Industrial Food Animal Production, Antimicrobial Resistance, and Human Health', *Annual Review of Public Health* 29: 151–69.

Smith, M. D., Asche, F., Guttormsen, A. G. and Wiener, J. B. (2010), 'Genetically Modified Salmon and Full Impact Assessment', *Science*, 330: 1052–3.

Smith, W. R. (1899), *Lectures on the Religion of the Semites*, New York: Appleton.

Sobo, E. (1997), 'The Sweetness of Fat', in C. Counihan and P. Van Esterik (eds), *Food and Culture: A Reader*, 256–71, New York: Routledge.

Staples, J. (forthcoming), 'Beef and Beyond: Exploring the Meat Consumption Practices of Christians in India', *Ethnos*.

Staples, J. and Klein, J. A. (eds) (forthcoming), 'Special Issue: Consumer and Consumed: Humans and Animals in Globalising Food Systems', *Ethnos*.

Stone, G. D. (2002), 'Both Sides Now: Fallacies in the Genetic-Modifications Wars, Implications for Developing Countries, and Anthropological Perspectives', *Current Anthropology*, 43(4): 611–30.

Striffler, S. (2005), *Chicken: The Dangerous Transformation of America's Favorite Food*, New Haven, CT: Yale University Press.

Striffler, S. and Moberg, M. (eds) (2003), *Banana Wars: Power, Production, and History in the Americas*, Durham, NC: Duke University Press.

Strom, S. (2013a), 'Major Grocer to Label Foods with Gene-Modified Content', *New York Times*, 8 March 2013.

Strom, S. (2013b), 'Report on U.S. Meat Sounds Alarm on Resistant Bacteria', *New York Times*, 16 April 2013.

Strom, S. (2015), 'Chipotle To Stop Serving Genetically Altered Food', *New York Times*, 26 April 2015.

Sumner, D. A. (2014), 'American Farms Keep Growing: Size, Productivity, and Policy', *Journal of Economic Perspectives*, 28(1): 147–66.

Sun, C. (2015), 'Dog Meat Restaurant in Guangzhou Closes amid "Falling Demand"', *South China Morning Post*, 18 May 2015.

Sutton, D. and Beriss, D. (2015), 'Teaching Restaurants', in C. L. Swift and R. Wilk (eds), *Teaching Food and Culture*, 147–67, Walnut Creek, CA: Left Coast Press.

Thu, K. M. and Durrenberger, E. P. (eds) (1998), *Pigs, Profits, and Rural Communities*, Albany: State University of New York Press.

Tierney, R. K. and Ohnuki-Tierney, E. (2012), 'The Anthropology of Food', in J. M. Pilcher (ed.), *The Oxford Handbook of Food History*, 117–34, Oxford: Oxford University Press.

Tracy, M. (2010), 'The Mutability of Melamine: A Transductive Account of a Scandal', *Anthropology Today*, 26(6): 4–8.

Ulijaszek, S. (2007), 'Bioculturalism', in D. Parkin and S. Ulijaszek (eds), *Holistic Anthropology: Emergence and Convergence*, 21–51, New York: Berghahn Books.

Veeck, A., Yu, H. and Burns, A. C. (2010), 'Consumer Risks and New Food Systems in Urban China', *Journal of Macromarketing*, 30(3): 222–37.

Vegan Future (2007), 'The Vegan Future, Interview with Matt Ball', Veganoutreach.org.

Visser, O., Mamonova, N. and Spoor, M. (2012), 'Oligarchs, Megafarms and Land Reserves: Understanding Land Grabbing in Russia', *Journal of Peasant Studies*, 39(3–4): 899–931.

Vogeler, I. (ed.) (1982), *The Myth of the Family Farm: Agribusiness Dominance in U. S. Agriculture*, Boulder, CO: Westview Press.

Watson, J. L. (ed.) (2006a), *Golden Arches East: McDonald's in East Asia*, 2nd edn,
    Stanford, CA: Stanford University Press.

Watson, J. L. (2006b), 'Update: McDonald's as Political Target: Globalization and Anti-
    Globalization in the Twenty-First Century', in J. L. Watson (ed.), *Golden Arches East:*
    McDonald's in East Asia, 2nd edn, 183–97, Stanford, CA: Stanford University Press.

Watson, J. L. (2006c), 'SARS and the Consequences for Globalization', in A. Kleinman
    and J. L. Watson (eds), *SARS in China: Prelude to Pandemic?*, 196–202, Stanford, CA:
    Stanford University Press.

Watson, J. L. (2011), 'Feeding the Revolution: Public Mess Halls and Coercive
    Commensality in Maoist China', in E. Zhang, A. Kleinman and Tu Weiming (eds),
    Governance of Life in Chinese Moral Experience: The Quest for an Adequate Life,
    33–46, London: Routledge.

Watson, J. L. (2014), 'Meat: A Cultural Biography in (South) China', in J. A. Klein and
    A. Murcott (eds), *Food Consumption in Global Perspective: Essays in the Anthropology*
    of Food in Honour of Jack Goody, 25–44, Basingstoke: Palgrave Macmillan.

Watson, J. L. and Caldwell, M. L. (eds) (2005), *The Cultural Politics of Food and Eating*,
    Malden, MA: Blackwell Publishing.

Weis, T. (2013), 'The Meat of the Global Food Crisis', *Journal of Peasant Studies*, 40(1):
    65–85.

Weismantel, M. J. (1988), *Food, Gender, and Poverty in the Ecuadorean Andes*,
    Philadelphia: University of Pennsylvania Press.

West, H. G. (2013), 'Appellations and Indications of Origin, *Terroir*, and the Social
    Construction and Contestation of Place-Named Foods', in A. Murcott, W. Belasco
    and P. Jackson (eds), *The Handbook of Food Research*, 209–28, London: Bloomsbury
    Academic.

Williams, N. (2003), 'Death of Dolly Marks Cloning Milestone', *Current Biology*, 13(6):
    R209–10.

Wiley, A. S. (2015), 'Just Milk? Nutritional Anthropology and the Single-Food Approach',
    in C. L. Swift and R. Wilk (eds), *Teaching Food and Culture*, 77–95, Walnut Creek,
    CA: Left Coast Press.

Wilk, R. (1999), '"Real Belizean Food": Building Local Identity in the Transnational
    Caribbean', *American Anthropologist*, 101(2): 244–55.

Wilk, R. (2006), *Home Cooking in the Global Village: Caribbean Food from Buccaneers to*
    Ecotourists, Oxford: Berg.

Wines, M. (2014), 'Invader Batters Rural America, Shrugging Off Herbicides', *New York*
    Times, 11 August 2014.

Wissler, C. (1926), *The Relation of Nature to Man in Aboriginal America*, New York:
    Oxford University Press.

Wong, E. (2013), 'Rice Tainted with Cadmium is Discovered in Southern China',
    New York Times, 21 May 2013.

Wong, E. (2014), 'One-Fifth of China's Farmland is Polluted, State Study Finds',
    New York Times, 17 April 2014.

Xiu, C. and Klein, K. K. (2010), 'Melamine in Milk Products in China: Examining the
    Factors that Led to Deliberate Use of the Contaminant', *Food Policy*, 35: 463–70.

Yan, Y. (2002), 'Unbalanced Reciprocity: Asymmetrical Gift Giving and Social Hierarchy in Rural China', in M. Osteen (ed.), *The Question of the Gift*, 67–84, London: Routledge.

Yan, Y. (2005), 'Of Hamburger and Social Space: Consuming McDonald's in Beijing', in J. L. Watson and M. L. Caldwell (eds), *The Cultural Politics of Food and Eating*, 80–103, Malden, MA: Blackwell Publishing.

Yan, Y. (2012), 'Food Safety and Social Risk in Contemporary China', *Journal of Asian Studies*, 71(3): 705–29.

Yates-Doerr, E. (2012), 'Meeting the Demand for Meat?' *Anthropology Today*, 28(1): 11–15.

Yates-Doerr, E. (2015), *The Weight of Obesity: Hunger and Global Health in Postwar Guatemala*, Berkeley: University of California Press.

Yates-Doerr, E. and Mol, A. (2012), 'Cuts of Meat: Disentangling Western Natures-Cultures', *Cambridge Anthropology*, 30(2): 48–64.

Zhan, M. (2008), 'Wild Consumption: Relocating Responsibilities in the Time of SARS', in L. Zhang and A. Ong (eds), *Privatizing China: Socialism from Afar*, Ithaca, NY: Cornell University Press.

Zhang, J. (2014), *Puer Tea: Ancient Caravans and Urban Chic*, Seattle: University of Washington Press.

Zhang, Q. F. and Donaldson, J. A. (2008), 'The Rise of Agrarian Capitalism with Chinese Characteristics: Agricultural Modernization, Agribusiness and Collective Land Rights', *The China Journal*, 60: 25–47.

PART ONE

Food, Self and Other

CHAPTER ONE

Culinary Stereotypes: The Gustatory Politics of Gastro-Essentialism

MICHAEL HERZFELD

Stereotypes often focus on food habits. Indians eat curry, we are told; the French consume enormous quantities of red wine and smelly cheese; Americans are known in the rest of the world as the ultimate consumers of fast foods. These are examples of what I propose here to call *gastro-essentialism*. This phenomenon, like all forms of essentialism, is an attempt to deny the changes that time brings in its train – to claim an eternal authenticity for what, historically speaking, is but a single rendition of a variable set of practices.

FOOD AND STEREOTYPING: ANALYTICAL ISSUES

The stereotypes themselves are liable to change. As stereotypes harden under conditions of conflict, the attributions that are associated with them also change. Thus, during a period of tense Franco-American relations over the Iraq war, 'French fries' became 'freedom fries', a brief retrogression reminiscent of similar steps during the First World War when hamburgers and frankfurters were similarly renamed. Despite this long and obvious association, and despite the turn since the 1990s towards ethnographies 'of the senses' (e.g., Classen 1993; Howes 1991; Seremetakis 1996), some of it oriented to the learning of taste associations in early life (notably Seremetakis 1993), there seems to have been relatively little in the way of a sustained attempt to explore the role of taste and odour in the social life of stereotypes (but see Classen, Howes and Synnott 1994; Stoller 1989).

The relative absence of accounts of the linkage between cooking and stereotyping is especially strange because ideas about food pervade a huge variety of stereotypes – class, ethnic, national, gender-based, religious and many more.[1] This is clear from the widespread discussion of gastronomic 'authenticity' by both its aficionados and its critics. Cutting across the basic categories of stereotype, there are two idioms of their use in social relations that especially concern us here. On the one hand, entire groups can be metonymically represented by what are assumed to be their preferred foods

and food-related habits: all Frenchman and Italians like garlic, English food is stodgy
and tasteless, Russians drink enormous quantities of vodka, men like meat and women
like salads. Some of the stereotypes are of obvious political inspiration. There is a
Greek ditty, popular in the years after the Second World War, that says, 'The English
and the French [or: Germans] are potato eaters; Italians are spaghetti-eaters; Greeks
are brave men!'[2] Class stereotypes also take on a teleological cast, as when Romans,
many of whom still affect a working-class identity even when they have improved
their economic situation, insist that the Roman predilection for offal sprang from the
Papal authorities' monopoly of the best meat cuts for their own personal enjoyment.

Like all stereotypes, these assumptions about what entire groups of people eat take
an element of reality and blow it vastly out of proportion. On the other hand, however,
the consumers of food themselves have stereotypes about the rules for the preparation
of their national or regional dishes. The Italian disapproval of drinking milky coffee
in the afternoon, or of mixing garlic and cheese in the same dish, exemplifies this kind
of stereotype. (Some of the alleged rules are themselves products of stereotyping, as in
the case of the apparently apocryphal American claim that Italian cooks test whether
the pasta is sufficiently *al dente*, or chewy, by throwing it at the wall and seeing
whether it sticks – and rejecting it when it does not.) Stereotypical representations
of 'our own' food preferences and eating habits are useful for identifying strangers
and for expressing exasperation or even disgust at their culinary obtuseness. Roman
waiters complain bitterly, for example, about American customers who demand that
their pasta be cooked for longer than it is for local customers, protesting that they
are being asked to turn good Italian pasta into 'mud' (*fango*). Those claims might
superficially seem amusing, but the phrase 'good Italian pasta' echoes the words of
the far-right former mayor of Rome Gianni Alemanno, who appealed to growing
anti-immigrant sentiment by arguing that immigrant children were not to be served
'ethnic' food in Roman schools but were instead to be treated to a diet that might,
perhaps, transform them into true Romans themselves.[3]

Stereotypes are the basis of discrimination. Foreigners may be challenged to eat
foods that are known to contravene their ideas of acceptability. In Italy, in certain
areas a cheese that is wriggling with live worms (and known appropriately as
formaggio ai vermi, cheese with worms) may be offered as a test to visitors; the
proverbial sheep's eye functions in this way in pastoral societies throughout the
Balkans and the Middle East; and raw meat or fish is often used in this way as
well. A distinguished French anthropologist once invited me to dinner, saying that
he would cook some beef and asking how I liked to eat it; when I told him that
I preferred it *bleu*, he reacted with some astonishment, saying, 'But you are English!'
When the dinner had materialized and a delicious joint had rapidly shrunk under
our hungry depredations, he asked me as I was taking my leave, 'Do you know
what you have eaten? It was horse!' Apparently even an anthropologist is not proof
against stereotyping, and he was evidently quite taken aback by my calm response
that the meal had indeed been delicious![4]

Instead of simply listing the features of stereotypes and then condemning them as
false, which has long been the dominant perspective, we should pay close attention

to the ways, contexts and idioms in which they are used. As I have argued elsewhere (Herzfeld 2005: 201–9), some stereotyping characterizes all social relations. By examining this phenomenon as a social process instead of pre-emptively condemning it as a moral error, we will understand more fully how prejudice itself works, but also how people of different cultural backgrounds initiate the exploration of each other's worlds. Nowhere is this more apparent than in culinary encounters. And those encounters do often begin with expressions of surprise and even horror. When I was a schoolboy, one of the girls in my class fell sick; my mother brought her and her sister home with me to await their mother and prepared supper, asking whether the sister liked spaghetti. Responding to that young lady's enthusiastic affirmation, my mother, who had grown up in Germany and had travelled extensively in Italy, prepared a dish of Italian-style spaghetti, only to be astonished at the girl's horrified realization that what she was expected to eat was not a plate of canned Heinz spaghetti![5] Such experiences have continued all my life. When I first went to an anthropology conference in the United States, my American room-mate and I came down, in a large hotel in Houston, to a buffet breakfast styled as 'English'. But the staff could not understand why I wanted hot mustard for breakfast, and nor could my friend, whereas I was horrified that he was pouring maple syrup onto the same plate on which he had sausages and bacon. We are still good friends; gastronomic disgust is not always fatal to social relations. But although we had known each other as fellow graduate students in Greece, it was not until we were sharing a context closer to his own cultural setting that we, as anthropologists, were confronted with our own culinary prejudices.

These relatively minor encounters illustrate the flexibility of cultural assumptions about what food habits mean. They remind us of the importance of focusing – ethnographically, even in such everyday experiences of our own – on practice rather than on the rules alone. Structural arguments, appealing though they often are (see, e.g., Douglas 1966; Goody 1982), fail to account for such individual variation. People learn the rules of their cultures and often adopt the food prejudices of their close relatives because these prejudices, buttressed on occasion by pseudo-medical arguments, are confirmed by the vast majority of others they meet in the course of their everyday lives. But the prejudices themselves, although they may seem to conform to notions of unchanging tradition, do vary over time, individual predilection and social context.

Stereotypes are about form; and form – whether of appearance, smell or taste – is central to culinary rule-making. Social interaction entails a constant play with form – the *inventive* 'de-formation' of social *convention* that I call 'social poetics'.[6] Everyone has a stake: those who cook, those who consume, those who merely comment. If we examine 'gastro-politics' (Appadurai 1981) from this dynamic perspective, we find that the rules themselves become the focus of the negotiation of ideas, not only about food, but also about the people involved in the interaction. This also harmonizes with Watson's (2006) critique of models of globalization – exemplified in discussions of McDonald's worldwide – that superficially accept the homogeneity of form instead of examining the uses to which form is put.

STEREOTYPES AND HISTORY

The two varieties of stereotype that I have suggested here – the representation of the Other in standardized terms and the insistence on adherence to one's own 'authentic' rules – come together in moments of conflict and forced contrast. This convergence should alert us to the fact that all stereotypes also represent the complex effects of historical processes of encounter. Each group insists on adherence to its alleged cultural rules with a rigidity that often does not apply in the intimate cultural spaces of its own everyday life, and does not seem to inhibit their capacity for disrespecting the rules of others. In the film *Big Night*, in which two Italian brothers attempt to open a restaurant in an American city, the American who demands 'spaghetti with meatballs' violates a rule – itself more idealized than realized – that pasta should not be served on one plate with large pieces of meat or fish, and serves to dramatize the mutual incomprehension of the hilariously stereotypical representatives of the two cultures, the brash American customer and the histrionic Italian chef. We could consider the culinary obstinacy of each of these two men as a metonym of his larger cultural identity, an identity that in turn has acquired its stereotypical form through cultural and social conflicts of often considerable duration.

Both kinds of stereotype must therefore be examined in their historical contexts. They represent the sedimentation of attitudes that are often of great age, although they do also change over long (and sometimes brief) periods of time. A good example of such a change in the material dimensions of culinary stereotypes is the way Thai food has come to be regarded as dominated by variants of the chilli pepper. It is clear that this is the source of its searing heat today, but the origins of the Thai use of chilli, a New World vegetable, lie in the activities of Portuguese and perhaps Iranian merchants soon after the European voyages of discovery; it is not by mere chance that what Thais call 'Thai pepper' (*prik thai*) today is actually the same black pepper that is also consumed in Europe, and that plays a relatively minor role in the symphony of taste sensations that characterizes modern Thai cooking. Few foreigners are aware of this surprising fact, believing instead that the authenticity of Thai food depends specifically on the presence of powerful chillies. In China, much the same can be said of the distinctive Sichuan cuisine (*Chuancai*).

Sugar, too, has a specific history that has shaped both its uses and the attitudes that it evinces. Mintz's magisterial *Sweetness and Power* (1985) has shown how the provision and consumption of sugar became a mark of political control and authority, in part because it established itself as a necessity among the poorer social classes as well. Spices, too, were clearly the object of considerable political clout, if only because the long distances they had to be transported in order to be available to the emergent colonial masters in Europe guaranteed both prestige and high expense.[7] These associations are filtered through a wide variety of different cultural ideologies. In societies where women's power appears to be enormously circumscribed, for example, sweetness is associated – in both literal (dietary) and metaphorical terms – with the female sex and with femininity.[8] The ability to consume extremely spicy food, while commonly associated with masculinity, is also viewed in some cultural contexts in Thailand and elsewhere as a mark of working-class taste and even of uncouthness.

At first sight, these facts – and they are also very *common* facts – would seem to be irremediably paradoxical. That, however, is only true if we view the associations of different tastes on a single plane, rather than multi-dimensionally. An important index of the complexity of the politics of gustation lies in the rhetorics of bodily self-control found in various cultural settings. As someone who has worked in one place (Greece) where most people express deep distaste for very spicy food, and in another (Thailand) where, on the contrary, the capacity to eat food at an extreme of spiciness is seen as a mark of being *kaeng* (excellent at doing something, and especially something that is seen as a cultural norm), I have long been intrigued by such variations in the interplay of sweetness and hot spice, as well as by the clear evidence that, whatever the prevailing norms in each setting, there is also a considerable degree of individual variation internally.[9]

It is important to recognize this variation, because in most culinary stereotypes it is hidden behind generalizations such as the statement that all Thais like hot food. I personally know Greeks who revel in spicy foods (although admittedly they are in a small minority) and Thais who cannot stomach them (perhaps a higher proportion, for reasons that will appear shortly). The interest of such statements, however, lies less in their inaccuracy than in their popularity. Why does it matter that some clusters defined by culture, social class or gender exhibit this or that gustatory preference?

We can embark on our exploration of this question with Mary Douglas's (1966) well-known definition of dirt, or symbolic pollution, as 'matter out of place'. Culinary stereotypes, no less than other similarly over-generalized attributes, feed both solidarity and prejudice. Solidarity is not simply a matter of commensality, important though it also is to experience 'breaking bread' together; it entails acknowledging shared food preferences in a more generic sense – a gustatory equivalent, as it were, of Anderson's (1983) notion of the 'imagined community' of a nation. People do not only share food; they share ideas *about* food. Conversely, those who do not accept such conventions are regarded with some nervousness.

Individuals have no way of knowing how others actually experience a taste, which is a psychological inner state akin to belief (see Needham 1972), but that does not prevent them from pontificating about what the correct taste of a wine or cheese should be. Indeed, the actual content of such pronouncements may count for less than the fact that one knows how to make them sound authoritative. The rhetoric of shared taste standards, especially in its most dramatic incarnation – the sometimes mysteriously descriptive language of wine aficionados – provides a form of the 'phatic communion' that Malinowski (1936: 314–316) recognized as essential to establishing a sense of common social ground. It may be reinforced by body posture and gesture, which, being non-linguistic,[10] reinforces phatic communion by creating a sense of familiarity and comfort; in the form of table manners, gesture may signal a foreigner's willingness to abide by local rules of commensality and standards of taste.[11]

Since eating is both a social and a personal activity, it provides a sensitive arena for judging who belongs and who does not. Being able to talk knowledgeably about food and drink is one major criterion on which that discrimination turns, at least in European and European-derived societies. The performance of expertise articulates a right to be at the table. But there are other, perhaps less obtrusive and less self-aware ways of gaining access to the convivial circle. Success and failure in the largely unconscious adaptation to local bodily habits generally determines the local degree of willingness to engage the ethnographer as an insider (Herzfeld 2009; cf. Kondo 1990: 11–26). Eating and serving conventions are but one part of this gestural context; their correct adoption is particularly important because, like the language of gastronomic and oenological knowledge, it legitimates implicit claims of entitlement to expertise in specific cuisines – even while it may distinguish the foreigner, who is too careful to 'get it right', from the productively insouciant insider.[12]

This last point requires a brief explanation, which is best provided by means of an example. To a member of the English upper classes, a visitor's failure to eat peas on the top of the tines of the fork demonstrates a lamentable lack of skill – of a bodily skill that expresses and instantiates what is fundamentally more important, a social skill. But among others of similar class background, our snobbish Englishman may almost make a point of shovelling peas into his mouth as if the public convention had not existed. The spaces of cultural intimacy permit many such socially poetic violations of established convention; but they must be performed in a way that demonstrates what the others present already know – that the individual in question would behave properly in a more public venue (or, by not doing so, might be indicating his disdain for lesser beings). In that intimate setting, such apparent misdemeanours reinforce rather than undermine the claim of class membership.

In a society that likes to imagine itself as classless, this principle is reversed. In Greece, it is a common and – for obvious reasons – male axiom that three things should be consumed with the hands: chicken, fish and women. This is consistent with the common Greek insistence that formal manners are a sign of insincerity, which is regarded as an un-Greek characteristic. Perhaps a similar, culturally intimate logic informs the ordinance of Gainesville, Georgia, where it is allegedly illegal to eat chicken except with the hands.[13] Since Greece joined the European Union, and at a time when class differences have become vastly more visible than before the 1967 military coup, there has, in fact, been a gradual 'Europeanization' of the culinary scene. While the fight against the Brussels bureaucrats to maintain the stuffed intestine dish (*kokoretsi*) that is an Easter tradition succeeded, one no longer finds the plates (*pikilies*, literally 'varieties') of greasy little tidbits – a piece of liver, a slice of spleen, a fried shrimp, a dollop of Russian salad – that were once the tastiest food in town. But outside the privileged areas of the cities, where the wealthy can enjoy playing European at such misnamed establishments as *Cucina Povera* ('poor [people's] cuisine', in Italian!), an insistence on social equality produces a constant self-reproduction of the folksy Greek who disdains the manners and Westernized tastes of the elite. A waiter may sit down with an angry customer, treating the latter to a bottle of wine, simply to show that a good fight means that the two combatants are indeed social equals.

Such performances usually entail a measure of conviviality; they conjure up a context of equality in which all parties can be assumed to like roughly the same things. By the same token, however, objecting to an assumed collective standard of taste entails some social risk; offending against the conventions of taste and smell invites derision, or even hostility. In North America, something as simple as disliking chocolate, a moral deficiency akin to lacking a driver's license (this writer is guilty of both failings!), triggers a reaction of disbelief. That disbelief does not usually translate into hostility; the matter is too trivial. But it is the tip of an attitudinal iceberg with a much more sinister base: the exclusion of those who are different.

Exclusion can take the form of a self-justifying hostility. That is what happens when people attribute a 'bad smell' to others on the ostensible grounds that these outsiders eat different food. The prohibition of using public transport or entering a theatre within four hours of eating garlic, an edict that allegedly was on the law books of Gary, Indiana, at least until late in the twentieth century,[14] was probably an attempt to restrict the movement of migrant workers around the city. Probably a similar form of discrimination inspired a state law – in West Virginia, where people may take roadkill home for supper – that still makes it illegal to cook cabbage or sauerkraut, supposedly because of the odours these produce.[15]

Nor are such exclusions unique to Westerners.[16] Japanese people often object to Westerners' body smell on the grounds that this comes from their consumption of meat. (The recent Japanese shift to a more meat-oriented diet may have reduced that particular accusation.) Such complaints are reciprocated by equally generalized (although somewhat less uniform) complaints by Westerners about Japanese body odour.[17] Even when people are aware that their own preferred foodstuffs cause offence to others, as in the case of Thai and Hong Kong hoteliers (and in Thailand even taxi drivers) who post signs prohibiting the presence of fresh durians, the message is clear: smell divides – as, indeed, do manners, food choices and the evidence of taste in the more cerebral sense celebrated in Bourdieu's (1984) concept of class-based taste as 'distinction'.

But just *how* these senses divide people from each other is a difficult question. We cannot automatically assume that smells deemed offensive index only what is disorderly or foreign to the prevailing social order. Bubandt (1998), for example, has shown how, among the Buli of Indonesia, bad odours index the origins of the social order itself, creating anxiety and at the same time reassurance – a culturally specific understanding of what a bad odour signifies. The same holds true for food tastes; I have argued elsewhere that the palpable changeability of Thai flavours at the moment of consumption, for example, matches a pattern of political ambiguity in which authoritarian and egalitarian impulses are constantly in tension with each other (see Herzfeld 2011, 2015).

Individual odours or tastes do not have universal meanings. In the present age of global marketing, we too easily forget that superficial resemblances may mask wide semantic and semiotic divergences – precisely the point that Watson (2006) has made central to his critique of globalization theory. For that reason, the lability of terms such as 'ethnic food' should not surprise us; the superficially similar form of foods produced in global fast-food outlets masks very different local interpretations of what those foods mean to their respective sets of local consumers. High-end restaurants, although they often cultivate an aura of originality and creativity, also adhere to certain conventions, without which the discussion of their offerings could not produce the phatic communion that is unquestionably an important part of the *cachet* they enjoy. Not for nothing do we hear jokes about 'beds of wilted lettuce' and the 'amusing presumption' of a bottle of wine. These are recognizable because they crop up frequently. The most original restaurants of all could not survive without the stereotyping that these locutions imply. The extreme instantiation of this principle is the former Tel-Aviv restaurant Café Ke'ilu (roughly, Café Make-Believe), where no actual food was served, but where the staffers were trained to explain what they were serving so elegantly.[18] Anthropologically speaking, they were serving up pure phatic communion – although the restaurant's eventual failure suggests that the sense of sharing did not live up to the proprietor's fond hopes for what he called 'conceptual dining'.

SPICE BOYS: THE HIDDEN DYNAMICS OF GLOBALIZED FOOD TRADITIONS

The Make-Believe Café also fits another observable pattern, albeit in an eccentric way. The explosion of 'ethnic' cuisine in the West and the proliferation of upscale Western foods in non-Western countries have clearly reinforced a global hierarchy of taste and value.[19] This hierarchy ensures that the cultural specificity on which the global hierarchy depends will not be threatened with disappearance, although there may be subtle modulations and accommodations. Lunching with a distinguished Thai politician and intellectual in an Italian restaurant in Bangkok, for example, I was not surprised by his preference for *penne all'arrabbiata*, a pasta dish laced with dried chilli, because, as he himself remarked, he liked its spiciness. Indeed, in a country where food is typically very spicy but where spiciness itself is seen by many as marking lower-class taste, an Italian restaurant – a prestigious establishment – offered a subtle compromise.

For a Thai, such spiciness is not particularly associated with 'anger' (*rabbia*), as it is, at least in a literal sense, for Italians.[20] For those who (unlike my lunch companion) identify themselves as Buddhists, however, it is nevertheless inconsistent with religious precepts enjoining the avoidance of sensual excitement, which is what foreign visitors and indeed most Thais seem to associate with typically Thai flavours. The difference is that, for the Thais, this apparent disobedience reflects the pragmatics of social life, an accommodation to the reality that flawed human beings still enjoy exciting sensations and conviviality and are not yet ready for the complete annihilation of the senses in Nirvana (see Herzfeld 2011, 2015), whereas for foreigners visiting the country, the spicy food – insofar as they feel able to eat it – is part of the exotic experience they feel it is legitimate to crave and indeed is a large part of what they were seeking when they arrived.

Italian restaurants in the United States are the borderline between ethnic and 'high' cuisine, straddling a border that conceptually reproduces the division between north and south in Italy itself; 'northern Italian cuisine' is considered 'high', whereas southern Italian food is usually treated as its humble, street-food compatriot. The hybrid 'ethnic cuisine' has come to reflect a measure of political correctness in the past two decades, but, in the past, 'ethnic' unambiguously signified a 'lower' class of cooking. That discrimination, interestingly, is still strong in Italy, especially among supporters of the political right wing who argue that 'ethnic restaurants' should be banned from traditional city centres because they undermine the promotion of the national or regional heritage.[21]

The fear that 'ethnic' restaurants might change the 'centuries-old culinary traditions' (to quote a newspaper article on Forte dei Marmi, cited in note 21, above) is not without foundation – because the very idea of a centuries-old tradition is an example of the prejudicial 'allochronism', the banishing of the exotic other to a different time, that Fabian (1983) has criticized in anthropological writing itself and that is a commonplace of the exoticism we encounter in much journalism as well. Food practices do change precisely because they are practices, not sets of rules written in stone. This is where a social poetics can help us link the incremental changes that occur as one cook gives instruction to another (see Sutton 2001), linking memory-talk to present habits and possible changes, to those more substantial shifts that we can discern over the *longue durée*.

Negotiating food during fieldwork offers a useful point of entry into this process. When I did fieldwork in a pastoralists' village high in the mountains of west-central Crete in the 1970s, the main staple was huge amounts of cold or lukewarm boiled mutton, seasoned, if at all, with salt and a bit of black pepper. But this food was the object of great adulation, because the shepherds were also animal rustlers, and, if one boils a stolen sheep instead of roasting it, the thief is less likely to get caught because there would be much less smoke. Speed, rather than gustatory ornament, was the general rule; there was nothing to indicate that anyone in the village had the slightest interest in spice.

And yet my wife and I had in our possession some curry powder, which we used to disguise the less attractive tastes that came with local meat on occasion, when we were cooking at home. We also used it to produce a passable version of Hong Kong's famous Singapore Rice Sticks (except that we did it with Greek spaghetti[22]). The women in the village would have nothing to do with what to them clearly smelled more like a dangerous poison than a meal.

The men, on the other hand, were anxious to try it – and showed every sign of enjoying it hugely. They referred to the curry as our 'pepper' (*piperi*) and, years later, recalled with amusement how they had shown they could handle it. These men are formidably tough. They carry knives and guns, and use them – on one recent occasion they shot down a police helicopter that was showing too much interest in their activities. But clearly it was the advent of curry that meant, for some of them at least, that the acme of manhood had now been discovered, thanks to us (and no matter that my wife, whom they evidently regarded as a delightful eccentric, would eat it as happily as any man). In a village where women also drank sweet liqueurs but rarely touched the real firewater (see also Cowan 1990: 87), the pattern was clearly established before our Indian curry powder reached their noses and gave them a new arena for their displays of gastro-masculinity. And they welcomed it with, as it were, open mouths.

Now this curry was not, by Indian standards, particularly hot. To these Cretan shepherds, it was highly exotic, and that meant that tackling it was already sufficient adventure. Yet I think some of them found it very hot indeed. These Cretan shepherds shared with American males, especially with those of the more stereotypically tough Texan or Appalachian varieties, an obsession with the eating of meat. They had their own tests of masculinity; among themselves, prowess at stealing sheep was the truest mark of male valor (Herzfeld 1985). Another important test of masculinity, even if it was not actually carried out very often by the time I came to live in the village, included eating the dense white fat (*knisari*) that encloses an animal's kidneys – and eating it raw. So spice was not the only food-based test of masculinity by any means. But the idea of eating high spice in a form created in a completely different part of the world does seem to have appeared to them, with suggestive immediacy, as the ideal mode of demonstrative maleness. American men, on the other hand, even many Texans, would almost certainly baulk at eating any part of an animal raw; steak tartare is not an American favourite. But they delight in hot sauces – Louisiana has made a fortune out of this proclivity – and, faced with an Indian or Thai restaurant, are likely to tell the waitstaff that they want their food as hot as it could be made.

This is where we can see even more clearly that spiciness and its significance are not stable signs. I have heard from staff members of Indian and Thai restaurants in the United States that they experience a great deal of trouble with young American men who come swaggering in and demand the hottest food in the house. If they get what they asked for, they often become angry and abusive, claiming that no one could eat such food. And so the restaurateurs have learned to pursue a policy of discretion: they verbally accede to these young men's demands, but serve them food that, by the standards of the national cuisine in question, is in fact deliberately rather mild. In this way, the customers' concern with masculinity paradoxically creates a space for reducing the level of spiciness through performances of cultural incomprehension, incredulity and even affront. Those of us who genuinely 'like it hot' often, as a result, have to deal with a deep reluctance on the part of waitstaff to serve up food that really does meet our expectations.

In my own case this has sometimes required a good deal of patience. In Thai restaurants, where I am able to order in Thai, the reaction can vary. If the waiter produces a menu written in Thai – it is not uncommon for Chinese and Thai restaurants to operate parallel and partly different menus – the problem is quickly resolved: if you can read Thai, so the implicit logic goes, you can probably eat real Thai food too. But there are frequently situations in which even speaking Thai does not do the trick – not, at least, until one has returned after the initial visit and asked for the food to be made spicier than on that earlier occasion. That seems to be a good way to establish oneself as a regular customer with known and perhaps unusual tastes. Only on one occasion that I can recall did something rather different occur. On that occasion, a Thai waitress took down my order and then asked how spicy I wanted the food to be. I told her; she asked, 'You mean Thai style (*baep thai*)?' 'What language are we speaking?' I joked back. At this, she lit up, and went to place the order. When the food came, it was both ambrosial and ferocious. And when the bill arrived at the end of the meal, I saw why: 'Thai people (*khon thai*)', the waitress had written on the order, thereby confirming my suspicion that a double standard was in operation, albeit one that with a bit of luck one might be able to breach.

Most of the time, however, the difficulty of persuading Thai restaurants abroad to serve genuinely spicy food seems to be reinforced by two things. On the one hand, there is the experience of dealing with infuriated males that I have just described. On the other there is the global hierarchy of value, already mentioned, in which the assumptions that Asian restaurateurs in Western countries make about Western capacities – assumptions that may well be justified by the reactions they register – converge with the persistent idea that spicy food reflects working-class taste and is inconsistent with, in particular, Buddhist values enjoining the avoidance of physical excitement. If Western gastronomies generally avoid heavy spice altogether, the emergence of a strong bourgeoisie in countries like Thailand has produced a somewhat similar discomfort with heavily spiced food. Some who share this perspective prefer to cite local religious values, but there is also a sense of emulating an idealized West as a place where subtlety rather than ferocity marks the height of gastronomic achievement; and this either produces or reinforces the development of a parallel class structure, in which emulation of the West provides the degrees of achievement. In the Thai case, this is a well-documented process that began in earnest with the pursuit of being *siwilai*, civilized, in the reign of Rama V Chulalongkorn (Thongchai 2000), and results in a very carefully tamed rendition of Thai food for both tourist consumption in Thailand and the presentation and content of what is served as Thai food abroad.

Thus, in one encounter in a Thai restaurant in Paris, I had suggested to the owner and (as far as I could see) sole waitperson that, since some of the group I was with might not share my taste for strong Thai food, he might want to provide us with some *phrik nam plaa* (fish sauce laced with bird's eye chillies) for those who did. He agreed, pleasantly enough; the conversation was in Thai. When the food had mostly arrived but the sauce (after three attempts to remind him) had not, I very politely asked him one more time; he immediately became very hostile, probably because he felt his competence had been called into question, and pointed by said in English that patience was important in Thai culture! That this sneering reaction was a violation of both Thai ideals of *marayaat* (etiquette) and Anglo-Saxon (and French) good manners was less relevant, I suggest, than the probability that what we saw here was an illustration of the same principle that, in my view, guides the Thai table manners: a system that ostensibly represents 'Thainess' (the rule that one does not put one's fork in the mouth) but does so in a manner that both claim a Western standard of being civilized (by replacing the use of hands with Western-derived silverware). This system allows Thais to reciprocate the disdain that some perceive in Western attitudes towards them.

Thus, an ethnographic understanding – even an anecdotally ethnographic view – of the presentation of Thai food must include attention to the social context in which it takes place. Much of what is done in Thai restaurants conforms to what Peter Jackson has so aptly called the 'regime of images', a system that links Western bourgeois values and aesthetics to an invocation of ancient Thai values, all brought together in the respectful representation of Rama V – whose portrait indeed frequently appears in Thai restaurants both at home and abroad, and whose edict was responsible for the requisite use of fork and spoon and for the attendant rules of how to use them (which completely reverses American practice in particular). I have narrated two attempts of my own to negotiate the assumptions that are made about Westerners and spicy food, and I suggest that a comparison of the two moments (the latter was admittedly unique in my experience!) shows how emotions of irritation and resentment as well as great pleasure may variously greet foreigners' attempts to emulate what is increasingly seen as a lower-class variety of Thainess (and thus as a space of that embarrassing zone I have called 'cultural intimacy'). It is possible that the genders of the respective individuals also played a role. In a way, moreover, both responses illustrate the awkwardness that comes with knowing that, on the one hand, one is representing one's country abroad but, on the other hand, doing so under debatable premises – since surely one must be aware of the chasm that separates what is served up from what one eats at home. When pressed, a Thai restaurateur can refuse to speak Thai, with a logic not unlike the common Greek observation that the Greek language is too difficult for foreigners: if you get too close, we may have to exclude you. The sweetness of much Thai food served in North America and Europe, which surpasses the already increased use of sugar in more bourgeois establishments in Thailand, might signify – in an interesting variant of Sidney Mintz's argument – a shift in the balance of power, but one that is still accompanied by great uncertainty and therefore by a sense of awkwardness that sometimes creates real discomfort.

Whether Western global power is waning or not, the old assumptions that equated Westernness with superior values are no doubt now more under attack than ever. But countries that were never formally under the colonial yoke – and therefore cannot play the post-colonial card without risking derision – are still stuck with those old standards. Interestingly enough, Thailand and Greece both belong to that category. And both, although in very different ways, have flirted with Western ideas about cuisine that reflect both bourgeois and, concomitantly, international aspirations.

For the Greeks, as for some other Europeans, Thai food is still an exotic rarity. It is thus presented with a caution that makes its doubly bourgeois character all too evident. It suits both the Thai bourgeois predilection for sweetness and the Greek aversion to heavily spiced food. The only Thai meal I ever ate in Greece was served in a wealthy Athens suburb by an entirely Filipino staff; it was bland, sweet, and yet vaguely recognizable as 'Thai', a worthy exemplar of a cultural trend that, under Thaksin Shinawatra's government, actually became a form of cultural ambassadorship overseas.[23] The regime that took power in a military coup in January 2014, and that has subjected recalcitrant citizens to something it euphemistically calls 'attitude adjustment', is clearly keen on managing not only hearts and minds but also stomachs: engaging on a campaign of what we might call culinary absolutism, it has developed a robot that allegedly can tell if the Thai food served in a foreign-based restaurant is authentic or not, and gives a percentage mark to indicate the degree of success. On the other hand, I was also recently served a reasonably well-spiced meal in an upscale restaurant in Bangkok, a cooking school specializing in Thai food, by a Filipino waitress who was deeply embarrassed to admit that she did not speak any Thai. She had, however, learned to describe the dishes in perfect English. Migration creates new global circumstances in which gastro-essentialism, analytically unsustainable though I hope to have shown it to be, is rapidly gaining rhetorical ground.

WHITHER GASTRO-ESSENTIALISM?

The ethnographic questions that these examples raise require further 'inquisitive observation' (Bestor 2003: 41–2, 317) and, without question, further forays into restaurants around the world. In addition to trying the food, the fieldwork entails listening to conversations and analysing what actually goes into the phatic communion these conversations create. Discussions can also be quite contentious. For example, Thais often emphasize, especially in reaction to foreign commentary, that Thai food is not exclusively spicy; its currently distinctive feature is a wide range of tastes, often blended together in complex harmonies. Such statements are themselves a micro-political arena, prompting questions about the status implications of spiciness, complexity and sweetness.

What actually does get noticed about a particular cuisine is the pivotal element in the dynamics I have been discussing here. Ethnographic research that focused entirely on the reception of different food traditions would doubtless reveal endless variations on this theme of variability. But an accumulation of examples would not in itself provide much insight. What is the theoretical benefit that we seek?

By refocusing attention on the practices, not only of food consumption and production, but also of food talk and the phatic communion through which it permits the sensation of shared cultural identity, we can understand authenticity as a negotiable (and often usefully vague) good. Although negotiability appears to contradict the very idea of authenticity, and although conflict often appears to surround its claims, the approach from social poetics allows us to see that all these arguments over the long haul shape what people understand by authenticity in particular places and under particular cultural and political conditions. The small but incremental changes that a cook, a food reviewer or a restaurant customer introduce into the production of a particular dish are likely to have more observable effects over the long haul than the stability sought by bureaucracies (Ceccarini 2014) or even by robots. Caldwell's (2004) discussion of the Russian domestication of 'French fries' to the point where the McDonald's version had come to seem authentically Russian illustrates the point to perfection.

Gastro-essentialism is arguably a travesty of what we experience in our everyday social lives. We may (and I do!) nevertheless treat certain dishes as more or less authentic, by which we imply something about our own personal foibles and perhaps also seek to establish a claim on expertise. But even as we do so, we should be aware that such claims participate in a larger and highly durable discourse, one that is linked to larger political processes and pressures (as the robot demonstrates). Food talk presents authenticity as reassuringly stable (see Klein 2007: 514; Mintz 2001: 104) – except, to be sure, in the high-end world of fusion and other 'innovative' or 'creative' food regimes (where one might argue that the insistence on originality was itself a claim to a consistent and permanent standard). In this respect, food stereotypes follow the pattern of all other idioms of stereotyping, and similarly serve political and interactional ends. To treat food outside its contexts of consumption and discussion – restaurants, domestic settings and acts of hospitality – is to ignore its double-edged role. Food can mediate social and cultural change, even as, and precisely because, it claims to represent age-old tradition.

NOTES

1. Note my use of the gerund 'stereotyping', in place of the simple noun 'stereotypes'. This conveys the action/practice orientation that is the crux of my argument here.
2. In Greek: *Angli-Galli patatadhes, Itali makaronadhes, Ellines pallikaradhes.*
3. See, for example, Tiziana Guerrisi, 'Alemanno e il menu etnico: "Da mal di pancia ai bimbi"', *La Repubblica*, Rome section, 19 July 2008, p. 1; http://www.06blog.it/post/3339/via-il-menu-etnico-dalle-scuole-si-torna-alla-carbonara; for a petition against Alemanno's policy, see http://www.petizionionline.it/petizione/no-allabolizione-del-menu-etnico-dalle-mense-scolastiche-comunali-di-roma/2755. (Both URLs, posted in 2008, were still accessible on 16 February 2015.) This was a true tussle over the stomachs of the young.
4. Many North Americans would blanch at the Beijing restaurant that advertises, in English, 'donkey burgers'. Elsewhere in China, special restaurants serve donkey meat as a popular delicacy.
5. See also Caldwell's (2004: 17) experience of presenting a Russian four-year-old with local-style fried potatoes, which provoked a shriek of horror: 'But they're not McDonald's!'
6. For a full discussion of cultural intimacy and social poetics, see Herzfeld (2005), especially pp. 32, 46–7.
7. Helms (1988) argues that in many societies the distance goods have to travel is constitutive of their symbolic and material value.
8. Some gender inflections of the senses lead to different ways of structuring such ideas; see, for example, Bubandt's (1998: 58) discussion of the Buli (Indonesia) association of the *smell* of (menstrual) blood with women, as opposed to the *taste* of greasy foods recalling semen as a male attribute.
9. An early attempt to analyse the relationship between sweet and savoury flavours, specifically in the context of British eating habits, is Douglas (1975: 252–60).
10. Note that I avoid the popular but misleading term 'body language'.
11. On table manners as a marker of a foreigner's adaptability to local codes of conduct, see Herzfeld 2011; on the similar role of food talk, see Klein 2007: 514; Mintz 1996: 92–105.
12. I use the notion of 'productive insouciance' to relieve it of the burden of intentionality implied by Malaby's (2002: 296) extremely useful concept of 'instrumental nonchalance' – an implication that he justifies for the particular case he discusses, that of appearing with a relaxed physical posture while balancing a tray of coffee, but that for many people in other situations may not be accompanied by the self-awareness he reports for his Cretan informants. There is a parallel here with foreigners, notably in Italian contexts, who give themselves away by a too-precise adherence to the rules of syntax.
13. See http://www.ticketsarasota.com/2011/10/14/outlawed-foods-what-were-they-thinking/, last accessed 15 February 2015.

14. See http://en.metapedia.org/wiki/Garlic_%28contra%29#Laws_against_eating_garlic, last accessed 15 February 2015. According to the same source, riding on a streetcar after eating garlic is forbidden on Sundays in Toronto, while ministers cannot deliver sermons after eating garlic in Marion, Oregon.

15. See http://www.ticketsarasota.com/2011/10/14/outlawed-foods-what-were-they-thinking/, last accessed 15 February 2015.

16. I use the term 'Western' in full awareness of its limitations, but in this essay it serves to denote what Western Europeans and North Americans might reasonably claim to recognize as common cultural features.

17. See, characteristically, http://forum.gaijinpot.com/forum/living-in-japan/health-fitness/14491-do-non-japanese-stink, last accessed 15 February 2015.

18. See *The Item* (Sumter, N.C.), 17 April 1998, p. 6B, available at: http://news.google.com/newspapers?nid=1980&dat=19980417&id=GtYvAAAAIBAJ&sjid=paoFAAAAIBAJ&pg=1259,4316827, last accessed 16 February 2015.

19. On the global hierarchy of value, see, for example, Herzfeld (2005: 51–7).

20. Even in Thailand, however, the bird's eye pepper (or 'mouse shit pepper', *prik khi nu*, as it is called in Thai) is sometimes used as a metaphor for an explosive personality.

21. See, for example, http://www.telegraph.co.uk/foodanddrink/foodanddrinknews/8827721/Italian-town-bans-any-new-kebab-shops-or-other-ethnic-food.html, last accessed on 16 February 2015, on such a ban in the Tuscan towns of Forte dei Marmi and Lucca. Predictably, perhaps, this website of a British newspaper known for its conservative political views, puts a relatively positive 'spin' on the ban, which is nevertheless widely perceived in Italy as part of a concerted and racist attack on Third World immigrants. In Italy such concerns surface in the moderate leftist press as clear expressions of right-wing prejudice; see 'Lucca, stop ai ristoranti etnici – "Salvaguardare la tradizione"', *La Repubblica*, 'Cronaca', 26 January 2009.

22. Interestingly enough, in Greek, spaghetti is *makaronia*, while *lazania* means something in strips like Italian *tagliatelle* rather than the large sheets of *lasagna*. But then in the United States, the term *entrée* means 'main course' rather than 'appetizer' (its meaning in the original French)! These examples of semantic lability nicely illustrate my concluding paragraph in this essay.

23. The Thaksin government invested considerable effort in promoting Thai food abroad. On the robot, see http://www.nytimes.com/2014/09/29/world/asia/bad-thai-food-enter-a-robot-taster.html?_r=1, last accessed 16 February 2015. The robot does look like an extreme instance of the reductionism of audit culture (Strathern 2000) as it tries to control something that had hitherto been left to the judgement of individual tasters; it also implies, again, that food standards never change.

REFERENCES

Anderson, B. (1983), *Imagined Communities: Reflections on the Origins and Spread of Nationalism*, London: Verso.

Appadurai, A. (1981), 'Gastro-politics in Hindu South Asia', *American Ethnologist*, 8: 494–511.

Bestor, T. C. (2003), *Tsukiji: The Fish Market at the Center of the World*, Berkeley: University of California Press.

Bourdieu, P. (1984), *Distinction: A Social Critique of the Judgement of Taste*, translated by R. Nice, Cambridge, MA: Harvard University Press.

Bubandt, N. (1998), 'The Odour of Things: Smell and the Cultural Elaboration of Disgust in Eastern Indonesia', *Ethnos*, 63(1): 48–80.

Ceccarini, R. (2014), 'Food Bureaucracy and the Making of Authentic Pizza', in R. Cobb (ed.), *The Paradox of Authenticity in a Globalized World*, 23–34, New York: Palgrave Macmillan.

Caldwell, M. L. (2004), 'Domesticating the French Fry: McDonald's and Consumerism in Moscow', *Journal of Consumer Culture*, 41: 5–26.

Classen, C. (1993), *Worlds of Sense: Exploring the Senses in History and across Cultures*, London: Routledge.

Classen, C., Howes, D. and Synnott, A. (eds) (1994), *Aroma: The Cultural History of Smell*, London: Routledge.

Cowan, J. K. (1990), *Dance and the Body Politic in Northern Greece*, Princeton, NJ: Princeton University Press.

Douglas, M. (1966), *Purity and Danger: An Analysis of Concepts of Pollution and Taboo*, London: Routledge & Kegan Paul.

Douglas, M. (1975), *Implicit Meanings: Essays in Anthropology*, London: Routledge & Kegan Paul.

Fabian, J. (1983), *Time and the Other: How Anthropology Makes its Object*, New York: Columbia University Press.

Goody, J. (1982), *Cooking, Cuisine, and Class: A Study in Comparative Sociology*, Cambridge: Cambridge University Press.

Helms, M. W. (1988), *Ulysses' Sail: An Ethnographic Odyssey of Power, Knowledge, and Geographical Distance*, Princeton, NJ: Princeton University Press.

Herzfeld, M. (1985), *The Poetics of Manhood: Contest and Identity in a Cretan Mountain Village*, Princeton, NJ: Princeton University Press.

Herzfeld, M. (2005), *Cultural Intimacy: Social Poetics in the Nation-State*, 2nd edn, New York: Routledge.

Herzfeld, M. (2009), 'The Politics of Gesture: Reflections on the Embodiment of Ethnographic Practice', *Ethnography*, 10: 131–52.

Herzfeld, M. (2011), 'The Politics of the Thai Table: Food, Manners, Values', *Education about Asia*, 16(3): 46–8.

Herzfeld, M. (2015), 'Serving Ambiguity: Class and Classification in Thai Food at Home and Abroad', in K. O. Kim (ed.), *Re-Orienting Cuisine: East Asian Foodways in the Twenty-First Century*, 186–200, New York: Berghahn.

Howes, D. (ed.) (1991), *The Varieties of Sensory Experience*, Toronto: University of Toronto Press.

Klein, J. A. (2007), 'Redefining Cantonese Cuisine in Post-Mao Guangzhou', *Bulletin of the School of Oriental and African Studies*, 70(3): 511–37.

Kondo, D. K. (1990), *Crafting Selves: Power, Gender, and Discourses of Identity in a Japanese Workplace*, Chicago: University of Chicago Press.

Malaby, T. M. (2002), 'Odds and Ends: Risk, Mortality, and the Politics of Contingency', *Culture, Medicine, and Psychiatry*, 26(3): 283–312.

Malinowski, B. (1936), 'The Problem of Meaning in Primitive Languages', in C. K. Ogden and I. A. Richards (eds), *The Meaning of Meaning*, Supplement I: 296–336, London: Routledge.

Mintz, S. W. (1985), *Sweetness and Power: The Place of Sugar in Modern History*, New York: Viking Penguin.

Mintz, S. W. (1996), *Tasting Food, Tasting Freedom: Excursions into Eating, Culture, and the Past*, Boston, MA: Beacon Press.

Needham, R. (1972), *Belief, Language, and Experience*, Oxford: Blackwell.

Seremetakis, C. N. (1993), 'Memory of the Senses: Historical Perception, Commensal Exchange and Modernity', *Visual Anthropology Review*, 9: 2–18.

Seremetakis, C. N. (ed.) (1996), *The Senses Still: Perception and Memory as Material Culture in Modernity*, Chicago: University of Chicago Press.

Stoller, P. (1989), *The Taste of Ethnographic Things: The Senses in Anthropology*, Philadelphia: University of Pennsylvania Press.

Sutton, D. E. (2001), *Remembrance of Repasts: An Anthropology of Food and Memory*, Oxford: Berg.

Thongchai, W. (2000), 'The Quest for "Siwilai": A Geographical Discourse of Civilizational Thinking in the Late-Nineteenth-Century and Early-Twentieth-Century Siam', *Journal of Asian Studies*, 59: 528–49.

Watson, J. L. (2006), 'Introduction: Transnationalism, Localization, and Fast Foods in East Asia', in J. L. Watson (ed.), *Golden Arches East: McDonald's in East Asia*, 2nd edn, 1–38, Stanford, CA: Stanford University Press.

CHAPTER TWO

Muslim Foodways

MARIS GILLETTE

It's a warm, sunny Saturday afternoon in late August 2013, and in the San Francisco Bay area, the season's summer fairs are ongoing. Art and crafts, history, gardening, music, dance, classic cars – from Memorial Day to Labor Day, there are hundreds of festivals to choose from, as the *San Jose Mercury News* reports (http://www.mercurynews.com/ci_23300287/summer-festivals-2013-your-guide-bay-area-fairs). Today, August 17th, you're planning to visit an event in Newark, California. There's a Super Slide and rides for the kids, stalls selling jewellery, toys and clothing, jazz and vocal music performances, cooking and skateboarding demonstrations and best of all, lots of delicious food. Hot dogs, pizza, tacos, grilled corn, falafel, chicken and waffles, prawn skewers, brisket, shaved ice, cupcakes – the list goes on. When you arrive at the lot between Sears and Macy's at 2.00 pm, the place is packed. Long lines for food, traffic jams over parking, crowd of all ages and ethnicities – it's an amazing scene. Later, reading the paper, you see that 10,000 people showed up, five times more than the organizers had expected (http://www.mercurynews.com/fremont/ci_23920272/first-halal-festival-draws-crowd-10-000).

So what was this popular gathering? Halal Fest. Every food item served at the festival was halal, or permissible for Muslims to eat. As one of the organizers, Irfan Rydhan, told *Illume Media*, he got the idea for organizing a festival after seeing halal food carts and trucks in New York City (http://www.illumemagazine.com/zine/articleDetail.php?California-Muslims-Launch-the-Nation-s-First-Halal-Food-and-Eid-Festival-14446). Whether he knew it or not, Rydhan and a group of seven other self-described Muslim foodies living in California were following in the footsteps of Sameer Sarmast of New Brunswick, New Jersey, who organized what appears to be the United States' first halal food festival on 26 August 2012 (http://www.nbcbayarea.com/news/local/Californias-Halal-Food-Fest-Victim-of-Success-220199551.html, http://centerformuslimlife.org/event/first-annual-halal-food-fest/). Rydhan told the press that the organizers sought 'to promote halal food options to Muslims, people of faith and the greater community and to promote Muslim-owned businesses and nonprofits that serve the community in the area' (http://www.mercurynews.com/fremont/ci_23920272/first-halal-festival-draws-crowd-10-000). The crowds overwhelmed the festival's capacity – as one participant jokingly tweeted, '#halalfest got more Muslims together than hajj or a half off sale at the dollar store' (http://www.nbcbayarea.com/news/local/Californias-Halal-Food-Fest-Victim-of-Success-220199551.html). Those who couldn't get the food they wanted visited Muslim restaurants nearby, Rydhan noted, so the event was good for local businesses.

Newark's Halal Fest highlights key aspects of Muslim foodways. As the festival's name suggests, halal is a foundational concept for Muslim eating. Halal means 'permissible' or 'lawful' in Arabic. The Qur'an, God's revelation, is the source for what is or is not halal. Yet while the Qur'anic guidelines appear simple, Muslims around the world, and at particular historic moments, interpret them differently. Given the size and diversity of Muslim populations, the many debates over religious observance and the numerous schools of jurisprudence and interpretation, it should not be surprising that Muslims differ in how and what they eat.

Anthropologists who have studied Muslim food and eating in specific contexts convey the richness of Muslim foodways. If we compare this scholarship we see areas of widespread convergence, and can identify divergence, among Muslim populations. I add to this comparison by drawing on my ethnographic research with Muslims in three different contexts: Chinese Muslims (Hui) in the city of Xi'an, Iranian Muslims in the city of Karaj and American Muslims in the city of Philadelphia.[1] I see a few widely shared food avoidances and eating practices, as well as many differences.

As Newark's Halal Fest suggests, today's food producers, of all sizes and backgrounds, use halal as a market brand. Transnational corporations and government agencies vigorously pursue what they characterize as 'a critically important playground for marketers, with the halal segment alone worth $2.1 trillion, and growing by $500 billion annually' (Ogilvy and Mather 2010: 1). As transnational companies produce Muslim food, halal becomes partly 'delocalized' (Fischer 2011: 69). Muslims no longer rely solely on personal relations or local authorities, or on both, to determine what is halal. Over the last decade, we find Muslim food scientists and engineers using advanced food-testing techniques to categorize foods as permitted or prohibited; formal halal certification processes administered by governments and private organizations; organic, ecologically friendly and sustainable halal food movements; gourmet halal grocery stores, restaurants and food offerings; and an online world of blogs and websites on food, health and Islam. Muslim states, companies and individuals have initiated boycotts of foods considered anti-Muslim, and movements to promote consumption of foods specifically marketed as pro-Muslim.

In the early twenty-first century, most Muslims' foodways blend local ideas and practices with transnational commodities, many specifically targeted at Muslim consumers by corporations and governments eager to profit from what they consider a growing market sector. Muslims around the world adapt, adopt, reinvigorate and reaffirm their eating practices in relation to products and trends originating from various commercial, cultural and religious sites. As an Iranian Muslim businessman I know put it, halal is a living tradition.

THE QUR'AN ON FOOD AND EATING

The Qur'an instructs Muslims on core beliefs, proper living, Islam's relationship to other religions, the nature of prophecy and the afterlife. The Qur'an is God's word and God's communion with humanity (Aslan 2006: 158). Translations from Qur'anic Arabic can only be approximations.[2] For many Sunni Muslims, no other religious source, including the sayings of the Prophet Muhammad (hadith), the writings of Muslim clergy and scholars or the schools of jurisprudence that arose to interpret the Qur'an and guide religious practice, is as authoritative. For most Shia Muslims, the Prophet Muhammad's legitimate successors, the fixed number of Imams who will appear before Judgement Day, must interpret the hidden meanings of the Qur'an for the Muslim community (Aslan 2006: 181–5).

In general, the Qur'an instructs Muslims that the earth and the animals and plants growing on it are good, and enjoins Muslims to eat of the good foods that God provides (Surah 2:21–22, 2:168, 2:172, 13:2–4, 24:18–21, 24:51, 80:24–32). The Qur'an links eating good food to enjoyment, righteous works and worship (2:172, 24:51, 80:32). Only four foods are forbidden to Muslims: carrion, blood, pig flesh and food dedicated to anyone other than God (Surah 2:173, 5:3–4, 6:145). Muslims who must eat these foods to avoid starvation or by force of necessity may do so without sin (ibid.). The Qur'an does not, however, explain why these foods are prohibited.

Many Muslims also consider alcohol forbidden (haram). Pew's 2013 report, based on face-to-face interviews with 38,000 Muslims in more than 80 different languages and 39 countries, found that medians of at least 60 per cent described drinking alcohol as immoral (Pew Research Center 2013: 3–4). The Qur'an is somewhat ambiguous on this subject. For example, in Surah 16:64–67, intoxicants made from dates and grapes are included in a list of God's provisions for believers and as signs of God's greatness. In Surah 2:219, God says that there is benefit for some in wine and gambling, but for most, great sin. In Surah 5:90–91, the Qur'an states that drinking intoxicants and gambling incite enmity and hatred among the faithful, which is the work of Satan.

The Qur'an explicitly prescribes fasting for Muslims during the month of Ramadan, and encourages voluntary fasting for those who can endure it without excessive hardship (Surah 2:183–187). Fasting is for the glory of God, to help Muslims be grateful for God's gifts and to become righteous. During the month of Ramadan, Muslims must fast every day from the break of dawn until sunset. They must also be sexually abstinent during this period. Muslims who are ill or on a journey during Ramadan are excused from fasting, but are told to compensate by fasting at a later date. Based on my field research and the anthropological literature, it is a widespread, if not universal, practice among menstruating women to abstain from fasting (they should, however, make up for the missed days later). Although not explicitly stated in the Qur'an, many Muslims understand women to be impure during menstruation, as God tells men to avoid (sexual congress with) their wives when they are menstruating (Surah 2:222).

DEMOGRAPHY

According to a 2009 study, there are 1.57 billion Muslims in the world, making up 23 per cent of the global population (Pew Research Center 2009: 1). The Middle East and North Africa region has the most countries with Muslim majority populations, but, in fact, only 20 per cent of the world's Muslims live there. More than 60 per cent of Muslims live in Asia. The Pew Research Center (2009: 5) identifies the four biggest Muslim populations by country, in ranked order, as Indonesia (202,867,000 Muslims), Pakistan (174,082,000), India (160,945,000) and Bangladesh (145,312,000). Of these countries, only Pakistan is officially a Muslim state. More than 300 million Muslims live in countries where Islam is not the majority religion.

The Pew Research Center projects that the world's Muslim population will grow at twice the rate of the non-Muslim population over the next two decades (2011: 1–2). The international marketing and public relations agency Oglivy Mather predicts that more than half of the world's population will be Muslim by 2050 (2010: 2). Pakistan, Indonesia, India and Bangladesh will continue to host the largest national populations of Muslims, with Pakistan overtaking Indonesia in numbers (Pew Research Center 2011:2). The world's Muslim population will remain youthful as compared to the non-Muslim population, with a median age of thirty in 2030 (Pew Research Center 2011: 13; see also Oglivy Mather 2010: 2). Nine countries are projected to have more than 100 percentage points of growth in their Muslim populations in the next two decades (http://features.pewforum.org/muslim-population/growth.php?sort=Percent2010). Of these, eight countries are from Europe and North America.[3]

Not long after the Prophet Muhammad's death in 632 CE, the Muslim community split over who should lead the ummah.[4] Many believed that Muhammad, during his final pilgrimage to Mecca, had publicly chosen his son-in-law and cousin Ali as his successor (Aslan 2006: 112). Others believed that Abu Bakr, Muhammad's close friend and the first convert to Islam, should become the new secular leader (caliph). Aslan argues persuasively that several clans resisted Ali's succession because they did not want to see the Banu Hashim clan, to which Muhammad and Ali belonged, become more powerful (2006: 117). Ultimately, disagreements over who should lead the ummah resulted in war, Ali's assassination and the Muslim community's sectarian division between Sunni and Shia (see Aslan 2006: 114–36). Sunni and Shia Muslims accept the Qur'an as God's revelation, Muhammad as God's final prophet, and the five pillars of Islam (the profession of faith, prayer, fasting, alms-giving and the pilgrimage). However, they diverge on Ali's position in Islam, who can interpret the Qur'an, and the role that traditions about what Muhammad said or did, and what his companions said or did, should play in directing observance.[5] The very words that Muslims use to profess the faith mark their sectarian affiliation: Sunni Muslims say there is no God but God and Muhammad is his prophet; Shia Muslims add that Ali is the protector (wali) of God.

Typically, scholars and the media state that the vast majority of contemporary Muslims are Sunni, as many as 87–90 per cent, according to the Pew Research Center's 2009 study (2009: 1, 8, see also 38). The rest are Shia, 70–80 per cent of whom live in Iran, Pakistan, India and Iraq (2009: 1, 8–11). However, when Pew conducted interviews with Muslims in 2008–9 and 2011–12 (Pew Research Center 2012: 18–21), many rejected a sectarian affiliation (2012: 4). Pew interviewed 38,000 Muslims, and majorities in Central Asia, Southern and Eastern Europe, and Indonesia chose to describe themselves as 'just a Muslim', rather than labelling themselves Sunni or Shia. I have frequently heard Muslims in China, Iran and the United States deny groups and/or individuals membership in the ummah: Sunnis who claim Shias are not Muslims, Huis who claim Uyghurs are not Muslims, Salafis who claim non-Salafis are not Muslims – I could give many more examples. Given the historical and contemporary disagreements about who is a real or true Muslim, Pew's finding is remarkable (and reaffirmed by the diverse crowd at Newark's Halal Fest).

Although Sunni–Shia is Islam's only sectarian division, numerous factions exist within this basic distinction, and there is a mystical tradition, known as Sufism, among both Sunni and Shia Muslims. (Sufis, too, have often been accused by non-Sufis of not being Muslim.) Sunni Islam has four main schools of jurisprudence: Hanafi, Shafii, Maliki and Hanbali. The Salafi movement, sometimes called Wahhabism or 'fundamentalist Islam' in the media, is also a Sunni faction. Sunni juridical schools differ about what Muslims are allowed to eat, with the Hanafi (which has the most adherents) being more restrictive, and the Maliki (predominant in North Africa), the least (see Chehabi 2007: 17; cf. Fischer 2011: 81). Shia Muslims include Twelvers (dominant in Iran and Iraq), Zaydis, Ismailis, Alevis and Alawites. Among Sunni and Shia are groups whose food customs resemble those mapped by the Jewish kosher rules. Some scholars have also related Shia eating to pre-Islamic Zoroastrian food customs (see Gignoux 1994: especially 30–1). Factions such as the Ahmadiyya, Aliran Kepercayaan, Druze, Kharijites, Moorish Science Temple and Nation of Islam cannot easily be classified as Sunni or Shia. Some of these groups promote distinctive dietary practices.

Local practices shape factional adherence. For example, Hui in the Xi'an Muslim district are Sunni Muslims. In over twenty years of ethnographic research in this neighbourhood, I have never heard anyone ever speak about following a particular school of jurisprudence, including intellectuals (one of whom was a scholar of Hui history) and clergy (*ahong*). However, residents frequently talked about three local factions: Gedimu, Sunnaiti and Salafi. They described mosques as belonging to, and families as adhering to, one of the three factions. The word 'Gedimu' comes from the Arabic word for ancient (*qadim*). Locals characterized Gedimu as the traditional faction. A Hui historian from the Muslim district argued that Gedimu observance was the closest religious practice to the Islam of the Prophet Muhammad and his companions, as it is the oldest faction in China and developed in relative isolation. Gedimu adherents had some distinctive food habits. One was the practice of making and distributing a fried oil cake, called *youxiang*, for death date remembrances. The bereaved family took *youxiang* to relatives, friends and neighbours of the deceased on a number of dates, including one week, thirty days, forty days and one year after the death. Members of the two other factions, which derived from reform movements, did not distribute *youxiang*, though they might receive them. Gedimu regarded giving *youxiang* as a way of accumulating merit for the deceased; Sunnaiti and Salafi rejected this as an innovation or heresy. From the 1990s through the first decade of the 2000s, the Gedimu's practice of using *youxiang* to remember death dates changed. Fewer families made *youxiang*, instead buying steamed or baked breads (*mantou, tu'ermu*) to distribute. By 2013, many families would give cooking oil and rice instead.

SHARED PRACTICES IN THE ETHNOGRAPHY OF MUSLIM FOODWAYS

When we look at all those who identify themselves as Muslim – which includes substantial numbers of secular Muslims – we find that no aspects of Muslim foodways are truly universal. For example, many Malaysian Muslims view dog as equally polluting as pig, and the Malaysian government officially adopts and promotes this position (see MS 1500 2009). Yet I've heard American Muslims state that dogs are loyal companions who deserve kind treatment, pointing to the Qur'anic passage that describes dogs protecting the faithful (Surah 18: 18). Iranian Muslims regard shellfish as haram, while restaurants in Singapore serve halal shellfish (see http://thehalalfoodblog.blogspot.se/2012/10/aquamarine.html). Kazakhs and other Central Asians view *kumiss*, fermented mare's milk, as halal, but the Illinois-based non-profit educational organization entitled Muslim Consumer Group, founded by a South Asian-American Muslim food scientist, classifies kumiss and other fermented dairy products as prohibited (Muslim Consumer Group 2007). Chinese Muslims in Xi'an believe fish with teeth are haram, though one Hui scholar told me this derived from a Chinese belief that you become like what you eat (e.g. if you eat an ugly and fierce animal, you will resemble that creature). Uyghurs in Ürümqi believe Hui food is not halal (Cesaro 2002: 152–85). Malays in London think Chinese food is not halal, even when it is halal-certified (Fischer 2011: 82). When we look at the broad range of foods that people could eat, Muslims from different backgrounds, and at different times, classify halal and haram foods differently.

In my experience, pork is the food prohibition that Muslims most consistently observe. None of the Muslims I worked with in Philadelphia or Karaj felt as strongly anti-pig as the Muslims living in the Xi'an Hui district. There, many locals refuse even to say the word pig, or use it only for cursing (cf. Gladney 1996: 272–3). By contrast, African-American Muslims in Philadelphia typically have non-Muslim relatives who eat ham and/or bacon, and encounter pork at family or neighbourhood celebrations. Nevertheless, even very secular Muslims who I know in Philadelphia and Karaj would never eat pork, in contrast to secular Jews.

The Pew Research Center reports general agreement among Muslims around the world that drinking alcohol is immoral (2013: 10; Chapter 3). However, Pew found countries (Afghanistan, Albania, Azerbaijan, Bosnia-Herzegovina and Chad) where one-fifth to one-third of the population did not consider consuming alcohol a moral issue (2013: Chapter 3, 3–4). Pew's study describes beliefs rather than practice. Buitelaar reports that residents of the two Moroccan communities she worked with told her that wine is as haram as pork, yet some drank wine (1993: 107; see also CNN 2003 on Moroccan wines). In China, Iran and the United States, some Muslims drink beer, wine or other forms of alcohol, while others are adamantly against such consumption. I've seen such differences in families and in neighbourhoods. During the 1990s, for example, residents living on the western side of the Xi'an Muslim district led a vigorous anti-alcohol movement, in which food stall owners refused to allow alcohol on their premises, let alone sell or consume it. On the east side, Hui entrepreneurs allowed customers to bring alcohol into Hui food stalls and restaurants, though they did not sell it. In one family, three of the brothers strictly abstained from alcohol, while another drank and sold alcohol in his suburban restaurant – a restaurant that he widely advertised as a halal, 'pure and true' (*qingzhen*) restaurant.[6]

In addition to abstaining from pork, and considering alcohol immoral, most Muslims fast during the month of Ramadan. The Pew Research Center's survey of Muslims in thirty-nine countries found Ramadan fasting to be the single most widely shared Muslim ritual (2012: 9). In Southeast Asia, South Asia, sub-Saharan Africa and the Middle East and North Africa, 94–99 per cent of respondents reported that they fasted during Ramadan. In Southern and Eastern Europe and Central Asia, majorities of Muslims also said they fasted. Marjo Buitelaar's study of Ramadan in Marrakech and Berkane during the late 1980s is the most comprehensive research on Muslim fasting to date (1993). While other anthropologists mention Ramadan, and provide some details of local practice (e.g. Murphy 1986: 101–3, Rouse 2004: 24–5, 106–7, 210–11), Buitelaar is the only ethnographer to do an in-depth study and analysis. Her book details the activities leading up to Ramadan and Ramadan observance (which includes nightly feasting) in two urban communities. She pays particular attention to women. For the Moroccans she studied, Ramadan fasting is the key marker of being Muslim, far more important than prayer, alms-giving (though in fact women regularly give alms on behalf of their families during Ramadan) or making the hajj (1993: 77–96). Buitelaar describes how Ramadan fasting creates a sense of identity and community among Muslims. The foods that locals use to break the fast, and the media broadcasts during the month (some of which feature the King of Morocco as the Commander of the Faithful), also impart a specifically Moroccan identity. Buitelaar argues persuasively that the nightly meals which break the fast, and the Feast of the Breaking of the Fast (Eid al-Fitr) at the end of the month, are times of heightened sociability that provide more opportunities for women to participate in collective religious observance than they have at other times.

Gendered religious practice is characteristic of many Muslim communities. Muslim women are far less likely than men to worship collectively at the masjid, since collective prayer is not obligatory for women (men must pray together at Friday jumma). Gender segregation at meals is also common (e.g., Cesaro 2002: 136–51; Tapper and Tapper 1986: 67; Sarroub 2005: 46–58). Muslims in Xi'an and Karaj always ate segregated by gender at formal events, such as weddings and funerals. Ethnographies from Central Asia, China, Morocco, Niger, Saudi Arabia and the United States all describe how Muslim women are responsible for provisioning and feeding the family (Buitelaar 1993; Cesaro 2002; Fischer 2011; Gillette 2000; Popenoe 2004; Rouse 2004; Rouse and Hoskins 2004; Yamami 1994). Keeping a halal kitchen, raising children to eat as observant Muslims and cooking special food for Muslim feast days tend to be women's domain. Muslim women in dramatically different cultural contexts view cooking and feeding as a form of religious observance (e.g., Buitelaar 1993: 57–8, 118, 127–8; Gillette 2000: 120–1, 145–7; Popenoe 2004: 41–7; Rouse 2004: 108–9; Rouse and Hoskins 2004: 226–7).

Also widespread is a tendency for Muslims to equate the cuisine of their local group with halal and purity (tayyib). For many Muslims, ethnic identity and religious identity are inextricably intertwined (e.g., Cesaro 2002: 152–85; Fischer 2011: 109–35; Fischer 2007; Gillette 2000: 114–44; Kaya 2005; Popenoe 2005: 54–9; Tapper and Tapper 1986: 65). The unity of religious and ethnic identity means that group members trust food made by members of their in-group. This sentiment does not necessarily translate to food made by Muslims across ethnic boundaries. Cesaro, working with Uyghurs in Ürümqi (2002), and Fischer, working with Malays in London (2011), both give examples of Muslims declining to eat halal food that did not belong to their own ethnic group. American Muslims may be a notable exception to this trend. Journalists in New York City report that 'halal food' and 'halal food trucks' are synonymous with chicken and rice with white sauce, and garner customers from Bangladesh, Pakistan, Afghanistan, Southeast Asia and New Jersey (e.g., Brooks 2009; Fazel 2009; Knafo 2007). In Philadelphia, I have seen Muslims of various ethnic backgrounds regularly eating halal Middle Eastern food. To me, it seemed that Philadelphia Muslims, regardless of their own ethnic background, automatically regarded Middle Eastern food as halal. Pakistani cuisine also drew Muslims from diverse backgrounds. Somewhat less frequently, I have seen American Muslims eating other ethnic cuisines, such as Afghani, African-American and Persian.[7] The success of halal food festivals in California and New Jersey suggests that American Muslims are willing to eat across ethnic boundaries.[8]

DIVERGENCE IN THE ETHNOGRAPHY OF MUSLIM FOODWAYS

In addition to halal and haram classification, we find many other differences in Muslim eating practices. Some communities use eating as a key disciplinary mechanism. For example, Loukia Sarroub describes how Yemeni-American Muslim students enforced gender segregation in their public high-school lunchroom during the late 1990s and early 2000s (2005: 46–58). While females felt that their male classmates enforced segregation (particularly those who were recent migrants), the girls themselves actively policed one another's behaviour to ensure they were viewed as modest. In the Xi'an Muslim district, residents' views about pollution maintained barriers between Hui and non-Muslims (Gillette 2000: 117–32). Xi'an Hui would not even drink out of a glass that belonged to a non-Muslim because it was not clean, religiously and in all respects (purity and cleanliness were understood as related). Because Hui and Han Chinese 'could not eat together' (*chi bu dao yikuar*), they could not engage in reciprocal social relations, marry (unless the non-Muslim converted), or even live comfortably in the same neighbourhood. Elsewhere, however, Muslim communities do not use eating to separate themselves from ethnic others. Christopher Murphy describes Muslims in Delhi who eat with Hindus (1986: 96–101, 103–10). The Muslim residents of Old Delhi invited Hindu guests to wedding feasts, sometimes employing Hindu cooks to make the meal for both Muslim and Hindu guests (the food was vegetarian). Muslims welcomed Hindus into their homes to eat sweets at the end of Ramadan. Murphy writes that locals saw the Eid al-Fitr 'as a day of amity when even Hindus could come to greet their Muslim friends and eat sawaiyan [made from vermicelli, milk, and sugar], which, being a sweet, non-meat dish, is suitable to be offered to vegetarians' (Murphy 1986: 104).

Food-based hospitality is another area where Muslim communities diverge. Ethnographers working with Uyghurs, Meccans and rural Jordanians write that these groups see hospitality expressed through food and eating as an essential group characteristic (Antoun 1968; Cesaro 2002: 108–35; Yamami 1994). Muslims in Karaj also emphasized hospitality. Hosts prepared lavish dinners for guests, with multiple dishes, and verbally encouraged visitors to eat. Guests, in their turn, brought pastries when they came to visit, whether they came for a meal or simply stopped by for a conversation. In the families I know, it is common for a person to offer food to the person beside her before taking some for herself. One woman prepared small plates of food for workers who came to do repairs on her house, and for drivers when she took a taxi. By contrast, I experienced less food-based hospitality in Philadelphia, even though participants in the Muslim Voices community history project were welcoming.

Muslim communities have different views on how much food to consume. Rebecca Popenoe examines female fattening among the Azawagh Arabs living in Niger (2004, 1999). Her research shows that many Saharan Muslim populations, including Tuareg, Brakna Moors, Bardama and the Azawagh Arabs, practised female fattening over many centuries (Popenoe 2004: 33–50). Popenoe describes how fattening allows Azawagh Arabs to emphasize differences between men and women, enhancing gender distinctions that they locate in the Qur'an and Islam. Through fattening, women create bodies that are more closed and pure. Fattening dampens female desire, which is viewed negatively, and awakens male desire, leading to procreation, which is positive. Girls who are fattened reach womanhood more quickly than other girls, allowing them to realize their proper social and religious roles sooner. Yet elsewhere, Muslims stress moderation in consumption. For example, the founders of HealthyMuslim.com, Amjad bin Muhammad Rafiq and Saeed bin Salid (both of whom have PhDs in biochemistry) cite the fourteenth-century theologian Ibn al-Qayyim to demonstrate that Muslims have a religious obligation to eat in moderation (http://www.healthymuslim.com/articles/xqmwqaloz-eat-less-and-live-longer.cfm). They write that Muslims should eat 'wholesome nutritious foods', ensure a 'balance of quality and quantity' and ameliorate 'the consequences of bad diet' (http://www.healthymuslim.com/about.cfm). Their website, which is based in Birmingham, England, provides information on findings from food research published in medical journals and other media. Their view is that Muslims should 'remember that with all foods, moderation is the key' (http://www.healthymuslim.com/articles/ossuo-dark-chocolate-in-moderation-is-beneficial.cfm).

Ingesting the Qur'an is another practice that varies across communities. Some Muslims ingest Qur'anic text for its curative properties. Lambek describes Muslims in Mayotte who copy text from the Qur'an, dissolve it in water and drink the water

(1995). Zadeh discusses this practice in early Muslim groups, along with related customs such as writing the Qur'an on sweets to be eaten (2009:464). In other cases, Muslims have ingested Qur'anic text copied on paper to dispose of it when burning was not possible (http://www.slate.com/articles/life/faithbased/2005/05/quranic_etiquette.html). Yet there are also communities that do not have such traditions, such as the Xi'an Muslim district.

One of the most significant areas of difference is the attention, or lack thereof, that Muslims devote to eating halal. Some Muslims are extremely fastidious, while others are relatively unconcerned. Johan Fischer, in his multi-sited research on transnational Malaysian halal foods, describes diaspora Malays in London who spent significant amounts of time researching halal foods online, checking the credentials of halal-certifying bodies and reading ingredient lists to be certain that foods they purchased had no haram substances (2011: 69–88). Yet others ate halal simply by not intentionally violating Qur'anic prescriptions. As one man put it, 'You just have to shut one eye' (2011: 84). Generally speaking, Fischer's research shows higher levels of concern among Malays in London than Malays in Kuala Lumpur (see also 2011: 134). In part this is because the Malaysian government has regulated halal since the late 1970s, and halal is part of the national curriculum in Malaysia (2011: 31–68).

I see two social factors affecting the attention that Muslims pay to halal (individual practices must also be considered in relation to personal biographies). The first is whether or not groups live in a Muslim state. I include under this rubric governments that are officially secular but take Islam 'as the religion of the country', as we find in Malaysia (Fischer 2011: 32). In states where the government associates itself with Islam, for example Iran, Malaysia and Saudi Arabia, citizens are unlikely to scrutinize the goods they consume to check if they are halal. The families I know in Karaj, for example, had never discussed halal until I raised the issue with them. When I asked whether the packaged foods they bought at the grocery store had halal trustmarks on them, they were surprised; it had never occurred to them to check. The basic assumption was that the food they purchased and ate was halal.

The fact that adult Iranians had seen foods switch from haram to halal did not alter this disposition. For example, H. E. Chehabi describes how caviar and sturgeon became halal during the early years of the Islamic Republic (2007). After Mossadegh nationalized Iranian fisheries on the Caspian Sea, the Pahlavi government marketed caviar, despite the fact that Shia clergy considered sturgeon (and its roe) haram, since sturgeon do not have scales (2007: 18–21). When Iran became an Islamic Republic, government officials wanted to retain revenues from the very lucrative caviar industry, but would not produce or sell haram foods. In September 1981, Shia clergy in Khomeini's office in Qom inspected specimens of the Caspian's three types of sturgeon, and agreed that they had scales near the tail and fins (2007: 22). Khomeini then issued a fatwa that fish with any scales, including near the tail, were halal. Shortly after the ruling, Iranians circulated jokes about people who had eaten caviar getting out of hell, but by 2005 consumption had increased so much that Caspian sturgeon were near extinction. When I asked Karaj urbanites about this history, some remembered that these events had happened before the Islamic

Republic was founded. Others pointed to shark meat, which Khameini proclaimed halal in 1995 (see also Orlando Sentinal 1995). High demand for shark fin in East Asia drove the reexamination of that fish's halal status. These reclassifications did not result in anxiety. Some saw them as a point of pride, showing that Shia Islam was dynamic in contrast to what they viewed as a more static Sunni Islam.

The second crucial factor influencing groups' fastidiousness about halal is the relationship between the Muslim population and other local populations. For example, the Chinese Muslims I studied regarded the majority Han population as hostile to Muslims. Historical records show anti-Muslim government policies, for example during the late Qing and Cultural Revolution, and Han Chinese communities who used pigs to provoke and punish Chinese Muslims (see, e.g., Gillette 2008). Hui regularly accused Han of using pigs to insult and degrade Muslims (e.g., Christian Science Monitor 1993; Mehra 2002; Fang 2010). The key boundary for Xi'an Hui was between them and Han. They did not worry about mass-produced Western foods (unlike the Illinois-based Muslim Consumer Group, for example).

African-American Muslims in the United States are a contrasting case. Rouse writes that the African-American Muslims she studied in Los Angeles told her eating halal was easy, not very different from the American diet (2004: 125). Studies of African-American Muslims in Philadelphia, New Jersey, and other parts of the northeast indicate that these groups do not stress food as an element of religious observance (Elmasry 2010; Lee 2010). Rouse argues that among the African-American converts she studied, Sunni Islam was a 'framework for challenging racism, sexism, and economic exploitation' (2004: 216). She characterizes adherents' relations with non-Muslim Los Angelenos as relatively open (2004: 215). In Philadelphia, African-American Sunni Muslims were not invested in differentiating themselves from non-Muslim African-Americans (the Nation of Islam is a somewhat different case). They located themselves in the context of African-American history and, unlike Chinese Muslims, did not regard themselves per se as a target of hostility and prejudice.

DELOCALIZED MUSLIM FOODWAYS

Johan Fischer draws our attention to the Malaysian government's efforts to make Malaysia a 'global halal hub' and turn Malaysian halal certification into a global standard (Fischer 2008, 2011, 2012; see also MS 1500; Othman, Sungkar and Hussein 2009). Fischer reports that the Malaysian government began regulating halal in response to the dakwah movement of the 1970s. Officials also promoted the production of halal foods to stimulate economic growth. After the European Union barred Malaysia from marketing meat there, the Malaysian government encouraged local and transnational entrepreneurs to pursue government halal certification for a wide range of foods, pharmaceuticals, toiletries and other products (2011: 37–41). Fischer calls this process, in which the concept of permissibility and consumability is applied to new commodities, halalization (2011: 32).

Fischer links halalization to the delocalization of Muslim foodways (2011: 69). Delocalization results from the rise of an 'international agro-food system' that supplies, creates and distributes food across multiple locations (Ward and Almås 1997). It is broadly characteristic of mass-produced foods. Consumers know little about who made mass-produced foods, how they were made or the settings where such foods were created. Yet, in many Muslim communities, 'the drivers for halal lie in someone being a Muslim', as marketing researchers Jonathan Wilson and Jonathan Liu put it (2010: 110). Many Muslims believe whether or not a food is good to eat depends as much, or more, on who, how and where as on what (e.g., Cesaro 2000: 152–85; Gillette 2000: 114–44; cf. Murphy 1986). For example, during my first months of ethnography in the Xi'an Muslim district, I quickly learned that local Hui saw all food made by other Hui as pure and good to eat, and all food made by Han Chinese, or by other non-Muslims (regardless of whether or not they were 'people of the book'), as never pure or good to eat, even if the food was vegetarian and contained no haram substances.[9] Trust in the halalness of food, or lack thereof, was personal, depending mostly on who made the food. When Muslims eat mass-produced foods, however, they are not secured by personal, face-to-face relationships between producer and consumer.[10]

Halal certification is a response to the delocalization of food. Halal certification refers to the practice of organizations (including but not limited to government bodies) identifying a set of specific guidelines for halal, and then applying those guidelines to adjudicate whether specific foods or other commodities are halal or haram. The Malaysian government's halal standard, MS 1500, is a good example, but there are many others. As of late 2013, there were dozens of halal-certifying groups around the world, from private non-profits to government organizations (see, e.g. Ahlul Bayt 2013; Andolu Agency 2013; Fischer 2012; Gooch 2010; halaladvocates. net n.d.; Halalworld.org n.d.; Henley 2013: 7; Osburne 2011; The Nation 2011; South China Morning Post 2008). Typically, a halal-certifying organization charges a fee to producers who seek certification and conducts an examination of the product in question. The examination includes investigating product ingredients, production site and production methods. If the commodity meets the organization's guidelines, the organization allows the producer to place its halal trustmark on it. A simple online search for 'halal logo' produces images of halal certification trustmarks from around the world. Most of these include the word halal written in Arabic. Individuals and groups have called for the creation of a unified international halal standard (e.g. Ahlul Bayt News Agency 2013; Andolu Agency 2013; Anuga 2013; Donovan 2009), but since Muslims do not share a single set of criteria for halal, this goal is unlikely to be realized.

According to the World Halal Council, an international group of halal-certifying organizations founded in Jakarta in 1999, halal certification began in the United States during the 1960s (http://www.worldhalalcouncil.com/about-us). JAKIM, the Department of Islamic Development Malaysia, states that they issued their first halal certification letters in 1974 (http://www.halal.gov.my/v3/index.php/en/corporate/halal-history). The Halal Food Council, established in 1984 in Salisbury, Maryland (USA), dates the first halal certification to the late 1970s (http://halalfoodcouncil. info/history.html). While the date for the first halal certification of mass-produced food remains uncertain, these websites, and scholars of halal commodities, agree that halal certification was a response to the transnational circulation of foods (Fischer 2011; Wilson and Liu 2010: 111).

The proliferation of halal certification, or halalization, must be understood not only as a means for Muslims to eat the products of an international agro-food system, but also as a capitalist profit-making strategy. Transnational marketing agencies have identified the 'new Muslim consumer' as the next big market for entrepreneurs (Oglivy Mather 2010; Oglivy Noor n.d.). Newspaper reports from England, Hong Kong, Thailand, Malaysia, Turkey, Germany and elsewhere all discuss the size of Muslim populations and their annual spending on food (e.g., Anuga 2013; The Nation 2011; South China Morning Post n.d.; Schröder 2009). Food entrepreneurs use halal as a 'brand', co-brand or brand component in pursuit of economic gain (Wilson and Liu 2010: 108, 111; see also Oglivy Noor n.d.: 10–11, 18–24). They hope to sell products by appealing to religious sentiments and 'Muslim pride' (Oglivy and Mather 2010; Oglivy Noor n.d.). When we see products such as halal-certified toothpaste (Tom's of Maine), eye cream (One Pure) and deodorant (Syahirah), among other non-food goods, we see companies pursuing revenues by targeting a (large) niche market.

The behaviour of Muslim consumers can have a significant impact on the profitability of mass-produced goods. For example, when Nike used a decoration on their shoes that resembled the word 'Allah' in Arabic calligraphy in 1997, Muslims around the world boycotted their shoes (Harrington 1997; Oglivy Noor n.d.: 10). Nike apologized, donated money to fund a playground at a Muslim elementary school, discontinued the shoe and diverted those produced away from the Middle East to 'less sensitive' markets (Harrington 1997). When a Danish newspaper published satirical cartoons of the Prophet Muhammad, many Muslims responded by boycotting the Danish company Arla Foods (BBC 2006). Reduced sales caused Arla to furlough employees, as the company lost up to USD $3.2 million per day as Muslims avoided Danish foods (ibid.; Oglivy Noor n.d.: 11). By contrast, when Best Buy included a congratulatory message about the Feast of Sacrifice with its Thanksgiving promotional materials in 2010, their sales increased by 13 per cent, as Muslims and liberals supported the company by buying goods there (Oglivy Noor n.d.: 18, 22).

Halal-certifying organizations directly influence Muslim consumption by labelling products halal, haram or mashbooh (dubious, and so best avoided). At times these groups recommend product boycotts, such as when the Muslim Consumer Group asked Muslims to boycott Sara Lee because the baking company refused to use vegetable-fat-based dough conditioners (Muslim Consumer Group 2009), and to quit buying Laxmi products because the company included an image of a Hindu goddess on their packaging (Muslim Consumer Group 2010a). They direct Muslim consumers towards companies that produce goods that meet the group's halal standards by producing lists that name products that are halal and the companies that produce them (e.g., http://www.muslimconsumergroup.com/personal_care_products.html). According to newspaper reports, Muslims are particularly likely to patronize Lipton and Nestlé (Thomas 2010). Of course, which halal-certifying organization companies patronize, and government bodies recognize, as a proper certifying body, has significant financial repercussions for that organization (e.g. Muslim Consumer Group 2012).

Some Muslims express concern with the methods used to process mass-produced food. Two key issues are how meat is slaughtered and whether alcohol is used for food processing. Individuals and organizations debate what constitutes a halal method of slaughter (see, e.g. Asian Express 2012; Elliott 2005; Henley 2013; MS 1500; Osburne 2011). Some argue that for slaughter to be halal, a man must recite the blessing and wield the knife on each individual animal. Others believe that if a Muslim is present during slaughter, the slaughter is necessarily halal. Some halal slaughterhouses play a recording of the blessing over loudspeakers and use mechanical methods (e.g., Henley 2013; Osburne 2011). Muslims debate whether it is permissible for animals to be stunned prior to slaughter, as is common with mass-produced meat. Some Muslims argue stunning is permissible as long as the process does not kill the animal. In the United Kingdom, the two major halal certification groups disagree about this question, with the Halal Monitoring Committee disallowing any form of stunning for halal meat, and the Halal Food Authority permitting stunning when it does not kill the animal (Hasan 2012; Henley 2013). The Malaysian government has adopted the latter position in its halal standard (see MS 1500: Annex A, on stunning). There are also many debates about whether stunning is more or less humane for the animal, in which halal slaughter has figured prominently (see, e.g. Berg 2011). Some argue these debates are a cover for Islamophobia (e.g. Hasan 2012).

For some halal certification bodies and Muslim consumers, halal slaughter is not simply about which meat Muslims can eat. Also relevant is whether mass-produced foods contain animal fats. Animal fats regularly appear in mass-produced foods as gelatin and magnesium stearate (e.g. Canadian Halal Foods 2013; Muslim Consumer Group 2013b; IFANCA n.d.). Some Muslims avoid mass-produced food that contains animal fats as an ingredient in order not to consume anything from an animal that was improperly slaughtered (sometimes called non-*zabiha* animal products) or pork products. Halal certification groups such as Canadian Halal Food and the Muslim Consumer Group urge Muslims to reject all foods that do not use either fish gelatin or vegetable-based gelatins, for example, to be certain that the gelatins are not made from pork or animals that were not slaughtered according to Islamic dietary prescriptions.

The use of alcohol in food processing is another major concern for some Muslims. For example, ethyl alcohol is used to produce flavour extracts (including vanilla), concentrates for soft drinks and foods, distilled white vinegar, mouthwash, hairspray, astringents, perfumes and other products (http://www.grainprocessing. com/alcohol/). While food corporations such as Nestlé, Post Foods and Gatorade (Pepsi) argue that the alcohol in their food evaporates during production, some Muslims and halal certification groups consider any commodities made with ethyl alcohol to be haram (e.g. Muslim Consumer Group 2013b; Sunni Forum 2004, 2007). Alcohol-free beverages are another area of debate. For example, many Iranian Muslims drink alcohol-free beverages, which are readily available in restaurants and stores. Iranian alcohol-free beers such as Delster, by Iran Behnoush Company, or Istake, by Arpanoosh Company, etc., have halal certification. However, the American Muslim Consumer Group argues that because such beverages are made from alcoholic substances and contain some alcohol, they are haram (Muslim Consumer Group 2010b).

Some of the Muslim consumer advocacy groups involved in debates over whether or not mass-produced foods (and other commodities) are halal use advanced food science techniques to adjudicate whether these goods are permissible, thus turning some of the techniques of the agro-food industry to religious purposes. For example, after the French newspaper *Le Monde* reported that soft drinks such as Coke, Pepsi and 7up contained alcohol, the Muslim Consumer Group conducted its own tests, sending samples to an independent laboratory in Chicago (Santi 2012; Muslim Consumer Group 2013a). They used a 'sophisticated method of residual solvents identification' called USP 35 to determine whether and how much alcohol was present in a range of sodas. On the basis of the lab reports, the Muslim Consumer Group determined that Coca-Cola and 7up were haram because they contained alcohol, but Pepsi was halal, because it did not. In some cases, industrial food scientists founded such groups: Rasheeduddin Ahmed, who founded the Muslim Consumer Group, worked as a senior food scientist at Kraft Foods (http://www. muslimconsumergroup.com/about_us.html).

Websites like that of the Muslim Consumer Group can be considered another aspect of Muslim food's delocalization. Halal-certifying groups join food corporations in using the worldwide web to reach Muslim consumers in far-flung locations. Halal certification groups are key players in processes of halalization: some groups now argue that Muslims should consume no food that lacks a halal trustmark.

There are other Muslim advocacy groups that use the web to influence how Muslims should eat. For example, websites such as healthyMuslim.com and Muslimhealthnetwork.org address diet, nutrition, chronic diseases and exercise, and provide advice about how to eat and live better, drawing on data and information produced by modern food science. The people behind these sites aspire to promote healthy eating practices to non-local Muslim audiences, and frame their efforts as aligned with Islamic principles. Individuals also weigh in on Muslim eating and health, in blogs such as Gluten Free Salafi (http://glutenfreesalafi.com/). In this particular example, the author wants to live according to the Qur'an and Sunnah and be strictly gluten-free. She provides recipes, talks about illness and remedies and discusses women's health. All of these websites contribute to the delocalization of Muslim foodways by promoting food and eating practices across and outside of face-to-face communities.

REPERSONALIZATION OF MUSLIM FOODWAYS

Though most, if not all, of the world's Muslims now eat delocalized foods, they continue to make and eat local halal food too. Muslim foodways are not, and show no signs of becoming, completely delocalized. Fischer himself describes how Malays in London prefer to eat meat slaughtered by local butchers, rather than buying halal-certified meat in supermarkets (Fischer 2011: 91–4). Others have reported similar findings (Ahmed 2008). Contextually specific in-group notions about halal and purity, such as the idea that Chinese food cannot be halal even if it is halal-certified, continued to influence London Malays' food and eating choices (Fischer 2011: 82, see also 89–107). Fischer also observes that home cooking and home eating 'translated' less secure foods into beneficial, pure Muslim foods (2011: 134). Even while consuming delocalized foods, Muslims still eat foods made by people they know. Local cultural ideas about what is good to eat still affect Muslim eating practices. And personal relations, including who makes the food, still influence how Muslims perceive what they eat.

New movements to repersonalize food are a consequence of globalization and the agro-food industry (see also West, Chapter 19, this volume; Avieli, Chapter 6, this volume). For example, in 1986, Carlo Petrini founded the Slow Food movement in Italy to promote local cuisines, sustainable agriculture and small-scale food businesses. In addition, movements to promote organic food, community-supported agriculture and locally sourced foods followed. These developments depart significantly from the mass-production model of food and eating. Participants in these efforts often use translocal technologies such as the worldwide web and other media to attach names, faces, biographies and places to food.

Halal versions of this new gastronomy are relatively recent. Over the past five years, a significant number of Muslims have been promoting small-scale, ecologically sustainable, organic and gourmet halal food. This includes Muslims who blog or maintain websites about food without any apparent profit motive, as well as entrepreneurs with goods to sell. A few restaurateurs in England and France have opened gourmet establishments, where top chefs serve halal haute cuisine to middle and upper class Muslims (Al-Arabiya 2009; Henley 2013; Qureshi and Smithers 2009). Some entrepreneurs have founded small-scale, gourmet halal food companies. For example, Abraham Natural Produce is a family business in Kent, England, that sells organic, ecologically friendly halal meat and fair-trade olives, dates and other products (see www.organic-halal-meat.com). Norwich Meadows Farm is a small business in upstate New York selling organic produce and 'eco-halal meat' from pasture-raised, halal slaughtered chickens, turkeys, sheep, goats and cattle (www.norwichmeadowsfarm.com; see also Koenig 2008). Crescent Foods sells locally sourced, organic halal chicken as part of what it calls a 'farm to fork' movement (http://crescenthalal.com/).

Whether restaurants or small producers, these ventures present themselves in profoundly personal ways. Their websites feature the names of founders, biographical sketches, photographs and mission statements. They self-consciously position themselves as an alternative to anonymous, industrial, globalized food. They seek to persuade Muslims that eating organic, local, Fair Trade and ecologically friendly food aligns with the Qur'an and Islamic values. They work to create the sentiment, if not the reality, of a personal relationship between producer and consumer.

A number of Muslim blogs and websites also promote gourmet, organic, local and ecologically sustainable halal food and eating. Some have commercial elements, such as My Halal Kitchen (myhalalkitchen.com), whose founder writes cookbooks and teaches. Others appear to be solely educational. For example, Beyond Halal (beyondhalal.com) was founded by New England educators with a commitment to making sure Muslims know where their food came from. The website discusses food ethics and Islam, supports small-scale halal businesses that share the founders' values and provides links to media about sustainable agriculture, animal rights, cookbooks and other topics. Websites such as these feature photographs; author biographies; editorials; personal testimonies; recipes; reflections on Muslim eating; descriptions of DIY food and eating projects; and evaluations of Muslim food companies such as Crescent Food, Nature's Bounty Meats and Whole Earth Meats. These online resources put a personal spin on Muslim foodways and seek to counter the agro-food industry.

Muslim food activism, such as food boycotts and 'buy-cotts', can be considered ways to repersonalize food and eating too. Boycotts and buycotts separate Muslim foodways from a broadly standardized transnational economy of consumption. Muslims publicly identify themselves as distinctive kinds of consumers through such food activism. They claim, and create, community on the basis of shared goals.

Many Muslim boycotts and buycotts are political protests. For example, Fischer reports on Malaysian Muslims who boycotted American foods to protest the US invasion of Afghanistan in 2001, and other Malaysians who responded to such calls by advocating that Malaysian Muslims consume more (Fischer 2007). In 2002, Muslims in the United Arab Emirates and Saudi Arabia boycotted American foods in support of the Palestinian *intifada* (Islam Online 2002; Mroue 2002). The Muslim boycott of Arla Foods was a political protest; although the Danish government had no input on the newspaper's decision to publish caricatures of the Prophet Muhammad, many Muslims held it accountable (Fox News 2006). Of course, nation-states are not the only targets of political protests. We also find examples of boycotts where Muslims seek to separate themselves from broader social formations. For example, an Egyptian Salafi group recently posted on Facebook that tomatoes were 'Christian food' and Muslims should not consume them (Hurriyet Daily News 2013).

A few food entrepreneurs have sought to capitalize on exclusively Muslim market sectors by promoting foods that align with political agendas, a corporate form of food activism that nevertheless speaks to particular interests and values. For example, an Egyptian manufacturer made Abu Ammar Corn Chips, named after a nom de plume of Yassar Arafat (BBC 2002). The package had an image of Arafat on the front, and was meant to familiarize Egyptian children with the Palestinian cause. The manufacturer donated the revenue from one in twenty-five packages of chips to the Palestinian cause (ibid., see also Economist 2012b). A related example is the Dubai company that makes Hero Chips: around the same time as Abu Ammar chips came out, Hero Chips were marketed with an image of a boy throwing a stone at an Israeli tank (Economist 2012b). Presently, Hero Chips retain their name, but have a 'new look' and no longer reference the Palestinian cause (www.herocrisps.com/about-us.php). When many Middle Eastern Muslims boycotted US goods during 2002, Iran's Zamzam Cola presented itself as the Muslim soft drink, and saw a major increase in sales (Islam Online 2002; Mroue 2002; Theodoulou, Bremmer and McGrory 2002).

Muslim hunger strikes are a form of political activism that can also be understood as an extreme form of food repersonalization. While hunger strikes are a political strategy employed around the world, they are also deeply personal. Activists who refuse to eat call attention to themselves as individuals, and to the groups and causes that they represent. Perhaps the best-known Muslim hunger strikers are the Muslims detained at Guantanamo Bay Naval Center, who are refusing food to protest their imprisonment and ill-treatment by the US military (Reilly 2013). More than 100 of the 166 detainees are on hunger strike (Townsend 2013). Some of these men have been forcibly fed, a practice the UN Human Rights Commission condemns as torture. Muslim political detainees have also gone on hunger strikes elsewhere. In 2012, a group of Tunisian Salafi arrested on suspicion of attacking the US embassy in Tunisia went on hunger strike to protest prison conditions and delayed sentencing (Daily Star 2012). In 2013, a Muslim detained in an Irish prison carried out a hunger strike to protest degrading treatment, including abuse specifically directed at him as a Muslim (O'Loughlin 2013). There are many other examples from sites around the world, including Israel, Iran, Morocco, Algeria and Bahrain.

MUSLIM FOODWAYS AND THE FUTURE

Muslims use food to materialize, embody and affirm who they are, what they believe in, where they came from and where they want to go. Researchers and scholars should pay more attention to Muslim foodways. It is a dynamic field where influential social trends play out and where we can learn about processes essential to individual life, families and communities. Muslim foodways are rich in possible research topics, yet only a few anthropologists are working towards understanding and analysing them. I hope this essay provokes many more researchers to work in this field.

Muslims are already, and will continue to develop as, a target market for transnational corporations. More foods and other products will be certified as halal, creating controversies along a number of fronts. Some will embrace this trend, while others will protest, boycott or even ignore it (see, e.g., Economist 2012a; Gammanpila 2013; Geller 2011; Fischer 2011).

Delocalizing and repersonalizing trends will continue to characterize Muslim foodways in the future. We can expect Muslims to participate actively in global trends, such as the Slow Food movement or the transnational business of the agro-food industry. Muslims will take advantage of global technologies, such as the worldwide web, media and food activism, for personal and local purposes. As the population of Muslims grows in Muslim-minority settings, we are likely to see many more people organizing events that encourage Muslims from different backgrounds to share food, support Muslim entrepreneurship and meet one another. Islamic practice will continue to be diverse, and so will Muslim foodways – though they undoubtedly will be differently diverse in the future.

ACKNOWLEDGEMENTS

The author would like to thank James L. Watson, Eriberto P. Lozada, Melissa Caldwell, Mohsen Ghodsi and research participants in Xi'an, Philadelphia and Karaj for their contributions to this work. Most of the research was funded by Haverford

College and the European Institute for Advanced Studies Fellowship Program. The author gratefully acknowledges the support of the Swedish Collegium for Advanced Study, where she wrote this chapter.

NOTES

1. I have published regularly on Hui Chinese Muslims, including a recent book chapter on women's empowerment in the Xi'an Muslim district (Gillette 2015). Over the past eight years, I have done ethnographic research on both diasporic and Karaj-based Iranian Muslims, largely through opportunities provided by visiting my in-laws. I am working on a documentary about changes to Iranian women's lives over the past century. My research on Philadelphia Muslims came about through a community history project that I co-directed and facilitated with Louis Massiah of Scribe Video Center. I worked closely with members of the Ahmadiyya community and African-American Muslims for two years while we ran a pilot programme entitled Muslim Voices of Philadelphia.
2. I cannot read Qur'anic Arabic. My knowledge of the Qur'an comes from reading Chinese and English translations, instruction from religious students and clergy, secondary scholarship and hearing the recitation of Qur'an.
3. The countries with percentage increases greater than 100 are Ireland (191), Canada (183), Finland (150), Norway (149), New Zealand (146), United States (140), Sweden (120), Niger (105) and Italy (102).
4. See Aslan (2006: 57–9) for a discussion of this word, which originates in the Qur'an. Aslan notes that ummah was the term used for the followers of Islam during Muhammad's life; 'Muslim' is a later usage. Following other scholars, Aslan argues we should think of the ummah as a radically new kind of social organization based on an Arab tribal paradigm.
5. I focus on religious differences here. There are enormous political ramifications to this division. Politics played a part in the split from the beginning.
6. *Qingzhen*, or pure and true, is the Hui word that encompasses the idea of halal. As the translation suggests, its meaning goes far beyond 'permissible' to encompass ideas of purity and goodness. Hui typically equate *qingzhen* with being Hui – that is, being a member of the Hui ethnic group or nationality, and being a Muslim.
7. This topic merits systematic research. Particularly important in the US context is whether and how often non-African-American Muslims eat soul food, and how Muslims view African-American food. My impression is that South Asian halal food is popular across a wider spectrum of Muslims than African-American halal food. With regard to Persian or Afghani cuisine, one could argue that fewer Philadelphia Muslims eat this food because there are fewer restaurants. On the other hand, such practices could relate to Shia–Sunni differences, negative American perceptions of Iranians, etc.
8. London hosted the UK's first halal festival in late September 2013. Food offerings included North African, Spanish, South American, Turkish, South Asian, Palestinian, North American, Japanese, French and other foods. See http://halalfoodfestival.com/who-is-exhibiting.php. I have not been able to find reports on the number of attendees.
9. The Qur'an identifies food made by people of the book (Jews, Christians) as lawful to eat. See Surah 5:5.

10. I was surprised to find that Hui considered some categories of mass-produced food, such as candy and children's snacks, permissible (see Gillette 2000: 145–7). Hui did not make these foods and they did not have 'pure and true' trustmarks. Given how assiduous residents of the Xi'an Muslim district were in monitoring the border between Hui and non-Hui, why should these mass-produced foods be edible? I argue that the answer related to the values such foods represented, and the aspirations that adults had for their children. See Gillette (2000: 145–66).

REFERENCES

Ahlul Bayt (2013), '16 More Restaurants in Taiwan Obtain Halal Certification', *Ahlul Bayt News Agency*. http://www.abna.ir/data.asp?lang=3&Id=404722.

Ahmed, A. (2008), 'Marketing of Halal Meat in the United Kingdom', *British Food Journal*, 110(7): 655–70.

Al-Arabiya (2009), 'French Halal Restaurants Try Gourmet Cuisine', *Al-Arabiya News*. http://www.alarabiya.net/articles/2009/12/18/94559.html.

Andolu Agency (2013), '4th International Food Fair Begins in Istanbul', *Andolu Agency*. http://www.aa.com.tr/en/news/224748--4th-international-halal-and-healthy-food-fair-begins-in-istanbul.

Antoun, R. (1968), 'The Social Significance of Ramadan in an Arab Village', *The Muslim World*, 58: 36–42.

Anuga (2013), 'Anuga 2013: One Halal – One Certification'. http://halalfocus.net/eu-one-halal-one-certification-we-create-values-on-anuga-2013/?utm_source=rss&utm_medium=rss&utm_campaign=eu-one-halal-one-certification-we-create-values-on-anuga-2013.

Aslan, R. (2006), *No God But God: The Origins, Evolution, and Future of Islam*, New York: Random House.

BBC News (2006), 'Boycott Costing Arla £1m per Day', *BBC News*. http://news.bbc.co.uk/2/hi/business/4676614.stm.

BBC News (2002), 'Egypt Offered a Crispy Taste of Arafat', *BBC News*. http://news.bbc.co.uk/2/hi/middle_east/2009628.stm.

Berg, R. (2011), 'Should Animals Be Stunned Before Slaughter?' *BBC News*. http://www.bbc.co.uk/news/magazine-14779271.

Brooks, Z. (2009), 'What's in the White Sauce? He Doesn't Want To Know', *The New York Times*. http://dinersjournal.blogs.nytimes.com/2009/06/02/whats-in-the-white-sauce-he-doesnt-want-to-know/?_r=0.

Buitelaar, M. (1993), *Fasting and Feasting in Morocco*, Oxford: Berg.

Canadian Halal Foods (2013), 'Alerts'. http://www.canadianhalalfoods.com/alerts.html.

Cesaro, M. C. (2002), *Consuming Identities: The Culture and Politics of Food among the Uyghur in Contemporary Xinjiang*, PhD thesis, University of Kent at Canterbury.

Chehabi, H. E. (2007), 'How Caviar Turned out to be Halal', *Gastronomica*, 7(2): 17–23.

Christian Science Monitor (1993), 'Muslims in China Protest Children's Book', *The Christian Science Monitor*. http://www.csmonitor.com/1993/0901/01141.html.

CNN (2003), 'Morocco: Medieval and Modern Juxtaposed', *CNN.com*. http://archive.is/NiNGX.

Crescent Foods (2013), *Crescent Foods* website. crescenthalal.com.

Daily Star (2012), 'Tunisian Islamists End Hunger Strike', *The Daily Star Lebanon*. ttp://www.dailystar.com.lb/News/Middle-East/2012/Dec-28/200208-tunisian-islamists-end-hunger-strike-activists.ashx#axzz2kRI5jqjh.

Donovan, M. (2009), 'Halal Food Makes Business Sense', *South China Morning Post*. http://www.scmp.com/article/700012/halal-food-makes-business-sense?login=1.

The Economist (2012a), 'Boundaries and Turkeys', *The Economist*. http://www.economist.com/blogs/democracyinamerica/2011/11/religion-public-life.

The Economist (2012b), 'Speak Low if You Speak God', *The Economist*. http://www.economist.com/node/21559940.

Elliott, A. (2005), 'A Halal Slaughterhouse Provides Nourishment for a Far-Flung Culture', *The New York Times*. http://www.nytimes.com/2005/03/09/nyregion/09butcher.html?_r=0.

Elmasry, S. (2010), 'The Salafis in America: The Rise, Decline and Prospects for a Sunni Muslim Movement among African Americans', *Journal of Muslim Minority Affairs*, 30(2): 217–34.

Fang Xiao (2010), 'Muslims Protest Selling of Fake Goat Meat in Northwest China', *The Epoch Times*. http://www.theepochtimes.com/n2/china-news/muslims-protest-selling-of-fake-goat-meat-in-northwest-china-38564.html.

Fazel, M. (2009), 'Where the Club Crowd Eats at 4 a.m. on the Weekend', *The New York Times*. http://cityroom.blogs.nytimes.com/2009/08/11/where-the-club-crowd-eats-at-4-am-on-the-weekend/.

Fernandez, L. (2013), 'California's Halal Food Fest, Victim of Success', *NBC Bay Area*. http://www.nbcbayarea.com/news/local/Californias-Halal-Food-Fest-Victim-of-Success-220199551.html.

Fischer, J. (2007), 'Boycott or Buycott? Malay Middle-Class Consumption Post 9/11', *Ethnos*, 72(1): 29–50.

Fischer, J. (2008), 'Religion, Science and Markets: Modern Halal Production, Trade and Consumption', *EMBO Reports*, 9(9): 828–31.

Fischer, J. (2011), *The Halal Frontier: Muslim Consumers in a Globalized Market*, New York: Palgrave Macmillan.

Fischer, J. (2012), 'Branding Halal: A Photographic Essay on Global Muslim Markets', *Anthropology Today*, 28(4): 18–21.

Fox News (2006), 'Muslim Boycotts Hurt Danish Firms', *Fox News*. http://www.foxnews.com/story/2006/02/16/muslim-boycotts-hurt-danish-firms/.

Gammanpila, U. (2013), 'Halalization and the End of Sri Lankan Food Culture', *Ceylon Today*. http://www.ceylontoday.lk/76-25154-news-detail-halalization-and-end-of-sri-lankan-food-culture.html.

Geller, P. (2011), 'Happy Halal Thanksgiving', *American Thinker*. http://www.americanthinker.com/2011/11/happy_halal_thanksgiving.html.

Gignoux, P. (1994), 'Dietary Laws in Pre-Islamic and Post-Sassanian Iran: A Comparative Survey', *Jerusalem Studies in Arabic and Islam*, 17: 16–42.

Gillette, M. (2000), *Between Mecca and Beijing: Modernization and Consumption among Urban Chinese Muslims*, Stanford, CA: Stanford University Press.

Gillette, M. (2008), 'Violence, the State, and a Chinese Muslim Ritual Remembrance', *Journal of Asian Studies*, 67(3): 1011–37.

Gillette, M. (2015), 'Women's Empowerment in the Xi'an Muslim District', in H. Ahmed-Ghosh (ed.), *Contesting Feminisms: Gender and Islam in Asia*, 69–88. Albany, NY: SUNY Press.

GIMDES (n.d.), *GIMDES: About Us.* http://www.halalcertificationturkey.com/en/about-us/.

Gladney, D. (1996), *Muslim Chinese: Ethnic Nationalism in the People's Republic*, Cambridge, MA: Council on East Asian Studies, Harvard University.

Gluten Free Salafi (n.d.), *Gluten Free Salafi* website. glutenfreesalafi.com.

Gooch, L. (2010), 'Malaysia Seeks to Export Its Halal Credentials to China', *The New York Times*. http://www.nytimes.com/2010/12/22/business/global/22chinahalal.html?pagewanted=all&_r=0.

Grain Processing Corporation (2013), *Grain Processing Corporation*. www.grainprocessing.com.

Halal Advocates of America (n.d.), *Halal Advocates of America*. halaladvocates.net.

Halal Food Blogspot (2012), 'Aquamarine', *The Halal Food Blog*. http://thehalalfoodblog.blogspot.se/2012/10/aquamarine.html.

Halal Food Council (n.d.), *Halalfoodcouncil.info*. http://halalfoodcouncil.info/history.html.

Halal World Center (n.d.), *Halal World Center*. http://en.halalcenterrussia.ru/main/about-us/.

Halalworld.org. (n.d.), *Halalworld Institute: Islamic Chamber Research and Information Institute*. http://www.halalworld.org/home?lang=en#.UoIoZrt77II.

Harrington, J. (1997), 'Nike Recalls Disputed Logo: Company Apologizes to Offended Muslims', *The Cincinnati Enquirer*. http://www.enquirer.com/editions/1997/06/25/bus_nike.html.

Hasan, M. (2012), 'Halal Hysteria: The British "Debate" about Meat, Animal Cruelty, and Ritual Slaughter Has Become a Proxy for Deeper Fears', *The New Statesman*. http://www.newstatesman.com/politics/politics/2012/05/halal-hysteria.

HealthyMuslim.com. (2013), *HealthyMuslim.Com: Your Guide to Health, Fitness, and Longevity*. http://www.healthymuslim.com/index.cfm.

HealthyMuslim.com. (n.d.), 'Eat Less and Live Healthier and Longer?' *HealthyMuslim.com*. http://www.healthymuslim.com/articles/xqmwqaloz-eat-less-and-live-longer.cfm.

HealthyMuslim.com. (n.d.), 'Dark chocolate in Moderation is Beneficial', *HealthyMuslim.com*. http://www.healthymuslim.com/articles/ossuo-dark-chocolate-in-moderation-is-beneficial.cfm.

Henley, J. (2013), 'Halal Food: Why is it So Hard to Find in Britain?' *The Guardian*. http://www.theguardian.com/lifeandstyle/2013/sep/25/halal-food-why-hard-find-britain?CMP=twt_gu.

Hero Chips (2012), *Hero Fresh Potato Chips Promo Page*. www.herocrisps.com.

Hurriet Daily News (2013), '"Tomatoes are Christian", Egyptian Salafi Group Warns', *Hurriet Daily News*. http://www.hurriyetdailynews.com/tomatoes-are-christian-egyptian-salafi-group-warns--.aspx?pageID=238&nid=23713.

IFANCA (n.d.), 'FAQs: May we eat gelatin?' *IFANCA* website. http://www.ifanca.org/faq/faqs/detail/4ca2fa8c-b848-4c0e-8e85-593c1b830f0c.

Illume Media (2013), 'California Muslims Launch the Nation's First Halal Food and
    Eid Festival', *Illume Media*. http://www.illumemagazine.com/zine/articleDetail.
    php?California-Muslims-Launch-the-Nation-s-First-Halal-Food-and-Eid-Festival-14446.

Islam Online (2002), 'Iran's Zamzam-Cola to Quench Pilgrims' Thirst in Makkah',
    IslamOnline.net. http://archive.is/YQ5fq.

JAKIM, the Department of Islamic Development Malaysia (2011), *Halal Malaysia*. http://
    www.halal.gov.my/v3/index.php/en/corporate/halal-history.

Kaya, I. (2005), 'Identity and Space: The Case of the Turkish Americans', *Geographical
    Review*, 95(3): 425–40.

Knafo, S. (2007), 'Decline of the Dog'. *The New York Times*. http://www.nytimes.
    com/2007/07/29/nyregion/thecity/29hala.html.

Koenig, L. (2008), 'Keeping the Faith', *Gastronomica*, 8(1): 80–4.

Lambek, M. (1995), 'Choking on the Qur'an: And Other Consuming Parables from the
    Western Indian Ocean Front', in W. James (ed.), *The Pursuit of Certainty*, 258–81,
    London: Routledge.

Lee, V. (2010), 'The Mosque and Black Islam: Towards an Ethnographic study of Islam in
    the Inner City', *Ethnography*, 11(1): 145–63.

Mehra, C. (2002), 'Chinese Muslims Protest Persecution', *The Nation*. http://wwrn.org/
    articles/13185/?&place=united-states&section=islam.

Mohammed, A. (2013), 'First Halal Festival Draws Crowd of 10,000', *San Jose Mercury
    News*. http://www.mercurynews.com/fremont/ci_23920272/first-halal-festival-draws-
    crowd-10-000.

Mroue, B. (2002), 'Arab Countries Boycott U.S. Goods Over Mideast Policies', *Los
    Angeles Times*. http://articles.latimes.com/2002/jul/29/business/fi-boycott29.

Murphy, C. (1986), 'Piety and Honor: The Meaning of Muslim Feasts in Old Delhi', in
    R. S. Khare and M. S. A. Rao (eds), *Food, Society and Culture*, 85–119, Durham, NC:
    Carolina Academic Press.

Muslim Consumer Group (2005–12), *Muslim Consumer Group Website*. www.muslim
    consumergroup.com/.

Muslim Consumer Group (2007), 'Kefir is not Halal', *Muslim Consumer Group Alerts*,
    posted 20 October 2007. http://www.muslimconsumergroup.com/alerts.html.

Muslim Consumer Group (2009), 'Publix Brand Breads are Not Halal', *Muslim Consumer
    Group Alerts*, posted 17 December 2009. http://www.muslimconsumergroup.com/
    alerts.html.

Muslim Consumer Group (2010a), 'Do Not Bring Laxmi Products To', *Muslim Consumer
    Group Alerts*, posted 16 April 2010. http://www.muslimconsumergroup.com/alerts.html.

Muslim Consumer Group (2010b), 'Facts about Non-Alcoholic Wine', *Muslim Consumer
    Group Alerts*, posted 4 August 2010. http://www.muslimconsumergroup.com/
    alerts.html.

Muslim Consumer Group (2012), 'Malaysia JAKIM is Violating US Fair Business Practices
    Act of 1974 By Approving Only Two Halal Certifying Organizations out of Many So
    That They Can Monopolize Halal Certification Business in USA', *Muslim Consumer
    Group Alerts*, posted 18 March 2012. http://www.muslimconsumergroup.com/
    alerts.html.

Muslim Consumer Group (2013a), 'MCG's Analysis of Alcohol in US-made Soft Drinks Will Be Same in Other Countries If the Ingredient Statements are Same', *Muslim Consumer Group Alerts*, posted 28 July 2013. http://www.muslimconsumergroup.com/alerts.html.

Muslim Consumer Group (2013b), 'Halal-haram-mashbooh ingredients', http://www.muslimconsumergroup.com/halal-haram-mushbooh_ingredients.html.

MS 1500 (2009), *Halal Food – Production, Preparation, Handling and Storage – General Guidelines*, second edition, Jalan Usahawan, Malaysia: Department of Standards Malaysia.

The Nation (2011), 'Thailand Urged to Cash in on Halal Products', *The Nation (Thailand)*. http://www.nationmultimedia.com/2011/01/28/business/Thailand-urged-to-cash-in-on-halal-products-30147385.html.

O'Loughlin, A. (2013), 'Jail Conditions Forced Muslim into Hunger Strike', *The Irish Examiner*. http://www.irishexaminer.com/archives/2013/0719/world/jail-conditions-forced-muslim-into-hunger-strike-237304.html.

Ogilvy and Mather (2010), 'Brands and the New Muslim Consumer Executive Summary: Landmark Ogilvy & Mather Study Identifies "New Muslim Consumer"'. http://www.slideshare.net/OgilvyAsia/brands-islam-and-the-new-muslim-consumer-executive-summary.

Oglivy Noor (n.d.), 'A Little Empathy Goes A Long Way: How Brands Can Engage the American Muslim Consumer'. http://americanmuslimconsumer.com/2013/wp-content/uploads/2013/09/Ogilvy-Noor_A-Little-Empathy-Goes-A-Long-Way.pdf.

Orlando Sentinal (1995), 'Iranian Leader Drops Ban On Eating Of Shark Meat', *Orlando Sentinel*. http://articles.orlandosentinel.com/1995-02-17/news/9502170663_1_shark-meat-islam-ayatollah-ali-khamenei.

Osburne, J. (2011), 'Food for Islamic Diets Big Industry Here', *Philadelphia Inquirer*, republished in *Muslim Voice Community Newspaper*. http://www.azmuslimvoice.info/index.php?option=com_content&view=article&id=911:food-for-islamic-diets-big-industry-here&catid=24:politics&Itemid=28.

Othman, P., Sungkar, I. and Hussein, W. S. W. (2009), 'Malaysia as an International Halal Food Hub: Competitiveness and Potential of Meat-based Industries', *ASEAN Economic Bulletin*, 26(3): 306–20.

Pew Research Center (2009), *Mapping the Global Muslim Population*, Washington, DC: Pew Research Center's Forum on Religion and Public Life. http://www.pewforum.org/2009/10/07/mapping-the-global-muslim-population/.

Pew Research Center (2011), *The Future of the Global Muslim Population*, Washington, DC: Pew Research Center's Forum on Religion and Public Life. http://www.pewforum.org/2011/01/27/the-future-of-the-global-muslim-population/.

Pew Research Center (2012), *The World's Muslims: Unity and Diversity*, Washington, DC: Pew Research Center's Forum on Religion and Public Life. http://www.pewforum.org/2012/08/09/the-worlds-muslims-unity-and-diversity-executive-summary/.

Pew Research Center (2013), *The World's Muslims: Religion, Politics and Society*, Washington, DC: Pew Research Center's Forum on Religion and Public Life. http://www.pewforum.org/2013/04/30/the-worlds-muslims-religion-politics-society-exec/.

Popenoe, R. (1999), 'Islam and the Body: Female Fattening among Arabs in Niger', *ISIM Newsletter*, 4(99): 5.

Popenoe, R. (2004), *Feeding Desire: Fatness, Beauty, and Sexuality among a Saharan People*, London: Routledge.

The Qur'an (n.d.), *The Noble Qur'an*. http://quran.com/.

Qureshi, H. and Smithers, R. (2009), 'Halal Food No Longer a Minority Taste', *The Guardian*. http://www.theguardian.com/lifeandstyle/2009/sep/18/halal-food-taste.

Reilly. R. J. (2013), 'Guantanamo Hunger Strike Will Lead to Multiple Deaths, Says Military's Muslim Adviser', *The Huffington Post*. http://www.huffingtonpost.com/2013/04/18/guantanamo-hunger-strike-deaths_n_3110642.html.

Rouse, C. (2004), *Engaged Surrender*, Berkeley: University of California Press.

Rouse, C. and Hoskins, J. (2004), 'Purity, Soul Food and Sunni Islam: Explorations at the Intersection of Consumption and Resistance', *Cultural Anthropology*, 19(2): 226–49.

Sarroub, L. (2005), *All American Yemeni Girls: Being Muslim in a Public School*, Philadelphia: University of Pennsylvania Press.

Schröder, D. (2009), 'Halal is Big Business: Germany Waking Up to Growing Market for Muslim Food', *Spiegel Online International*. http://www.spiegel.de/international/germany/halal-is-big-business-germany-waking-up-to-growing-market-for-muslim-food-a-653585.html.

Smith, L. (2005), 'Quranic Etiquette: Why My Egyptian Doorman Ate My Homework', *Slate*. http://www.slate.com/articles/life/faithbased/2005/05/quranic_etiquette.html.

South China Morning Post (2008), 'TDC Ensures That Muslim Guests Will Feel at Home', *South China Morning Post*. http://www.scmp.com/article/643700/tdc-ensures-muslim-guests-will-feel-home.

Sunni Forum (2004, 2007), 'Use of Ethyl Alcohol in Food/Drinks and its Permissibility', http://www.sunniforum.com/forum/showthread.php?31590-Use-of-Ethyl-Alcohol-in-Food-Drinks-and-Its-permissibility!.

Tapper, R. and Tapper, N. (1986), 'Eat This, It'll Do You a Power of Good: Food and Commensality among Durrani Pashtuns', *American Ethnologist*, 13(1): 62–79.

Theodoulou, M., Bremmer, C. and McGrory, D. (2002), 'Cola Wars as Islam Shuns the Real Thing', *The Times*. http://www.thetimes.co.uk/tto/news/world/article1972859.ece.

Thomas, L. (2010), 'List of the World's Most Muslim Friendly Brands Published', *Muslim Village.com*. http://muslimvillage.com/2010/11/06/7150/list-of-worlds-most-muslim-friendly-brands-published/.

Townsend, M. (2013), 'BMA Urges Obama to Stop Doctors Force Feeding Guantánamo Prisoners', *The Guardian*. http://www.theguardian.com/world/2013/jul/27/bma-says-end-guantanamo-force-feeding.

Ward, N. and Almås, R. (1997), 'Explaining Change in the International Agro-Food System', *Review of International Political Economy*, 4(4): 611–29.

Wilson, J. and Liu, J. (2010), 'Shaping the Halal into a Brand?', *Journal of Islamic Marketing*, 1(2): 107–23.

World Halal Council (2013), *WHC World Halal Council*. http://www.worldhalalcouncil.com/about-us.

Yamami, M. (1994), 'You Are What You Cook: Cuisine and Class in Mecca', in S. Zubaida and R. Tapper (eds), *Culinary Cultures of the Middle East*, 173–84, London: I.A. Tauris.

Young, G. (2013), 'Summer Festivals 2013: Your Guide to Bay Area Fairs and Outdoor Fun', *San Jose Mercury News*. http://www.mercurynews.com/ci_23300287/summer-festivals-2013-your-guide-bay-area-fairs.

Zadeh, T. (2009), 'Touching and Ingesting: Early Debates over the Material Qur'an', *Journal of the American Oriental Society*, 129(3): 443–66.

CHAPTER THREE

Food, Commensality and Caste in South Asia

JAMES STAPLES

INTRODUCTION

Das, a Tamil Brahmin and my sometime research assistant, was candidly recounting to me his relationship, forty years previously, with a Dalit[1] prostitute he had met in a Bombay slum. Young, far from home and lonely, he had taken comfort in the fact that she, like him, originated from the city of Madras, on India's opposite coastline. 'If you stayed the whole night, had sex once or twice and ate food there, it would cost around Rs100',[2] he explained, adding that although he may have slept over in her hut a few times, he had always declined her offers of food. He was prepared to take coffee, or a bottled soft drink purchased from outside, but not food that she or her family had prepared at home. 'Maybe [it was] a non-vegetarian household,' he said, a tad sheepishly, as if to acknowledge the contradictions inherent in what he was saying. 'Even in Bombay, I wouldn't take food unless I knew the people quite well.'

The extent to which caste identity affects who might eat together in South Asia, or what they might eat, where and when, is complex, contingent and highly variable, with considerable variations noted across regions, time periods and shifting social contexts. Das's intuitive sense that to eat food prepared by someone of lower ritual status than himself was riskier than to have sexual intercourse with them may well have been contested by some of his Brahmin peers. Indeed, several commentators argue that food-sharing rules are often relaxed ahead of other markers of caste status, including with whom one might have sexual relations (Klass 1980: 34). What his story illustrates, however, is not only how fraught cross-caste exchanges of food might be – with some consumables relatively more acceptable than others – but also that distinctions based on relative purity or Hindu 'transactional thinking' (Marriott 1976: 109) might be insufficient as predictors of who might accept what food from whom. In Das's case, it appears, the fact that her cooking utensils might have been used to prepare meat dishes was as at least as significant as the cook's caste identity (although the two were, of course, deeply interrelated).

I begin with this vignette, drawn from a much longer series of life-history interviews with Das (Staples 2014a), as a device to highlight the ambivalence surrounding how food rules might be read, reconstituted and acted upon in India, both now and in the past. Social rules governing whom one might accept particular kinds of cooked food from are now further complicated by statutes that outlaw caste discrimination and offer positive discrimination for the ritually lowest-ranking castes. This means that the simple reading off of caste hierarchy from the observation of public food transactions envisaged by an earlier generation of ethnographers is no longer possible, if indeed it ever was. As Adrian Mayer pointed out in relation to his fieldwork in a central Indian village in the 1950s, answers to his questions about which castes would eat, drink or smoke together were rather notional, since 'much inter-caste commensality had never been tested by actual invitations to eat together' (1996: 35; see also Staples 2007: 134). In addition, as I will demonstrate, seemingly static rules are regularly manipulated, reinterpreted or just plain broken, across a range of different contexts.

I begin by reviewing and contextualizing the anthropological literature on food and its relation to caste in India. I then consider – with reference to more recent material, including my own fieldwork in Andhra Pradesh, on India's south-east coastline – the ways in which caste and food continue to be intertwined in social contexts increasingly shaped also by class, environmental concerns and a liberalization of trade. New kinds of food and styles of preparation also serve to challenge an overly simplistic, singular or constant reading of relations between caste and food. First, however, for the benefit of non-South Asianist readers, some background on the notion of 'caste' itself, and the historic connection between caste and food, is called for.

DEFINING CASTE

What Béteille calls the 'book view' (1991: 8) of caste traces its roots back to Hindu creation stories recorded in the verses of the *Rigveda* – one of the canonical sacred Hindu texts, thought to have been written 3,000–3,500 years ago (Fuller 1992a: 12). According to the *Rigveda*, humanity was created out of the sacrifice of Purusha, the primordial man, into four distinct, hierarchically ordered categories or *varnas*. Brahmins, the priestly *varna*, emanated from Purusha's mouth; the Kshatriyas, as warriors and rulers, from his arms; the Vaisyas, the merchants and traders, from his thighs; and the Shudras, there to serve the other three *varnas* above them, from his feet (ibid.).[3] The origins of the 'Untouchables' – or Scheduled Castes (SC) as they are now officially known – are less clear, although there are numerous additional myths to account for their later arrival at the bottom of the social hierarchy (see, e.g. Deliége 1993). Over the centuries, as the roles of each *varna* were elaborated in the *Dharmashastras* (Hindu sacred law books), each were further divided into separate *jatis*, or castes. There are, for instance, numerous Brahmin *jatis*. But in its most straightforward form, to summarize Dumont's interpretation of the caste system as set out in his classic, *Homo Hierarchicus* (1980),[4] Brahmins, as the most inherently pure *varna*, came top in a hierarchy of ritual status, followed respectively by Kshatriyas, Vaisyas and Shudras, each of whom were relatively less pure than those who preceded them, their relative impurity defined in relation to the purity of those above them and *vice versa*. The status of the Brahmin, from Dumont's perspective, was wholly reliant on the opposing ritual status of the Untouchable. The *jatis* within each *varna* were also ordered hierarchically, although here the ordering was more contested and regionally variable.

Dumont's structural analysis of caste as a holistic, relational system based on the principles of relative purity and impurity, where ritual status trumped (or, in Dumont's terms, encompassed) political power, has been subjected to sustained critique over the nearly five decades since the publication of *Homo Hierarchicus*. Here is not the place to reenact the various arguments.[5] It suffices to state that they centre around Dumont's perceived failure to take adequate account of actual caste practices on the ground that would have contradicted his grand theoretical schema; his Brahmin-centric perspective that blinded him to alternative orderings of the *varna* system (Dirks 2001; Quigley 1999; Burghart 1978); his inadequate recognition of the role colonialism played in shaping caste into something rather different to that imagined in the *Rigveda* (Appadurai 1986, 1988; Béteille 1991; Dirks 2001: 5); and an overcommitment to Western dualistic models as opposed to Hindu categories (Marriott 1976: 113). The ethnographic observation that priestly Brahmins are often afforded lower status than non-priestly ones (Parry 1994; Fuller 2007), for example, casts doubt over the validity of Dumont's neat correlation of purity and ritual status. Where Dumont's analysis remains useful, however, is in its assertion that the ordering of castes is relational (Mosse 1999), which means that castes derive their status not only on the grounds of their inherent attributes – from being born, for example, into a particular caste, or engaged in a particular caste-based occupation – but also on the basis of their interactions with other castes. It is here that food becomes significant.

CASTE BOUNDARIES AND FOOD TRANSACTIONS

The importance of food transactions to maintaining caste boundaries has long been recognized. An essay written by Célestin Bouglé in 1908 (translated into English by David Pocock in 1971) records that 'it is above all from food that contamination is feared. It can only be eaten amongst caste-fellows; it should not be even be touched by a stranger, whose glance is sometimes sufficient to pollute it' (Bouglé 1971: 23; see also Dubois 1906: 181–9). Émile Senart noted in his 1930 book on caste that people would refuse food prepared or even touched by those they considered their inferiors, while O'Malley, a couple of years later, reported in *Indian Caste Customs* that one of the most salient features of caste was that 'members of the same caste eat and drink together but not with members of an inferior caste' (1932: 1). So fraught was the business of avoiding food prepared by those ranked lower than oneself that, according to O'Malley, a college hostel in Allahabad had required thirty-seven cooks to cater for just 100 students (1932: 106–7). For anthropologists of the 'village studies' era in the years that followed Indian independence, these rules of public dining appeared relatively stable. Classics of the village studies era, such as Srinivas's *Religion and Society among the Coorgs of South India* (1952) and Dube's *Village India* (1955) – both based on rural ethnographic fieldwork in the South – routinely record Hindus' resistance towards accepting cooked food prepared or offered to them by anyone from a lower caste (Srinivas 1952: 27; Dube 1955: 37–8). Béteille, a little later, likewise noted that 'the common meal expresses symbolically both the unity of those who eat together and the cleavages between those who are required to eat separately' (1965: 56). Brahmins in the area of his fieldwork – Tanjore District of Tamil Nadu, in India's south-east – usually dealt with this by not attending the wedding feasts of non-Brahmins, although if they did they would be given consumables such as betel leaves, areca nuts and fruit: items that were not seen as inherently polluted (1965: 58). Like my research assistant Das, some of the more 'progressive' Brahmins might also have accepted coffee (ibid.), while sweetmeats prepared from sugar, milk and ghee – as long as they are unbroken – have long been widely acceptable (see, e.g. O'Malley 1932: 41).

McKim Marriott and his Indianist colleagues at the University of Chicago accepted Dumont's assertion that caste distinctions were observable in public commensality, but were also highly critical of what they saw as Dumont's reading of caste through Western categories rather than through Hindu ones (Marriott 1990: xiii; 1976: 13; see Fuller 1992b for a critique of Marriott). In proposing an ethnosociological approach to understanding India (a move that prefigured the later 'ontological turn' in Anthropology), Marriott attempted to explain that food transactions were not simply about the maintenance of social boundaries or of cultural difference – reducible to the binary opposition of purity and impurity. Rather, food exchanges were literally about protecting or transforming diners' moral qualities. Unlike Western persons, who, Marriott claimed, perceive and experience themselves as relatively stable, self-contained units or individuals, Hindus experience themselves as what he termed 'dividual': that is, composed of unstable, transferable atoms and, therefore, potentially transformed through their interactions with other people and things. In Marriott's own words:

> Dividual persons absorb heterogeneous material influences. They must also give out from themselves particles of their own coded substances – essences, residues, or other active influences – that may then reproduce in others something of the nature of the person in whom they have originated. (1976: 111)

From this perspective, receiving 'highly particulating substances' (Daniel 1987: 186) – such as cooked food or water – posed particular risks to the diner's bodily and moral integrity: cooked rice, because it was boiled in water, absorbed the qualities of the cook during preparation, which were subsequently passed on to those who ate it. Such foods, as previous authors had documented (e.g. Cantlie 1981; Khare 1976, 1992), were known as *kacca*, which were contrasted to *pucca* dishes: less risky consumables, fried in ghee (which, as a product of the sacred cow was harder to contaminate) rather than boiled in water.[6] Cooking pots and other vessels were also more or less susceptible to absorbing pollution: metal pots were apparently less absorbent than earthen vessels, for example (Cantlie 1981: 50; Dubois 1906: 181; Senart 1930: 39), while disposable tableware – such as plates made from stitched-together leaves – were often used to feed outsiders and those of lower status to avoid contamination from those whose substance-code was incompatible. O'Malley's further observation that the Brahmin ate in such a way as to avoid even contact between his own hand and his mouth – 'he rolls his rice into a ball of convenient size and, holding his head back, pops it into his open mouth without his hand touching the latter' (1932: 114) – might appear overly orthodox by today's standards, but given that nearly all the people I have worked with, across all castes, studiously avoided putting a glass or a bottle to their lips when they drank water, it seems highly plausible (see also Achaya 1994: 63; Srinivas 1952: 103). Tamil Brahmins, in particular, favoured using two vessels – a deep stainless steel saucer and a small matching tumbler – to serve coffee so that the coffee could be poured back and forth between each until, as it was explained to me, it was cool enough to pour into one's open mouth without having to touch the glass to one's lips. In addition, cooks would avoid tasting a dish during preparation with any utensil that would again come into contact with the food, and even water used to rinse the mouth should be spat out rather than swallowed (Guha 1985: 141). None of this is simply a technical matter of hygiene. 'Food in India', as Khare summarizes it rather nicely, 'is ... never simply a material substance; it is never only what the eyes see. The unseen karma and dharma of the giver and receiver energize it, circulate it, and colour it' (1992: 6).

Behaviours to minimize risk of contamination still appeared to form part of most Hindus' (and, indeed, converted Christians') embodied repertoire – even when it was no longer explicitly articulated in those terms – with arrangements altered to accommodate or obscure from view these enduring dispositions rather than challenge them directly. In the central Indian village where Mayer conducted fieldwork, for example, transformations in commensal relations between certain castes over the last few decades had been made possible not by challenging beliefs in the fluidity of personal bodily boundaries, but by changing the kinds of foods offered at feasts. Whereas in 1954 a range of both *kacca* and *pucca* dishes were served (roasted wheat balls [*batti*] and dhal – both *kacca* – and sweetmeats, which were considered *pucca*), by the time Mayer revisited nearly forty years later, the feast menu – of *puri* (deep-fried wheat breads), vegetable curry and sweetmeats – was comprised entirely of what were seen as *pucca* items (1997: 36–8). Likewise in Kerala, Osella and Osella note that hosts often arranged functions at which only bakery items would be served in order that castes higher than themselves would be able to attend (2000: 241). Such dietary modifications enabled, in contemporary settings, the avoidance of acknowledging perceived differences in relative purity. In the case described by Osella and Osella, for example, although men from differently ranked castes emphasized gender and class solidarities by sharing alcoholic drinks together in public spaces as friends, consumption in each other's homes was avoided. 'For a Nayar man to hold hands with his Izhava friend on the street requires only external contact', they explain, 'and that too in a neutral, public space; consumption – a symbolic taking into oneself of the other – implies internal contact, and assimilation of alien substance' (2000: 230).[7]

CASTE AND TYPES OF FOOD

Valentine Daniel, one of the few South Asianist anthropologists to apply an ethnosociological approach across an entire monograph, noted that as well as reproducing themselves through their transactions with one another, castes also maintained their 'substance-codes'[8] through the *kinds* of food they ate (1987: 186). Drawing on Marriott's classification of 'transactional strategies' (1976: 109), he demonstrated ethnographically that those Marriott dubbed 'minimal transactors' – castes who avoid both giving and receiving *kacca* food – find 'cooling foods' most compatible with their substance, whereas 'maximal transactors' – castes prepared to receive as well as to give food to other castes – tend to favour 'heating foods' (1984: 70–1; see Marriott 1976: 125–9). 'The hot castes', Daniel tells us, 'more readily, willingly and customarily eat hot foods than do the cool castes' (1987: 186). Some foods are widely recognized as hot or cold: onions and garlic, for example, are nearly always referred to as heating and, as such, should be avoided by cool castes and certain categories of people, such as widows, in whom they might inappropriately inflame passions (see, e.g. Lamb 2000). Conversely, consumed by the appropriate people, hot foods such as wild meat and alcohol might positively be transformed 'into outputs of greater gifts, payments, sexual power and violence' (Marriott 1976: 123; see, e.g., Carstairs 1957: 84, 188; Mayer 1960: 44–5; Beck 1969). Daniel acknowledges that there is no definitive classificatory system into which hot and cool foods might be separated: buffalo milk is considered hot by Telugu Brahmins of Kalappur, for instance, but not by the Parayans of the same village. The relative appropriateness of particular foods to particular people might also vary seasonally and according to factors beyond caste – such as gender, stage in the life cycle or individual substance-code. As Daniel shows, for example, food grown from the soil of one's natal home, or water drawn from its wells, will always be considered more compatible than food consumed in other places. Cantlie (1981), drawing on fieldwork with Hindus in Assam, notes also that young boys and premenstrual girls are less open to the dangers of pollution through food than their more senior peers – an insight which helps to explain why children's taste for meat is often pandered to in otherwise vegetarian houses in urban West Bengal and Tamil Nadu (Donner 2008a; Caplan 2008). Both examples remind us of the significance of the diner's position in the life cycle as well as his or her caste.

Some of the rules recorded map quite well onto the hot/heating versus cold/cooling categories Daniel sets up, while others require additional frames of reference. *The Laws of Manu*, for example, forbade the so-called twice-born castes (Brahmins, Kshatriyas and Vaisyas) to consume 'domestic fowls, onions and garlic, turnips and carrots, salted pork and mushrooms' (O'Malley 1932: 116), while 'other castes abhor lentils and tomatoes because their colour resembles blood' (1932: 118). Mushrooms were still considered risky by some of my own higher-caste informants in South India, perhaps as a corollary of earlier injunctions, noted by Dubois (1906: 87), to avoid vegetables, like mushrooms, whose roots or stems grew into 'the shape of a head', presumably because to have eaten them would have symbolized cannibalism. Since mushrooms were anyway rare in the South – at

least in coastal Andhra where I worked – my informants' ambivalence might also
have been shaped by the problem of incorporating new or seldom encountered foods
into their existing classificatory models. When potatoes were first introduced into
Bengal in the mid-eighteenth century, for example, they were seen as unacceptable,
at least for Brahmins, although they later became well incorporated into the cuisine
(O'Malley 1932: 119; Achaya 1994: 129). In much of contemporary India, as I will
explore further below, new European- and East Asian- inspired dishes such as pizzas,
vegetarian burgers and stir-fried noodles have provoked classifications beyond (or in
addition to) those made between *pucca/kacca* or cold/hot, which draw as much on
class as on caste identities.

But perhaps the most significant distinction drawn in terms of *what* people eat
is that made between vegetarianism and non-vegetarianism, distinctions that –
at least in large parts of the southern states of Andhra Pradesh, Tamil Nadu and
Karnataka – correlate fairly well with caste distinctions. As Fuller puts it, 'The
pronounced opposition between the two great categories – Brahmins versus non-
Brahmins and Harijans – also tends to be assimilated to that between vegetarians and
non-vegetarians' (1992a: 93). As he also notes, however, this correlation becomes
weaker in the north of India – especially in states where meat-eating Rajputs, of the
Kshatriya *varna*, are dominant – and also in Kerala and West Bengal. In Kashmir
Brahmins have been noted to eat meat (Srinivas 1952: 52), and similar observations
have been made in Kerala, with some high-status castes – such as the Nayars – even
consuming the more generally prohibited flesh of the cow (Osella and Osella 2000:
320). In West Bengal, too, Brahmins have long since rationalized the consumption
of meat, and, especially, fish. The eleventh-century Bengali scholar and politician
Bhatta Bhavadeva wrote, in relation to the Hindu sacred texts: 'All this prohibition
is meant for the prohibited days ... so it is understood there is no crime in eating fish
and meat' (cited in Achaya 1994: 128). Other texts of the era (see, e.g. Sachua 2005;
Achaya 1994: 56–7), by contrast, note a more widespread vegetarianism based on
ahimsa – the order not to kill – which applied in particular to Brahmins. As Achaya
notes, however, there was perhaps a materialist basis for this as well as a ritual or
spiritual one, since in ancient India there was an unparalleled abundance of non-
meat foodstuffs available: 'It is perhaps no exaggeration to say that nowhere else
in the world except in India would it have been even possible to be a vegetarian in
1000 BC' (1994: 57; see also Harris 1989 for an ecological rationalization of the
Hindu taboo on cattle consumption).

While the split between vegetarians and non-vegetarians correlates crudely with
the distinction drawn between Brahmins and non-Brahmins, however, variations
within the camps dividing those who eat or do not eat meat are perhaps more
telling of the finer distinctions drawn along caste lines. Among meat-eating castes,
for example, there was a sharp division between those who openly admitted to
eating beef – some Dalit castes, in particular – and those of the dominant Shudra
castes, who ate chicken, goat and fish, but saw beef consumption as defiling. 'I would
rather die rather than eat beef,' Atal Behari Vajpayee, the then prime minister, was
reported as saying, when posters accusing him of being a beef eater appeared in
his home state of Madhya Pradesh.[9] This move, by a right-wing Hindu nationalist
party, forcefully linked the high-caste taboo on beef with patriotic behaviour,

marginalizing non-Hindu Indians (Muslims and Christians in particular) and Dalit castes (see O'Toole 2003).

At the same time, the conscious rejection of beef – and, for some castes, meat altogether – had also been a powerful strategy in terms of social mobility. Such actions may have been seen as part of the process of what Srinivas – drawing on his work with the Coorgs of South India – called Sanskritization (1952; see also Bailey 1957: 271; Charsley 1998). As Srinivas defined it, Sanskritization is a process by which lower castes adopt the practices and ideologies, including those relating to food and commensality, of the higher castes. Similar moves have been recorded among low-caste converts to Christianity. For the Paraiyar Catholics described by Mosse (1999) in Tamil Nadu, for example, conversion to Christianity was seen as symbolizing a shift from practices seen as unclean – beef-eating among them – to those worthy of respect. This resonates with the rejection of beef by Madiga (leatherworker Dalits) converts in the 1920s – also in South India – who were persuaded to change their eating habits to encourage other castes to convert alongside them (Harper 2000: 278). 'To move upwards', as Goody neatly summarizes it, 'meant changing one's diet, usually by becoming more vegetarian' (Goody 1982: 115).

Recent work by Desai (2008) among a Hindu sect in central India, however, challenges the view, inherent in Srinivas's Sanskritization thesis, that low-caste adoption of vegetarianism simply apes high-caste practice in order to achieve social mobility. Desai argues instead that his subaltern informants see eschewing meat as a spiritually transformative act in itself.[10] Whatever motivates people to give up meat, however, my central point here is the same: such choices disrupt a straightforward correlation between caste and vegetarianism. Changing one's diet as a strategy either of social mobility or of religious transformation is also compatible, at least theoretically, with the ethnosociological argument that one's bodily substance is materially altered through consumption: it allows those who embrace vegetarianism, for example, to claim that they have *literally* changed in the process. Where Marriott's Hindu categories are less successful is in providing an explanation for changes in the opposite direction, which is what I begin with in the next section.

FROM THE ONTOLOGICAL TO THE POLITICO-ECONOMIC

For the mostly low-caste Christian converts I worked with in coastal Andhra Pradesh, the consumption of meat – and, for many of them, of beef in particular – was represented not as a source of shame or defilement, classified according to Hindu categories, but as a positive marker of a celebrated and socially cohesive counter identity. It also demarcated them, as they described it, as modern and progressive; a direct snub to those they saw as their upper-caste Hindu oppressors. As I summarized it elsewhere:

> Christians … attempted to invert the negative symbols of their former low caste status, transforming them into positive aspects of a Christian identity. Meat consumption, therefore – especially of beef – had become a quiet celebration of

their shared Christianity *and* an illustration that they did not accept their Hindu-imposed classification as ritually impure. (Staples 2008: 43)

Such inversions of the meanings applied to meat are also recorded elsewhere in India. Although, as noted above, many Christian converts in Tamil Nadu were reported to have given up beef at the point of conversion, Mosse's more recent work on Dalit Christianity describes how Jesuit schools in some areas of the state have, conversely, begun promoting beef-eating as 'a provocative, conflict-generating, dramatic act of protest and the denial of shame' (Mosse 2010: 254; Arun 2004). The increasing politicization of beef festivals – at which the consumption of beef is publicly celebrated – on university campuses in, for example, Hyderabad and Kolkata might likewise be seen as a response to the rise in Hindu nationalism (see, e.g. Gorringe and Karthikeyan 2014).

In a more general sense, what these examples show is that food rules and their manipulation are as much about politics and oppression – what Appadurai dubbed 'gastro-politics' (1981) – as they are about distinctive Hindu ontologies. This recognition chimes with the approaches of anthropologists such as Mencher (1974), Berreman (1979) and Mitra (1994), all of whom, to greater and lesser extents, theorize the differences in cross-caste practices – including those relating to the consumption and sharing of food – in terms of the economic and political struggles between castes rather than ritual purity or cosmological concerns. 'From a bottom-up perspective,' writes Mencher, 'caste has functioned as a very effective system of economic exploitation' (1974: 469) – a system which Berreman compared with apartheid in South Africa (Berreman 1972). Appadurai, more subtly, has also argued that difficult ecological conditions and inequalities over access to food – particularly grains – helped to form the historical context against which more abstract Hindu ideas about sharing, distribution and power have come to be expressed by food (1981: 495).

While Marriott moved us away from the structural functionalism to which Dumont was intellectually bound, his work does imply a certain homogeneity in the ways Hindus think, radically opposed to 'Western' thinking. As such, he implicitly equated Hindu with upper-caste thought, and so was less successful in directing us from the Brahminical, top-down perspective that Mencher, Berreman and others have rightly been critical of. Both Dumontian and ethnosociological approaches implied that Indians across caste groups bought, more or less uniformly, into the 'book view' of Hinduism and plotted out their transactions, like 'lexicographers' (Parry 1991), in accordance with official Hindu orthodoxies. The understanding and experience of meat-eating as celebratory, however, suggests that many in India deploy explanatory frameworks that extend far beyond the limitations of models that either situate purity as the ideological foundation of the caste system (Dumont 1970) or 'transactional thinking' (Marriott 1976: 109) as the determinant of what or how people eat.

A positive spin on beef-eating is not the only exception that challenges the widespread applicability of these rules. Even as far back as the 1930s, we are told that, in urban areas, 'educated men of different castes will eat and drink together at private parties and will not scruple to eat forbidden food at hotels and restaurants' (O'Malley 1932: 118). Siegel (2010) suggests that people, men especially, also became less particular about *what* they ate when they dined outside the home. At the end of the nineteenth century, urban food culture in India 'was one of somewhat surreptitious and profane indulgence, of snacks grabbed informally in *galis* [alleyways] and at stalls, out of the view of polite company' (Siegel 2010: 77). Many, it seemed, were less concerned with literally maintaining the purity of their bodily substance than their outwardly recognized status.

My own, more recent research similarly indicated that food rules weakened the further one travelled from home. 'Even in the old days it wasn't always so strict,' my friend Gopi, a member of one of the dominant Shudra castes, told me during a field visit in 2013. I was discussing with him and some of his friends, all of them in their 60s and 70s, the changes they had seen in food consumption patterns over the years. 'If my father went to the market and had to take food outside,' he continued, 'he'd eat at the food stalls and canteens there when he had to, and people didn't ask questions about who had cooked the food, they just ate!' The others nodded. 'That's the same thing now,' said Subbaiah, who was from a comparable caste. 'In Hyderabad, where my nephews live, the Kammas, the Brahmin, even the Madiga, they might all eat together. But back in the village, the same Brahmin will still tell the Madiga to get off the bed and sit on the floor!'

Other informants were keen to regale me with stories of Brahmins and other high-status castes surreptitiously purchasing beef from the market and asking them to prepare it for them. One Dalit woman told me, in hushed tones: 'Even Brahmins will come and ask us to cook it [beef] for them sometimes. [They are] afraid to ask their own wives to prepare it, so will come to us instead!' In the diaspora, despite certain foods remaining forbidden, culinary distinctions based on caste appear to have been dropped even more comprehensively, as suggested in ethnographic reports from Guyana (Smith and Jayawardena 1967: 62); South Africa (Kuper 1967: 255–6); and Kenya (Bharati 1967: 288, 385).

Such variations, and the apparent ease with which rules are flouted away from the gaze of one's village (or one's wife), put a strain on Marriott's thesis that Hindus perceive themselves as *literally* transformed – morally and physically – through the consumption of cooked food. They also lend support to Mencher's claim that ideas about purity are little more than a smoke screen that allows for the social and economic exploitation of the lower castes by those ranked above them. Engaging with such ideas also alerts us to the political and economic aspects of food and commensality, leaving us more open to the idea that not only might ideas of relative purity be used to exploit those at the bottom, but also that the lower castes themselves might manipulate such ideas for their own ends. During my fieldwork in coastal Andhra, for example, my cook would often argue that particular dishes were unsuitable for our respective constitutions at particular times, but, as a forensic examination of my field notes later made clear, these claims were actually as much about satisfying her own culinary tastes as they were about stabilizing our bodily equilibriums (Staples 2008).

As the above example suggests, the possibilities of thought that Mencher's thesis gives rise to also reveal some of the fault lines in her argument: the relationship between food and caste cannot be reduced to a relationship only of socio-economic exploitation. First, for materially poor members of high castes, the restrictions

---

imposed both on what they might eat and whom they might accept it from can be disabling as well as indicative of status. The Bengali Brahmin widows Lamb describes, for instance, find their diets (as well as their dress and their movements) more restricted than that of their lower-caste peers, in ways that might arguably be seen as disempowering rather than unambiguously expressive of their higher status. At the same time, however, the maintenance of strict dietary rules by the upper castes might also be seen as a symbolic means of retaining their superiority *despite* material impoverishment; a strategy comparable to those deployed by the European aristocracy in response to the rise of the bourgeoisie in the nineteenth century (Mennell 1985: 209–10).

In other contexts, the fear of being accused of 'caste feeling' (Staples 2007: 145–7) in itself made for fraught commensal situations, particularly in the contemporary mixed caste contexts that some of my informants found themselves in. 'When we're staying at the college hostel,' one male student told me, 'we don't know the castes of other people, nor who has cooked the food. But if we say no to something that we are offered by a fellow student – even if we don't want it because it's something we don't like or because we are not hungry – it can be quite awkward. If you make some excuse and don't take the food you are offered you risk offending them.' A non-meat eater myself, I could empathize with the student's position: as I have analysed elsewhere (Staples 2008), when a middle-class Christian Dalit who invited me to dinner offered me beef and I declined, her sense was not simply that I was a vegetarian on the grounds of personal choice, but that I was affiliating myself with the high-caste Hindus who, she said, had exploited people like her for generations. To refuse food can be as problematic as accepting it.

The above-mentioned student was from a middle-ranking caste and like me claimed not to be overly concerned with classical rules about purity and pollution. Nevertheless, he did confess, when pressed, to some reticence about dining in the houses of others beyond his family and his community – an oblique reference, I felt, to not wishing to dine with other castes. Struggling for a form of words that he thought might be acceptable to me, he concluded: 'It's not that they are dirty, necessarily, or that I think something bad will happen to me if I eat their food, but it's just that it's not our habit, that we take care by only eating at home. Different people also eat different things, things that might not be suitable for us. Too much sharing is risky, no?'

Osella and Osella (2000: 230) capture very nicely the dangers that gastro-politics posed to what appeared outwardly as strong relationships between members of differently ranked castes in Kerala, when they recount the story of Izhava (low-caste) Satyapalan and his high-caste friend Rajasekharan. Although both men had regularly bought one another tea and snacks at local *hotels*, they never visited each other's homes until the day Rajasekharan's motor scooter unexpectedly ran out of petrol close to Satyapalan's house. Their friendship never recovered from what happened next. In the Osellas' words:

Luckily Satyapalan was at home, and elder brother's motorbike stood outside. Rajasekharan siphoned off enough petrol to get home and spat vigorously several times to get rid of the taste, wiping his mouth with his handkerchief. Satyapalan invited him, 'Come inside and have some lime-water to rinse the petrol out of your mouth.' As Rajasekharan … hesitated, Satyapalan's expression changed. He entered the house and returned with a glass of lime-water which he held out, in view of (Izhava neighbour) onlookers, to Rajasekharan: 'You have petrol in your mouth, take it.' Rajasekharan, embarrassed and flustered, tried to cover himself. 'No, really, it's alright now: I can't taste anything.' Satyapalan held the glass challengingly in outstretched hand. Rajasekharan took it and quickly swigged off less than half, grimacing, before handing it back saying, 'That's enough thanks, it's okay now.' (2000: 230)

Such stories nuance the suggestion that food rules are part of an upper-caste conspiracy to keep those who serve them in their place. Rather, the quotidian experience of such rules also constrains food-sharing behaviours of people from across the caste spectrum, sometimes adversely affecting those towards the top as well as discriminating against those at the bottom. They also suggest that embodied notions of relative purity – fractured, partial and inconsistently applied though they are – still exert influence over commensality that go beyond relations of socio-economic exploitation.

BEYOND CASTE

Since the 1980s, the spotlight has shifted away from caste and on to other forms of social differentiation – such as class and gender – that were arguably under-represented in the earlier regional ethnography. This shift overlapped with (and it was in part a consequence of) the broader disciplinary turn from structure to agency. These developments, which in some ways also responded to empirical changes in post-colonial South Asia in relation to globalization and, from the early 1990s, economic liberalization, demanded that we focus on food beyond caste and collective dining. Broadly speaking, this has happened in two main ways. First, we have started to explore how people in India might engage with food and food sharing not only in relation to caste, but in relation to other, cross-cutting identities, including gender, kinship and class. Recognition of a new or 'emerging' middle class was particularly relevant here. Secondly – and not entirely separately from the first point – we have become much more open to the idea of caste not as an overarching, determining structure, but as a resource or a malleable feature of personal identity. In respect of both, forensic observation of the micro-practices that surround food – from subtle changes in the way food is presented to the mechanics of how people eat – has revealed subtly new ways in which food, caste and politics remain intricately intertwined.

Taking first the shift from structure to agency, or from the collective to the personal, Donner's work on food as it is consumed in the home has been particularly pertinent. Drawing on Khare's insight that food is interpreted in India on three different levels – what he calls the ontological and the experimental, the transactional and therapeutic, and the world critical (1992: 8) – Donner argues that an emphasis on public consumption of food had diverted our attention away from the equally significant, everyday dining context of the family home (2008b: 155; see also Caplan 2002, 2008). In such contexts, as she demonstrates, food is as much about intra-familial relations and personal self-control as it is about collective identity. The middle-class Bengali mothers she works with in Calcutta, for example, often adopted vegetarianism not only as a marker of their high caste, Brahmin status, but specifically in order to control their sexual urges and thus to limit the sizes of their families, while continuing, in some cases, to cook meat and fish for their husbands and children (Donner 1992: 157, 159).

Busby likewise demonstrates the significance of gender to familial eating practices when describing the significance of who cooks what for whom, in the fishing village in Kerala where she conducted fieldwork: 'While fish curry may be more easily shared [than cooked rice], so that a woman may make curry for her daughter and son-in-law, or a woman for her brother-in-law, the cooking of rice or tapioca, a watery and absorbent food, is almost always done individually by women for their own husbands' (2000: 128). In this case, the logic often applied to commensal relations between castes is seen to apply also to relations between different categories of kin: in the same way that those castes from which one should not accept cooked food are also those into which one should not marry, cooking rice for a man here implies an intimacy that is seen as proper only within marriage. Sex and food, in short, are closely linked.

While Busby's work nicely nuances earlier work on food and caste – demonstrating a wider nexus of relations, including kinship and gender, that help to configure who eats what and with whom – Donner's analysis also hints at a wider historical shift, one that sees a move from the collective, or caste, as the locus of one's identity, to the personal. For the middle-class mothers of her study, vegetarianism is reconfigured as a form of self-cultivation: a 'traditional' high-caste practice reinterpreted in relation to new consumption patterns. In some ways, such shifts in how people eat have been made possible by wider changes. The proliferation of takeaway stalls selling packets of readymade curries, even in the small towns like those I worked in, meant that individual members had greater choice over what they ate than they would have had in the past. I knew several women, for example, who could now avoid the beef their husbands demanded – even if they still cooked it for them – because the men could pick up a packet of *sambar* for them on the way back from the meat market. The increasing number of fridges in even village homes also gave families a greater flexibility over what could be served and when.

What was particularly notable, however, was a shift in the idioms that people used to talk about and justify their food choices. Meat, for example, was no longer envisaged just as a marker of low-caste status, as it had been in the past, but could also be configured as something of high class (because of its cost), sophisticated, modern and progressive. Eating chicken Manchurian (deep-fried balls of chicken served in a 'Chinese style' sauce) or egg fried noodles outside one of the Chinese food carts that now lined the main road into the town, as my younger informants told me, was fashionable among students from across caste groups, the areas around the carts becoming places to 'hang out' and be seen (see Staples 2014b). Much of the talk I heard about meat in recent years was also framed in terms of health rather than on caste *per se*. 'I grew up as a vegetarian,' one of my older male informants told me, 'but the doctor suggested to me that I should take up meat because I was anaemic and it would be good for me. It helps to keep me strong.' By contrast, several women who had previously eaten meat told me they had given it up, not (at least explicitly) as a strategy of elevating their status, but on medical advice to reduce their blood pressure. 'I stopped meat because of BP,' a Dalit Christian woman said, 'but, in the old days, meat was also tastier to eat than it is now, and better for you, too. Back then you didn't have all the pesticides on the crops that the animals eat, and they were farmed differently, so they had more bite and more flavour.' Use of idioms related to class, education, modernity and health gave people in contemporary India a language to talk about – and experience – food that went beyond caste and, certainly, a large number of accounts suggest that caste is also less important in terms of public dining than it once was.

That is not to say, however, that caste has become obsolete in relation to food in India. On the contrary, it remains important, but in many contexts – particularly in urban environments – the ways in which caste is engaged with has begun to shift. I know several Brahmins, for example, who remain strictly vegetarian and retain a pride in the kind of preparations they serve in the home which mark them out as Brahmins, but who are much less worried than they would have been in the past about who has cooked the food they eat in other contexts. In a similar, but more negative, way, people I worked with would regularly comment on what or how other people ate as symptomatic of their lower-caste status, referring, for example, to rough or heavy spicing as 'low caste preparations', or the style of throwing food into one's mouth (see Staples 2008, 2014b) as 'a very low caste way of eating'. Here, the language remained linked to caste, but the comments blurred the lines between caste and class – perhaps unsurprisingly, given that high-class status very often coincides with high-caste status (see, e.g. Fuller and Narasimhan 2007). In short, then, food remained a marker of both personal and caste identity; but as caste seemed only peripherally to be experienced in terms of ritual purity, particularly for younger informants, the relationship between food and caste was a changing one.

CONCLUSION

One of the things that has become clear in revisiting the literature to write this chapter is that shifts in how the relationships between food and caste have been understood by anthropologists have, at one level, been about broader epistemological shifts far away – literally *and* figuratively – from the Indian village contexts in which we have traditionally viewed these relationships. Structural functionalism, and the village studies of the 1950s that it spawned, gradually gave way to the dominance of French structuralism and, with it, Louis Dumont's theories of caste, which aimed to move beyond specific cases to view the wider system of which they were a part. Marriott's ethnosociological critique, in some respects, was in step with the turn from grand theory that marked the postmodern shift from structure to agency, and which foreshadowed the later 'ontological turn' (Pedersen 2012) in the discipline. Postmodernism, however, also critiqued the way we had exoticized 'otherness' to challenge the assumption – implicit in an ethnosociological approach – of difference, identifying anthropology's focus on caste as a reflection of our obsession with the exotic at the expense of the relationships and identities that shaped the lifeworlds of most Indians (see, e.g. Inden 1990). This, in turn, shifted caste away from the foreground, allowing newfound interests in class and other identities to flourish.

Although the trends I have described might be seen as independent of *actual* changes in the relations between caste, cuisine and commensality, the two are not entirely separate. The turns in disciplinary theory I have described also map on to, and were arguably responses to, transformations within India and elsewhere. The shift away from caste, for example, which followed the critique of anthropology as too orientalist, matched the increasing importance afforded to class that had been building since the Green Revolution of the 1960s (Frankel 1971) and accelerated by economic liberalization of the 1990s. The importance of class as a marker of identity grew in tandem with the increase in foods available – from noodles to pizzas – through which class distinctions, as opposed to caste differences, might be expressed.

However, we should not be too hasty in dismissing caste as a colonial relic. Although it has become increasingly unacceptable, at least among metropolitan elites, to reference caste in making claims to superiority (Pandian 2002), recent scholarship suggests that dominant castes continue to code their symbolic status through, among other things, food and commensality. A memo to staff at *The Hindu* newspaper's Chennai office in early 2014, for example, politely requested employees to refrain from eating meat in the staff canteen, because it 'causes discomfort to the majority of the employees who are vegetarian'. As Gorringe and Karthikeyan (2014) argue persuasively, such prescriptions – like the ban on beef on menus at the 2010 Commonwealth Games – may be presented as being about respect for cultural practices, but in fact allow upper castes both to hide and practice caste at the same time. Presenting meat-eating as culturally taboo in a nation where up to three-quarters of the population eat meat both demonstrates the continuing persuasiveness of Brahminical practices in the public sphere, and 'reveals how the unmarked and abstract Indian citizen is still – all too often – modelled on an upper-caste norm' (2014: 21). While we are right to take seriously identities beyond caste, understanding how food, commensality and caste relate to one another remains, as I hope to have demonstrated, vital to understanding South Asia.

NOTES

1. Dalit is the self-ascribed and currently favoured term for the castes formerly referred to as untouchables or, in official government terminology, Scheduled Castes (SC).
2. Although this was the figure Das gave, I suspect it had been inflated in relation to current day costs.

3. See online version of Griffith's (1896) translation of the Rigveda – downloadable from http://www.sanskritweb.net/rigveda/griffith-p.pdf (retrieved 4 August 2014). The relevant passage is verse 12 of hymn XC: 'The Brahmin was his mouth, of both his arms was the Rajanya [the Kshatriya] made. His thighs became the Vaisya, from his feet the Sudra was produced' (1896: 469).
4. See, for a neat summary of Dumont's arguments, Quigley (1994: 35).
5. See, for example Appadurai (1986, 1988), Heesterman (1971), Mencher (1974) and Khare (1984).
6. For a more detailed taxonomy, see Achaya (1994: 62, 65), who draws on Khare (1976) to draw out in finer detail the distinctions between *kacca* and *pucca* foods, which both of them correlate with the domestic and public spheres, respectively. Ritual distinctions between foods that are *anna*, or cultivated (such as rice, wheat, barley and lentils), and those that are *phala* (wild grains, vegetables and fruit) are also significant, with the latter considered more appropriate for auspicious ceremonies.
7. Note here, incidentally, that food transactions are interpreted as symbolic rather than literally transformative in the way Marriott has described, although the outward practice remains the same in either case.
8. A term coined by Marriott (1976: 110) to denote that code and substance cannot be assumed to be separable, because Hindu thought does not separate actors from their actions in the way that Western philosophical traditions do.
9. See http://news.bbc.co.uk/1/hi/world/south_asia/2945020.stm (accessed 8 September 2011).
10. See also Osella and Osella (2008: 184) who, in turn, argue – contra Desai – that contemporary vegetarianism in India can never be separated from its links to Hindu fundamentalism.

REFERENCES

Achaya, K. T. (1994), *Indian Food: A Historical Companion*, Delhi: Oxford University Press.
Appadurai, A. (1981), 'Gastro-politics in Hindu South Asia', *American Ethnologist*, 8(3): 494–511.
Appadurai, A. (1986), 'Is Homo Hierarchicus?', *American Ethnologist*, 13(4): 745–62.
Appadurai, A. (1988), 'Putting Hierarchy in its Place', *Cultural Anthropology*, 3(1): 36–49.
Arun, C. J. (2004), *From Outcaste to Caste: The Use of Symbols and Myths in the Construction of Identity; A Study of Conflict between the Paraiyars and the Vanniyars in Tamil Nadu, South India*, PhD thesis, University of Oxford.
Bailey, F. G. (1957), *Caste and the Economic Frontier: A Village in Highland Orissa*, Manchester: Manchester University Press.
Beck, B. E. F. (1969), 'Colour and Heat in South Indian Ritual', *Man* (N.S.), 4(4): 553–72.
Berreman, G. (1972), 'Race, Caste and Other Invidious Distinctions in Social Stratification', *Race*, 23(4): 385–414.
Béteille, A. (1965), *Caste, Class and Power: Changing Patterns of Stratification in a Tanjore Village*, Oxford: Oxford University Press.
Béteille, A. (1991), *Society and Politics in India: Essays in a Comparative Perspective*, London: Althone Press.

Bharati, A. (1967), 'Ideology and Conent of Caste Among the Indians of East Africa', in
    B. M. Schwartz (ed.), *Caste in Overseas Indian Communities*, 283–320, California:
    Chandler Publishing Company.

Bouglé, C. (1971), *Essays on the Caste System*, translated by D. Pocock, Cambridge:
    Cambridge University Press.

Burghart, R. (1978), 'Hierarchical Models of the Hindu Social System', *Man* (N.S.),
    13(4): 519–36.

Busby, C. (2000), *The Performance of Gender: An Anthropology of Everyday Life in a
    South Indian Fishing Village*, New Brunswick: Althone Press.

Cantlie, A. (1981), 'The Moral Significance of Food Among Assamese Hindus', in
    A. C. Mayer (ed.), *Culture and Morality: Essays in Honour of Christoph von Fürer-
    Haimendorf*, 42–64, Delhi: Oxford University Press.

Caplan, P. (2002), 'Food in Middle-class Madras Households from the 1970s to the
    1990s', in K. Cwiertka and B. Walraven (eds), *Asian Food: the Global and the Local*,
    46–62, Oxford: Routledge.

Caplan, P. (2008), 'Crossing the Veg/Non-Veg Divide: Commensality and Sociality
    among the Middle Classes in Madras/Chennai', in C. Osella and F. Osella (eds), *Food:
    Memory, Pleasure and Politics*, Special Issue of *South Asia: Journal of South Asian
    Studies*, 31(1): 118–42.

Carstairs, G. M. (1957), *The Twice Born: A Study of a Community of High-Caste Hindus*,
    London: Hogarth Press.

Charsley, S. (1998), 'Sanskritization: The Career of an Anthropological Theory',
    Contributions to Indian Sociology, 32(2): 527–49.

Daniel, V. E. (1987), *Fluid Signs: Being a Person the Tamil Way*, London: University of
    California Press.

Desai, A. (2008), 'Subaltern Vegetarianism: Witchcraft, Embodiment and Sociality in
    Central India', in C. Osella and F. Osella (eds), *Food: Memory, Pleasure and Politics*,
    Special Issue of *South Asia: Journal of South Asian Studies*, 31(1): 96–117.

Donner, H. (2008a), 'New Vegetarianism: Food, Gender and Neo-Liberal Regimes in
    Bengali Middle-Class Families', in C. Osella and F. Osella (eds), *Food: Memory,
    Pleasure and Politics*, Special Issue of *South Asia: Journal of South Asian Studies*, 31(1):
    143–69.

Donner, H. (2008b), *Domestic Goddesses: Maternity, Globalization and Middle-Class
    Identity in Contemporary India*, Aldershot, Hampshire: Aldgate.

Dirks, N. B. (1971), 'The Brahminical View of Caste', *Contributions to Indian Sociology*
    (NS), 5: 16–23.

Dirks, N. B. (1987), *The Hollow Crown: Ethnohistory of an Indian Kingdom*, Cambridge:
    Cambridge University Press.

Dirks, N. B. (2001), *Castes of Mind: Colonialism and the Making of Modern India*,
    Princeton, NJ: Princeton University Press.

Dube. S. C. (1955), *Hindu Village*, London: Routledge & Kegan Paul.

Dubois, A. J. A. (1906), *Hindu Manners, Customs and Ceremonies*, translated by
    H. K. Beauchamp, 3rd edn, Oxford: Clarendon Press.

Dumont, L. (1980), *Homo Hierarchicus: The Caste System and Its Implications*, Chicago
    and London: The University of Chicago Press.

Frankel, F. R. (1971), *India's Green Revolution: Economic Gains and Political Costs*, Princeton, NJ: Princeton University Press.

Fuller, C. J. (1992a), *The Camphor Flame*, Princeton, NJ: Princeton University Press.

Fuller, C. J. (1992b), 'Review of "India Through Hindu Categories"', *Journal of Asian Studies*, 51(2): 432.

Fuller, C. J. (2007), *Servants of the Goddess: The Priests of a South Indian Temple*, Cambridge: Cambridge University Press.

Fuller, C. J. and Narasimhan, H. (2007), 'Information Technology Professionals and the New-Rich Middle Class in Chennai (Madras)', *Modern Asian Studies*, 41(1): 121–50.

Goody, J. (1982), *Cooking, Cuisine and Class: A Study in Comparative Sociology*, Cambridge: Cambridge University Press.

Gorringe, H. and Karthikeyan, D. (2014), 'The Hidden Politics of Vegetarianism: Caste and *The Hindu* Canteen', *Economic and Political Weekly*, 49(20): 20–2.

Griffith, R. T. H. (1896), *The Hymns of the Rigveda*, translation, 2nd edn, online, available from http://www.sanskritweb.net/rigveda/griffith-p.pdf (accessed 4 August 2014).

Guha, D. S. (1985), 'Food in the Vedic tradition', *India International Centre Quarterly*, 12(2): 141.

Harper, S. B. (2000), *In the Shadow of the Mahatma: Bishop V. S. Azariah and the Travails of Christianity in British India*, Richmond: Curzon Press.

Harris, M. (1989), *Cows, Pigs, Wars and Witches: the Riddles of Culture*, New York: Vintage Books.

Heesterman, J. C. (1971), 'Preisthood and the Brahmin', *Contributions to Indian Sociology*, 5: 43–7.

Inden, R. (1990), *Imagining India*, Oxford: Basil Blackwell.

Khare, R. S. (1976), *The Hindu Hearth and Home*, New Delhi: Vikas Publishing House.

Khare, R. S. (1984), *The Untouchable as Himself: Ideology, Identity and Pragmatism Among the Lucknow Chamars*, Cambridge: Cambridge University Press.

Khare R. S. (ed.) (1992), *The Eternal Food: Gastronomic Ideas and Experiences of Hindus and Buddhists*, Albany: State University of New York Press.

Klass, M. (1980), *Caste: The Emergence of the South Asian Social System*, New Delhi: Manohar.

Kuper, H. (1967), 'Changes in Caste in South African Indians', in B. M. Schwartz (ed.), *Caste in Overseas Indian Communities*, 237–65, California: Chandler Publishing Company.

Lamb, S. (2000), *White Saris and Sweet Mangoes: Aging, Gender, and Body in North India*, Berkeley: University of California Press.

Marriott, M. (1976), 'Hindu Transactions: Diversity Without Dualism', in B. Kapferer (ed.), *Transaction and Meaning*, 109–42, Philadelphia: Institute for the Study of Human Issues.

Marriott, M. (1990), 'Introduction', in M. Marriott (ed.), *India through Hindu Categories*, xi–xvi, New Delhi: Sage.

Mayer, A. C. (1960), *Caste and Kinship in Central India*, London: Routledge and Kegan Paul.

Mayer, A. C. (1996), 'Caste in an Indian Village: Change and Continuity 1954-1992', in C. Fuller (ed.), *Caste Today*, 32–64, Delhi: Oxford University Press.

Mehta, R., Nambia, R. G., Singh, S. K., SuBrahminyam, S. and Ravi, C. (2002), *Livestock Industrialization, Trade and Social-Health-Environmental Issues for the Indian Poultry Sector*, Rome: Food and Agriculture Organization.

Mencher, J. (1974), 'The Caste system Upside Down, or the Not-So-Mysterious East', *Current Anthropology*, 15: 469–93.

Mennell, S. (1985), *All Manners of Food: Eating and Taste in England and France from the Middle Ages to the Present*, Oxford: Blackwell.

Mosse, D. (1999), 'Responding to Subordination: The Politics of Identity Change Among South Indian Untouchable Castes', in J. R. Campbell and A. Rew (eds), *Identity and Affect: Experiences of Identity in a Globalising World*, 64–104, London: Pluto Press.

Mosse, D. (2010), 'The Catholic Church and Dalit Christian Activism in Contemporary Tamil Nadu', in R. Robinson and J. M. Kujur (eds), *Margins of Faith: Dalit and Tribal Christianity in India*, 235–62, New Delhi: Sage.

O'Malley, L. S. S. (1932), *Indian Caste Customs*, Cambridge: Cambridge University Press.

Osella, F. and Osella, C. (2000), *Social Mobility in Kerala: Modernity and Identity in Conflict*, London: Pluto Press.

Osella, F. and Osella, C. (eds) (2008), *Food: Memory, Pleasure and Politics*, Special Issue of *South Asia: Journal of South Asian Studies*, 31(1).

O'Toole, T. (2003), 'Secularising the Sacred Cow: The Relationship between Religious Reform and Hindu Nationalism', in A. Copley (ed.), *Hinduism in Public and Private*, 84–109, Delhi: Oxford University Press.

Pandian, M. S. S. (2002), 'One Step Outside Modernity: Caste, Identity Politics and Public Sphere', *Economic & Political Weekly*, 17(18): 1735–41.

Parry, J. P. (1991), 'The Hindu Lexicographer? A Note on Auspiciousness and Purity', *Contributions to Indian Sociology* (N.S), 25(2): 267–85.

Parry, J. P. (1994), *Death in Benares*, Cambridge: Cambridge University Press.

Pedersen, M. A. (2012), 'Common Nonsense: A Review of Certain Recent Reviews of the "Ontological Turn"', *Anthropology of This Century*, 5, URL: http://aotcpress.com/aticles/common_nonsense

Quigley, D. (1994), 'Is a Theory of Caste Still Possible?', in M. Searle-Chatterjee and U. Sharma (eds), *Contextualising* Caste, 25–48, Oxford: Blackwell.

Quigley, D. (1999), *The Interpretation of Caste*, New Delhi: Oxford University Press.

Sachua, E. C. (2005), *Alberuni's India*, vol. 2, Marston Gate: Elibron Classics.

Searle-Chatterjee, M. and Sharma, U. (1994), *Contextualising Caste: Post-Dumontian Approaches*, Sociological Review Monograph Series.

Senart, É. (1930), *Caste in India: The Facts and the System*, translated by Sir D. Ross, London: Methuen.

Siegel B. (2010), 'Learning to Eat in a Capital City: Constructing Public Eating Culture in Delhi', *Food, Culture and Society: An International Journal of Multidisciplinary Research*, 13: 71–90.

Smith, R. T. and Jayawardena, C. (1967), 'Caste and Social Status Among the Indians of Guyana', in B. M. Schwartz (ed.), *Caste in Overseas Indian Communities*, 43–92, California: Chandler Publishing Company.

Srinivas, M. N. (1952), *Religion and Society among the Coorgs of South India*, Oxford: Oxford University Press.

Staples, J. (2007), *Peculiar People, Amazing Lives. Leprosy, Social Exclusion and Community-Making in South India*, Delhi: Orient Longman.

Staples, J. (2008), '"Go on, just try some!": Meat and Meaning-Making among South Indian Christians', in C. Osella and F. Osella (eds), *Food: Memory, Pleasure and Politics*, Special Issue of *South Asia: Journal of South Asian Studies*, 31(1): 36–55.

Staples, J. (2014a), *Leprosy and a Life in South India: Journeys with a Tamil Brahmin*, Lanham, MD: Lexington Books.

Staples, J. (2014b), 'Civilising Tastes: From Caste to Class in South Indian Foodways', in J. A. Klein and A. Murcott (eds), *Food Consumption in Global Perspective: Essays in the Anthropology of Food in Honour of Jack Goody*, 65–86, New York: Palgrave Macmillan.

CHAPTER FOUR

Jewish Foods at the Turn of the Twenty-First Century

JOËLLE BAHLOUL

As the lifeblood of daily material life and of the socialization of the body, food occupies a crucial place in the Judaic religious system and, as a result, in the experience of Jews in history and culture. In exploring food consumed by Jews, a major distinction needs to be made between Judaism as a religion and Jewish culture in history. Applying the Saussurian linguistic approach (de Saussure 1968) to Jewish food is helpful in this endeavour, by enabling us to distinguish the *langue* of Jewish food from its *parole*. Because the Judaic system of religious laws, inscribed in the Bible and in rabbinical legislation, has regulated diet among Jews for centuries before the modern period and secularization, I will consider it as the register of *langue* with its complex set of food prescriptions and prohibitions. The domain of *parole* is constituted by the observances and culinary traditions, even if they are partial, of these religious prescriptions by Jews throughout history and in the diverse contingent experiences of Jewishness in specific historical settings. This chapter focuses on the relationship between the Judaic religious dietary laws and the actual food practices among Jewish immigrants from North Africa established in France since the late 1950s and early 1960s.[1]

The historical context is that of the decolonization of North Africa and of the massive waves of migration resulting from the achievement of national independence in Morocco, Algeria and Tunisia. My two main questions will be: How did the religious traditions of food and table manners survive the experience of historical migration? How were these traditions and manners adjusted to the post-colonial experience of secularization and Westernization, which has characterized the mid-twentieth-century history of the Jews of North Africa?

FAITH AND FOOD: 'EATING THE BOOK'

The end of the twentieth century was a period of prolific contribution in the social anthropology of Jewish dietary laws, pointing to the central place of food in religion and its practice, and in society and culture. Following in the footsteps of structuralist thinkers such as Mary Douglas (1966; see also Soler 1979) and Edmund Leach (1969), Gérard Haddad's (2013) volume, *Eating the Book*, develops a psychoanalytical reading of Jewish dietary laws. According to Haddad, such laws regulate acts of food as acts of faith devoted to reproducing and transmitting the major precepts of patriarchal Judaism.

The *Book*, more specifically the Pentateuch or Torah in Hebrew, and in its core the eleventh chapter of Leviticus – among others – indicates to every Jew how she or he should select his or her foods while also participating in the specific cosmic and social order dictated by the Mosaic revelation. A number of later additional rabbinical texts have also dealt with the regulation of food rituals within a similar spirit of ingestion of the divine word.[2]

Judaic sacred texts relating to food place a special emphasis on the consumption of animal flesh, and are thus profoundly connected to the biblical definition of life and of its suppression for nutritional purposes. These rules organize the *selection of animals* whose flesh can be consumed (detailed in Leviticus XI), but also the specific *slaughtering operation* preceding the marketing of kosher meat (detailed in Deuteronomy XII: 21). The meats considered *kosher*, or edible by Leviticus law, are typically (a) the flesh of cloven-hoofed, ruminant mammals, with pig flesh thereby excluded as the pig is not a ruminant; (b) the flesh of non-carnivorous birds such as poultry, pigeons, pheasants, geese, ducks and other granivores; and (c) the flesh of specified fish whose anatomy features scales and fins. Leviticus thus excludes, as *taref*[3] meat, the flesh of rabbits and related rodents (as non-ruminants and non-cloven hoofed), camels as non-cloven hoofed and a number of crawling shellfish and cartilaginous sea creatures, many of which have been defined as carnivorous animals.[4] In addition, Leviticus does not allow eating the flesh of animals that crawl or jump on the surface of the earth or in water, such as frogs, snakes and shrimp. One exception to this rule concerns certain species of locust. The spirit of Leviticus is to match the Jewish diet with the mythological order described in Genesis, according to which life and death are processes of a divine conception, and all animals need to fit in their natural element.[5] Leviticus's style and narrative suggests an overall vegetarian spirit. One of the narrative mythological consequences of this spirit is the prohibition, specified in Deuteronomy (XII: 23) of the consumption of blood in human and animal diet.[6]

The dietary exclusion of blood can also be found in the strict biblical regulation of the slaughtering of animals for consumption. *Shechitah*[7] has to be performed by a certified rabbinical slaughterer and consists of a rapid incision in the neck arteries and organs (aorta, trachea and oesophagus). Rabbinical authorities view this surgical procedure as one that allows the rapid loss of blood and consciousness, and thus avoids the animal's suffering and awareness of life loss. Jewish law does not consider slaughtering after stunning as a kosher procedure.[8]

The rules have two major consequences for the *culinary* process. First, before any cut of meat is cooked, a maximum amount of its blood component has to be drained off. This procedure, operated by both butchers and domestic cooks, consists in washing and salting the meat prior to cooking, for about two hours. Second, the combination of dairy and meat ingredients in the same dish and on the same menu is strictly prohibited, under Exodus XXIII: 19 and Deuteronomy XIV: 21. This prohibition's outcome is the complex organization of kitchenware. In Orthodox families who strictly observe dietary laws, the kitchen space has to include two separate sets of dishware and cooking utensils, two separate sinks and, often, two separate dishwashers as well. One side of the kitchen is the dairy side; the other, the meat side.[9] Between these two categories of dairy and meat,[10] one finds *parve* food, which includes a number of ingredients that include neither a dairy nor a meat element. These ingredients can be associated with both dairy or meat dishes and preparations. Fish-based products are considered *parve* and are not affected by the prohibition of meat/dairy culinary combination.[11]

Hebrew dietary laws include additional prohibitions. One of these rules concerns the prohibited consumption of the sciatic nerve in mammals' meat such as beef and lamb.[12] In a wide-ranging kosher market such as that which exists in the American and European cities with large Jewish populations, the difficulty associated with the removal of the sciatic nerve has resulted in the sole marketing of the front part of the animal in kosher stores.[13] Finally, some Judaic dietary laws are observed on a time-bound basis. In this category is the prohibition of leavened foods during the eight days of the spring holiday of Passover. The forbidden foods include primarily grain-based ingredients that have been fermented in the cooking process, such as bread and various types of baked foods, but also beer (in some communities) and fermented cheese. This prohibition's rationalization is located again in the biblical sacred narrative as it relates the important episode of the exodus from Egypt and its Pharaohs.[14] Its consequence is the designation of the *matzah* (or unleavened bread) as the perfect food for Passover. The time-bound Passover diet obligates strictly observant and traditional Jews to clean their house for a month prior to the holiday, and to remove any trace of leavened food ingredient (the Hebrew concept of *chametz*). Special care is given to the kitchen area.

Ritual fasts, such as the Yom Kippur fast and the fast of Esther before the Purim holiday, are other types of time-bound practices involving food or its rejection, all of which are regulated in the biblical or rabbinical sacred literatures. By the end of the twentieth century, the most observed ritual fast was that of Yom Kippur. In the following part, I will place these food rituals, beliefs and regulations within a specific historical context.

THE COLONIAL AND POST-COLONIAL REPUBLICAN CONTRACT IN THE KITCHEN AND ON THE TABLE

Political domination was the major part of the French colonial system in North Africa, but colonialism has been associated with related forms of domination, from language to dress to other types of bodily control (see Memmi 1965: 24–5). In colonial society, the imposition of European food, taste and diet, among other bodily practices, has been part and parcel of the mission to civilize selected colonized populations. Jews in North Africa have experienced these various forms of colonial domination since the middle of the nineteenth century, to which they have generally responded by assimilating to the dominant French culture. The whole process eventually culminated in their massive and progressive adoption of French culture in the first half of the twentieth century and in their immigration to France in the 1950s and 1960s.[15] Through colonial domination, these Jews acquired their political and social emancipation in the twentieth century, while having to give up a certain number of religious traditions and cultural assets. The early phase of the process of Europeanization included the progressive adoption of the French language with the schooling of Jewish children in the French public educational system.[16] Secularization followed, as well as progressive integration into the colonial European community. Both of these historical processes eventually resulted in major transformations in private and domestic life, from family relationships to the organization of ritual menus.[17]

Since the mid-1960s and their wide-scale establishment in France, North African Jews have made up the majority of the French Jewish population, and constitute the world's second largest Sephardic population, after the Israeli Sephardim. A large proportion of this population's eldest segments were born in North Africa. They experienced the major tragedies of the twentieth century and, in particular, the decolonization of North Africa and immigration to France from the late 1950s to mid-1960s. At the dawn of the third millennium, their integration into French society and culture has long been successfully completed. Yet a relatively small amount of social scientific information exists on the details of this integration (though see Bensimon-Donath 1971; Bahloul 1984, 1992 and 1996; Lasry and Tapia 1989).

This massive migration process was experienced as the completion of the migrants' emancipation and Europeanization since the early twentieth century. Migration came into effect as the culmination of a century-long social and cultural transformation. Once they became full-fledged citizens of French major cities, they organized a complex scenario of integration that included the maintenance of *some* North African traditions while giving up others. The challenges of migration were monumental. It is not easy for anyone to leave a house, a neighbourhood, a country, a landscape where family life has evolved over decades of collective memory. For many women of the generation born after World War I, the family house, table and kitchen offered a favourable setting to implement their balanced system of integration and cultural survival. There, they had wide control over their progeny and over the household organization. There, they inventively used their domestic powers to help their families integrate in the European culture without sacrificing the bulk of their native North African traditions.

To be sure, the challenges associated with the integration into French society have been sharpened, at least in the first decades after immigration, by the fate of Jewish dietary laws and the threat of secularization (or an excessive version of it). Should they be given up in order to ensure integration into French civil society, or should they be 'accommodated' to the constraints of new urban lifestyles? The popular responses to these dramatic dilemmas have been found in the history of French Jews' access to citizenship and civil society.

The recourse to the Napoleonian system of French citizenship was to be strictly enforced in compliance with the rules of the Republic (Schwarzfuchs 1979; Malino and Wasserstein 1985; Birnbaum 1996). Under these rules, the Jews are integrated as equal citizens of the French nation and are obligated by the 'Republican contract'. This contract ideologically stipulates that all aspects of particular ascription, whether religious, linguistic or ethnic, should be displayed within the limits of private life, that is, the domestic and family domain. Outside of this private realm, that is, in public life, the adopted citizens have to demonstrate their belonging to French civil society and its secular culture. This Republican contract has generated various forms of 'Marranism' among French Jews who, in the past century and a half, have complied strictly with the rules of distinction between the private and the public, and have retained their religious observance within the limits of the domestic and family domains. For some, becoming secular was the easiest way to the Republic.

For North African Jewish immigrants, the Republican contract has become a condition to their recognition as full-fledged French citizens. As a result, religious observance, often abandoned altogether by their Ashkenazi coreligionists, has withdrawn into the core of domestic life, represented most strikingly by the stove and the pots.[18] The kitchen and the table are, therefore, used as creative terrains of expression and (re)formation of Jewish and French identities. There, historical roots in North Africa are also inventively maintained or 'reinvented' (Hobsbawm and Ranger 1992; Goldberg 1992). The boiling stew is a social, historical and cultural venue that has the advantage of being flexible and adjustable to regular – sometimes profound – changes.

So how do these Jews inscribe, in their cuisine and eating habits, their relationship to the French Republic?[19] The system is, in fact, structured to establish distinctive *boundaries* between the core of Jewishness and the representation of the outsider (French, Gentile, 'them'). The boundary between the world of Sephardic Jewishness and that of French citizenship allows this Jewish identity to evolve by crossing it in both ways, depending on alternative strategies of reproduction and integration. This boundary system is multifaceted. It operates as follows:

- A *temporal distinction* between ordinary meals of the week and festive meals of Sabbath and ritual family reunions allows consumers to move between secular and ritual time by switching from French taste to traditional Sephardic taste in a timely fashion.
- A *flavour boundary* is established between the contents, in ingredients and culinary styles, of ordinary menus and those of ritual festive menus.
- The *cooking labour division* of the two different cuisines differentiates between the home cooking of traditional festive Sephardic recipes and the food served on ordinary days and cooked outside the home kitchen by non-members of the family.
- The *distinction between kosher* dishes, cooked and served during religious holidays, and *non-kosher* dishes consumed, even at home, during ordinary

meals of working weekdays is one of the key structural principles of this
French Sephardic diet.

- *Translating* Judeo-Arabic culinary terms into the French culinary
  terminology is a structural principle that creates a direct link between food
  and language, two important areas of the Westernization of Sephardic
  culture and politics.

- *Collective memory* plays an instrumental role in the preservation of
  traditional Sephardic taste and cuisine and thus offers a variety of identity
  strategies in the integration of Sephardic Jews in French culture.[20]

WHAT IS 'TRADITIONAL' SEPHARDIC FRENCH CUISINE?[21]

'Traditional cuisine' is that which has been 'reinvented' as *traditional* in immigrant
culture. It is an uprooted cuisine that, by way of collective memory, is performed
in compliance with its original gastronomic structures. I use the concept of
'performance' because the cooking and consumption of traditional cuisine, usually
scheduled in highly ritualized meals and family gatherings, unfolds as a mnemonic
performance, or as the dramatization of remembrance of the native landscape and
culture.[22] In North African Jewish representations, this cuisine is distinct in its
ingredients and cooking techniques. It goes without saying that the designation
of the cuisine as 'traditional' does not prevent changes to kitchen habits. Changes
have indeed been introduced by the historical alteration resulting from the
Europeanization of North African Jewish private lifestyles. The main symbolic
process, though, is that which associates traditional and modern cuisines to specific
periods in Sephardic historical consciousness. Traditional cuisine is believed to be
that which has flourished in North Africa before emigration. By contrast, modern
cuisine is believed to be that which our Sephardic eaters have adopted as they
became Europeanized and after their immigration in France. Ethnographic details
on ingredient contents and cooking techniques will provide further insight on this
symbolic process.

Ingredients

These include a majority of ingredients of the Mediterranean market place that are
now found in France, either as a result of importation or of the growing presence
of these products in French agro-industry. Vegetables, grains, fruits, herbs and spices
are the core of this repertoire, as they represent the embodied memory of the native
landscapes and sensory cultures. Typical examples of North African vegetables used
in Jewish cuisine are cardoons and artichokes, spinach and Swiss chard, olives, fresh
and dried fava beans, coriander, mint, cumin, chick peas, grapes, pomegranates,
almonds, quinces, dates and figs.

While the artichoke is an import from Italian Renaissance Jewish cuisine, the most
prestigious vegetables in this Sephardic cuisine are products of the farming culture

of the Ancient Middle East and can be found in biblical mythological narratives. This is not a minor reason for their dominant presence in religious ritual menus: the connection is easily made, at least from a symbolic viewpoint, between their modern nutritional significance and their mythological functions. Displaying those ancient biblical fruits on twenty-first century tables creates a ritual connection with biblical mythology and with the native North African sensory scenery.

Yet some other similarly crucial vegetables have been introduced in more recent times and do not have this mythological status. In this category one can find a variety of ingredients that are native to the New World or to Asia and that have been introduced in Mediterranean cuisines by the medieval Arab and European transoceanic commerce of food and spices.[23] Citrus fruits, tomatoes and peppers, eggplants and potatoes are such ingredients. It is worth noting that traditional cuisine rarely includes fruits, herbs and vegetables that have recently been introduced in the North African Jewish diet such as broccoli, basil and Brussels sprouts.

By contrast, the meat repertoire of traditional cuisine has included some meat ingredients that were not popular in North Africa before emigration. Beef has long been the supreme meat ingredient in traditional Sephardic (and Jewish) cuisine and it has maintained this status in recent decades.[24] Chicken and fish have had an important presence as well, while lamb (and not mutton) has been present in traditional cuisine in some time-bound ritual holiday menus, in particular in some grilled and boiled recipes of Passover and Rosh Hashana dinners. By contrast, veal has made a recent entry in this traditional cuisine as a lean replacement for some fat lamb or beef cuts.

The presence of veal and leaner meat products in some ritual dishes thus represents the historical changes experienced by North African Jews as they progressively Europeanized their lifestyles and integrated into French society and culture after immigration. It also points to the change in the representation of the female body aesthetics, notably among the baby boomer generation in their early adult years in the 1960s. The ingredient change also signifies the upward mobility that North African Jews have experienced in their integration in French society, allowing them to afford more expensive meat cuts, such as veal.

Despite this trend, the absence of turkey meat in this cuisine is significant, as it has made a rare intrusion in Mediterranean cuisine in general. One exception to that rule is the status of turkey meat in late twentieth-century Israeli cuisine. The famous *schnitzel*, a fried turkey cutlet and the successor of its Viennese veal version, is an example of that culinary process. As a national culinary item brought to the young state of Israel by Eastern and Central European Jewish immigrants, it has progressively been integrated into all ethnic Jewish cuisines, both in Israel and among diaspora Jewish communities (Roden 1996: 205). The Jewish transnational market of kosher meats has made turkey meat available, in cutlet or deli format, in world kosher stores, especially in France. That is why it can be found on Sephardic Orthodox tables.

One notable characteristic in traditional Sephardic cuisine is its strict compliance with Jewish dietary laws. Indeed, the presence of non-kosher meats and food ingredient combination is an unthinkable category in traditional Sephardic cuisine because of the high status of kosher food in religious ritual and festive menus.

Cooking Techniques

Couscous, steamed grain, is a native North African dish unique in its cooking technique. It occupies a central place in traditional French Sephardic cuisine as it is also a festive dish in most Maghrebi cuisines, be they Jewish, Muslim or Christian. It is festive because of its combination of diverse vegetable, legume and meat ingredients, and because it is viewed as a complete meal in itself. As a result, the Sephardic tradition assigns couscous in the most important holidays of the religious calendar and in sabbatical meals most specifically. Equally ranked is the *dafina*, also called *t'fina* or *s'china*, an overcooked dish, and another culinary representation of nutritional wholeness in its composition. Its Arabic name and culinary character endow this dish with a prestigious status on Sabbath and main holiday meals. The Judeo-Arabic terminology refers to its long slow cooking: *s'china* means 'warm' in Arabic, and both terms, *dafina* and *t'fina*, mean 'buried' and refer to an old culinary technique consisting of burying the pot in the ground and inside burning charcoal to let it cook overnight from the beginning of Sabbath on Friday evening. The dish is usually served on Saturday lunch. Its cooking technique is the result of the prohibition of lighting fire (electricity or gas stoves) *during* the Sabbath hours and naturally qualifies it as a festive ritual dish.

In culinary technical hierarchy, traditional Sephardic cuisine accords much prestige to slow and prolonged cooking, as represented in these stews composed of a large variety of ingredients, meats and vegetables, and of a wide array of flavouring herbs and spices. The list of ingredients for a typical *t'fina* is a telling example of this culinary trope. Below are examples of the traditional culinary code, excerpted from recipe books and translated by the author:

Ingredients for *dafina*

> A pound of veal stew, two calf feet, one veal bone, five eggs in their shell, two pounds of potatoes, 300 grams of rice, a pound of chick peas, two onions, three garlic cloves, six prunes, two sugar cubes, one cup of vegetable oil, 50 grams of chicken fat, a dash of salt, pepper, cumin and ground nutmeg. *Preparation*: one hour and fifteen minutes. *Cooking time*: one hour and one night. (Raphaël et al. 1983: 101)

Ingredients for the Algerian *t'fina with spinach and Swiss chard*

> Two kilos of spinach or Swiss chard, one kilo of beef shoulder, preferably gelatinous, one beef bone, three spoonfuls of peanut oil, one bay leaf, six smashed garlic cloves, one pound of cooked chick peas, a dash of paprika, salt and pepper. (Jaffin 1980: 100)

This dish is served on the Saturday lunch menu or on the eve of Rosh Hashana dinner, for which the Eastern North African table tradition requires the display of the green colour. This preferred colour constitutes a culinary symbol of natural renewal at this time of the year cycle, and is used similarly in Muslim traditional cuisines (see Rodinson 1965). The persistence of this dish on Jewish holiday menus is a clear testimony to its eaters' desire to symbolically reconstitute their native landscape and cultural codes around ritual family gatherings.

Ingredients for the Rosh-ha-Shana Algerian lamb head stew with cardoons

> One lamb's head, one kilo of cardoons, one pound of chick peas, some peanut oil, four garlic cloves, one bay leaf, and a dash of paprika, salt and pepper. (Jaffin 1980: 28)

The presence of the head in this dish is a reference to the linguistic ritual blessing, recited in Hebrew before that dinner. It is the expression of a wish to always be at the 'head' (the top) of everything and not at the bottom.[25] The ritual synchronization of the nutritional and linguistic aspects of this festive meal is very specific to Jewish ritual structures and can also be found in other holiday menus such as the Passover Seder. It indeed has an educative function, especially designed for children, that consists in eating sacred words by ingesting ingredients which name reminds of a Hebrew blessing word.

A CALENDAR OF JEWISH EATING

The boundary system established in the Sephardic French diet is first and foremost inscribed in the temporal flow of quotidian life. It creates an opposition between the ordinary days of the weekly cycle and the extraordinary schedule of sabbatical and religious food reunions. The distinction between the secular lifestyle of the week's working days and the sacred time of Sabbath and religious holidays is particularly forceful in the menus' contents. The system – which does not apply to the most observant families, who keep a kosher diet at all times – operates as follows.

FIGURE 4.1: A basket of *challah* rolls stored in a kitchen corner in preparation for a bar-mitzvah celebration. (Photograph by author, Marseilles, late 1970s)

During the week, as one is involved in professional experiences and social relationships with Gentile friends and colleagues, the diet tends to be Frenchified. This goes as far as allowing non-kosher food items in the diet (such as ham or charcuterie), pointing to the fact that this part of daily life belongs to the register of the secular, or perhaps that of the non-religious/non-sacred. Among the least observant households, French food items (often non-kosher ones) would even enter the home kitchen and menu, especially when Gentile friends are invited around the table. This would be the case, for example, for French national cheeses (Camembert and Roquefort) and even shellfish.[26] The statistical recurrence of these French food items on the household's diet is an indication of the extent of its members' social network among Gentile circles of friends and colleagues. It also is a dietary response to the desire for political integration as French citizens. In order to be considered an equal citizen of the French Republic, a Jew needs to sit and eat at his fellow Gentile Frenchmen's table, even if the food is 'impure'.[27]

This political and ideological requirement prevails in public life. It does not apply to private dinners, as we have discussed above. Thus, sabbatical and holiday menus, generally served within the limits of domestic circles, are strictly kosher. They are also composed of dishes of the traditional North African Judeo-Arabic culinary repertoire. The distinction between ordinary days and sacred Sabbath and religious holidays consists, at least every week, in associating the resting time of the Sabbath (end of the week) with the sacred time of Jewish religious identity. Festive food practically and symbolically associates the density of the social network of consumers around the table, most of whom are related through kinship, with the density of the dishes cooked and served at ritual tables (Figures 4.1 and 4.2). Food density equals density of the family social fabric.

It should be noted here that ritual density (of the dishes and of their consuming community) is paced by the cycle of the ritual calendar. This means that some of the treasured recipes of traditional cuisine are served only once or twice a year, in the festive menus of the religious holidays they are assigned to. Sweet couscous is a striking example of this calendar of taste. It is usually served in Moroccan and Algerian families at the *Mimuna* dinner consecrating the termination of the ritual week of Passover food restrictions (see Goldberg 1978). The steamed wheat grain is combined with dried fruits such as raisins and almonds, abundant amounts of sugar, cinnamon and butter, as well as buttermilk and honey. The culinary and social density that characterizes ritual tables is thus often represented by traditional North African rich and overcooked stews that include a fair amount of fat and a larger variety of ingredients, from meats, root and leaf vegetables, potatoes and even grains or some sort of starchy item.

The temporal distinction between food consumed in ordinary days and that served on festive religious tables thus has a sensory effect: private domestic life is vested with a sacrality that is nutritionally formulated in the rich flavours, odours and sounds of family reunions. The temporal dimension of this articulation reinforces the synesthetic operation of identity and transforms identity into a bodily experience.[28] Temporally moving from one sensory register to another ultimately consists in moving from one identity register to another, from one culture to the

FIGURE 4.2: The weekly home baking of *challah* (in French, *pain juif*) on Friday morning. (Photograph by author, Nice, mid-1970s)

other, from one historical register to another. In food lies the complex articulation of the politics of Jewish identity in French history and culture.

The dietary distinction between the weekdays and Sabbath is characteristic of the average North African family in France, that is, those located in the middle class rather than in the social ladder's extremities, and also those observing a 'traditionalist' religious lifestyle rather than an Orthodox one. This type of religious observance has been identified in recent social scientific research as the one that characterizes the majority of the French Jewish population (Cohen 2002).

THE SEPHARDIC VERSION OF THE 'RAW AND THE COOKED': THE DIVISION OF LABOUR OF COOKING, MENU PREPARATION AND CONSUMPTION

Another aspect of the distinction between the secular public life and the sacred private world is its correspondence with the distinction between inside and outside the home. Sephardic homes have a tendency to preserve traditional cuisine in their core, while French foods are preferably cooked and consumed outside the home. Though some French recipes would be allowed inside the house during weekdays, and most certainly outside the family home, traditional cuisine is imperative in Sabbath and holiday menus prepared and eaten inside the home dining room. Early twenty-first century festive traditional cuisine is different from what it was half a century ago, in both its ingredient composition and its cooking techniques. For various reasons linked to the now wider presence of Sephardic women in the labour force and to the evolution of culinary taste in favour of a leaner and lighter cuisine, traditional dishes have lost some of their fat and spice components.

Despite these changes, Sephardic traditional festive cuisine is most often prepared at home by members of the family, typically adult women (Figure 4.3). I say 'most often' to point to a new development in the Sephardic cuisine scene. In the past fifteen to twenty years, Sephardic homemakers have enjoyed the products of an increasing market of prepared kosher North African traditional cuisine, usually sold in kosher butcher shops and groceries or by kosher caterers, especially in cities like Paris, Lyon and Marseilles where the Sephardic population is statistically substantial.[29] This market, run largely by North African Jewish entrepreneurs, has not drastically changed the pattern of home preparation of traditional menus. The dishes sold in this food industry are generally prepared by female relatives of the grocer or the butcher, or of the caterer. They are generally sold frozen before religious holidays.

Nevertheless, traditional festive cuisine is not only prepared at home; it is also consumed at home and primarily by family members gathered for these occasions. It is worth noting that, when non-kosher food is consumed during weekdays at home, it would most certainly *not be cooked at home* but purchased as prepared food items. So the home kitchen and family pots very rarely allow non-kosher items in their core, underlining the distinction between home/sacred/traditional and non-domestic/secular/French as a separation between the cooked and the raw, to refer to the Lévi-Straussian culinary dual opposition (Lévi-Strauss 1983). The cooked here represents the sacredness of the home, while the raw stands for the French side of Sephardic identity.

FIGURE 4.3: Preparation of the traditional couscous for Friday dinner. (Photograph by author, Nice, mid-1970s)

THE TRANSLATION EFFECT:
FROM JUDEO-ARABIC TO FRENCH

The correlation between culinary and linguistic structures, analysed by Claude Lévi-Strauss within the context of the analysis of myth (ibid.), finds an interesting application in late twentieth-century North African Jewish cuisine in France. At home, traditional dishes are more likely to be called by their past Judeo-Arabic names. So our Sephardic eaters do not only eat traditional cuisine, they also eat words of traditional language and communication. But with the progressive passing of the generation of native Judeo-Arabic speakers, these names will eventually fade away. One has to notice, though, that food names are the last native words to disappear. They function like memorial linguistic and cultural lexicons.

In some cases, some Judeo-Arabic food names have been translated into French. One typical case, observed over many years in my ethnographic culinary quests, is the conspicuous *blanquette de veau*. The original dish is in fact a lamb soup, simply cooked with garlic, in which a beaten egg mixed with fresh mint is thrown seconds before serving. Its original Judeo-Arabic name (of Eastern Algeria) is *m'hatsar*. Although it does look white like the classic French *blanquette*, it definitely belongs to a different culinary category, as a soup first, and as a dish including lamb, while the former typically features veal. The French version of *blanquette* also includes butter and cream, as opposed to the kosher lamb soup that does not allow the combination between meat and dairy.

What has happened here, I believe, is a process of linguistic legitimization of a dish that is usually served during the dinner of Rosh Hashana, and as such is a prestigious and festive dish. So the analogy with *blanquette* consists in identifying the traditional dish to one of the most prestigious French culinary items. Another evidence of the legitimization at work here is the switch from lamb to veal, the latter being viewed as a modern meat, less fat than lamb, though still strong in flavour. As a matter of fact, many cooks have indeed replaced lamb with veal in traditional cuisine, following a recently developed health-oriented attitude towards diet.

RECENT DEVELOPMENTS:
GLOBALIZATION OF JEWISH CUISINE

The twenty-first century's first two decades have seen new developments in the culinary structures revealed above.

First, with the increasing dominance of Israeli suppliers of kosher groceries on the French market, some Israeli and Ashkenazi Eastern European ingredients and culinary items have been introduced in French Sephardic cuisine, especially among the youngest and the most religious.[30] In France, the youngest cooks have often 'Sepharshkenized'[31] their kitchen, combining recipes and ingredients of both Jewish traditions, and introducing these dishes in their religious festive menu repertoire. Sephardic cuisine has been globalized and now includes the Israeli culinary scene. In the Parisian Jewish quarter, around subway station St. Paul and the Marais district, tourists and visitors can enjoy falafels[32] and hummus salads in the several competing kosher restaurants along rue des Rosiers (Figure 4.4). The Israeli cuisine is one of the diasporic Jewish cuisines offered in the Jewish Marais. A number of Jewish visitors come to the area either before Sabbath or immediately after, to run errands for their home rituals or to enjoy a family dinner in a district that they clearly consider their own. The ethnic restaurant scene in this area and in other districts with substantial Jewish populations has become a key element in the transformation of the neighbourhood into a Jewish one. A majority of the restaurant industry owners are Sephardic Jews from North Africa.

Second, since the early 2000s, another phenomenon has spread with the increasing usage of the Internet by many ethnic and cultural associations. Traditional Sephardic cuisines, the transmission of which is now under threat due to the increasing passing of the first generation of North African immigrant cooks, have become memorialized by a diversity of communication tools. This has happened through the creation of community websites named after Judeo-Arabic food names and featuring key sections on cuisine and recipes.[33] This recent trend has supplemented the wide-ranging publication, in the 1970s and 1980s, of a number of Sephardic (and more generally Jewish) cookbooks. The websites are unique forms of communication, in that they are formed by cultural associations of immigrants from specific North African countries and are used to ensure the transmission of the immigrant culture in an epoch characterized by the fear of identity loss. The fact that these sites are named after ritual culinary items is indicative of the necessary salvaging of

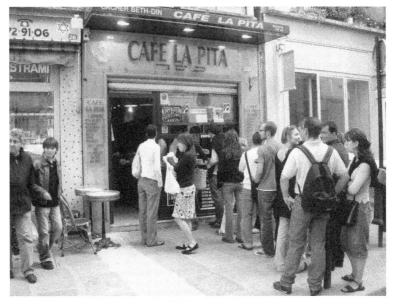

FIGURE 4.4: The crowd in front of a falafel restaurant on Rue des Rosiers in Paris, on a Sunday afternoon. (Photograph by author, 2005)

traditional cuisine as identity marker and thus as a pleasurable channel of cultural transmission. The 'chat room' sections in these Internet sites, and more typically on some of the communities' Facebook pages,[34] are worth examining. In addition to featuring photographs of festive dishes posted by Internet users, they allow the latter to exchange comments about the 'authenticity' of the posted recipes. Jews are not the only users of these sites, which also encourage Arab-Muslim correspondents to intervene and provide their own versions of the discussed recipes, who do so in addition to offering good wishes for religious holidays to their Jewish interlocutors. On these sites, the original cultures and cuisines are exposed, reminisced, debated and transmitted.

BY WAY OF CONCLUSION: THE POLITICS OF RELIGIOUS FOOD AND IDENTITY

Since the beginning of the twenty-first century, anti-Semitism has been on the rise in several West European nations and has been specifically focused on religious dietary laws and practices among Jews of all origins. As Robin Judd (2007) explores it, this has been present in German politics towards the Jews since the late nineteenth century. Several institutions of Western European democracy are now targeting specific religious observances. This is particularly true in France, where the separation between Church and State and the ideology of *laïcité* have been defining aspects of the country's national identity and Republican ideology.

For the first time in half a century, two major rituals related to bodily practices have been criticized or even banned in some countries: circumcision and ritual slaughtering (*shechitah*). Circumcision's legal validity has been questioned by activist groups advocating in defence of the male body's integrity. The ritual in both Judaism and Islam is now viewed as an offence to the male body by virtue of religious beliefs now presented as archaic and contrary to secular democratic values. Anti-circumcision lobby groups, both in the United States and in Western Europe, claim that the ritual should be banned as a violation of human rights, similarly to female excision.[35]

The ritual slaughter of animals in Judaism and Islam is criticized as cruelty to animals by various animal rights activists in the United Kingdom, Denmark, the Netherlands and France, deploying ideological rationales similar to the blatantly anti-Semitic, Nazi attacks of the 1930s against these rituals.[36] At the beginning of the twenty-first century, ritual slaughter has returned to political and ideological debates that seem to be focused on the blood aspect in these rituals, in a move that is reminiscent of the old anti-Semitic obsession with Jews as bloodthirsty. In political discourse, those rituals are attacked as pertaining to an archaic past and as having no place in modern democracy. In this vein, France's then prime minister, François Fillon, expressed in 2012 his 'personal sentiment' in regard to Jewish and Muslim ritual slaughter as being obsolete in a world that provides sanitary protection to food consumers.[37]

On 7 January 2015, a series of Islamist attacks in Paris included a hostage crisis in the city's largest kosher supermarket that killed four customers in their last-minute shopping before the Sabbath. Combined with an attack that killed a large part of the satirical magazine *Charlie Hebdo*'s editorial board, the violence at the *Hyper Cacher* store associated the cartoons against the Prophet with kosher challah breads, pointing to the fact that, according to Leon Wieseltier's (2015) comments, both are the products and symbols of democracy that the attackers wished to destroy. So eating kosher food and reading an abrasive satirical cartoon magazine, despite the fact that the users of these two public 'services' have no social connection whatsoever, pertain to the same right of French citizenship. Indeed, in January 2015 (if not before), kosher food has, in a sense, entered public life (if so tragically), marking a turn in the expression of the French bicentennial Republican contract, and exiting the realm of private kitchen and family tables. Now many French citizens in their vibrant efforts to defend the values of the Republic can and do advocate for the right to distribute, eat and cook kosher food, probably as some others advocate for the right to consume pork.

NOTES

1. This chapter is based on ethnographic data collected among Sephardic immigrants in France between the mid-1970s and the early 2000s. My usage of the term 'Sephardic' is ethnographically based. In French Jewish ethnic terminology, this term includes all Jews of non-Ashkenazic origins established in France in the past several centuries, that is, descendants of Jews of the Comtat Venaissin (today's Provence region), Jews of North African origins and Jews originating in the Ottoman Empire and the Balkan region. In addition to the usage of French as their daily language, the main languages spoken or partially used by these communities are, or used to be, Judeo-Arabic and Arabic, Berber, Ladino, Turkish or Spanish.
2. Most of these post-biblical rules have been recorded primarily in the Babylonian Talmud.
3. The Hebrew term for 'impure', or the opposite of 'kosher'. This term is better known in the United States by its Yiddish pronunciation as '*treif*'.
4. Examples include shark, ray, eel, catfish and sturgeon. The latter is allowed for consumption in the United States under Conservative rabbinical ordinance, while it is forbidden among British Ashkenazi authorities but allowed among many Sephardic communities in the United Kingdom. The consumption of swordfish is also debated, being allowed in some communities while forbidden among others.
5. This is what Mary Douglas proposes as the anthropological analysis of that specific rule (1966: 54–6). The permission of locust consumption has frequently been interpreted as the exception treated by rabbis as a necessary move in times of locust invasions and consequent famines.
6. Any animal whose diet includes the flesh of another animal will not be considered kosher. This is an additional reason for the dietary exclusion of the pig, which is an omnivore.
7. The Hebrew term for ritual slaughter.
8. This aspect of Jewish laws of slaughtering purity is similar to Muslim religious law and has resulted in a political debate in recent years, in several European countries.

9. This observance rule has been ethnographically scrutinized by Fishkoff (2010). In
   particular, she points to the persistence of Orthodox families who use the services of
   companies whose goal is to provide counsel to new home owners in their desire to
   kasher ('purify') their kitchen (2010: 24–7).
10. In Hebrew: *halavi* versus *basari*.
11. For details on this selective prohibition, as well as the entire system of Jewish dietary
    laws, see Geffen and Rabinowicz (2007).
12. This prohibition refers to Jacob's wound in his thigh, received during a fight with an
    angel, a biblical episode detailed in Genesis XXXII: 25–33.
13. The reference to the biblical narrative mentioned in the previous note has often been
    mentioned by my interviewees in response to my enquiry about the religious meaning
    of the exclusion of hind cuts.
14. This special Passover diet is narratively and historically rationalized in Exodus,
    chapter 12, especially its last verses.
15. The majority of these Jewish populations immigrated in France, but a substantial
    part (especially among Moroccan Jews) also went to Israel and North and Latin
    America (Canada in particular). For details on this history, see: Ageron (1979);
    Chouraqui (1972); Eisenbeth (1936); Heller-Goldenberg (2004); Hirschberg
    (1974–81); Laskier (1994).
16. In his *Monolingualism of the Other*, Jacques Derrida (1998) elaborates on the
    philosophical and psychoanalytical effects of this linguistic transformation, as he
    relates to his own personal experience (among others) as a Jew in colonial Algeria.
17. For details on this process of 'civilization' among North African Jews, see Shreier
    (2010); Bahloul (1983).
18. This subtle, dialectical articulation has been particularly significant for Algerian Jews,
    whose French citizenship had been denied during the sombre years of the Vichy
    government (see Abitbol 1989). In the aftermath of the Second World War, these
    Jews have made every effort to retrieve their French identity, within both the public
    and the private domains.
19. In what is to date the most sophisticated historical study of the politics of Jewish
    religious food in France, political historian Pierre Birnbaum (2013) retraces the
    Voltairian philosophical approach to the attribution of French citizenship to the
    Jews of the late eighteenth century, as asserted by the famous Abbé Grégoire just
    before the French Revolution. Jews were to abandon their backward religious rituals,
    especially those around the table, and were to share food with other French citizens,
    as recognition of their willingness to actively participate in the companionship and
    conviviality inherent to the French nation.
20. The embodiment of collective memory has been finely explored in recent
    anthropological literature, for example, Sutton (2001) and Connerton (1989:
    72–104). The prestigious *Oxford Symposium on Food and Cookery* devoted its 2000
    meeting on the topic of 'Food and Memory', resulting in a remarkable collection
    of ethnographic and historical studies of the role of collective memory in the
    construction of taste (Walker 2001).
21. For details of this cuisine, see the following selected cookbooks: Jaffin (1980);
    Benbassa (1984); Nathan (2010); Chiche-Yana (1990); Hazan-Arama (1987);

Karsenty (1974); Taïeb (1998); Roden (1996). An exhaustive inventory and analysis of Jewish cookbooks published in France since the early twentieth century can be found in Assan and Nizard (2014).

22. The proliferation of published Sephardic cookbooks in France in the 1980s and 1990s is another cultural form of memorialization of traditional Sephardic cuisines (see note 21). A similar process was at work in that period on Ashkenazic cuisine.

23. The major impact of Arab medieval food commerce in North African Jewish cuisine has to be underlined here. For details on the history of this trade and culinary activity, see Rodinson (1949, 1965). More details can be found in Waines (2011).

24. This status can be observed in culinary terminology as well. Many of my interviewees of the 1970s and 1980s used the term 'meat' to actually mean 'beef'. In vernacular culinary language, the ultimate meat, that which has to be absolutely served on most ritual meals, especially on the Sabbath table, is beef.

25. The recited Hebrew blessing is as follows: '*ba rosh ve lo bazanav*' (at the head and not at the tail). The term '*rosh*' is a reference to the Hebrew name of the Jewish New Year.

26. It is among those Jews, who maintain a minor ritual observance, that shellfish would be served on the secular New Year's Eve dinners, especially when they are shared with non-Jewish friends.

27. Pierre Birnbaum (2013) has forcefully demonstrated how the debate over the recognition of Jews as French citizens since the eighteenth century has often been focused on the requirement that they abandon their dietary laws, believed to be a handicap in their participation in civil society. To this day, some French Jews have been zealous in demonstrating that they have complied with this Republican requirement by indeed partially giving up their religious food rituals. This debate and political situation is still vibrant in twenty-first century France.

28. On the synesthesia of cultural identity, see Sutton (2001: 90–2).

29. The business of kosher catering has prospered dramatically in the past two decades due to the changes in domestic gender roles. Major French kosher caterers offer their services for holidays of the life-cycle (weddings, bar- and bat-mitzvah), but also for holidays of the year-cycle such as Passover and the Jewish New Year.

30. This development can be observed in particular among those Sephardic or mixed Sephardic-Ashkenazic families who have joined the ultra-Orthodox Lubavitcher movement in the past two or three decades (see Podselver 2010).

31. This neologism is a favourite among some French Jews who like to point, ironically, to the recent matrimonial integration between Ashkenazim and Sephardim in their country.

32. Falafel is a sandwich typically stuffed with fresh-cut vegetables and fried pureed chickpeas croquettes. It is a Middle Eastern specialty but has for several decades been viewed as a national culinary dish in Israeli popular culture.

33. www.harissa.com (Community website of Tunisian Jews), www.dafina.net (Community website of Moroccan Jews) and www.zlabia.com (Community website of Algerian Jews) are examples of such websites.

34. See, for example, the Facebook page of *La dafouineuse*.

35. For details, see www.circinfo.net.

36. See: Anonymous (2014); Shafi and Arkush (2014); Tagliabue (2011).

37. In: *Le Monde*, 5 March 2012.

REFERENCES

Abitbol, M. (1989), *The Jews of North Africa during the Second World War*, Detroit: Wayne State University Press.

Ageron, C.-R. (1979), *Histoire de l'Algérie contemporaine*, Paris: Presses Universitaires de France.

Anonymous (2014), 'Lettre ouverte de Bardot au gouvernement sur l'abattage rituel et l'hippophagie', *RTL numérique/Agence France Presse*, 8 September. Available at: www.rtl.fr.

Assan, V. and Nizard, S. (2014), 'Les livres de cuisine juive: à la recherche d'un monde perdu?'*Archives Juives*, 47(1): 113–31.

Bahloul, J. (1983), *Le culte de la Table Dressée: rites et traditions de la table juive algérienne*, Paris: Éditions A.M. Métailié.

Bahloul, J. (1984), *Parenté et ethnicité: la famille juive nord-africaine en France*, Paris: Ministère de la Culture.

Bahloul, J. (1992), 'La famille sépharade dans la diaspora du XXème siècle', in S. Trigano (ed.), *La Société juive à travers l'histoire*, Paris: Fayard.

Bahloul, J. (1996), 'The Sephardi Family and the Challenge of Assimilation: Family Ritual and Ethnic Reproduction', in H. Goldberg (ed.), *Sephardi and Middle Eastern Jewries: History and Culture in the Modern Era*, 312–24, Bloomington: Indiana University Press.

Benbassa, E. (1984), *Cuisine judéo-espagnole: recettes et traditions*, Paris: Scribe.

Bensimon-Donath, D. (1971), *L'intégration des juifs nord-africains en France*, Paris: Mouton.

Birnbaum, P. (1996), *The Jews of the Republic: A Political History of State Jews in France from Gambetta to Vichy*, Stanford, CA: Stanford University Press.

Birnbaum, P. (2013), *La République et le cochon*, Paris: Éditions du Seuil.

Chiche-Yana, M. (1990), *La table juive: recettes et traditions de fêtes*, Aix-en-Provence: Edisud.

Chouraqui, A. (1972), *La Saga des Juifs en Afrique du Nord*, Paris: Editions Hachette.

Cohen, E. H. (2002), *Les Juifs de France, valeurs et identité*, Paris: FSJU.

Connerton, P. (1989), *How Societies Remember*, Cambridge and New York: Cambridge University Press.

Derrida, J. (1998), *Monolingualism of the Other*, translated by P. Mensah, Stanford, CA: Stanford University Press.

Douglas, M. (1966), *Purity and Danger*, New York: Praeger.

Eisenbeth, M. (1936), *Les juifs de l'Afrique du Nord: démographie et onomastique*, Algiers.

Fishkoff, S. (2010), *Kosher Nation*, New York: Schocken Books.

Geffen, R. M. and Rabinowicz, H. (2007), 'Dietary Laws', in M. Berenbaum and F. Skolnik (eds), *Encyclopaedia Judaica*, 2nd edn, vol. 5, 650–59, Jerusalem: Keter Publishing.

Goldberg, H. E. (1978), 'The Mimuna and the Minority Status of Moroccan Jews', *Ethnology*, 17(1): 75–87.

Goldberg, H. E. (1992), 'Religious Responses Among North African Jews in the Nineteenth and Twentieth Centuries', in J. Wertheimer (ed.), *The Uses of Tradition: Jewish Continuity in the Modern Era*, 119–44, New York and Jerusalem: JTS Press.

Haddad, G. (2013), *Eating the Book,* London: Seahorse Editions.

Hazan-Arama, F. (1987), *Saveurs de mon enfance: la cuisine juive du Maroc*, Paris: Robert Laffont.

Heller-Goldenberg, L. (2004), 'Judeo-Moroccan Memory in Québec', in S. Ireland and P. J. Proulx (eds), *Textualizing the Immigrant Experience in Contemporary Québec*, 149–60, Westport, CT: Praeger.

Hirschberg, H. Z. (1974–81), *A History of the Jews in North Africa*, 2 vols, Leiden: E. J. Brill.

Hobsbawm, E. and Ranger, T. (eds) (1992), *The Invention of Tradition*, New York and Cambridge: Cambridge University Press.

Jaffin, L. (1980), *150 Recettes et Mille et Un souvenirs d'une juive d'Algérie*, Paris: Éditions Encre.

Judd, R. (2007), *Contested Rituals: Circumcision, Kosher Slaughtering, and Jewish Political Life in Germany, 1843-1933*, Ithaca, NY: Cornell University Press.

Karsenty, I. and Karsenty, L. (1974), *Cuisine Pied-noir*, Paris: Denoël.

Laskier, M. M. (1994), *North African Jewry in the Twentieth Century: The Jews of Morocco, Tunisia, and Algeria.* New York and London: New York University Press.

Lasry, J.-C. and Tapia, C. (eds) (1989), *Les Juifs du Maghreb: diasporas contemporaines*, Paris and Montreal: Les Presses de l'Université de Montréal/L'Harmattan.

Leach, E. (1969), *Genesis as Myth, and Other Essays*, London: Jonathan Cape.

Lévi-Strauss, C. (1983), *The Raw and the Cooked (Mythologiques*, vol. 1), Chicago: The University of Chicago Press.

Malino, F. and Wasserstein, B. (eds) (1985), *The Jews in Modern France*, Hanover, NH and London: Brandeis University Press and University Press of New England.

Memmi, A. (1965), *The Colonizer and the Colonized*, Boston, MA: Beacon Press.

Nathan, J. (2010), *Quiches, Kugels, and Couscous: My Search for Jewish Cooking in France*, New York: Knopf Publishing Group.

Podselver, L. (2010), *Retour au Judaïsme? Les Loubavitch en France*, Paris: Editions Odile Jacob.

Raphaël, F., Fisch, J., Koscher, J. and Bodenheimer, F. (1983), *Les recettes de la table juive: Alsace/Europe de l'Est/Israël/Afrique du Nord*, Strasbourg: Librairie Istra.

Roden, C. (1996), *The Book of Jewish Food*, New York: Knopf.

Rodinson, M. (1949), 'Recherches sur les documents arabes relatifs à la cuisine', *Revue des Études Islamiques*, 17: 95–165.

Rodinson, M. (1965), 'Ghidha', in *Encyclopédie de l'Islam*, vol. 2, Paris: Maisonneuve et Larose.

de Saussure, F. (1968), *Cours de linguistique générale*, Paris: Éditions Payot.

Schreier, J. (2010), *Arabs of the Jewish Faith: The Civilizing Mission in Colonial Algeria*, New Brunswick, NJ: Rutgers University Press.

Schwarzfuchs, S. (1979), *Napoléon, the Jews, and the Sanhedrin*, London: Routledge & Kegan Paul.

Shafi, S. and Arkush, J. (2014), 'Jewish and Muslim methods of slaughter prioritize animal welfare', *The Guardian*, 6 March.

Soler, J. (1979), 'The Semiotics of Food in the Bible', in R. Foster and O. Ranum (eds), *Food and Drink in History*, 126–38, Baltimore, MD: Johns Hopkins University Press.

Sutton, D. E. (2001), *Remembrance of Repasts: An Anthropology of Food and Memory*, Oxford and New York: Oxford University Press.

Tagliabue, J. (2011), 'Bill on Humane Slaughter Yields New Front for Muslim Tensions', *The New York Times*, 26 June 2011.

Taïeb, D. (1998), Les *fêtes juives à Tunis racontées à mes filles*, Paris: Simonot.

Waines, D. (2011), *Food Culture and Health in Pre-Modern Islamic Societies*, Leiden and Boston, MA: Brill.

Walker, H. (ed.) (2001), *Food and the Memory: Proceedings of the Oxford Symposium on Food and Cookery 2000*, Totnes, Devon: Prospect Books.

Wieseltier, L. (2015), 'We Are Hyper Cacher', *The Atlantic*, 20 January 2015.

CHAPTER FIVE

Approaches to Food and Migration: Rootedness, Being and Belonging

EMMA-JAYNE ABBOTS

INTRODUCTION

Food plays a significant role in the social lives of diasporas: it can create a sense of continued belonging and reiterate affiliations to 'home'. Following debates on food, identity, ethnicity and commensality, food preferences have been demonstrated to facilitate the construction of discrete migrant subjectivities and group identities by both inclusion – in that they reaffirm relations between migrants – and exclusion – in that others in the host region do not share migrant tastes. Variations on this theme address the role that food plays in negotiating interactions between migrants and hosts, particularly its potential to change attitudes to, and the political economic situation of, migrant groups, the creativity of migrants and the formation of hybridized foodways. Building on an established body of literature on household hierarchies and gender, an additional topic has been the investigation into how food labour relations within migrant households shift in accordance to the new social and environmental context in which they find themselves.

This chapter initially surveys and reflects upon this literature, indicating how it engages with broader themes within the anthropology of food. In particular, I wish to point to how studies of food and migration can make a significant contribution not just to the anthropology of food, but also to our understanding of the ways in which the globalized movement of people, objects, narratives and ideas is experienced and negotiated. The broader themes discussed include the ways in which food, and ideas about food, travel; memory and nostalgia; the assertion of regional, place-based foods; the practices of everyday food provisioning; and the ways that food can reveal political divisions and economic inequities, as much as it can show community and cohesion. However despite its engagement with these wider questions, I wish to suggest that the scholarship on food and migration has also been somewhat contained, and indicate possible future directions for research that could enhance its wider contribution. These new directions and developments can, I hope to demonstrate, broaden the scope of investigation by encompassing both the migrant 'in situ' and their 'home' community, as well as considering the movements of foods and food practices. I further contend that a renewed focus on 'the body' can deepen analysis.

Throughout, I focus on work that addresses migration from the global south to north as, paralleling scholarship on migration more generally, the anthropology of food and migration has concentrated its efforts in this area. However, a small but emerging field of work is drawing attention to privileged migration and the experiences of those moving from north to south (see, e.g., Fechter 2007), although little of this material engages with food explicitly. This, I suggest, is an oversight. Although small in number, privileged migrants and expatriates often have the political and economic capital to potentially significant shape food markets and practices in their host country. Further explorations into the ways their food encounters are negotiated and experienced (see Abbots 2013) thereby has the promise of deepening our understanding of the relationship between food and migration, as well as migratory processes more broadly.

In the latter sections of this chapter, I explore the possibilities of these emergent areas of research. Drawing on my ethnography from the Ecuadorian Andes, I argue that food exchange networks between migrants and those at home play a pivotal role in anchoring migrants and contend that the recent emphasis on food practices of migrants in situ obscures the labour of those who remain in the home communities. I consider the ways that food gifts not only remind migrants of their obligations to their home household, but also, through the sharing of dishes across time and space, socially and physically (re)make them as members of that household. Thus, I aim to elucidate the manner in which migrants' food practices are governed from afar, as well as how migration can influence and change food practices 'at home'. Within this argument the body is central, and one of my aims in this chapter is to draw out the threads of embodied food practices that are often implied in accounts of food and migration, but rarely developed. Invoking Strathern (1988), I show how home foods constitute migrant bodies by acting as a counter to the 'exogenous' foods of their host environment, and reflect on how familiar smells, tastes and textures can facilitate imaginings of place – effectively transporting migrants back home. As such, I hope to highlight food's capacity to potentially stem loss and promote continuities in a migratory context, as well as suggesting the tensions to which these processes can give rise.

BEING AND BELONGING: MIGRANT FOOD SPACES

Migrant food practices are not uncommonly analysed through the framework of ethnic belonging and the construction of identities (Chapman and Beagan 2013; Kalcik 1984; Harbottle 2000; Ray 2004; Vallianatos and Raine 2008). As Caplan points out, there has been a preoccupation with 'food as a marker of difference' and identity (1997: 9), and the well-established argument, that commensal relations and the consumption of specific foods enact group and individual identities, has been a productive lens for scholars of food and migration. Migration places an individual's sense of being and belonging into a state of flux; as they become pulled in multiple directions and subjected to a range of influences and changes in their everyday lives, they have to (re)construct their identities and relations. Food, as will become evident, has been demonstrated across a number of ethnographic contexts to play a significant role in 'anchoring' a migrant, while also enabling the creation of new subjectivities and orientations. Consequently, food frequently becomes viewed as a marker of ethnic identity (Vallianatos and Raine 2008: 365).

One of the most nuanced texts on this topic is Ray's (2004) study of first and second generation middle-class Bengali-Americans. *The Migrant's Table* articulates how modern and traditional, ethnic and universal and the local and global intersect (2004: 10). Ray explains that certain meals and patterns of eating are subject to change, whereas some remain stringently Bengali and others are Bengali 'traditions' invented in the United States. He further elucidates how migrants construct culinary identities and assert gustatory boundaries in relation to 'others' – in this context, Bengali in Bengal, Indian in the United States and American (2004: 78–9). This theme of 'commensal sociality' is similarly found in the work of Renne (2008: 616) who shows how West Africans in the United States use foods, which, although different in terms of their production, remain ideologically similar, to maintain and reproduce social relations with families, 'hometown associations' and religious groups. She further draws attention to the significant role of speciality grocery stores in enabling the reproduction of West African social relations and reinforcement of their identities (ibid.).

Migrants interact with speciality groceries and restaurants at multiple levels. They are, as I discuss further below, historically a source of labour, employment and income – and potentially a site of exploitation – as well as being a space of definition between migrants and hosts. They are also a stopping point on the routes along which foods travel. Whether they are direct imports or have travelled through globalized networks and associated with home by other means (Renne 2008), a number of the foods consumed by migrants are sourced via speciality groceries. Mankekar (2005), among others (Charon Cardona 2004; Diner 2001; Hage 1997; Saber and Posner 2013), reflects upon how 'ethnic' grocery stores reproduce home, both materially and discursively. She examines Indian groceries in the San Francisco Bay area and argues that they 'form a crucial node in the transnational circulation and consumption of commodities and discourses about India' (Mankekar 2005: 210). The stores, she explains, are not just locations to purchase 'Indian' food, but are also 'social spaces' in which migrants 'might forge identity and community' (2005: 207) – a process that is reassuringly familiar to some and stiflingly claustrophobic for others. The stores are also assemblages in which food, the arrangement of products, the 'customer service', the advertisements, the decoration and the music serve to (re)produce India in the United States in a manner that invokes powerful and contested notions of gender, class, family and nation. Mankekar thereby reminds us not only that the production of home culture is a polyvocal process, but also that responses to home can be deeply ambivalent and as divisive as they are cohesive.

Yet places of migrant belonging can also traverse previously entrenched social boundaries and foster solidarity between minority groups within a wider diaspora. Tuomainen (2009) demonstrates how, in their efforts to construct and uphold a

Ghanaian or African subjectivity, Ghanaian migrants in London diminished regional and ethnic contrasts by consuming foods previously associated with other ethnic groups (see also Beyers 2008 and Diner 2001). Likewise, Saber and Posner's (2013) sensitive account of Eritrean and Sudanese asylum seekers' experiences in Tel Aviv elucidates how their restaurants, while being perceived as 'traditional', are also sites of cultural hybridization and transnationality in which familiar experiences are shared and diasporic identities forged from multiple ethnic identities. Referring to such restaurants as 'culinary safe havens' (2013: 198), Saber and Posner argue they provide asylum seekers with a sense of familiarity, security, empowerment and certainty and stress the critical importance of familiar foods in everyday survival strategies. Foods and food spaces are thus coping mechanisms for migrants that can also cut across social and ethnic divisions.

Mankekar and Saber and Posner further emphasize the embodied experiences of migrants' food spaces and the ways that multi-sensory cues – such as visual displays, textures and smells – create a familiar home environment that can provide both security for some and unease for others. In so doing, they move beyond discussions of 'taste' and remind us not only that purchasing, preparing and consuming food is experienced through all the senses, but also that these practices can effectively transport migrants back 'home'. Food, then, transcends space and time. As such, these accounts resonate with the anthropology of the senses (see Stoller 1989) and work on food and memory (see Holtzman 2006), as well as indicating how we can approach 'the body' in a migratory context. Arguably one of the most influential accounts within the genre is Sutton's ethnography of food and embodied memory in Kalymnos, Greece. I discuss this, together with the ways work on food and migration can engage with the body, below, but first I turn to relations between migrants and hosts.

ACCULTURATION, APPROPRIATION AND HYBRIDIZATION: INTERACTIONS BETWEEN MIGRANT AND HOSTS

Spaces of migrant foods are not produced in isolation but are interwoven with that of the host country. Whether it is Sydney-siders enjoying 'ethnic' restaurants (Frost 2008) or migrants incorporating new foods into their diets, the interactions between host and diaspora have just as much salience as those between migrants. Given the dominance of debates over globalization, homogenization and creolization in the anthropology of food (see Abbots 2012a, 2014a; Caldwell 2004; Ritzer 2010; Watson 2006), and the discipline more widely (Hannerz 1987), it is not surprising that questions of acculturation, incorporation, hybridization and rejection have framed many of these discussions (see Beyers 2008; Caplan 1997; Harbottle 2000; Jamal 1996; Tuomainen 2009; Vallianatos and Raine 2008). An extension of this theme also demonstrates that food habits are one of the last cultural traits to change among migrants (Charon Cardona 2004; McIntosh 1996) and often point to the way that the main meal of the day, and festive and weekend meals, have the greater continuity (Bradby 1997; Ray 2004).

Scholarship on how migrants' food practices adapt and change can also indicate structural disparities and environmental factors (Charon Cardona 2004; Hage 1997; Jamal 1996), and demonstrate migrant agency and creativity in the production of hybrid dishes (Renne 2008). It can further suggest broader political and economic dynamics. Tuomainen (2009), for example, situates her discussion of Ghanaian food practices in London within the historical context of Britain's colonial relations with Ghana and explains that many Ghanaians regarded British culinary habits as part of their own food culture *before* migration, even though these foods were primarily restricted to socially elite groups (2009: 544). Upon migrating, Ghanaians discovered that they could access these, once elite but still high status, foods easily and could thus emulate the privileged. This demonstrates, Tuomainen argues, that Ghanaians have a more positive view of colonialism than, for example, the Irish migrants to the United States discussed by Diner (2001), who rejected the foodways of their occupiers.

The ways in which food practices and knowledges become markers of difference (and similarities) between hosts and migrants is further expounded by Frost (2008). Her ethnography of a group of Indonesian migrant women in Sydney traces the ways they adapted their domestic culinary knowledge for public consumption by running a successful cookery course for a local adult education college. This, Frost explains, enabled the women to confirm their commonality while concomitantly reiterating their differences to their hosts, as their lack of knowledge of how and what to eat as an Australian was brought into sharp relief. But this distance was also a point of intersection. Frost reveals how the women had a 'deeply strategic knowledge of the Sydney cityscape' (2008: 180) that was premised on their ability to source 'their' foods, and this enabled them to engage, critique and 'mildly subvert' the dominant culture of their host country (2008: 180–1). Although cautious of the ways in which host desires for 'ethnic' food and rubrics of multiculturalism can potentially essentialize migrants, Frost thus shows how food can be a mechanism of 'empowerment and exploration' for a marginalized group (2008: 187).

The extent that ethnic restaurants and multicultural food spaces facilitate cohesion and community between migrants and hosts has been subject to some debate. A body of related literature also assesses whether celebrations of multicultural foods deflect attention away from structural inequalities or provide the locus for cross-cultural understandings and identity (Cook, Crang and Thorpe 1999; Harbottle 1997). In the context of the Netherlands, van Otterloo (1987) argues that relations between migrants and their Dutch hosts were more confrontational in other contexts than 'at the table', whereas Hage (1997) argues that the celebration of migrants' food is a form of gastro-tourism which requires little to no engagement between hosts and migrants. His account of middle-class Australians' enthusiasm for 'authentic' Vietnamese cuisine, and the collusion of Vietnamese migrants in presenting their food in this manner, points to how moments of encounter can be based upon stereotyped caricatures. Hage concludes this form of 'multicultualism without migrants' (1997: 118) has little to no consequence to the hegemonic Anglo-Australian identity (see also Flowers and Swan 2015). Moreover, while Frost suggests that ethnic food may offer a route of economic advancement for migrants, others (Baxter and Raw

1988; Kalra 2004) have pointed to the ways in which the catering industry, and the food sector more generally, thrives from cheap migrant labour and can be sites of significant exploitation, discrimination and the reiteration of economic and social disparities.

It is not, however, just gastro-tourists who potentially essentialize and reify migrant food practices. Whether focused on migrant communities or the interactions between migrants and hosts, the risk remains that anthropological analysis, despite its best intentions, invokes a static and dichotomous relationship between their 'food from there' and 'our food from here' – a process that, in turn, treats identities, and those of migrants in particular, as singular and fixed. Chapman and Beagan (2013) raise this point in their study of two Punjabi-Canadian families. Drawing on influential theorists of transnationality and migration (Ong 2003; Rouse 1995; Schiller, Basch and Blanc 1995), and the fluid understandings of identities that emerge from this work, they emphasize that migrant subjectivities are multiple and demonstrate that food practices can simultaneously constitute, and reflect, a range of, sometimes contradictory, attachments that intersect with ethnicity, class, gender, age and nationality. They also highlight how migrants can establish affiliations to multiple nation-states. Chapman and Beagan are, then, highly critical of the accounts of migrant food practices that centre on acculturation and the gradual loss (or retention) of culinary patterns of home, concluding that

> theoretical conceptualizations of food and migration that focus on acculturation or resistance – in which ethnic identity is either retained or lost after migration – do not adequately capture the reality of transnational experiences. (2013: 381)

This perspective is supported by Renne (2008), who demonstrates that the subjectivities of West African migrants are as multiple and hybridized as their foods. Moreover, just as the foods within host environments change, so do those from home, with Collins (2008) reminding us that a neat line cannot be drawn between 'traditional' foods from home and hybrid foods in migrants' host contexts. This indicates how the framing foods from home as place (or ethnicity) based and traditional is an artificial construct, that is often founded upon a nostalgia or imagining of home (see also Tuomainan 2009). Thus, we have to remember that just as people and food (and their narratives) travel and circulate, so do the meanings attached to them.

UPHOLDING HOME: GENDER, GENERATIONS AND FOOD LABOUR

The recognition that migrant subjectivities are multiple and that culinary practices are subject to myriad influences and changes, raise questions as to which individuals shoulder the responsibility of (re)producing migrant identities, as well as the ways multiple influences are negotiated. Accounts sculpted by these questions are often, although not exclusively, framed by gender, generations and household hierarchies (see Ray 2004). As such, they commonly engage with a wider body of work on the gendered dimensions of food knowledge and labour (see also Sutton, Chapter 16, this volume, and R. Watson, Chapter 15, this volume). The ways that women are the primary performers of food work within the home, and the extent that this can be a site of empowerment and agency, have been well documented outside migratory contexts (Counihan and Kaplan 1998; Pilcher 1998; Weismantel 1988), as have discussions of how women privilege other family members' needs, tastes and preferences above their own (Counihan 1999; DeVault 1991; Murcott 1983). Given that migration, of both individuals and households, affords the opportunity for gender roles to be reconfigured (Abbots 2012), it is perhaps not surprising that concerns over who feeds and cares for a migrant household, and, in turn, (re)produces migrant foodways, emerge.

As Frost's (2008) ethnography suggests, migrant women's capacity to source food forms the basis for many of their social interactions outside the domestic sphere (see also Mankekar 2005), and food can provide one of the key mechanisms for interacting with their hosts and other migrants. It is also, as Flowers and Swan (2015) point out, a mechanism through which gender, as well as race and ethnicity, is essentialized and reified. The 'primary carer' role that women continue to play within migratory contexts is further examined in Vallianatos and Raine's (2008) account of Arabic and South Asian female immigrants in Canada. They reveal the fluidity and renegotiation of gender roles within migrant families, and the ways this is informed by broader economic and social pressures, such as the time men are required to spend at work. Nevertheless, they also point to the ways that both Arabic and South Asian women's self-definitions continued to be fixed upon being mothers and wives, and that provisioning food and cooking remain critical to their own gendered identity. Due to these continuing responsibilities, Vallianatos and Raine refer to such women as 'gatekeepers' who inculcate 'family and community values via traditional foods and cuisines' while brokering 'outside' influences (2008: 357). As suggested above, Vallianatos and Raine's analysis can be criticized for the manner it dichotomizes 'food from here' with 'food from there', but it does draw attention to ways that food practices are mediated within migrant households, the pressures to which primary food-provisioners are subjected and the tensions that emerge from this process. Of these tensions, generational differences emerge as one of the most significant aspects in Vallianatos and Raine's discussion, a theme further addressed by Harbottle (2000) in her account of Iranian migrants in Britain (see also Chapman and Beagan 2013; and Ray 2004).

Thus, one of the primary questions that emerge from explorations of the interplays between food and migration is 'who does the work of (re)producing migrant identities and mediating between host and home, and to what extent does this change over time?' The oft-implied, but rarely articulated, assumption of this question, and work on food and migration more broadly, is that migrants' practices – and their pre-migration food practices – are at risk of being lost. Food, the argument goes, can help stem that loss by maintaining continuities and (re)embedding the migrant in their home community (however that may be defined), while also enabling change to occur and facilitating the creation of new relations of being and belonging. Notions of loss can be further discerned in discussions of assimilation and nostalgia, and it is perhaps a concept, along with gain, that warrants more considered attention, at the very least from migrants' perspectives.

Loss, continuities and change are themes in Strathern's (1988) synthesis of Melanesian anthropology, *The Gender of the Gift*. The relationship of this text to the topic of food and migration may not be immediately self-evident, but I would like to suggest that the arguments put forward by Strathern provide a productive jumping-off point for broadening the scope of this particular field of study. Similar to the accounts above, Stathern makes the point that, in migratory contexts, it is women who emerge as specifically 'social in their orientations' and 'become visible reminders of enduring norms of social conduct' (1988: 76–7). Women, as such, become the upholders of culture. Drawing on the ethnography of Jolly, situated in a *kastom* village in the Vanuatu peninsula, Strathern explores how foodways in this context are both gendered and related to social status, with yams being associated with masculinity. Male migration is consequently understood to weaken men's bodies as, instead of ingesting yams, they consume the 'foreign' foods of rice, tinned fish and corned beef. Yet, this weakening, Strathern explains, can be replenished during the yam harvest. She thereby elucidates how a symbolically resonant food from home can counteract potentially dangerous exogenous foods and help minimize the loss of migrants' bodies to European influences. Moreover, in helping ensure male migrants' (re)rootedness to home through yams, women, who are actively prevented from accessing the 'outside world', ensure the continuation of *kastom*.

The reasons I draw attention to this work are twofold. First, it further reiterates the gendered dimension of food labour and women's role in (re)producing culture and stemming loss in a migratory context. Second, it indicates that, in analysing the interplays between food and migration, we should be taking into account the broader social networks that traverse host and home. In other words, it throws into sharp relief that most works on food and migration are ironically limited in geographical and analytical scope. These limitations, I would like to suggest, have also inhibited the topic's contribution. The examples I have discussed thus far, while wide-ranging in subject, have one clear commonality – they focus on migrants in situ. This may be the obvious starting point, but migrants do not necessarily sever their ties to home but rather, instead, actively maintain them. Likewise, as Strathern's discussion suggests, those at home may proactively nurture continuities with migrants. Households, however geographically and physically dispersed, can remain symbolically and socially united (Abbots 2011, 2014b, 2015). The social lives of migrants, then, are not just enacted in their host locations but instead played out with, and influence, the lives of those who remain at home. Here and there are mutually entangled.

RETHINKING FOOD AND MIGRATION: THE FLOWS BETWEEN HERE AND THERE

For a subject ostensibly addressing movement, work in the anthropology of food and migration has hence been arguably confined by geographical location and straightjacketed by locale. In this section I would like to offer an alternative analytical frame that addresses the flows between home and host as part of broader networks of exchange. In particular, I argue that a focus on the actions of individuals at home warrants just as much attention as migrants' activities in situ.

The village of Jima in the Southern Ecuadorian Andes, where I have conducted long-term fieldwork, is a community significantly affected by sustained migration to predominantly the United States. Migration of primarily, although not exclusively, men is a long-term household strategy for many, and remittances have dislodged small-scale agriculture, waged labour and petty entrepreneurship as the main sources of income. Migration, and the economic benefits it brings, has thus transformed the organization of social life and the enactment of cultural practices. As such, Jimeño foodways, as I have discussed elsewhere (Abbots 2011, 2012a, b), are subject to change. Yet they also play a critical role in enabling the (re)production of cultural continuities and the perpetuation of household relations across space.

It is through the broader networks of exchange between migrants and their kin at home that the capacity of food in ensuring continuity comes to the fore. As with Strathern's discussion of Vanuatu migrants, in Jima there is a risk that migrated men will be 'lost' while in the United States and to mitigate against this, the women who remain look to continually remake their male kin as Jimeño and root them back into the village and their household. They achieve this through food packages. But these packages do not contain just any foods, nor are they sent randomly. Rather they contain *cuy* (roast guinea pig) and *mote* (white hominy), which, as I have argued previously, are locally framed as 'typical' foods laden with symbolic meaning (see Abbots 2011, 2012a). *Cuy*, in a domestic context, is subject to a number of commensal restrictions in that it travels through limited networks of exchange and is only eaten with intimate members of a household's social network – and, as such, helps define those relations – while *mote* is firmly rooted to Jima through oral histories that reaffirm its specificity to the locale. Moreover, packages of *cuy* and *mote* are commonly mailed to migrants during ritual and festive events in both the wider community's and the household's calendars, thereby enabling the migrant to participate in the celebration, albeit at a geographical distance (Abbots 2011: 213).

Food packages do not travel, however, in isolation. Instead they articulate with the flows of other objects and remittances that are sent by migrated men back to Jima. Packages of culturally important food, then, form part of a broader process of transnational exchange through which affective relationships are enacted and maintained within a geographically dispersed household, and through which physically absent men are made symbolically present (Abbots 2014b, 2015). These exchanges are based on reciprocal labour relations and the mutual reproduction of the household, with migrated men transforming their labour into remittances, and their female kin producing food (Abbots 2011: 212). This process of perpetual gifting thereby maintains a continual cycle of obligation, indebtedness and reciprocity that practically remind men of their obligations to their household, as well as serving to physically and symbolically (re)root them within that household, a point to which I return below.

The broader, more holistic approach to food and migration that I present here demonstrates that food cannot be considered in isolation but has to be situated in a wider context of movement, travels and flows across space. It further shows how we can deepen our understanding of (gendered) food labour, agency and power in a migratory context if we take these broader networks into account. Much of the literature I have discussed thus far has addressed migrants' actions and their agency (or disempowerment) vis-à-vis their hosts. But this, I contend, is only part of the story. The ethnography from Jima shows that there are other actors involved in the reproduction and reinvention of migrant food practices, but these individuals and their actions are commonly obfuscated by frameworks that assume that migrants are the ones performing and (re)creating culture and identities. This is not to deny migrant actions – for in the Jimeño context men sometimes request *cuy* from home and thus seek to remake themselves as Jimeño – but rather to advocate an approach to food and migration that encompasses and brings to the foreground the food labour of those that are, at best, treated as 'off-camera' and, at worst, overlooked entirely.

A focus on the flows between home, migrant and host further draws our attention to how migration can shape and inform food practices in the sending community, thereby helping ensure that these are not falsely reified and portrayed as static. One of the most significant aspects of this process is the receipt of remittances and their power to potentially transform lives. The ways that remittances are and should be used have been subject to some debate, both within anthropology and more widely. On the one hand, reports show that remittances are channelled into agricultural production and the continuation of rural livelihoods (Durand et al. 1996; Vasco 2011); on the other, it is evident that remittances facilitate a significant change in social and cultural life, including foodways. It is this second scenario that is, to some extent, being played out in Jima.

Newly acquired remittance prosperity, the low social status of the peasantry, the loss of agricultural knowledge, not to mention labour power, and the resultant breakdown of reciprocal labour agreements have all contributed to the rejection of small-scale agricultural production in Jima. As remittance prosperity has increased and is seen to be secure, agricultural yields have diminished. This is not to state that smallholding has disappeared entirely: many households still maintain a small plot and grow symbolically important maize for domestic use, although, when resources allow, this is now worked by a waged labourer. People also still raise *cuy*, albeit in a separate space in the garden as opposed to within the house, as historically practised. Cooking practices within the home have also changed. The introduction of waged domestic workers into newly-prosperous households have changed food labour practices and created new household hierarchies, although these remain gendered (see Abbots 2012b). Remittances have further transformed food spaces, especially the kitchen. As the arrival of domestic appliances, purchased in the United States and installed in Jimeño homes, becomes a social signal of migratory success and continuing transnational kinship relations (Abbots 2013, 2015), methods of food preparation change – as do modes of eating, with the building of formal dining rooms and the construction of spacialized divisions between domestic workers and family members (Abbots 2012b). On the other hand, some food labour practices are consciously continued, especially in relation to *cuy* and maize products, and domestic workers are excluded from the familial preparation and consumption of *cuy*. To fully understand these processes, I suggest, we cannot view them in isolation but have instead to situate them within the context of ongoing affective relations with migrants and the remaking of them as Jimeño (see Abbots 2011).

Moreover, outward migration can encourage changes in food consumption practices at home, as those who remain have the resources to purchase food from different stores, produce less of their own foods, and look to emulate the food practices of the 'more modern' migrant kin. In Jima, this most evidently plays out in the popularity of global fast-food chains (Abbots 2012a). These changes can, of course, have consequences on dietary health, although we have to be cautious that we do not assume causal connections between changing methods of food production and sourcing, consumption and health; the interplays between these are complex and subject to multiple factors and influences.

Food practices in Jima, both 'traditional' and 'new', can thus be intimately related to affective relations with migrants. As well as more public displays of mobility, new foods and kitchen equipment (and new kitchens) can consequently also be interpreted as public representations of continuing intimate relations with migrants. At times, these statements are made during cultural fiestas, with equipment being taken out of the kitchen and publicly displayed. This practice subverts the intended attempt to promote cultural continuities and food traditions by highlighting change and 'modern food'. And, while the display of material wealth and technology and its relation to social position and aspirations is not a new insight, the way migration enables this process, and the different meanings that are overlaid onto food and kitchen paraphernalia as a result, is a potentially productive line of enquiry. Just as we ask how migrants adapt their food practices to new social and material environments, so too can we examine how they change the environments back home. This can interrogate how the foods and the food-based objects associated with migrants come to 'stand in for' the physically absent migrant and produce their symbolic presence. Thus, to fully unpack the shifting meanings of foods and food stuffs in relation to migration, we should be traversing both public life and domestic life and looking to expound how food can enact the intimacies of physically dislocated kinship, as well as examining how migration informs food's role in the (re)construction (and contestation) of social hierarchies.

In ethnographic contexts that are being affected by migration, we can then ask what food practices are subject to change, what is allowed to change, what do individuals strive to maintain, and how do they negotiate the multiple influences and discourses to which they are subject. As explored above, these questions have been asked, to variable effect, in host sites, both from the perspective of the migrant and the host. However, those accounts have rarely considered the consequences of migration on the sending communities, which also experience, and have to negotiate, new food influences and tastes. This question of how 'traditional' local food is changing and being reinvented in relation to global processes is not a new one within the anthropology of food, and migration is not the only factor. But, perhaps somewhat surprisingly, the recognition that it is a factor has often been overlooked in favour of more structural processes such as the expansion of supermarket retailing and the extended reach of the fast-food industry. I would like to suggest that the ethnography from Jima suggests that development of individual, community and regional migratory networks that span multiple locales and food spaces forms a significant aspect of these global dynamics. Migration also informs the way these structural factors are experienced and managed at a local level. To give an example, I have argued that one cannot fully comprehend the significance of major US-based fast-food chains in Southern Ecuador without taking outward male migration to the US and transnational households into consideration (Abbots 2012a). This wider perspective, then, can aid our understanding of how and why the foods from 'home' change and adapt (or not) and how migrants can sculpt these processes. I now conclude by turning to look at how this is experienced through the body.

MIGRATION, FOOD AND THE BODY

The body is a recurring, although often implied, theme, in work on food and migration, and I would like to propose that this is another research direction that has the potential to be developed. Returning to Strathern briefly, she shows us how foreign food is understood in Vanuatu to weaken migrated men's bodies, and how women work to replenish those bodies. Invoking Strathern, I have made similar arguments in relation to packages of *cuy* (Abbots 2011), arguing that its consumption physically and socially (re)constitutes Jimeño migrants living in the United States as Jimeño and as kin, and examining the ways the dish, and the moral values with which it is associated, is juxtaposed against those of the host country. Thus, we can see that those at home can govern what is ingested from afar as they look to (re)make the bodies of migrants. Migrants can, of course, reject, accept and request these foods. The ways that these embodied attempts to re(root) and disentangle migrants are experienced and negotiated (by both migrants and those at home), as well as the tensions that can emerge from those potentially disciplining procedures, further indicates the import of attending to the relationships between migrants and the individuals at home, as opposed to framing 'home' in a more abstract, oblique manner.

The ways that migration is an intensively embodied experience is also evident in accounts that are concerned with the sensory experiences of food and the ways that they can transport migrants 'back home', in a manner that is both pleasurable and disconcerting (see Mankekar 2008). As Sutton's (2001) study of food and memory in Kalymnos demonstrates, the embodied act of eating enables individuals to look backwards to past meals while enjoying those in the present and anticipating food events in the future. As such, Sutton not only highlights food's 'memory power', as grounded in the embodied and sensory experience of consuming, tasting and smelling, but also demonstrates its rhythms and rituals, and the ways these maintain connections between places, events and people. Eating can thus be accorded to remembering both home and the people contained within it. Similarly, Ben-Ze'ev (2004) elucidates the processes through which taste and smell are central to the retrieval of memories among migrants and traces the processes through which these embodied experiences of food become abstracted and codified. This account thereby details the ways in which narratives, the senses and food's materialities interplay in creating a collective identity among diasporas, with Ben-Ze'ev concluding that tastes and smells (and their discourses) can provide the foundation on which belonging is constructed.

Ethnographic accounts of memory and the senses thereby show how food can move an eating ingesting body beyond the confines of its physical locale and transcend space. Yet, as with most work on food and migration, the focus remains on migrant experience, not on how, for example, those who remain at home form memories and construct narratives of migrants through food. We can, however, use this literature as a starting point from which to explore the ways that food can bring together bodies that are dispersed in space, and examine the ways that eating the same foods but in different places produces coterminous bodies that are 'made' of the same substances. The anthropological study of food has arguably concentrated its efforts on the political economy and symbolic meanings to the detriment of the body (Abbots and Lavis 2013), but the fact remains that food is ingested and brought into the body. It is this process of incorporation, drawing on Fischler (1988), that makes it a particularly powerful medium in the constitution of personhood. This making of coterminous bodies was evident in my research participants approaches to *cuy*, in that they expressed the view that consuming the dish would constitute individuals as Jimeño (Abbots 2011). Personhood was therefore not fixed and static but somewhat mutable and made through the ingestion of substances that were deemed to be of the locale. In the context of migration this process continues through the sending of *cuy* packages, with families 'sharing' meals and substances despite being in different locations – an argument that develops and extends Carsten's (1997) conclusion that individuals are made as kin through shared meals. The ways in which the bodies of migrants are connected back to home and are also linked to other bodies at home through shared substances are, then, research directions that have plenty of scope for expansion.

Finally, returning to migrants in situ we can also further explore how migration is experienced through the body. There has been some work on this topic but, as indicated above, much of it tends to focus on the familiar tastes, smells and images of foods from home. We can, however, ask how unfamiliar foods are experienced and examine not only the ways in which these encounters are felt through the body, but also, in turn, how these embodied experiences shape perceptions and understandings of both 'foreign' places and the people living within them. Just as sharing substances can create coterminous bodies, a refusal to ingest the food of others can remove oneself from potential social entanglements. It was this perspective that I have adopted in my attempt to better understand how privileged North American migrants respond to moving to Ecuador.

As I have discussed elsewhere (Abbots 2013), privileged migration in this context is lifestyle motivated, with my research participants desirous of a 'simple life' and 'simple food' that is produced outside of the agro-industrial complex. However, their lived reality is characterized by their distancing from local foods as they struggle to source food that, in their terms, is risk and anxiety free. Many privileged migrants consequently sourced their food from 'modern' supermarkets and imported it from home. In interrogating these tensions and contradictions, I have sought to elucidate how they are shaped by migrants' visceral reactions and looked to demonstrate how focusing on these embodied responses can illuminate how migrants construct themselves in relation to the 'foreign bodies' – microbes, foods and local people – they encounter. Arguing that privileged migrants' views of their Ecuadorian hosts are informed by their own, often violent, bodily responses to the local food they consume, I have documented not only how concerns over bodies, specifically their physical health and well-being, are a motivating 'push' factor that encourages their migration in the first instance, but also how these concerns – and the embodied risky realities of eating food to which the body is not accustomed – limit migrant integration. In order to protect their bodies from harm, the privileged migrants with whom I conducted my research withdrew from Ecuadorian foods and food spaces – and people – and retreated into food practices that they deemed to be 'safe' and trustworthy. As such, this ethnography shows that the body plays a critical role in shaping not just migrant food practices, but also their experience of migration more widely. We thus ignore the embodied interactions of migration at our peril.

CONCLUSION

The topic of food and migration is broad and cannot be considered in isolation, but should be situated within broader questions of the interplays between food and ethnicity, identity, globalization, memory, kinship and the body, to name but a few areas I have highlighted in this chapter. People, foods and ideas about foods, as well as food's material culture, travel. They are also continually (re)rooted and embedded. One of the challenges facing studies of food and migration is developing theoretical frameworks and approaches that account for both movement and the establishment of new roots. To date, much work has focused on the second part of this equation and one of the key concerns has been on how food practices facilitate the reiteration of established, and the construction of new, ways of being and belonging among migrants. Whether focused on upholding ethnic identities, cutting across previous social boundaries in the making of new collectivities, or the creation of new hybridized, multifaceted and shifting subjectivities, this body of scholarship has demonstrated that food plays a critical role in migrants' everyday lives. Sourcing, preparing and consuming food, together with feeding others, are some of the most immediate and pressing concerns migrants face and, as the ethnography demonstrates, these processes can be a mechanism for security, empowerment, and affiliation with others, just as much they can be a site of difference, marginalization and uncertainty.

Regardless of its specific subject orientation, approach or ethnographic context, the anthropology of food and migration further highlights that migrants do not live in a vacuum, but are instead entangled in networks of relations, all of which potentially shape their food practices and, in turn, inform those of others. Some may prefer to focus on relations within migrant groups or those that cut across such divisions as part of wider diasporas, whereas others may focus on the interactions between hosts and migrants or between migrants and the sending communities. But what is of central importance is that we recognize that these relationships are interwoven, and that neither the foodways 'from here' nor the foodways 'from there' are static, but are instead subjected to multiple influences and change. In this chapter, I have made a particular plea for more attention to be directed towards the dynamics between migrants in situ and their sending communities, and advocated a broader framework that incorporates these relations. I have also encouraged an approach that recognizes the consequences of migration on the sending community, as a way of emphasizing these dynamic interplays and processes. I have further signalled that the embodied experience of migration, while subject to some discussion, is an emergent area of research that has significant potential to provide new insights into the relationship between food and migration. This is not to disparage, or diminish the contribution, of work that has focused on the ways that migrants (re)establish their own food practices in their host contexts and (re)produce identities through food. Rather it is to state that this trope of literature, while providing a solid foundation for the anthropology of food and migration, is treading a rather well-worn path. Studies of food and migration have a significant contribution to make to the ways in which we understand the flows of people, objects and narratives and the ways individuals – both those who are 'on the move' (Renne 2008: 623) and those who appear to be staying 'at home' – experience and negotiate these movements. I hope to have indicated some possible directions that could augment and enhance this contribution.

REFERENCES

Abbots, E.-J. (2011), '"It Doesn't Taste as Good from the Pet Shop": Guinea Pig Consumption and the Performance of Class and Kinship in Highland Ecuador and New York City', *Food, Culture and Society*, 14(2): 205–24.

Abbots, E.-J. (2012a), 'The Celebratory and the Everyday: Guinea Pigs, Hamburgers and the Performance of Food Heritage in Highland Ecuador', in M. McWilliams (ed.), *Celebrations: The Proceedings of the Oxford Symposium on Food and Cookery 2011*, 12–23, London: Prospect Books.

Abbots, E.-J. (2012b), 'In the Absence of Men? Gender, Migration and Domestic Labour in the Southern Ecuadorean Andes', *Journal of Latin American Studies*, 44(1): 71–96.

Abbots, E.-J. (2013), 'Negotiating Foreign Bodies: Migration, Trust and the Risky Business of Eating in Highland Ecuador', in E.-J. Abbots and A. Lavis (eds), *Why We Eat, How We Eat: Contemporary Encounters Between Foods and Bodies*, 119–38, Aldershot: Ashgate.

Abbots, E.-J. (2014a), 'The Fast and the Fusion: Class, Creolization and the Remaking of *Comida Típica* in Highland Ecuador', in J. Klein and A. Murcott (eds), *Food Consumption in Global Perspective. Essays in the Anthropology of Food in Honour of Jack Goody*, 87–107, Houndmills, Basingstoke, Hants: Palgrave Macmillan.

Abbots, E.-J. (2014b), 'Investing in the Family's Future: Labour, Gender and Consumption in Highland Ecuador', *Families, Relationships and Societies*, 3(1): 143–8.

Abbots, E.-J. (2015), 'Buying the Ties that Bind: Consumption, Care and Intimate Investment among Transnational Households in Highland Ecuador', in E. Casey and Y. Taylor (eds), *Intimacies, Critical Consumption and Diverse Economies*, 36–59, Houndmills, Basingstoke, Hants: Palgrave Macmillan.

Abbots, E.-J. and Lavis, A. (2013), 'Introduction: Mapping the New Terrain of Eating: Reflections on the Encounters between Foods and Bodies', in E.-J. Abbots and A. Lavis (eds), *Why We Eat, How We Eat: Contemporary Encounters Between Foods and Bodies*, 1–12, Aldershot: Ashgate.

Baxter, S. and Raw, G. (1988), 'Fast Food, Fettered Work: Chinese Women in the Ethnic Catering Industry', in S. Westwood and P. Bhachu (eds), *Enterprising Women: Ethnicity, Economy, and Gender Relations*, 58–75, London: Routledge.

Ben-Ze'ev, E. (2004), 'The Politics of Taste and Smell: Palestinian Rights of Return', in M. Lien and B. Nerlich (eds), *The Politics of Food*, 141–60, Oxford: Berg.

Beyers, L. (2008), 'Creating Home: Food, Ethnicity and Gender among Italians in Belgium since 1946', *Food, Culture and Society*, 11(1): 7–27.

Bradby, H. (1997), 'Health, Eating and Heart Attacks: Glaswegian Punjabi Women's Thinking about Everyday Food', in P. Caplan (ed.), *Food, Health and Identity*, 213–33, London: Routledge.

Caldwell, M. L. (2004), 'Domesticating the French Fry: McDonald's and Consumerism in Moscow', *Journal of Consumer Culture*, 4(1): 5–26.

Carsten, J. (1997), *The Heat of the Hearth: The Process of Kinship in a Malay Fishing Community*, Oxford: Clarendon Press.

Caplan, P. (1997), 'Approaches to the Study of Food, Health and Identity', in P. Caplan (ed.), *Food, Health and Identity*, 1–31, London: Routledge.

Chapman, G. E. and Beagan, B. L. (2011), 'Food Practices and Transnational Identities: Case Studies of Two Punjabi-Canadian Families', *Food, Culture and Society*, 16(3): 367–86.

Charon Cardona, E. T. (2004), 'Re-encountering Cuban Tastes in Australia', *The Australian Journal of Anthropology*, 15(1): 40–53.

Collins, E. L. (2008), 'Of Kimchi and Coffee: Globalisation, Transnationalism and Familiarity in Culinary Consumption', *Social and Cultural Geography*, 9: 151–69.

Cook, I., Crang P. and Thorpe, M. (1999), 'Eating into Britishness: Multicultural Imaginaries and the Identity Politics of Food', in S. Roseneil and J. Seymour (eds), *Practising Identities: Power and Resistance*, 223–48, Basingstoke: Macmillan.

Counihan, C. M. (1999), *The Anthropology of Food and the Body: Gender, Meaning and Power*, New York: Routledge.

Counihan, C. M. and Kaplan S. L. (1998), *Food and Gender: Identity and Power*, Amsterdam: Harwood.

DeVault, M. L. (1991), *Feeding the Family: The Social Organisation of Caring as Gendered Work*, Chicago: University of Chicago Press.

Diner, H. R. (2001), *Hungering for America: Italian, Irish and Jewish Foodways in the Age of Migration*, Cambridge, MA and London: Harvard University Press.

Durand, J. Kandel, W., Parrado, E. A. and Massey, D. S. (1996), 'International Migration and Development in Mexican Communities', *Demography*, 33(2): 249–64.

Fechter, A.-M. (2007), *Transnational Lives: Expatriates in Indonesia*, Aldershot: Ashgate.

Fischler, C. (1988), 'Food, Self and Identity', *Social Science Information*, 27: 275–92.

Flowers, R. and Swan, E. (2015), 'Multiculturalism as Work: The Emotional Labour of Ethnic Food Tour Guides', in E.-J. Abbots, A. Lavis, and L. Attala (eds), *Careful Eating: Bodies, Food and Care*, 25–44, Farnham, Surrey: Ashgate.

Frost, N. (2008), '"Strange People But They Sure Can Cook!" An Indonesian Women's Group in Sydney', *Food, Culture and Society*, 11(2): 173–89.

Hannerz, U. (1987), 'The World in Creolization', *Africa: Journal of the International Africa Institute*, 57(4): 546–59.

Harbottle, L. (1997), 'Fast Food/Spoiled Identity: Iranian Migrants in the British Catering Trade', in P. Caplan (ed.), *Food, Health and Identity*, 87–110, London: Routledge.

Harbottle, L. (2000), *Food for Health, Food for Wealth: The Performance of Ethnic and Gender Identities by Iranian Settlers in Britain*, New York and Oxford: Berghahn Books.

Hage, G. (1997), 'At Home in the Entrails of the West: Multiculturalism, Ethnic Food and Migrant Home-Building', in H. Grace, G. Hage, L. Johnson, J. Langsworth and M. Symonds (eds), *Home/World: Space, Community and Marginality in Sydney's West*, 99–153, Annandale, NSW: Pluto Press.

Holtzman, J. D. (2006), 'Food and Memory', *Annual Review of Anthropology*, 35(1): 361–78.

Jamal, A. (1996), 'Acculturation: The Symbolism of Ethnic Eating among Contemporary British Consumers', *British Food Journal*, 98(10): 12–26.

Kalcik, S (1984), 'Ethnic Foodways in America: Symbol and the Performance of Identity', in L. Keller Brown and K. Mussell (eds), *Ethnic and Regional Foodways in the United States: The Performance of Group Identity*, 37–65, Knoxville: University of Tennessee Press.

Kalra, V. S. (2004), 'The Political Economy of the Samosa', *South Asia Research*, 24: 21–36.

Mankekar, P. (2005), '"Indian Shopping": India Grocery Stores and Transnational Configurations of Belonging', in J. L. Watson and M. Caldwell (eds), *The Cultural Politics of Food and Eating: A Reader*, 197–214, Malden, MA: Blackwell.

McIntosh, W. A. (1996), *The Sociologies of Food and Nutrition*, New York: Plenum Press.

Murcott, A. (1983), '"It's a Pleasure to Cook for Him": Food, Mealtimes and Gender in some South Wales Households', in E. Garmanikow, D. Morgan, J. Purvis and D. Taylorson (eds), *The Public and the Private: Social Patterns of Gender Relations*, 78–90, London: Heinemann.

Ong, A. (1999), *Flexible Citizenship: The Cultural Logics of Transnationality*, Durham, NC: Duke University Press.

Pilcher, J. M. (1998), *Que Vivan Los Tamales!: Food and the Making of Mexican Identity*, Albuquerque: University of New Mexico Press.

Ray, K. (2004), *The Migrant's Table: Meals and Memories in Bengali-American Households*, Philadelphia: University of Pennsylvania Press.

Renne, E. P. (2007), 'Mass Producing Food Traditions for West Africans Abroad', *American Anthropologist*, 109(4): 616–25.

Ritzer, G. (2010), *McDonaldization: The Reader*, Los Angeles, CA: Pine Forge Press.

Rouse R. (1995), 'Questions of Identity: Personhood and Collectivity in Transnational Migration to the United States', *Critique of Anthropology*, 15: 351–80.

Saber, G. and Posner, R. (2013), 'Remembering the Past and Constructing the Future Over a Communal Plate', *Food, Culture and Society*, 16(2): 197–222.

Schiller, N. G., Basch, L. and Blanc, C. S. (1995), 'From Immigrant to Transmigrant: Theorizing Migration', *Anthropological Quarterly*, 68: 48–63.

Stoller, D. (1989), *The Taste of Ethnographic Things: The Senses in Anthropology*, Philadelphia: University of Pennsylvania Press.

Strathern, M. (1988), *The Gender of the Gift: Problems with Women and Problems with Society in Melanesia*, Berkeley: University of California Press.

Sutton, D. (2001), *Remembrance of Repasts: An Anthropology of Food and Memory*, Oxford: Berg.

Tuomainen, H. M. (2011), 'Ethnic Identity, (Post) Colonialism and Foodways: Ghanaians in London', *Food, Culture and Society*, 12(4): 525–54.

Vasco, C. (2011), *The Impact of International Migration and Remittances on Agricultural Production Patterns, Labor Relationships and Entrepreneurship: The Case of Rural Ecuador*, Published thesis, Kassell, Germany: Kassell University Press.

Vallianatos, H. and Raine, K. (2008), 'Consuming Food and Constructing Identities among Arabic and South Asian Immigrant Women', *Food, Culture and Society*, 11(3): 355–73.

Van Otterloo, A. H. (1987), 'Foreign Immigrants and the Dutch at Table, 1945-1985: Bridging or Widening the Gap?' *Netherlands Journal of Sociology*, 23: 126–43.

Watson, J. L. (ed.) (2006), *Golden Arches East: McDonalds in East Asia*, 2nd edn, Stanford, CA: Stanford University Press.

Weismantel, M. J. (1988), *Food, Gender and Poverty in the Ecuadorian Andes*, Philadelphia: University of Pennsylvania Press.

CHAPTER SIX

Local Food, Local Specialties and Local Identity

NIR AVIELI

Both the antiquity of movement of humans and foods, and the abiding importance of place –locality – deserve to be kept firmly in mind.

(Sidney Mintz, 'Food and Diaspora', 2008: 514)

Food only becomes local when outsiders arrive.

(Binh, a chef specializing in the dishes of his hometown Hoi An, Vietnam, 2009)

Food is often invoked in popular, promotional and professional articles, TV programmes and websites as an expression of the locale. Visitors and locals are tempted to sample the unique produce, dishes and beverages of specific regions and places as a way of experiencing them, and local specialties are presented as tourist attractions. Heated professional debates over *terroir*, a concept originally coined for the French wine industry but enthusiastically adopted in many other culinary realms, highlight the importance of the localness of food among amateur and professional gastronomes and foodies. Struggles over culinary copyrights and cultural ownership, such as the case of the Greek feta cheese (Lichfield 2010) or the recent 'Hummus Wars' (Avieli and Grosglik 2013), highlight (among other things) the economic value of food associated with specific spatial contexts (see West, Chapter 19, this volume). Local food is widely acknowledged as an important marker of local identity.

Anthropologists and other social scientists have long noted that food is strongly associated with identity (Wilk 2006; Mintz 2008; Moon 2008). Although anthropological attention has been paid mainly to the interface of food and national (Narayan 1997; Watson 1997), ethnic (Tuchman and Levine 1993; Poe 2001), gender (Counihan 1999, 2004) and class (Goody 1985; Mennell 1985) aspects of identity, 'local food' and its relation to local identity have also been studied (Bell and Valentine 1997; Freidberg 2003). However the term 'local food' remains vague.

One of the main difficulties concerns the spatial scope of the 'local'. It is sometimes used to denote regions (Everett and Aitchison 2008; Cavanaugh 2007; Tregear 2003) and even national territories and cuisines. O'Connor, in her analysis of Hawaiian *luau*, uses 'local' to denote things Hawaiian (e.g. 2008: 167), while Wilk (2001) in places uses *local* to refer to the culinary traditions of specific locales in Belize (e.g. 2001: 246), and elsewhere to denote Belize and Belizean cuisine as a whole.

The food industry, too, finds it hard to define the local. In 2008, the US Congress passed Resolution H.R.2419, in which 'locally' and 'regionally' were grouped together and defined as 'the locality or region in which the final [food] product is marketed, so that the total distance that the product is transported is less than 400 miles from the origin of the product', or 'the State in which the product is produced' (http:/thomas.loc.gov/cgi-bin/query/z?c110:h2419:), stretching the 'local' to include vast areas, while conceiving of 'food' as a product rather than artefact, that is, disregarding the cultural context and highlighting production modes.

Approaching the 'local' is further complicated by the fact that the term is attributed interchangeably to autochthonous or indigenous populations and to those physically present at a specific geographic location, whether a village, a region, a nation or even a continent (as in Castillo and Nigh 1998). O'Connor (2008: 167) points out that 'being "Hawaiian" can mean being of Hawaiian ethnic background. Yet "Hawaiian" is a term that is also used ... to mean being "local" – born and brought up in the islands, although not ethnically Hawaiian.' O'Connor leaves out newcomers, expats, tourists and other Simmelian sojourners (Siu 1952), though some stay for a long time and may be conceived by both natives and short-term visitors as locals. The contributors to Watson's (1997) insightful *Golden Arches East*, an edited collection of ethnographies conducted at McDonald's branches in cities throughout East Asia, show how the locale always influences the food consumed at certain places, even in institutions such as McDonald's, which boast uniformity and universal standards. The volume convincingly shows how the food and foodways in each McDonald's branch display localness as one of their key features.

'Local food' therefore denotes a space that extends between original fare eaten in distinctive locations by the indigenous populations from time immemorial – all the way to the food eaten at certain, potentially huge, territories by anyone present therein.

In this chapter I develop and complicate the understanding of the ways in which local food interacts with local identity by focusing on foods that ethnographers of everyday life are well placed to discuss and which can provide rich insights into the complexities of local identities, but which have received far less attention in the anthropological literature than they should: dishes presented and termed by the dwellers of certain places as their 'local specialties', prepared in specific locations from local ingredients with unique methods, and into distinctive artefacts that are presented by the locals as important components of the locale.

These dishes echo Sidney Mintz's (2008) definition of local food as a culturally specific food system prepared in a particular territory with its own seasons, flora and fauna, soils, hydrology, farming and processing techniques, preservation and storage systems and distinctive division of labour. Yet the 'local specialties' I discuss are also attributed with social endorsement and meanings by those who prepare and consume them.

In what follows I show how these artefacts express in minute detail and with great sensitivity the social and cultural complexities of the locale, well beyond the explicit definitions made by locals and outsiders. Further, I show how different local specialties in certain locales may convey different and even contradicting ideas regarding the meaning of local identity. I discuss also how these ideas are deciphered differently by different consumers. Furthermore, I show that local specialties, even when presented by the locals as important collective representations, are not always consumed by the locals. The meanings of these local specialties are therefore complex and often stem from discursive practices that transcend the apparent materiality of food.

THE LOCAL SPECIALTIES OF HOI AN

Whenever asked what exactly I was doing in Hoi An, a small town in Central Vietnam, I used to answer that I was studying the town's eating and drinking culture (*nghien cuu van hoa am thuc Hoi An*). The most frequent response was: 'Ah, have you had *cao lau* yet?'. For many Hoianese, be it professional cooks and restaurateurs, tourism entrepreneurs and guides, business people or simply those with whom I happened to chat over a bowl of noodles in a street stand, researching the town's culinary culture meant exploring its local specialties (*dac san Hoi An*).

Local specialties had a noticeable presence in Hoi An. There was hardly a street in and around the historic centre of town that did not feature at least one noodle stand with a sign reading *cao lau* or *mi Quang*. Many of the cooked-food stands in the municipal market served them too, along with other local specialties such as *banh xeo* (sizzling [pan]cakes) and *banh it la gai cu lau Cham* (Cham Island rice cakes). *Com ga* (chicken rice) was also a ubiquitous local specialty, sold at numerous stalls, while the main street on the islet of Cam Nam was packed with restaurants serving *hen tron* (stir-fried baby clams), *banh dap* (broken rice crackers) and *che bap* (sweet corn porridge).

When I inquired about the exact meaning of the term *dac san*, Thau, the owner of a small restaurant, explained: '*Dac san* is a dish that can be found only in a specific place. For example – *cao lau* is *dac san Hoi An*, because you can only find it in Hoi An … .' Thau suggested a straightforward definition: local specialties are dishes prepared only in a specific locale.

The town's local specialties were also endorsed officially. The first book ever published by the municipal research centre was called *Dac San Hoi An* (*The Local Specialties of Hoi An*, Tran 2000), and was a catalogue of the town's local specialties, featuring some thirty dishes. The book stirred some controversy as according to its critics, some of the dishes discussed in the book were not unique to Hoi An nor to the province of *Quang Nam*. There were also some reservations regarding the names and terms, as well as the modes of preparation, as they appeared in the book. Some of my friends were quite critical about this project as a whole. Nonetheless, there was no debate regarding the prominence and importance of *dac san* as icons of the local culinary culture and of the town.

What I found most intriguing about this book, however, was the fact that a small market town in a district of merely eighty thousand people, mostly countryside dwellers, boasted over thirty dishes treated as 'local specialties'. If this ratio is true for the whole country, Vietnam might feature tens of thousands of local specialties. Florence and Storey's (1999: 126) suggestion of '500 unique Vietnamese dishes' is therefore very conservative, even when considering that many local specialties are nuanced variations. In any case, it is clear that these dishes are very specific markers of locales throughout the country.

In the next pages I discuss three dishes that define and/or express specific facets of Hoianese identity. As we shall see, some of these dishes are only consumed by those who permanently live in town, while others are intended for different kinds of outsiders. I also show that the preparation and consumption of these dishes, along with the meanings they convey, are dynamic and in constant flux, despite the conservative stability attributed to the idea of local specialties, making them even more accurate representations of the locale which, like all human projects, is fluid and ever-changing.

BANH BAO BANH VAC AND THE HOIANESE-CHINESE IDENTITY

Anh (brother/Mr) Trang's great-grandfather came to Hoi An from Beijing in the early twentieth century, married a Vietnamese woman and established a dumpling business. A large painting of this forefather, wearing a pale blue Chinese tunic, was hanging on the wall by the family altar at Mr Trang's house. Standing in front of his ancestor's painting, Mr Trang proudly patted the shoulder of his plump thirteen-year-old son and told me: 'He will be the fifth generation of *banh bao* makers.'

The working day regularly started at 5.00 am, when Huong (Trang's wife) would go to the market and purchase shrimps, spring onions, mushrooms and bean sprouts. Mr Trang would mix a few kg of rice flour with water, and pound the mixture in a large stone mortar to make the dough. He was very clear about the special qualities of his dumplings: 'The real secret is in the pounding – how to make the dough. No one in Hoi An knows how to make the dough properly besides me, and I learned it from my mother. I always pound the dough early in the morning, inside the kitchen, windows closed, and I don't allow anyone in, this is our family secret.'

Most of the work and the greatest expertise, however, were invested in the shaping of the dough into dumplings. The dish, in English called 'white rose', consisted of a combination of two kinds of dumplings: the flower-shaped *banh bao* ('plump cake') and the shell-shaped *banh vac* ('flat cake'). The first stage of preparation was similar for both: a small ball of dough was flattened with the palm on the working table and an index finger dipped in oil was used to shape the dough into a cup. A pinch of the pink shrimp paste was used as the 'heart' of the white rose, while the thin dough was folded into white 'petals'. The *banh vac* were simply filled with the shredded vegetables and closed. The dumplings were then steamed for a few minutes. Each order consisted of ten dumplings: seven *bao* and three *vac*. They were served on a plate, garnished with deep-fried shallots and *nuoc mam cham* (fish sauce flavoured with lime, sugar, chilli and garlic). The correct way to eat white rose was with a spoon: the sauce was poured over the dumplings, which were then scooped with the deep-fried shallots.

My Hoianese interviewees were clear about the origins of this dish: it came from China and was one of the contributions of the Chinese immigrants (*Hoa* or ethnic Chinese) to the local culinary scene. The poetic name, 'white rose', however, was neither traditional nor Chinese: it was coined by a French tourist who had had them at one of the first tourist-oriented restaurants in the early 1990s and had suggested that they looked like white roses. The name was adopted into the English menus of tourist-oriented restaurants instead of the otherwise untranslatable *banh bao banh vac*.

Though similar dumplings may very well be eaten in China, *banh bao banh vac* are unique in several ways. First, the combination of *nuoc mam cham* (fish-sauce dip) and deep-fried shallots is distinctively Vietnamese. Second, the unique shape and colour combination of these dumplings can be found only in Hoi An, at least according to their maker and his town's people. Finally, they are prepared by a single Chinese-Hoianese family. This dish, therefore, expresses several aspects of the Hoianese local identity that call for some elaboration.

First and foremost, this dish can be found only in Hoi An, as my Hoianese friends emphasized repeatedly. In one case, when a Hoiaenese woman married a man from a neighbouring Danang (both ethnic Vietnamese), 'white rose' dumplings were brought to the feast by the bride's family, indicating the bride's origin to their new relatives, a point that was confirmed by the bride's sister, when I asked her about this unusual addition to the wedding menu.

Most white rose consumers, however, are out-of-town visitors, Vietnamese, overseas Vietnamese and non-Vietnamese tourists, who eat the dumplings in the numerous tourist-oriented restaurants that offer them under the 'local specialties' heading in their menus. For these outsiders, eating *banh bao banh vac* means eating a dish that can be found in only one place in the world – Hoi An. For outsiders, then, just like for the Hoianese, this dish indicates localness or 'Hoianeseness', a local specialty (*dac san*) indeed, though the Chinese context is unknown to most non-Vietnamese visitors, while most Vietnamese tourists are unaware of the fact that a single family produces them for all the restaurants.

When it comes to the locals, however, their perception of white rose is broader than just a marker of local identity. Quite a few interviewees told me that they 'don't like it so much' and that it was 'too expensive' (5,000 dong or $US 0.50 per portion in 1999 and up to 15,000 dong or over US $ 1.00 in 2008). They also insisted that *banh bao banh vac* were Chinese, and often mentioned in this context the presence and prominence of the ethnic Chinese dwellers of town.

This acknowledgement should not be taken for granted: though official historiography and local versions of oral history boast the successful and peaceful integration of the *Hoa* (ethnic Chinese) with the *Kinh* (ethnic Vietnamese) in Hoi An (a name that reads 'The Peaceful Congregation' of, as I was repeatedly told: 'Vietnamese, Chinese, Japanese and Westerners'), the relationship between the Vietnamese and Chinese was not always that peaceful, and soured considerably in the first decade after national reunification in 1975, when official policies targeted the ethnic Chinese, resulting in a huge wave of ethnic Chinese 'boat people' fleeing the country, and the practical depletion of the Hoianese-Chinese community.

Hoi An has been marketed in the last two decades by the local and national authorities as a 'Chinese' town. Chinese shop houses and temples are the main features underlying UNESCO's decision to enlist the town's ancient quarter as a World Heritage Site. Paradoxically, the celebration of the town's Chinese character took place only once most of the Chinese left. Acknowledging and stressing the Chinese character of *banh bao banh vac* is yet another way of dealing with this paradox, which is a main feature of contemporary Hoi An: a Chinese town with very few Chinese around.

Indeed, the most important identity aspect expressed by white rose is that of the Hoianese-Chinese. This ethnic group evolved in Hoi An as a consequence of marriages between male migrants from various regions in Southeast China and local women. Though the regional origin of each of the Chinese communities is acknowledged and maintained through membership in one of the five Chinese assembly halls, intermarriage, assimilation and the gradual adoption of Vietnamese language and culture seem to have overshadowed many of the specific regional variations and replaced them with a more general Hoianese-Chinese identity.

This new identity is represented, among other things, by Chinese dishes that are not marked as regional Chinese (e.g. Cantonese, Fukienese or Hainanese) and that feature specific culinary inflections that makes them both local and unique. A good example is *hoanh thanh chien* (fried wontons) another Hoianese local specialty. Wontons, the well-known Chinese dumplings, are generally served in soup and found in Chinese restaurants worldwide. In Vietnam, they are available in this form in Hanoi's Old Quarter and Saigon's Cho Lon (the city's Chinatown).

In Hoi An only two families made *hoanh thanh* in the early years of the millennium: one was originally from *Phouc Kien* (Fujian in Southeastern China) and the other was Vietnamese, yet the father told me that he learned how to prepare *hoanh thanh* 'from a friend who worked for the Chinese'. The point is that in Hoianese restaurants the wontons are not boiled or served in a soup, but fried (*chien*) and served with a sweet-and-sour sauce made with vegetables and shrimp, flavoured with fish sauce. Hence, a pan-Chinese food item is given a local twist to create a distinctive Hoianese-Chinese dish.

ON SIZZLING PANCAKES AND BEING LOCAL

'I am hungry and it is late,' said *Co* (teacher/miss) Dung. 'Let's eat *ram cuon Ba Le* ("Mrs Le's spring rolls").' We walked up the alley that leads to *Ba Le* (Madame Le's) well and stopped by the restaurant: a cluster of low plastic tables and chairs in the alleyway, where the occasional motorbike riders literally rubbed shoulders with the customers. A plastic sheet loosely hung over the alley, providing some kind of shelter for the diners. The unpaved dirt floor was almost entirely covered by used napkins, shredded greens and other leftovers. The table was smeared with oil, and Dung, mumbling '*ghe qua ...*' (so disgusting), wiped it with napkins, which she then discarded on the floor.

I recognized a few of the diners who nodded or smiled at me, while Dung and her colleague Ti, both school teachers, went through a quick, low-voiced gossip session concerning a couple sitting with their backs to us.

Mrs Thuy, the owner, came to greet us and take our order: 'Haven't seen you for a while,' she remarked. We ordered *banh xeo* (sizzling pancakes), *thit nuong* (grilled meat) and *ram* (spring rolls). As she was leaving, Ti whispered in my ear: 'She amassed a fortune selling *banh xeo*, now she is rebuilding her house.' I looked in disbelief at the crude setting and the local clientele, but Ti shot a confirming glance as Mrs Le returned and set some plates on our table: a large tray of lettuce leaves, herbs, bean sprouts, shredded banana flower, sliced pineapple, unripe star fruit and green banana, another plate of rice paper and bowls of thick dipping sauce.

Le's daughter was sitting amidst a battery of small frying pans, sizzling over kerosene stoves. She poured a spoonful of oil into each cast-iron pan and added a shrimp and a piece of pork fat into the smoking oil. Then she poured a ladleful of thin batter made of rice flour, duck eggs and water, which crusted instantly. She added a bunch of bean sprouts, folded the pancake in two, added some more oil, turned it over for some more frying and placed it over a bamboo grid to drain the oil. Another girl was rolling shrimp, meat and spring onion in rice paper into 'three friends spring rolls' (*ram tam huu*), deep-frying them in a large wok. A third girl was grilling pork skewers.

I returned to the table where everyone were preparing their first roll. Half a pancake, torn with the chopsticks, placed over the semicircular rice paper, along with a fried spring roll, some grilled meat, a bunch of greens and the crucial shears of tannin green banana and tart star fruit. The rice paper was tightly rolled (*cuon* means 'rolled') and dipped in the thick.fermented bean sauce. Even great expertise did not prevent the oil from staining one's fingers and dripping over the table and clothes – hence the great amount of used napkins.

The young couple who were the subject of gossip rose to leave. When they noticed Dung and Ti, their teachers, they hesitantly approached our table, crossed their hands over their chests and bowed their heads in a very respectful greeting. The two teachers grunted in approval and watched their students leave after bidding polite farewells to the proprietor and some of the other customers.

Eating *cuon* is unique to Vietnam. This eating style is apparently the outcome of the active cultural synthesis (or mediation) between the chopsticks of Eastern Asia and the South Asian use of the right hand fingers for eating. The event described here belongs exclusively to the Vietnamese culinary sphere.[1]

Banh xeo is common in Quang Nam Province, and places that serve *banh xeo* in other parts of the country present it as a local specialty of Quang Nam (*dac san Quang Nam*). Nevertheless, variations of this dish can be found in many places in the Center and South. The Hue version, *banh khoi* ('smoking pancake'), is almost identical, though thicker and always with egg in the batter (in Hoi An, the batter usually only has rice flour and is, therefore, cheaper and 'not as tasty'). In several places in *Cuu Long* (Mekong Delta) I had much larger pancakes made from similar ingredients, which were not eaten rolled.

Though these may seem minor nuances, they are noticed by the consumers and denote specific locations. Chi, a local chef, quoted the Vietnamese saying: 'The size of *banh xeo* is equivalent to the size of one's heart.' She pointed out that the pancakes in Quang Nam are the smallest in the country and explained that the Center is the poorest area of the country ('with only one crop of rice per year') and therefore dishes sold in Quang Nam are often smaller and cheaper than those made elsewhere in the country.

The most important feature of eating *ram cuon* at Ba Le's was the fact that this place was considered distinctively Hoianese, that is, local, by the locals. The prices were cheap even by local standards, the setting was informal and relaxed. People of all classes and of varying status, young and old, poor and rich, single, married and accompanied by children, frequented the place. Though beer was served and some male customers got drunk, this was not a *quan nhau* ('rice-alcohol shop', male drinking joints that offer spicy snacks along with the liquor), and women of all classes (e.g. respectable high-school teachers) did not hesitate to eat there.

The location was such that it prevented outsiders from stumbling upon it accidentally, further enhancing its local character. Even visitors from neighbouring Danang and Tam Ky, who actively searched for hidden local specialties, were rarely familiar with this place. As for foreign tourists, they wandered sometimes into these narrow back alleys, but when they did, the rough setting, unfamiliar dishes and eating mode, as well as the fact that the owners and most of their customers spoke only Vietnamese, made a culinary venture into this place almost impossible. I asked the owner several times if she had any foreign clients and she responded that the few that came were usually invited by local hosts. When going to *Ram Cuon Ba Le*, one would meet only friends, neighbours and acquaintances but rarely a stranger. Eating in this place made for a sense of 'Hoianeseness' that was unparalleled in any other eating venue in town: if you knew this place and ate here, you were really a part of the local scene.

Nevertheless, this kind of local identity – not that of a 'dweller of an ancient international port town', a 'Chinese', or a 'Central-Vietnamese', but one that encompasses the idea of *living here*, the most immediate and non-reflexive of identities – is the hardest to pinpoint or describe, and the one that most of interviewees refused to discuss or even acknowledge. When I asked some of my friends 'Why do you go to eat *Ram Cuon Ba Le*?' they found this question most peculiar and impossible to answer. Even the common response for most other dishes – 'because it is tasty!' – was rarely suggested in this context. One of them said: 'Yes, the place is so dirty and the service is very rude but I like eating there.' Another neatly summed up the local attitudes by saying: 'We go to eat there because it is *vui*' (fun, happy, *joie de vivre*).

In fact, I was invited by local friends to eat at *Ram Cuon Ba Le* more than to any other food venue in town, sometimes by people whom I didn't expect to meet in such a rough-and-ready and unhygienic setting. In a small town sometimes overrun by outsiders, here was a space where locals could feel at ease, while outsiders did not disrupt the local intimacy. Ironically, it represented the utmost expression of the romantic tourist notion of 'the real authentic place where locals eat' while manifesting its inaccessibility to outsiders: the few foreigners who ate at *Ram Cuon Ba Le* were accepted as 'locals' of sorts.

It is important to note that the localness embedded in *Ram Cuon Ba Le* was more about the dining experience than the food itself. *Ram cuon* are available around the province and 'variations on the theme' can be found throughout the Center and South. This culinary experience was made local by the circumstances: only permanent dwellers of town frequented it, while the setting was such that turned outsiders away, even when accidentally stumbling upon it. As such, *Ram Cuon Ba Le* sets the boundaries of localness, practically allowing only those living permanently in town, creating and maintaining a sense of 'us' even in a tourist destination like Hoi An, in which on certain days, visitors outnumber the locals.

STRANGERS AT HOME: THE LOCAL SPECIALTIES OF THE NEXT DOOR VILLAGE

Cycling to Cam Nam village, we crossed the bridge that connects town with this densely inhabited sandbank, deposited by the silting Hoi An River. The view from the bridge was always picturesque: the small boats bustling around the fish market, the coconut-lined pier, and some of the river-front Chinese merchant houses of the old town. In the distance loomed the odd-looking *My Son* ('Beautiful Mountain'), the sacred mountain of the bygone Cham. Eastward, the fishing boats of *Cam Chau* village were docked by the trees and bamboo lined river bank. Flocks of ducks paddled in the shallow water and large lever fishing nets were hanging loosely in the wind.

We cycled along the islet's main street, lined with riverside restaurants featuring large terraces perched on stilts just above the water. The signs all read: *Hen-Tron, Banh-Dap, Che-Bap Cam Nam* (Baby-Clams, Broken Rice Crackers and Sweet Corn Soup of Cam Nam Village). As we cycled by, the female proprietors leapt from whatever they were doing and beckoned us into their restaurants. But we stopped at our favourite place and chose a table overlooking the river and the wobbly bamboo bridge that connected the islet with a smaller shoal, where corn and watermelons were intensively cultivated in the spring and early summer.

It was a sunny March afternoon and dozens of farmers were irrigating the green corn stalks with tins carried on shoulder poles. At the adjacent table some high-school students were hanging out. A young couple from Danang was sitting at another table, easily identifiable by their stylish clothes, sunglasses, and the mobile phones left nonchalantly yet conspicuously on the table. Hien, the proprietor, came smiling to our table with a bottle of sparkling water and two glasses. We ordered a set: baby-clam salad, broken rice crackers and sweet corn soup.

The tiny clams (*hen*) were dug from the riverbed with special pitchforks and boiled to open the shells. The morsels of black flesh were then stir-fried in peanut oil, fish sauce, onion and *rau ram* (rice paddy herb). Once cooked, they were seasoned with lime juice and garnished with deep-fried shallots, fresh mint and crushed peanuts. The salad-like dish (*tron*, or 'toss') was served in a small saucer with a crunchy rice cracker (*banh trang day*) and fresh red chilli.

The 'broken crackers' had three layers: a fresh, soft, steamed rice paper, (*banh uoc*) fastened in-between two similar rice papers that had been dried and grilled to become crisp and brown. The soft rice paper was glutinous and sticky, and so clung to the crunchy crackers. The dish was brought to the table on a plate, and then 'broken', pressing it down with the palms till it cracked. The broken crackers were served with a semi-fermented, unfiltered fish sauce (*mam cai*) made in the village, seasoned with sugar, chilli, pineapple slices and deep-fried shallots. The sweet corn soup was made of fresh corn boiled with sugar and young coconut pulp.

The sun was slowly descending and the colours were deepening. It was high tide, and the river rose almost to the height of the terrace. We could still see the conical hat of a clam fisherman. Neck-deep in the water, he was shaking the long pole of his pitchfork in the muddy riverbed, sending small ripples in the dark water around him.

This romantic setting housed yet another complex, multi-levelled and labour-intensive set of local specialties. Here again we see how a wide variety of inexpensive local ingredients and taste-agents are combined into culinary creations that are rich and complex in flavour. The 'broken crackers' stress the Vietnamese culinary tendency to produce textures and play with them, using the same ingredient in different states of preparation so as to fuse contradicting textures into perfect combinations.

These three special dishes were not considered *dac san* of Hoi An, but rather of the relatively small village of Cam Nam, with only 5,000 inhabitants. The local nature of these dishes was further indicated by the signs stating the name of the Cam Nam village as a marker of uniqueness. As a matter of fact, all three dishes, but especially the sweet corn soup and the *mam cai* fish sauce, are widely available throughout Vietnam. I was told, however, that 'you can find similar dishes but not the same ones. Here they have a special taste that is better than anywhere else'. It is important to note that most of my interviewees admitted at the time that they had never gone further than the neighbouring provinces and therefore could not tell if differences existed. But when discussing local identity, these facts were not really important. What did matter were the claims for distinctiveness and excellence.

Another important point concerns Cam Nam restaurants as a hub for local tourists. An afternoon in Cam Nam is popular among Hoi An's urban dwellers: high-school students as well as their teachers and many other middle-class townspeople frequent these rural venues, set amidst the refreshing riverscapes. There, they might meet different outsiders, mainly from neighbouring cities of Danang, Tam Ky and Hue, and occasional international tourists.

Crossing the bridge, the Hoianese themselves become tourists on their way to enjoy the local specialties of the next door village. In the open-air restaurants of Cam Nam, they feel comfortable and even fashionable, just like their neighbours from the metropolis of Danang, who often look down on them as *nha que* (country bumpkins). In Cam Nam, the Hoianese, who systematically avoid the much lauded specialties of their own hometown, are happy to consume the local specialties of their own sub-district, so long as these dishes come under the heading of Cam Nam and not Hoi An.

This tendency turns the idea of 'local specialties' as vessels for the expression of local identity into a sociological paradox: as soon as a practice is identified, named and marked as 'local' by outsiders, it becomes a representation of their 'external identity' – 'their identity in the eyes of the world' (Cohen 2000: 28). It then becomes a commodity that is marketed for a profit, yet hardly represents the 'internal identity' of the locals, that is, the way in which they perceive themselves. As this vacuum has to be filled, new dishes are chosen so as to maintain the 'internal' local identity. These dishes can fulfil their role so long as they stay unmarked. The discovery and exposure of these new dishes and their tagging as 'local specialties' commodify and hollow them out, as it were, of the internal identity.

For outsiders, however, such 'local specialties' offer new and exciting possibilities for the construction of their own identities as 'non-tourists' and, to a certain extent, even as 'locals'. In our case, the Hoianese negotiate a sophisticated urban identity through their consumption of Cam Nam dishes, in line with their own rejection of the 'ancient town' and 'Chinese town' facets of identity.

Yet the Hoianese do not consume Cam Nam dishes without reservation: whenever I suggested a visit to Cam Nam or reported a visit there, the immediate response was: 'an hen dau buom' ('[when] eating baby clams, [one's] stomach hurts'). Some people insisted that the clams should be consumed only in the morning, when they are still fresh, as they tend to spoil by the afternoon. Others said that this is but a matter of luck (and good relations with the proprietors): the clams spoil easily and often cause digestive upsets.

As a matter of fact, we have had the clams quite a few times with locals and outsiders and have never had any digestive mishaps. The Hoianese ambivalence towards the clams seems to reflect deep-rooted suspicions harboured by townspeople towards the countryside and its dwellers. When the Hoianese say that the clams in Cam Nam village upset their stomachs, they are suggesting that the food is potentially spoiled and the kitchens are dirty – just like the people who live there and serve it.

Cam Nam dishes are special in another aspect – their connection to the surrounding ecosystem or *terroir*: the baby clams are harvested in the river, right beneath the restaurants, the corn is cultivated just around them, and the rice crackers and fermented fish sauce are made locally too. As pointed out earlier, the 'local nature' of local specialties is often embedded in the local ecology.

My interviewees often pointed to the setting of the Cam Nam restaurants as their key attraction, and praised the products for being 'local' in the most immediate way possible: the distance from the source to the plate does not exceed fifty metres. In these venues, the *local* nature of the 'local specialties' is stressed: one can find *che bap* in Hoi An and in many other places, yet rarely does one eat corn porridge surrounded by the green stalks from which the fresh corn cobs were harvested.

Nevertheless, this neatly presented, context-specific 'localness' should not be taken for granted. A few months after the visit described above I took a foreign visitor to eat the local specialties of Cam Nam. It was just before the beginning of the rainy season and the river was extremely shallow. A few miserable-looking dry corn stalks were the only remnants of the lush fields of previous summer. There were no farmers or clam harvesters in sight.

I ordered clams and broken crackers. Hien asked if we would like some sweet corn soup too. I asked, 'How can you have the corn soup if there is no corn?' Hien explained that she buys fresh corn in Hoi An market and that the corn comes from the vegetable-growing centre of Dalat (some 750 km away). I inquired about the price of the clams and Hien said that it came to approximately 4,500 dong a kilo.

When I asked why they were so expensive, she said that there are no more clams in Hoi An River, so they were harvested in Tam Ky, some 60 km away. 'How about the *mam cai*?' I asked cautiously. 'No problem with that,' she said, adding, '*Mam cai* can keep for a long time.'

This episode raises several questions concerning the role of space as a marker of local identity: if local products can be replaced by imported ones so easily, what exactly is the importance of local produce? Is this just a process of commercialization or does it change the attitude of the consumers? Michael Paolisso (2007), in his study of the depletion of the Chesapeake Bay blue crabs and their replacement by crabs imported from South America and Southeast Asia, suggests that the increasing import of crabs led to a shift in their perception and description from a natural resource (crabs) into a local specialty (crab cakes) with the twofold result of '"localizing" imported crab meat and replacing traditional producers with traditions of local food preparation and hospitality' (2007: 655), thus 'regionalizing the foreign' (2007: 660).

Hien was making a similar argument: since the taste of local specialties is maintained even when using ingredients from elsewhere because of the cooking techniques and skill, they remain special *and* local. Like the Chesapeake crab cakes producers, she shifted the emphasis from the produce to the product.

Here again we face the paradox embedded in local specialties such as white rose, which are no longer consumed by locals: what exactly do they stand for? Are they local? Are they special? And what do they teach us about local identity? Hien, however, admitted that corn and clams were only seasonally imported from elsewhere, further supporting the idea that the product, rather than produce, was local. Chi, a Hoianese chef I consulted, added that this was a modern market-oriented phenomenon: 'When I was a child, you could eat corn porridge only in the summer, when it was harvested in Cam Nam, and clams only when the conditions and season allowed. But, today, this is a big business. People make money and so they must ensure regular supply. Don't worry, next summer you will have the local clams and corn again.'

When I mentioned this incident to other Hoianese friends, they found it somewhat amusing but immediately reverted to 'when eating clams one's stomach hurts', emphasizing that now, when the clams come from so far, the danger is even greater. This fear of pollution reflects the prevalent suspicion that outsiders and their food are polluted and polluting. Here we touch upon food avoidances and taboos, which are usually discussed in the context of religious and ceremonial eating (e.g. Douglas 1957, 1966; White 1992). But since we are dealing with daily fare, the rejection is not total, the explanations not cosmological or theological, and the 'punishment' for deviation is mild (a possible stomach upset).

THE VARIOUS MEANINGS OF 'LOCAL FOOD'

In a world where communities are imagined (Anderson 1991), food is exceptional. In his influential book, Anderson argued that printed texts – newspapers, books and maps – are the means through which masses of people who may live thousands of miles apart, who have never met and who will probably never meet, imagine that they belong to a bounded community and share qualities, values, tastes and preferences with the other community members. Anderson could not have predicted that the Internet would create ever larger and more 'imagined' communities.

Food and foodways make a unique contribution to this process of imagination, as they bridge the gap between the imagined and the concrete. The materiality of food, the tastes, aromas and textures of ingredients and dishes allow diners/consumers to experience the materiality of the community. The tens or hundreds of millions who consume 'national dishes' (e.g. *mansaf* in Jordan (Howell 2003) or tamales in Mexico (Pilcher 2001)), sometimes in specific moments (turkey at Thanksgiving in the United States (Siskind 1992), or New Year rice cakes in Vietnam (Avieli 2005)), taste, smell and feel the food which they imagine their compatriots to be eating at the very same time, thus adding a material dimension to the process of imagination, attributing it with a sense of reality and removing it from the realm of fantasy.

But when it comes to dishes presented and termed by the dwellers of certain places as 'local specialties' (i.e., dishes prepared in specific locations from local ingredients with unique methods and into distinctive artefacts), imagination seems to be redundant. Here we are dealing with places such as Hoi An: small, *gemeinschaft* communities, whose members know personally many other community members and experience on a daily basis the similarities in lifestyle. Food, and particularly local specialties, are mundane and taken-for-granted components of this experience in such contexts. When my Hoianese interlocutors told me that I should concentrate on the town's local specialties, they were suggesting a one-to-one identification of the locale with its specialties, pointing to white rose dumplings and suggesting: 'this is us'. Later on, they indicated that the clams, crackers and corn porridge from Cam Nam are 'them' and 'not us' (cf. Ohnuki-Tierney 1993).

However, the ethnographic process of exposing layers of meaning revealed a more complex relationship between the locale and its local specialties: the thin and superficial façade constructed for outsiders gave way to several versions of history, exposed dilemmas and contradictions, and defined a nuanced and, indeed, more accurate portrayal of the ways in which the dwellers of Hoi An perceive of their town and of themselves. In this respect, local specialties express or represent the locale in modes that are much more complex and accurate than the locals expect. Local specialties embed intricate histories, express tensions, contradictions and conflicts and expose power relations. In many ways, local specialties are the most sensitive reflections of localness.

Another important feature of local specialties of Hoi An has to do with the fact that the culinary construction of local identity may be material and embodied, as in the case of the pancakes at *Ba Le* well, but also discursive, as in the case of 'white rose' dumplings. Indeed, Binh's argument, quoted at the onset of this chapter: 'food only becomes local when outsiders arrive', was echoed in the words of those interviewees who commented about the dumplings: 'We don't like them so much.' In fact, 'white rose' dumplings were mainly (if not entirely) consumed by outsiders, be it international tourists, Vietnamese visitors from out of town or guests in a wedding conducted in another city. 'White rose' dumplings were hailed in the book dedicated to the town's local specialties (Tran 2000) and feature in the menu of practically every tourist-oriented restaurant in town, and as such were clearly defined and promoted by the locals as 'our local specialties'. At the same time, the locals did not eat them. 'White rose' dumplings were consumed discursively but not physically by the locals. It is interesting to turn again to the Chesapeake Bay crabs. Paossolio (2007) does not report whether the locals go on consuming the now imported crabs. He only describes how they developed a new discourse that justifies the substitution of a local ingredient (crabs) by imported one, so as to protect the (profitable) status of the dish (crab cakes) as a 'local specialty'. My findings suggest that the dwellers of Chesapeake Bay probably display a similar attitude: brag about the crab cakes and avoid them at once.

Another attribute of local specialties is that they may involve ambivalence, as in the case of the clams, crackers and porridge of Cam Nam. These dishes provided Hoianese diners with a sense of cosmopolitanism, superiority and power associated with tourism, but always with a measure of caution and contempt, evident in their almost Pavlovian verbal (i.e., discursive) response that the clams cause upset stomachs. It is precisely the localness of the food or dish that makes it both authentic *and* dangerous.

My concluding argument is that local specialties are paradoxical artefacts: they are deeply embedded in local ecologies, histories and sociologies and at the same time are often (possibly always?) produced and maintained in the dynamic contexts of tourism and migration, in relation to flows of people and goods. As such, they stand for stability, age-old traditions and respectable conservatism, but thrive in conditions of globalization and change.

NOTE

1. Dung, who is a university professor and teaches Vietnamese culture told me that some Vietnamese scholars argue that rice paper and fish sauce, two essential and iconic ingredients of the Vietnamese cuisine, are actually of Cham origin. 'Thus,' she pointed out, 'cuon, even if unique to Vietnam, is not originally Vietnamese.' If this is correct, a whole range of questions should be raised regarding the origins of the Vietnamese culture, challenging, for example, the official definition of North Vietnamese culture as the original, pure sources of contemporary Vietnamese culture (see Taylor [1998] and Wheeler [2006] for claims along similar lines). Since Hoi An was a Cham port for most of its existence, the rolled pancakes are local even if they are Cham and not Vietnamese.

REFERENCES

Anderson, B. (1991), *Imagined Communities: Reflections on the Origin and Spread of Nationalism*, London: Verso.

Avieli, N. (2005), 'Vietnamese New Year Rice Cakes: Iconic Festive Dishes and Contested National Identity', *Ethnology*, 44(2): 167–87.

Avieli, N. and Grosglik, R. (2013), 'Food and Power in the Middle East and the Mediterranean: Practical Concerns, Theoretical Considerations', *Food, Culture & Society*, 16(2): 181–95.

Bell, D. and Valentine, G. (1997), *Consuming Geographies: We Are Where We Eat*, New York and London: Routledge.

Castillo, R. and Nigh, R. (1998), 'Global Processes and Local Identity among Mayan Coffee Growers in Chiapas, Mexico', *American Anthropologist*, 100(1): 136–47.

Cavanaugh, J. (2007), 'Making Salami, Producing Bergamo: The Transformation of Value', *Ethnos*, 72(2): 149–72.

Counihan, C. M. (1999), *The Anthropology of Food and Body: Gender, Meaning and Power*, New York and London: Routledge.

Counihan, C. M. (2004), *Around the Tuscan Table: Food, Family and Gender in Twentieth-Century Florence*, New York: Routledge.

Everett, S. and Aitchison, C. (2008), 'The Role of Food Tourism in Sustaining Regional Identity: A Case Study of Cornwall, South West England', *Journal of Sustainable Tourism*, 16(2): 150–67.

Florence, M. and Storey, R. (1999), *Vietnam: Travel Survival Kit*, Hawthorn: Lonely Planet Publications.

Freidberg, S. (2003), 'Not all Sweetness and Light: New Cultural Geographies of Food', *Social & Cultural Geography*, 4(1): 3–7.

Goody, J. (1985), *Cooking, Cuisine and Class: A Study in Comparative Sociology*, Cambridge: Cambridge University Press.

Howell, S. (2003), 'Modernizing Mansaf: The Consuming Contexts of Jordan's National Dish', *Food and Foodways*, 11(4): 215–43.

Lichfield, G. (2010), 'Food Fight: A Look inside the Middle East's New Weapons of Mass Consumption', *Foreign Policy*, 15 January. http://www.foreignpolicy.com/articles/2010/01/15/food_fight (accessed 12 June 2015).

Mennell, S. (1985), *All Manners of Food: Eating and Taste in England and France from the Middle Ages to the Present*, Oxford: Blackwell.

Mintz, S. W (1986), *Sweetness and Power: The Place of Sugar in Modern History*, New York: Viking.

Mintz, S. W. (1997), 'Afterword: Swallowing Modernity', in J. L. Watson (ed.), *Golden Arches East: McDonald's in East Asia*, Stanford, CA: Stanford University Press.

Mintz, S. W. (2008), 'Food and diaspora' (School of Oriental and African Studies Food Forum Distinguished Lecture)', *Food, Culture & Society*, 11(4): 509–23.

Moon, S. (2008), 'Buddhist Temple Food in South Korea', *Korea Journal*, 48(4): 147–80.

Narayan, U. (1997), *Dislocating Cultures: Identities, Traditions and Third-World Feminism*, New York and London: Routledge.

O'Connor, K. (2008), 'The Hawaiian *Luau*: Food as Tradition, Transgression, Transformation, and Travel', *Food, Culture, and Society*, 2(2): 149–72.

Ohnuki-Tierney, E. (1993), *Rice as Self: Japanese Identities through Time*, Princeton, NJ: Princeton University Press.

Pilcher, J. M. (1998), *¡Que vivan los tamales! Food and the Making of Mexican Identity*, Albuquerque: University of New Mexico Press.

Paolisso, M. (2007), 'Taste the Traditions: Crabs, Crab Cakes, and the Chesapeake Bay Blue Crab fishery', *American Anthropologist*, 109(4): 654–65.

Poe, T. N. (2001), 'The labor and Leisure of Food Production as a Mode of Ethnic Identity Building Among Italians in Chicago, 1890-1940', *Rethinking History*, 5(1): 131–48.

Siskind, J. (1992), 'The Invention of Thanksgiving: A ritual of American Nationality',
   Critique of Anthropology, 12(2): 167–91.
Siu, P. (1952), 'The Sojourner', *The American Journal of Sociology*, 58(1): 34–44.
Tran, V. A. (ed.) (2000), *Van Hoa Am Thuc o Pho Co Hoi An (The Culinary Culture of the
   Ancient Town of Hoi An)*, Hanoi: Nha Xuat Ban Khoa Hoc Xa Hoi Hanoi.
Tregear, A. (2003), 'From Stilton to Vimto: Using Food History to Re-think Typical
   Products in Rural Development', *Sociologia Ruralis*, 43(2): 91–107.
Tuchman, G. and Levine, H. G. (1993), 'New York Jews and Chinese Food: The Social
   Construction of Ethnic Pattern', *Journal of Contemporary Ethnography*, 22(3):
   382–407.
Van Den Berghe, P. L. (1984), 'Ethnic Cuisine: Culture in Nature', *Ethnic and Racial Studies*,
   7(3): 387–97.
Visser, M. (1999), 'Food and Culture: Interconnections', *Social Research*, 66(1): 117–30.
Watson, J. L. (ed.) (1997), *Golden Arches East: McDonald's in East Asia,* Stanford, CA:
   Stanford University Press.
Wheeler, C. (2006), 'One Region, Two Histories: Cham Precedents in the History of Hoi
   An Region', in Nhung Tran and A. Reid (eds), *Viet Nam: Borderless Histories*, 169–93,
   Madison: University of Wisconsin Press.
Wilk, R. (2006), *Home Cooking in the Global Village: Caribbean Food from Buccaneers to
   Ecotourists*, London: Berg.
Wilson, T. (2006), 'Food, Drink and Identity in Europe: Consumption and the Construction
   of Local, National and Cosmopolitan Culture', *European Studies: A Journal of European
   Culture, History and Politics*, 22: 11–29.
Winter, M. (2003), 'Embeddedness, the New Food Economy and Defensive Localism',
   Journal of Rural Studies, 19: 23–32.

PART TWO

Food Security, Nutrition and Food Safety

CHAPTER SEVEN

Observer, Critic, Activist: Anthropological Encounters with Food Insecurity

JOHAN POTTIER

ANTHROPOLOGY, HUMAN RIGHTS AND ACTIVISM

After the Universal Declaration of Human Rights was published, and until the mid-1980s, anthropologists showed little interest in human rights. Then followed a time of reengagement, marked by prominent lectures and calls for action. Activism within anthropology was gaining ground. From the mid-1990s, however, concerned anthropologists moved away from the idea of actively promoting rights in order to focus on the social practice of rights claims. Mark Goodale looks back:

> The heart of the ethnographic approach is descriptive [in that it demonstrates] ... how human rights actually function empirically, what human rights mean to different social actors, and, finally, how human rights relate – again, empirically, not conceptually – to other transnational assemblages. (Goodale 2006: 4)

Description did not mean abandoning activism. In 1999, the American Anthropological Association (AAA) launched its Declaration on Anthropology and Human Rights, urging that anthropologists use their knowledge of cultural processes and power relationships to commit themselves to

> the promotion and protection of the right of people and peoples everywhere to the full realization of their humanity, which is to say their capacity for culture. When any culture or society denies or permits the denial of such opportunity to any of its own members or others, the American Anthropological Association has an ethical responsibility to protest and oppose such deprivation. (AAA 1999)

Since the AAA Declaration also stressed that judgement required detailed empirical evidence, Goodale proposed a Third Way path by suggesting that the discipline needed to be both critical and engaged in public service.

Regarding the right to food, a lot remains to be done. At the turn of the last century, it was clear that technological advances in agriculture and food distribution had not benefitted the world's poor. Hunger and malnutrition were on the increase even in advanced industrialized countries.

Polarized positions on the role of anthropology in human rights contexts – description or prescription – have been successfully reconciled in anthropology's encounter with assisted development. Since the 1990s, anthropologists have found a way through the impasse by accepting that 'to argue *for* or *against* engagement represents something of a false choice' (Crewe and Axelby 2012: 40). The authors continue:

> No longer able to maintain a position of pure detached objectivity, all anthropology, in some way, concerns itself with questions of change and development. ...
>
> Anthropology is now recognised in the dark corners of many official agencies as valuable both for the analysis and the practice of development. (2012: 40)

A major focus in the study of food security is the global expansion of agribusiness and the costs to local economies (Phillips 2006: 42). Costs relate to farmers losing land for food production, losing plant diversity through monoculture, and losing the right to reproduce their own seed. All are grave concerns. As Keith Hart puts it, 'The aggressive privatization strategies of the leading biochemical corporations undermine one of the key planks of the cultural commons – *our right* to borrow the means of growing food from each other' (Hart 2004: 216; emphasis added). Scholarly analysis can help inform activists about what should be done.

Swift and Hamilton (2001) reached a similar position regarding pastoral food insecurity in sub-Saharan Africa. They show how fine-grained ethnography of seasonal and market vulnerabilities, including pastoralists' *varied* responses, has resulted in project and programme support to pastoral food security. The most successful examples have protected 'tenure and other conditions which favour mobility and flexibility, which encourage livelihood diversification, and which intervene to protect pastoral terms of trade in a crisis' (2001: 75). Empirical research, the authors point out, has revealed that food insecurity at the household level arises from several causes (environmental risk, market risk, poverty and increasingly conflict), and is most devastating when several causes converge (2001: 67).

In this chapter I show how ethnographic approaches contribute to debates on food and livelihood security. The following themes will be considered: food security as concept; agribusiness and livelihoods (including: the power of transnational food corporations; land tenure and the poor; gendered struggles over crops, household labour and budgets); GMOs and food safety; food security in protracted crises; and urban food security. For the last of these I shall draw on my recent fieldwork in Lilongwe (Malawi) and Kampala (Uganda).

FOOD (IN)SECURITY DEFINED AND MEASURED

How do global institutions define food security? The term was first used in the early 1970s when it referred to food availability at national levels; countries needed to have enough food. Today, the debate has shifted to local levels – the household and the individual – but with an acknowledgement that 'local' and 'global' constitute a blurred binary. Since 1996, the FAO World Food Summit has adopted the definition that food security exists 'when all people, at all times, have physical and economic access to sufficient, safe and nutritious food to meet their dietary need and food preferences for an active and healthy life' (FAO 1996). The Summit also acknowledged that the concept needed broadening to encompass livelihood security.

There is now agreement – among donors, governments, development organizations and academics – that food security has three basic dimensions: availability, access and adequacy. Food availability means that the supply of food must be sufficient in terms of quantity, quality and variety. Food should also be accessible: that is home-grown or affordable as a commodity. Affordability becomes problematic when commodity prices rise unexpectedly or infrastructure is lacking. In the policy literature, however, accessibility is mostly approached in terms of 'household purchasing power'; individual entitlements are not routinely considered. In contrast, anthropologists have long insisted that the notion of 'household purchasing power' needs unpacking. Thirdly, food must be adequate (utilizable) in quantity and quality. What matters are the safety of food and water, and the provision of primary health care and environmental hygiene, all of which, when available, minimize gastrointestinal infections and enhance the benefits of a nutritious diet. It is with food access and the role of markets that anthropologists have been most concerned, especially since the rise of the 'neoliberal food regime' (McMichael 2009).

How do global institutions measure food security? Interestingly, recent assessments are pitched at the national level and appear to pay only lip service to the three basic dimensions. The current WFP methodology, for example, uses a questionnaire approach in which enumerators ask household heads about the food household members have eaten in the week preceding the interview. In WFP's recent assessment of food security in Uganda, for example,

> the response for each food on the [questionnaire] list was simply the number of days, in the week prior to the interview, that it had been consumed *by one of the members of the household*. The information gathered ... [was then] analysed by calculating the Food Consumption Score (FCS) and, subsequently, assigning [each household to] a Food Consumption Group. (WFP 2009: 55; emphasis added)

Three groups are used: households can have a 'poor', 'borderline' or an 'adequate' consumption profile.

The FCS approach does not appeal to anthropologists. The job of the anthropologist is to disaggregate and examine evolving relationships and rights, and to learn about how they are negotiated. The reason for this is simple: food security is context specific and may mean different things to different people, in different spaces and times. To highlight these important distinctions, it is necessary to work with historically informed, location-specific ethnography. To stay with Uganda, the importance of location and historical context is effectively conveyed in an article on Tororo district, where a 'cotton-cereals farming system' introduced in colonial times had become traditional by the late 1960s (Whyte and Kyaddondo 2006). Following the collapse of the cotton industry under Idi Amin and subsequent launch of a Chinese-run irrigated rice project, still going strong today, Michael Whyte and David Kyaddondo explored location-specific, contrasting responses to the rice scheme. What the authors tell us about food (in)security draws on a detailed examination of multiple contexts: how farming systems and land use changed over time; how trade in food crops emerged; how discourses about food and food security took on new contours and what the changes meant for 'the gender-based division of labour in family production, and [for] the interdependence of families and individuals as expressed in social exchange' (2006: 173). The anthropological approach reaches well beyond food consumption scores.

The gap between local and international discourses on food insecurity, which has been illustrated (see Pottier 1999), is evident also in the way soil scientists use a biophysical lens to measure the health of agricultural systems. Such scientific understandings, their underlying assumptions and their incompatibility with local perceptions have recently caught the attention of anthropologists. Ramisch's fieldwork in south Mali, for example, has allowed him to outline the partiality of the knowledge embedded in the scientific discourse of nutrient balance (Ramisch 2010). He became aware that scientists who used the nutrient balance methodology were oblivious to those phenomena that mattered to Fulani farmers – the practical arrangements with regard to land, labour and livestock – which needed constant attention and negotiation (2010: 25). What farmers found easy to make 'visible' in their own terms was hard to fathom for the scientists. And vice versa, the soil scientist's idea of identifying negative nutrient balances in order to identify farming systems or cropping practices that were 'at risk' was beyond the grasp of local farmers (2010: 28). Ramisch's observations warn that 'simply casting light upon a particular, biophysical component of soil fertility' comes nowhere near revealing the complexities surrounding the food (in)security of a region or household (2010: 45).

AGRIBUSINESS AND LIVELIHOODS

This section covers: the rise, power and impact of transnational food corporations; land tenure, land access and the poor and gendered struggles over crops, household labour and budgets.

The Rise, Power and Impact of Transnational Corporations

Philip McMichael (2009) refers to the launch of the World Trade Organization (WTO) in 1993 as the beginning of the third food regime. From here on, an expanding corporate agriculture sector, in tandem with the WTO, ensured 'the continued export of subsidized grain from the global north, and the rise of non-traditional food export (fruits, vegetables, and meats) from the global south, produced for agribusiness' (2009: 148). Trade agreements brokered by the WTO also ensured that farm subsidies in the global North would be preserved, while southern states were forced to drop such protection. Measures to prevent states from regulating their own food systems had been in place since Structural Adjustment Programmes (SAPs) were imposed by the World Bank and the International Monetary Fund (IMF) in the

1980s and 1990s. SAPs cut public sector expenditure and state subsidies, removed price controls and paved the way for neoliberal globalization.

Anthropological approaches to the study of globalization, including the globalization of food commodities, insist on placing the debate in culturally and historically appropriate contexts. Full contextualization safeguards against the making of sweeping, downright negative generalizations. Hence, in addressing food insecurity, the spotlight must rest not just on worldwide structural constraints and injustices (the fall-out of decisions imposed by the IMF/World Bank and the WTO), but also on the resilience and the ingenuity with which farmers have *responded* to conditions of imposed hardship and deprivation. However, since achieving an analytical balance is far from easy, some anthropologists have cautioned against over-celebrating local people's agency and ingenuity (see Peters 2004). It is feared that globally imposed, structural constraints are getting more difficult to circumvent, as will be seen in relation to intellectual property rights.

The rise and spread of neoliberal trade agreements have made farmers vulnerable to the vagaries of the global marketplace. The concentration of key agricultural commodities and finance in the hands of a small number of 'agribusiness giants' now threatens livelihoods the world over. Intellectual Property Rights (IPR) legislation and global discourses about 'food safety' have resulted in local crops and produce being banned. For example,

> in 1998, India's indigenous edible oils from mustard, coconut, sesame, linseed and groundnut processed in artisanal cold press mills were banned, using 'food safety' as an excuse. Restrictions on the import of soya oil were simultaneously removed and ten million farmers' livelihoods were threatened. (Shiva 2013: 197)

The challenge for anthropology is to study globalization in a contextualized manner, both from above and below, but without getting caught in the web of a simplistic local–global binary, which assumes that 'the local south' is invariably acted upon by 'the global north'. Inspired by the work of Anna Tsing (2000) and drawing on her fieldwork in the Tehuacán Valley, Mexico, Elizabeth Fitting (2011) spells out what the challenge involves. She invites anthropologists to foster an awareness of how

> globalization, like any moment in the history of capital, takes form through particular spaces, interacting with and remaking natural environments, social relations, and cultural meanings. This process includes interactions between humans and the natural environment. Transgenes, agricultural pests, and soil fertility, for example, interact with each other and humans in an active and unpredictable manner. This anthropological approach insists upon a historical perspective (the history of particular places and 'what is historically sedimented here') and multiple scales of analysis, not simply the local and the global. (2011: 28)

Transcending the local–global binary opens the door for an appreciation of how 'ordinary' people have the potential to affect top-down processes and policies. Tehuacán Valley producers are indeed affected by processes of a global magnitude, 'but they also make decisions about how best to respond to them, they build political alliances, and they make requests and demands for support from regional state officials'. Although the agro-food corporations exert their influence on the Mexican government and have influenced the design of its Biosafety Law, 'peasants respond, resist, and react, and Mexican activists and their international networks pressure politicians and state officials to address the problems surrounding GM corn imports and field trials' (2011: 27).

This kind of approach 'opens up lines for inquiry that challenge the idea of globalization as a predominantly economic, hegemonic, or singular process' (Phillips 2006: 40).

Land Tenure, Land Access and the Poor

One reason why land tenure and land access are linked to food security is that women are still by and large responsible for food provisioning. Women are interested not just in the volume of food they need for the household, but also in its quality. This makes women interested in biodiversity – a topic long neglected in food security debates, despite its potential benefits for nutrition (Mackenzie 2003; also Khadka and Verma 2012). Observations of how women maintain biodiversity have now rekindled anthropology's interest in gender and land rights.

Land is known to be socially embedded; it is the site of an intricate interlocking of both rights and contestations. Here again, simple binaries (e.g. the powerful male versus the submissive female) have limited explanatory value. In one of her illustrations from Murang'a, Kenya, Fiona Mackenzie shows how women reacted to being poorly rewarded for tending their husbands' coffee farms – they abandoned the farms and took up contract work on nearby estates. Not only did men then agree to pay their wives, but they also agreed – partly through an intervention of the Murang'a District Farmers' Cooperative Union (MDFCU) – to change their personal union accounts 'from individual (male) accounts to joint (spousal) accounts' (Mackenzie 2003: 260). Similar observations have been made for Ghana's Akan region, where women overturned 'customary' inheritance practices to secure rights to their husbands' land in the case of divorce or death (Quisumbing et al. 2001: 158). And they negotiated better terms as well – claiming 'sweat money' – for the labour they, along with their children, expended on their husbands' cocoa farms. Pressures from women, again with some institutional backing, then resulted in a substantial increase in 'gift transactions' of land, now the 'most important mode of land acquisition for women' (2001: 176). Such progress notwithstanding, Akan women still faced credit and other constraints that made it hard for them to properly invest in land.

Ethnographic research has made anthropologists recognize that statutory and 'customary' laws are more interconnected than is generally realized. 'In practice, people, including women, sustain their claims to resources by employing arguments from both the statutory and so-called customary law' (Whitehead and Tsikata 2003: 95). But while there are examples of women securing co-ownership in land with their husbands, the more common observation is still that women lose their claims when individualized proprietorship develops. Bina Agarwal conveys this in her argument that Indian women farmers need to reconnect with the land but without the conditions of insecurity they have experienced in the past (Agarwal 2003). Indian women, Agarwal explains, hope to access arable land via three avenues: the state, the family and the market. Regarding the first two options, women nearly always face insurmountable obstacles since the government and local state authorities typically allot land to male household heads, a biased practice that then reinforces similar discriminatory practices at the local level. The situation for women, especially widows, is not rosy (2003: 202). The third path to accessing land – which is to purchase and cultivate land on a group basis – is more hopeful. Agarwal lists several advantages when poor women work in groups to lease or purchase land, one being that they then qualify for government credit to develop the land. Group ownership also lessens the pressures exerted by conservative family members.

But the importance of land for survival and food security has now been challenged by powerful international bodies. Thus in 2005, in its report on *The State of Food and Agriculture*, the FAO argued that land was no longer the key to survival. What would lift the rural poor out of poverty were not the small plots they cultivated, but the advent of a commercially vibrant agricultural sector from which benefits would trickle down to the poor. The FAO urged donors and governments to promote policies that would enable the poor to exit from the land and take advantage of (what the FAO called) their most valuable asset: their own labour (FAO 2005).

Rwanda became a showcase for implementing this new vision. The post-genocide Government of Rwanda has been restructuring its economy away from 'subsistence' farming towards a 'professionalized' agriculture from which the land-poor will exit. Backed by international donors, DFID (UK) and USAID especially, the vision of a prosperous agricultural sector devoid of poor peasant farmers has been justified on the grounds that large-scale monocropping on *consolidated* plots will boost non-farm employment and thus lift the rural poor out of poverty. Despite the country's poor track record with creating off-farm employment, the new vision became enforceable by law in 2005 with the introduction of the Organic Land Law, 2005 (for review and commentary, see Pottier 2006). Inflated claims about employment generation are a feature also of the narratives surrounding large-scale land deals (see e.g. Li 2011).

A particularly interesting experiment with land consolidation in Rwanda is the government's ambition to 'revolutionize' marshland agriculture. To ensure 'food security for all the population', the government has taken steps to develop marshlands for the production of high-value crops such as rice, sugar cane and maize (Government of Rwanda 2007: 65). Again, the assumption is that technology and private entrepreneurship will get the poor out of poverty. The Rwandan government has made swampland, which is state property, available in concessions either to private investors or local authorities. The recipients then allocate plots to farmer groups, who cultivate collectively. An example of the first scenario is Kabuye Sugar Works (KSW), which in 1997 was bought by the Uganda-based Madhvani Group, a conglomerate with Indian roots. Despite strong opposition from local farmers who stood to lose their access to this valuable land, Madhvani was granted a fifty-year land lease on approximately 3,150 hectares of swampland. By 2007, KSW employed some 5,000–6,000 manual labourers.

To begin to understand how resource-poor farmers were affected, and what this might mean for household relations and food security, it is informative to consider the field observations by Murison and Ansoms (2012), who reflect on what the transformation has meant for household food sufficiency and women's workloads. Having researched both forms of swampland development (by private investors and local authorities), Murison and Ansoms conclude that the 'new agriculture' approach with its emphasis on monocropping is having a negative impact on households. Monocropping has reduced the variety of food crops that smallholders produce, while there is also a virtual ban on growing sweet potatoes. The loss of diversity has meant that the market price of several foodstuffs has escalated. Price hikes, moreover, have not been matched by an increase in household incomes, so that farmers now struggle to buy the food they used to cultivate. This is a major concern, since women remain solely responsible for biodiversity and keeping their households food secure.

The second form of marshland cultivation in Rwanda, whereby local authorities allocate swampland to farmer cooperatives, has also resulted in poor(er) peasant farmers being squeezed out of the marshlands. Farmer cooperatives, Murison and Ansoms show, impose taxes which smallholder farmers find difficult to pay. For one cooperative they researched, it was estimated that around one-third of peasants had already lost access. The taxation system meant that only better-off farmers could work several plots, a far cry from earlier times when the poor cultivated multiple plots, including marshland plots, as an important risk-coping strategy. The practice, when I researched it in the mid-1980s, was supported by loosely structured cooperatives in which gender issues such as women's workload and remuneration could be openly discussed (Pottier 1989). None of this continues today.

The research on Rwanda's marshland exploitation is one example of how anthropologists have begun to turn their attention to the new phenomenon of large-scale land deals, popularly known as 'land grabs'. At this stage in the debate, we are still waiting for ethnographies that fully contextualize how exactly such deals are struck and on what scale and what impact they have on local livelihoods and the right to land and food. There is a lot for anthropologists to engage with. As recent review papers suggest, topics on which anthropological expertise is required, and which are already being addressed, include: the causes of land grabbing; the crisis narratives that frame the justification for land deals (e.g. discourses on global food and environmental/fuel insecurity); the impact on patterns of rural social differentiation; and narratives around resistance and the construction of alternatives (see Fairhead, Leach and Scoones 2012; White et al. 2012). Theoretical–empirical research to date confirms that 'the standard narrative that those involved in such deals are simply foreign companies from the North appropriating land in the South' is in need of unpacking (White et al. 2012: 628).

Gendered Struggles Over Crops, Labour and Budgets

When anthropologists first developed an interest in household dynamics and gender, discussions focused on the impact of cash cropping and technological innovation. Findings sometimes highlighted the increase in employment opportunities, but they spoke mostly of gender imbalances and struggles over workloads and remuneration. Women not only routinely faced longer working days for scant reward, but also their absences from home and lack of negotiating power often impacted negatively on their personal food security and that of their households.

In recent times, gender imbalances in workload and remuneration have become more complex, as have the linkages to food security. At the household level, food security still rests by and large on women's ability to successfully combine food production with received income. In this respect, a central research question is as follows: how do men and women negotiate responsibilities for food provisioning, if they do so at all? Sometimes it does, indeed, seem that husbands – like in decades past – still have not come to terms with the notion of sharing in the burden of supplying food or of assuming a larger share when new needs emerge. Miriam Goheen's (1996) restudy of life in the Nso' chiefdom in Cameroon, first researched by Phillis Kaberry in the 1940s and 1950s, is instructive. As wives, Nso' women produce virtually all the food crops a household needs, and they perform (with daughters and young sons) a fair amount of coffee-related labour. Yet it is the men who decide how the income from coffee should be spent, which is mostly on items not essential to nutrition (1996: 35–6, 91). Women, moreover, complain that men have become lax. Having researched budget negotiations in some detail, Goheen concludes:

> The prejudice against women handling money [in the 1940s] meant that husbands assumed responsibilities for virtually all cash purchases. Today, women's household obligations have expanded with increased demands on their incomes brought about by changes in the rural standard of living. Women complain that in the past men purchased household necessities such as palm oil and salt, but today they expect women to assume these responsibilities. (Goheen 1996: 90)

Men do not see nutritional welfare as their social responsibility. It is 'women's food crops and cash contributions [which] provide for most household necessities' (1996: 90–1). Household budgeting in relation to food purchases is a topic anthropologists must continue to investigate in all its historical and localized complexity (see e.g. Thorsen 2002); it is also a topic to which food policy makers need to pay more attention. Further down, I shall illustrate this with reference to research on improved cassava varieties.

The need to paying more attention to household budgets relates also to scenarios where men seek their fortunes in international migration. This new type of 'cash cropping' and its consequences for regional and household food security was recently researched by Adhikhari and Hobley (2011) in the context of male outmigration from Khotang District (Nepal) to the Gulf and Malaysia. In this case study, the effects of male outmigration on livelihoods are multiple and socially varied. Not only is there a reduction in male labour in agriculture, but the range of food crops has also shrunk. Local maize, for example, is disappearing and making way for cheap rice imports. Productivity decline is felt also in the livestock sector, where 'large livestock are replaced by small, less labour-intensive livestock (goats, chickens and pigs) that can be sold faster to provide small amounts of money for immediate household consumption' (2011: 14). On the positive side, the decline in labour availability and productivity has boosted wage-labour rates and arrangements for sharecropping, which has brought some benefit to poorer sections of the community, Dalits ('untouchables') in particular.

But what of the women who stay behind? Women with migrant husbands, recently married wives especially, face serious well-being difficulties. For a start, women's stress levels are very high when remittances fall below expectation or fail to materialize. The first years are particularly stressful since moneylenders pressurize women to pay off the loans their husbands took out to initiate the migration. Wives who stay behind are also expected to carry out more agricultural tasks, participate in village committees, hire male labour and take agricultural surpluses to market – all activities that make household budgeting more difficult and add to the psychological pressure women endure (2011: 20). Here is the catch. While there is clear evidence that most migrant households in Khotang benefit economically from international migration, which will continue as a chief livelihood strategy, the wives and daughters left behind experience longer working days, and heightened levels of risk, scrutiny and anxiety.

That women's control of household budgets is crucial for food security will not surprise anyone. What may surprise, however, is that households are still being treated as units when agricultural scientists or food policy makers consider the food security benefits they expect from new technology. The issue here is that questions about resource allocation and power at the household level are not always addressed, even when bold claims are made. This is apparent from publications like *The Cassava Transformation* (Nweke, Spencer and Lynam 2002), in which the authors argue that commercial cassava has become a 'powerful poverty fighter'. The book synthesizes the results of the Collaborative Study of Cassava in Africa (COSCA), carried out from 1989 to 1997 in villages in six African countries, and expresses the hope that these results 'will be used to help develop improved food policies and research and extension programs in order to accelerate the cassava transformation and ultimately increase food security and incomes of the people of Africa' (2002: 13–14).

The COSCA study is particularly insightful in its demonstration of how men become interested in cassava production when new technologies materialize along with the promise of cash. The reader is, therefore, urged to drop the conventional wisdom that 'cassava is a woman's crop' (2002: 150) and invited to consider important 'Gender Surprises'. One such surprise is the 'evidence that as cassava is transformed into a commercial crop, both men and women play significant roles in production and processing', even though 'women [continue to] play the dominant role in food preparation' (2002: 17). For Nigeria, where much commercial cassava is now produced for urban consumption, it is observed that 'men were involved in cassava processing in more than 50 per cent of the COSCA villages with mechanized graters that prepared *gari* for sale. ... This finding implies that men increase their labor inputs in cassava processing where the crop is mainly produced for urban consumers' (2002: 149). But while this finding is significant, it will not surprise anthropologists and hardly qualifies as a 'gender surprise'. The discovery of men's interest in commercial cassava reminds me of Zambia in the 1980s, when its government put a price on cassava and women feared that if they were to make money from cassava, their previously undisputed control over the crop would be challenged by men. Men were likely to claim that growing cassava was now a cash-oriented activity, like growing maize, and thus within the male domain (Gatter 1993: 163).

The COSCA study highlights gendered shifts in household labour (fair enough), but does not appear to have considered whether there is evidence to show that any of the money men made from growing and processing high-yielding cassava found its way into the budget for food provisioning. Even should men verbally accept to make regular contributions, the claim still needs to be examined empirically before it can be ascertained that improved cassava has gained the status of a 'powerful poverty fighter' capable of contributing to 'improved food policy' (2002: 13, 198).

On a somewhat similar note, it is insufficient to praise women for their contributions to maintaining and furthering biodiversity, as is done, for example, in the Convention on Biological Diversity (1992), and to leave it at that. Praise is justified, but hard questions need to be asked as well, something anthropologists have started to do. In a literature review of recent research on biodiversity, the International Centre for Integrated Mountain Development (ICIMOD, Kathmandu) shows why researchers and planners must move beyond praise: 'merely mentioning women in CBD documents is not enough to strengthen their access to biological diversity' (Khadka and Verma 2012: 8). To strengthen their access, women must actively participate at every level of policymaking. This need relates directly to their responsibilities for food and livelihood security.

> Biodiversity loss, caused by the modernization of agriculture, globalization, land grabbing, and changes in land use practices, often reduces women's access to, and use of, biodiversity resources, increasing the time and energy spent by women to collect the resources they need for food and for cultural, social, and environmental purposes. (2012: 8–9)

Khadka and Verma also confirm that the connections between gender, biodiversity conservation and management, on the one hand, and livelihood security, on the other, are particularly pronounced in the context of male outmigration. With case studies from the Himalayan region, they show that outmigration has resulted in a significant increase of women's workloads, has reduced livestock keeping and dented food security (2012: 10) – similar outcomes are also reported in the above-mentioned study on Nepal. Khadka and Verma add that when women lose access to land, they not only experience 'a loss of income and food security, but also a loss of autonomy and a feeling of disempowerment' (2012: 13). Such observations make it imperative that women gain better control over decision-making (and policy making) with regard to biodiversity.

GLOBAL CAPITALISM AND THE DEBATE ON GM CROPS

When farmers enter into contract relations with the corporate sector, they are legally bound to conform to corporate demands regarding the use of seeds and chemicals, and even production timeframes. The restrictions may lead to farmers losing income, paying higher food prices, and losing some of their autonomy and right to intellectual property. Fighting its corner, agribusiness will strive for the moral high ground with the promise that its engineered products can 'feed the world', a claim activists dismiss as cynical justification for corporate control (Lawrence and Grice 2009: 90).

Anthropology's initial take on the GM debate has been to show how it is riddled with assumptions (Scoones 2006). To move forward, Scoones proposed that the debate be delinked from the corporate claims about 'feeding the world', and moved to geographical areas considered at risk. Protagonists needed to 'recognize that contexts do matter, and that technology design and promotion cannot be dissociated from social, economic and ecological settings' (2006: 329). A livelihood focus was required. Unless the debate moved to ground level, there would be insufficient evidence to either promote or condemn GM technology. Kloppenburg (2004) agreed, but was emphatic that the GM industry needed slowing down. He was persuaded by plant pathologist Robert Goodman's argument that the random insertion of transgenes by genetic engineering techniques could be likened to 'throwing a grenade into the genome' (Goodman 2002, cited in Kloppenburg 2004: 311). Kloppenburg concluded: 'while there is no consensus [on risk], a significant number of scientists *unbeholden to the [biotechnology] companies and without close ties to activist groups* have found good reason to question the headlong rush to deployment of GM crops' (2004: 312; emphasis added). More recently, activists have themselves brought independent evidence of harm caused by GM technology. In *Making Peace with the Earth* (2013), scientist-turned-activist Vandana Shiva has an update. She reports, for example, that the government of Kerala has banned Endosulfan insecticide after its health department identified 4,000 victims who suffered from 'reproductive disorders and congenital malformation' (2013: 150–1). She also points to independent laboratory tests on pregnant women in Canada, which showed that 'traces of Bt. toxin from Monsanto Bt. corn were found in the blood of 93 per cent women and in 80 per cent of their umbilical cord and foetal blood' (2013: 180).

Corporate agribusiness also harms livelihoods, not in the least through the promotion of legislation about intellectual property rights. Plant Breeders' Rights (PBR) legislation, now adopted in countries around the globe, functions 'to constrain the traditional modes of farmer-to-farmer germplasm exchange by which crop diversity has been so productively maintained for so long' (Kloppenburg 2004: 323). Activist Pat Mooney (ETC Group) argues that farmers have been let down by the 1992 Convention on Biological Diversity (CBD), which has made genetic resources a national property. This has opened the door for 'Seed Giants' to use 'appropriationist initiatives' and gain a steady foothold (2004: 336). In the worst-case scenario, as with activist Shiva's portrayal of India as a once-sovereign country whose food chain has been broken, it is claimed that entire nations have become food insecure because governments uphold and protect the corporate rights to profit (Shiva 2013: 130). As a result, 'the majority of Indians have grown poorer because they have lost their land and livelihoods' (2013: 135). Particularly harmful is that 'new IPR laws are creating monopolies over seed and plant genetic resources, and *redefining seed saving and seed exchange that are the basic freedoms of farmers*' (2013: 167; emphasis added).

How should anthropologists engage? As with the debate on land, a conscientious anthropologist should research both the structural constraints that make farmers food insecure *and* farmers' resilience and ingenuity, but without over-celebrating human agency and inventiveness. On the one hand, anthropologists need to provide 'thick description' of the damage corporate agribusiness and so-called free trade regimes inflict on poor farmers; on the other, they must fully document how 'farmers at risk' grapple with that fast-changing world on which, activists claim, they are losing their grip. How do farmers understand the structural constraints (imposed by seed companies, lawyers, politicians, moneylenders, etc.) that surround them? Is all perceived as negative or do farmers see advantages too? And do women and men, the young and the old, the rich and the poor have a shared understanding of what agribusiness represents? While Shiva's examples of 'GM dictatorship' and its effects are truly shocking, it is difficult to assume that Indian farmers would perceive the challenges they face as simply a question of 'bad' GM versus 'good' biodiversity. Life's choices tend to be more complex and framed in different ways; people face paradoxes; and different generations may not see eye to eye. The anthropologist's ambition to probe complexities and paradoxes, and scrutinize the contextualized ways that frame debates, should not be dismissed as academic indulgence. Activists too can learn from such empirical (somewhat 'detached') insights and use them to boost their own efforts to restore biodiversity.

One foray into the complexities and paradoxes that mark poor farmers' livelihoods can be found in Elizabeth Fitting's account of Mexico's Tehuacán Valley, where she carried out ethnographic research in 2001–2 and 2005. Fitting proposes that the challenge of conserving in situ biodiversity goes beyond the technical issue of regulating GM food imports. The threat to biodiversity, she argues, comes not from the presence of GM crops alone but from the economic hardships that have led to high levels of outmigration – hardships that to some extent, but not entirely, have been inflicted by the neoliberal corn regime (2006: 20). But farmers' reactions are varied. Confronting the crisis, younger migrants (in their twenties or younger) who return from the USA are now turning their backs on agriculture, preferring instead to work in the valley industries; only older migrants continue to work in corn production. The latter have switched to growing *elote* – white maize, monocropped and sold as corn on the cob.

Although Fitting's research remains a rare example in anthropology, it shows that the discipline has moved on since the early days of the GM debate. In taking the debate to the communities affected, Fitting appreciated not only that small-scale producers are 'actors who react to and engage rural policy and state bureaucrats and experts' (2011: 4–5), but also that there are unfair constraints on their choices in life. Indeed, it is one of Fitting's main arguments that

> although small-scale agricultural producers are always faced with a degree of uncertainty, under the neoliberal corn regime the struggle to maintain or improve

their livelihoods has intensified. Moreover, *I believe* that those campesinos who want to remain on the land should have the ability to do so. The anthropologist Armando Bartra (2008) refers to this as the right *not* to migrate, 'the right to stay at home'. (2011: 5; emphasis added)

To fulfil their ethical obligations, anthropologists, like activists, should be bold enough to declare that they too *believe* in rights that must be upheld.

FOOD SECURITY IN PROTRACTED CRISES

Protracted crises, whether driven by conflict or famine conditions, commonly result in mass displacements, livelihood disruptions and institutional dysfunction or collapse. For humanitarians wishing to intervene, the chaos raises difficult questions about priorities and timescales.

Anthropological research on Africa's 'New Wars' and 'New Famines' illustrates the exceedingly complex nature of contemporary emergencies (Devereux 2006; Richards 2005). While the use of food as a weapon in war (destruction of crops, harvests and markets) is well established in the literature, social analysts are increasingly aware that access to land and other assets may be reconfigured in the course of conflict. Social groups, as Peter Little shows for Jubba, southern Somalia, may move in and out of poverty – a dynamic with huge implications for intervention (Little 2008). By tapping into local discourses of survival and food insecurity, anthropologists have responded to the challenge of how best to bridge the gap between short-term emergency relief and longer-term development assistance. Invariably, they begin with a contextualized reading of the political and economic landscape.

In his assessment of the livelihood and food insecurity situation in Jubba, which he analysed for 1995–2005, Little highlights that market access, livelihood diversification and assets enabled certain households to adjust to a highly unstable environment while others became more vulnerable. Arguing that empirical research must precede intervention, Little proposes that researchers examine how 'households move in and out of different states of poverty and food insecurity in response to various kinds of shocks, including conflicts, droughts and market disruptions' (Little 2008: 108). Such asset-based inquiry is of value to development agencies interested in 'devising strategies that help to rebuild household and community assets to levels that are sustainable in the medium to long-term (5–10 years)' (2008: 123). When agencies lack this kind of information, they typically engage in short-term humanitarian action and lose sight of the longer-term programmes that can bring peace and stability.

The critique that agencies lack crucial information can be extended to other crisis settings. In his account of food insecurity in eastern DRC, where he conducted fieldwork in the immediate aftermath of the Congolese war, Vlassenroot (2008) also notes how *shifting local conditions* were not understood by intervening agencies, which, in any case, preferred to respond within a short-term framework by providing food aid, seeds and tools distribution, and setting up nutrition centres.[1] Vlassenroot argues that land tenure security ranked much higher among local priorities than food aid or seeds and tools, because so many people had been displaced by politico-military elites who used land to reward their supporters (2008: 218). A strategic framework for strengthening people's access to vital assets would have served the population better. Agency ignorance about conditions on the ground was a problem also in the immediate aftermath of war and genocide in Rwanda, when the same short-term measures were on offer. Farmers welcomed the seeds and tools they received, but were more concerned about the restoration of opportunities for seasonal wage work, which was essential to the rehabilitation of the agricultural sector. Restoring these opportunities meant restoring the internal flow of seasonal migrant labour, which in turn would stimulate the circulation of cash and seeds (Pottier 1996: 69–70).

The perspective that agrarian injustice may lie at the heart of conflict, with land reform being the key to ending the violence, also runs through Paul Richards's reflections on the wars in Sierra Leone and Liberia, where hundreds of thousands of youth were vulnerable to militia mobilization even as hostilities appeared to be ending (Richards 2005). Richards urged that the two countries introduce thorough land reforms (along with new marriage laws for Sierra Leone) to end the long centuries of agrarian injustice. He addressed human rights campaigners directly, telling them to concentrate on the protection of young people's tenancy rights. Without such protection, post-conflict training in rural skills would bear no fruit. The reform of tenancy rights was 'as urgent an issue as tracking the gun-runners or diamond- and timber-smugglers' (2005: 588).

The academic discourse around 'new famines' shares a rights focus with the 'new wars' literature – a focus on how rights violations lie at the root of famine crises, and what this means for intervening agencies if they are to become more accountable. Analytically, the challenge is that of a paradigm shift away from viewing famine as a failure of access to food towards an acknowledgement that famine is political. The famines of the twenty-first century (e.g. Malawi 2002; Niger 2006; Somalia 2012) became famines because they were *allowed to become famines*. The centrality of politics in the 'new famines' thinking calls for attention to the "black hole of unaccountability" within the international relief system, with national governments, international donors and NGOs indulging in mutual recriminations whenever emergency food is not delivered in time' (Devereux 2006: 8). Malawi's 2002 famine illustrates the problem. Leaving aside the controversy over whether available crop estimates for maize were reliable, once the crisis broke, donors were slow to react. It is difficult to explain their slow reaction. Donors may have been 'genuinely unaware of the severity of the impending crisis'; on the other hand, many maintained fractious relationships with the government of the day (Devereux 2002: 75).

The North Korean famine of the 1990s is another illustration of how contemporary famine conditions are *allowed* to emerge and develop. Sandra Fahy's research with famine survivors shows that when food shortages turned severe, the North Korean regime placed heavy restrictions on people talking about famine, hunger and starvation, and meted out harsh punishments for those who broke them. The regime used state media, the print media in particular, to convince citizens that their hardship matched that of the heroic 'March of Suffering' (Manchuria 1938) during which Kim Il Sung's guerrilla army defeated Japanese imperialism. The regime's recourse to metaphoric description appeared convincing in the eyes of the people and the world, initially at least, and turned the famine into a slow, silent and invisible process, especially inside North Korea (Fahy 2012: 536). Despite the stringent government controls on the flow of information, North Koreans developed 'a vibrant lexicon' to engage in subtle 'coded communication', often using the very terms government provided, but with their meanings remade (2012: 539). It was not until the famine had reached an advanced stage 'when its affects were finally visible in Pyongyang, [that] informants who lived in those areas were shocked to find famine dead on their doorsteps. Prior to this high visibility, it was easier to deny the famine' (2012: 542).

A recent analysis of the 2011 Somalia famine also identifies the drivers that *allowed* this famine to gather momentum. According to Bradbury and Maletta (2012), the famine attested 'not only to the culpable failures of internal governance, but also to the failure of the system of international governance and politics' (2012: 131). When America's post-9/11 antiterrorism legislation led to the suspension of major humanitarian programmes in Somalia, notably those of the WFP, the sudden reduction in food aid – and in remittances from the diaspora – made the famine inevitable. It is not only local players who use famine to further their own agendas.

URBAN FOOD SECURITY

The conditions that prevail in low-income urban neighbourhoods – overcrowding, below-standard housing, poor or non-existent sanitation and so on – make it impossible for the urban poor to utilize their food intake to maximum benefit. When safe drinking water, environmental hygiene and primary health care are lacking, gastrointestinal infections annul the benefits of even the most nutritious diet. Among other concerns regularly voiced is that city dwellers tend to be net buyers of food, and therefore vulnerable to price hikes. These predicaments, and the conundrum that locally grown grains are usually more expensive than imports, have resulted in a policy interest in urban and peri-urban agriculture. While city authorities may still disapprove of urban agriculture, capital cities like Kinshasa and Kampala have benefitted from official endorsements.

Ethnographic studies of urban food security in Africa reveal that the 'urban poor' are an adaptive, resilient social category whose ways of dealing with hardship deserve research and policy attention (e.g. Khouri-Dagher 1996; Lourenço-Lindell 2002; Maxwell 1999; Tollens 2004). Ethnographers appreciate that multifaceted, grassroots initiatives keep cities food secure. Initiatives include urban and peri-urban farming, and often involve dynamic rural–urban interactions. In Kinshasa, for example, the rural–urban trade in foodstuffs has adapted spectacularly during the recent war, while the impoverished population has also created new strategies to stave off hunger. In response to such dynamic scenarios, researchers now pay attention to practices of food supply and distribution, to the quest for livelihood diversity and to the social networks that connect city and countryside.

Two of Kampala's peripheral wards were the venue for a brief study I conducted in July and September/October 2012 (Pottier 2015). Aiming to achieve a broad understanding of what it meant to be food insecure, I concentrated on how 'the urban poor' (a slippery term) perceived their food insecurity, what their food intake was like at the time of my research, whether and how food intake related to seasonality and what strategies were deployed to stay food secure. The data I collected revealed that food-insecure households dropped, or significantly decreased, the consumption of 'cooking' bananas (*matoke*) as soon as their availability started to go down (in July) and the market price shot up. The dietary shift was gradual for households with secure assets, but food-insecure households moved fairly quickly to a diet of a stiff maize porridge (*posho*) and beans, and survived on just one meal a day. The adults in food-insecure households worked in poorly remunerated, informal sector activities. Many such households were headed by grandparents, single grandmothers especially, but the widespread existence of three-generational households was not in itself a sign of insecurity. The majority of grandparent-headed households *were* food secure, either because they had regular income from paid work or rentals, or because they received direct contributions – produce or money – from *rural* family farms, or because they received assistance from within the extended family to help with the cost of food and school fees for the children in their care. A secure income and access to produce from a family farm 'at home' gave stability also to households that were less complex in their social make-up. Nearly half of the heads of household I interviewed said it was their access to rural family land (*kibanja*), governed under so-called customary law, which made them food secure. The one complicating factor was that siblings who inherit land *negotiate* the terms on which the land is to be allocated and used. Since *kibanja* cannot be formally divided, the negotiations often fail to satisfy all parties. One informant, who gave vent to his frustration that he was not getting any produce from the rural farm his brother and sister cultivated, said of the hunger he knew in the city: 'Food shortage starts at home' (*bula lyemmere litandi kira ku kyalo*). Farming or not farming a piece of *rural* family land could make a difference to *urban* food security.

The interest in *urban* agriculture in Kampala varied considerably between and within the two wards I researched. In one ward, where slum conditions and regular flooding prevailed, the interest was virtually non-existent. In the other ward, in contrast, many residents had a keen interest in both cultivation and small livestock, which was beneficial to their food security. These variations between wards, and inside them, were a reminder that 'the urban poor' is a catch-all phrase that may obscure significant socio-economic differentiation.

The situation in Kampala showed up some parallels with the low-income wards in Lilongwe, Malawi, where I had previously carried out similar research (Pottier 2014). Lilongwe residents, too, depended on low wages or casual/seasonal work (*ganyu*), and shopped daily for their food. Food insecurity was perceived as the inability to secure adequate maize supplies during the hunger months (*mwezi wa njala*) from December till mid-March. People who did *not* suffer a drop in staple consumption during those months and had the means to continue to buy sufficient relish considered themselves as food secure. Food-insecure households, in contrast, restricted their diet to one meal a day, using a stiff maize porridge (*nsima*) as base. Lilongwe's urban poor not only reduced their food intake and downgraded its quality, but they also strategized to avoid making these adjustments. Besides trying to earn extra cash from *ganyu*, many relied on urban–rural ties, women especially, to maintain gardens in the villages from where they originated. Residents in the wards I researched came predominantly from southern Malawi, where women inherit land. Farming at home contributed directly to the urban household's food supply and, significantly, also created the conditions for a smooth change of residence should unforeseen circumstances drive migrants out of the city. Urban agriculture was an option, but one that only well-established migrants could afford. This was further evidence that urban agriculture tends to benefit better-off, better-connected households rather than poor ones (Lee-Smith 2010: 487).

CONCLUSION

Although the right to adequate food is recognized in the Universal Declaration of Human Rights (1948), in the International Covenant on Economic, Social and Cultural Rights (1966) and in the 'Voluntary Guidelines on the Right to Food' (2004), this right is only an economic right, and hence does little more than *encourage* states to take responsibility (Marcus 2003). Unsurprisingly, most states feel under no obligation to act. And likewise, members of the international community hesitate to intervene when the right to food is denied; they fear violating sovereignty.

A similar hesitancy about engaging still exists for those anthropologists who, in the words of Anthony Good, find 'the line between balanced assessment and advocacy … uncomfortably blurred' (Good 2003: 114). Engagement may bring the risk of manipulation. Increasingly, though, anthropologists accept that fieldwork leads to an ethical obligation to promote the well-being of the people who collaborate in research; they understand that anthropology, too, is inherently political. This awareness does not diminish the commitment to close observation and detached scrutiny, but it does make anthropologists more amenable to engaging with activists and policymakers so that valuable empirical insights add to the conversations of those whose job it is to prescribe and steer other people's lives.

NOTE

1. We may well ask what appetite the international community had for taking on land tenure insecurity in the DRC, where land rights were/are virtually non-existent because of the legacy of President Mobutu's patrimonial practices. When I put this question to Louis Michel, then European Commissioner for Development and Humanitarian Aid, at a roundtable discussion in Westminster, he agreed that land tenure insecurity was at the root of the conflict, but could not see how land reform would make it onto the agenda of any high-level donor meeting. (Roundtable discussion on Building Stability in DR Congo, Portcullis House, Westminster, 17 January 2008.)

ABBREVIATIONS

AAA	American Anthropological Association
CBD	Convention on Biological Diversity
COSCA	Collaborative Study of Cassava in Africa
DFID (UK)	Department for International Development (United Kingdom)
DRC	Democratic Republic of Congo
FAO	Food and Agriculture Organization (of the United Nations)
FCS	Food Consumption Score
GM	Genetically Modified
GMO	Genetically Modified Organism
ICIMOD	International Centre for Integrated Mountain Development
IMF	International Monetary Fund
IPR	Intellectual Property Rights
KSW	Kabuye Sugar Works
MDFCU	Murang'a District Farmers' Cooperative Union
NGO	Non-Governmental Organization
PBR	Plant Breeders' Rights
SAP	Structural Adjustment Programme
USAID	United States Agency for International Development
WFP	World Food Programme (of the United Nations)
WTO	World Trade Organization

REFERENCES

Adhikhari, J. and Hobley, M. (2011), *'Everybody is Leaving – Who will Sow our Fields?' – Effects of Migration from Khotang District to the Gulf and Malaysia*, On behalf of the Swiss Agency for Development and Cooperation (SDC). Available at http://www.swiss-cooperation.admin.ch/nepal/en/Home/Important_Documents (accessed 5 October 2014).

Agarwal, B. (2003), 'Gender and Land Rights Revisited: Exploring New Prospects via the State, Family and Market', *Journal of Agrarian Change*, 3(1/2): 184–224.

American Anthropological Association (1999), *Declaration on Anthropology and Human Rights*. Available at http://www.aaanet.org/about/Policies/statements/Declaration-on-Anthropology-and-Human-Rights.cfm (accessed 5 October 2014).

Bartra, A. (2008), *The Right to Stay: Reactivate Agriculture, Retain the Population*, San Francisco, CA: Global Exchange.

Bradbury, M. and Maletta, R. (2012), 'When State-Building Fails: Famine, Counterterrorism, and the Politicization of Humanitarian Action in Somalia', in A. Donini (ed.), *The Golden Fleece: Manipulation and Independence in Humanitarian Action*, 109–35, Bloomfield, CT: Kumarian Press.

Crewe, E. and Axelby, R. (2012), *Anthropology and Development: Culture, Morality and Politics in a Globalised World*, Cambridge: Cambridge University Press.

Devereux, S. (2002), 'The Malawi Famine of 2002', *IDS Bulletin*, 33(4): 70–8.

Devereux, S. (ed.) (2006), *The New Famines: Why Famines Persist in an Era of Globalization*, London: Routledge.

Fahy, S. (2012), 'Famine Talk: Communication Styles and Socio-Political Awareness in 1990s North Korea', *Food, Culture & Society*, 15(4): 535–55.

Fairhead, J. Leach, M. and Scoones, I. (eds) (2012), *Green Grabbing: A New Appropriation of Nature?* Special Issue of *The Journal of Peasant Studies*, 39(2): 237–61.

Fitting, E. (2006), 'Importing Corn, Exporting Labor: The Neoliberal Corn Regime, GMOs, and the Erosion of Mexican Biodiversity', *Agriculture and Human Values*, 23: 15–26.

Fitting, E. (2011), *The Struggle for Maize: Campesinos, Workers and Transgenic Corn in the Mexican Countryside*, Durham, NC: Duke University Press.

FAO (1996), *Synthesis of the Technical Background Documents, World Food Summit, 13-17 November 1996*. Rome: FAO. Available at http://www.fao.org/docrep/003/w2612e/w2612e00.HTM (accessed 5 October 2014).

FAO (2005), *Agricultural Trade and Poverty: Can Trade Work for the Poor?* Rome: FAO, The State of Food and Agriculture Report 2005. Available at http://www.fao.org/docrep/008/a0050e/a0050e00.HTM (accessed 5 October 2014).

Gatter, P. (1993), 'Anthropology in Farming Systems Research: A Participant Observer in Zambia', in J. Pottier (ed.), *Practising Development: Social Science Perspectives*, 153–86, London: Routledge.

Goheen, M. (1996), *Men Own the Fields, Women Own the Crops: Gender and Power in the Cameroon Grassfields*, Madison: The Wisconsin University Press.

Good, A. (2003), 'Anthropologists as Expert Witnesses', in R. A. Wilson and J. P. Mitchell (eds), *Human Rights in Global Perspective: Anthropological Studies of Rights, Claims and Entitlements*, 93–117, London: Routledge.

Goodale, M. (2006), '"Introduction" to "Anthropology and Human Rights in a New Key"', *American Anthropologist*, 108: 1–8.

Goodman, R. M. (2002), Personal Communication in Kloppenburg (2004).

Government of Rwanda (2007), *Economic Development and Poverty Reduction Strategy, 2008-2012*, Kigali: Ministry of Finance and Economic Planning.

Hart, K. (2004), 'The Political Economy of Food in an Unequal World', in M. E. Lien and B. Nerlich (eds), *The Politics of Food*, 199–220, Oxford: Berg.

Khadka, M. and Verma, R. (eds) (2012), *Gender and Biodiversity Management in the Greater Himalayas: Towards Equitable Mountain Development*, Kathmandu: Centre for Integrated Mountain Development (ICIMOD).

Kloppenburg Jr., J. R. (2004), *First the Seed: The Political Economy of Plant Biotechnology, 1492-2000*, Cambridge: Cambridge University Press, especially Chapter 11 (only in Second Edition).

Lawrence, G. and Grice, J. (2004), 'Agribusiness, Biotechnology, and Food', in J. Gremov and L. Williams (eds), *A Sociology of Food and Nutrition: The Social Appetite*, 78–95, Oxford: Oxford University Press.

Lee-Smith, D. (2010), 'Cities Feeding People: An Update on Urban Agriculture in Equatorial Africa', *Environment and Urbanization*, 22(2): 1–17.

Li, T. (2011), 'Centering Labour in the Land Grab Debate', *Journal of Peasant Studies*, 38(2): 281–98.

Little, P. (2008), 'Livelihoods, Assets and Food Security in a Protracted Political Crisis: The Case of the Jubba Region, Southern Somalia', in L. Alinovi, G. Hemrich and L. Russo (eds), *Beyond Relief: Food Security in Protracted Crises*, 107–26, Rugby, Warwickshire: Practical Action Publishing and FAO.

Mackenzie, F. (2003), 'Land Tenure and Biodiversity: An Exploration of the Political Ecology of Murang'a District, Kenya', *Human Organization*, 62(3): 255–66.

McMichael, P. (2009), 'A Food Regime Genealogy', *Journal of Peasant Studies*, 36(1): 139–69.

Marcus, D. (2003), 'Famine Crimes in International Law', *The American Journal of International Law*, 97: 245–81.

Maxwell, D. (1999), 'The Political Economy of Urban Food Security in Sub-Saharan Africa', *World Development*, 27(11): 1939–53.

Murison, J. and Ansoms, A. (2012), 'De la prospérité à "Saudi" à la noyade au "Darfour": L'histoire d'un marais au Rwanda', in F. Reyntjens, S. Vandeginste and M. Verpoorteren (eds), *L'Afrique des Grands-Lacs Annuaire, 2012–13*: 375–96.

Nweke, F. Spencer, D. and Lynam, J. (2002), *The Cassava Transformation: Africa's Best-Kept Secret*, East Lansing: Michigan State University Press.

Peters, P. (2004), 'Inequality and Social Conflict over Land in Africa', *Journal of Agrarian Change*, 3(1/2): 269–314.

Phillips, L. (2006), 'Food and Globalization', *Annual Review of Anthropology*, 35: 37–57.

Pottier, J. (1989), 'Debating Styles in a Rwandan Cooperative: Reflections on Language, Policy and Gender', in R. D. Grillo (ed.), *Social Anthropology and the Politics of Language*, 41–60, London: Routledge.

Pottier, J. (1996), 'Agricultural Rehabilitation and Food Insecurity in Post-War Rwanda: Assessing Needs, Designing Solutions', *IDS Bulletin*, 27(3): 56–76.

Pottier, J. (1999), *Anthropology of Food: The Social Dynamics of Food Security*, Cambridge: Polity Press.

Pottier, J. (2006), 'Land Reform for Peace? Rwanda's 2005 Land Law in Context', *Journal of Agrarian Change*, 6(4): 509–37.

Pottier, J. (2014), 'Urban Hunger and the Home Village: How Lilongwe's Migrant Poor Stay Food Secure', in N. Domingos, J. Sobral and H. West (eds), *Food Between the Country and the City: Ethnographies of a Changing Global Foodscape*, 107–25, London: Bloomsbury.

Pottier, J. (2015), 'Coping with Urban Food Insecurity: Findings from Kampala, Uganda', *Journal of Modern African Studies*, 53(2): 217–41.

Quisumbing, A. Payongayong, E. Aidoo, J. B. and Otsuka, K. (2001), 'Women's Land Rights in the Transition to Individualised Ownership: Implications for Tree-resource Management in Western Ghana', *Economic Development and Cultural Change*, 50(1): 157–81.

Ramisch, J. (2010), 'Beyond the Invisible: Finding the Social Relevance of Soil Nutrient Balances in southern Mali', in L. German, J. Ramisch and R. Verma (eds), *Beyond the Biophysical: Knowledge, Culture, and Power in Agriculture and Natural Resources Management*, 25–48, Dordrecht, Netherlands: Springer.

Richards, P. (2005), 'To Fight or to Farm? Agrarian Dimensions of the Mano River Conflicts (Liberia and Sierra Leone)', *African Affairs*, 106(417): 571–90.

Scoones, I. (2002), 'Agricultural Biotechnology and Food Security: Exploring the Debate', *Institute of Development Studies Working Paper*, 145.

Scoones, I. (2006), 'Can GM Crops Prevent Famine in Africa?' in S. Deveureux (ed.), *The New Famines: Why Famines Persist in an Era of Globalization*, 312–35, London: Routledge.

Shiva, V. (2013), *Making Peace with the Earth*, London: Pluto Press.

Swift, J. and Hamilton, K. (2001), 'Household Food and Livelihood Security', in S. Devereux and S. Maxwell (eds), *Food Security in Sub-Saharan Africa*, 67–92, London: ITDG.

Thorsen, D. (2002), '"We help our husbands!" Negotiating the Household Budget in Rural Burkina Faso', *Development and Change*, 33: 129–46.

Tollens, E. (2004), 'Food security in Kinshasa: Coping with adversity', in T. Trefon (ed.), *Reinventing Order in the Congo: How People Respond to State Failure in Kinshasa*, 47–64, London: Zed.

Tsing, A. (2000), 'The Global Situation', *Cultural Anthropology*, 15(3): 327–60.

Vlassenroot, K. (2008), 'Land Tenure, Conflict and Household Strategies in the Eastern Democratic Republic of the Congo', in L. Alinovi, G. Hemrich and L. Russo (eds), *Beyond Relief: Food Security in Protracted Crises*, 197–221, Rugby, Warwickshire: Practical Action Publishing and FAO.

Whitehead, A. and Tsikata, D. (2003), 'Policy Discourses on Women's Land Rights in Sub-Saharan Africa', *Journal of Agrarian Change*, 3(1/2): 67–112.

White, B., Borras, S. M., Hall, R., Scoones, I. and Wolford, W. (2012), 'The New Enclosures: Critical Perspectives on Corporate Land Deals', *Journal of Peasant Studies*, 39(3/4): 619–47.

Whyte, M. A. and Kyaddondo, D. (2006), '"We are Not Eating our Own Food here": Food Security and the Cash Economy in Eastern Uganda', *Land Degradation and Development*, 17: 173–82.

World Food Programme (2009), *Uganda: Comprehensive Food Security & Vulnerability Analysis*, Rome: World Food Programme, VAM Food Security Analysis.

CHAPTER EIGHT

Feeding Farmers and Feeding the Nation in Modern Malaysia: The Political Economy of Food and Taste

FRANCESCA BRAY

What does it take to feed a nation? Is it enough to provide sufficient foodstuffs at affordable prices? Or are symbolic and ideological nourishment a latent part of the calculus when politicians, economists and agronomists plan and regulate a nation's food supply? Today the political economy of food attracts attention across the social sciences, for the complex logics and linkages of food systems encapsulate many characteristic tensions of the modern technoscientific world order: tensions, for instance, between biology and politics, local and global, ethical choice and economic rationality, and national sovereignty and transnational regulation. Anthropology brings crucial insights to the critical analysis of food systems, not least by tracing how extra-economic, extra-caloric value is assigned to or created by particular foodstuffs or food practices. Locating these processes precisely in their specific social and historical context, anthropologists of food reveal vital dimensions of the role and power of food in governance, state formation and national as well as personal or social identity.

Three foundational anthropological studies of the political economy of food and taste came out in around 1980. Two were studies of colonial and post-colonial food systems in the shaping of global power relations. Goody's comparative study of West African and Eurasian foodways, *Cooking, Cuisine and Class* (1982), was informed by Marxist theory of the articulation of modes of production. Mintz's study of sugar and slavery in the emergence of industrial capitalism and mass consumption, *Sweetness and Power* (1985), fused classic and cultural Marxism. In *La distinction* (1979) Bourdieu wove eating and drinking styles into a Weberian analysis of the reproduction of class identities and relations in prosperous post-war France.

Long before the recent boom in food studies in the Anglophone world, European anthropologists continued to develop critical approaches to food, taste and power that interwove material, social, historical and symbolic analyses (e.g. Grignon, Aymard and Sabban 1989). In the Anglophone academy, anthropologists of rural society and of development continued to investigate systems of food production, offering perceptive insights, for instance, into the complex consequences of the Green Revolution (GR), but they rather ignored crops as food. Meanwhile few cultural anthropologists were interested in food. The field became more receptive to taking food seriously, however, as theories of consumption gained purchase in the interpretation of culture. The publication of Ohnuki-Tierney's *Rice as Self* (1994), a study of rice in the production of modern Japanese nationhood and identity, heralded a new and enduring anthropological obsession with food as culture, where material analysis typically focused less on relations or processes of production than on the phenomenology of consumption.

More recently, conditions of production have been reintegrated into the anthropology of food, which has once more taken a turn towards political economy. Food is both a revealing lens and an appealing theme for anthropologists investigating contemporary issues like the articulations of global assemblages (Dunn 2005); geographies of inequality (Fêo Rodrigues 2008); state legitimacy, state collapse and its aftermath (Jung, Klein and Caldwell 2014); risk governance and the impact of disaster (Assmann 2013; Lora-Wainwright 2013); or the tensions between national sovereignty, community rights and transnational regulatory regimes (McAllister 2009). In the political economy of food, tastes and technology, landscapes and laws, identity and nourishment, corporations and families, commensality and nationhood are intimately entangled: production and consumption cannot be considered separately, the material resources for producing, preparing and distributing food have to be treated as culturally and politically saturated, while the making of meaning must be understood as simultaneously an interpretative and a concrete, material process.

REPRODUCING THE MODERN PEASANTRY

A century ago Lenin declared the peasantry doomed to imminent extinction; Chayanov countered that peasant farming could adapt to the needs of modernization. Social scientists have debated ever since whether the peasantries they encountered were chance survivals or the way of the future (Bernstein 2009). The received wisdom of most economists and planners is that peasant-scale farming is wasteful and inefficient. A fascinating paradox of late-capitalist food systems, then, is the frequency with which states invest to protect or encourage small-scale, peasant farming.

It is neither cheap nor easy for modern industrialized nations to support a class of smallholder farmers. Most of the price consumers pay for an item of food covers processing, packaging, transport, advertising and retailing; just a tiny fraction goes back to the farmer. Add the penetration and ruthless competition of global markets and it becomes clear that, unless they are producing fine craft wines or other high-value niche products, small producers are at a distinct disadvantage compared to big farms, where economies of scale reduce production costs and raise profit margins (see also West, in this volume). Cereals like wheat or rice are the least suitable crops for commercially viable small-scale farming: consumers expect their staple food to be affordable, and there are few obvious opportunities for farmers themselves to add value to the grain they grow. Yet against this logic of consolidation many nations, rich and poor, from Ecuador to Zambia to Japan, strive to maintain 'traditional' family farms or smallholdings, sometimes in the name of food sovereignty, sometimes in the name of heritage, national taste or social justice.

Japan is probably the best-known case of a wealthy post-agrarian country whose government has chosen to ensure self-sufficiency in rice, the national staple food, by providing costly subsidies to peasant-scale farms (Ohnuki-Tierney 1994; Cwiertka 2006). To the untutored eye, Japan's rice sector appears to be an island of backwardness in an otherwise highly advanced economy – but in fact it is a thoroughly contemporary product of targeted technological and financial development. The Malaysian case is less well known but equally striking. In Malaysia as in Japan, a political commitment to support and preserve peasant-scale rice farming has remained in force for decades, through the nation's transformation from a predominantly rural society into an envied 'economic tiger'. Critics of Malaysia and Japan decry the wastefulness of paying smallholders to grow expensive rice when big farms would be more efficient, and when cheap rice is plentifully available on international markets. But are such policies just self-indulgent folly? As the Japanese literature demonstrates, the value of rice in Asian nations, where people understand themselves as being constituted socially, physically, spiritually or morally by their staple food, cannot be reduced to dollars and cents. Anthropology offers revealing insights into this contemporary conundrum.

This chapter explores the motives, costs and benefits of the Malaysian state's heavy and sustained investment in preserving peasant rice farming, through the vicissitudes of a 'Long Green Revolution'[1] now entering its fifth decade. The case of padi farmers in the poor East Coast state of Kelantan (Figure 8.1) illustrates the historical unfolding of this complicated and costly arrangement, and its many-layered contribution to national unity. To understand the long-term engagement between the powerful Malaysian state and some of its most vulnerable citizens, we need to consider why rice and rice farmers matter, in a web of values that meshes a local symbolism of rice as self, political responses to multi-ethnic tensions, and a keen sense of geopolitical vulnerability. Highly specific as the Malaysian case may be, it suggests more general anthropological insights into the many forms of sustenance that a staple food offers, and into the dilemmas that nations face, the complex and often costly bargains and sacrifices that must be made, to secure their food needs in the face of the logic of markets and the mounting fragility of global and local food supply.

Ever since Independence in 1957, the Malaysian government has poured resources into modernizing and supporting the national rice industry. Its twin goals have been to grow enough rice to make the nation self-sufficient in its staple food, and to eliminate poverty among the Malay peasants who were the nation's rice growers, and who constituted one of the poorest groups in Malaysian society.

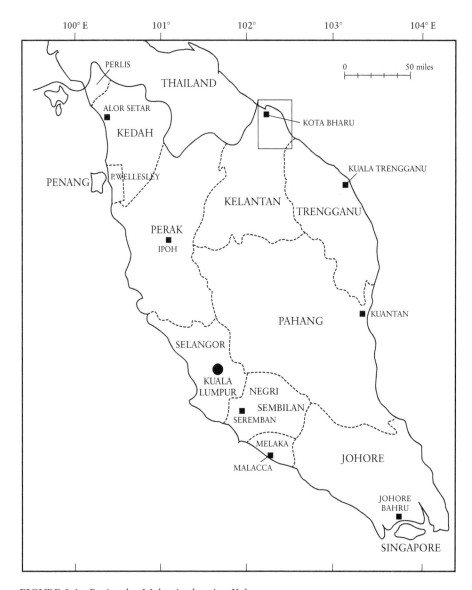

FIGURE 8.1: Peninsular Malaysia showing Kelantan.

Yet despite actively taking up the technological and economic opportunities on
offer, the peasant beneficiaries of these government policies have never emerged
from poverty, nor has the predominant form of padi farming switched from tiny
smallholdings to more productive or profitable units of management. Forty years
after first adopting GR technologies, it costs twice as much to produce a tonne
of rice in Malaysia as it does to import it; yet padi farmers' profit margins are

tiny and as a social group they still represent troubling 'pockets of poverty' in Malaysia's largely prosperous, middle-income society (*Ninth Malaysia Plan*: 89; Hill 2013: 251).

It might seem paradoxical that the Malaysian government, whose succession of detailed and minutely managed Five Year Plans all include lavish investment in the rice industry, has spent so much money and effort merely to preserve an impoverished peasantry. How should we explain this striking case of unequal development? It is clearly not the result of neglect. Rather, I argue, it stems from deep-rooted assumptions about the significance of rice, both as crop and food, in the constitution of post-Independence Malaysian identity. It reflects a very Malaysian social contract, an unshakeable determination by the post-Independence government that Malaysian citizens should eat rice grown in Malaysia. The state thus undertook to feed its rice farmers so that they, in return, could shoulder the burden of feeding the nation.

In 1976–7 I spent a year in a Kelantan village, Bunut Susu, studying rice farming and the impact of newly introduced GR technology. I returned briefly in 1981 and 1982, but stopped keeping up systematically with Malaysian affairs in the mid-1980s and did not visit Kelantan again. When I began work on this chapter in 2013, however, I found that the challenges of rice farming had been an enduring national obsession through the whole period. I thus had no difficulty in amassing a profusion of newspaper and research articles and official reports on the state of rice farming in Malaysia and in Kelantan through the intervening years and up to the present. Though by no means consistent or comparable in what they document or how they measure it, these sources unequivocally confirm that through five decades of spectacular national growth and transformation, with a continual flow of resources devoted to modernizing Malaysia's rice industry, padi farming has remained a peasant activity, barely profitable and exclusively Malay.

In the following section, *Getting by in Kelantan* I set the scene, showing how everyday life was organized around and through rice in the village where I did fieldwork before the introduction of GR technologies. In *Rice as Self* I describe how exchanges and sharing of rice nourished closeness and reciprocity in Malay village life, and show how these values of closeness and reciprocity were mobilized by the state to justify costly interventions in the development of peasant rice farming as a way to build national unity. In *Kelantan's Long Green Revolution* I show how the padi farming peasantry has been kept afloat and in place through forty years of 'development' by a sequence of government interventions and technological and managerial improvements.

GETTING BY IN KELANTAN: PADI FARMING BEFORE THE GREEN REVOLUTION

In 1972 the government established the Kemubu Agricultural Development Authority, KADA, to bring the GR and double-cropping of rice to Kelantan. The *daerah* or district of Bunut Susu lies within the KADA irrigation unit of Lemal/Pasir

Mas (Figure 8.2). About 15 km distant from the state capital, Kota Bharu, Bunut
Susu includes several villages and hamlets and covers about 20 km². In 1976 it had
around 10,000 inhabitants (KADA 1976).² There was a metalled road to Kota Bharu
as well as a much older railway halt; since there were few cars or trucks around,
most people took their produce to market by train. The straight new road, which
I travelled daily on my Honda scooter, ran along the main irrigation canal banked up
several feet above the fields (Figure 8.3). Here I puttered past an open sluice where

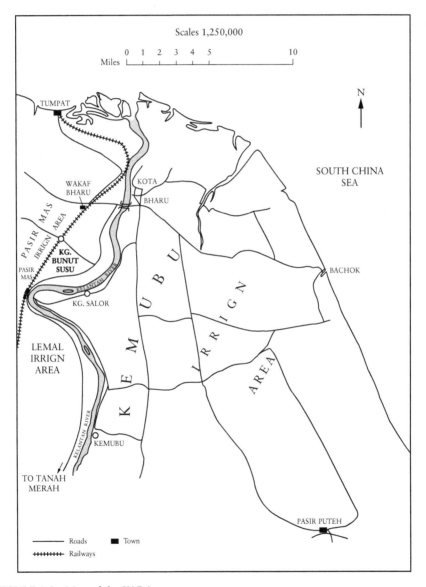

FIGURE 8.2: Map of the KADA area.

water gurgled into the fields, there past a tall green noticeboard with an irrigation schedule painted in white. Telegraph poles followed the road and kingfishers sat poised on the power lines. The padi fields furthest from the road, not having been levelled, were often too dry or too swampy for the new rice varieties. The drier fields were mostly planted with tobacco or vegetables; in the boggy low fields water buffalo grazed and wallowed luxuriously. Beyond the bright-emerald padi fields, dark-green thickets marked the fringes of the higher *kampung* land with its house plots, gardens, orchards and rubber groves.

Until 1972 the farming households of Bunut Susu used their *bendang* (dyked padi fields) to grow a single crop of transplanted rice (*padi cedong*) during the monsoon season. They planted traditional, slow-ripening varieties, chosen for yield or flavour and according to the type of soil, the level or the exposure of the field. Some dry rice was grown on upland fields, dibbled in (*tugal*), not transplanted. *Bendang* were ploughed and harrowed with water buffalo; weeding was done with hoes or by hand; for reaping a harvesting knife (*ketaman*) was used, cutting the grain one stem

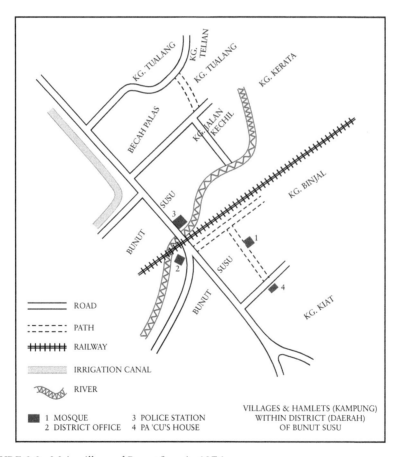

FIGURE 8.3: Main village of Bunut Susu in 1976.

at a time (Bray and Robertson 1980; Hill 2012). Men and women both worked in the fields. Most work could be managed easily by the farming couple, but extra labour was brought in for two urgent tasks: transplanting and harvesting. This was managed either through labour exchange, or by paying workers in rice (see *Rice as self* below).

There were no distinct landowning, tenant or landless classes in Bunut Susu. At some stage in their lives most people owned padi land, and at some stage most rented land out or leased it in. Although the average household size at the time was six people, padi farms were very small; they varied little in size, consisting usually of several plots, the total averaging 0.7 ha (see Table 8.1). In 1977 the three richest men in Bunut Susu each owned a total of about 4 ha, of which between 2.4 and 3.2 ha were padi land; they farmed some themselves and rented the rest out (Bray and Robertson 1980: 215). Couples with several children, some old enough to work in the fields, were always on the lookout for extra plots of land to rent; owners with more land than they could work, widows for instance, were always on the lookout for tenants. Ninety-six per cent of tenancies for rice land were sharecropping agreements, *pawah* (Hill 2013: 107). Depending on the quality of the plot and the relative needs and resources of owner and tenant, the harvest would be divided into two (*bagi dua*) or three (*bagi tiga*), and the owner would take a third, half or two-thirds of the harvested *padi* back to his or her barn.

Before KADA introduced double-cropping, households aimed to produce enough rice for their own needs but did not always succeed. If kin were not able to help them out, they had to buy rice. Since local surpluses were small, this usually meant cheap Thai rice from the village store. Malnutrition among children was quite common. According to a FELCRA (Federal Land Consolidation and Rehabilitation Authority) survey of 1975, of 23,800 Kemubu households just prior to the adoption of GR technology, 28 per cent reported having insufficient land to meet their livelihood needs. 77 per cent fell into the category of 'poor', earning under M$ 1,500 (US$535) a year, 23 per cent subsisted on less than M$600 (US$215) and only 5.4 per cent earned more than M$3,000 (US$1070). For most families this income came from several sources. Only a third grew nothing but padi: others also sold rubber or tobacco to the agents of big companies like Anglo-American Tobacco, and almost all took vegetables, *sireh*[3] (Figure 8.4), fruit or other garden produce to market. A few families declared income from renting land, and 15 per cent said they worked as farm labourers (FELCRA 1976: Tables 5, 6, 8 and 14). Padi farming took at most three or four hours a day except at transplanting and harvest; tapping rubber took only an hour or so and a child could do it; market gardening on *kampung* land was easily combined with padi cultivation, and during the off-season months *bendang* too were often used for cash crops. After the rice harvest many men sought labouring jobs, locally or as far away as Singapore, while groups of women would sometimes travel over to Kedah on the West Coast, where the monsoons came later, to earn cash as harvesters.

In other words, before KADA built its irrigation scheme and introduced double-cropping, Bunut Susu families combined padi farming with many other forms of

TABLE 8.1 Padi farming in KADA, 1976–2010*

	1976	1979	2006	2010
KADA total area	57,000 ha			65,000
Non-farmland	3,600			18,000
Total farmland	53,400			47,000
– Padi	32,000			38,000
– Rubber	7,300			12,200
– Coconut	3,700			600
– Mixed crops/orchard	27,000			14,000
Popn. size	200,000			460,000
Farming families	45,000			54,000
Av family size	approx 6			5.4
Av age of farmer	approx 50			56
Rice area planted	32,000 ha			38,000 ha
Irrigated rice area	22,000 ha			31,000 ha
Av rice-farm size	0.7 ha			0.7 ha
– Owner operator	32%			7.4%
– Owner+tenant	50%			61.7%
– Tenant only	18%			30.9%
Av rice yield	2.49 t/ha	3.65 t/ha	3.56 t/ha	3.97 t/ha
Total rice output	106,000 t	154,000 t	181,000 t	201,000 t
Av annual hh income	**M$ 1,500		M$ 13,000	M$ 19,500
Income fr. rice			M$ 8,000	M$ 14,000
Other income			M$ 5,000	M$ 5,500

* Based on KADA 1976, 1980, 2014; Siwar *et al.* 2014. I include the columns for 1979 and
2006 because they indicate the rise in yield and output in the late 1970s, the stagnation of rice
yields between the late 1970s and the mid-2000s (though total output increased with irrigation
improvements and a greater acreage of double-cropping), and the rapid increase in both yields and
income since the crisis of 2007.
** M$: the Malaysian dollar or *ringgit*, Malaysia's national currency since 1967, was and remains
roughly equivalent to US$4.

work, none of them well paid. Though farming required almost no cash inputs,
it generated few profits and farmers often failed to grow enough food for their
needs. With little formal education, scarcity of land and no local industries to offer
alternative employment, marginal or desperate families had to leave. Large numbers
migrated to factories in other states; others signed up with FELDA, the Federal Land
Development Authority, which offered poor households a new life as shareholder-
workers in oil-palm plantations deep in the hills (Robertson 1984). In just one

FIGURE 8.4: Threading sireh leaves for market. (Photograph by author)

parish of Bunut Susu, I was told in 1976, thirty families had recently taken up
FELDA tenancies: this was one of the main outlets through which land came on
the market at the time. But there were also opportunities for upward mobility: with
improvements in school access and a steady expansion in public administration
jobs for Malays under the New Economic Policy (NEP) (see *Kelantan's Long
Green Revolution* below), some younger people got jobs as teachers or government
employees, enviable permanent positions where they 'ate a salary' (*makan gaji*),

enabling them to help their parents back in the *kampung*. By 1977 couples in Bunut Susu confided with a mixture of pride and apprehension that their children were unlikely to be content with the muddy occupation of farming (Bray and Robertson 1980: 217; Fujimoto 2004).

The introduction of GR technologies had an immediate impact on the rice-farming life in Bunut Susu. But before proceeding to the twists and turns of national padi-farming policies and their impact in Kelantan, I address the specific symbolic and emotional importance of rice in Malay, and in Malaysian, society.

RICE AS SELF IN MALAYSIA: FEEDING, SHARING AND RECIPROCITY

In her study of Malay housekeeping, conducted in a fishing village on the Kelantan coast during 1939–40 and 1963, Rosemary Firth noted that the value set on rice far surpassed its importance as the indispensable daily staple: exchanges of rice circulated like blood through the body, not only between close kin but also between neighbours and more distant relatives, nourishing and fortifying as they flowed (Firth 1966: 58–71).[4]

That food nourishes not only the bodies of the individuals who consume it, but also the social relations that make them who they are, is a central premise of the anthropology of food. In her landmark study of food, substance and the processual nature of kinship in Langkawi, an island off the West Coast of Malaysia, Carsten shows that for village Malays feeding (understood as both the giving and taking of food or nourishment) was a 'vital component in the long process of becoming a person and participating fully in social relations' (1995: 223). 'Food', Carsten continues, 'creates both persons in a physical sense and the substance, blood, by which they are related.' Children are nourished in the womb by their mother's blood, and after birth by the milk from her breast, formed from her blood. Blood is created in the body from food, and the primary food, the substance of any real meal, is cooked rice, *nasi*. '*Darah, daging mari pada nasi*, "Blood, flesh come from cooked rice," people say' (1995: 228), and the sharing of meals of rice builds relatedness between all those living around one hearth, just as drinking milk from the same woman's breast makes infants into siblings.

In Bunut Susu too, before the advent of KADA, rice pulsed through village life, nourishing social bonds and a sense of community. Sometimes the rice was cooked (*nasi*), equally often it was still in the husk (*padi*), or milled but raw (*beras*). Guests at weddings or circumcisions brought *beras* for their hosts to cook and serve as *nasi* at the communal feast. Friends who helped with tasks like rebuilding a house were given *padi* or *beras*; giving cash would have denied the closeness and permanence of the relationship. Two forms of exchange were involved in transplanting and harvesting, the times of peak labour demand when extra hands were needed. The first was *berderau*, where groups of families exchanged equal quantities of work on each others' fields. The second was *pinjaman*, where the farmer provided a midday meal of *nasi* and curry to kin or neighbours who turned out to help. Although most seasonal labour needs were met through exchange, there were also opportunities for the landless, who could turn up to help at harvest and were paid one bundle of *padi* for every twenty they reaped.

One could think of these *kampung* transfers of rice at once as a form of currency for payment, a celebration of people working together and a nourishing of long-term relations, a mutual feeding that built solidarities and redistributed resources. The redistributive element was especially clear in the arrangements for access to padi land. While *kampung* land was always rented for cash, padi tenancies were all sharecropping agreements: the rent was transferred at harvest time, dividing up the bundles of rice between landlord and tenant in a ratio agreed upon at the beginning of the contract. There was scope for considerable flexibility within the terms of the initial agreement: though *bagi dua* and *tiga* restricted the actual shares of the crop to two-thirds, half or a third, responsibilities for ploughing, seed-grain and other inputs were also part of the deal, which took into account the quality of the land and also the respective needs of both parties. It might seem that the scarcity of padi land would always advantage owners, but because it was rented only between households within the *kampung* and the terms were common knowledge, generosity largely prevailed. Frail elders got a bigger share from their tenants, couples with small children were charged less. Sharecropping redistributed the scarce resources of land and labour and shared the risks and benefits of unpredictable yields (Bray and Robertson 1980). The ethos was so marked that some researchers spoke of 'income-sharing' as the basic principle of *kampung* economic life (Fujimoto 1983).

Let me now turn to the rationale behind another notable form of Malaysian 'income-sharing': the reciprocal feeding of state and padi farmers through a system of development and support which has evolved, but endured, for several decades.

By 1976, when I arrived in Kelantan, Malaysia was justifiably confident of a bright future as an economically successful and politically stable nation, and it could well afford to invest large sums in a GR. Through the period of the Second Malaysia Plan (1971–5), despite a hiccup during the oil crisis of 1973–4, Malaysia maintained an enviable average growth rate of 5.9 per cent per annum, which showed no signs of flagging. The expansion of the Malaysian economy was prudently balanced across a wide range of activities, comprising urban-based sectors like the electronics assembly industry, construction and a new and ambitious finance sector, as well as natural resource extraction and plantation agriculture. Natural resources included tin-mining, timber and the oil and gas industry, much of which was reorganized into a national company, PETRONAS, in 1974. Estate-grown export crops like rubber and oil palm also added considerably to local employment and to the national coffers. By 1976 Malaysia had indisputably entered the club of modern nations.

The previous years, however, had not gone so smoothly: ethnic and geopolitical tensions threatened the new nation's survival for over a decade. At Independence in 1957, Malays numbered about 55 per cent of the population, Chinese 35 per cent and Indians 10 per cent. Occupational segregation was marked, with most businesses, large and small, owned by Chinese and almost all land and senior government and military posts in Malay hands. Most capital was still controlled by foreign companies, but the Chinese share, at around 35 per cent, was much greater than the 2 per cent in Malay hands, though poverty was widespread among urban working-class Chinese and rural Malay farmers alike. Tensions between the two communities over political control and perceived inequalities in wealth and opportunity ran high, and events kept fanning the flames.

The first prime minister of independent Malaya, Tunku Abdul Rahman, coined the term *bumiputra*, 'sons of the soil', to distinguish ethnic Malays and other indigenous groups from 'recent immigrants', that is to say, Chinese and Indians. With the First Malaysia Plan, the government began a programme of affirmative action to improve the economic position of the *bumiputra* – in effect, Malays. The plan was much resented by non-Malays and even the Malays themselves considered the programme to be ineffectual. In 1963 Malaya expanded to become Malaysia, incorporating the sparsely populated but resource-rich Borneo territories of Sabah and Sarawak, and the densely populated island city of Singapore. Malay fears of the political impact of largely Chinese Singapore joining the nation led to race riots in 1964 and to the expulsion (some say secession) of Singapore in 1965. In the elections of May 1969 the opposition polled more votes than the Malay-majority coalition. This led to further traumatic race riots and the declaration of a state of emergency. A new coalition government under Tun Abdul Razak devised a detailed national framework, the NEP, to promote national unity.

> The NEP had two prongs, namely 'poverty eradication regardless of race' and 'restructuring society to eliminate the identification of race with economic function'. The NEP was supposed to create the conditions for national unity by reducing interethnic resentment due to socioeconomic disparities. (Jomo 2004: ii)

Among the primary targets of the NEP were padi farmers, 88 per cent of whom were classified as poor in 1970 (Fujimoto 1991: 436).[5]

Since Independence the rice-farming sector had become a key focus of government policy, initially with the goal of raising output to make the nation self-sufficient in this staple food. This quest reflected prevailing geopolitical tensions.

Under British rule self-sufficiency was debated but dismissed: it was cheaper and easier to import rice from Burma to feed the mining and plantation workers who powered the economy. Padi was quite extensively grown in the northern Federated Malay States, but by farmers producing mostly for their own needs and earning income from other crops. Ways to increase local rice production were often discussed. But Malay rulers and British administrators alike doubted that rural Malays would willingly sacrifice time and income to grow more rice; schemes to modernize production with irrigation and mechanization were too costly to develop far, while attempts to coax Chinese entrepreneurs into setting up as commercial rice farmers failed. Overall it made sense for Malaya to import the bulk of its rice supplies (Kratoska 1982; Hill 2012).

Padi farming in the Federated Malay States remained essentially a subsistence activity, contributing little to the national economy or to urban food supplies. Yet it was the foundation for the livelihood of millions of rural Malays, and steps were taken to support and protect a social group viewed as both vulnerable and entitled. In

1913 the Malay Reservation Enactment came into force: designed to protect Malays against dispossession by (mostly Chinese) moneylenders, it prohibited the transfer to non-Malays of Malay Reserve Land, which included most farm land. Meanwhile the Rice Lands Enactment of 1917 prohibited, in principle if not always in practice, any alienation to other crops or uses of land suitable for padi farming (Kratoska 1982).[6] Padi farming and Malay identity thus became inseparably entwined.

By Independence, the calculus of how best to secure the national food supply had changed. Prospects for reliable rice imports looked grim. Burma was no longer a sister state within the British Empire, indeed after the 1962 coup it disappeared from the map of international trade. 1962–6 saw an undeclared war (*Konfrontasi*) with Indonesia, which objected to the Borneo territories of Sabah and Sarawak joining Malaysia. Indochina was plunged in war, and Asian as well as Western leaders feared that Thailand and Indonesia would soon succumb to the Communist menace. It was clear that the new nation must try to feed itself. The government declared a goal of 100 per cent self-sufficiency in rice, and went all out for a programme to boost production through irrigation, extension of the padi area, and investment in fertilizers. A Guaranteed Minimum Price (GMP) policy, first introduced in 1949, was raised to encourage farmers to put more rice on the market (Fujimoto 1991: 431–2). In 1960 the nation produced 54 per cent of its rice needs; by 1970 this had risen to 80 per cent self-sufficiency level (SSL). Total output, cultivated area and average yield all increased by about half during this decade, yet rural poverty actually increased, although 40 per cent of all the considerable sums invested in national development were spent on agriculture (Peacock 1981: 641; Siwar et al. 2013: 713; Vengedasalam, Harris and MacAulay 2011: Table 1, 2).

Padi farming was by now identified in the national mind as a quintessentially Malay occupation. In the peninsular states the proportion of Malay farmers was (and remains) over 90 per cent (Alam et al. 2010: 252).[7] Furthermore, 'with independence and democracy came the realization that the rice-growing peasantry represented a substantial power bloc for whom it was both politically and economically desirable to do something' (Hill 2013: 111). At that point two-thirds of votes were generated in the rural sector, and padi farmers were a fifth of the national labour force (Peacock 1981: 641, 643). The NEP aimed to eradicate poverty and to promote national unity and strength. How better to do this than by raising the incomes of the farmers, supporting and feeding them in return for the onerous responsibility of growing rice to feed the nation? As Fujimoto notes, the NEP marked a significant shift in state policy, from increasing rice production to increasing the income of padi farmers (1991: 432).

In *kampung* reciprocity, and notably in sharecropping arrangements, land, labour and rice were exchanged in ways that helped all families to eat, work and survive. In NEP reciprocity, the padi farmers contributed their land and labour, while the state (on behalf of the nation) made massive investment in infrastructure, credit, subsidies and technical know-how. This exchange was intended to assure not simply the well-being but the very survival, as modernization progressed, of an economically marginal yet symbolically potent group. The poor Malay padi farmers, voters all, were constituted as the quintessential subjects of the NEP *bumiputra* policy of redistributing wealth and capital assets to Malays from the wealthy, largely non-Malay, business and industrial sectors. This transfer was to be effected by the government, in the name of securing supplies of the food that all Malaysians, Indians, Chinese and Malays alike, shared as their staple.

The long-term official investment in supporting Malay padi farmers was declared by the government, and interpreted by social scientists, as both pro-*bumiputra* and a tool for fostering national unity and building solidarity across ethnic and urban–rural boundaries. Government and media continually stressed the precarity of national rice supplies, fretting over SSLs achieved and targeted, the risk of depending on imports and the challenges of increasing national output. This discourse has undoubtedly fostered a sense of shared risk among the general public, helping them to accept the necessity for considerable investments of taxpayers' money. Translated into the symbolic logic of the *kampung*, if all Malaysian citizens, whatever their ethnicity, partake of the *nasi* provided by *bumiputra* farmers, this sharing of nourishment, and the exchange of resources that its production entails, builds visceral solidarities between individuals and groups whose interests and identities would naturally differ, diverge or even conflict.

Unlike in Japan – and not surprisingly given the long dependence of Malaysia's urban population on rice imports – government insistence that Malaysians should eat rice grown in Malaysia did not translate into similar beliefs about 'rice as self' to those expressed in Japan, where it is held that native rice varieties are uniquely suited not only to preparing Japanese cuisine but to nourishing Japanese bodies and spirits. Nevertheless, the NEP policy was not simply a pragmatic move to protect marginal Malays while securing supplies of basic food, but a biological nation-building project.

Though quantity was an important element in the calculus of state interventions in the padi sector, quality, in the sense of the preservation of a valued landscape, was an overriding consideration. As 'the basis of culture and tradition of the Malays' (*National Agricultural Plan 3*, quoted in Daño and Samonte 2003: 190), tiny padi farms are treated as the anchor of 'traditional' *kampung* landscapes and all that they represent emotionally and ethically as well as politically. For forty years economists, agronomists and officials have all agreed that tiny padi farms are inherently inefficient. Yet rather than allowing the scale economies of GR technologies to follow their natural course, replacing peasant holdings with large farms, the Malaysian government has concocted a continuously evolving portfolio of inputs, resources and interventions tailored to keep smallholdings afloat and to retain padi farmers on the land. As Malaysia has surged ahead into high-tech modernity and prosperity, Malay padi farming appears increasingly anachronistic. Yet the sector continues to support the same number of peasant farmers as it did forty years ago. Increases in rice yields and total output have at least matched population growth, and although they are still one of the poorest groups in Malaysia, padi farmers can still get by. Meanwhile the cost of the state intervention that enables them to subsist is no longer a significant share of GNP but a mere drop in the ocean of the booming national economy, a 'sacrifice' all the more necessary and acceptable as threats of climate change sharpen the sense of national vulnerability (Khor 2008; Alam et al. 2010).

KELANTAN'S LONG GREEN REVOLUTION

Kelantan had the largest area of established padi lands of any Malaysian state after Kedah; it was also the most rural of any of the peninsular states, and had the highest poverty levels. It is not surprising, then, that Kelantan was high on the priority list for GR-based development, organized around the Kemubu Irrigation Scheme. There had been development initiatives in Kelantan before, but nothing approached the institutional density or lavish financing of the programme that began under the NEP.

In 1969–70 the Ministry of Agriculture established a dense network of new institutions to develop and protect Malay padi farming (Daño and Samonte 2003: 198–206; Hill 2013: 263–4). These included MARDI (Malaysia Agricultural Research and Development Institute), BMP (Agricultural Bank of Malaysia) and LNP (later BERNAS, the National Rice and Padi Institute). MARDI provided the science, BMP offered credit to smallholders through Farmers' Associations. BERNAS took over control of the national rice market, providing subsidies and financial incentives to encourage padi farmers to increase their crops and the amount they sold; furthermore, it was mandated to ensure fair and stable prices both for farmers and for consumers. In the name of price stabilization and secure food supply, BERNAS therefore disbursed huge sums to support minimum farm-gate prices for padi farmers and maximum retail prices for milled rice. The organization displaced almost all private enterprise in the milling and storage industry, and in the rice trade. BERNAS also decided upon levels of SSL and regulated imports and exports of padi.

Although levels of support have fluctuated since the 1970s, all the basic programmes are still in place today, as are the institutions that provide them. With increasing pressure to reduce state ownership and support coming from multilateral organizations like WTO and AFTA (ASEAN Free Trade Association), organizations from the oil company PETRONAS to BERNAS have been notionally privatized in recent years. BERNAS went private in 1996, but as Daño and Samonte note, its links to the ruling party remain as strong as ever (2003: 301). Table 8.2 gives an idea of some of the incentives provided to small padi farmers over the years.

The lynchpin of GR development in padi farming, however, was irrigation. With a reliable water supply and using hybrid varieties bred for high yields, quick ripening, and positive response to chemical fertilizers, farmers could double-crop padi, using their *bendang* for a crop in the off season as well as the traditional crop transplanted just after the monsoon rains. Although padi farmers throughout Malaysia were being encouraged to improve output by using modern inputs, in the 1970s the focal points for full GR innovation were the two Integrated Agricultural Development Authorities (MADA in Kedah, KADA in Kelantan), organized around irrigation schemes built at great cost in two of the largest traditional heartlands of Malay padi farming.

TABLE 8.2 Direct subsidies and incentive payments in rice production*

	1976	mid-1980s	2009
Price subsidy	None; GMP of **M$ 248/t	M$168/t + M$ 530 GMP	M$248/t
Fertiliser subsidy	Farmer pays M$10/20 kg sack	100% free up to M$200/ha for small farms	240 kg/ha NPK, 80 kg/ha organic
Yield increase incentive	No	No	M$650/t over yield of base year
Padi production incentive	No	Yes	Tractor M$100/ha extra fertiliser M$140/ha
Additional fertiliser	No	No	NPK 150kg/ha
Pesticide/herbicide subsidy	Yes	Yes	M$200/ha
Tractor subsidy	Yes	Yes	M$100/ha

* Based on KADA 1980, 2014; Fujimoto 1991, 2004; Hill 2013: 264, Table 12.1.

When I arrived in Bunut Susu in 1976 the irrigation canals had just recently been extended as far as the *daerah*, and KADA extension officers were working with the local Farmers' Associations (FAs) to encourage everyone to learn to farm the new way, and to take advantage of the subsidized seeds, fertilizers and tractor hire on offer, as well as other forms of credit.[8] Since it cost only a token M$5 per share to join the FA every household belonged to it[9]; a number of FA members worked actively with KADA staff on schemes for improving rubber, peanut or banana cultivation as well as padi. Since KADA staff were mostly locals, discussions with farmers – some on KADA or FA premises, others at the living-room table or the coffee-stall in the village centre – were frequent, informal and definitely two-way.

All but one or two of the local farming households had adopted the new GR technologies with enthusiasm, albeit with a critical eye. Indeed, refusing to participate was not an option for anybody whose fields lay within the irrigated area (though at the borders many fields were still not irrigated). Once the pumps were switched on ten kilometres away in Lemal, every field in the unit had to follow the strict schedule promptly and exactly. As I mentioned earlier, tall timetable boards stood in prominent positions in the fields, and flyers in Arabic script were distributed to remind everyone which operations had to be carried out when. The changes entailed were systemic. With only a couple of weeks between main- and off-season crop, farmers had no time for ploughing with buffaloes and so had to switch to hiring tractors. Nor was there time to reap with a knife: everybody switched to sickles. Since everyone had to transplant and reap at the same time, the old labour exchanges became impossible and farmers had to hire labourers – but labour was now very scarce.

As part of the GR package, farmers now had to purchase seeds of the new high-yielding varieties (HYVs), along with the chemical inputs they needed to prosper. At that point most farmers still tried to keep a plot of two of the old varieties, which were tastier (*sedap*) and more resistant to pests and diseases. But these traditional rices, whose seeds were selected at harvest and passed between friends and neighbours, ripened too slowly to fit in the double-cropping schedule. Furthermore, as farm-gate prices and rice retail subsidies rose, it made sense to sell one's whole crop of padi and buy commercial milled rice to eat. By the mid-1980s Fujimoto noted that the old varieties had almost entirely disappeared (2004: 61).

In 1976 most Bunut Susu farmers were happy to be growing so much more rice, and were looking forward to a more secure and prosperous future. Double-cropping had more than their doubled annual output, allowing them to feed their families and then sell any surplus through the FA at the guaranteed farm-gate price – though this was not an obligation if private dealers offered better prices. Nevertheless, being accustomed to mixed farming and multiple sources of income, the Bunut Susu farmers were weighing the costs and benefits of focusing on double-cropped padi.

KADA policies were explicitly pro-poor and tailored to maintaining peasant-scale farming. The KADA economist, Rohaini bt Zakariah, told me: 'It is essential to recognize that the smallest and most indebted farmers are the ones whose need for subsidies, government and other services is greatest.' Though the cash costs of padi production had risen steeply, most inputs were subsidized and cheap credit was available to all FA members on the same terms, regardless of how much land or other collateral they possessed. Since all farmers had equal access to inputs, the size of farm in itself did not affect padi yields. Profits typically increased with farm size, but the scarcity of labour hampered anyone trying to set up a larger operation. The one or two ambitious folk who tried running 4 ha or even 10 ha padi farms soon gave up and invested their entrepreneurial energies elsewhere (Fujimoto 1991: 451).[10]

Did the new hybrid rices, like the old varieties, pulse like blood through the veins of the kampung? One immediate effect of the new GR system was that agricultural labour exchange became impossible; furthermore rice no longer circulated as a quasi-currency in lieu of cash payments. Yet the reciprocities of sharecropping did persist for several years. The shares were made still more flexible: in addition to *bagi dua* and *tiga*, a new division into five parts, *bagi lima*, allowed landlord and tenant to divide 60:40 or 40:60, along with a spectrum of agreements about who would bear the costs for which inputs, from tractor ploughing to hiring labour for transplanting or paying for pesticides. By the mid-1980s, however, fixed, cash rents had become the norm (Fujimoto 1996: 285). Either farmers felt more confident in assessing their resources, or now that most padi was sold to the FA, not taken home to the household granary, preliminary exchanges of grain between tenant and landlord were simply inconvenient and had lost all their earlier meaning. 'Paddy is no longer a good for exchange among the villagers, indicating the enormous extent to which the social role of rice production has been drastically modified' (Fujimoto 2004: 70).

RESOLVING CRISES

In the first few years after the introduction of GR technologies, padi yields and total output rose sharply (Table 8.1), justifying the optimism of farmers and of KADA staff. The initial impact was indeed revolutionary: it doubled the quantity of rice produced each year, rebuilt the rural landscape around an irrigation system, and thoroughly commercialized a rural economy where hitherto reciprocity had played a key role in redistributing resources, and rice had circulated much like a currency. What had *not* undergone revolutionary change, however, was the basic unit of production, the peasant padi farm. Over the next four decades the padi farming sector in Kelantan, and in Malaysia generally, confronted a series of crises. In each case the government intervened, and in each case the measures taken were designed to preserve peasant farming as the foundation of the padi sector.

The first crisis, incipient in the late 1970s and full blown by the 1980s, was a crisis of unused land. The challenges of timetabling and labour shortages, added to short-ages of irrigation water, soon made themselves felt, and padi production slumped in the early 1980s. Economists and agronomists argued that the only rational and viable solution was to encourage or create large farms that would use resources more effi-ciently and clear larger profits. The government, however, sought new solutions that would preserve peasant farming while increasing the nation's food supply. In KADA as elsewhere, additional tractors and other machinery were brought in and farmers were encouraged to give up the highly labour-intensive practice of transplanting rice. Instead they were given mechanical drills for direct seeding. This technology actually reduced yields,[11] but in combination with a generous new padi production subsidy, introduced in 1991, overall padi output increased. In 1993 national output once again reached the 2.1 million tonnes first achieved in 1981, remaining at roughly this level until 2006. For the time being, a new equilibrium was achieved – the nation was producing enough rice to meet its security needs, and production incentives were sufficient to keep farmers growing padi, even though they did not make them rich.

Between 1991 and 2006 the padi sector trundled along without any notable hitches. With the technical improvements padi farmers' total incomes initially rose; they then stagnated for over a decade, yet the government felt no need to go beyond minor repairs to the system, like tinkering with subsidies and improving local-level irrigation facilities.

The next crisis, in 2007, was externally generated. From 1970 to the early 1980s Malaysian padi farmers had consistently provided 80 per cent or more of national rice needs, reaching an astonishing 92 per cent in 1980. Although Malaysia's population was growing steadily (from 11 million in 1970 to 20 million in 2010), as people became more prosperous and diets diversified annual per capita rice consumption fell, from 125 kg in 1970 to 75 kg in 2010. In 1990 the government lowered its SSL target to 65 per cent, an amount that Malaysia's padi farmers regularly surpassed by 5 per cent even though productivity had stagnated. But 2007 saw a global collapse in cereal harvests. Thailand and Vietnam, the main sources of Malaysia's rice imports, were badly affected. Rice prices in Bangkok rose 30 per cent, and there were food riots in Ho Chi Minh city (Fahmi, Abu Samah and Abdullah 2013: 178).

Even in good years only 7 per cent of the total world rice crop enters global markets, so the collapse of Thai supplies severely shook the complacency of the Malaysia government. Its immediate response was a new National Food Security Policy aimed to reduce imports from 30 per cent to 20 per cent by 2010; in 2010 the SSL target for 2015 was set at 85 per cent (Siwar et al. 2014: 713, Table 1). How was this to be achieved? Despite heavy subsidies, yields in Malaysia were lower than in most of its tropical neighbours: in 2007 yields averaged 3.5 t/ha in Malaysia compared to 4.7 t/ha in Indonesia and 4.9 t/ha in Vietnam; although Thai yields, at 2.7 t/ha, were significantly lower, so too were production costs. Experts agreed that there was little hope of fine-tuning the existing technical and social system to wring out higher surpluses. It was also evident that climate change must now be taken into account: the areas that could be reliably double-cropped were shrinking as water shortages became more frequent, while increased temperatures were starting to reduce yields (Siwar et al. 2014: 714).

The solutions proposed were of two kinds. The first called for heavy investment in plant breeding and allied research, to develop higher-yielding but hardier rices that would need less water, land, fertilizer and pesticide (Looi 2013). Like the technologies of the first GR, those of the proposed environment-friendly second GR are perfectly compatible with a continuation of smallholder farming if they are, as agronomists propose, 'supported with an extensive package and incentives development, skills development among farmers and provision of infrastructure facilities' (Siwar et al. 2014: 719).

The second strategy was to revive earlier experiments with large padi farms. But this did not mean a shift to consolidated, commercial farming. Any form of rationalization has to respect the Malay Reservation Enactment, which forbids the sale of Malay-own land to non-Malays, and the Padi Lands Enactment, which forbids the use of rice land for other purposes. The farm structures are, furthermore, carefully designed to create scale economies without dispossessing small farmers. Like the other granary areas, KADA revived and greatly expanded its hitherto languishing Padi Mini Estate (MEP) programme, whereby farmers pool their padi land into one large, well-equipped unit worked cooperatively under KADA supervision. The 9th Malaysia Plan had declared that MEPs would significantly raise yields and double farmer income from padi (2006: 3.72), but so far there are no signs of such dramatic improvement. KADA also doubled the area under 'Independence Estates', *Ladang Merdeka*, consolidated landholdings with improved irrigation, drainage, roads and other infrastructure. They include processing facilities as well as farmland, and are run like businesses. The workforce includes landowner/shareholders, but is supplemented by contract arrangements for tasks requiring special equipment. Elderly farmers who contribute land are paid rent by the collective, but no longer work in the fields. 'An "on farm development" model converts the unsystematic work practices into a work culture that emphasizes estate management which is far more advanced and possesses high productivity' (KADA 2014): the goal is to build human capital as well as improving output and farmer incomes. KADA online reports suggest that both yields and profits have risen dramatically on its *Ladang Merdeka* (KADA 2014). If sustainable, this dramatic improvement will certainly have boosted confidence among KADA officers and given many struggling padi farmers hope for a better future and incentives to join up with an estate farm.

Let us now consider how KADA farmers' incomes fared through the long GR (Table 8.3). Over the last forty years KADA padi farmers have been raised from absolute to relative poverty. As Jomo notes (2004: 5), national definitions and measures of poverty are highly political. Usually padi farmers are swallowed up into a general category of 'agricultural labour' or *bumiputra* so that the figures are far from clear. Yet undoubtedly most peninsular Malay padi farmers, including those in relatively poor Kelantan, are materially better off now than they were in 1970, when 88 per cent of them were reckoned poor. Although they still earn only less than half the average household income, over the years KADA farmers have acquired electric light and running water, TVs and motorbikes; their houses now have concrete foundations and tiled roofs, their children are properly nourished, go to school and often get good jobs. Bunut Susu is now a dormitory town for Kota Bharu where farming families live next to salary earners. The tiny prayer house is now a fine mosque and the village boasts a Technical College as well as a school.

Over the last few decades padi farmers have been guaranteed a relatively secure if modest livelihood, completely shielded from market fluctuations, though not from government decisions to adjust subsidies. Under different circumstances this dependency might have caused resentment or resistance, but in the Malaysian context padi farmers were well aware just how large a share of national resources was devoted to their support and seem therefore to have trusted the state, through

TABLE 8.3 Average household income of KADA farmers by source, 1968–2010 [from Rabu 2013, with permission]

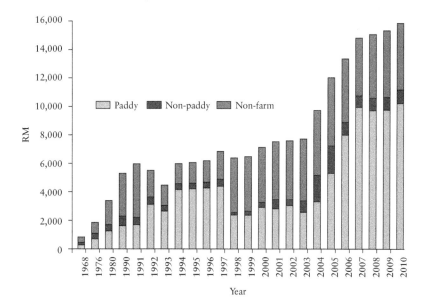

thick and thin, as being on their side. Without state support they simply could not survive: in 2009 it was estimated that 74 per cent of padi farmers' income came from government support measures (Man and Sadiya 2009: 142).

But what if the government chooses or is obliged to reduce support? Malaysia, like most of its neighbours, has so far staved off AFTA requirements to eliminate import tariffs by classifying rice as a 'highly sensitive' product (Vengedasalam et al. 2013: 2). Economist Deviga Vengedasalam and her colleagues echo the region's geopolitical and political sensibilities in assessing the value of rice not in simple economic terms but as a national good:

> Although full liberalization increases net welfare and government revenue, due to the *national interest in food security issues*, the partial liberalization of rice trade with WTO and AFTA compliance would be recommended. *Removing production based subsidies and replacing them with income support*, would not only generate greater government revenue but also reduce the taxpayers' burden and *improve the livelihood of farmers*. (2013: 15, emphases added)

This recommended switch from production subsidies to what is essentially an occupational wage follows a similar logic to that of the Mini Estates and *Ladang Merdeka* projects: the state undertakes to preserve peasant padi farmers as a social group, while reorganizing production so that they effectively become wage-workers for the collective. Throughout the Long Green Revolution the Malaysian government has never faltered in its commitment to protecting Malay padi farmers as a class, whatever the nature of the problems facing the sector. In the latest, most creative turn, although KADA farmers are being urged to remake themselves as entrepreneurs, a term implying that some will succeed while others will fail, in fact it seems that the collective reorganization of land, labour and capital resources on the new estates will continue to maintain peasant padi farmers as a status group, if no longer as a category of workers, by conferring on them the coveted status of *makan gaji*, salaried workers paid by the government.

CONCLUSION

The story of how life for rice farmers in Kelantan 'stood still' while the Malaysian nation around them surged forward as a prosperous tiger economy neatly illustrates a twofold challenge facing many nations in an era of international development programmes, free trade regulatory regimes and heightened awareness of the precarity of global food markets. Internationally, the challenge lies in justifying a policy of food security as a legitimate exception to prevailing free trade regulations and economic and scientific orthodoxies; domestically, the government has to maintain public support for costly policies supporting a sector of ostensibly 'inefficient' or 'backward' small farmers. I have applied anthropological approaches to food as a social, political and cultural nourishment to show how the Malaysian government has responded to these challenges by skilfully mobilizing local meanings of rice, creating a regime of value that constitutes a convincing alternative, or rather complement, to strictly economic calculus.

The puzzle of the reproduction of the Malaysian rice-farming peasantry pinpoints some characteristic entanglements of embodiment, sociality, economics and imaginaries as they play out in food policy in the contemporary world. Today, prompted by the global food crisis of 2008, an increasing number of national governments are choosing to pursue the goals of food security, food sovereignty and small-farmer support, although they fly in the face of free market and productivist logic. It is no longer left to transnational small-farmer alliances like Via Campesina to preach the virtues of peasant farming. National governments in countries as diverse as Bolivia, Zambia, South Korea and the People's Republic of China are protecting or promoting small-scale farming. A 2014 scientific report for the United Nations and World Bank declares that 'Business as usual is not an option!', advocating urgent support for small farmers on the grounds of environmental sustainability, social justice and long-term efficiency in maintaining food supplies (IAASTD 2014). From an anthropological perspective this optimism requires tempering: even if small farmers can produce enough to meet humanity's growing needs (Bernstein 2009), it is naive to presume that models or values, let alone tastes or qualities, can cross frontiers unchanged (Dunn 2005). Nevertheless, there are important resources that can be mobilized here, both for better understanding and for social action. Food systems and food practices are both *good to think with* and *good to act with*: they illuminate the deep articulations of power and belief, and serve as a powerful moral vehicle for activists and critics operating in the world outside the academy, fusing the role of subject or consumer with that of citizen (see also Luetchford, in this volume). As practised by anthropologists today the political economy of food, with its meticulous unpacking of what constitutes 'good food' or 'ethical eating' in a specific context (Jung, Klein and Caldwell 2014), has an important role to play in furthering the project of social justice.

NOTES

1. Term taken from Patel (2012), who argues that the GR must be understood in *longue durée* terms as a succession of phases within a specific regime of accumulation, initially anti-Communist in its agenda, which both depends upon and supports high levels of state intervention.
2. In 2010 it was 15,000 (Census of 2010, quoted http://en.wikipedia.org/wiki/Pasir_Mas, accessed 11 March 2014). Bunut Susu has become a dormitory town for Kota Bharu, just a few minutes away by car; it now has its own school and clinic and the mosque has been considerably expanded.
3. Sireh was one of the most profitable garden crops in Bunut Susu. The leaves of the sireh vine (Piper betle) are an essential component of the betel quid, still a popular stimulant throughout Southeast Asia today. The sireh leaves are wrapped around slivers of areca nut and smeared with lime to form the quid. In the 1970s smoking was starting to rival betel as a routine stimulant in Kelantan. But women mostly preferred betel; furthermore, cigarettes lacked the cultural significance of betel, which played an important role in weddings and other rituals, and was offered to guests as a sign of hospitality.

4. This was not a metaphor Firth used herself: her style, even for the time, was notably dry.
5. This compared to about 50 per cent for the population at large. See Jomo (2004) on the definitions and statistical assessments of poverty in the Malaysia Plans.
6. Both laws are still in force today (Md. Arifin 2013).
7. In Sabah and Sarawak upland rice is widely grown by other indigenous groups who, like Malays, qualify as bumiputra, but unlike Malays have been encouraged by the government to discontinue padi farming in favour of other commercial crops.
8. My own ethnographic observations in Bunut Susu, detailed in Bray and Robertson (1980) and Bray (1977, 1986), are supported, supplemented and extended into the 1990s by Fujimoto (1983, 1991, 2004), who conducted long-term research with padi farmers in Kampung Hutan Cengal, just south of Bunut Susu.
9. In 1979 roughly a sixth of the 17,400 FA members in KADA were women (KADA 1980: Table 5.1); they were likely widowed or divorced, since when a couple farmed together, as household heads, the husband typically signed up as the official member. In 2011 women were about 30 per cent of a total 39,000 members (KADA 2014). This suggests a feminization of farming, a process common throughout Asia as alternative occupations open up for men in nearby towns.
10. In the other granary regions too, despite early indications that land was becoming concentrated in the hands of a few rich farmers (e.g. Scott 1983), farm size gradually reverted to peasant scale. A 2010 study of three rice regions, MADA in Kedah, BLS in Selangor and KETARA in Terengganu put average farm size at 3.3, 2.5 and 3.1 ha respectively, with the largest farm in each case at 11.5, 14.6 and 16.2 ha (Terano, Zainalabidin and Golnaz 2013: 76).
11. Ironically, a recent study has recommended a return to transplanting as 'the key factor in increasing gross return from rice farming' (Terano, Zainalabidin and Golnaz 2013: 80).

ABBREVIATIONS

AFTA	ASEAN Free Trade Area
ASEAN	Association of Southeast Asian Nations
BERNAS	Padi Beras Nasional Berhad(National Rice and Padi Institute)
BMP	Agricultural Bank of Malaysia
FA	Farmers' Association
FELCRA	Federal Land Consolidation and Rehabilitation Authority
GMP	Guaranteed Minimum Price
GR	Green Revolution
HYV	High-Yielding Variety
KADA	Kemubu Agricultural Development Authority
MARDI	Malaysia Agricultural Research and Development Institute
MEP	Mini Estate Padi
NEP	New Economic Policy
SSL	Self-Sufficiency Level
WTO	World Trade Organization

REFERENCES

Alam, M. M., Chamhuri, S., Murad, M. W., Molla, R. I. and Toriman, M. E. (2010), 'Socioeconomic Profile of Farmer in Malaysia: Study on Integrated Agricultural Development Area in North-West Selangor', *Agricultural Economics and Rural Development*, 7(2): 249–65.

Assmann, S. (2013), 'Reassessing Food Safety, Risk and Globalization in China and Japan', *Food, Culture & Society*, 16(1): 7–19.

BERNAS (Padi Beras Nasional Berhad) (2014), www.bernas.com.my (accessed 20 March 2014).

Bernstein, H. (2009), 'V. I. Lenin and A. V. Chayanov: Looking Back, Looking Forward', *Journal of Peasant Studies*, 36(1): 55–81.

Bourdieu, P. (1979), *La distinction*, Paris: Éditions de Minuit.

Bray, F. (1977), 'A Comparative Study of Padi Cultivation in Kelantan, Malaysia', Unpublished report for KADA, the British Academy, and the Royal Society, Cambridge: East Asian History of Science Library.

Bray, F. (1986), *The Rice Economies*, Oxford: Blackwell, and Berkeley: University of California Press (second edition, 1994).

Bray, F. A. and Robertson, A. F. (1980), 'Sharecropping in Kelantan, Malaysia', in G. Dalton (ed.), *Research in Economic Anthropology* 3, 209–44, Greenwich, CT: JAI Press.

Carsten, J. (1995), 'The Substance of Kinship and the Heat of the Hearth: Feeding, Personhood, and Relatedness among Malays in Pulau Langkawi', *American Ethnologist*, 22(2): 223–41.

Cwiertka, K. J. (2006), *Japanese Cuisine*, London: Reaktion Books.

Daño, E. C. and Samonte, E. D. (2003), 'Public Sector Intervention in the Rice Industry in Malaysia', Southeast Asian Regional Initiatives for Community Empowerment (SEARICE): 185–216; published online: www.zef.de/module/register/media/2692_6MALAYSIA.pdf.

Dunn, E. C. (2005), 'Standards and Person-Making in Eastern Europe: A Tale of Two Sausages', in A. Ong and S. J. Collier (eds), *Global Assemblages*, 173–93, Oxford: Blackwell.

Fahmi, Z., Abu Samah, B. and Abdullah, H. (2013), 'Paddy Industry and Paddy Farmers' Well-Being: A Success Recipe for Agricultural Industry in Malaysia', *Asian Social Science*, 9(3): 177–81.

FELCRA (Federal Land Consolidation and Rehabilitation Authority) (1976), *Kemubu Socio-Economic Survey*, unpublished manuscript, Kuala Lumpur.

Fêo Rodrigues, I. P. B. (2008), 'From Silence to Silence: The Hidden Story of a Beef Stew in Cape Verde', *Anthropological Quarterly*, 81(2): 343–76.

Firth, R. (1966), *Housekeeping among Malay Peasants*, London: University of London, The Athlone Press.

Fujimoto, A. (1983), *Income Sharing among Malay Peasants*, Singapore: Singapore University Press.

Fujimoto, A. (1991), 'Evolution of Rice Farming under the New Economic Policy', *The Developing Economies*, 39(4): 431–54.

Fujimoto, A. (2004), 'Transformation of Rice Farming and Rural Life in a Kelantan Village', *Journal of the Rural Life Society of Japan*, 27(2): 55–74.

Goody, J. R. (1982), *Cooking, Cuisine and Class*, Cambridge: Cambridge University Press.

Grignon, C., Aymard, A. and Sabban, F. (eds) (1989), *Le temps de manger*, Paris, Éditions EHESS.

Hill, R. D. (2012) *Rice in Malaya*, 2nd edn, Singapore: NUS Press (first edition, Oxford: Oxford University Press, 1977).

Hill, R. D. (2013), *Agriculture in the Malaysian Region*, 2nd edn, Singapore: NUS Press (first edition, Budapest: Akademia Kiado, 1982).

IAASTD (International Assessment of Agricultural Knowledge, Science and Technology for Development) (2014), *Agriculture at a Crossroads*. http://www.globalagriculture. org/ (accessed 20 March 2015).

Jomo, K. S. (2004), *The New Economic Policy and Inter-Ethnic Relations in Malaysia*, Identities, Conflict and Cohesions Programme Paper Number 7, Geneva: UNRISD.

Jung, Y., Klein, J. A. and Caldwell, M. L. (eds) (2014), *Ethical Eating in the Postsocialist and Socialist World*, Berkeley: University of California Press.

KADA (Kemubu Agricultural Development Authority) (1976), *Rumusan Perangkaan-Statistical Digest (1970-1975)*, Lundang, Kota Bharu.

KADA (1980), *Rumusan Perangkaan-Statistical Digest 1979*, Lundang, Kota Bharu.

KADA (2014), *KADA (Lembaga Kemajuan Pertanian Kemubu)*.http://kada.gov.my/en (accessed 10 January 2014).

Khor, G. L. (2008), 'Food Production Strategies for Improving Household Food Security amidst Rising Food Prices: Sharing the Malaysian Experience', *International Food Research Journal*, 15(3): 249–57.

Kratoska, P. H. (1982), 'Rice Cultivation and the Ethnic Division of Labor in British Malaya', *Comparative Studies in Society and History*, 24(2): 280–314.

Looi, S.-C. (2013), 'Cost-Efficient, High-Yielding Padi Variant Now Grown in Terengganu, Perak, Pahang', *New Straits Times*, 22 August 2013, http://www.nst.com.my/latest/cost-efficient-high-yielding-padi-variant-now-grown-in-terengganu-perak-pahang-1.342351 (accessed 11 April 2014).

Lora-Wainwright, A. (ed.) (2013), *Dying for Development*, Special Issue, *China Quarterly*, 214.

McAllister, C. (2009), 'Seeing Like an Indigenous Community: The World Bank's *Agriculture for Development Report* Read from the Perspective of Postwar Rural Guatemala', *Journal of Peasant Studies*, 36(3): 645–51.

Man, N. and Sadiya, S. I. (2009), 'Off-Farm Employment Participation among Paddy Farmers in the Muda Agricultural Development Authority and Kemasin Semerak Granary Areas of Malaysia', *Asia-Pacific Development Journal*, 16(2): 141–53.

Md. Arifin, S. (2013), 'Malay Reservation Land – Unleashing a Century of Trust', *International Surveying Research Journal*, 3(2): 1–28.

Mintz, S. W. (1985), *Sweetness and Power*, New York: Viking.

Ninth Malaysia Plan 2006-2010 (2006), Putrajaya: Economic Planning Unit.

Ohnuki-Tierney, E. (1994), *Rice as Self*, Princeton, NJ: Princeton University Press.

Patel, R. (2012), 'The Long Green Revolution', *Journal of Peasant Studies*, 40(1): 1–63.

Peacock, F. (1981), 'Rural Poverty and Development in West Malaysia (1957-70)', *The Journal of Developing Areas*, 15(4): 639–54.

Rabu, M. R. and Mohd Shah, M. D. (2013), 'Food and Livelihood Security of the Malaysian Paddy Farmers', *Economic and Technology Management Review*, 8: 59–69.

Robertson, A. F. (1984), *People and the State*, Cambridge: Cambridge University Press.

Scott, J. C. (1983), 'Everyday Forms of Class Struggle between Ex-Patrons and Ex-Clients: The Green Revolution in Kedah, Malaysia', *International Political Science Review*, 4(4): 537–56.

Siwar, C., Idris, M. D. M., Yasar, M. and Morshed, G. (2014), 'Issues and Challenges Facing Rice Production and Food Security in The Granary Areas in the East Coast Economic Region (ECER), Malaysia', *Research Journal of Applied Sciences, Engineering and Technology*, 7(4): 711–22.

Terano, R., Zainalabidin, M. and Golnaz, R. (2013), 'Farm Management Analysis in Paddy Granary Areas in Enhancing On-Farm Income', *Agris on-line Papers in Economics and Informatics*, 5(1): 73–81.

Vengedasalam, D., Harris, M. and MacAulay, G. (2011), 'Malaysian Rice Trade and Government Intervention', Paper presented at the 55th Annual Conference of the Australian Agricultural and Resource Economics Society, http://ageconsearch.umn.edu/bitstream/100726/2/Vengedasalam.pdf (accessed 4 March 2014).

CHAPTER NINE

Children's Food

JENNIFER PATICO AND ERIBERTO P. LOZADA Jr

INTRODUCTION

Claude Lévi-Strauss suggested long ago that food is good to think (1963: 89). In this review of the anthropological literature on children's food, we suggest that some foods, especially those identified as children's food, are particularly good to think with in that they embody the wider conflicts, resolutions and other cultural issues faced by different societies throughout the world. Children's food illustrates wider social concerns because children themselves are pivotal in the structuring of modernity, as Sharon Stephens (1995) has illustrated, in that much of the work of parents' imagination is embodied in their children. Children's food makes children – through food's nutritive properties (or lack of), through its role in socialization and family dynamics, and due to the centrality of both food and children in political discourse and economic consumption. Issues in food safety become more socially charged when the victims are mostly children. While such symbolic, social and political issues are of central concern to anthropological studies of food in general, we will illustrate how they become more evocative and more diagnostic in the case of children's food because they involve social understandings of the past and negotiations about the future.

HOW 'CHILDREN'S FOOD' MAKES CHILDREN

While childhood as a distinct life stage developed during the dawn of the modern era in the seventeenth century (Aries 1962), food identified as primarily for children's consumption did not develop as a cultural category until the twentieth century with industrial food production and the growth of processed foods, nutritional science and most importantly home economics (Bentley 2014). Vileisis (2010) dates the rise of modern food – processed, packaged and distributed over wide spatial and social distances – to the passing of the Pure Food and Drug Act of 1906 and the birth of the FDA. Vileisis sees the rise of the industrial food system in the United States as a growing divergence of food from nature and the loss of 'kitchen literacy' – a basic understanding of where food comes from. This loss of food knowledge in the cities in turn spawned the home economics movement, where science was deployed to address wider social concerns over the proper feeding of children by urban women, which further stimulated the acceptance and consumption of manufactured food.

Helen Veit (2013) concludes that this rationalization of foodways, when linked with other progressive era ideologies such as eugenics and euthenics (the improving of living conditions that addressed the environmental effects on race) and the asceticism of food consumption with the First World War , resulted in food consumption becoming endowed with a sense of morality. In 1917, Herbert Hoover and the newly established US Food Administration put children at the heart of their campaign to manage wartime food reserves. Mothers were taught about 'calories, vitamins, and minerals so that they might scientifically raise families without wasting food needed for the war effort' (Haley 2009: 79). As will be discussed later, scientific approaches to children's food play a parallel but distinct role in other historical contexts, including the postsocialist transformations of the late twentieth and early twenty-first centuries. More generally, as we shall see, this moralizing of food, when linked to the care of children, has a profound impact on gender roles, the family and other wider social issues.

This morally charged, science-based social climate gave rise to the category of children's food in the United States. Prior to the early twentieth century, food was not specifically produced for children. Children's menus, for example, did not exist in American restaurants prior to the Volstead Act (Prohibition) in 1919. In the late nineteenth century, children rarely ate in restaurants; restaurants were mostly places for wealthier adults to entertain themselves. In fact, social activists like Jane Addams specifically charged that restaurants were corrupting places for children, and discouraged taking children out to eat (Haley 2009: 73). When children did eat out (wealthy families who indulged their children, or families who ate at restaurants run by immigrants or black owners that welcomed children), they were simply fed smaller or simpler versions of adult meals. With the loss of adult entertainment space due to Prohibition, however, restaurants gradually turned to welcoming families to make up for the lost revenue, developing menu items that ideologically used scientific criteria spelled out by Dr. Louise Stanley, chief of the Bureau of Home Economics (Haley 2009: 86). Humes refers to this conflation of science and ideological concerns as the 'hodgepodge of medicine and morality that informed the first 20 years of children's menus' (Humes 2013; see also Bentley 2014). By the end of the Second World War and with the expansion of the middle class in America, both the restaurant business as a whole and the children's menus in particular grew tremendously as Americans ate out more regularly.

The post-war discovery of the child consumer (see also Cook 2004) and the targeted marketing of food to children in the media resulted in more products identified as 'children's foods' (colloquially labelled since the 1970s as 'junk foods'). Differential value is given to children's and adults' foods; 'value' can be understood here both in terms of the qualitative characteristics attributed to particular food items and in terms of assessments of their relative aesthetic or nutritive worth (Graeber 2001; Batada and Borzekowski 2008). These evaluations illuminate how children themselves are positioned and qualified vis-à-vis adults in specific cultural and historical settings. For example, James (1998) observes that 'kets', cheap mass-produced candies for children in Britain, are defined by adults as junky or 'rotten' (in the Lévi-Straussian sense) non-food (Lévi-Strauss 1997;

Curtis, James and Ellis 2010). The disparaging ways in which these candies, and thus children's tastes and judgements, are portrayed by adults bespeak how children are socially demarcated from adults. By the same token, in valuing these highly processed, brightly coloured, inexpensive foods, James argues, British children themselves are creating a children's world that stands in opposition to the world of adults.

Curtis, James and Ellis (2010), again working in Britain, highlight that 'children's foods' are understood to fall outside of family time and proper meals – once more foregrounding how children (and their tastes and judgements) are being defined vis-à-vis adults more generally, since foodstuffs marked by their association with children are given a special yet negatively valued place in relation to the family unit and its norms (see also James, Curtis and Ellis 2009: 5–6). In short, these studies from British and US contexts demonstrate how, in highly commercialized food cultures, 'children's foods' and 'children' define one another, reflecting one another's presumed qualities – particularly their inadequacies – vis-à-vis adult rationality and aesthetics.

Others have examined this process through direct attention to the marketing strategies through which the food industry hails children as consumers. Here we see how all sorts of food have been packaged and marketed to represent childhood fun or 'eatertainment' (Elliott 2008, 2010). But whereas Elliott frames the 'fun food' trend as troubling insofar as it contributes to the obesity crisis (see below), Cook (2009a, b) reminds us that mothers actively use commercial messages and products as they craft their mothering practice. He frames commercialism not as a foreign invader but as intimately interconnected with mothers' meaning-making practices. Notably, while advertising pitches are geared towards play and fun when directed at children, they can also centre around anxiety when directed to mothers.[1]

To add further complexity, as Namie (2011) has illustrated, foods that adults understand to be of low or negative nutritional value may simultaneously be valued for their usefulness as chits of motherly affection. Namie notes that 'junk food' symbolizes both 'good' and 'bad' mothering for US mothers; 'feeding children junk suggests you are unconcerned with your children's health, yet not allowing your child to indulge marks you as a mother who does not care about your child's happiness. Acquiescence and denial are equally problematic' (2011: 406–7). Patico (2013) observes that while many middle-class Atlanta parents worry about the sugary and fatty foods their children might consume, particularly while out of their direct care (e.g. when at school purchasing items from vending machines), they are also critical of parental over-control when it is seen to limit children's enjoyment of childhood rituals, their autonomy and their developing abilities to make their own 'good' food choices. Thus junk food indexes childhood but also mediates ambivalence about what it means to show proper care for a child, given that protecting health is often in conflict with other parenting goals and that adults wish both to move children towards adulthood and to provide space for the carefree pleasures they associate with childhood.

Looking beyond Euro-American settings, ethnographers link commercialism and its attendant anxieties more closely with local socio-economic developments, particularly processes of modernization and rapid commoditization. Jing (2000a, b), for example, describes how under the one-child policy, China's singleton children have become a target of intensive commercial messages. Under post-Mao commercialism, children's food is shaped by multinational corporations such as Heinz, and advertisements position western products as superior to Chinese ones through their use of science. In the Chinese context, these messages compete and collude with state messages that frame child-feeding as an element of 'superior childrearing', aimed at increasing the 'population quality' of China (see also Chee 2000; Gillette 2000). 'Modern science is characterized as an ultimate yardstick of what is good for the family while the state casts itself in the double image of compassionate proponent of both modern science and children's welfare' (Jing 2000a: 146).

In other postsocialist contexts, foods are similarly linked with reconceptualizations of childhood, teenagehood and individual success. Dunn (2004) examines how 'youth' are (re)constructed as a category in postsocialist Poland, in part through marketing of a special fruit drink that is supposed to be both appropriate for and desirable to youth. The new beverage indexes the kind of person wanted for postsocialist capitalism: flexible, active and choosy – the antithesis of (what is now understood as) the stodgy socialist consumer. Here, as in the Chinese studies, we see how ethnographies focused on particular food products, especially branded foods, can illuminate the complex ways in which age categories and desirable personal qualities are reconstructed and propagated in the context of major political economic transformations. State and corporate agendas intersect, working both to raise and to address adults' anxieties about the future and about their children's success in a swiftly changing economic and cultural landscape.

HOW FOOD DEFINES FAMILIES AND PARENTHOOD

Anthropologists have long been interested in the social and symbolic properties of food: the ways that food works as a medium of social and cognitive organization (Lévi-Strauss 1997; Douglas 1966). In particular, they have recognized that food defines social identities, categories and relationships. For example, Mintz argues that cross-culturally, food, because it is ingested, tends to carry a strong moral charge as it is substantiated or incarnated in the person one becomes; food, moreover, 'is a basis for linking the world of things to the world of ideas through one's acts, and thus also a basis for relating oneself to the rest of the world' (1996: 70). Punch, McIntosh and Emond affirm that food must be seen not only as sustenance but as symbolic – 'as something that can come to stand for thoughts, feelings, and relationships' (2010: 227).

More particularly, many recent and classic works recognize that food makes kinship. For example, anthropological scholarship based in Melanesia has observed how food production and exchange are intimate social processes that create the 'substance' of a person, such that a person's social being is intermingled with the foods they produce, share and consume. Food distribution and feeding result in social ties and, in these societies, are a primary means through which close kinship and other forms of social alliance are created and maintained (Barlow 2010; Meigs 1997; Munn 1986; see also Carsten 1995; Schieffelin 1990). Most of the recent scholarship in the ethnography of children and food, by contrast, is based in industrialized and urban settings and tends to focus on the management of food in nuclear households, where individualistic food preferences are emphasized (even as commensality is valued as a sign of the integrity of the family unit). These studies – which cross the disciplines of anthropology, sociology and geography – nonetheless mirror classic anthropological approaches to food, sociality and kinship insofar as they ask how the family meal works to create the family itself, in both social and symbolic terms.

James, Curtis and Ellis (2009), for example, highlight that in Britain, a 'proper meal' is considered to be characteristic of a 'proper family'. In other words, the very existence of the family as a unit is to some degree dependent on the food practices that are understood to define it. Wilk (2010) emphasizes the ideological weight of the nuclear family meal, which is seen in the United States as being under threat but also tends to be naturalized as a seemingly timeless aspect of how family life has and must be organized – notwithstanding the fact that cross-cultural examples show other configurations for how commensality and kinship can interrelate. Fear of losing the family meal (and by extension, the integrity of the family) is not limited to United States: Hungarians hold similar concerns, which are linked with their experiences of social and economic upheaval in the wake of postsocialist capitalist transition (Haukenes 2007). These studies point to how family food practices carry ideological weight in the face of broader economic, social and political uncertainties, potentially representing stability, normalcy and the cohesion of the social fabric in the face of threats to the same.

'Family' is made not only through commensality, but also in mundane practices of provisioning: Miller (1998) emphasizes that shopping (particularly grocery shopping) is a key means through which Londoners (particularly mothers) create a sense of relatedness. For Miller, shopping is a ritual through which a mother enacts love and comes to know her relationship with those in her care. Coming at the same question from a different angle, Bell-Kaplan (2000) highlights that middle-school children in a middle-class American community view their adult caretakers through the lens of the foods they provide, such that their perceptions of their mothers' 'goodness' are informed and expressed through family food practices. Likewise, Bell-Kaplan (ibid.) observes, growing children gain competence in providing care through the act of feeding their families.

In short, food has been recognized as a material practice that is central to family life, where food consumption and socializing around food are the means through which the abstract reality of the family is made concrete for the individuals who are part of it. The works discussed above also highlight how meals work as potent representations of family life, such that social actors define and judge parents and families according to the presence or absence of meals considered normative. Further, recent ethnographic research by anthropologists and sociologists focuses on how the rules and relationships that structure family life are constructed from day to day through food practices in the home.

For example, a number of studies examine how child-feeding relates to normative motherhood. Two main points are made in these discussions: that food practices, especially child-feeding, define motherhood in an intense way; and that in the process, discourses and practices surrounding children's food operate to reproduce gender inequalities. In one of the most famous examples, DeVault (1991) looks at how, in their work as wives and mothers, 'women quite literally produce family life from day to day, through their joint activities with others' (DeVault 1991: 13). DeVault examines family-feeding in the United States as a form of care work, asking how women's felt and practised responsibility for it ends up naturalizing gender roles, in the process obscuring class-specific challenges and differences.[2] Szabo (2011) takes a particularly cautionary perspective on North American women's involvement in time-intensive food preparation, noting that recent, seemingly progressive calls for families to 're-engage food' (to cook from scratch, to grow one's own food, to buy from local producers and so on), though well intended, involve labour that falls disproportionately on mothers and which would require changes to the structure of labour in the United States to become practicable.

Two anthropologists of Japan have highlighted how mothers' food-related labour does not only locate them within the home but also positions them vis-à-vis more public worlds and institutions. These works point to ways in which their responsibility for feeding children can be both a source of personal and aesthetic satisfaction for mothers and a constraint on their time and self-imaginations. Allison (1991) shows this through an ethnographic analysis of the bento boxes (*obentō*) Japanese mothers sent to school with their preschoolers in the 1980s. Students were expected to finish their lunches and responsibility for this lay with the mothers, who bore the onus of creating meals that were visually appealing as well as tasty. Using Althusser's terminology, Allison describes the bento box as an 'ideological state apparatus' that disciplined not only children but also mothers into the roles they were expected to play in Japanese society and its economy; for while many women took pleasure in the aesthetic aspects of this work, Allison argues, its time-consuming nature served to discourage women from entering or re-entering the work force while their children were young.

In a more recent account, Seddon (2011) examines contemporary Japanese women's bento blogs. Bloggers not only express themselves through the bentos they create, but also, Seddon argues, make a public claim for the import of this work of familial care. In this way, we can consider not only how the work of providing children's food cements normative gender identities and disciplines women and children into state-sanctioned social and economic roles, but also how new communication technologies provide media through which women experience and articulate the social and political significance of children's food (and their own).

Finally, it is worth noting that the connection between normative gender roles and child-feeding is not limited to heterosexual families. Carrington (2013) demonstrates that food constitutes family in lesbian and gay families in the United States in a way similar to what DeVault describes for heterosexual families. Carrington draws attention to how these couples attempt to create a sense of egalitarianism in their descriptions of how cooking and shopping labour is carried out in their households, sometimes minimizing the amount of labour that actually goes into these tasks in order to help family members maintain desirable gender roles and the appearance of labour parity. The 'link of feeding with the production of womanly status [even when men perform it] persists and presents dilemmas for lesbigay families' (Carrington 2013: 200).

CHILD SOCIALIZATION AND POWER

Other scholarship looks beyond the question of women's work and the gendering of food provisioning to focus on the more immediate interpersonal relationships and hierarchies that can be revealed through close analysis of transcriptions of mealtime conversation. These works often attend, in particular, to how child socialization is achieved through familial interactions around food. Some especially notable contributions draw upon research conducted at the UCLA Center for the Everyday Lives of Families (CELF) (e.g. Ochs and Fasulo 1996; Paugh and Izquierdo 2009; Ochs and Shohet 2006; Kremer-Sadlik and Paugh 2007). These analyses primarily draw upon video recordings of self-identified middle-class families in Los Angeles, California; each family's household interactions were captured for a period of one week, and the anthropologists who worked on the project often focus in on close details of mealtime interaction using linguistic anthropological methods.

Ochs and Fasulo (1996), for example, offer a comparison of US and Italian mealtime socialization, illustrating how parents in the two settings socialized different attitudes towards food as well as shaping different familial relationships. In the United States, parents socialized children into the sense that they are expected not to like many things; there was an ongoing power struggle between parents and children, where parents were generally trying to get children to eat things they did not like. Here nutrition was emphasized as the primary value of food, and children were marked off clearly from adults both in their putative tastes and in their social positioning at mealtime. In Italy, by contrast, socialization focused on development of personal taste and a sense of affection towards foods, with pleasure emphasized above other aspects of eating; parents' assumption was that developing a child's taste in food was a matter of developing personality. Ochs and Fasulo thus link mealtime interaction not only with taste in food, but also with basic cultural socialization and models of personhood (see also Ochs and Shohet 2006; James, Curtis and Ellis 2009).

Related studies home in on conflicts and power struggles in the family that are revealed through family mealtimes. Paugh and Izquierdo (2009) analyse food interactions in dual earner middle-class households in Los Angeles, with a focus on the politics of parent–child negotiations such as bargaining for replacement foods, setting limits on food consumption and other resolutions of children's desires. In this manner, even as parents seek control in their mealtime interactions with children, they use food choices to socialize individualism, such that they express ambivalence about the process and outcomes of child-feeding and about their own authority versus the autonomy of their children (see also Patico 2013).

Similarly, drawing on interviews with mothers in the United States, Cook (2009b: 323) examines how they frame children's desires and demands as interfering with good nutrition, such that 'grappling with children's subjectivities and agency' involves significant 'emotional, physical and semantic labor' (2009b: 323). Backett-Milburn et al. (2010) show how these dynamics can vary by class: Scottish working-class parents are more resigned to the inevitability of their teens eating the things they want; food choices rank lower in these parents' hierarchy of worries than they do in middle-class households, where teens are more subject to active regulation of eating by parents. For middle-class parents, overseeing their children's food intake is part of fashioning a middle-class adult (2010: 312; see also Wills et al. 2009). Either way, food is shown here as one medium through which the general socialization of children – including their relative independence from or subjection to parents, their moral guidance and their models of social acceptability – is negotiated. Moreover, examination of these practices provides a window onto the concrete, material and interactive means through which class sensibilities are socialized and enacted in family life.

Other studies focus on matters of discipline, resistance and subjectivity, with special attention to children as potentially powerful social agents. Grieshaber (1997: 653) espouses an explicitly Foucauldian approach in her study of Australian families: specific aspects of household organization – 'power/knowledge relationships' and 'techniques of normalization' – act to create docile subjects of both parents and children (1997: 652, 665). Grieshaber considers how children (and adults) are both subjects and objects of discourses, and she points to the ways in which children resist adult-set rules, to some extent creating themselves as subjects with authority within the family. Ochs and Shohet likewise examine child resistance as it was evidenced in their transcriptions of family mealtime conversations in the United States, Italy and elsewhere, observing that 'because food is saturated with emotional meanings, children across many of the world's communities use it as a medium of resistance, including habitually refusing food as an extreme form of social control' (2006: 47).[3]

While many of the studies mentioned above rely on passive observation of family mealtime interactions, other researchers engage more directly with children as research subjects. For example, Bell-Kaplan (2000) interviews and conducts focus groups with American middle-schoolers to gain understanding of their perceptions of the adequacy of the care provided by their mothers, specifically as it is represented through food. In a usefully meta-methodological move, Sobo and Rock (2001) examine the impact of the presence of a guardian on responses from children about food recall. Gillette (2000) learns about an eleven year old's spending and eating practices by asking him to complete a food journal. Chee (2000) takes up food as a means of looking at family relations and childhood experiences in Beijing under the one-child policy, drawing upon interviews with children eight to eleven years old and their parents. This method allows Chee to investigate not only familial but also key peer relationships pertinent to food choices: trendy foods constitute signs of prestige and wealth and are pivotal in practices of peer competition, having a clear impact on social inclusion and exclusion.

A few studies attend to material culture and uses of space in connection with food: Curtis, James and Ellis (2010) notice that certain foods are marked off and associated with different roles – for example, foods that are kept for adults and away from kids and stored on special, separate shelves. 'These micro-geographies are therefore both constitutive of the distinction between children's and adults' foods and eating practices and of the different statuses of child and adult within the family' (2010: 295). In other words, foods are linked with social roles and identities through divisions and demarcations of space. In connection with the CELF project mentioned above, Ochs and Beck (2013) present visual evidence of household consumer practices, with special attention to the stockpiling of food that often happens in Los Angeles households (as well as the prominence of child-centred material objects, such as toys, and images in these households) (see also Arnold et al. 2012).

THE POLITICS OF CHILDHOOD OBESITY

In the last ten years, children's food has become a worldwide focus for political discourse because of the childhood obesity crisis. Worldwide, the World Health Organization (WHO) reports that 'childhood obesity is one of the most serious public health challenges of the 21st century' (WHO 2014), with over 42 million children under the age of five (35 million of these in developing countries) defined as obese. Simultaneously, children are suffering from being stunted (162 million) or underweight (99 million) (UNICEF 2014), though unlike obesity, these trends are globally declining. In the United States, according to the Center for Disease Control and Prevention, obesity has more than doubled in children and quadrupled in adolescents, resulting in more than one-third of children and adolescents who are overweight or obese (CDC 2014). Children with obesity face both immediate and long-term health risks, including risk of cardiovascular diseases, type 2 diabetes and different types of cancers, and are more likely to be obese as adults. This epidemic of childhood obesity is taking place in both developed and under-developed nations and in both cities and countryside, resulting from the acceleration of a number of trends in children's foodways.

First, marketing campaigns using radio, television and now digital media have heightened their efficacy in targeting children with advertising for calorie-dense, low-nutrient foods. For example, in the United States, 'more than 98% of the television food ads seen by children and 89% of those seen by adolescents are for products high in fat, sugar, and/or sodium' (Harris et al. 2009: 213). With greater capacity to reach target audiences through specific channels (and supplemented by digital media) that cater to children (Story et al. 2008), children's food companies have integrated marketing communications to build relationships between children and specific brands that evoke positive emotional experiences, even when children are aware of this marketing purpose (Breiner et al. 2013; see also Elliot 2010). In addition to the food being advertised, the behaviours depicted in the ads are of concern to public health specialists. For example, snacking, which is understood to contribute more to obesity problems, is featured much more prominently than food eaten in kitchens, dining rooms or restaurants (Harris et al. 2013).

Second, disadvantaged children are particularly susceptible to obesity because of racial issues, poverty and food insecurity. In the United States, low-income children in American Indian, Latino and African-American communities are disproportionately suffering from obesity and poor nutrition (Slocum 2006). These communities are often found in food deserts – 'urban neighbourhoods and rural towns without ready access to fresh, healthy, and affordable food' (USDA 2014), which the USDA further refines as low-income communities (poverty rate of 20 per cent or greater) and low-access communities (33 per cent of the community live more than one mile from a supermarket/large grocery store in the cities, ten miles in rural areas). Sources of food in food deserts are convenience stores, bodegas and other small stores that either feature junk food or lack affordable nutritious food. Even when controlling for income, 'the availability of chain supermarkets in African American neighborhoods was only 52% that of their counterpart white neighborhoods' (Story et al. 2008: 259).

Third, the relative cheapness of low-quality foods targeted at children (and adults) has greatly contributed to the epidemic of childhood obesity. Children's food provides the greatest amount of calories at the lowest cost, which make such purchases appealing to families with limited resources: 'Fresh fruits and vegetables are more expensive on a per calorie basis than are fats and sugars' (Story et al. 2008: 263). The relative cheapness of low-quality foods has its roots in farm policies that have subsidized commodity crops (i.e. corn) while neglecting healthy fruits and vegetables which receive little government support. This pattern of agricultural subsidies 'may have indirectly influenced food processors and manufacturers to expand their product lines to include more fats and sweeteners in their products' (Story et al. 2008: 262). These US federal subsidies, moreover, have ramifications beyond American borders. For example, the popularity of the products of American food companies such as Coca-Cola, Kraft, Mars and many others in China has contributed to a 'nutrition transition' – 'as incomes have grown, consumers have begun to eat more meat, fish, vegetable oils and processed foods, and fewer basic grains such as rice' (Hawkes 2008: 154). This, in turn, has resulted in alarming changes in the rate of increase of overweight children and childhood obesity in China (Chen 2008).

In response to the obesity crisis, various international and national organizations have attempted to curb junk food marketing to children, all with limited success. In 2004, the WHO and the Food and Agriculture Organization of the United Nations (FAO) reported that junk food marketing to children should be addressed by all stakeholders in a manner that put children's health at the centre of regulations (Hawkes 2004). Since then, with a few exceptions individual nations, not least the United States, have had limited success in establishing regulatory policies. The US example illustrates the contentious nature of the public debate on children's food; like climate change, there are many stakeholders with vested interests in curbing efforts to solve the childhood obesity problem with policy, even in a limited fashion such as voluntary marketing restrictions.

Although the Institute of Medicine established the Standing Committee on Childhood Obesity in 2008, there were limited political efforts to solve the issue until the Obamas moved into the White House in the spring of 2009 and established a vegetable garden on the South Lawn of the White House as a way to symbolically encourage Americans to make healthier food choices, especially for their children. Later that same year, Congress established the Interagency Working Group on Food Marketed to Children (Working Group) to study and develop recommendations for standards in marketing food to children (Breiner et al. 2013). More visibly, in 2010, Michelle Obama announced the *Let's Move!* campaign to end childhood obesity, with President Obama also establishing the White House Task Force on Childhood Obesity. The goals of the task force are: (a) ensuring access to healthy, affordable food; (b) increasing physical activity in schools and communities; (c) providing healthier food in schools and (d) empowering parents with information and tools to make good choices for themselves and their families (White House 2010). The non-profit organization Partnership for a Healthier America was created to involve various stakeholders (foundations, activist organizations and corporations) in developing strategies.

Children's health and food activists were ecstatic over the prominent attention given to addressing childhood obesity. The spring of 2010 was described as a 'season of promise that the blight of childhood obesity – which is on track to make today's kids the first generation of Americans to live shorter lives than their parents – might still be beaten back' (Huber 2012: 11). Later that year, the Healthy, Hunger-Free Kids Act was signed into law that gave the Department of Agriculture the power to regulate foods sold in schools. In the spring of 2011, however, as the Working Group released a draft on voluntary guidelines for marketing food to children for public comment, food and media companies (including those who were members of the Partnership) criticized the proposed rules, leading to Congress delaying action on the Working Group's guidelines later in 2011 by tasking the Working Group (and the FTC in particular) to do a cost–benefit analysis of voluntary guidelines (Dietz 2013).[4] Since then, there have been no meaningful attempts to enact national policy or regulation on the marketing of food to children in America, and *Let's Move!* shifted away from marketing efforts to exercise.

In 2012, New York Mayor Michael Bloomberg attempted to take direct action in reducing childhood (and adult) obesity by limiting the size of sugar-sweetened drinks to sixteen ounces in restaurants, delis, movie theatres and sports stadiums through the city's Board of Health. Before the plan could take effect, the law was invalidated by a New York State Supreme Court judge, a ruling that was appealed by the city. On 26 June 2014, the New York Court of Appeals ruled that the Board of Health had exceeded their regulatory scope, effectively killing the NYC Big Soda Ban. Beverage companies had heavily mobilized to fight this law, because they 'feared that their products could be widely branded as a threat to public health' (Grynbaum 2014).

As such statements reflect, the battle over childhood obesity is replete with the fear-inducing rhetorics characteristic of moral panics. Indeed, critical scholars have highlighted that interpreting the statistical data that supports the existence of a rapidly expanding 'epidemic' in childhood obesity can be a slippery task, one that takes part in the cultural politics of the moment as much as empirical observation. As medical anthropologist Moffatt (2010) argues, careful and balanced attention must be paid both to the undeniable health effects of industrialized food production upon children and to the discursive aspects of the 'epidemic'.

Few countries have attempted either direct regulation of children's food or indirect regulation by limiting advertisements. Sweden does not allow any promotions to young children, while the United Kingdom, Ireland, South Korea and a few other nations have regulations on television marketing of high-fat/sugar/salt foods to children (Breiner et al. 2013: 46–7). While there has been limited success over the airwaves, as seen in the passage of the Healthy, Hunger-Free Kids Act in the United States, the battle over children's food and childhood obesity continues to be fought in the schools.

THE POLITICS OF SCHOOL FOOD

Schools provide contexts in which some researchers engage children away from their parents, sometimes making use of creative and innovative elicitation techniques. For example, Dryden et al. (2009) asked schoolchildren in the United Kingdom to describe their 'dream' and 'nightmare' lunchboxes. The authors argue that children were doing 'identity work' in constructing and narrating their boxes; analysis of these revealed children's understandings of individualism as well as popular nutritional discourses and their moral content. Counihan (1999) attempted to ask children abstract questions about what constituted good or bad food, but they were little interested. She ended up, instead, recording stories they told and then looking for food symbolism in those tales, locating themes such as food as control, food as symbolic of familial identifications and conflict, and food as connected with expressions of anger and greed.

More to the point, anthropologists have begun to intervene in debates concerning the politics of school food. They have approached the issue both from a health perspective – how can school food programmes better address the nutritional needs of children and provide more equitable access to nourishing foods for children across the socio-economic spectrum? – and through other lenses of cultural critique: how do well-intended school policies and practices work to exacerbate, rather than ameliorate, gender and class inequalities or to shore up exclusionary visions of national identity?

Contestation surrounding school-provided lunches is not particularly new, as Levine's (2009) and Poppendieck's (2010) recent histories demonstrate for the United States. Since the inception of the National School Lunch Program in the 1940s, debates have centred around issues such as how school lunches can or should be used to address persistent poverty as well as how best to balance the nutritional needs of children with concerns about local and federal financial outlays. As Levine (2009: 5–6) describes, the programme has deeper roots in early twentieth-century Americanization movements; school menus provided an opportunity to educate new Americans about proper eating and were conceived as 'basic civics training'. In recent years, mass media have reported on the 'cupcake wars' in which US parents disagree about whether to ban birthday cupcakes and other sweet, fatty foods from school celebrations (Schulte 2006; Isoldi et al. 2012).

Patico's current research in Atlanta charter schools is exploring how, where parents contribute snack or special occasion foods for the consumption of an entire class of children, administrators and parents alike may be concerned to regulate the health of those contributions (preferring fresh fruits and vegetables and other whole foods) while also monitoring themselves for intolerance of some families' cheaper, 'unhealthy' choices (such as mass-produced, orange-powdered cheese puffs). In this way, foods offered at school provide adults with ways of perceiving socio-economic and taste distinctions within their communities and of testing the nature and limits of their own interest in 'diversity'.

Some scholars are interested to show how school food programmes are, indeed, contributing to the childhood obesity epidemic. For example, Crooks (2003) takes a biocultural approach in examining the sale of snack foods in a Kentucky Appalachian school and how it contributes to overweight and compromised nutritional status. (Unsurprisingly, Crooks finds that the school's administration chooses to sell such foods because it provides additional revenue that assists in providing for highly valued educational objectives.) Through interviews with white and Mexican American teenagers in the United States, Taylor (2011) reports that teens express feeling powerless to resist fattening foods they encounter at school. Thus schools have been recognized, in both popular and scholarly contexts, as settings in which children's eating habits are shaped – not necessarily for the better – and where political, economic and ideological forces converge to encourage children's consumption of foods considered less than optimal for their health.

Poppendieck (2010) in particular examines the state of school food through interviews with school food personnel and participant observation in a school kitchen as well as cafeterias and food service conferences around the country. Poppendieck shines light on the complex interplay of financial pressures, government regulations and understandings of children's food preferences that lead schools to make the decisions they do about what to offer in the cafeteria. She describes the 'kids-are-customers model' that many cafeteria managers apply, arguing that when adults claim that they must succumb to their customers' preferences even when they are unhealthful, 'there is an abdication of adult authority and responsibility' (2010: 272).

Poppendieck further observes that the stigma associated with school food ends up constraining the profits and thus the options of school cafeterias (see also Persson Osowski, Göranzon and Fjellström 2010).[5] While a few extremely dedicated activists have made important strides in improving cafeteria food in their own communities, they must combat obstacles that require time and other resources to overcome. Ultimately, Poppendieck argues that the best way to improve the nutrition of children across the board may be to provide free school food to all public school children, thereby alleviating the stigma that leads fewer children to participate in school food programmes and impacts the quality and cost of the foods poorer children can access.

What is clear is that school food debates in the United States tap into not only disagreements about childhood nutrition and battles over scarce resources, but also fundamental conflicts between state-led and consumer-led approaches to reform, between laissez-faire and paternalistic approaches to child socialization and nutrition, and between desires to eradicate and to sustain markers of class inequality. Even the most 'progressive' efforts at school lunch reform have been critiqued for the roles they play in exacerbating class inequality or reinforcing abdications of state responsibility for child welfare. Thus Allen and Guthman (2006: 401) argue that farm-to-school movements ultimately reinforce neoliberal trends by emphasizing 'contingent labor relationships, private funding sources, and the devolution of responsibility to the local, all of which have serious consequences for social equity' (2006: 401). More research is needed that explores how school food programmes, and the broader cultures of food developed in schools, work to further – or conceivably to challenge – unequal distributions of resources among families as well as class-inflected food aesthetics and identities.

Other researchers investigate in more intimate ethnographic detail the forms of governmentality that are achieved through food management during and surrounding the school day. Allison (1991) describes lunchboxes as an 'ideological state apparatus' in Japan – a means through which both mothers and children are disciplined, and where the lines between private and state concern are fuzzy. Similarly, Pike and Leahy (2012) examine how school food debates position mothers as targets of public pedagogy, working to regulate mothers and moralizing food. Other recent ethnographic work draws on Foucauldian perspectives to explore how schools are spaces whose uses and meanings are contested by various actors, not least through food. Jo Pike (2008, 2010) purports to look beyond passive approaches to children as targets of school food policy, instead focusing on how power relationships between adults and kids are negotiated in school spaces. Not only does the organization of space shape and constrain children's lunchtime activity (Pike 2008), but teachers, lunchroom staff and children, respectively, are positioned in terms of their relative class positions and authority within the institutional lunchroom and its social/physical space (Pike 2010; see also O'Connell 2010). Daniel and Gustaffson (2010) observe that school policies in London disregard the significance of lunchrooms as children's spaces; the authors foreground children's desires for spaces for autonomous social engagement – goals that are distinct from adults' agendas for these spaces (see also Dorrer et al. 2010; Kohli, Connolly and Warman 2010).

Finally, recent ethnographies of schools strive to illuminate not only how power struggles between children, parents and schoolteachers play out around food, but also how national, ethnic and class identities are constructed, defended and enforced in classrooms and lunchrooms. Karrebaek (2012, 2013) examines how interactions between minority students and majority teachers in Danish schools establish certain foods as traditional and superior, shaming children who bring other foods to school and defining their lack of respectability. Similarly, Golden (2005) looks at how foods are defined as Israeli in Israeli schools and how food events are managed in the service of a sense of national and civic identity. Salazar (2007) records Mexicano adults' memories of school food in the United States, examining changing food habits, processes of cultural assimilation and emotional responses to unfamiliar school foods (see also Srinivas 2013). When Nukaga (2008) observes US children's cafeteria food exchange practices, she finds that they reproduce ethnic boundaries in ways that are distinct from adults' practices. Brembeck (2009) describes how Bosnian and Iraqi children living in Sweden attempt to fit in through their adoption of local sweet foods; their sweet teeth may be harmful to their health, but they also represent an experience of cultural integration.

GLOBALIZING CHILDREN'S FOOD

Fast food is the children's food *par excellence*. Unlike other types of children's food, such as the high sugar/salt, low-nutrient processed snack foods discussed above, fast food is a total experience (Watson 1997a: 36); children enter fast-food restaurants and make a selection of what they want to eat, sometimes and in some places dining in the restaurant, and in other times and other places, taking it away. In a study of Kentucky Fried Chicken in China, Lozada (2000), following Strathern's (1992) conclusion that choice has become the hallmark of modernity, argues that the availability of *choice* in the case of fast food, unlike in the case of meal times at home, is one of the main reasons why children find fast food desirable.[6]

Children are also desirable for fast-food companies. In a pioneering ethnographic study of McDonald's, Watson concludes that 'McDonald's was one of the first corporations to recognize the potential of the children's market; in effect, the company started a revolution by making it possible for even the youngest consumers to choose their own food' (Watson 1997b: 100). Even in France, with its noted *patrimoine culinaire*, McDonald's has been able to succeed due to its focus on children and the family (Fantasia 1995).

As children in different parts of the world find themselves in distinct cultural environments, fast-food restaurants similarly have very different experiences from place to place; this is why Watson (1997a) prefers to call McDonald's a 'multilocal' company instead of a multinational one. Even within a particular region such as East Asia, fast-food restaurants find themselves having to adapt to the local needs of their customers (children *and* their parents). For example, McDonald's in Hong Kong and Japan are clearly perceived of as local, almost indigenous, to people who have grown up with it all their lives; by contrast, in the different social and historical contexts of China and Korea, McDonald's is clearly seen as foreign (Watson 1997a). In China, McDonald's is valued because of its association with American modernity (Yan 1997); in Honduras, customers enjoy the experience in McDonald's *despite* its connection to American cultural and economic imperialism (Schortman 2010).[7] In France, José Bové used a tractor to dismantle a McDonald's, while during the NATO bombing of Belgrade, Serbians used rocks to attack the McDonald's because of its American connection.

Fast-food restaurants in different parts of the world have been seen as challenging traditional culture, globalization-induced changes that become more salient as parents and grandparents watch children become enamoured of new foodstuffs and styles of eating. Fast food, and children's food more generally speaking, are indexical of the impacts of globalization and wider social and cultural changes. While Korean children may enjoy hanging out at McDonald's, their parents face a wider dilemma of how to be simultaneously nationalistic and global (Bak 1997: 137).[8]

Bak illustrates how many people in Seoul believe that Korean children are meant to eat Korean food – food grown by Korean farmers on Korean land – through the political discourse of *sint'oburi:* 'Human bodies and their native environments are so closely linked that people should eat what is produced locally in order to maintain cosmic harmony' (Bak 1997: 154). *Sint'oburi* was the slogan of the National Agricultural Cooperative Federation (NACF), an organization that mobilized people in debates about the trade negotiations on the Korean import ban on foreign rice (especially American rice) in the 1990s.

At the same time, a noted survey found that Korean children preferred the taste of hamburgers and pizza over *kimchi* (spicy, fermented vegetables) – a national symbol (Han 2000). *Kimchi* is both essential and marginal to Korean meals: 'A [Korean] meal is not proper without it, yet *kimchi* is not considered a main dish' (Bak 2014: 2). Primarily home-made (but gradually becoming commodified), *kimchi* is the stuff of childhood memories, as is *kimjang* – the late-November gathering of generations of family members (especially women) who make *kimchi* together (Bak 2014). But eating *kimchi* is an acquired taste, something that Korean children learn to like over time, as is clear in Korean adults' consumption of *kimchi*. The battle between traditional foodstuffs like *kimchi* and new, global children's food like hamburgers takes place all over the world. In Guatemala, for example, Green (2003) describes a scene where a Mayan mother and daughter have a fight over *tamales* (traditional Mesoamerican dish made of *masa*, a corn-based starchy dough): the daughter wants to eat hot dogs, and doesn't understand why her mother insists on making *tamales*. In Fiji, the introduction of commodified foods has even changed patterns of kinship, as seen in who eats at the Sunday family meal (Toren 2007). Family meals are not only highly charged recreations of the family, as discussed earlier – they are also contestations over cultures and modernity.

Children are not always the instigators introducing new foods; parents do their share of bringing in non-local commodities and practices into the domestic sphere. Milk has become a global children's food *sine qua non* (see Wiley 2011, and Chapter 10, this volume). In the past 30 years, milk production has increased by more than 50 per cent, driven by a doubling of milk consumption in developing countries (FAO 2014): 'It turns out that, along with zippy cars and flat-panel TVs, milk is the mark of new money, a significant source of protein that factors into much of any affluent person's diet' (Arnold 2007). Milk has been promoted for children's consumption as the unique food item that can make the individual and the nation strong: 'One cup of milk can strengthen a nation' (Chen 2003).

In 2008 in China, however, milk was transformed into something toxic. That year, dairy products (baby formula, ice cream bars, etc.) from the Sanlu Group (a joint-venture dairy in China) were found to be contaminated with melamine – an industrial chemical used to make plastic and to tan leather, but added to milk to increase its apparent protein content. After the Chinese government's discovery of melamine in Sanlu products, nationwide testing found 22 out of 109 firms also had products contaminated with melamine, including two other top Chinese dairies (Yili and Mengniu). Estimates vary, but Yan reports that this scandal 'stands out as one of the worst cases of poisonous food, causing six deaths, 51,900 hospitalizations of children with serious kidney problems, and 24,900 cases of children suffering from other problems' (Yan 2012: 717).[9] At the wider social level, this has led to more widespread social distrust and insecurity, a potentially highly destabilizing situation for both Chinese children and parents.

WHITHER CHILDREN'S FOOD?

As Klein notes, concerns over food safety (especially children's food) in China is generating ambivalence towards modernity: 'the country's food safety issues are also typical of a globalizing food system in which food supplies have become ever more divorced from their regional moorings and dependent on long distance trade and intensified production methods' (Klein 2013: 377). In his examination of how Chinese food shoppers cope with issues of food safety, Klein (2013) finds that shoppers and food purveyors have forged new connections of trust that have revalorized the local in ways that are driven by the traditional cultural idea that good food is the source of family happiness. While conducting fieldwork for his current research on sustainable aquaculture, Lozada is finding many Chinese urbanites who are creating a 'parallel modernity', one resistant to commercialism, to provide a more sustainable, better life for their children. Like Michelle Obama's starting a vegetable garden at the White House to help educate her daughters about proper food choices, these new farmers have an ideological basis for their return to traditional farming and distribution techniques. They are a highly educated group – former urban professionals who use information technology and other modern resources in their farming (Zhang and Zhang 2012). Sacha Cody refers to this as 'exemplary agriculture': 'a philosophy and approach to agriculture that emphasizes sustainable farming techniques ... [and] a nostalgic appreciation for China's agrarian history and the depth of indigenous knowledge about farming' (Cody 2014). This movement is centred on local, organic food products, farmers' markets and community-supported agriculture (CSA).

Started in Japan in 1971 by a group of women concerned about chemicals in their food (*teikei* movement), CSA was transplanted to the United States in the late 1980s and has gradually grown in the United States and elsewhere as a global movement, a response to industrialized agriculture. CSA members initially purchase a share of a farm prior to planting, and receive a share of the harvest; members effectively share the risks and rewards with the farmer. Some CSAs include shared labour as part of their membership; others participate in farm management (Cone and Myhre 2000). One of the key characteristics of CSAs is that members get to know the farmers and gain access to the farm itself. This is interpreted as building trust, building community and reconnecting with nature, food and the land. Many CSAs have programmed educational activities designed to teach children about farming, nutrition and other food-related issues. Cone and Myhre (2000) further conclude that CSAs tend to be gendered, where women assume much of the responsibility for CSA management and activities. Janssen (2010) sees CSA initiatives as part of social networks of support beyond members and farmers that include media and organizations, a type of 'civic agriculture'.

In terms of children's food, the integration of children into the production and distribution of food is reminiscent of the nature-study movement from the late nineteenth and early twentieth century, a time when progressive educators and naturalists felt that urban children may grow up not knowing where food comes from. School gardens were a common outcome of the nature-study movement (Vileisis 2010). In his own work with a local CSA in North Carolina, Lozada observed his youngest son (then aged eight) participate in a similarly themed 'food camp' organized by the CSA manager. While visiting farms around Shanghai, Lozada was surprised to see similar activities being organized for Shanghai children – surprised given the well-known cultural emphasis on cramming academic activities into the lives of Chinese children in preparation for success in the notorious college entrance exam (*gaokao*). Lozada also discovered that many of his students at Fudan University were involved in organizations like Jane Goodall's Roots and Shoots (a learning programme that helps students learn about environmental conservation) and also had experience in sustainable agricultural practices such as rooftop gardening, urban agriculture or other activities like the ones organized by the Chinese CSAs. Lozada plans to continue fieldwork on this issue in China, exploring how children's engagement in the food system shapes their consumption practices and attitudes towards environmental conservation.

In urban Atlanta, Patico observes middle-class families – again, often highly educated professionals or (in the case of stay-at-home mothers) former professionals – for whom good health, practices such as urban gardening or chicken raising, and a sense of locality and community are intertwined. Children of such families absorb these post-industrial, anti-commercial food values, even as they may lobby for more sweet treats or fast foods; indeed, such styles have become part of a class-inflected urban sensibility. This sensibility, Patico finds, often includes both significant concern for parents to limit overly processed, especially sugary, foods *and* the desire to be seen as laid-back (rather than overly controlling) in one's parenting and food practices: a good role model, but not a 'food Nazi' (see Patico 2013). In this context, children often are considered to thrive when given choices (whether among different foods, different after-school activities or different courses of action) and chances to learn to make their own 'good' and 'healthy choices' rather than have all of their options determined by adults. Yet the provision of such choices is not just a concession to children's desires; rather, it often is also understood implicitly as a management tool, since being able to make a choice is said to make children more engaged, invested and thus compliant rather than resistant. Thus discussions and strategies related to children's food speak not only to nutritional debates but to fundamental questions of personhood and power in the neoliberal United States, helping to define acceptable modes of self-presentation and of social relationship.

These two ongoing studies exemplify one of the most striking directions in contemporary anthropological approaches to children's food (which are undeniably, as this essay has demonstrated, varied and rich): that children's food mediates parents' reactions to a global modernity. Just as children's food has been a means through which modernity is defined and enacted in industrializing countries, so we must continue to explore how children's nutrition now provides a medium for anti- or postmodernizing approaches worldwide. In the process, people articulate visions of family and community even as they may make use of the languages of individualism and entitlements to consumer choice. Because these two research projects in very different geographical and cultural locations involve both the everyday decisions made by parents as they provide for their children and more abstract cultural conceptions of raising children, they share the potential for depicting contemporary cultural strategies for coping with what parents – and, as active consumers, children – see as the primary challenges to living the good life.

NOTES

1. Coutant et al. (2011) investigate how yogurt commercials in several European countries craft their messages for mothers using a 'tensive' rhetoric that targets worries about children's health, their cognitive development and success, and their feelings towards their mothers. That is, they play to mothers' desires to be loved and appreciated by their children (see also Cook 2011).
2. Cook (2011) considers how mothers are positioned in US advertisements, observing that ads work to reinforce a sense that motherhood is defined by a woman's single-minded focus on her child (see also Hays 1996).
3. Similarly, Cantarero (2001) considers how children living in a youth home in Spain enact resistance by refusing food. Through the 'language' of food resistance, 'children indicate their desire to belong in a specific age group, they vindicate their ethnic difference, they show their wish to relate or not to other mates or to the staff, they express the need to be attended' (paragraph 54; see also Kohli, Connolly and Warman 2010).
4. Dietz (2013) also reviews the 1978 FTC rule-making incident known as KidVid, where in crafting a rule to restrict highly sugared foods to children, Congress then removed the FTC's authority to regulate unfair advertising to children (but not adults) in 1980.
5. Similar sentiments have been observed in Sweden by Persson Osowski, Göranzon and Fjellström (2010), who use qualitative 'ethnological' surveys to gather open-ended responses concerning Swedes' perceptions of school food. Swedish respondents associated school food with the national welfare state, and as such they accorded it status as a 'second-class' food.
6. When Lozada conducted the research in the 1990s, he used McNeal and Yeh's (1997) insights into Chinese children as consumers to understand how their fast-food consumption fit into a wider range of family choices that Chinese children were able to influence. In an update to their earlier findings, McNeal and Yeh (2003) found not only that Chinese children had more money to spend, but also that they had even more influence on family expenditures.
7. Schortman's (2010) article lists Guatemalan-based Pollo Campero among the usual suspects of fast-food restaurants, further stressing the multilocality aspect of fast food. She notes that meals purchased from comedores (local eateries) are more likely to be takeouts than meals from fast-food restaurants.

8. Bak's (1997) article highlights the different challenges between fast food and other foreign food imports – the 'total experience' of fast food versus the domestication of other imported foods such as instant coffee, Spam and Coca-Cola, which takes place in homes, offices and other local spaces.

9. Yan (2012) reviews many different cases of food safety problems, including food adulteration, food additives, pesticides and fake foods – eggs made out of chemicals, soy sauce made out of human hair, etc. Yan argues that China has become a 'risk society' (following Ulrich Beck's idea that modernization has produced a society that manufacturers its own dangers), albeit one with Chinese characteristics such as the continued presence of natural risk, fragmentation and social distrust.

REFERENCES

Allen, P. and Guthman, J. (2006), 'From "Old School" to "Farm-to-School": Neoliberalization from the Ground Up', *Agriculture and Human Values*, 23(4): 401–15.

Allison, A. (1991), 'Japanese Mothers and *Obentōs*: The Lunch-Box as Ideological State Apparatus', *Anthropological Quarterly*, 64(4): 195–208.

Aries, P. (1962), *Centuries of Childhood*, New York: Vintage Books.

Arnold, J., Graesch, A., Ragazzini, E. and Ochs, E. (2012), *Life at Home in the Twenty-First Century: 32 Families Open Their Doors*, 1st edn, Los Angeles: The Cotsen Institute of Archaeology Press.

Arnold, W. (2007), 'A Thirst for Milk Bred by New Wealth Sends Prices Soaring', *The New York Times*, 4 September, sec. Business/World Business. http://www.nytimes.com/2007/09/04/business/worldbusiness/04milk.html.

Backett-Milburn, K., Wills, W., Roberts, M.-L. and Lawton, J. (2010), 'Food and Family Practices: Teenagers, Eating and Domestic Life in Differing Socio-economic Circumstances', *Children's Geographies*, 8(3): 303–14.

Bak, S. (1997), 'McDonald's in Seoul: Food Choices, Identity, and Nationalism', in J. L. Watson (ed.), *Golden Arches East: McDonald's in East Asia*, 1st edn, Stanford, CA: Stanford University Press.

Bak, S. (2014), 'Food, Gender, and Family Network in Modern Korean Society', *Asian Journal of Humanities and Social Studies*, 2(1): 22–8.

Barlow, K. (2010), 'Sharing Food, Sharing Values: Mothering and Empathy in Murik Society', *Ethos*, 38(4): 339–53.

Batada, A. and Borzekowski, D. (2008), 'SNAP! CRACKLE! *WHAT?*: Recognition of Cereal Advertisements and Understanding of Commercials' Persuasive Intent Among Urban, Minority Children in the US', *Journal of Children and Media*, 2(1): 19–36.

Bell-Kaplan, E. (2000), 'Using Food as a Metaphor for Care Middle-School Kids Talk About Family, School, and Class Relationships', *Journal of Contemporary Ethnography*, 29(4): 474–509.

Bentley, A. (2014), *Inventing Baby Food: Taste, Health, and the Industrialization of the American Diet*, Oakland: University of California Press.

Breiner, H., Parker, L., Olson, S., Standing Committee on Childhood Obesity Prevention, Food and Nutrition Board, and Institute of Medicine (2013), *Challenges and Opportunities for Change in Food Marketing to Children and Youth: Workshop Summary*, National Academies Press.

Brembeck, H. (2009), 'Children's "Becoming" in Frontiering Foodscapes', in A. James, A.-T. Kjørholt and V. Tingstad (eds), *Children, Food, and Identity in Everyday Life*, 130–48, New York: Palgrave Macmillan.

Cantarero, L. (2001), 'Eating in a Home for Children. Food Resistance in the Residence Juan de Lanuza', *Anthropology of Food* (online), http://aof.revues.org/1024?lang=en.

Carrington, C. (2013), 'Feeding Lesbigay Families', in C. Counihan and P. Van Esterik (eds), *Food and Culture: A Reader*, 3rd edn, 187–210, New York: Routledge.

Carsten, J. (1995), 'The Substance of Kinship and the Heat of the Hearth: Feeding, Personhood, and Relatedness among Malays in Pulau Langkawi', *American Ethnologist*, 22(2): 223–41.

Center for Disease Control and Prevention (2014), 'CDC – Obesity – Facts – Adolescent and School Health', http://www.cdc.gov/healthyyouth/obesity/facts.htm (accessed 8 July).

Chee, B. (2000), 'Eating Snacks and Biting Pressure: Only Children in Beijing', in J. Jing (ed.), *Feeding China's Little Emperors: Food, Children, and Social Change*, 48–70, Stanford, CA: Stanford University Press.

Chen, C. M. (2008), 'Overview of Obesity in Mainland China', *Obesity Reviews*, 9 (March): 14–21.

Chen, K. (2003), 'Got Milk? The New Craze in China is Dairy Drinks', *Wall Street Journal*, 28 February, sec. News, http://online.wsj.com/news/articles/SB1046383693546800623.

Chernin, A. (2008), 'The Effects of Food Marketing on Children's Preferences: Testing the Moderating Roles of Age and Gender', *The ANNALS of the American Academy of Political and Social Science*, 615(1): 101–18.

Cody, S. (2014), 'Can Young Chinese Farm?' *The China Story*, http://www.thechinastory.org/2014/07/can-young-chinese-farm/.

Collins, F. L. (2008), 'Of Kimchi and Coffee: Globalisation, Transnationalism and Familiarity in Culinary Consumption', *Social & Cultural Geography*, 9(2): 151–69.

Cone, C. A. and Myhre, A. (2000), 'Community-supported Agriculture: A Sustainable Alternative to Industrial Agriculture?' *Human Organization*, 59(2): 187–97.

Cook, D. T. (2004), *The Commodification of Childhood: The Children's Clothing Industry and the Rise of the Child Consumer*, Durham, NC: Duke University Press.

Cook, D. T. (2009a), 'Children's Subjectivities and Commercial Meaning: The Delicate Battle Mothers Wage When Feeding Their Children', in A. James, A.-T. Kjørholt and V. Tingstad (eds), *Children, Food, and Identity in Everyday Life*, 112–29, New York: Palgrave Macmillan.

Cook, D. T. (2009b), 'Semantic Provisioning of Children's Food: Commerce, Care and Maternal Practice', *Childhood*, 16(3): 317–34.

Cook, D. T. (2011), 'Through Mother's Eyes: Ideology, the "Child" and Multiple Mothers in US American Mothering Magazines', *Advertising & Society Review*,

12(2). http://muse.jhu.edu/journals/advertising_and_society_review/summary/
v012/12.2.cook.html.

Counihan, C. (1999), 'Fantasy Food: Gender and Food Symbolism in Preschool
Children's Made-Up Stories', in C. Counihan, *The Anthropology of Food and the Body:
Gender, Meaning, and Power*, 129–55, New York: Routledge.

Coutant, A., de La Ville, V.-I., Gram, M. and Boireau, N. (2011), 'Motherhood,
Advertising, and Anxiety: A Cross-cultural Perspective on Danonino Commercials',
Advertising & Society Review, 12(2): 1–19.

Crooks, D. L. (2003), 'Trading Nutrition for Education: Nutritional Status and the Sale of
Snack Foods in an Eastern Kentucky School', *Medical Anthropology Quarterly*, 17(2):
182–99.

Curtis, P., James, A. and Ellis, K. (2010), 'Children's Snacking, Children's Food: Food
Moralities and Family Life', *Children's Geographies* 8(3): 291–302.

Daniel, P. and Gustafsson, U. (2010), 'School Lunches: Children's Services or Children's
Spaces?' *Children's Geographies*, 8(3): 265–74.

DeVault, M. L. (1991), *Feeding the Family: The Social Organization of Caring as Gendered
Work*, Chicago, IL: University of Chicago Press.

Dietz, W. H. (2013), 'New Strategies To Improve Food Marketing To Children', *Health
Affairs*, 32(9): 1652–8.

Dorrer, N., McIntosh, I., Punch, S. and Emond, R. (2010), 'Children and Food Practices
in Residential Care: Ambivalence in the "Institutional" Home', *Children's Geographies*,
8(3): 247–59.

Douglas, M. (1966), *Purity and Danger*, New York: Routledge.

Dryden, C., Metcalfe, A., Owen, J. and Shipton, G. (2009), 'Picturing the Lunchbox:
Children Drawing and Talking About "Dream" Lunchboxes in the Primary School
Setting', in A. James, A.-T. Kjørholt and V. Tingstad (eds), *Children, Food, and Identity
in Everyday Life*, 69–93, New York: Palgrave Macmillan.

Dunn, E. (2004), *Privatizing Poland: Baby Food, Big Business, and the Remaking of Labor*,
Ithaca, NY: Cornell University Press.

Elliott, C. (2008), 'Marketing Fun Foods: A Profile and Analysis of Supermarket Food
Messages Targeted at Children', *Canadian Public Policy*, 34(2): 259–73.

Elliott, C. (2010), 'Eatertainment and the (re) Classification of Children's Foods', *Food,
Culture and* Society, 13(4): 539–53.

Fantasia, R. (1995), 'Fast Food in France', *Theory and Society*, 24(2): 201–43.

Gillette, M. (2000), 'Children's Food and Islamic Dietary Restrictions in Xi'an', in J. Jing
(ed.), *Feeding China's Little Emperors: Food, Children, and Social Change*, Stanford,
CA: Stanford University Press.

Golden, D. (2005), 'Nourishing the Nation: The Uses of Food in an Israeli Kindergarten',
Food and Foodways, 13(3): 181–99.

Graeber, D. (2001), *Toward a Theory of Value: The False Coin of Our Own Dreams*,
New York: Palgrave.

Green, L. (2003), 'Notes on Mayan Youth and Rural Industrialization in Guatemala',
Critique of Anthropology, 23(1): 51–73.

Grieshaber, S. (1997), 'Mealtime Rituals: Power and Resistance in the Construction of
Mealtime Rules', *The British Journal of Sociology*, 48(4): 649–66.

Grynbaum, M. M. (2014), 'New York's Ban on Big Sodas Is Rejected by Final Court', *The New York Times*, 26 June. http://www.nytimes.com/2014/06/27/nyregion/city-loses-final-appeal-on-limiting-sales-of-large-sodas.html.

Haley, A. P. (2009), 'Dining in High Chairs: Children and the American Restaurant Industry, 1900–1950', *Food and History*, 7(2): 69–94.

Han, K. (2000), 'Some Foods Are Good to Think: Kimchi and the Epitomization of National Character', *Korean Social Science Journal*, 27(1): 221–35.

Harris, J. L., Pomeranz, J. L., Lobstein, T. and Brownell, K. D. (2009), 'A Crisis in the Marketplace: How Food Marketing Contributes to Childhood Obesity and What Can Be Done', *Annual Review of Public Health*, 30: 211–25.

Haukanes, H. (2007), 'Sharing Food, Sharing Taste? Consumption Practices, Gender Relations and Individuality in Czech Families', *Anthropology of Food*, no. S3. http://aof.revues.org/1912.

Hawkes, C. (2008), 'Agro-food Industry Growth and Obesity in China: What Role for Regulating Food Advertising and Promotion and Nutrition Labelling?' *Obesity Reviews*, 9 (March): 151–61.

Hawkes, C. (2004), 'Marketing Food to Children', *The Regulatory Framework. Geneva: World Health Organization*. http://www.who.int/entity/dietphysicalactivity/regulatory_environment_CHawkes07.pdf.

Hays, S. (1996), *The Cultural Contradictions of Motherhood*, New Haven, CT: Yale University Press.

Hemme, T. and Otté, J. (2010), *Status and Prospects for Smallholder Milk Production: A Global Perspective*, Rome: Food and Agriculture Organization of the United Nations.

Huber, B. (2012), 'Michelle's Moves Has the First Lady's Anti-obesity Campaign Been Too Accommodating Toward the Food Industry?' *NATION*, 295(18): 11–17.

Humes, M. (2013), 'Feeding the Kiddie', *Slate*, 7 August. http://www.slate.com/articles/life/food/2013/08/children_s_menu_history_how_prohibition_and_emmett_holt_gave_rise_to_kid.html.

Isoldi, K. K., Dalton, S., Rodriguez, D. P. and Nestle, M. (2012), 'Classroom "cupcake" Celebrations: Observations of Foods Offered and Consumed', *Journal of Nutrition Education and Behavior*, 44(1): 71–5.

James, A. (1998), 'Confections, Concoctions and Conceptions', in H. Jenkins (ed.), *The Children's Culture Reader*, New York: New York University Press.

James, A., Curtis, P. and Ellis, K. (2009), 'Negotiating Food', in A. James, A.-T. Kjørholt and V. Tingstad (eds), *Children, Food, and Identity in Everyday Life*, 35–51, New York: Palgrave Macmillan.

James, A., Kjørholt, A.-T. and Tingstad, V. (2009), 'Introduction: Children, Food, and Identity in Everyday Life', in A. James, A.-T. Kjørholt and V. Tingstad (eds), *Children, Food, and Identity in Everyday Life*, 1–12, New York: Palgrave Macmillan.

Janssen, B. (2010), 'Local Food, Local Engagement: Community-Supported Agriculture in Eastern Iowa', *Culture & Agriculture*, 32(1): 4–16.

Jing, J. (2000a), 'Food, Nutrition, and Cultural Authority in a Gansu Village', in J. Jing (ed.), *Feeding China's Little Emperors: Food, Children, and Social Change*, 135–58, Stanford, CA: Stanford University Press.

Jing, J. (2000b), 'Introduction: Food, Children, and Social Change in Contemporary China', in J. Jing (ed.), *Feeding China's Little Emperors: Food, Children, and Social Change*, 1–25, Stanford, CA: Stanford University Press.

Karrebaek, M. S. (2012), '"What's in Your Lunch Box Today?": Health, Respectability, and Ethnicity in the Primary Classroom', *Journal of Linguistic Anthropology*, 22(1): 1–22.

Karrebaek, M. S. (2013), 'Lasagna for Breakfast: The Respectable Child and Cultural Norms of Eating Practices in a Danish Kindergarten Classroom', *Food, Culture and Society*, 16(1): 85–106.

Klein, J. A. (2013), 'Everyday Approaches to Food Safety in Kunming', *The China Quarterly*, 214: 376–93.

Kohli, R. K. S., Connolly, H. and Warman, A. (2010), 'Food and Its Meaning for Asylum Seeking Children and Young People in Foster Care', *Children's Geographies*, 8(3): 233–45.

Kremer-Sadlik, T. and Paugh, A. L. (2007), 'Everyday Moments: Finding "Quality Time" in American Working Families', *Time & Society*, 16(2–3): 287–308.

Levine, S. (2009), *School Lunch Politics: The Surprising History of America's Favorite Welfare Program*, Princeton, NJ: Princeton University Press.

Lévi-Strauss, C. (1963), *Totemism*, Boston, MA: Beacon Press.

Lévi-Strauss, C. (1997), 'The Culinary Triangle', in C. Counihan and P. Van Esterik (eds), *Food and Culture: A Reader*, 1st edn, 28–35, New York: Routledge.

Lozada, Jr., E. P. (2000), 'Globalized Childhood? Kentucky Fried Chicken in Beijing', in J. Jing (ed.), *Feeding China's Little Emperors: Food, Children, and Social Change*, 114–34, Stanford, CA: Stanford University Press.

McNeal, J. U. and Yeh, C.-H. (1997), 'Development of Consumer Behavior Patterns Among Chinese Children', *Journal of Consumer Marketing*, 14(1): 45–59.

Meigs, A. (1997), 'Food as Cultural Construction', in C. Counihan and P. Van Esterik (eds), *Food and Culture: A Reader*, 1st edn, 95–105, New York: Routledge.

Miller, D. (1998), *A Theory of Shopping*, Ithaca, NY: Cornell University Press.

Mintz, S. W. (1996), *Tasting Food, Tasting Freedom: Excursions into Eating, Culture, and the Past*, Boston, MA: Beacon Press.

Moffat, T. (2010), 'The "Childhood Obesity Epidemic": Health Crisis or Social Construction?' *Medical Anthropology Quarterly*, 24(1): 1–21.

Munn, N. (1986), *The Fame of Gawa: A Symbolic Study of Value Transformation in a Massim (Papua New Guinea) Society*, Durham, NC: Duke University Press.

Namie, J. (2011), 'Public Displays of Affection: Mothers, Children, and Requests for Junk Food', *Food, Culture and Society*, 14(3): 393–411.

Nukaga, M. (2008), 'The Underlife of Kids' School Lunchtime Negotiating Ethnic Boundaries and Identity in Food Exchange', *Journal of Contemporary Ethnography*, 37(3): 342–80.

O'Connell, R. (2010), '(How) Is Childminding Family Like? Family Day Care, Food and the Reproduction of Identity at the Public/private Interface', *The Sociological Review*, 58(4): 563–86.

Ochs, E. and Beck, M. (2013), 'Dinner', in E. Ochs and T. Kremer-Sadlik (eds), *Fast Forward Family: Home, Work, and Relationships in Middle Class America*, 48–66, Berkeley: University of California Press.

Ochs, E., Pontecorvo, C. and Fasulo, A. (1996), 'Socializing Taste', *Ethnos*, 61(1–2): 7–46.

Ochs, E. and Shohet, M. (2006), 'The Cultural Structuring of Mealtime Socialization', *New Directions for Child and Adolescent Development*, 2006(111): 35–49.

Patico, J. (2013), 'The Real World in a Honey Bun', *Gastronomica: The Journal of Food and Culture*, 13(3): 42–6.

Paugh, A. and Izquierdo, C. (2009), 'Why Is This a Battle Every Night?: Negotiating Food and Eating in American Dinnertime Interaction', *Journal of Linguistic Anthropology*, 19(2): 185–204.

Persson Osowski, C., Göranzon, H. and Fjellström, C. (2010), 'Perceptions and Memories of the Free School Meal in Sweden', *Food, Culture and Society*, 13(4): 555–72.

Pike, J. (2008), 'Foucault, Space and Primary School Dining Rooms', *Children's Geographies*, 6(4): 413–22.

Pike, J. (2010), '"I Don't Have to Listen to You! You're Just a Dinner Lady!": Power and Resistance at Lunchtimes in Primary Schools', *Children's Geographies*, 8(3): 275–87.

Pike, J. and Leahy, D. (2012), 'School Food and the Pedagogies of Parenting', *Australian Journal of Adult Learning*, 52(3): 434–8.

Poppendieck, J. (2010), *Free for All: Fixing School Food in America*, Berkeley: University of California Press.

Punch, S., McIntosh, I. and Emond, R. (2010), 'Children's Food Practices in Families and Institutions', *Children's Geographies*, 8(3): 227–32.

Rock, M., McIntyre, L. and Rondeau, K. (2009), 'Discomforting Comfort Foods: Stirring the Pot on Kraft Dinner® and Social Inequality in Canada', *Agriculture and Human Values*, 26(3): 167–76.

Salazar, M. L. (2007), 'Public Schools, Private Foods: Mexicano Memories of Culture and Conflict in American School Cafeterias', *Food & Foodways*, 15(3–4): 153–81.

Schieffelin, B. (1990), *The Give and Take of Everyday Life: Language Socialization of Kaluli Children*, New York: Cambridge University Press.

Schortman, A. (2010), '"The Children Cry for Burger King": Modernity, Development, and Fast Food Consumption in Northern Honduras', *Environmental Communication*, 4(3): 318–37.

Schulte, B. (2006), 'Once Just a Sweet Birthday Treat, the Cupcake Becomes a Cause', *The Washington Post*, 11 December, sec. Metro. http://www.washingtonpost.com/wp-dyn/content/article/2006/12/10/AR2006121001008.html.

Seddon, K. (2011), 'Bento Blogs: Japanese Women's Expression in Digital Food Culture', *Women & Performance: A Journal of Feminist Theory*, 21(3): 301–19.

Segal, A. (2010), 'Food Deserts: A Global Crisis in New York City Causes, Impacts and Solutions', *The Journal of Sustainable Development*, 3(1): 197–214.

Slocum, R. (2006), 'Anti-racist Practice and the Work of Community Food Organizations', *Antipode*, 38(2): 327–49.

Sobo, E. J. and Rock, C. L. (2001), '"You Ate All That!?": Caretaker-Child Interaction During Children's Assisted Dietary Recall Interviews', *Medical Anthropology Quarterly*, 15(2): 222–44.

Srinivas, T. (2013), '"As Mother Made It": The Cosmopolitan Indian Family, "Authentic" Food, and the Construction of Cultural Utopia', in C. Counihan and P. Van Esterik (eds), *Food and Culture: A Reader*, 3rd edn, 355–75, New York: Routledge.

Stephens, S. (1995), *Children and the Politics of Culture*, Princeton, NJ: Princeton University Press.

Strathern, M. (1992), *Reproducing the Future: Essays on Anthropology, Kinship and the New Reproductive Technologies*, New York: Routledge.

Szabo, M. (2011), 'The Challenges of "Re-engaging with Food": Connecting Employment, Household Patterns and Gender Relations to Convenience Food Consumption in North America', *Food, Culture and Society*, 14(4): 547–66.

Taylor, N. L. (2011), 'Negotiating Popular Obesity Discourses in Adolescence: School Food, Personal Responsibility, and Gendered Food Consumption Behaviors', *Food, Culture and Society*, 14(4): 587–606.

Toren, C. (2007), 'Sunday Lunch in Fiji: Continuity and Transformation in Ideas of the Household', *American Anthropologist*, 109(2): 285–95.

UNICEF (2014), 'Childinfo: Statistics by Area/Child Nutrition'. http://www.childinfo.org/malnutrition_progress.html (accessed 8 July).

USDA, Agricultural Marketing Service (2014), 'Food Deserts'. https://apps.ams.usda.gov/fooddeserts/foodDeserts.aspx (accessed 8 July).

Veit, H. Z. (2013), *Modern Food, Moral Food: Self-Control, Science, and the Rise of Modern American Eating in the Early Twentieth Century*, Chapel Hill: The University of North Carolina Press.

Vileisis, A. (2010), *Kitchen Literacy: How We Lost Knowledge of Where Food Comes from and Why We Need to Get It Back*, 1st edn, Washington, DC: Island Press.

Watson, J. L. (1997a), 'McDonald's in Hong Kong: Consumerism, Dietary Change, and the Rise of a Children's Culture', in J. L. Watson (ed.), *Golden Arches East: McDonald's in East Asia*, 1st edn, 77–109, Stanford, CA: Stanford University Press.

Watson, J. L. (1997b), 'Transnationalism, Localization, and Fast Foods in East Asia', in J. L. Watson (ed.), *Golden Arches East: McDonald's in East Asia*, 1st edn, 1–38, Stanford, CA: Stanford University Press.

White House (2010), 'Presidential Memorandum – Establishing a Task Force on Childhood Obesity'. http://www.whitehouse.gov/the-press-office/presidential-memorandum-establishing-a-task-force-childhood-obesity (accessed 12 February).

Wiley, A. S. (2011), 'Milk for "Growth": Global and Local Meanings of Milk Consumption in China, India, and the United States', *Food & Foodways*, 19(1–2): 11–33.

Wilk, R. (2010), 'Power at the Table: Food Fights and Happy Meals', *Cultural Studies↔ Critical Methodologies*, 10(6): 428–36.

Wills, W., Backett-Milburn, K., Lawton, J. and Roberts, M.-L. (2009), 'Consuming Fast Food: The Perceptions and Practices of Middle-Class Young Teenagers', in A. James, A.-T. Kjørholt and V. Tingstad (eds), *Children, Food, and Identity in Everyday Life*, 52–68, New York: Palgrave Macmillan.

World Health Organization (2012), 'Prioritizing Areas for Action in the Field of Population-based Prevention of Childhood Obesity', World Health Organization. http://www.who.int/iris/bitstream/10665/80147/1/9789241503273_eng.pdf?ua=1.

World Health Organization (2014), 'Childhood Overweight and Obesity', World Health
  Organization. http://www.who.int/dietphysicalactivity/childhood/en/ (accessed 8 July).
Yan, Y. (1997), 'McDonald's in Beijing: The Localization of Americana', in J. L. Watson
  (ed.), *Golden Arches East: McDonald's in East Asia*, 1st edn, Stanford, CA: Stanford
  University Press.
Yan, Y. (2012), 'Food Safety and Social Risk in Contemporary China', *The Journal of
  Asian Studies*, 71(3): 705–29.
Zhang, Z. and Zhang, S. Y. (2012), 'Leveraging Micro Blogging to Build Trust by
  Community Supported Agriculture (CSA) Pioneers in China', *GlobDev 2012*,
  December. http://aisel.aisnet.org/globdev2012/15.

CHAPTER TEN

Cow's Milk as Children's Food: Insights from India and the United States

ANDREA S. WILEY

INTRODUCTION

The idea that children have different nutritional needs and hence require a different diet than adults is relatively recent in biomedical science, having developed alongside the emergence of nutritional science and the medical specialty of paediatrics in the early twentieth century (Halpern 1988; Levenstein 1988). In Northern European countries and others such as the United States, these new areas of expertise were accompanied by public health efforts to address undernutrition through food assistance programmes and nutrition education, and widespread use of growth monitoring as a way of assessing child nutritional status. Amidst these initiatives, milk emerged as a particularly appropriate food for children, one that would meet their needs for calories, protein and micronutrients and enable their growth. Over the course of the twentieth century, it became widely assumed that milk drinking was inherent to childhood, as evidenced by the establishment of school feeding programmes, which invariably featured milk, and various milk-industry promotions that linked milk drinking to child growth and health. By the twenty-first century, these ideas had achieved global spread, appearing even in countries without long-standing dairy traditions (Wiley 2011, 2016).

The idea that children should drink milk makes intuitive sense – the first and only food of infants is mother's milk, and so substituting another kind of milk for breast milk, augmenting the diet of a nursing infant, or transitioning a baby or toddler to another animal's milk after weaning, seems like a reasonable way to approach the feeding of children. But the role that other mammalian milk has played or *should* play in the diets of older children is less well understood and likely to vary cross-culturally. In this chapter, I trace the establishment of the normative status of milk consumption among post-weaning age children in two countries: India and the United States. Milk refers to cow, water buffalo or goat milk rather than human breast milk. I argue that the childhood milk practices may be understood in relation to the perceived biological effects of this peculiar food. But biological outcomes such as growth in height are embedded in cultural contexts; so goals for child growth and health are likely to shape policies and practices around childhood milk consumption. I briefly consider the evidence deployed to support assertions that milk is essential to adequate child growth and focus on how this connection came to be culturally meaningful.

A comparative approach is particularly helpful in this analysis because it can shed light on how a single food may have different cultural meanings, and reveal how food is intimately connected to other aspects of social life. Additionally, in the case of milk, its biological effects – whether imagined or measurable – may contribute to different consumption patterns and human biological variation. It is important to recognize at the outset that historically milk had a limited distribution in diets across the world, as it was consumed only in those populations with histories of dairying (Europeans and their descendants, pastoralists from Africa to Central Asia, and South Asians). This variation in exposure to milk left its mark in human biology: only in these populations are there high frequencies of the mutation (lactase persistence) that allows for lifelong digestion of lactose – the sugar found only in milk. Although it is widely acknowledged now that most humans do not possess this mutation, milk drinking is still largely considered a normal – and normative – practice, as evidenced by its presence in contemporary dietary guidelines in many countries (Wiley 2007). But even among populations with relatively high rates of lactase persistence, such as the United States and India (especially in the north), fresh milk was not commonly consumed as milk historically was fermented (the primary mode in India) and/or separated into its component parts for preservation (i.e. cheese, *ghee*). Thus fluid milk consumption among children is culturally and historically contingent, even while associations between fluid milk and growth may be related to the biological characteristics of milk itself, as the sole source of nutrition for rapidly growing infant mammals.

The comparison between India and the United States is apt for a variety of reasons. India and the United States both have well-entrenched dairy cultures, with India's total production and consumption of fluid milk now exceeding that of the United States, which had previously held the top rank (United States Department of Agriculture 2015). Per capita intake is much lower however (Figure 10.1), and there are steep socio-economic and regional gradients in milk intake that are not seen in the United States (National Nutrition Monitoring Bureau 2002; Sebastian et al. 2010). Most surveys report rising milk intake in India, especially among middle-class urbanites, (Ministry of Women and Child Development n.d.). Opposing trends are evident in the United States. While consumption rose in the first half of the twentieth century, it peaked during the Second World War and has been declining ever since. This drop has been especially precipitous among children.

Ideas about milk as particularly beneficial to children are well entrenched in both countries, and supported by dietary guidelines and, in the United States, school feeding programmes that extend milk's usage among older children (Wiley 2014). But the different consumption trends suggest that milk is tethered to different social and cultural processes such as economic constraints, conditions of the dairy industry, medical systems (inclusive of nutrition) or religion (i.e.

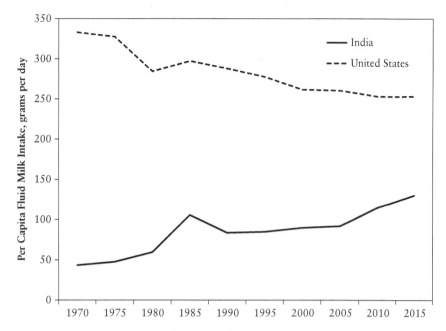

FIGURE 10.1: Per capita intake of milk and changes over time in India and the United States. (United States Department of Agriculture, 2015)

Hinduism in India and the cow's sacred status), and that milk's meaning as a food for children may be variable across the two countries. I consider how ideas about milk's contributions to growth came to the fore in the twentieth century in both places, how they have been shaped by local social and cultural forces and how milk is currently understood as a children's food. This also requires a look at the ideals and meanings surrounding variation in body size and conceptualizations of childhood in each context.

HISTORICAL CONTEXT: MEDICAL SYSTEMS, MILK AND THE FEEDING OF YOUNG CHILDREN

Dairying has a deep history in India, having become well established during the early Indus Valley civilization around 5,000 years ago. The Vedas, a body of texts in Sanskrit compiled around 1500–500 BCE and forming the foundational texts of Hinduism, are a rich source of evidence for normative views of food consumption. They contain numerous references to milk and articulate the importance of dairy products in the diet. These texts provide evidence to suggest that feeding children milk is an ancient practice – infants were given their first solid food of boiled rice, milk, sugar and honey starting at around six months of age (Achaya 1994). The later texts of Susruta (~300–500 CE), which form the basis of contemporary Ayurvedic medical practice, have an elaborate and systematic discussion on paediatrics that includes recommendations for child feeding. Honey and clarified butter (*ghee*) were advised within the first few days of life, and while breast milk was considered 'the natural food of an infant', if it was not available, cow and goat's milk were considered appropriate substitute (Kutumbiah 1959).

The Ayurvedic texts differentiate children into age groups based on their normative diet: milk alone (breast milk, or cow/goat's milk if substituted; up to one year); milk and boiled rice (one to two years); boiled rice alone (older than two years) (Bhishagratna 1911). The process of child growth was thought to extend up to twenty years, but there was no recommendation for consumption of milk beyond two years of age or an assignment of an appropriate time to wean from breast milk to other forms of milk. Of course these are guidelines, and how actual behaviour conformed to them is not known.

We know that milk was introduced into the Americas through European colonization; however, we lack sufficient information on the role that animal milk had in the diets of children throughout European history (Wiley 2016). Evidence from Roman Egypt suggests that cow's milk could be added from six months up to eighteen months (Lefkowitz and Fant 1982), but beyond that there is little characterization of children's diets after weaning (Prowse et al. 2010; Wiley 2014). In the United States, the idea that children of post-weaning age have 'special' dietary needs that reflect their biological distinctiveness compared to adults is relatively new. Along with the emergence of paediatrics in the 1920s, there was a trend towards a more 'child-centred' society in the United States, prompted by anti-child labour laws and compulsory education, which also served to lengthen the life stage recognized as childhood (Levenstein 1988; Calvert 2003; Cunningham 1998). Paediatricians began to articulate the ways in which children faced health issues that were quite different from those of adults, and there was greater professional oversight of child health, especially feeding practices and growth (Halpern 1988).

The central role that milk came to have in paediatric dietary recommendations stemmed from a nineteenth-century surge in milk production and the emergence of the National Dairy Council (NDC) in 1915 as the marketing arm of the dairy industry. Urban infants of working mothers were the first market for fresh milk; but as the volume of milk production increased, distribution networks developed and methods of preservation were more widely adopted, raising the demand for milk became a goal of the emerging US dairy industry (DuPuis 2002). The target market identified was older children, who were after all, still growing, albeit at a slower rate than infants. The NDC became the primary institution promoting milk to children and set about creating educational campaigns to extol the benefits of milk consumption to child growth.

But this new commercial enterprise seemed to rest on existing assumptions about cow's milk being the 'natural' food for children. Robert Hartley, the evangelical social reformist who crusaded for safety in the milk supply in the mid-nineteenth century when adulteration and contamination were rampant, based his efforts on the claim that cow's milk was a natural drink for children: milk is 'the chief aliment of children of all ages in all places where the population is condensed in great numbers;

it is the nourishment chosen and relied upon to develop the physical powers and impart vigour to the constitution during the most feeble and critical period of human life.' (Hartley 1977[1842]: 109, 136). The roots of this belief in American or European culture are not well understood, but may have been part of an intuitive understanding: since infants consume milk and grow rapidly, milk must be providing the needed resources. These could be easily extended to post-weaning age children living in societies with traditions of dairying. Notably, fluid milk, rather than dairy products more broadly, were the focus of such recommendations. Fermented dairy products that had long been produced were ignored, possibly because of their reliance on bacterial fermentation during a time when the germ theory of disease was becoming widely accepted (Mendelson 2008), but also perhaps because rapidly growing nursing infants consume fluid breast milk and that as a drink, milk could be easily added to the diet without needing to substitute for other foods.

MILK AND CHILD GROWTH: MEANINGS IN THE EARLY TWENTIETH CENTURY

It was through milk's association with child growth that milk was to become entrenched in children's diets in the United States, and this linkage has had broad salience in India as it moved towards, and then beyond, Independence in the mid-twentieth century and became a central player in the global economy in the early twenty-first century. As knowledge about nutrition and the effects of nutrients on human biology grew in the 1910s and 1920s, there were parallel interests in child growth, and milk was positioned as the 'natural' mediator of relationships between the two. In the United States, early-twentieth-century milk advertisements claimed that milk 'builds up the body – brains – bones – and muscles – and promotes growth of the entire system'. The milk-growth linkage was exploited extensively by the NDC and other institutions promoting milk, basing their claims on widely cited studies of children in urban working-class households in the United Kingdom in 1926–8 (Orr 1928; Leighton and Clark 1929). Three cohorts of school children, ranging between five and thirteen years of age, were given 0.75–1.25 pints of milk each school day, a biscuit of similar caloric value, or nothing, and they were measured at the beginning and at the end of two seven-month periods. The results showed consistent differences between the milk-supplemented groups and both the control group and those getting the biscuit. The children who received skimmed milk grew 0.20–0.42 inches (0.51–1.07 cm) more than the biscuit-supplemented children, raising the question of whether differences in growth would be even more accentuated if the additional milk had been consumed for longer periods of time, or throughout childhood (see Pollock 2006 for a critique of these trials). Regardless, these studies provided the evidence to back up claims about milk's 'special' effects on growth in height and positioned milk as central to a variety of public health, and paediatric, parental and commercial endeavours.

School feeding programmes also took up the charge to encourage milk consumption among school children. Some cities had special school milk programmes established in the 1920s, subsidized by local charitable organizations such as the Red Cross or Anti-Tuberculosis Association (Crumbine and Tobey 1929). In some areas, milk was dispensed for both infants and older children in the context of regular growth monitoring (Halpern 1988). Children identified as underweight were eligible for additional milk and children were often served it in the classroom 'while the teacher tells them about this wholesome product ... [and] ... to cultivate a taste for milk as the one best food for growth' (Crumbine and Tobey 1929: 155). A pamphlet published by the Child Health Organization for the Bureau of Education in 1922 declared: 'American parents and children must be taught the nutritional value of milk ... because milk is the best and most important food in the diet of the school child. No other food can take its place. It contains the elements necessary for the growth of the different structures of the body' (Reaney 1922: 4, 8). To this end a variety of educational activities were proposed in which milk was featured in every subject and students charted their daily milk consumption while their weight and height were tracked across the school year.

School milk programmes became federally supported in 1946 with the National School Lunch Act: 'as a measure of national security, to safeguard the health and well-being of the Nation's children and to encourage the domestic consumption of nutritious agricultural commodities' (Gunderson 1971). Fluid milk must be offered as part of school meal programmes in order to receive reimbursement from the government. Such efforts expanded in the early 1970s with the Special Supplemental Program for Women, Infants and Children (WIC), which provides vouchers for a set list of foods for low-income pregnant women and new mothers and their children up to the age of five; children are allocated sixteen quarts of milk each month (~ 500 ml/day). Milk has also been a routine part of the Dietary Guidelines for Americans since the earliest food guides of the late nineteenth and early twentieth centuries (United States Department of Agriculture Food and Nutrition Information Center 2011), and remains a cornerstone of the current guidelines (United States Department of Health and Human Services and United States Department of Agriculture 2015). Two to three cups (~500–750 ml) are recommended for children, depending on age.

Thus through the evolving confluence of government mandates, and philanthropic organizations, the professionalization of paediatrics and a well-organized dairy industry producing ever-greater quantities of milk and fostering close links to the government agencies charged with the development and implementation of food and nutrition policies, child health, growth and milk became one package, one that upwardly mobile families in the early- and mid-twentieth-century United States were eager to embrace. It became increasingly difficult to imagine how children of all ages could be healthy – defined through gains in height and weight – without drinking milk (Figure 10.2).

Milk's position in relation to growth played out somewhat differently in India, where concerns about food scarcity, undernutrition and poverty have predominated well into the twenty-first century. British colonial administrators had expressed no real concern about nutritional conditions of Indians until the 1930s, when the Nutrition Research Laboratories were established (Arnold 2000). The NRL's first

FIGURE 10.2: A young child with the ideal meal, 1916. (Source: Hunt, 1916)

director, W. R. Aykroyd, was tasked with ascertaining nutritional status among Indians and developing some affordable means of improving it. He had been involved in trials of milk and growth in the United Kingdom, and came to India well versed in the current knowledge of micronutrient deficiencies as well as the work on milk and growth (Arnold 2000). He and his Indian colleagues conducted surveys on milk consumption and child height and weight in South India. Compared to a sample of well-off US children measured during the same period, the Indian children were found to be 3.5–7.5 inches shorter than the American children of similar age, and the absolute differences became more accentuated with age (Aykroyd and Krishnan 1936; Aykroyd and Rajagopal 1936; Richey 1937).

Aykroyd and his co-workers went on to conduct some small-scale milk intervention studies among mostly adolescent hostel students similar to those that had been carried out in the United Kingdom (Aykroyd and Krishnan 1937). They found that adding one cup of reconstituted powdered skim milk to the diet of boys resulted in significantly greater gains in height and weight than a calorically equivalent supplement of millet. The study of girls did not include a control group that received millet, but those receiving a milk supplement grew more in both height and weight compared to girls who ate a similar baseline diet. Thus research in India contributed to the understanding that milk seemed to enhance growth compared to other foods, and, as a result, furthered the cause of enhancing access to milk as a way of enhancing growth.

Concluding that 'the value of milk as food for children is recognized even by the illiterate, but over great areas of the country whole milk is scanty and beyond the reach of the poor', Aykroyd linked the lack of access to milk to problems of production: 'Unquestionably, it is preferable that Indian children should consume whole milk locally produced. ... It remains questionable whether, in many areas, demand for milk can create an adequate local supply. It will be some time before cheap standard skimmed milk products, locally produced, become available in quantity in India' (Aykroyd and Krishnan 1937: 1105). In keeping with the pessimism about Indian food productivity at the time, there seemed to be no means to provide children with sufficient milk. Despite his studies of milk's benefits to child growth, Aykroyd conceded that it would simply be too costly to recommend even one cup (~250 ml) of milk per day for children.

The idea that milk was a particularly good food was apparently entrenched in the South Indian villages surveyed by Aykroyd, but supply and economic constraints could not meet demand, and consumption consequently was low. In the 1930s, family budget studies, diet surveys conducted by Imperial [subsequently Indian] Council of Medical Research, and national sample surveys consistently reported very low levels of milk intake, ranging between 25 and 50 g (1–2 ounces) of milk and milk products per day (Sinha 1961). This is in stark contrast to the United States, where the dairy infrastructure was elaborated and the problem was getting people to consume more of the abundant supply. Indeed a study of Iowa school children in the 1950s bemoaned the finding that boys and girls were not meeting the one-quart-per-day requirement, as they were consuming 'only' between 2.2–3.3 cups (~540–800 ml) per day (Eppright and Swanson 1955)!

In an attempt to ensure better diets, and as a result better physical and cognitive growth and development among children, India has experimented with school meal programmes, with the first one introduced in Madras in 1925 (Chutani 2012). Free school lunches were offered in Tamil Nadu in the 1960s and expanded in the 1980s. In 1995 the federally funded 'National Programme for Nutritional Support to Primary Education' (commonly known as the 'Midday Meal [MDM] Programme') was inaugurated and provided 100 g of food grains per student per day. This scheme was converted into an entitlement for a cooked meal in 2001, and meals generally included a grain, pulses, vegetables and, when possible, fruit (Chutani 2012).

Compared to the US school meal programme, the MDM programme is notable for its lack of milk, reflecting the fact that the programme in the United States was strongly motivated by a desire to find an outlet for the surplus domestic supply of milk. In India there is no such excess, and the government has been unwilling to commit to buying up or importing milk for its school children. Critics have chided both the MDM programme and in the Integrated Child Development Scheme Supplemental Nutrition Program (ICDS-SNP), which provides additional food, mostly grains and pulses, for preschool age children for not including milk (Mishra, Panda and Gonsalves 2009; Working Group on Children under Six 2007).

Milk and milk products are mandated in the 2010 (and previous editions) National Institute of Nutrition Dietary Guidelines for Indians, which recommend 200–300 g/day for children (National Institute of Nutrition 2010). 'Milk that provides good quality proteins and calcium must be an essential item of the diet, particularly for infants, children and women. Include in the diets, foods of animal origin such as milk, eggs and meat, particularly for pregnant and lactating women and children.' For children and adolescents, 'plenty of milk and milk products' should be consumed, primarily for their calcium content, and milk and milk products are among the 'body building and protective' foods.

Similar to Aykroyd's comments over seventy-five years ago, however, the National Institute of Nutrition report acknowledges that the current Indian milk supply would not be able to provide sufficient for all Indians to meet this recommendation. Thus the bemoaning of an inadequate food supply, especially with regard to milk, has been a constant in India over the twentieth century: domestic food production cannot meet recommendations, and widespread poverty precludes access to nutrient-rich foods. In the context in which average intake is recognized as less than 100 g (lower amounts of ~50 g have been reported for children up to age eighteen years living in rural India, National Nutrition Monitoring Bureau 2002), recommending even a cup of milk (250 g) is still recognized as suboptimal, but 'even a little milk is better than none' for children, as 'milk is an ideal food for infants and children' (Gopalan, Rama Sastri and Balasubramanian 1984: 42).

Even if milk was readily available, it is not clear that Indian children would be selectively chosen for milk provisioning. Ethnographers and the psychoanalyst Sudhir Kakar have noted the importance of the corporate household in Indian society, and the subjugation of individual interests to those of the larger family unit (Kakar 2012; Mandelbaum 1948; Seymour 1999; Trawick 1992). Describing her research on childrearing in Orissa, Susan Seymour writes that the principal goal is to have children learn '*interdependence* – the understanding that they are one among many, are *not* unique individuals' (Seymour 1999: 71). This contrasts with a more atomistic approach to individual roles in US households and a clear mandate that children – regardless of age – should get milk above all others (McIntyre, Williams and Glanville 2007). A recent short story from Bengal reveals how milk can be at the centre of Indian family conflicts in households with limited income. 'A Drop of Milk' by Narendra Mitra (2007) centres around a poor family who can afford milk only to meet the 1.5 pints (~750 g) required to fulfil the needs of the eighteen-month-old daughter. The father would like milk for his tea, the mother to relieve her digestive 'acidity', the son to focus on his schoolwork, the brother-in-law for the fortitude to get a job. The story ends with each household member acknowledging the greater need of the other and ultimately directing the coveted glass of milk to an undernourished classmate of the son. Consistent with the Ayurvedic principles, the toddler has the first claim on milk, but beyond that there is no clear privileging of the school-age son. Children's needs compete with those of other household members.

BODY SIZE AND MILK: MEANINGS OF GROWTH

If milk is promoted or fed to children for its 'special' growth-enhancing qualities, it is important to understand the meanings attached to growth in both countries. What does height symbolize? Individual children's health is assessed by their achieved height for age, and average height has long been used as a major index of population health (Tanner 1982; Steckel 2009). Rates of child stunting (having a height for age that is two standard deviations lower than the mean of a growth standard), as well as average adult heights, correlate well with standards of living and overall life expectancy across countries (Deaton 2007). Wealthier – and more politically and economically powerful – countries generally have taller citizens, and within countries, height is strongly positively correlated with educational attainment and income (Deaton and Arora 2009; Case and Paxson 2008). More rapid growth in height during the early childhood period has also been linked to better cognitive performance (Yang et al. 2011; Murasko 2013), including among children in India (Spears 2012). Thus the conditions that impact early growth can have long-term consequences for life chances, and parental as well as governmental concerns about child growth are well warranted.

Average height is strikingly different between India and the United States, and the differences described for boys in the earlier part of the twentieth century persist in the present. Compared to those in India, adult heights in the United States currently average 22 cm higher for men (~177 vs. ~155 cm) and ten cm higher for women (~162 vs. ~152 cm) (McDowell et al. 2008, Deaton 2008). According to the 2005–6 Indian National Family Health Survey, almost half of the children under the age of five years were stunted in height compared to the World Health Organization growth standards (WHO Multicentre Growth Reference Study Group 2006), and this percentage is similar across childhood age groups (Gopalan and Ramachandran 2011). Urban children were less likely to be stunted than rural children (40 per cent vs. 51 per cent, Kanjilal et al. 2010). These indices all contrast markedly with those from the United States, where stunting occurs among less than five per cent of children, although there too there are differences by poverty status (Markowitz and Cosminsky 2005; Lewitt and Kerrebrock 1997). Importantly, these differences in height are not the result of fixed genetic differences; South Asian children raised in the United States or Europe grow to the same size as local children (Deaton 2007).

The links between height and political and economic status and power were not lost on either those in the subcontinent agitating for independence from Britain or on the American presidents and nutritionists in the first half of the twentieth century. In their 1929 book, *The Most Nearly Perfect Food: The Story of Milk*, Samuel Crumbine and James Tobey wrote:

> The races which have always subsisted on liberal milk diets are the ones who have made history and who have contributed the most to the advancement of civilization. As was well said by Herbert Hoover in an address on the milk industry delivered before the World's Dairy Congress in 1923, 'Upon this industry, more than any other of the food industries, depends not alone the problem of public health, but there depends upon it the very growth and virility of the white races.' (Crumbine and Tobey 1929: 77–8)

Of course this rhetoric about milk's contributions to the political and economic success of the United States – and the 'virility of the white races' – conveniently ignored the long-standing dairy traditions of India. India is mentioned as a place where pastoralist peoples of the remote Himalaya had a 'magnificent physique' with 'unusual virility and fertility', attributable to their diet of goat's milk and vegetables. But only those living in 'the few good dairy regions of that country are always vastly superior to the more numerous natives who live only on cereal grains' (Crumbine and Tobey 1929: 9–10). Thus there would be no competing, and non-'white' large-scale dairy-based civilization to compete with the Euro-American mythology, which causally linked Western political and economic success, body size and dairy culture.

But the same rhetoric was deployed by the nascent Indian independence movement, which merged ideas about milk as a food that promoted physical growth and strength with accusations about food scarcity aimed at the British, and the need to protect cows to serve both ends. As Charu Gupta noted, 'The cow was now [in the 1920s] more directly linked with building a strong nation, a nation of Hindu men who had grown weak and poor from lack of milk and *ghee*. For a body of healthy sons, cows became essential. … Like a mother, she could feed her sons with milk, making them stronger' (Gupta 2001: 4296). Protection and improvement of cows were needed to produce sufficient milk and to strengthen 'the poor physique of many of the population' (Home Poll 1922, quoted in Gupta 2001: 4296). The stunted growth of Hindus was attributed to the shortage of cows, created by the British predilection for beef and Muslim sacrifice of cows in celebration of Bakr 'Id (Adcock 2010). Cow's milk could also trade on its purity; in a society with sharp caste boundaries marked by restrictions on food sharing, food items cooked in milk or *ghee* (clarified butter) were rendered pure and thus invulnerable to lower-caste pollution (cf. Staples, in this volume). As such it could unify the disparate members of Indian society and transform them into citizens of a new 'pure' nation (Uberoi 2003).

Thus links between cow's milk, national strength and physical growth were articulated as India moved towards nation-statehood. It is important to note, however, that cows have not been the primary producers of milk in India. Instead, water buffalo's milk makes up the majority of the milk supply. Water buffalo produce not only more milk, but also milk that is higher in fat and economically more valuable. But while shortages of milk were decried, buffalo were not embraced as the means to improve this situation. The buffalo does not share the cow's sacred status among Hindus; indeed as the vehicle of Yama, the god of death, buffalo are inauspicious as well as perceived as dull-witted. Mahatma Gandhi himself denigrated buffalo's milk (Gandhi 2001[1942]), and as a politician from a nationalist Hindu party has recently argued, 'Cow's milk is the elixir of life. Those who consume it become energetic and smart unlike buffalo's milk, which produces lazy people' (Ghatwai 2008). This suggests that milk consumption practices are more complex in India, as different milk types may have different meanings, and may be used to achieve varying biological ends.

As those agitating for independence were aware, body size – especially height – not only describes the physical size of a country's citizenry, but also its strength and power. The growth metaphor remains a powerful one in the early twenty-first century: India has had a rapidly expanding economy and global political influence. India's upwardly mobile urban citizens are embracing milk, as evidenced by more household expenditures and consumption (Ali 2007). Milk advertisements tend to feature the salutary effects of milk drinking on child growth to encourage milk purchases among this rising demographic. A particularly direct one by the national milk cooperative Mother Dairy features a variety of children dressed in oversize adult professional clothing with the following statement in bold font: 'The Country Needs You! Grow Faster.' Mother Dairy's ads were noted as among the first in India to directly target children as consumers and for their lack of the usual references to health or purity (Rai 2006). Complan, a fortified milk powder sold by Heinz, comes with a height measuring guide on its packaging, and its website's FAQ on child growth and nutrition explicitly states: 'Complan has 16% protein which is 100% milk protein and it is critical for a child's growth' (http://www.heinz.co.in/nutrition-space/complan-faqs.aspx).

Milk advertisements in India also frequently use cows, usually Holsteins, the classic black and white cow breed that was domesticated in Northern Europe, rather than the beloved humped zebu cattle that are native to South Asia. Holsteins are a much larger and heftier breed than the ubiquitous zebu and are more prolific milk producers. The larger size of Holsteins may be the key symbol in these ads: bony zebu dairy cows are not compelling if milk is being singled out for its growth-promoting abilities. This size differential also corresponds to Holsteins' European origins. In the wake of new economic policies in India enacted in the 1990s that opened the doors to multinational corporations, milk, which is largely still a domestic product, could use Western motifs as a way of 'modernizing' or 'globalizing' its image. This has the further effect of decoupling milk from its traditional or religious roots, instead linking it to India's full-fledged emergence into global political economy.[1]

Larger, more productive cows and larger, wealthier citizens distinguish India and the United States and countries in Northern Europe. But do Indian parents perceive milk as a means for their children to attain larger sizes? My ongoing research on the relationship between milk consumption and different aspects of child growth in Pune, a rapidly growing urban centre in the state of Maharashtra, provides some insight into this question. Parents (mainly mothers) of seventy-six children aged five to six years, who had been part of an ongoing study on maternal and child diet and growth, were interviewed about their child's milk consumption habits as well as their own understandings of milk's relationship to child growth and development.

Asked about what benefits milk might have for their children, the most common answer was that it enhanced cognitive development (26 per cent). Over 15 per cent noted that it would enhance growth in height, and slightly more (17 per cent) referenced strength and strong bones. When queried directly about whether they thought that milk enhanced physical growth, over 90 per cent said yes. Specific benefits of milk were articulated largely in terms of nutrients: calcium, energy or micronutrients, but almost none mentioned protein. Calcium was most often listed in association with 'strong bones'. If a child does not drink milk, almost one-third said, the child would be weak, would lack strength or have weak bones, and almost one quarter said their growth in height would be compromised.

Over three quarters of the children in the study did drink milk regularly, with similar numbers drinking cow's milk and buffalo's milk. Few drank either both or goat's milk. There was considerable variability with respect to which milk was reported as 'better'; almost half of the caretakers said that cow's milk was preferable, while 35 per cent considered buffalo's milk as better and almost one-fourth noted goat's milk as a superior milk for children. Few households had access to goat's milk and so consumption was rare. But it was also the case half of the mothers who reported that milk was good for cognitive development also thought that cow's milk was better for children, while only 10 per cent thought buffalo's milk was better. In contrast, among those who said that milk promoted physical growth and strength, more thought buffalo's milk was better (37 per cent) compared to cow's milk (26 per cent). This is consistent with expressed sentiments that cow's milk can make you smarter, while buffalo's milk can make you bigger, but dumber, much as buffalo are considered to be less intelligent than cows. A substantial percentage (20–25 per cent) of mothers who noted either cognitive or physical growth benefits asserted that goat's milk was actually better for children. This is likely related to perceptions of goat's milk as more nutritious due to the fact that goats eat lots of herbs and shrubs, and that it was more easily digested. Thus it would appear that in this sample of rural and urban mothers, most view milk consumption as important to the growth and development of their children, especially in the domains of height, strength and intellect. Nutritionist messages seem to have caught on here as well, with many specifically referencing nutritive qualities of milk (such as calcium or vitamins) as the source of growth- and health-enhancing effects (Scrinis 2013; cf. Paxson, in this volume). Although there were not specific questions asked about other dairy products in this study, they were not mentioned by mothers in the discussions of child growth.

Somewhat surprisingly, more traditional motifs related to Krishna, the Hindu god most often associated with milk, did not emerge in the interviews with the mostly Hindu study participants. Krishna is commonly represented as a plump baby with a glint in his eyes and his hand in the butter vessel. Tales of his childhood are replete with ideals for motherhood – unconditional love, nurturance and indulgence all playing out amidst an abundance of dairy products (Figure 10.3). Krishna's fatness is symbolic of his penchant for all things dairy – especially butter – but also his mother's devotion. Subsequently his youth was spent frolicking with the cows and cowherds in idyllic pastures before an adulthood spent vanquishing various evils and defending *dharma*. But although Krishna is associated with cows, milk and butter, stories about him carry no moral imperative for children to drink milk, and he is not held up as particularly tall, large or strong, and his plumpness is limited to infant representations.

It may be that the status of milk as a 'good' food is reinforced by its association with Krishna, who stands on the side of the virtuous, but at the same time, Krishna's idealized masculine adult form does not seem to translate into gender differences in milk's perceived benefits or patterns of consumption. Over 90 per cent of caretakers in the study stated that milk had equal benefits for boys and girls, and that one sex did not require more than the other. In a country known for gender discrimination manifesting in gender differences in child nutrition (Miller 1987), this was a surprising outcome, given that milk is an expensive commodity.

FIGURE 10.3: A young Krishna is milking a cow, while his parents Yasoda and Nanda stand nearby. (Rajasthan, late 18th century, © Trustees of the British Museum)

What do parents expect from greater size and cognitive performance among their children? Greater height is a highly desirable trait for males *and* females, particularly among the upwardly mobile middle class looking for marriage partners for their children (Wiley 2011). Marriage is a means by which families may enhance their social and economic status (for females by marrying up the caste hierarchy; for males by acquiring a large dowry). Height is a measure of the success of individuals and their families, and especially reflects on the quality of a mother's care (R. Parameswaran, personal communication). Given the way in which it serves as a symbol of distinction between wealthy and poor countries, height is a potent metaphor for and marker of status differentials, which have currency at the individual, household and national levels. Moreover, in India, the linkage between cognitive performance and height is more than twice as strong as it is in the United States, suggesting that better nutrition in childhood is crucial (Spears 2012). Cognitive performance is, in turn, linked to greater job opportunities and upward mobility. That milk might enhance both of these in one glass is a powerful motivator to provide children with milk.

But what about these associations in the United States? Here too the wealthier are generally taller than the poorer (Deaton and Arora 2009), but milk consumption among children is not differently patterned by socio-economic status (Sebastian et al. 2010). Beliefs about milk enhancing child growth and building 'strong bones' are ubiquitous. Advertisements in the late 1900s and early 2000s were as blatant as the Mother Dairy ads: 'Got milk? Get Tall! Want your kids to grow? The calcium in milk helps your bones grow strong. So give them a tall glass.' The milk–calcium–strong bones link has become so well known that milk has become associated in the minds of many Americans that most people can articulate the view that children need to drink milk to 'build strong bones' (Wiley, unpublished data). Yet declines in milk consumption have been particularly dramatic among children since the 1970s (Sebastian et al. 2010).

Why are children not drinking their milk in America? Most are drinking some amount of milk, with average consumption among two- to eleven-year-olds being just over one- and one-quarter cups (~320 ml) per day, which is well below recommended amounts. Do American parents not care about gains in height? Average height increased among Americans who were born up through the mid-twentieth century, but these gains levelled off, and the relationship between height, education and income has remained relatively stable (Komlos and Baur 2004). Thus Americans are not growing taller, and while they were the tallest national population prior to the Second World War, there have been greater height gains among Northern European countries subsequently, and now the United States lags behind these countries substantially. Some have suggested that this differential is related to differences in health care access and social safety nets across countries (Komlos and Baur 2004). Others have suggested that declining milk consumption may have contributed to the lack of increases in height in the United States, because milk consumption did not drop as markedly in Northern Europe, especially in the Netherlands, where average height increased the most (de Beer 2012). Regardless, Americans are now much taller than they were in the early part of the century, while milk consumption has remained the same or lower (Wiley 2016).[2]

Despite widespread understanding of milk as a 'good food' for children, and its associations with growing strong bones, these health messages do not seem to bring urgency to milk purchases or consumption. As a result, advertisements seem to have turned away from a focus on young children and growing strong bones. Those advertisements that are aimed at children have hitched themselves to public health initiatives encouraging physical activity to prevent childhood obesity (e.g. www.fueluptoplay60.com is currently the most active milk promotion). At the same time, however, the demographic featured in milk advertisements is adults, mostly women, as milk positions itself 'for all ages' (Wiley 2011). With declining fertility and an aging baby-boom population, and with a tired message that milk enhances strong bones or height, milk processors are desperate to find a new market. Concerns about 'excess growth' manifesting as rising rates of obesity and chronic disease, the message that 'milk makes children grow' no longer packs the rhetorical punch that it did in the early twentieth century (Wiley 2011).

The opposing milk consumption trends among children in India and the United States represent children's entry into the world of consumers, able to articulate their preferences and influence family purchasing patterns (Curtis, James and Ellis 2010; Elliott 2011). In the United States this takes the form of choosing other drinks, with supermarket aisles devoted to fruit drinks and soda, a lavish selection that is cleverly and widely advertised, branded, brightly coloured and sweet – clamouring for children's attention. Flavourings, sweeteners and colour have been added since the early twentieth century to make milk more attractive and palatable to children, but milk can no longer keep up with the sheer variety and novelty of other drinks. Yet milk retains a place in children's diets through school milk programmes, where chocolate milk is the bestseller, and through its status as the 'original' kid's food with its inherently healthier nutrient profile and entrenched views about its benefits to children's bodies.

We are just beginning to have some insight into how these forces might be playing out in India. The Mother Dairy ads speaking directly to children suggest that children might be able to assert more authority over household food purchases. There is concern that 'Western' foods are replacing traditional foods eaten by children, and that these contribute to the growing problem of child overweight and obesity (Sharma, Grover and Chaturvedi 2011), especially among urban and wealthier families (Bhardwaj et al. 2008). Milk appears to be part of the mix of 'Western' foods but whether it will maintain its status among them remains to be seen, or whether its identity as a 'traditional' food will be re-established. Sweetened and coloured milk is marketed to children and adults alike: 'Amul Kool Koko is fun, nourishing drink with chocolate.' (Amul Kool Milk Shake is milk and sugar blended with fruit or almonds and 'the product has calcium, protein, carbohydrates, vitamins, etc. for healthy growth of a human body. ... This product can be consumed by all people irrespective of their age.' www.amul.com). The 'fun' has crept into milk products along with nutrients; although they are not specifically targeted to children, 'healthy growth of a human body' certainly links them to the young.

CONCLUSION

India and the United States are currently the world's top milk producers, they share an identity as 'dairying cultures', and privilege milk as a food. While dairy products had long been consumed, fluid milk achieved a new status as a growth- and strength-promoting food in the context of the two countries' respective nation-building projects in the early to mid-twentieth century, as the unique physiological needs of children came to be understood in the scientific community. Thus efforts to encourage milk consumption by embedding it within the needs of growing children served a variety of political, economic and public health ends. These goals were able to capitalize on the seemingly intuitive link between milk's unique properties as a food and child growth. The widespread assumption that post-weaning age children should drink milk is of relatively recent origin even in dairying societies, and most populations around the world did not consume bovine milk beyond the weaning period.

Childhood milk consumption has become well established as a normative principle both among individuals and in official dietary guidelines, but the ideal is not attained in either India or the United States. Instead, milk-drinking practices are influenced by other values and social structures. In India, consumption desires are constrained by limited per capita production and widespread poverty, but are enthusiastically indulged by the burgeoning urban middle class as a marker of, and means to enhance, household status. Beliefs about the sanctity of the cow or Krishna's affection for all things dairy are likely to be weak motivations among Indian Hindus, as most milk comes from the less auspicious water buffalo. Milk is part of official dietary recommendations, but with a limited supply and unmet demand, the dairy industry does not need to take a central role in milk promotion. In contrast, the dairy industry in the United States is heavily invested in sustaining demand for its abundant supply of milk and it creates most of the discourse around milk. Milk consumption is not a marker of socio-economic status in the United States (Sebastian et al. 2010) and there are food assistance programmes to encourage childhood milk intake among the poor and these have the parallel effect of supporting the dairy industry. Furthermore, with children now viewed as consumers with preferences of their own, milk has lost ground amidst the myriad sweetened and coloured beverages marketed to them. Its normative status as something children 'should' drink has changed; children are now encouraged by marketers to choose what they 'want' to drink. Whether milk will similarly lose its lustre among India's children remains to be seen.

Milk's association with growth makes sense given its biological functions to support infant growth, but milk-feeding practices for children need to be understood in relation to family or national goals for body size. Claims that milk consumption enhances height continue to have a great deal of traction in India, as Indians are among the shortest populations in the world, a stature incommensurate with their growing 'Asian Tiger' economy. Taller, larger bodies are a sign of wealth and health and are characteristic of the modern, powerful citizenry that contemporary children are poised to join. These characteristics were similarly linked to milk in the twentieth-century United States when child undernutrition was common, but in the ageing United States, children are a shrinking demographic, and there is widespread concern about food overconsumption and them being 'too large'. Instead, milk is being repositioned as a food for 'all ages' and a salve for later-life chronic diseases, but milk's biological link to growth may prevent its taking on this new meaning.

In sum, the comparison of childhood milk consumption practices can be used to demonstrate how food is deeply embedded in social and cultural life. Milk is indeed a nutrient-rich food of benefit to those with poor nutritional status and the ability to digest its lactose. Even while its nutritional components have been highlighted as key to its 'goodness', milk has been imagined both in India and the United States as much more than that. The 'naturalization' of childhood milk drinking has served a variety of social purposes in these two large dairy cultures; but despite this shared tradition, the two countries are experiencing contrasting consumption trends as milk takes on new meanings in each.

NOTES

1. Early advertisements and milk labels in the United States also tended to feature such large, placid cows grazing in verdant pastures, before images of plump and equally placid children began to be featured after the Civil War (DuPuis 2002). The link between milk and the strong (white), large body became more direct, with the large cows receding into the background.

2. A recent meta-analysis suggests that there is a modest positive relationship, which may be stronger when children are undernourished and among adolescents, who are growing rapidly. Relationships seem to be restricted to fluid milk rather than dairy products in general (de Beer 2012, see also Wiley 2012). Thus while promotions attributing greater height to milk appear to resonate well with, and 'make sense' to, consumers, the current scientific literature does not provide unambiguous support for these statements.

REFERENCES

Achaya, K. T. (1994), *Indian Food: A Historical Companion*, New York: Oxford University Press.

Adcock, C. S. (2010), 'Sacred Cows and Secular History: Cow Protection Debates in Colonial North India', *Comparative Studies of South Asia, Africa and the Middle East*, 30: 297–311.

Ali, J. (2007), 'Structural Changes in Food Consumption and Nutritional Intake From Livestock Products in India', *South Asia Research*, 27: 137–51. doi: 10.1177/026272800702700201.

Arnold, D. (2000), *Science, Technology and Medicine in Colonial India*, Cambridge: Cambridge University Press.

Aykroyd, W. R. and Krishnan, B. G. (1936), 'Diet Surveys in South Indian Villages', *Indian Journal of Medical Research*, 24: 667–88.

Aykroyd, W. R. and Krishnan, B. G. (1937), 'The Effect of Skimmed Milk, Soya Bean, and Other Foods in Supplementing Typical Indian Diets', *Indian Journal of Medical Research*, 24: 1093–115.

Aykroyd, W. R. and Rajagopal, K. (1936), 'The State of Nutrition of School Children in South India Part II Diet and Deficiency Disease in Residential Hostels', *Indian Journal of Medical Research*, 24: 707–25.

Bhardwaj, S., Misra, A., Khurana, L., Gulati, S., Shah, P. and Vikram, N. K. (2008), 'Childhood Obesity in Asian Indians: A Burgeoning Cause of Insulin Resistance, Diabetes and Sub-Clinical Inflammation', *Asia Pacific Journal of Clinical Nutrition*, 17(Suppl 1): 172–5.

Bhishagratna, K. L. (1911), *The Sushruta Samhita: An English Translation Based on Original Sanskrit Text*, vols I–III, Calcutta: Wilkins Press.

Calvert, K. (2003), 'Patterns of Childrearing in America', in W. Koops and M. Zuckerman (eds), *Beyond the Century of the Child: Cultural History and Developmental Psychology*, 62–81, Philadelphia: University of Pennsylvania Press.

Case, A. and Paxson, C. (2008), 'Stature and Status: Height, Ability, and Labor Market Outcomes', *Journal of Political Economy*, 116: 499–532. doi: 10.1086/589524.

Chutani, A. M. (2012), 'School Lunch Program in India: Background, Objectives and Components', *Asia Pacific Journal of Clinical Nutrition*, 21: 151–4.

Crumbine, S. J. and Tobey, J. A. (1929), *The Most Nearly Perfect Food: The Story of Milk*, Baltimore, MD: The Williams & Wilkins Company.

Cunningham, H. (1998), 'Histories of Childhood', *The American Historical Review*, 103: 1195–208.

Curtis, P., James, A. and Ellis, K. (2010), 'Children's Snacking, Children's Food: Food Moralities and Family Life', *Children's Geographies*, 8: 291–302. doi: 10.1080/14733285.2010.494870.

de Beer, H. (2012), 'Dairy Products and Physical Stature: A Systematic Review and Meta-Analysis of Controlled Trials', *Economics & Human Biology*, 10: 299–309. doi: http://dx.doi.org/10.1016/j.ehb.2011.08.003.

Deaton, A. (2007), 'Height, Health, and Development', *Proceedings of the National Academy of Sciences*, 104: 13232–7. doi: 10.1073/pnas.0611500104.

Deaton, A. (2008), 'Height, Health, and Inequality: The Distribution of Adult Heights in India', *American Economics Review*, 98: 468–74.

Deaton, A. and Arora, R. (2009), 'Life at the Top: The Benefits of Height', *Economics & Human Biology*, 7: 133–6. doi: http://dx.doi.org/10.1016/j.ehb.2009.06.001.

DuPuis, E. M. (2002), *Nature's Perfect Food: How Milk Became America's Drink*, New York: New York University Press.

Elliott, C. (2011), '"It's Junk food and Chicken Nuggets": Children's Perspectives on "Kids' Food" and the Question of Food Classification', *Journal of Consumer Behaviour*, 10: 133–40. doi: 10.1002/cb.360.

Eppright, E. S. and Swanson, P. P. (1955), 'Distribution of Calories in Diets of Iowa School Children', *Journal of the American Dietetic Association*, 31: 144–8.

Gopalan, C., Rama Sastri, B. V. and Balasubramanian, S. C. (1984), *Nutritive Value of Indian Foods*, Hyderabad, India: National Institute of Nutrition, Indian Council of Medical Research.

Gopalan, H. and Ramachandran, P. (2011), 'Assessment of Nutritional Status in Indian Preschool Children Using WHO 2006 Growth Standards', *Indian Journal of Medical Research*, 134: 47–53.

Gunderson, G. W. (1971), *National School Lunch Program (NSLP): Background and Development*, Washington DC: United States Department of Agriculture, Food and Nutrition Service.

Gupta, C. (2001), 'The Icon of Mother in Late Colonial North India: "Bharat Mata," "Matri Bhasha" and "Gau Mata"', *Economic and Political Weekly*, 36: 4291–9.

Halpern, S. A. (1988), *American Pediatrics: The Social Dynamics of Professionalism, 1880-1980*, Berkeley: University of California Press.

Hartley, R. M. (1977[1842]), *An Historical, Scientific and Practical Essay on Milk as an Article of Human Sustenance*, New York: Arno Press.

Hunt, C. L. (1916), 'Food for Young Children', *United States Department of Agriculture Farmers' Bulletin*, 717: 1.

Kakar, S. (2012), *The Inner World: A Psycho-analytic Study of Childhood and Society in India*, 4th edn, New Delhi: Oxford University Press.

Kanjilal, B., Mazumdar, P., Mukherjee, M. and Rahman, M. H. (2010), 'Nutritional Status of Children in India: Household Socio-Economic Condition as the Contextual Determinant', *International Journal for Equity in Health*, 9: 19.

Komlos, J. and Baur, M. (2004), 'From the Tallest to (one of) the Fattest: The Enigmatic Fate of the American Population in the 20th Century', *Economics & Human Biology*, 2: 57–74. doi: http://dx.doi.org/10.1016/j.ehb.2003.12.006.

Kutumbiah, P. (1959), 'Pediatrics (Kaumara Bhrtya) in Ancient India', *Indian Journal of Pediatrics*, 26: 328–37. doi: 10.1007/BF02989331.

Lefkowitz, M. R. and Fant, M. B. (1982), *Women's Life in Greece and Rome*, Toronto: Samuel-Stevens.

Leighton, G. and Clark, M. L. (1929), 'Milk Consumption and the Growth of School-Children', *Lancet*, 213: 40–3.

Levenstein, H. A. (1988), *Revolution at the Table: The Transformation of the American Diet*, New York: Oxford University Press.

Lewitt, E. M. and Kerrebrock, N. (1997), 'Population-Based Growth Stunting', *The Future of Children*, 7: 149–56.

Mandelbaum, D. G. (1948), 'The Family in India', *Southwestern Journal of Anthropology*, 4: 123–39.

Markowitz, D. L. and Cosminsky, S. (2005), 'Overweight and Stunting in Migrant Hispanic Children in the USA', *Economics & Human Biology*, 3: 215–40. doi: http://dx.doi.org/10.1016/j.ehb.2005.05.005.

McDowell, M. A., Fryar, C. D., Ogden, C. L. and Flegal, K. M. (2008), 'Anthropometric Reference Data for Children and Adults: United States, 2003–2006', *National Health Statistics Report No. 10*, www.cdc.gov/nchs/data/nhsr/nhsr010.pdf.

McIntyre, L., Williams, P. and Glanville, N. T. (2007), 'Milk as Metaphor: Low-Income Lone Mothers' Characterization of their Challenges Acquiring Milk for their Families', *Ecology of Food and Nutrition*, 46: 263–79. doi: 10.1080/03670240701407640.

Mendelson, A. (2008), *Milk: The Surprising Story of Milk through the Ages*, New York: Alfred A. Knopf.

Miller, B. D. (1987), 'Female Infanticide and Child Neglect in Rural North India', in N. Scheper-Hughes (ed.), *Child Survival: Anthropological Perspectives on the Treatment and Maltreatment of Children*, 95–112, Boston, MA: D. Reidel Publishing Company.

Ministry of Women and Child Development (n.d.), *India Nutrition Profile*, Ministry of Women and Child Development, Government of India.

Mishra, Y., Panda, G. R. and Gonsalves, C. (2009), *Human Rights and Budgets in India*, New Delhi: Human Rights Law Network.

Mitra, N. (2007), 'A Drop of Milk', in J. Thieme and I. Raja (eds), *The Table is Laid: The Oxford Anthology of South Asian Food Writing*, 273–81, New Delhi: Oxford University Press.

Murasko, J. E. (2013), 'Physical Growth and Cognitive Skills in Early-Life: Evidence from a Nationally Representative US Birth Cohort', *Social Science & Medicine*, 97: 267–77. doi: http://dx.doi.org/10.1016/j.socscimed.2012.12.006.

National Institute of Nutrition (2010), Dietary Guidelines for Indians, http://www.indg.gov.in/health/nutrition/dietary-guidelines-for-indians.

National Nutrition Monitoring Bureau (2002), Diet and Nutritional Status of Rural Population, NNMB Technical Report No. 21. Hyderabad, India: National Institute of Nutrition.

Orr, J. B. (1928), 'Milk Consumption and the Growth of School-Children', *Lancet*, 1: 202–3.

Pollock, J. (2006), 'Two Controlled Trials of Supplementary Feeding of British School Children in the 1920s', *Journal of the Royal Society of Medicine*, 99: 323–7.

Prowse, T., Saunders, S., Fitzgerald, C., Bondioli, L. and Macchiarelli, R. (2010), 'Growth, Morbidity, and Mortality in Antiquity: A Case Study from Imperial Rome', in T. Moffat and T. Prowse (eds), *Human Diet and Nutrition in Biocultural Perspective: Past Meets Present*, 173–96, New York: Berghahn Books.

Rai, A. R. (2006), 'Mother Dairy's BIG India Plans', *Rediff News*, 4 July.

Reaney, B. C. (1922), *Milk and Our School Children, Prepared for the Bureau of Education by the Child Health Organization of America*, Washington, DC: Government Printing Office.

Richey, H. G. (1937), 'The Relation of Accelerated, Normal and Retarded Puberty to the Height and Weight of School Children', *Monographs of the Society for Research in Child Development*, 2: i–67. doi: 10.2307/1165448.

Scrinis, G. (2013), *Nutritionism: The Science and Politics of Dietary Advice*, New York: Columbia University Press.

Sebastian, R., Goldman, J., Wilkinson Enns, C. and LaComb, R. (2010), 'Fluid Milk Consumption in the United States: What We Eat In America, NHANES 2005-2006', *Food Surveys Research Group Dietary Data Brief*, No. 3. http://ars.usda.gov/Services/docs.htm?docid=19476.

Seymour, S. C. (1999), *Women, Family, and Child Care in India: A World in Transition*, Cambridge: Cambridge University Press.

Sharma, R., Grover, V. and Chaturvedi, S. (2011), 'Recipe for Diabetes Disaster: A Study of Dietary Behaviors among Adolescent Atudents in South Delhi, India', *International Journal of Diabetes in Developing Countries*, 31: 4–8. doi: 10.1007/s13410-010-0009-8.

Sinha, R. P. (1961), *Food In India: An Analysis of the Prospects for Self-Sufficiency by 1975-1976*, New York: Oxford University Press.

Spears, D. (2012), 'Height and Cognitive Achievement among Indian Children', *Economics & Human Biology*, 10: 210–19. doi: http://dx.doi.org/10.1016/j.ehb.2011.08.005.

Steckel, R. H. (2009), 'Heights and Human Welfare: Recent Developments and New Directions', *Explorations in Economic History*, 46: 1–23. doi: http://dx.doi.org/10.1016/j.eeh.2008.12.001.

Tanner, J. M. (1982), 'The Potential of Auxological Data for Monitoring Economic and Social well-being', *Social Science History*, 6: 571–81.

Trawick, M. (1992), *Notes on Love in a Tamil Family*, Berkeley: University of California.

Uberoi, P. (2003), '"Unity in diversity?" Dilemmas of Nationhood in Indian Calendar Art', in S. Ramaswamy (ed.), *Beyond Appearances?: Visual Practices and Ideologies in Modern India, Contributions to Indian Sociology No. 10*, 191–232, Thousand Oaks, CA: Sage Publications.

United States Department of Agriculture (2015), *Production, Supply, and Distribution Online*, Foreign Agricultural Service, available from http://apps.fas.usda.gov/psdonline/ (accessed May 21 2015).

United States Department of Agriculture Food and Nutrition Information Center (2011), *Historical Dietary Guidance*, Washington, DC: USDA National Agricultural Library.

United States Department of Health and Human Services and United States Department of Agriculture (2015), *Dietary Guidelines for Americans*. USDHHS/USDA 2015, available from http://health.gov/dietaryguidelines/2015/guidelines/ (accessed 21 February 2016).

WHO Multicentre Growth Reference Study Group (2006), WHO Child Growth
    Standards: Length/height-for-age, weight-for-age, weight-for-length, weight-for-
    height and body mass index-for-age: Methods and development. http://www.who.int/
    childgrowth/standards/technical_report/en/index.html.
Wiley, A. S. (2007), 'The Globalization of Cow's Milk Production and Consumption:
    Biocultural Perspectives', *Ecology of Food and Nutrition*, 46: 281–312.
Wiley, A. S. (2011), 'Milk for "Growth": Global and Local Meanings of Milk
    Consumption in China, India, and the US', *Food and Foodways*, 19: 11–33.
Wiley, A. S. (2012), 'Cow Milk Consumption, Insulin-Like Growth Factor-I, and Human
    Biology: A Life History Approach', *American Journal Of Human Biology*, 24: 130–8.
    doi: 10.1002/ajhb.22201.
Wiley, A. S. (2014), *Cultures of Milk: The Biology and Meaning of Dairy Products in India
    and the United States*, Cambridge, MA: Harvard University Press.
Wiley, A. S. (2016), *Re-Imagining Milk*, 2nd edn, New York: Routledge.
Working Group on Children under Six (2007), 'Strategies for Children under Six',
    Economic and Political Weekly, 42: 87–101. doi: 10.2307/40277131.
Yang, S., Tilling, K., Martin, R., Davies, N., Ben-Shlomo, Y. and Kramer, M. S. (2011),
    'Pre-Natal and Post-Natal Growth Trajectories and Childhood Cognitive Ability and
    Mental Health', *International Journal of Epidemiology*, 40: 1215–26. doi: 10.1093/ije/
    dyr094.

CHAPTER ELEVEN

Food, Borders and Disease

JOSEPHINE SMART AND ALAN SMART

INTRODUCTION

In 1862, a ship from San Francisco arrived in Victoria (British Columbia, Canada) and unleashed a smallpox epidemic throughout British Columbia that killed an estimated 20,000 people within a year, most of whom being First Nations people (Belshaw 2013). Major nodes of transit, whether they are port cities like Hong Kong and San Francisco, or inland metropolis like Mexico City and Toronto (Canada), are particularly vulnerable to contagions from afar, which arrive as invisible passengers sheltered within the bodies of human and animal carriers or as silent riders in commodities both organic and inorganic. The paths of cross infection are diverse and often devastating, and increasingly global in their reach as evident from the recent incidents of avian flu, Severe and Acute Respiratory Syndrome (SARS), and swine flu. In this chapter, we concentrate on the movement of food across borders, with emphasis on the health risks arising from emerging infectious diseases and contamination that pose significant public health threats.

Food, defined in the broadest sense as a collection of consumables both processed and raw, is essential to our survival. There exists a large and rich body of work, both academic and popular, on food and its relevance to human existence across temporal and geographical frames in its full complexity of procurement methods, preservation and preparation, nutritional value, symbolisms, and meanings of gender, power, imperialism, modernity, identity/ethnicity and culture (see Anderson 1988; Belasco and Scranton 2002; Counihan 1999; Macbeth 1997; Harris 1989; Revel 1982; Toussaint-Samat 1992; Wilk 2006). Research that examines the relationship between health and food is highly diverse and may be loosely grouped into several categories. Foremost among these are the studies of indigenous medical knowledge and practices in health management involving the use of selected flora and fauna and specific prescribed behavioural protocol. The use of guinea pig in broth and other forms to diagnose and treat health problems in Ecuador is a good example (Archetti 1997: 86–111). Pillsbury's discussion of Chinese post-partum food and behavioural rules among Taiwanese women in the United States is another example of this genre (Pillsbury 1978). Another category involves studies of changing dietary patterns and food choices/preference that have health implications, both immediate and long term. Sidney Mintz's influential book on the social history of sugar tells a powerful story of how sugar, once an item afforded only by the elites, became a daily necessity among the working class in Britain during the height of British imperialism in the 1800s (Mintz 1985). His work, using a political economy approach, shows how the entanglements of capitalism, imperialism, slavery, commodity marketing, war and trade policies supported a global increase in the use of sugar in human diet (Mintz 1996, 2009; Mintz and Du Bois 2002). Today we are just beginning to unravel the full implications of sugar consumption and its role in a wide range of 'modern' health problems such as obesity, high blood pressure, diabetes and even cancer. The cultural politics of food and globalization, the economic implications and public health impacts have attracted a lot of public attention and interest in recent years (see Freidberg 2004; Rampton and Strauber 2004; Scholsser 2001; Watson and Caldwell 2005).

A third category of food studies addresses specifically the relationship between food safety and health problems. The global circulation and production of food is viewed by many as a celebrated triumph for businesses that draw profits through the strategic relocation and/or industrialization of production, and a triumph for consumers who can get food at lower costs and increasingly free of seasonal constraints. It is a win-win situation. Others are critical of the implications of industrial agriculture, chief among which is the increasing separation between production and consumption, leaving consumers increasingly ignorant of how and where their food comes from, and what is in their food. Consumers become increasingly distrustful of the quality of their food, and begin to voice their concerns about food safety and how undisclosed chemicals and contaminants in their food may affect their health. Pollan's 2006 book *The Omnivore's Dilemma* effectively expresses the concerns of a large segment of consumers. He advocates a return to a bygone era when buyers purchased directly from the producers in a long-standing relationship of mutual trust and transparency.

Food globalization is influenced deeply by emotional responses ranging from fear and disgust through to desire and addiction. Food is mobile, but it is also subject to restrictions and rejections. Surprising sources for localization of food choices emerge when we start to consider consumers and their cultural logics for consumption. While publications tend to emphasize ethical and environmental rationales for 'locavorism', fear may be a stronger motivation for many. Xenophobia, in the wider sense of fear of non-humans as well as humans from elsewhere, can also play a part, increasing distrust and often disgust over issues like cannibal cows and disguised horse meat. The global landscape of eating is not just about industries, capital markets and food miles; it is deeply affected by cultural logics of food preferences and consumption that may preserve local foodways or selectively reject translocal cuisine items, overemphasize certain food safety factors and undermine other food risks that are equally real. Food safety risk is as old as human existence, but its power to inflict large-scale security risk is no longer contained within a delimited geographical boundary in our current global configuration based on time–space compression.

The impact of foodborne disease can be massive. Avian flu was first identified in Hong Kong in 1997 and was subsequently traced back to southern China as the source. The 1997 avian flu (strain H5N1) was a zoonotic disease that affected both poultry and humans and was highly pathogenic with a mortality rate among the infected at around 33–50 per cent (Nerlich and Halliday 2007: 47). A massive culling of nearly two million chickens in 1997 seemed to be effective in suppressing the spread of avian flu. But in 2003 avian flu (strain H5N1) re-emerged in Hong Kong and China, and in 2004 it was identified in Southeast Asia. The most recent re-emergence of avian flu comes in the form of a H7N9 strain and was found in two patients in Hong Kong in early December 2013 (*Ming Pao*, 8 December 2013: A12). Given that avian flu is transmitted through close contact between/among animals and humans, this latest re-emergence of avian flu in south China reactivated a series of well-established protocols involving animal culling and various border bio-security measures to minimize the risk of a major pandemic.

Avian flu is among more than two hundred zoonotic diseases identified by the World Health Organization.[1] Effective management of these zoonotic diseases involves multiple and diverse measures such as animal culling, quarantine and isolation of infected patients, enhanced port health inspection systems, surveillance of arrivals (re: people, livestock, meat products), fumigation of luggage/container/ aircraft cabins, animal and product traceability systems, new food safety protocols to prevent cross infection at points of processing and transport, strict rules regarding removal of SRMs (specified risk materials from parts of an animal) from the human food chain, and vaccine development (Crump, Murdock and Baker 2001: 768; Onodera and Kim 2006: 1–11).

The technical/medical interventions and outcomes are central to the changing configurations in global public health management, in particular the growing awareness and practice of the 'one-health' approach which is premised on the understanding that the effective management of human health must include a comprehensive understanding of the intimate interactions between human and non-human flora and fauna (Rock et al. 2009: 991–5). These human/non-human interactions are entangled in ecology, culture, technology and other forces both natural and man-made.

Caballero-Anthony (2006: 106–7) further suggests that emerging and re-emerging pandemics are no longer simply medical issues but are 'major security threats' in their nature as 'global public goods'. Effective policy interventions should be coordinated through a more inclusive participation involving a wide range of actors across geographical borders, political boundaries and disciplinary specializations. This logic of public health as a security issue is relevant in the context of a growing anxiety among consumers worldwide that many globally circulated food products may be health threats due to the lack of transparency about food safety standards in the country of origin or an indifference among distant producers about the welfare of the consumers of their goods (see Pollan 2006). In recent years, made-in-China products have suffered a significant loss in consumer confidence after a number of highly publicized problems with food safety in that country, such as the melamine-tainted baby formula in 2008 and the recycling of 'gutter oil' for domestic and commercial uses in the past few years (Barboza 2008; *The Economist* 2011).

This chapter uses the Hong Kong–China boundary region as a geographic filter to examine the changing entanglements of politics, trade governance, food safety, public health, consumer behaviour and diseases. We take a political economy approach with an aim to show how 'an ensemble of forces – technological, economic, political ... could effectuate large-scale changes' (Mintz 2008: 25). Not only do we wish to identify the multitude of factors involved and the complex ways they are 'entangled' to produce consequences that may or may not be intended, we also try to make explicit the 'rules of engagement' that empower or restrain the actors' roles and participation in the processes, and which direct the outcomes in certain ways.

The two zoonotic diseases covered in this chapter are relatively new members on the zoonoses list. The first one, Bovine Spongiform Encephalopathy (BSE), was first identified in the United Kingdom in 1986. A human form of it, known as variant Creutzfeldt–Jacob disease (vCJD), was confirmed in 1996.[2] It is a disease without known cure at this time. The second zoonotic disease discussed in this chapter is SARS, which first appeared in Hong Kong in 2003 and quickly spread worldwide within the year to infect over 8,000 people, with a mortality rate at nearly 10 per cent. The third case study in this chapter is the 2008 melamine-tainted baby formula scandal in China and its most unexpected consequence in the form of a global phenomenon in parallel trading of infant formula. These three cases are very different by nature of the disease/health risk, its local and global impact, the types of intervention that arise and their consequences. What they share in common is that they are global in reach and their threat to public health is real and greatly feared. The data presented in this chapter point to the need to recognize the interplay between disease, food and public health as a complex issue beyond the purely medical and technical dimensions. We must recognize that many social and cultural factors embedded in consumer preferences may work against scientific information and/or recommendations about particular food types and their direct link to health risk, thus creating unexpected barriers to the effective management of public health risk.

BOVINE SPONGIFORM ENCEPHALOPATHY (BSE)

A deadly disease known as *kuru* first surfaced in the Fore region in highland Papua New Guinea (PNG) in the 1920s. In the 1960s, anthropologists Glasse and Lindenbaum identified a link between the disease and the adoption of cannibalistic mortuary rites. *Kuru* is a lethal form of neurodegeneration affecting both the old and young. Typical symptoms are loss of motor-coordination, steady loss in weight and eventually death. These symptoms are very similar to those known today in vCJD patients, a form of zoonotic disease that is known as BSE (more commonly known as 'mad cow disease') in cattle (see Lindenbaum 2001; Rampton and Stauber 2004: 37–52). *Kuru* was transmitted from human to human through the mortuary ritual of consuming the brain and muscle of the diseased by close relatives, as observed by Glasse and Lindenbaum in the 1960s. Subsequently, the Australian government outlawed this practice and *kuru* is no longer found in PNG. *Kuru* remained an exotic oddity associated with PNG that was little known among the public until the outbreak of BSE in Britain and Europe in the 1990s.

On 19 December 1993, a six-year-old cow in Alberta, Canada was confirmed to have BSE. By then, the BSE situation in the United Kingdom since 1986 had shown other cattle-producing countries the potentially high economic and political costs of BSE as measured in terms of the erosion in consumer confidence in food safety, decline in the public trust of the government's effectiveness in public health management, and the tremendous social-psychological burden on the affected farmers and farming communities associated with the widespread culling of cattle herds and the uncertainty of an end to the terrible animal disease. Fortunately for Canada, it managed to bypass a potentially costly situation by pointing to the British origin of the infected animal, which was one of 175 animals imported from the United Kingdom before 1990 (Romahn 1993: B7). By highlighting the foreign origin of the animal, and carrying out a massive culling of all cattle imported from the United Kingdom between 1982 and 1990 (Campbell 1993: C2), Canada achieved the strategic transformation of the first BSE case from a potential economic disaster into a mere inconvenience. The next BSE case in Canada was confirmed on 20 May 2003. This time, there was no escape. Within two hours of the initial announcement of the confirmation of BSE in the morning of 20 May, all international borders were closed to Canadian beef, livestock, breeding products and beef product imports. Cattle producers in Alberta went into instant shock and despair. It was estimated that for every day the international trade ban was in effect, the Canadian economy suffered a loss of CAD$11 million and many jobs in a wide range of sectors linked to the cattle industry (Le Roy and Klein 2005; Government of Alberta 2006; CBC New Online Indepth 2006). The estimated total economic impact of BSE on the Canadian economy was estimated to be CAD$7–11 billion. In 2012, China and South Korea were the last two countries to reopen their market to Canadian beef imports (MCEC 2012; Government of Canada 2012).

In total, twenty cases of BSE in Canada were confirmed between 2003 and 2011 (CFIA 2011). In the global context, the United Kingdom ranks first with nearly 200,000 infected animals identified since 1986. Both France and Portugal have close to 1,000 cases of BSE confirmed since 1991 and 1990, respectively. BSE is found in many European countries. Japan, the only Asian country known to have BSE, had thirty-six confirmed cases between 2001 and 2009 (OIE no date). In the United States, three cases of BSE are known so far. BSE has not been identified in Africa, Central Asia, India, Southeast Asia, East Asia (except Japan) or Latin America.

Following China's announcement in 2012 of the reopening of its market to Canadian beef, the export value in the first six months of 2013 reached CAD$35 million, or 10,088 tonnes of Canadian beef (Canada Beef Inc. 2012). While this resumption of exports to China is impressive in its magnitude and future potential, it is what happened between 2003 and 2011 during the trade ban that tickles our curiosity. The export data documented by the Department of Agriculture and Rural Development (Government of Alberta) show that despite the imposition of the first BSE-induced trade ban in 2003, bovine semen and beef products continued to be exported to China (Government of Alberta, No Date a). Hong Kong rose in rank to become one of the major markets for Canadian beef exports after 2003 (Government of Alberta, No Date b). In a PowerPoint presentation given by the

Alberta Government (Government of Alberta, No Date c), the value of Alberta beef exports to Hong Kong grew substantially from CAD$1.67 million in 2003 to CAD$38.2 million (2004), CAD$76.38 million (2005), CAD$56.59 million (2006), CAD$90.40 million (2007), CAD$79.33 million (2008), CAD$66.42 million (2009) and CAD$55.35 million (2010). It should be noted that the export value of Canada beef to Hong Kong in 2002 was CAD$2.96 million and it was CAD$7.10 million for China (including Macau). In a parallel development, the import of Canadian beef also rose sharply in Macau from CAD$1.23 million in 2007 to CAD$14.76 million in 2008, CAD$27.06 million in 2009 and CAD$39.36 million in 2010.

What is behind the quantum leap in Canadian beef exports to Hong Kong and Macau after 2003? How do we explain the tremendous increase in the volume and value of Canadian beef in both markets? There is nothing written about this spectacular spike in the import of Canadian beef in Hong Kong or Macau after 2003, nor is there any identifiable major shift in consumption habits or demographics in these two Special Administrative Regions after 2003 that can possibly explain this increase in beef import from Canada. Thus, we can only offer a speculative but plausible explanation based on what we know about Hong Kong and China since we first conducted ethnographic research in the region in the mid-1980s. China is Hong Kong's biggest trading partner: nearly 50 per cent of Hong Kong exports are destined for China, and nearly 50 per cent of all imports to Hong Kong are from China (*Economy Watch* 2010). It is a similar situation in Macau. It is likely that some or most of the imported Canadian beef after 2003 was re-exported to China to meet niche market demands, in clear violation of China's policy to ban Canadian beef. We note that Hong Kong reopened its market to Canadian beef in 2004 while China upheld the trade ban on Canadian beef import until 2012. Macau reopened its market to Canadian beef imports in 2007. Even though Hong Kong was returned to Chinese sovereignty in 1997 and Macau in 1999, the 'one country, two systems' formula promises each city special status, which appears to have been upheld for public health management. Yet, the boundaries between China, Hong Kong and Macau are highly porous, especially for goods and people travelling into China from Hong Kong and Macau.

The exact cross infection pathways between the consumption of BSE-infected beef products and the development of vCJD in human have not yet been fully identified. So far the total number of people who have died from vCJD is modest. The United Kingdom had 175 cases between 1996 and 2011 (WHO, No Date). Worldwide there are only just over 200 known vCJD cases. While the numbers are low, the fear factor is high for this disease without known cure from which patients die within months after diagnosis. It is not in China's interest to allow an open gap in its health risk management policy in future trade bans by exempting Hong Kong and Macau from compliance as it did for Canadian beef in the context of BSE/vCJD. Such an open gap makes a mockery of its trade ban policy, and allows for possible free entry of contagion that may incur tremendous future health risk and erosion in people's confidence in the government's ability to safeguard their health and safety.

SEVERE ACUTE RESPIRATORY SYNDROME (SARS)

SARS was first identified in 2003 in Hong Kong, but it originated in China (see Kleinman and Watson 2006). The virus subsequently spread around the world and killed hundreds of people in China, Hong Kong, Canada, Southeast Asia and Europe, despite the quick response by health officials and governments to isolate and quarantine suspected cases (see Table 11.1 below). The economic impact was devastating. It brought global travel to a near standstill for several months in the summer of 2003 and plunged Hong Kong into a deep economic recession.

The virus was subsequently found in civet cats, foxes and other animals, which are highly prized animals for Chinese tonic foods and which were readily available in many restaurants in southern China within easy distance from Hong Kong. A major culling of civet cats and a ban on trade in civet cats were imposed in an effort to curb the spread of the disease. Government information and media coverage cautioned citizens against contact with and consumption of suspect animals. As the surveillance and trade ban protocols were enforced, a black market in civet cats, foxes and other exotic animals emerged in direct contradiction to the public messages that identified these animals as a possible health risk and as carriers of SARS. In order to understand this seemingly 'irrational' behaviour among some consumers in China at the height of the SARS outbreak in 2003 and 2004, we must move away from science and medicine to examine a cultural concept known as 'tonic food' (*bupin* 补品), which is deeply embedded within the Chinese cultural logic of food choices and food consumption.

The high degree of inclusiveness in food choices among the Chinese and many other Asian populations have a direct relevance to emergent infectious disease risks. In particular, the accepted and even esteemed practice of using exotic and rare animals in tonic food multiplies the risk factor many fold. When these animals are brought into close contact with human populations, new opportunities for cross-species infections are created. The transport of these animals also creates new opportunities of cross infecting other animal species in the same market or storage area. The SARS experience in China shows the weakness of the infectious disease control policy which supported a comprehensive culling of all known civet cats, both wild and farmed, as a means to eradicate the known host for the SARS virus. On the surface, the policy was effective in containing the spread of SARS. Does it guarantee that future SARS infection will not occur or that new viruses will not jump from animal to human?

The answer is negative on both counts for the following reasons. First, the policy nearly eradicated one particular animal species (i.e. civet cats) that was linked to SARS; this was good in the context of its intended purpose. What about all the other animal and bird species that are hosts to viruses and which therefore may infect human beings in the future under certain conditions of mutation and contact opportunities? Short of killing off all other life forms except human beings, we have no foolproof protection against future emergence of new viruses similar to SARS or the avian flu.

TABLE 11.1 Number of probable SARS cases, mortality figures, number of imported cases, and date of first onset for the SARS 'outbreak period' from November 1, 2002 until July 31, 2003.

Country	Total # of cases	Number of deaths	Case fatality ratio (%)	Number of imported cases (%)	Date onset first probable case
Australia	6	0	0%	6 (100%)	26-Feb-03
Canada	251	43	17%	5 (2%)	23-Feb-03
China	5327	349	7%	Not Applicable	16-Nov-02
China, Hong Kong Special Administrative Region	1755	299	17%	Not Applicable	15-Feb-03
China, Macao Special Administrative Region	1	0	0%	1 (100%)	5-May-03
China, Taiwan	346	37	11%	21 (6%)	25-Feb-03
France	7	1	14%	7 (100%)	21-Mar-03
Germany	9	0	0%	9 (100%)	9-Mar-03
India	3	0	0%	3 (100%)	25-Apr-03
Indonesia	2	0	0%	2 (100%)	6-Apr-03
Italy	4	0	0%	4 (100%)	12-Mar-03
Kuwait	1	0	0%	1 (100%)	9-Apr-03

(*Source*: Based on data updated December 31, 2003. Adapted from the WHO: http://www.who.int/csr/sars/country/table2004_04_21/en/index.html)

Second, the culling method does not by itself change people's eating habits and food choices, rooted in cultural logics of cosmic complementarity reinforced by centuries of ethnomedical practices. Despite the SARS outbreak and the government policy of banning the sale of civet cats in China, some people were still willing to buy and consume civet cats. A thriving black market emerged consequently to supply 'wild' and 'safe' animals at high costs. The policy of animal eradication alone is ineffective in modifying people's food consumption behaviour. Such a policy is limited in its effectiveness in eliminating the infectious disease risks, as can be seen in the black market for banned animals in the wake of the SARS outbreak. Cultural beliefs and practices are powerful forces and are rarely easily suppressed. Future policies pertaining to infectious disease risks should take into careful consideration the complex interrelationships between culture, food habits and infectious disease risks.[3] Policies of animal extermination as a disease control method should perhaps, under the appropriate conditions, be replaced by better policies of regulation to accommodate cultural practices.

The Chinese word *bu* 补 (sometimes transliterated as *pu*) means 'strengthening, supplementing, patching up' (Anderson 1988: 235). There is a well-documented body of knowledge on tonic food (*bupin*) that matches specific food items with identified health problems or health outcomes. This knowledge is disseminated in numerous publications ancient and contemporary, and is commonly passed from generation to generation via oral history and everyday practices in self-medication. The concept of tonic food is ancient, and the medical knowledge surrounding the concept is complex. The primary goal of food as medicine is prevention (Yang 1988: 6). A common misconception about tonic food is the uncritical assumption that more is better. If tonic food strengthens one's body and health, then a higher frequency of tonic food consumption must have greater accumulative effect. Within the Chinese worldview of cosmic complementarity, too much of a good thing can be bad because it upsets the balance of nature.

According to traditional Chinese wisdom, tonic food should only be used when one's system is weak or deficient. Tonic food should not be consumed without just cause; otherwise it may damage one's physiological well-being due to imbalance. Furthermore, care must be taken to identify the right kind of tonic food to target the particular deficiency or condition of the body. A mismatch will also cause harm. Too much 'heat' should be counteracted with food that is 'cold' or 'cooling' and vice versa. Lastly, tonic food cannot be used as a cure in extreme conditions of deficiency or serious illness. When a person's health is in a state of advanced weakness, it cannot handle the 'strengthening' properties and richness of tonic foods. The consumption of tonic food will cause harm to the body in the form of indigestion and insomnia (Yang 1988: 14).

Some tonic food work on the principle of sympathetic magic or what Anderson (1988: 237) calls the 'Doctrine of Similarities':

> Walnut meats have a reputation for strengthening the brain because they look like a brain; red jujubes and port wine are thought to strengthen the blood mainly because of their red color ... usually foods regarded as pu are not only appropriate

but also effective. The vast majority of pu foods are easily digestible, high-quality protein. Fowl – especially wild – are probably most used. Much stronger are sea cucumbers, birds' nests, raccoon-dogs, deer antlers, shark fins, pangolins, and many other wild animals and animal products. Many of these are famous worldwide as examples of the bizarre things human beings will eat and pay high prices for. … One of the most expensive is ginseng. (Anderson 1988: 236)

The common use of endangered and rare animals or plants in Chinese food is usually justified by their medicinal properties. The associated expressive function of conspicuous consumption in the use of these rare and expensive items is also a factor that should be considered. There is a common, though misleading, assumption that higher cost correlates with better quality or more valuable outcomes. Anderson makes the following observation:

> Rare, exotic, and unusual foods are considered *pu* not just because of cost and strangeness, though these are certainly factors, and conspicuous consumption is a very major part of their use … the striking appearance of such creatures as pangolins and raccoon-dogs is thought to indicate great energy or unusual energy patterns. Powerful creatures like eagles – to say nothing of the sexually hyperpotent deer – are also obvious sources of energy. (1988: 237)

Within the Chinese medical model, four major physiological areas are used to measure health: energy (*qi* 气), blood or circulation (*xue* 血), masculine vitality (*yang* 阳) and feminine vitality (*yin* 阴) (Hu 1990: 19–20; Yang 1988: 13). Tonic food is intended to address these areas with an ultimate goal of establishing a state of harmonious balance to support an optimal state of health (Yang and Zhang 1991: 3).

Food choices are shaped by many factors. The most readily observable are probably the marketing blitzes of consumer goods that saturate every medium of communication known to mankind today. This chapter deals with a silent but powerful source of influence in food choices called culture. The high degree of inclusiveness in Chinese cuisine is shaped by the Chinese worldview of cosmic complementarity and reinforced by ethnomedical approaches to health and wellness. A balance of *yin–yang* vitality is the foundation of good health, and imbalances cause problems. Food and herbs are effective agents of intervention to restore and maintain a harmonious balance of opposing but complementary forces in our body. All kinds of food, from the common to the exotic, are equally valuable and effective in such interventions when used appropriately. Thus food and medicine are one, and all food (plants and animals) are 'good' for their medicinal potentials. This cultural perspective on food and health provides the foundation to the practice of inclusiveness in Chinese cuisine. Chinese cooking uses everything and anything. These ideas and practices, developed over a course of several thousand years, have become highly normalized as everyday practices. People regularly administer self-medication through their daily food choices to counteract 'hot' with 'cold' and vice versa as a matter of 'doing my body good' or 'doing what my mother says is good for me'. Tonic food is a particular genre of Chinese food that are intended to strengthen the body.

Exotic and rare animals are often used in tonic food for their perceived potency, virility and high energy (*qi*). It is this aspect of Chinese food choices that deserves closer attention in the context of emergent infectious disease risks. When rare or exotic animals are used for human consumption, it creates new opportunities for cross-species infections, which are among the main conditions that support a pandemic (Specter 2005). Currently, one of the common policies to contain emergent infectious disease risks as in SARS and avian flu is a policy of host eradication. Civet cats were culled, so are chickens. This policy of host eradication, we argue, is ineffective in changing people's eating habits and food choices, which are deeply rooted in cultural ideas and practices. Policies of regulation may be considered to ensure that food sources are safe for human consumption so that the twin goals of containing emergent infectious disease risks and allowing the expression of cultural practices can be met.

INFANT FORMULA PARALLEL TRADING, 2008–13[4]

Throughout the 1980s and 1990s, there was a booming traffic of Hong Kong consumers in Shenzhen, the city closest to the Hong Kong–China border and one of the first Special Economic Zones created under the 1978 economic reform, to purchase cheap goods and services. Hong Kong housewives brought home cartloads of groceries (both dry and wet goods) on regular or even daily shopping trips, people had their clothing made-to-measure at a fraction of the cost in Hong Kong, nightlife in Shenzhen attracted young men and women, the sex industry became a strong magnet for Hong Kong men, and people flocked to the many restaurants in Shenzhen to feast on cheap and good food. Cross-border shopping trips became less common as price differentials between Hong Kong and Shenzhen for many commodities diminished, largely due to the appreciation of the Chinese currency, the *Renminbi*, aggravated by the depreciation of the US dollar to which the Hong Kong dollar is pegged at a fixed rate of 7.8. But cross-border shopping has not entirely disappeared as there are still many goods and services that are cheaper in China, including furniture, lights and household appliances, building materials, personal grooming services and real estate.

In 2003, in an effort to boost Hong Kong's economy which had declined under the impact of SARS, a new policy to issue more exit visas for PRC tourists to visit Hong Kong was put in place. It was known as the Individual Visit Scheme (IVS). The IVS was an economic godsend for Hong Kong. Newly rich PRC nationals are big spenders on gold, diamond and luxury branded goods. Beginning in 2008, infant formula became another item on the shopping list in response to the 2007 melamine scandal in China.

Western media first reported in 2007 the use of melamine in pet products, which cause kidney failure and other health problems. Melamine was subsequently found in baby formula produced by the Sanlu enterprise in China (a PRC–New Zealand joint venture) and over 300,000 babies were affected with varying degrees of distress due to kidney stones, malnutrition, urinary problems and other symptoms.

This melamine-in-baby-formula scandal in China became a focus of worldwide attention in September 2008 only after the government (after much delay) issued an official acceptance that it was a health problem caused by substandard baby formula products laced with melamine in a deliberate effort to boost the protein count to meet quality standards. Consumer confidence in China was greatly affected, aggravating an already established downward trend, which commenced probably as early as the mid-1980s, when the pollution problems caused by rapid industrialization in the early phases of the post-1978 economic reform first became a public concern.

Be it high levels of herbicides, pesticides and chemical fertilizer in vegetables, or carcinogenic malachite green in aquacultural products, or heavy metal in rice, or the repackaging of 'gutter oil' as 'clean' cooking oil for commercial and private uses (*Apple Daily*, 30 December 2012: A13; *The Economist* 2011), Chinese consumers have become increasingly suspicious of the safety of their food (Klein 2013; Yan 2012). It is within this context of ongoing distrust about the quality and safety of food in China that the trend among Chinese nationals to source 'safe' baby formula and other products from locations outside China since 2008 continues to grow in magnitude and reach. A recent *Apple Daily* report (4 January 2013: A30) described Chinese tourists in Australia hoarding two popular brands of baby formula – Karicare (from New Zealand) and Bellamy's (Australian) and causing shortages at retail outlets. A mother in Sydney could not get her preferred brand of baby formula at five supermarkets and pharmacies. At the sixth retail outlet, there were a few tins left on the shelf and she bought them all.

In the aftermath of the Sanlu baby formula scandal in 2008, the number of mainland Chinese tourists coming to Hong Kong increased sharply. When the IVS was introduced in 2003, only 7.3 per cent of all mainland visitors came under the new scheme, by 2007 it accounted for 55 per cent of all mainland visitors. The biggest increase was in the same-day trip category, which by 2008 made up nearly half of all visitor arrivals from mainland China on any single day (Chan 2008). In 2012, *The Wall Street Journal* reported a 66 per cent increase of mainland Chinese tourists in Hong Kong since 2008. Hong Kong received twenty-eight million mainland Chinese tourists in 2011, about two-thirds of all visitors that year. Since its inception in 2003, the IVS has expanded to include many more cities outside Guangdong. As a result, 270 million Chinese nationals are now eligible under the IVS scheme to visit Hong Kong and this number is expected to grow as the expansion of IVS continues to include more cities in China (*The Wall Street Journal* 2012). It is not clear how many Chinese tourists in Hong Kong stock up on baby formula in their personal luggage, but even a small fraction of twenty-eight million tourists means a lot of people.

The mainland Chinese visitors are not the only people engaged in the parallel import of baby formula. Hong Kong residents with families and relatives in China are also actively involved. While many travellers are bringing baby formula for 'self use', the strength of consumer demand in China for safe products has created a highly lucrative niche market for brand-name baby formula sourced through parallel trading. Many branded companies have set up manufacturing facilities in China to supply the Chinese market, but consumers are suspicious about the quality and safety standards. One Hong Kong medical doctor in private practice learned from her mainland Chinese patients that they refuse to buy international brand baby formula with simplified Chinese characters on the label, as this indicates China as its origin of production. Instead, they will pay more to buy the same branded product with traditional Chinese characters on the label, which indicates that it is an import from the United States or Europe via Hong Kong. Such is the depth and strength of the consumers' distrust of food safety in China.

Under the rubric of organized, profit-driven parallel trading networks, individuals are hired to do multiple daily trips bringing all sorts of parallel goods into Shenzhen (on the China side) and Sheung Shui and Fanling (on the Hong Kong side) for redistribution. The expanding scale of parallel traffic in baby formula since 2008, both for self-consumption and for payment as a form of informal economy (Hart 2010: 144–5), encouraged hoarding and stockpiling. This in turn caused frequent interruptions in the supply of baby formula at retail outlets in Hong Kong, especially at locations close to the Hong Kong–China boundary region (*China Daily*, 1 March 2011; Tsang and Nip 2013: A3). While these shortages in supply were always temporary, they did cause inconveniences. Furthermore, many retail clerks and shop owners in Hong Kong exploited this heightened demand to impose a surcharge and price hike on baby formula (*Apple Daily*, 4 December 2012: A12; *Ming Pao*, 24 January 2013: A4). With the increase in parallel trade and PRC tourist traffic on the Kowloon–Canton Railway (KCR) train line, linking Shenzhen and Kowloon, crowding on the train and in public spaces at and near the train station worsened. The situation eventually became explosive when affected parents and residents in the border region took to protests and confrontations (*Apple Daily*, 30 December 2012: A12, 6 January 2013: A6, 9 January 2013: A22; *Ming Pao*, 7 November 2012: A1; *Next Magazine*, 6 September 2012: 58–60, 20 September 2012: 42–6). The escalating moral panic expressed by the Hong Kong public eventually forced the Hong Kong Government to impose a new policy to limit the quantity of baby formula leaving Hong Kong as of 1 March 2013. An editorial in *Oriental Daily* (16 March 2013) describes this new policy as a correct and necessary response to the parallel goods trading problem in Hong Kong. Extraordinary conditions require extraordinary measures.

Public opinions have suggested that this newly enacted policy is not effective in curbing the parallel traffic in baby formula in Hong Kong. For as long as there is a demand for 'safe' baby formula sourced in Hong Kong, there will be a supply either through proper and legal channels or illegal ones. The parallel trading networks on both sides of the Hong Kong–China boundary seem to be well established and highly responsive to changing consumer demands. Thus the persistence of the employment of people – both Hong Kong permanent residents and PRC residents – in parallel trading is bound to continue. This provides evidence for Keith Hart's (2010: 144–5) suggestion that the formal and informal aspects of society have always been linked. This universal coexistence is true of neoliberal capitalism wherein people are supposed to optimize their economic well-being by seizing opportunities (both legal and illegal, as illegality becomes seen as simply another cost of doing business) as they arise. Parallel trafficking of niche products as a form of informal employment in the Hong Kong–China boundary region will thrive for as long as there is a consumer demand for these niche products – be it baby formula, branded luxury goods or exotic fauna and flora.

Furthermore, parallel import as a personal practice is bound to increase as more people cross borders and boundaries for business and leisure. Border studies in social sciences are predominantly anthropocentric, with an almost exclusive emphasis on human mobility. Yet what crosses borders – inter- and intra-species boundaries, physical, national borders by land/sea/air, and digital, 'borderless' highways – is mostly non-human in nature (Smart and Smart 2012). Trucks, container liners, animals/fauna, microbes, plants/flora, goods of all imaginable sorts are constantly moving through boundaries of one sort or another. People bring all sorts of things when they travel; the decisions leading to what type of goods one carries as personal luggage are often dismissive of regulations and laws, and greatly influenced by social and emotive elements. It may be a grandmother's best garlic sausage or meat pie, or home-made cheese by a loved one, a specialty meat that one cannot get elsewhere or a gift of dried seafood and cured meat from one's parents. Goods that travel are seldom selected purely on the basis of whether they are legal, safe or disease free. Consumption behaviour and human desires are by nature deeply embedded in affective and social meanings.

CONCLUDING COMMENTS

The world seems to be crawling with locavores struggling to find ways to live within the constraints of their self-imposed hundred-mile diet, attempting to combat the world-endangering growth of 'food miles', the vast distances that food items on average travel from production site to kitchen table. Or at least this would seem to be the case, judging from book titles and blog entries. An Amazon search locates seventeen books with the term locavore in the title, despite the term only having been coined by Jessica Prentice on World Environment Day 2005, while a Google search uncovers over one million results. One-hundred-mile diets, and their variants, account for nearly six million Google hits and eight books on Amazon. The desire to eat locally, and the related emphasis on slow food, appears to be the main defence against the general trend towards ever-greater distances between the places where food is produced and where it is consumed, even if the contest seems a classic case of David and Goliath.

We have argued in this chapter that there is another set of factors that have been acting, arguably with greater effect, against the global movement of food. Distant producers are widely thought to be less concerned about the consumers of their goods, and remediation of injuries is more difficult to achieve when exchanges are face-to-faceless than face-to-face. The use of import bans to protect public health has become much more common and influential in the last three decades. We have illustrated the dynamics of border-crossing concerning food and health risks with three case studies: BSE, SARS and tainted infant formula. Food and agricultural products raise concerns that are less heightened for mechanical products because of food's inherent association with organic materials that can spread infectious diseases, and its direct integration with the consumer's body and health. It appears that much of the desire for local food is not driven by environmental concerns, but by the belief that food from a distance raises greater health concerns.

Yet, local is not always trusted to be the best. Consumers in China harbour a deep distrust of the quality and safety of their locally produced food products, and the desire to source 'safe' infant formula (a specific item within a broader spectrum of food products) from Hong Kong and elsewhere has continued to expand significantly over time. We live in a time when multiple systems of food production and distribution coexist with seemingly infinite options of consumption preferences and forms. Food as an item of sustenance and a source of potential health threat creates tension in consumers' decisions about where to get their food, what kind of food is the best and safest and who to look to for the guarantee of food safety and guidance about healthy eating. In this chapter we have focused on import/export controls related to infectious diseases and food contamination. In doing so, we have shown that there are larger forces of entanglement – be they contagions, cultural logics of food preferences or trade policies – that structure the flows of food and choices of consumption beyond the individual and personal attributes that feed into the daily routine of consumption. Food is indeed a productive filter to understand human existence and the multilayered contradictions, regulations, contestations, compliances and creativity that make us human.

NOTES

1. Zoonoses or zoonotic diseases are generally defined as diseases shared by humans and other vertebrate animals. Rabies, Lyme disease and others are transmitted through vectors or hosts such as dogs and ticks, but others are transmitted directly between animals and humans through close contact or consumption as in the case of BSE/vCJD, avian flu and SARS. For a full list of known zoonoses, visit the World Health Organization website at www.who.int.
2. A worldwide ban on the export of British cattle and beef products was imposed after 20 March 1996 when the British government announced a link between vCJD in people and BSE-infected beef. The economic impact of this worldwide ban on Britain was tremendous; the British government tried to undo the damage by complaining that the ban was not justified, that it was not based on scientific evidence, but rather politically motivated. See Raude et al. (2005).
3. See Leung and Furth (2010) for historical data on the close linkages between culture, disease and public health management in East Asia, including chapters on SARS by Marta Hanson (2010) and Tseng and Wu (2010).
4. The term 'parallel goods' is written in Chinese as 水貨 (sui foh in Cantonese). The first character means 'water', the second character means 'goods'. The term is used in Hong Kong to denote the foreign origin of an item that can be bought at cheaper prices than the same item of the same brand carried in Hong Kong because it does not come with warranty and there is an element of risk about the quality.

REFERENCES

Archetti, E. P. (1997), *Guinea-Pigs: Food, Symbol and Conflict of Knowledge in Ecuador*, New York: Berg.

Anderson, E. N. (1988), *The Food of China*, New Haven, CT: Yale University Press.

Apple Daily 蘋果日報 (in Chinese), various dates.

Barboza, D. (2008), 'Chinese Destroyed 3,600 Tons of Tainted Feed: Officials Destroy Tons of Melamine-Laced Feed for Livestock', *New York Times*, 3 October 2008.

Belasco, W. and Scranton, P. (eds) (2002), *Food Nations: Selling Taste in Consumer Societies*, New York: Routledge.

Belshaw, J. D. (2013), 'The Lost Plague: Why We Have Forgotten One of Canada's Most Devastating Smallpox Epidemics', *The Walrus*, May: 19–20.

Caballero-Anthony, M. (2006), 'Combating Infectious Diseases in East Asia: Securitization and Global Public Goods for Health and Human Security', *Journal of International Affairs*, 59(2): 105–27.

Campbell, D. (1993), 'Entire Herd to Be Destroyed to Prevent Mad Cow Spread', *Calgary Herald*, 30 December: C2.

Canada Beef Inc. (2012), http://www.mancec.com/2012/03/19/canada-china-beef-trade-reopens/ (accessed 31 December 2013).

CBC News Online Indepth (2006), 'Mad Cow'. http://www.cbc.ca/news/background/madcow/timeline.html (accessed 9 April 2007).

CFIA (Canadian Food Inspection Agency) (2011), http://epe.lac-bac.gc.ca/100/206/301/cfia-acia/2011-09-21/www.inspection.gc.ca/english/anima/disemala/bseesb/surv/surve.shtml (accessed 31 December 2013).

Chan, S. (2008), 'Chinese Tourists Spend Big in Hong Kong', *Newsweek*, 23 July. http://www.businessweek.com/stories/2008-07-23/chinese-tourists-spend-big-in-hong-kongbusinessweek-business-news-stock-market-and-financial-advice (accessed 15 May 2013).

China Daily 中國日報 (in Chinese), various dates.

Crump, J., Murdock, D. R. and Baker, M. G. (2001), 'Emerging Infectious Diseases in an Island Ecosystem: The New Zealand Perspective', *Perspectives*, 7(5): 767–72.

Counihan, C. K. (1999), *The Anthropology of Food and Body: Gender, Meaning, and Power*, New York: Routledge.

The Economist (2011), 'Food Safety in China: In the Gutter', 29 October: 49–50.

Economy Watch (2010), http://www.economywatch.com/world_economy/hong-kong/export-import.html Published 15 March (accessed 31 December 2013).

Gewertz, D. B. and Errington, F. K. (2010), *Cheap Meat: Flap Food Nations in the Pacific Islands*. Berkeley, CA: University of California Press.

Government of Alberta (2006), http://www.gov.ab.ca/home/index.cfm?Page751 (accessed 4 May 2006).

Government of Alberta, Department of Agriculture and Rural Development (No Date a). http://www1.agric.gov.ab.ca/$department/deptdocs.nsf/all/sdd11872/$FILE/table45.pdf (accessed 13 December 2013).

Government of Alberta, Department of Agriculture and Rural Development (No Date b). http://epe.lac-bac.gc.ca/100/206/301/cfia-acia/2011-09-21/www.inspection.gc.ca/english/anima/disemala/bseesb/surv/surve.shtml (accessed 31 December 2013).

Government of Alberta, Department of Agriculture and Rural Development (No
    Date c), Power Point Presentation, Author Not Specified. http://www1.agric.gov.
    ab.ca/$department/deptdocs.nsf/ba3468a2a8681f69872569d60073fde1/e3fc081fe34
    5edab872572ce007439ea/$FILE/ngupdate_2008.ppt#283,9,CBEF Beef Exports and
    Projections (Million $) (accessed 31 December 2013).
Government of Canada (2012), http://www.agr.gc.ca/cb/index_e.php?s1=n&s2=
    2012&page=n120120 (accessed 31 December 2012).
Hanson, M. E. (2010), 'Conceptual Blind Spots, Media Blindfolds: The Case of SARS
    and Traditional Chinese Medicine', in A. K. C. Leung and C. Furth (eds), *Health and
    Hygiene in Chinese East Asia: Policies and Publics in the Long Twentieth Century*,
    228–54, Durham, NC: Duke University Press.
Harris, M. (1989), *Cows, Pigs, Wars, and Witches: The Riddles of Culture*, New York:
    Vintage Books.
Hart, K. (2010), 'Informal Economy', in K. Hart, J.-L. Laville and A. D. Cattani (eds),
    The Human Society: A Citizen's Guide, 142–53, Cambridge: Polity.
Klein, J. A. (2013), 'Everyday Approaches to Food Safety in Kunming', *The China
    Quarterly*, 214: 376–93.
Kleinman, A. and Watson, J. L. (eds) (2006), *SARS in China: Prelude to Pandemic?*,
    Stanford, CA: Stanford University Press.
Le Roy, D. G. and Klein, K. K. (2005), 'Mad Cow Chaos in Canada: Was It Just Bad Luck
    or Did Government Policies Play a Role?', *Canadian Public Policy*, 31(4): 381–99.
Leung, A. K. C. and Furth, C. (eds) (2010), *Health and Hygiene in Chinese East Asia:
    Policies and Publics in the Long Twentieth Century*, Durham, NC: Duke University Press.
Lindenbaum, S. (2001), 'Kuru, Prions, and Human Affairs: Thinking about Epidemics',
    Annual Review of Anthropology, 30: 363–85.
Macbeth, H. (ed.). (1997), *Food Preferences and Taste – Continuity and Change*,
    New York: Berghahn Books.
MCEC (Manitoba Cattle Enhancement Council) (2012), http://www.mancec.com/2012/
    03/19/canada-china-beef-trade-reopens/ (accessed 31 December 2013).
Ming Pao 明報 (in Chinese), various dates.
Mintz, S. W. (1985), *Sweetness and Power*, New York: Viking Penguin Inc.
Mintz, S. W. (1996), *Tasting Food, Tasting Freedom: Excursions into Eating, Culture, and
    the Past*, Boston, MA: Beacon Press.
Mintz, S. W. (2008), 'Food, Culture and Energy', in A. Nützenadel and F. Trentmann
    (eds), *Food and Globalization: Consumption, Markets and Politics in the Modern
    World*, 21–35, Oxford: Berg.
Mintz, S. W. (2009), 'Notes Towards a Cultural Construction of Modern Foods', *Social
    Anthropology*, 17(2): 209–16.
Mintz, S. W. and Du Bois, C. M. (2002), 'The Anthropology of Food and Eating', *Annual
    Review of Anthropology*, 31: 99–119.
Nerlich, B. and Halliday, C. (2007), 'Avian Flu: The Creation of Expectations in the
    Interplay between Science and Media', *Sociology of Health & Illness*, 29(1): 46–65.
Next Magazine 一周刊 (in Chinese), various dates.
(OIE) World Organization for Animal Health (No Date), http://www.oie.int/en/animal-
    health-in-the-world/bse-specific-data/number-of-reported-cases-worldwide-excluding-
    the-united-kingdom/ (accessed 31 December 2013).

Onodera, T. and Kim, C.-K. (2006), 'BSE Situation and Establishment of Food Safety Commission in Japan', *Journal of Veterinary Science*, 7(1): 1–11.

Oriental Daily 東方日報 (in Chinese), various dates.

Pillsbury, B. (1978), '"Doing the Month" – Confinement and Convalescence of Chinese Women after Childbirth', *Social Science and Medicine*, 12: 11–22.

Pollan, M. (2006), *The Omnivore's Dilemma: A Natural History of Four Meals*, New York: Penguin.

Rampton, S. and Stauber, J. (2004), *Mad Cow U.S.A.*, Nonroe, ME: Common Courage Press.

Raude, J., Fischler, C., Setbon, M. and Flahault, A. (2005), 'Scientist and Public Responses to BSE-Related Risk: A comparative study', *Journal of Risk Research*, 8: 663–78.

Revel, J.-F. (1982), *Culture and Cuisine: A Journey through the History of Food*, translated by H. R. Lane, Garden City, NY: Doubleday.

Rock, M., Buntain, B. J., Hatfield, J. M. and Hallgrímsson, B. (2009), 'Animal-Human Connections, "One Health," and the Syndemic Approach to Prevention', *Social Science & Medicine*, 68(6): 991–5.

Romahn, J. (1993), 'Mad Cow Disease Creates Problems for Area Exporters', *Kitchener-Waterloo Record*, 14 December: B7.

Schlosser, E. (2001), *Fast Food Nation: The Dark Side of the All-American Meal*, Boston: Houghton Mifflin Co.

Smart, A. and Smart, J. (2012), 'Life Across the Border: Biosecurity Quarantine and Zoonoses', in T. Wilson and H. Donnan (eds), *A Companion to Border Studies*, Oxford: Blackwell.

Specter, M. (2005), 'Nature's Bioterrorists – Is There Any Way to Prevent a Deadly Avian-Flu Pandemic?' *The New Yorker*, 28 February: 50–61.

Thow, A. M., Swinburn, B., Colagiuric, S., Diligolevud, M., Questede, C., Vivilif, P. and Leedera, S. (2010), 'Trade and Food Policy: Case Studies from Three Pacific Island Countries', *Food Policy*, 35: 556–64.

Toussaint-Samat, M. (1992), *History of Food*, translated by A. Bell, Oxford: Blackwell.

Tsang, E. and Nip, A. (2013), 'Traders Stockpile Milk Formula, Anger Mums', *South China Morning Post*, 25 January: A3.

Tseng, Y.-F. and Wu, C.-L. (2010), 'Governing Germs from Outside and within Borders: Controlling 2003 SARS Risk in Taiwan', in A. K. C. Leung and C. Furth (eds), *Health and Hygiene in Chinese East Asia: Policies and Publics in the Long Twentieth Century*, 255–72, Durham, NC: Duke University Press.

The Wall Street Journal (2012), 'Hong Kong Races for More Mainland Tourists', 29 August. http://blogs.wsj.com/chinarealtime/2012/08/29/hong-kong-braces-for-more-mainland-tourists/ (accessed 15 May 2013).

Watson, J. L. and Caldwell, M. L. (eds) (2005), *The Cultural Politics of Food and Eating*, New York: Blackwell Publishing.

WHO (World Health Organization) (No Date), http://www.who.int/mediacentre/factsheets/fs180/en/ (accessed 31 December 2013).

Wilk, R. (ed.) (2006), *Fast Food/Slow Food: The Cultural Economy of the Global Food System*, Lanham, MD: Altamira Press.

Yan, Y. (2012), 'Food Safety and Social Risk in Contemporary China', *The Journal of Asian Studies*, 71(3): 705–29.

Yang Lingling 杨玲玲 (1988), *Zen Yang Chi Zui Bu* 怎样吃最补, Taipei: Wenjing Chubanshe.

Yang Zhifu 杨智孚 and Zhang Feng 张峰 (1991), *Shi Bu Yu Yao Bu* 食补与药补, Taipei: Dujia Chubanshe.

CHAPTER TWELVE

Rethinking Food and its Eaters: Opening the Black Boxes of Safety and Nutrition

HEATHER PAXSON

You are what you eat. This familiar aphorism – a paraphrase of Brillat-Savarin's 1825 challenge, 'Tell me what you eat; I will tell you what you are' (1970: 13) – calls our attention to eating as an act of incorporation, of taking into the body elements of the surrounding world. Food substance is widely understood to carry in it not only material and sensory properties – nutrients, fluid, fats, flavours, properties of cooling or heat – but also symbolic, associative properties that may build up or deplete desired characteristics of an eater's mind, body and character (to take a North American example, consider red meat's association with masculinity). Anthropologists have often presumed that what 'food' *is*, culturally speaking, has to do with how people perceive and comprehend its intrinsic qualities – whether reductively, in terms of material components such as nutrients (cf. Harris 1985), or syntagmatically within classificatory systems of edibility (cf. Douglas 1966) – which qualities are then 'incorporated' into bodies. Either way, when food makes the eater, eating becomes a consequential act. After all, *eating well* is widely associated both with *being well* (health) and also with *doing good* (ethics).

In 'Food as a Cultural Construction', however, Anna Meigs (1987) challenges us to rethink 'food' by looking beyond eating as an act of incorporation. We should not, she argues, presume that what food *is* boils down to intrinsic qualities, culturally perceived. For the Hua of Papua New Guinea, she explains, food does not materially exist in and of itself. Instead, what food *is* – what qualifies edibility, sustenance, even taste – is to them inseparable from *who* tended the yam or raised the pig and what that person's relationship is to a potential eater. For the Hua, Meigs (1987: 104) writes:

> Foods are not inert objects, 'things' to be bought and sold. Rather, they possess the vitality and dynamism of living beings . . . They are alive; alive not only with their own contagious qualities (their rates of growth, textures, smells, and so forth) but also with the transmittable vitality, essence, *nu* of their human producers. Last but not least, foods are alive with the feelings, the emotional intents, of their producers (and to a lesser extent their preparers).

Taking up Meigs's challenge, in this chapter I want to rethink the relationship between food and eating as a straightforward one of incorporation; not only is incorporation anything but straightforward, food and eating can be otherwise conceptualized. Rather than presume an ontology of food and an agency of eating, I want to explore recent ethnographic work, my own and others', which pushes us to view food and eating as mutually constituted within particular cultural and political economic settings (cf. Mol 2008; Abbots and Lavis 2013; Guthman et al. 2014).

In calling into question both the ontological stability of what 'food' is and the biological singularity of 'the eating body', I highlight areas where the anthropology of food can benefit from insights drawn from Science and Technology Studies (STS), particularly in questioning the sociopolitical constitution of scientific objects and knowledge, such as nutrients, pasteurization, hygiene and standards. After all, nutrition science and public health initiatives have colluded in naturalizing the aphorism, 'We are what we eat,' through what Gyorgy Scrinis (2008, 2013) calls the ideology of 'nutritionism' and Jessica Mudry (2009) analyses as 'a discourse of quantification' through which people are taught that amino acids are our bodies' 'building blocks' and that Calcium and Vitamin D 'build strong bones', while calories are necessary 'fuel' burned by metabolism to 'run' bodies. While science studies shows us how 'nature' is often what science (a cultural practice) tells us it is, anthropology is well poised to track the movement of scientific objects and knowledges across social contexts, whether cross-culturally or transhistorically.

In this chapter, I explore how technoscientific means of food preservation – pasteurization, canning, aseptic packaging – and the nutritional tenets of biomedical dietary advice function as 'black boxes'. The term 'black box', defined in the mid-twentieth century by cyberneticians, has been adopted as a term of art by science studies scholars to refer to instruments or techniques that turn inputs into outputs through sets of processes whose logic and workings may be obscure to users (Latour 1987). Black boxes 'work' in so far as they are held together by contingent 'assemblages' of institutions, rules, social hierarchies and tacit understandings. Because of this, black boxes do not always travel smoothly from place to place or from one historical moment to another. Cracks may appear under the strain of new externalities, calling into question what is inside. Examination of how and why black boxes may be coming apart, or were put together in the first place, is useful for investigating the politics of food safety because it illuminates how 'packaged food products condense ideas of quality and safety through material and semiotic connections and exist as a kind of shorthand reference to assemblages of persons, places, and production' (Tracy 2013: 440). Investigation of food-related black boxes illuminates why the pervasive understanding of 'food' in terms of 'nutrients' has not actually translated into a healthier eating public, in the United States (Mudry 2009) or elsewhere (Yates-Doerr 2011, 2012). Indeed, insofar as the black boxes of pasteurization and other technoscientific 'fixes' have been presented as authoritative indicators, even guarantors, of 'good' (safe, healthy) foods, this itself has led to unintended, sometimes deleterious, consequences, including the production and consumption of unsafe food and seemingly poor nutritional choices.

While drawing throughout on other scholars' work on food safety and nutrition, this chapter is centred on my own ethnographic research into American artisanal cheese (cf. Paxson 2013). After undergoing a relentless process of industrialization and automation throughout most of the twentieth century, cheesemaking was returned to American farms in the 1970s by a handful of 'back-to-the-landers' who regarded handcrafted cheese as a quintessential 'natural' food, valued for its symbolic opposition to the bland homogenization and over-processing of industrial foods epitomized by plastic-wrapped, orange slices of processed 'American Cheese'. Since 2000, the number of artisan cheesemakers in the United States has grown exponentially. Moreover, more than half of the country's approximately 750 cheese making artisans today work with unpasteurized (raw) milk. The very quality that gives food safety officials pause about raw-milk cheese – that it is alive with an uncharacterized diversity of microbial life – makes handcrafting it a rewarding challenge for artisan producers, and consuming it particularly desirable for epicurean and health-conscious eaters drawn to its complex flavours and purportedly 'probiotic' aspect (Paxson 2008). Nutritionism, after all, has led to a dominant view of food as 'simultaneously alimentary and therapeutic – increasingly a tool for intervention in the health and character' of bodies (Landecker 2011: 168).

Given this context, it becomes especially important to understand how constitutionally unstable foods such as handmade cheeses – or the botulism-prone home canning that Elizabeth Dunn (2008) brilliantly analyses as reflective of the decaying post-Soviet Georgian state – are material embodiments of ecosocial worlds that are far from uniform, and are riddled with politics. By including beneficial microbes such as lactic acid bacteria, as well as the harmful *E. coli*, *Listeria monocytogenes*, *C. botulinum* and the like, in our accounts of food politics, exploration of *microbiopolitics* extends the scaling of agro-food studies into the body, into the gastrointestinal – and out into broader political ecologies and environments (Paxson 2008). How might regulation, not to mention everyday eaters, take account of such contingent materiality?

In addressing this question, here I examine the construction and fate of a number of black boxes embedded in contemporary foods and food supply chains having to do with efforts to ensure the health and safety of eaters. By no means is my aim to be comprehensive. Rather, I mean to offer emblematic cases concerning food production as well as consumption. I begin with cheese.

WHAT *IS* CHEESE?

Cheesemaking is an ancient means of preserving milk. Cheese is a good source of protein and calcium. Cheese is dangerously full of fat and cholesterol. Cheese is an animal product. Cheese is a dairy product. Cheese is comfort food. Cheese is an ingredient. Cheese is an industrially fabricated commodity good. Cheese is an artisanally crafted luxury. Cheese is alive with a diversity of microorganisms. Cheese is delicious. Cheese causes indigestion.

That these claims may simultaneously all be true calls into question what it is that we are talking about when we talk about 'cheese'. As a category of foodstuff, cheese names an interplay of substance and form: cheese results from acidifying and curdling milk and removing much of the watery whey; the remaining solids, rich with the *substance* of protein casein (whence the German word *Käse* and the English *cheese*) can be *formed* (whence the French *fromage* and Italian *formaggio*) into an infinite variety of shapes, sizes and types. Many of us 'know' cheese by specific types: Cheddar, Brie, mozzarella, etc., even if not all of us eat it. Abstention from a Brie-type cheese, for example, could be motivated on a number of grounds. The edibility of such a food may be called into question by a dairy allergy or lactase impersistence, or by commitment to an ethical stance such as veganism, or to a medicalized sense of well-being, as with cholesterol-free or low-fat diets.[1] Culinary context may matter: if the cheese is sliced and served atop a hamburger, an otherwise edible food can be made inedible for those following Kosher diets. Moreover, cheese's palatability may be compromised by an eater's particular sensitivity to odour, texture or flavour, as informed by prior exposure and association. 'Brie' cheese may be both edible and palatable for a particular person today but not in the future; edibility may be compromised by pregnancy (a discussion of cheese and pregnant eaters will be presented below), while palatability may vary from one cheese to another, or even from one day to the next with the very same wheel of cheese. After all, a cheese's 'becoming' is never completed. Teeming with bacteria, yeasts and moulds, cheese continues to ripen (or, from another perspective, decompose) until it is eaten, ingested, incorporated – or tossed out fully to rot.

Cheese's inherent instability, then, its resistance to standardization – particularly when made artisanally, without the standardization of ingredients and manufacturing process that characterizes industrial production (Paxson 2013) – draws our attention to its unfolding and contingent character and to the fact that edibility and palatability are *relations*. Those relations are not merely the outcome of cheese's place in various classificatory calculuses (as Mary Douglas might suggest: either pure or dangerous), but are instead entangled with broader social, agricultural and bio-cultural dynamics. The living substance of cheese continuously oozes through its discursive and technoscientific packaging. Cheese helps us to see how the 'goodness' of foodstuffs resists black boxing, whether it is the guarantee of safety (which I will address in the next section), or the rational promise of nutritional reductionism to maximize well-being (the focus of the subsequent section).

PROCESSING BLACK BOXES: THE HAZARDS OF ONE-SIZE-FITS-ALL REGULATION

In the United States, cheese safety is promoted through pasteurization. Since pasteurization kills virtually *all* naturally occurring microorganisms in milk, in order to make cheese, pasteurized milk must be reseeded with commercially available strains of lactic acid bacteria, called 'starter cultures', to set in motion the acidification and curding that leads to cheese. Pasteurization, introduced to American cheese factories beginning in the late 1920s, enabled larger quantities of milk to be pooled from more numerous and bigger dairy farms; the cheese industry adopted routine pasteurization in order to extend the shelf life of a perishable product and to expand its market reach – that is, more for economic than for strictly health and safety reasons.

In the United States, public health concern over cheese made from unpasteurized milk dates to the Second World War, when an outbreak of typhoid among overseas service people was traced to heat-treated (but unpasteurized) Cheddar contaminated with *Salmonella typhimurium*. After a subsequent laboratory study found that a sixty-day ageing period for Cheddar cheese made from unpasteurized milk is sufficient to knock out *Salmonella*, in 1949 a mandatory ageing period for cheese made from unpasteurized milk was written into the US legal Standard of Definition for 'cheese'.

The safety regulation of cheese, essentially unchanged since 1949, continues to rely on routine pasteurization; mandatory ageing – for a minimum of sixty days at a temperature of no less than 1.7°C – is a regulatory exception to accommodate cheese made from raw (unpasteurized) milk. The idea is that pathogenic control in cheese will be accomplished in one of two ways: by pasteurizing milk to knock out any pathogens before cheesemaking begins – the industry standard – or through ageing, the idea here being that as cheese (such as Cheddar) ages, it loses moisture and gains acidity, thus becoming increasingly inhospitable to pathogenic germs.

As a technoscientific approach to food safety, pasteurization is a key symbol of modernity's ability to dominate nature for human ends. In *The Pasteurization of France*, Bruno Latour (1988) argues that once Louis Pasteur *revealed* microbes in the laboratory, scientists believed their *control* would revolutionize social relations. Hygienists, government officials and economists laid the groundwork for what they believed to be 'pure' social relations, free of microbial interference and so amenable to rational order. By the end of the nineteenth century, markets and medicine were to be modernized through Pasteurian hygiene. Biopolitics, then, is joined by what I have called *microbiopolitics*: social regulation that is carried out through the control of microbial life (Paxson 2008, 2013). Microbiopolitics entails creating and popularizing categories of microscopic biological agents (*Penicillium*, *E. coli*, *Listeria monocytogenes*, *HIV*, etc.); evaluating such agents through an anthropocentric lens; and promulgating appropriate human behaviours and practices in view of our interrelationships with microbes that enable (or derail) human infection, inoculation and digestion.

For dairy scientists trained to optimize the safety and market standardization of industrially made cheese, the benefits of pasteurization have been and continue to be obvious and incontrovertible. Drawing on Bruno Latour's work, Colin Sage argues that, 'pasteurization has taken on the characteristics of a "black box" for many scientists for which it is simply unimaginable that it would be circumvented' (2007: 210). Latour has called our attention to the power of 'black boxes' to obscure the presumptions and operations of technoscientific knowledge. A black box encases 'a piece of machinery or a set of commands' deemed 'too complex' to grapple with, once efficacy has been established; 'In its place they draw a little box about which they need to know nothing but its input and output' (Latour 1987: 2–3). Heating milk at 72°C for 15 seconds or at 63°C for 30 minutes *kills* pathogens that may be present; that is what pasteurization *is*, say scientists. So thoroughly has this process been black boxed that pasteurization is legally confirmed in the United States by recording time/temperature treatments; it is not deemed necessary to test milk for residual microbial vitality (in order to be up to code, vat pasteurizers used by small-scale cheesemakers must be equipped with automated time/temperature recording devices; this piece of audit technology pushes the price tag for a small vat pasteurizer up to around US$28,000).

In practice, however, the outputs of black boxes, even when they would seem to 'work', exceed intended outcomes. In her study of China's modernizing dairy industry, Megan Tracy (2013) interprets ultra-high temperature (UHT) sterilization and aseptic packaging, when applied to milk produced in the remote 'grasslands' region of Inner Mongolia, not only as a technoscientific means of 'sealing out the bad' – microbes, air, light – but as doing double duty in 'sealing in' desired qualities including nutrients and flavour, but also what she names the 'terroir' qualities of 'purity' associated with the verdant grasslands on which the milk originated. In Tracy's analysis, control over the 'nature' of food substance is as discursive as it is technoscientific. Similarly in the United States, pasteurization of the milk used to make cheese not only 'seals out' unwanted, untrusted microbes, it also 'seals in' the symbolic virtue of modern progress. Untreated, 'naturally' unruly ruminant milk goes into the pasteurizer and comes out 'pasteurized': clean, pure and pathogen free – not only safe but also newly appropriate for human consumption. Within their black boxes, pasteurization and sterilization operate ideologically as well as microbiologically.

The black boxing of pasteurization in American cheesemaking does more than create confidence about the safety of pasteurized foods; it sheds doubt on the safety of foods whose manufacture employed any alternative to pasteurization. I once toured the research lab of a state university food sciences department that produces dairy products served on campus. Standing before a glass wall overlooking the automated processing plant gleaming with high-tech equipment, the lab manager responded to a question about raw milk's edibility with what seemed like genuine puzzlement that anyone in her right mind would want to risk drinking the stuff. 'We've done all this science over the last century,' he said. 'Why would you want to take a step backwards into the past? You take antibiotics, you get better. That's science.' Refusal to accept this black box, on his view, amounted to a repudiation of science itself.

But what the dairy scientist failed to recognize is that the black boxing of pasteurization not only reflects and reproduces faith in the progress of modern science, in this context it also fully presumes and works to legitimate an industrial food system. For food scientists to turn milk's pasteurization into a black box in the first place, Sage points out, milk must first be defined as essentially *in need* of technoscientific purification. Sage quotes a US food safety scientist as saying, 'There is no mystery about why raw milk is a common vehicle for salmonellosis and other enteric infections; after all, dairy milk is essentially a suspension of fecal and other microorganisms in a nutrient broth' (Sage 2007: 210, quoting Nestle 2003: 127). Industrial dairying practices – large-scale, automated, with technology separating farmers from the milking animals – are part of the constitutive assemblage of pasteurization's black boxing. On this view, which I have characterized elsewhere as a *Pasteurian microbiopolitics* (Paxson 2008, 2013), contamination is unavoidable, but eradicable through pasteurization. Pasteurians take the position that raw milk is by its very nature hazardous to human health. On drinking the stuff, the FDA is unequivocal: 'Raw milk is inherently dangerous and it should not be consumed by anyone at any time for any purpose.'[2] As the technoscientific backbone of the food industry's industrialization, pasteurization became a potent symbol of modern progress and invented 'raw-milk cheese' – like 'home-baked bread' (Bobrow-Strain 2013), an unmarked category prior to widespread industrialization of the food supply – as its devalued Other: backwards, obsolete, unnecessarily risky, even foolish.

To appreciate the symbolic implications of pasteurization in the American food system, it is useful to consider Elizabeth Dunn's (2008) analysis of canning in Soviet and postsocialist Georgia. During the Soviet era, a Ministry of Food Processing built numerous industrial canning operations outfitted with comprehensive technological standards to rationalize trade across the Soviet Union. The Soviet industrialization of the food system, Dunn argues, 'worked' not only to feed citizens and alter their tastes and culinary practices, but also to demonstrate the efficacy, and thus existence, of the Soviet state itself. Soviet eaters presumed the safety of food provisioned by a paternalistic state, which in turn reinforced their sense that the state in fact cared for them. Central to Dunn's argument is an understanding that Soviet efficacy relied, in part, on 'black-boxing' canning as an effective method of producing 'good' food. When the 'network of actors, objects, standards, and documents' whose orchestration constituted the practice of canning 'were confined to the factory and hidden away from the end users of the product', consumers simply learned to trust that 'canned food' was safe and good, without any real understanding of how canning occurs and what measures must, in fact, be taken to ensure safety (Dunn 2008: 247). All of this was made clear following the collapse of the Soviet system as Georgians began canning foods at home, seeking to sustain the tastes they had enjoyed under the relative economic and political certainty of Soviet rule. Notable outbreaks of botulism owing to improperly sterilized and sealed food jars revealed that, 'knowledge about safe canning had not traveled along with the canned food itself or with the taste for the food the state once made' (2008: 250). Once canning was removed from the assemblage of the state-run industrial factory, it failed to operate as people imagined it would. The black box did not transfer intact from factory to home. Black boxes often do not travel well, either temporally or spatially, precisely because their closures are held together by beliefs, institutions and practices that are embedded in wider social and political contexts.

While in the Soviet case, canning did not transfer as a black box from industrial to domestic spaces of production, in the United States the industrial black boxing of pasteurization – which lead the FDA to treat raw-milk cheese as inherently and fundamentally different from pasteurized-milk cheese – has blinded many food safety regulators to non-industrial possibilities of safe cheese production. In 2004, I spent ten days on a sheep dairy farm in Vermont, participating in nearly all aspects of farmstead cheese production, including milking sheep (see Paxson 2013, Chapter 2). I would not characterize the milk produced at this dairy and other cheesemaking farms I have visited as 'a suspension of fecal and other microorganisms in a nutrient broth.' Artisan cheesemakers who make cheese from unpasteurized milk, often on the dairy farms that supply the milk, challenge the founding assumption of Pasteurism by arguing that faecal matter is not naturally present in milk; it only gets in if humans are less than scrupulous in their dairying practices.

In contrast to the hyper-hygienic ethos that brought us the limitless shelf life of Velveeta, what I have called a *post-Pasteurian* approach to microbiopolitics embraces the idea that 'real' cheese, as a fermented food, is (rightly) teeming with living bacteria and moulds: that's what cheese *is*. In moving cheesemaking from the laboratory-like conditions of industrial factories, artisan cheesemakers have found that the black boxes of food science can produce unintended outputs. In Vermont, David and Cindy Major started the nation's first cheesemaking sheep dairy in the 1980s. In their early years of cheesemaking, after encountering problems trying to develop a protective natural rind on a cheese they were ageing, the Majors sought the advice of University of Wisconsin dairy consultants, who knew only industrial production: working with milk pooled from multiple farms, in automated factories, fabricating plastic-encased blocks of cheese that would mature, unattended, in refrigerated warehouses. Although the so-called natural rind on a cheese is the outcome of successive waves of bacteria and fungi colonizing its surface, the experts suggested that the Majors dip their cheeses in an antiseptic mould inhibitor. On their advice, David let off chlorine bombs in the ageing room to keep it sanitized! Not surprisingly, the hyper-hygienic strategy did not help the Majors solve their rind problem. Eventually, David drew an analogy between the cheeses and his sheep pastures, which suggested to him: 'Rather than sanitize, maybe we need to cultivate in the cave.' David came to perceive the cheese as a microbial ecosystem that requires him to cultivate and nurture a hospitable environment for the flourishing of those 'good' microbes that co-produce cheese with humans.

To be successful, post-Pasteurian food makers do not let microbes run wild. Repeatedly in my interviews with artisan cheesemakers, I heard that 80–90 per cent of cheesemaking is cleaning and sanitizing. Indeed, that is why I describe the artisanal microbiopolitical stance as *post*-Pasteurian rather than *anti*-Pasteurian: it *takes after* Pasteurism in acknowledging the importance of hygiene and sanitation, while moving *beyond* an antiseptic attitude to manage the microbial environment as a means of cultivating and enlisting 'good' microbes as allies that can outcompete 'bad' ones. In practice, this means monitoring and controlling the temperature and humidity of the rooms in which cheese is made and allowed to ripen, whether through automated sensors and computerized controls, or by opening and closing a window, hanging plastic sheeting in front of a wall of cheese racks, or throwing a bucket of water on the floor (see also West and Domingos 2012; West 2013).

In regulating cheese production to promote safety, the US Food and Drug Administration relies on a binary distinction, requiring one set of requirements for cheese – any cheese, regardless of type and method of fabrication – made from pasteurized milk, and another set of requirements for cheese – again, any cheese – made from unpasteurized milk. A number of problems follow from this. First, although US food safety officials never set out to establish the 'sixty-day rule' as an equivalent standard to pasteurization, many producers and consumers have come to view it as such. The black boxing of pasteurization, I suggest, has had the unintended output of creating a sort of shadow box around its constitutive outside, namely, the legal alternative of ageing cheese for a minimum of sixty days. Producers and consumers often approach the sixty-day rule as if it, like pasteurization, were supposed to be a black box. For example, one popular book showcasing Vermont cheeses declares, 'Cheesemakers need to choose between making raw-milk cheese, which must be aged for a minimum of sixty days to destroy the bacteria in it, or pasteurized cheese, which requires heating the milk to destroy bacteria beforehand' (Ogden 2007: 11). This statement is dangerously misleading on two counts. First, varieties of cheese do not fall into discrete, essential categories of being either 'raw-milk' or 'requiring' pasteurization – technically speaking, any cheese *can* be made from either raw or pasteurized milk. Second, ageing cheeses for sixty days does not 'destroy the bacteria in it' in any absolute sense; it merely contributes to a relatively inhospitable environment for microbes such as *Salmonella*, in cheeses such as Cheddar.

The problem with the sixty-day rule is that, microbiologically speaking, not all cheeses behave like Cheddar and not all pathogens behave like *Salmonella*. Because hard, dry, sharp Cheddar constitutes a fundamentally different microbial ecology, when it comes to pathogenic vulnerability, than soft, moist, low-acidity bloomy rind cheeses such as Brie, the sixty-day ageing period does not produce the same outputs when applied to each cheese; it does not travel as a black box between Cheddar and Brie. And consider *Listeria monocytogenes*, a bacterium that can cause listeriosis, an infection that may manifest as septicaemia, meningitis, or, in pregnant women, may result in spontaneous abortion or stillbirth. Although rare, listeriosis has a 20 per cent fatality rate and accounts for roughly one-fourth of deaths attributed to foodborne illness in the United States. Cheeses with a pH above 5.5 (meaning low acidity) are more likely to harbour *Listeria* than cheeses with higher acidity. Contradicting the premise of the sixty-day rule, ageing bloomy rind cheese such as Brie or a Camembert for sixty days turns out to *increase* its susceptibility to *Listeria* because, unlike Cheddar, as it ages its acidity actually declines (D'Amico, Druart and Donnelly 2008). Catherine Donnelly, a microbiologist at the University of Vermont whose lab pioneered methods of detecting *Listeria* in foods, said to me of the sixty-day rule, 'What's sad is, there are cheesemakers who read the letter of the law [and think] "Great! For a bloomy rind cheese [from raw milk], I'll just hold it for sixty days." And it's like, oh my *God*! We've got an accident waiting to happen. And they're perfectly within legal bounds to do that.' In fact, it is what the law currently requires of them.

Further complicating the microbiopolitical field, unlike the tubercular bacillus that can be carried from sickened cow to human through milk, or *E. coli*, which originates in manure and can enter the milk supply through insanitary milking conditions, *Listeria* is a ubiquitous environmental contaminant – you may have it on your shoes – and thus it is most likely to infect a cheese during manufacture, ageing or packaging. Pasteurizing milk prior to cheesemaking is no barrier to this sort of environmental contamination. In fact, Catherine Donnelly suggests that cheese made from pasteurized milk may be more susceptible to *Listeria* growth because it lacks the microbial diversity of raw-milk cheese – more diversity pits more of those 'good' microbes against possible baddies.

On 21 October 2010 federal agents locked the doors of the Estrella Family Creamery in Washington state, carrying out a court-ordered seizure in light of evidence presented by the US Food and Drug Administration of the 'persisting presence' of the potentially pathogenic bacterium *Listeria monocytogenes* in one of the ageing rooms where the family ripened cheese made from the raw milk of their own cows. In December of that same year, federal regulators demanded that pioneering cheesemaker Sally Jackson upgrade the jury-rigged cheesemaking equipment she had used for thirty years. Unable to afford the required modifications, Jackson retired after the Centers for Disease Control demonstrated a link between her raw-milk cheese and eight cases of illness due to enterohemorrhagic *E. coli* infection. Such cases have provided a warrant for the FDA to revisit the efficacy of the sixty-day rule (the regulation of raw-milk cheese is currently under review with government safety officials). At the same time, if outbreaks of botulism in Georgia bring to light a taste for socialist nostalgia and parallel suspicion of the postsocialist state's commitment to care for its citizens, the increasing appearance of *E. coli* O157:H7 and *L. mono* in raw-milk cheese and cheesemaking in the United States points to a counter-industrial taste for artisanally made foods as well as a distrust of one-size-fits-all federal oversight. When current regulations would seem irrational or, worse, ill-advised – and as there is clearly a consumer market for raw-milk products – some cheesemakers may be tempted to operate at the edges of the law, for example, selling under-aged raw-milk cheese at farmers' markets as 'pet food' or 'fish bait' rather than (wink-wink) for human consumption.

The sixty-day rule, put in place at the height of the cheese industry's industrialization, is becoming obsolete as a means of promoting public health. Obsolescence stems, first, from growing interest in producing and consuming raw-milk products. While in the 1950s, raw-milk cheeses were viewed as a holdover from the pre-industrial era, today they have new, positive value – still in opposition to industrial foods – as 'natural', 'authentic' or 'gourmet'. At the same time, the microbial field has transformed as pathogens of concern evolve apace with, and in opposition to, industrial agricultural practices. The Shiga toxin-producing O157:H7 mutation of *E. coli*, an intestinal bacterium included on the Centers for Disease Control list of bioterrorism agents, was first characterized in 1982 and may not have existed when the sixty-day rule was introduced. In 1949, *Listeria monocytogenes* had not yet been identified as a cause of foodborne illness.

Scrutiny of the sixty-day rule, through the work of Catherine Donnelly and others, is also, inadvertently, revealing the limitations of *pasteurization* in ensuring food safety. Both approaches to safety regulation, pasteurization as well as ageing, have been applied equally to processes of industrial and artisanal manufacture, and to a diversity of microbial ecologies we know as varieties of cheese. Such 'one-size-fits-all' regulation is being called into question by recognition that 'cheese' is not, in fact, reducible to a binary standard: pasteurization and its absence are insufficient classificatory distinctions. 'When standards change,' notes Susan Leigh Star, 'it is easier to see the invisible work and the invisible memberships that have anchored them in place' (1991: 44). Black boxes, the fully as well as semi-opaque, are coming open at their seams.

What is revealed is that food safety is largely relational and 'not an inherent biological characteristic of a food', as nutritionist Marion Nestle (2003: 16) writes. A given food may be safe for some individuals but not others (think of allergies as well as immunities), in small quantities but not large, or at one point in time but not another. Such contingency poses a challenge for food safety regulators, producers and consumers alike (see Solomon 2015 for an ethnographic examination of the unreliability of food safety in Mumbai). Neither 'raw-milk cheese' nor 'pasteurized cheese' are one: not equally well made, or equally risky or equally tasty. Some milk is cleaner than others. Some cheesemakers are more skilled and hygienic than others. And some cheese types are more susceptible to pathogenic infection than others. The challenge – for regulators, producers and consumers – is that these meaningful distinctions are not well captured by any of our conventional cheese categories.

SWALLOWING BLACK BOXES: THE INDIGESTIBILITY OF NUTRITIONAL GUIDELINES

The notion that 'food' conveys to 'the body' not only nutrition but also a potential for broader well-being is nothing new; beginning in the 1820s, the Presbyterian minister, Sylvester Graham, promoted feeding dietary fibre to the American people as a means of improving the moral fibre of the nation by curbing immoderate appetites – his Graham Crackers, invented in 1829, could be considered an early 'functional food', thought to have a positive effect on bodily health beyond basic nutrition (Schwartz 1986). Functional thinking underpins Scrinis's (2008) notion of *nutritionism*, an ideology of nutrition promoted by nutrition scientists, dieticians, public health authorities and, more recently, food marketers, which has encouraged eating publics, now around the world, to (1) regard foods primarily in terms of their nutritional composition: an apple *is* 100 calories; meat *is* protein; cheese *is* cholesterol and fat; (2) to draw causal connections between particular nutrients and aspects of physical health or illness: Vitamin D is good for bone strength; cholesterol leads to heart disease; and (3) to rationally deploy this reductive, functional thinking to put together 'nutritionally balanced', normatively 'good' diets, without culinary regard for meals. In practice, of course, people enact this ideological approach to food and eating to varying degrees, but it is difficult today not to be influenced by it. Nutritionism produces particular kinds of eating subjects: calculating, rationally reflexive and morally concerned about the outcome of their eating (Mudry 2009, 2013; Biltekoff 2013; Veit 2013). Most people struggle to 'stay on' rationalized diets precisely because that slice of chocolate cake is, in fact, irreducible to 'fat and sugar' and simultaneously retains the characteristics of 'reward, celebration, treat, deliciousness.'

To investigate a public health campaign against obesity in Guatemala, Emily Yates-Doerr examines what she calls 'nutritional black-boxing', defined as 'the process of consolidating technical and historically contingent ideas about nourishment and the myriad relationships surrounding dietary practices into seemingly unproblematic terms: a vitamin, a nutrient' (2012: 294). Nutrients, she demonstrates convincingly, are better viewed as black boxes than as coherent, autonomous things in the world: 'as they shift contexts, the information that they seem to hold in place transforms' (2012: 295). When nutritionists working in Guatemala present to schoolchildren and women what they believe to be straightforward lessons in identifying nutritionally 'good' and 'bad' foods – sugar, because it is sweet, is also bad and should be avoided; green vegetables, because they have vitamins, are good and should be eaten – the people who receive these lessons often draw from them unintended messages. Yates-Doerr tells, for example, of a school teacher who summed up a nutrition lesson by asking his class, 'What is a good source of iron?' and became frustrated by his students' response: 'Sugar!' Where had his lesson gone wrong? Why hadn't his lesson about the nutritional benefits of meat, beans and spinach sunk in? Yates-Doerr argues it was because his science lesson was disconnected from the students' extant understanding of 'food', which is first and foremost about taste, textures and the social relations of commensality, but which is also delivered to the kitchen table through assemblages other than the one that produced the nutrition 'facts' of the lesson. It turns out that Guatamala's government requires sugar fortification to prevent nutrition deficiencies; the box of sugar from which children (and their parents) convey sweetness to their drinks and food is clearly labelled, 'Sugar with Iron.' When pro-nutrient and anti-sugar lessons contradicted one another, it is little wonder that the children resolved the conflict by erring on the side of 'sugar-has-nutrients' (indeed, more than one adult explained to Yates-Doerr, as she watched them spoon sugar into their drinks, that it was 'for the vitamins' [2012: 297]).

What, then, of American cheese? As discussed above, the FDA regulates the *production* of all cheeses according to a binary division between raw-milk and pasteurized-milk cheese. But when it comes to FDA guidelines for the safe *consumption* of cheese, the agency introduces an additional category, *softness*, warning certain consumers to avoid 'soft' cheeses. While softness is not a nutrient, the government's dietary guideline concerning cheese safety shares features of nutritional black boxing.

The FDA directs its sternest warning concerning cheese-residing microbes at pregnant women, advising until recently against 'soft cheeses' such as 'Brie, Camembert, feta, blue-veined cheese, or Mexican-style cheeses such as queso blanco fresco.' Softness is intended to represent an indirect measure of moisture, high moisture being conducive to the growth of pathogens including *Listeria monocytogenes*, linked to stillbirth and miscarriage when ingested by pregnant women. But Brie, Camembert, Feta, blue-veined, Mexican-style cheeses are not self-evidently united by 'softness.' In addition, other cheeses would seem to be soft. What about them? Categorical lumping may appear to 'simplify' a public health message, but as with nutritional black boxing in Guatemala, such simplification can introduce, rather than mitigate, confusion and complications. In 2005, when my own pregnancy test came back positive, the first question I asked the nurse practitioner was, 'What about fresh mozzarella?' She had no idea so I went online. From participant observation as a pregnant cheese eater, I discovered that while many women have gotten the message to avoid 'soft' cheese, that message has generated quite a bit of confusion and erroneous information on pregnancy websites (see Paxson 2008). On Babycenter. com, for example, one woman asked, 'Does anyone know if those little Laughing Cow wedges are considered a soft cheese?' A pasteurized, process cheese that comes in foil-wrapped bite-sized wedges, Laughing Cow is undoubtedly *soft* but almost certainly pathogen free. In emphasizing a cheese's softness in its dietary guide for pregnant women, the FDA inadvertently drew attention away from the protective function of pasteurization.

In dietary warnings to pregnant women, 'soft cheese' is presented as a coherent type of food when in fact 'softness' obscures a heterogeneous set of risk factors. The high-moisture content of Brie and Camembert not only account for their softness but also contribute to their risk profile, while 'blue-veined' cheeses (which come in differing degrees of softness) make the list primarily owing to their pH. Taking acidity into account, the local ecology of Camembert, whose pH increases to 7.5 with ripening, is far more susceptible to *Listeria* than Feta (pH 4.4) – although equivalence is implied by their joint appearance on the warning list. Greek-Americans routinely defend Feta on pregnancy websites, citing as evidence fleets of relatives who survived pregnancy despite daily doses of the stuff (largely thanks to Feta, Greece boasts the highest per capital consumption of cheese in the world). The contraindication of experiential, bodily knowledge (as feminist medical anthropologists have argued regarding pregnancy and other biomedical care) may lead lay people to dismiss the abstract authoritative knowledge of a government agency as bankrupt, even beholden to industry interests (Abel and Browner 1998; Lock and Kaufert 1998).

'Mexican-style' cheeses are prominent on the consumer-warning list not because of their pH or moisture content (as a fresh cheese, the sixty-day rule already requires that *queso fresco* be made from pasteurized milk to be legally saleable). Instead, 'Mexican-style' cheeses are singled out because the United States' largest cheese-related outbreak of listeriosis (in the 1980s) was traced to *queso fresco* that was sold door-to-door and purportedly made in a bathtub (clearly, without a pasteurizer). The problem imagined here is not 'Mexican-style cheese' per se – this is not a matter of material reductionism – but instead the unruliness of a local microbial ecology that might flourish in a shadow economy of unlicensed commercial food production. Here, the FDA implicitly recognizes that food materializes particular social-material assemblages, but in overgeneralizing on a worst-case scenario it risks tainting a type of cheese with racist stereotypes.

Not only is the FDA diversifying its classification of cheese food beyond the pasteurized/unpasteurized divide, it is acknowledging a heterogeneity of 'eating bodies' – to some limited extent. In introducing 'soft', a sensory characteristic, as a classificatory cheese category in its dietary recommendations, the FDA acknowledges that eaters are not metabolically identical; they embody different risk profiles for foodborne illness. Pregnant women, the elderly and the immunocompromised are especially susceptible to listeriosis, and *Listeria monocytogenes* takes especially well to mould-ripened cheeses with low acidity, such as Brie and Camembert; as foods (rather than laboratory specimens), such cheeses are recognizably 'soft.' Hence, pregnant women (in particular) are advised to avoid consuming 'soft' cheeses.

However, the actual *occurrence* of food safety – that is, the avoidance of food poisoning (if not also allergies) – calibrates to a direct relationship between a particular food substance (*this* food, in *this* condition, right *now* today) and the bodily capacity of an individual eater to incorporate that substance, hitchhiking microbes and all. As Yates-Doerr demonstrates with regard to nutrition, '"health" is not a property that can be fixed within a food; existing instead in the specificities of dietary practices, it is a process to be enacted, not an object to hold' (2012: 307; see also Yates-Doerr and Carney 2015). Food safety is a contingent relationship; food classification, predicated on a discrete separation of food (with intrinsic qualities) and its eaters (who incorporate those qualities), cannot fully get at this. Although the occurrence of food safety is particular, the *regulation* of food safety operates by setting production standards calibrated to broad categories of food substance, not to particular substances of food. Those standards are set by anticipating *possible* encounters between types of foods and types of eaters. As such, regulatory categories are designed to cast a wide net of possibility, wider than would circumscribe most actual encounters; the gap between the two can be viewed, depending on one's perspective, as an abundance of caution or as over-regulation. Put differently, food safety officials regulate from the exception – from the exceptional consumer (e.g., pregnant or immunocompromised), but also from the exceptional producer (e.g., 'bathtub' cheese). As Susan Leigh Star noted, 'there are always misfits between *standardized* or *conventional* technological systems and the needs of individuals' (1991: 36). The deployment of broad classificatory categories obscures the specificities – or exceptions – on which regulation is based.

It also, of course, elides the organoleptic, commensal and emotional aspects of eating that can attach to particular foods simultaneous with medicalized understandings. While normative attention to edibility (is this something I should eat?) may overshadow appreciation for palatability and social value (is this something I want to eat?), it does not eradicate it. Yates-Doerr writes:

> Absent from the classificatory categories of nutrition is attention to taste, pleasure and awareness of all of the social relations inherent in the production and consumption of any meal. ... It is not that social context itself becomes irrelevant; rather it becomes obscured by the abstraction of a meal's value into its biochemical parts, parts that themselves come to appear as the whole source of a meal's value to the body. (2012: 304)

Borrowing from John Law (2004: 62), Bodil Just Christensen (n.d.) suggests we might best view 'food' as a 'fractional object': a 'material-semiotic assemblage consisting of layered meanings of many ontological kinds.' The social complexity of food and eating is ever-present and may resurface 'in the confusion that arises when people attempt to incorporate universalized food rules into the unpredictable and often-contradictory demands of everyday life' (Yates-Doerr 2012: 304–5).

BEYOND EATING AS INCORPORATION: MATERIALIZING LOCAL ECOLOGIES AND BIOLOGIES

In 1970, Margaret Mead described American ideas about nutrition as dominated by a Puritanical dichotomy between 'food that was "good for you, but not good"' and 'food that was "good, but not good for you"' (1970: 179). This view has underwritten and been reinforced by nutrition science, whose rational judgement of food's goodness presumes to be unswayed by any sensuous pleasures that food affords. Today, however, Mead's dichotomy is beginning to look as old-fashioned as Velveeta. More and more, I see Americans (and others) attempting to align various vectors of food's 'goodness' hoping to be pointed to perfect foods: healthy, tasty, safe, fair. Consumers seek guilt-free indulgence, and food corporations are eager to sell it to them (Mol 2009). Indeed, rather than presume that nutritionism in fact denies the body and its pleasures, as critics such as Michael Pollan (2009) lament, research by Bodil Christensen (n.d.) demonstrates that 'when food is practiced as nutrients', even by Danish gastric bypass patients and army conscripts trained to think and act within the 'logic of nutrients', eaters do not, in fact, lose their sensual appreciation for food. They may rationalize food choices on nutritional terms, but they describe the experience of eating with reference to taste, texture and satiation. Nutritional reductionism may obscure or de-prioritize other modes of apprehending and valuing food, but it does not erase them (Christensen n.d.). Amidst the dominance of nutritional reductionism, we are beginning to see a move towards embracing food as a 'fractional object', simultaneously embodying a variety of essences. Nutritionists in the Netherlands and France are beginning to emphasize the sensorial pleasures of eating as a means of mitigating the quantity of food intake (Vogel and Mol 2014; Sanabria 2015). What is more, an embrace of multiplicity in what qualities 'count' in foods occurs alongside new appreciation for diversity among eating bodies. Again, cheese offers an instructive example.

Cheese embodies the outcome of bacteria and fungi feeding on the proteins and sugars in milk to produce odorific decomposition; milk, in turn, is the outcome of domesticated cows, goats or sheep feeding on hay and pasture grasses containing cellulose, which ruminants digest thanks to the metabolic action of symbiotic microorganisms residing in their four-chambered guts. Cheese is the material legacy of ruminant and microbial bodies incorporating bits of their environment: eating, metabolizing. Put otherwise, cheese embodies *local ecologies*, by which I mean to point to a scaled-up version of what Margaret Lock has named *local biologies*. In Lock's work:

> *Local biologies* refers to the way in which the embodied experience of physical sensations, including those of well-being, health, illness, and so on, is in part informed by the material body, itself contingent on evolutionary, environmental, and individual variables. Embodiment is also constituted by the way in which self and others represent the body, drawing on local categories of knowledge and experience. (Lock 2001: 483)

In other words, bodies materialize tangible and semiotic elements of their natural and cultural environments, which may contain elements of both the 'local' and the 'global.' So too do foods. Recognition of this can be cause for celebration, as in claims to *terroir* foods and wine, valued for expressing distinctive characteristics said to be typical of their place of production (Barham 2003; Trubek 2008; Demossier 2011; Teil 2012; Rogers 2013). It can also be cause for alarm. Becky Mansfield (2011) reminds us that, owing to industrial waste runoff into waterways, the nutritional composition of fish today includes heavy metals; mercury has become part of what swordfish *is* materially, nutritionally.

How, through eating, do bodies materialize their environments? In rethinking obesity and diabetes by emphasizing the situated relationality of eating bodies, researchers are complicating the eating-as-incorporation paradigm by 'thinking metabolically' (Kendrick 2013: 237; see also Yates-Doerr 2012; Solomon 2015). Writing of the new fields of 'relational biology', including microbiome studies and nutritional epigenetics (a form of non-genetic inheritance), Hannah Landecker suggests that research scientists (if not yet nutritionists) are beginning to reconceptualize 'food' as 'a form of environmental exposure.' On this view, metabolism is more like tasting – in the sense of inquisitive sampling – than incorporation. Landecker writes, 'Today, diverse biomedical sciences of metabolism – from the study of intestinal bacteria mediating digestion to the reconceptualization of fat as an endocrine organ – are beginning to suggest that different individuals may process the same food very differently, and that different foods have potential to shape the metabolic interface in very different ways' (2011: 173). Landecker expands Brillat-Savarin's aphorism, quoted above: 'We cannot help but ingest and in the act of ingestion and digestion are drawn into the social, technical and political networks of food production, regulation and consumption. We are what we eat – but also what our parents and grandparents ate, and what we eat ate' – and metabolized, and incorporated (Landecker 2011: 187). 'It is not at all clear', writes Landecker of carnivorism, 'what the effect on metabolism is of eating bodies that themselves have had their metabolisms patterned by industrial agriculture.' If eating is relating (Bertoni 2013), then these nature–culture relations, often unseen, are far-reaching in space and time and unfold within political ecologies of production as well as consumption (cf. Baker 2013; Blanchette 2013; Heath and Meneley 2010; Weiss 2011; Yates-Doerr and Mol 2012).

Some evidence, however, points to a rise in the incidence of food allergies and autoimmune diseases. Both are understood to occur when a body's immune system has trouble distinguishing between 'self' or 'food' – that which can safely become incorporated into self – and 'non-self', that which is toxic or pathogenic to self (Martin and Cone 2003). The gut's immune system 'learns to recognize and accept ("tolerate") food, allowing it to be absorbed into the blood and lymph. It also learns to recognize dangerous pathogens and toxins ingested along with food and helps prevent them from being absorbed' – that is, by causing people to be sick (Martin and Cone 2003: 239). Immunologists have recognized that the immune system can be 'taught' to tolerate potentially dangerous substances through repeated low-dose exposure; ingesting small amounts of 'foreign' substance can 'train' the immune system to tolerate it – this is the reasoning behind ingesting local honey (full of environmental pollen) to reduce suffering associated with hay fever.

Taking inspiration from scientific recognition that 'the tasting body is not a natural category' but instead the outcome of cultural training, Annemarie Mol extends the notion of oral tolerance to entertain the possibility of 'teaching' a body to accept, even appreciate, food that is 'good' not only for the body (in terms of health) but that is 'good' in an ethical sense, for communities of producers or for the environment (2009: 277). I see this train of associations playing out in the recreational taste education that happens at food festivals and in boutique retail shops, in which connoisseurship – the cultivation of a knowing palate – is being reformatted to include knowledge about the means and methods of the production of comestibles, whether natural wine or pasture-raised meat or artisanally made cheese (Paxson 2013; Weiss 2011; Yates-Doerr and Mol 2012).

At the 2009 California Artisan Cheese Festival in Petaluma, Cowgirl Creamery's Sue Conley and Peggy Smith introduced a taste education session by explaining that they would 'talk about cheeses in terms of the place they're made in, and how place contributes to the cheese.' Their discourse points to how *good food* and *food that's good* are being brought together through a taste education that promotes artisanal practices as well as products. The first cheese we in attendance tasted was Cowgirl Creamery's fromage blanc, a simple, fresh cheese used primarily by chefs, which they selected 'to show the reflection of the milk' produced by the organic dairy of their neighbour in Point Reyes Station, Albert Straus. With this cheese, Conley and Smith wanted 'to showcase his hard work … how he's taken care of the land and his animals.' Straus's pastures are free of herbicides and chemical fertilizers; his cows are not treated with hormones or antibiotics to boost production volume. As tasters, we were meant to draw a causal connection between the 'good, clean' milk-flavour in the cheese we were tasting and Straus's 'good, clean,' environmentally conscious dairying practice (cf. Tracy 2013). Conley and Smith went on to describe in some detail Straus's newly installed methane digester, apparently without worry that our sensory apparatuses would then register suggestive hints of manure in the taste and odour of the cheese. Instead, we were meant to taste the goodness of greenhouse gas mitigation. Here, eaters with 'good taste' are enjoined to taste the 'good' qualities of food that materialize *elsewhere* – in the environmental ecologies of food production, say, including ruminant bodies – in much the way Annemarie Mol (2009) envisions the possibility of cultivating the good taste of a true consumer-citizen. This is telling of the new taste education.

When methane digesters become part of the 'taste of place' (Trubek 2008), eaters are enjoined to develop *socially aware* tastes. This is not strictly the taste of social distinction, in a Bourdieuian sense (although considering the high-priced recreational venues at which such taste education occurs, class is certainly a part of the story). Moreover, we are seeing the cultivation of a taste for food that's good to eat and *not incidentally* ethically good to make. In the new American taste education, artisanal cheese is said to taste good, in the first instance, because 'best practices' in farming and agricultural processing – from animal health, to a diversity of clean fodder, to sanitary milking and cheesemaking conditions, to a cheesemaker's craft skill – produce 'best quality' food and drink. On this view, an eater's enjoyment of a well-made cheese will therefore be heightened by knowing that the methods of production work to accomplish worthwhile ends beyond producing cheese: in keeping agricultural land out of the hands of developers, for example, or in the organic remediation of industrially farmed land, or sustaining the ability of a fourth-generation to continue family dairy farming. Recent sensory consumer research bears this out, at least in cheese-producing regions: focus-group surveys with cheese-buying consumers in Vermont indicate that 'the sensory experience of Vermont artisan cheese stems from a mix of intrinsic, organoleptic properties and extrinsic, socially embedded properties' including 'the farming practices of the cheesemakers' and an 'ethos of craftsmanship' in their production methods (Lahne and Trubek 2014: 132–3). Consumers 'confirm that their preferences for a particular taste also reflects their preference for a certain set of production and farming practices' which they credit with generating that taste (2014: 137).

Here, and not unlike what Meigs writes of the Hua of Papua New Guinea, questions of *who* makes food, *how* and within what nature–culture *relations*, are directly germane to what food 'is.' Living, metabolizing, microbially diverse cheese is upheld as a microcosm of the life-enhancing transformation of agricultural landscapes and regions in which artisan food-making wishes to participate. For this to be a persuasive claim, however, food makers must sort out microbial friend from foe – work (not faith) that produces the conditions through which a post-Pasteurian, counter-industrial diet might (for some) safely emerge. Microbiopolitics extends agro-food studies not only into the body of eaters, then, but also into the embodied knowledge of food producers.

'Microbes connect us through diseases,' Latour writes (1987: 37), 'but they also connect us, through our intestinal flora, to the very things we eat.' And through the things we eat, to wider ecologies and landscapes. At the beginning of the twenty-first century, as it comes to light that 90 per cent of what we think of as the human organism turns out to comprise microorganisms, the adage, 'We are what we eat,' gains new vitality. And if we are what we eat, then local biologies, local ecologies, can and should raise questions about environmental justice, agricultural labour politics and food safety regulation as well as further questions of health and illness. The new food politics, accompanied by a new taste education, aims not to consolidate 'black boxes' but instead to deliver something resembling CSA boxes: collections of foods whose nutritional and social values are meant to be open to eaters and feeders. To what extent it succeeds remains to be seen.

ACKNOWLEDGEMENTS

I am grateful to comments and suggestions on prior versions of this essay by Jillian Cavanaugh, Cristina Grasseni, Stefan Helmreich and Else Vogel. Thanks, too, to Jakob Klein and Woody Watson for the fun assignment and opportunity to be part of this volume.

NOTES

1. A more precise term than lactose intolerance, lactase impersistence refers to the tapering off of a body's production of the enzyme lactase, required for the digestion of lactose (Wiley 2011; see also Wiley, Chapter 10, this volume).
2. US Food and Drug Administration website, "Questions & Answers: Raw Milk." From 1 March 2007; updated on 26 March 2010. http://www.fda.gov/Food/FoodSafety/ ProductSpecificInformation/MilkSafety/ucm122062.htm. Accessed 16 June 2010.

REFERENCES

Abbots, E.-J. and Lavis, A. (eds) (2013), *Why We Eat, How We Eat: Contemporary Encounters between Foods and Bodies*, Farnham, UK: Ashgate.

Abel, E. K. and Browner, C. H. (1998), 'Selective Compliance with Biomedical Authority and the Uses of Experiential Knowledge', in M. Lock and P. A. Kaufert (eds), *Pragmatic Women and Body Politics*, 310–26, Cambridge, UK: Cambridge University Press.

Baker, K. (2013), 'Home and Heart, Hand and Eye: Unseen Links between Pigmen and Pigs in Industrial Farming', in E.-J. Abbots and A. Lavis (eds), *Why We Eat, How We Eat: Contemporary Encounters between Foods and Bodies*, 53–73, Farnham, UK: Ashgate.

Barham, E. (2003), 'Translating Terroir: The Global Challenge of French AOC Labeling', *Journal of Rural Studies*, 19: 127–38.

Bertoni, F. (2013), 'Soil and Worm: On Eating and Relating', *Science as Culture*, 22(1): 61–85.

Biltekoff, C. (2013), *Eating Right in America: The Cultural Politics of Food and Health*, Durham, NC: Duke University Press.

Blanchette, A. (2013), *Conceiving Porkopolis: The Production of Life on the American 'Factory' Farm*, PhD dissertation, Department of Anthropology, University of Chicago.

Bobrow-Strain, A. (2013), *White Bread: A Social History of the Store-Bought Loaf*, Boston, MA: Beacon.

Brillat-Savarin, J.-A. (1825 [1970]), *The Physiology of Taste*, translated by A. Drayton, London: Penguin Classics.

Christensen, B. J. (n.d.), 'Practicing Nutrients: Nutrition Facts and Eating Practices among Danish Obesity Surgery Patients and Conscripts in Military Service', unpublished manuscript.

D'Amico, D. J., Druart, M. J. and Donnelly, C. W. (2008), '60-Day Aging Requirement Does Not Ensure Safety of Surface-Mold-Ripened Soft Cheeses Manufactured from Raw or Pasteurized Milk When *Listeria monocytogenes* is Introduced as a Postprocessing Contaminant', *Journal of Food Protection*, 71(8): 1563–71.

Demossier, M. (2011), 'Beyond *Terroir*: Territorial Construction, Hegemonic Discourses, and French Wine Culture', *Journal of the Royal Anthropological Institute (N.S.)*, 17: 685–705.

Douglas, M. (1966), *Purity and Danger: An Analysis of the Concepts of Pollution and Taboo*, New York: Praeger.

Dunn, E. C. (2008), 'Postsocialist Spores: Disease, Bodies, and the State in the Republic of Georgia', *American Ethnologist*, 35(2): 243–58.

Guthman, J., Broad, G., Klein, K. and Landecker, H. (2014), 'Beyond the Sovereign Body', *Gastronomica*, 14(3): 46–55.

Harris, M. (1985), *Good to Eat: Riddles of Food and Culture*, Prospect Heights, IL: Waveland Press.

Heath, D. and Meneley, A. (2010), 'The Naturecultures of Foie Gras: Techniques of the Body and a Contested Ethics of Care', *Food, Culture and Society*, 13(3): 421–52.

Kendrick, R. (2013), 'Metabolism as Strategy: Agency, Evolution and Biological Hinterlands', in E.-J. Abbots and A. Lavis (eds), *Why We Eat, How We Eat: Contemporary Encounters between Foods and Bodies*, 237–54, Farnham, UK: Ashgate.

Lahne, J. and Trubek, A. (2014), '"A Little Information Excites Us": Consumer Sensory Experience of Vermont Artisan Cheese as Active Practice', *Appetite*, 78: 129–38.

Landecker, H. (2011), 'Food as Exposure: Nutritional Epigenetics and the New Metabolism', *BioSocieties*, 6(2): 167–94.

Latour, B. (1987), *Science in Action: How to Follow Scientists and Engineers through Society*, Cambridge, MA: Harvard University Press.

Latour, B. (1988), *The Pasteurization of France*, translated by A. Sheridan and J. Law, Cambridge, MA: Harvard University Press.

Law, J. (2004), *After Method: Mess in Social Science Research*, London: Taylor & Francis.

Lock, M. (2001), 'The Tempering of Medical Anthropology: Troubling Natural Categories', *Medical Anthropological Quarterly*, 15(4): 478–92.

Lock, M. and Kaufert, P. (eds) (1998), *Pragmatic Women and Body Politics*, Cambridge, UK: Cambridge University Press.

Mansfield, B. (2011), 'Is Fish Health Food or Poison? Farmed Fish and the Material Production of Un/Healthy Nature', *Antipode*, 43(2): 413–34.

Martin, E. and Cone, R. (2003), 'Corporeal Flows: The Immune System, Global Economies of Food, and New Implications for Health', in J. M. Wilce, Jr. (ed.), *Social and Cultural Lives of Immune Systems*, 237–66, London: Routledge.

Mead, M. (1970), 'The Changing Significance of Food', *American Scientist*, 58(2): 176–81.

Meigs, A. (1987), 'Food as a Cultural Construction', *Food and Foodways*, 2(1): 341–57.

Mol, A. (2008), 'I Eat an Apple: On Theorizing Subjectivities', *Subjectivity*, 22: 28–37.

Mol, A. (2009), 'Good Taste: The Embodied Normativity of the Consumer-Citizen', *Journal of Cultural Economy*, 2(3): 269–83.

Mudry, J. (2009), *Measured Meals: Nutrition in America*, Albany: State University of New York Press.

Nestle, M. (2003), *Safe Food: Bacteria, Biotechnology, and Bioterrorism*, Berkeley: University of California Press.

Ogden, E. E. (2007), *The Vermont Cheese Book*, Woodstock, VT: Countryman Press.

Paxson, H. (2008), 'Post-Pasteurian Cultures: The Microbiopolitics of Raw- Milk Cheese in the United States', *Cultural Anthropology*, 23(1): 15–47.

Paxson, H. (2013), *The Life of Cheese: Crafting Food and Value in America*, Berkeley: University of California Press.

Pollan, M. (2008), *In Defense of Food: An Eater's Manifesto*, New York: Penguin Books.

Sage, C. (2007), '"Bending Science to Match Their Convictions": Hygienist Conceptions of Food Safety as a Challenge to Alternative Food Enterprises in Ireland', in D. Maye,

L. Holloway and M. Kneafsey (eds), *Alternative Food Geographies: Representation and Practice*, 205–23, London: Elsevier.

Sanabria, E. (2015), 'Sensorial Pedagogies, Hungry Fat Cells and the Limits of Nutritional Health Education', *BioSocieties*, 10: 125–42.

Schwartz, H. (1986), *Never Satisfied: A Cultural History of Diets, Fantasies and Fat*, New York: The Free Press.

Scrinis, G. (2008), 'On the Ideology of Nutritionism', *Gastronomica*, 8(1): 39–48.

Scrinis, G. (2013), *Nutritionism: The Science and Politics of Dietary Advice*, New York, NY: Columbia University Press.

Solomon, H. (2015), 'Unreliable Eating: Patterns of Food Adulteration in Urban India', *BioSocieties*, 20(2): 177–93.

Star, S. L. (1991), 'Power, Technology and the Phenomenology of Conventions: On Being Allergic to Onions', in J. Law (ed.), *Sociology of Monsters: Essays on Power, Technology and Domination*, 26–56, London: Routledge.

Teil, G. (2012), 'No Such Thing as Terroir?: Objectivities and the Regimes of Existence of Objects', *Science, Technology & Human Values*, 37(5): 478–505.

Tracy, M. (2013), 'Pasteurizing China's Grasslands and Producing Terroir', *American Anthropologist*, 115(3): 437–51.

Veit, H. Z. (2013), *Modern Food, Moral Food: Self-Control, Science, and the Rise of Modern American Eating in the Early Twentieth Century*, Chapel Hill: University of North Carolina Press.

Vogel, E. and Mol, A. (2014), 'Enjoy Your Food: On Losing Weight and Taking Pleasure', *Sociology of Health & Illness*, 36(2): 305–17.

Weiss, B. (2011), 'Making Pigs Local: Discerning the Sensory Character of Place', *Cultural Anthropology*, 26(3): 438–61.

West, H. (2013), 'Thinking Like a Cheese: Towards an Ecological Understanding of the Reproduction of Knowledge in Contemporary Artisan Cheesemaking', in R. Ellen, S. J. Lycett, and S. E. Johns (eds), *Understanding Cultural Transmission in Anthropology: A Critical Synthesis*, 320–45, Oxford: Berghahn Books.

West, H. and Domingos, N. (2012), 'Gourmandizing Poverty Food: The Serpa Cheese Slow Food Presidium', *Journal of Agrarian Change*, 12(1): 120–43.

Wylie, A. (2011), *Re-Imagining Milk: Cultural and Biological Perspectives*, New York: Routledge.

Yates-Doerr, E. (2011), 'Bodily Betrayal: Love and Anger in the Time of Epigenetics', in F. E. Mascia-Lees (ed.), *A Companion to the Anthropology of the Body and Embodiment*, 292–306, Oxford: Wiley-Blackwell.

Yates-Doerr, E. (2012), 'The Weight of the Self: Care and Compassion in Guatemalan Dietary Choices', *Medical Anthropology Quarterly*, 26(1): 136–58.

Yates-Doerr, E. and Mol, A. (2012), 'Cuts of Meat: Disentangling Western Nature-Cultures', *Cambridge Anthropology*, 30(20): 48–64.

Yates-Doerr, E. and Carney, M. A. (2015), 'Demedicalizing Health: The Kitchen as a Site of Care', *Medical Anthropology*, published online 25 March 2015: 1–19.

CHAPTER THIRTEEN

Food Provisioning and Foodways in Postsocialist Societies: Food as Medium for Social Trust and Global Belonging

YUSON JUNG

AGONY AND DESIRE: FOOD PROVISIONING IN SOCIALIST AND POSTSOCIALIST EUROPE

Food provisioning and eating practices were central to the socialist projects in Eastern Europe and the former Soviet Union. They were one of the immediate and primary lenses through which the successes and failures of socialist policies were evaluated. They were also the basis for connecting citizens directly to the state. As Patterson (2009: 197) notes:

> Socialism had shifted ultimate responsibility for provisioning to the state, and the ongoing (and not always successful) effort to keep food and other necessities on the shelves was a government activity that connected most directly and most frequently with the lived experience of ordinary citizens.

Citizens in these socialist states grew increasingly dependent on the state for daily sustenance (Dunn 2008). Naturally, the socialist regimes were preoccupied with food science and food technologies and also introduced communal kitchens and public canteens that would allow socialist societies to achieve their ideals of progress and modernity (Glants and Toomre 1997; Caldwell 2009a; Shectman 2009).

One of the common memories that citizen-consumers in the postsocialist states of Eastern Europe recall are food provisioning practices that were triggered by a chronic shortage economy. As many scholars and witnesses of socialist Eastern Europe have reported, queuing and hoarding practices were a common feature of everyday life that were remembered by citizens as draining and time consuming, although the same people also recalled the sociality and communality that was formed while commiserating during the endless queuing (e.g. Caldwell 2009a; Bren and Neuburger 2012; Drakulic 1991; Dunn 2004, 2009; Fischer 2010; Patterson 2009; Ries 2009; Smith 2009; Verdery 1996).

Although agonizing, the shortage of food items was not necessarily an indication of famine conditions, as is often assumed and implied when evoking the imageries of the long queues for staples, such as bread and dairy, and empty shelves in the stores from the socialist era. On the contrary, because food was so central to the socialist projects, basic food items were also heavily subsidized and cheap, and ordinary citizens in Eastern Europe generally did not feel that they would be out of food to the point of starvation; (this, however, varies from country to country, and also in terms of time period – see Phillips 2002; Ries 2009; Dunn 2008; Massino 2012). My friends and colleagues in urban Bulgaria, for example, often pointed out to me that the fear of starvation only hit them during the economic crises in the 1990s after the fall of the socialist regime because of the plummeting of living standards and high inflation rates.

What the experience of the shortage economy during socialism did bring about, however, was the sense of *deprivation* of diverse and constant flow of goods, as well as the continued questioning of the *quality* of consumer items. Especially in the context of the Cold War, two political camps (capitalist West and communist East) competed against each other in realizing the promises of progress and modernity, thereby making consumption a highly politicized domain. Questions regarding deprivation and quality provoked consumer desire with which the socialist states had to deal in order to maintain the regime and establish political legitimacy and social stability. Although consumer desires did not directly translate into production under the Soviet system, many socialist states in Eastern Europe introduced 'everyday luxuries', such as ice cream and chocolate bars, to mitigate consumer desire and to assure some aspects of the regime's success of modernist foodways to all its citizens (Patico 2002; Smith 2009; see also Gronow 2003 on 'common luxury' in the Soviet Union). As Smith (2009: 142–3) describes of the Soviet Union, the same regime that forced its citizens to stand in line for staples, such as bread, milk, eggs and sugar, also made ice cream – once available only to the aristocracy – available to all citizens and it had become a ubiquitous and affordable product in major cities across the Soviet Union as early as the 1950s.

In Bulgaria, bananas and oranges were 'released' by the state[1] for special holidays such as the New Year. Although considered a rare luxury, any ordinary citizen could afford these tropical fruits as long as the supply did not run out. Similarly, the introduction of Western soft drinks such as Coca-Cola, as early as in the 1960s in Bulgaria,[2] and McDonalds in Yugoslavia and Hungary in the late 1980s (Caldwell 2004; Czegledy 2002) served as a way for the socialist states to respond to growing consumer desire and to allow citizens to experience a 'taste of freedom' (or 'small tastes of luxury') in the midst of highly ideologically charged, politically oppressive and economically challenging regimes. Food provisioning under socialism clearly reflected the paternalistic relationship between the state and society (Manning 2007; Verdery 1996).

Postsocialist food provisioning practices and foodways must be understood against this backdrop. Given the centrality of food in the socialist policies and governance, it is not surprising that the end of the Cold War in Eastern Europe highlighted food and eating practices as symbols for political and ethical discussions among the citizens in Eastern Europe (see also Jung, Klein, and Caldwell 2014). An impressive amount of literature and scholarship on postsocialist food practices has been produced over the past two decades by anthropologists, and they have greatly contributed in the scholarly debates on rapid social transformations in the era of globalization.

In this chapter, I focus primarily on studies that address food provisioning practices and foodways since the collapse of the socialist regimes in Eastern Europe and Soviet Union. While the focus is on Europe, the discussion here also has some significance for postsocialist and reform socialist states beyond Europe as they share many organizing principles regarding the systems of food provisioning. There are many themes and issues that have preoccupied postsocialist citizens regarding food. These include agricultural reform, subsistence economy, industrialized food systems, food safety, consumer identity, standardization, globalization, Europeanization, cultural heritage, memory and nostalgia, gender and class relations, migration and family relations, regulation and global capitalism, alternative food movements and the political economy of food and taste. In reviewing these studies, I will use my own research on food and culture in postsocialist Bulgaria since 1999 as a guide to provide a retrospective view on this evolving field of the anthropology of food in Eastern Europe. Furthermore, in the concluding section, I will offer some prospective overview on what I see as interesting points moving forward in the food practices of postsocialist societies in Eastern Europe and the former Soviet Union, and how they can widen our understanding of food practices more generally in the globalized twenty-first century.

EVERYDAY FOOD PRACTICES AFTER SOCIALISM: QUALITY, RISK AND CONSUMER COMPETENCE

My first trip to postsocialist Eastern Europe was in 1993 when I visited Budapest, Hungary. Arriving from Vienna, I remember how consumer items in Budapest looked more flimsy and were of cheaper (poor) quality than those in Vienna. The quality of these consumer goods stood in sharp contrast to the gorgeous and high-quality looking architectural legacy of the Habsburg Empire. Even the communist style concrete buildings looked sturdy and high quality, contrary to stereotypical descriptions of 'low quality' of things made during state socialism. Years later, when I visited Bulgaria for the first time in 1998, I was reminded of the consumer goods in Budapest in the early years of transition in Eastern Europe and how one had to be careful to not purchase substandard, potentially hazardous products, especially food.

One of the striking things I have noticed in Bulgaria since then was how my Bulgarian hosts and friends examined meticulously every consumer item, especially food items, that they bought – regardless of whether the items were sold in a self-service, 'Western-style' supermarket, in a more 'socialist-style' over-the-counter-service neighbourhood (corner) store or in an outdoor produce market. This marked a stark contrast to the grocery shopping behaviour in the United States where it seemed more like an automatic process (i.e. quickly grab a familiar food item and proceed to look for the next item). The locals explained such meticulous shopping practices in terms of avoiding *mente* products. As I have discussed elsewhere (Jung 2007, 2009, 2014a), *mente* refers to fake/fraudulent/adulterated goods that gradually permeated the postsocialist marketplace. Bulgarian consumers in the postsocialist period were obsessed with not buying *mente* goods to the point that a specialized magazine with the same title was published and became a popular reference to help consumers distinguish original (or real) goods from fake goods. Anything from cheese, milk, yogurt to soft drinks and alcohol could be *mente*.

To date, everyday food provisioning in postsocialist Bulgaria is often tangled with the discourse and experiences of *mente* food. These experiences became a critical foundation through which postsocialist citizen-consumers reorganized their food provisioning practices that required savvy shopping tactics involving price and quality. Whereas the socialist experience of coping with limited resources grounded their shopping practices, postsocialist citizens also had to learn how to bring 'price' into the equation because during socialism food prices were generally meaningless. In the planned economy, even with chronic shortage, prices stayed the same – one simply had to queue, hoard or barter, if necessary, to keep the household pantry stocked.

Navigating between the abundance of goods in the new consumerist society and poverty, many citizens in postsocialist Bulgaria complained that they felt deceived, confused and deprived. The initial excitement of seeing the stores filled with colourful consumer goods (especially compared to the homogeneous 'grey-colored' socialist products) gradually gave in to increasing consumer frustration in terms of affordability and reliability. These frustrations were pronounced even more acutely when procuring food, and I could often hear an infuriated cry by Bulgarian citizens, '*Moshenitizi!*' (Crooks!), indicating a deep sense of deception and disapproval of the newly developing market system.

The experiences with deception also coupled with a sense of deprivation both in the relative and literal sense. In the 1980s, many socialist citizens felt they were deprived of material abundance and good quality consumer goods compared to Western societies. Many ordinary postsocialist citizens continued to experience this sense of deprivation after 1989, as living standards plummeted and cost of living increased dramatically with the collapse of the socialist regime. Many of them, especially pensioners, simply struggled to survive in the postsocialist world (Jung 2014a; Mincyte 2009; Fischer 2010). Ordinary citizens often felt they could only afford the cheapest foods which were often of the poorest quality. In fact, my Bulgarian informants would refer to the poor quality foods they could afford under the new capitalist system as 'garbage' (*bukluk*) and sentimentally recalled the communist staples which, by comparison, seemed of better (decent) quality *and* affordable. What this meant for postsocialist citizens was that the poor quality stuff they could afford only reinforced the sense that one lost a dignified way of living by having to look at 'only the cheapest stuff', as my informants would lament. Few of them imagined that the collapse of state socialism would also bring about difficulty in affording decent quality food and products.

Quality, thus, has been an important index for postsocialist citizen-consumers in understanding and evaluating the ongoing social transformations. The planned economy system is often characterized as 'the economy of quantity' (Walker and Manning 2013), referring to the relative emphasis that the socialist planners put on quantity versus quality, the latter presumed to be more of a concern in the market-oriented capitalist system. To the surprise of many postsocialist citizen-consumers, however, they quickly learned that capitalism did not automatically guarantee higher quality. While the socialist planners did indeed focus on increasing output, quality was actually also a principal concern for the socialist policymakers because satisfying people's material needs was the very basis of the socialist legitimacy (Guentcheva 2012: 141). In fact, some consumer products from the socialist era in Bulgaria, such as furniture, clothing or kitchen appliances, were often pointed out by my informants as having lasting quality even though the design (the look) might not have been the most fashionable.

These perspectives applied also to food items. As Dunn (2008: 247) reports on Georgian canned foods that were produced industrially according to the Soviet system, Georgians fundamentally trusted the quality and safety of these industrially produced foods. They vaguely knew that the strong socialist state (Soviet Union) had standards for production and that those standards adhered to a certain level of quality (in other words, they were not 'garbage'). Although the same people also suspected that standards might not have been honoured all the time (see also Jung 2009), Dunn's (2004) observations in a formerly state-run food plant in Poland suggest that 'workers took the issue of food safety seriously and very often deployed craft knowledge to meet standards, not to evade them' (Dunn 2008: 247). This indicates that under the socialist regime citizen-consumers at least shared an assumption regarding basic food quality that is not hazardous. Discussing the sudden rise of botulism caused by home canning practices in post-Soviet Georgia, Dunn (2008: 249) explains a common agony (and irony) of the postsocialist context very aptly by using the words of her Georgian informant: 'For some people, commercially canned food is too cheap to be safe. For most people, others, it's too expensive to be affordable.'

It is not surprising to learn, therefore, how the postsocialist disappointment regarding quality also broke down a basic level of social trust that existed between citizens and the society at large, not to mention vis-à-vis the state (see also Yan 2012). One reaction to the weakening of social trust in the context of food provisioning was the rise of *food nationalism* as witnessed in Russia, for example. Caldwell (2002, 2004, 2006) points out how the influx of poor quality foreign products led Russian consumers to privilege the domestic (*nash*) products over imported ones (which at first were clearly popular with their novelty effect) in the post-Soviet period. She explains how quality was often cited as the primary factor for Russian consumers' preference for *nash* products (similarly, see also Patico 2002, 2008). Furthermore, the search for 'natural foods' and the strong attachment to *dacha* (Russian summer cottage), where Russians reconnected to nature and also grew their own food (Caldwell 2011), could also be understood as a Russian response to their search for quality and rebuilding social trust so that they could better cope with rapidly changing social realities.

Another response to the weakening of social trust in the newly evolving neoliberal capitalist environment was *nostalgia*. Many postsocialist citizens desperately
searched for both reliable and affordable higher quality foods and often found them
in food items that were presumed to be produced the same way as in the Soviet era.
Klumbytė's (2009; 2010) work on 'Soviet' sausages in Lithuania is a telling example,
explaining how quality and nostalgia intersect in the food provisioning practices of
the postsocialist era. Her study also shows how nostalgia for certain foods intimately relates to cultivating new political subjectivities where the longing for the past
does not have to be mutually exclusive with creating new postsocialist modernities.
In other words, the nostalgia for the socialist past does not necessarily mean citizens want to return to socialism, but rather it shows how they continue to explore
ways to enhance their consumer competence under the new market economy while
demanding a new social order that does not merely discount the past but bridges it
to the present and future.

The changing attitudes towards industrially produced canned food in postsocialist
Bulgaria, for instance, reflect this growing consumer competence (Jung 2009). During
my fieldwork in Bulgaria, I noticed among urbanites the gradual disappearance of
the traditional practice of canning to preserve fruits and vegetables. At first, this
tendency could be understood as a consequence of globalization and Westernization
in the postsocialist era, because in Bulgaria, industrially produced standardized
canned food was viewed with scepticism during the socialist period and was not
considered high quality.[3] This negative perception of factory-produced canned food,
however, started to change and more people began to buy standardized, industrially
produced canned food from the store. The local explanation for these changing
attitudes was that with more experience in the new capitalist system, people
were able to re-evaluate the meaning of standardization and eventually started to
embrace the normalization of standardized food. They repeatedly emphasized that
these changes were not simply because they trusted one system (capitalist) over the
other (communist) in producing canned food. This example shows the consumers'
rationalizing tendencies based on their own growing competence as consumers and
suggests how changing food practices can not only be explained in terms of external
influences but also need to be understood in terms of the cultural and historical
experiences of the local context.

Lastly, coping with the changes and making do as citizen-consumers in the
postsocialist world, many citizens also relied on the informal sector to procure
daily food. This may be surprising to some who associate the grey economy
with the black market under socialism, which presumably disappeared under
the new market economy. Raw milk in postsocialist Lithuania is a good example
that explains the circumstances and meanings of the informal sector within the
context of post-Soviet transformation. In Lithuania, which joined the European
Union in 2004, Mincyte (2009, 2014) noticed how the informal dairy markets
were popular in various Lithuanian towns. In spite of the potential risks that were
present regarding health and legality, the unofficial and unregulated raw milk (and
dairy products such as farmers' cheese, milk curd and sour cream) became part
of the staple diet among post-Soviet Lithuanians. Furthermore, even though the

Lithuanian public health agency was fighting fiercely to eliminate this informal sector (Lithuania's accession to the European Union demanded that uncertified food could not be tolerated in the common European market), the informal network of raw milk production, distribution and consumption only continued to thrive and gained further social, economic and political significance for those citizens who participated in this informal sector.

Another interesting aspect that Mincyte's study discovered was how gender was deeply implicated in these provisioning activities. She found that most producers, distributors and consumers in this raw milk economy were women. Often these women socialized in the dairy delivery points in various apartment complexes in urban Lithuania, strengthening their social ties and claiming safe public places for themselves within the deteriorating urban districts. Through these illegal raw milk activities, women also engaged in a kind of self-making project: this was their way of not only sustaining themselves but also making sure that they had a self-sufficient autonomy that allowed them to deal with the challenges posed by deepening social inequalities, globalization and a new regulatory regime imposed by the European Union.

These studies of food provisioning in Eastern Europe and the former Soviet Union provide illuminating insights into the complexities of procuring daily foods. Constrained by financial means and conflicted by the old and new value systems that came with rapid social transformation, postsocialist experiences show the importance of paying attention to the nuances in everyday practices that allow deeper understanding of lived experiences. Most importantly, these lived experiences are not merely structured by clear-cut dichotomies of either inherently socialist or capitalist values, even though they may be articulated by postsocialist citizens in those terms.

GLOBALIZING FOODWAYS IN POSTSOCIALIST EUROPE: IDENTITY POLITICS, VALUES AND MORALITY

The arrival of McDonalds behind the Iron Curtain has often been treated as a symbol of the end of the Cold War and the beginning of a new global era. The spread of the Golden Arches worldwide has been viewed as a sign of globalization that implied a sense of homogenization or Westernization. Against the popular perception of a homogenous world driven by corporate America in the era of globalization, anthropologists have argued how these so-called global symbols are experienced differently depending on the various local contexts (Watson 2006; Lozada 2000; Watson and Caldwell 2005).

New foods such as American fast-food joints or different 'ethnic restaurants' started to populate throughout the former Eastern Bloc following the collapse of the socialist regime thereby contributing to new foodways in this region. And these changes were undoubtedly a consequence of globalization led by neoliberal capitalism. The ways in which these new foods were introduced and experienced, however, varied from place to place (e.g. Blagoeva-Krasteva 2001; Caldwell 2004, 2006; Czegledy 2002; Velinova 2015), and the diverse meanings that postsocialist citizen-consumers attached to them have greatly contributed to challenging Western-centric assumptions about globalization and its impact on different cultures and societies.

When McDonalds arrived in Moscow in 1990, after fourteen years of negotiations with the Soviet authorities, the company quickly marketed its ordinariness and not its novelty or foreignness (Caldwell 2004). This resonated well with the local sentiments of *nash* (our own) that highlighted familiarity and intimacy, and McDonalds came to be domesticated in post-Soviet Russia. McDonalds' emblematic French fries (thin, long, crispy and soft), for example, replaced the more rustic local version of fried potato and came to be understood as 'our own'. Caldwell (2004) argues that for post-Soviet Russians, McDonalds was not about the interaction between the global versus the local, or the new versus the old. Rather, Russian consumers blurred the boundaries between the global and the local through domestication that involved Russian's flexible ideologies of trust, comfort and intimacy (Caldwell 2004: 181). The cultural logic behind this was that Russians tend to privilege the values they attach to things rather than the origins of things (2004: 184).

Consumption, and especially the consumption of commodities, was a significant domain through which ordinary people responded to dramatic and rapid social changes in Eastern Europe (Patico and Caldwell 2002; Bren and Neuburger 2012). This can be witnessed through the identity politics and identity formation expressed and fashioned through new foodways. The popularity of Chinese food in postsocialist Bulgaria in this regard offers an interesting example in understanding the relationship of food, identity politics and globalization.

Similar to how 'ordinariness' struck a chord with Russian consumers regarding McDonalds, I found that in Bulgaria the consumption of Chinese food was not so much about an exotic experience of 'the other' (Chinese/Asian) as much as a 'Western' experience indexing 'normal life'. Such understandings of Chinese food were partly grounded in Bulgarians' socialist experience of watching American films where ordinary people seemed to take out Chinese food as part of a normal lifestyle. The stories that were told by compatriots who were able to visit the Western world during socialism also contributed to such imagined associations. When Chinese food was introduced in Bulgaria in the early 1990s, therefore, Bulgarians were not simply attracted to its novelty but also to the fact that Chinese food indexed a 'normal life' and global belonging they felt deprived of during socialism. At the same time, as the novelty factor faded out and Bulgarian consumers experienced the decline of Chinese restaurants in terms of numbers and quality in Bulgaria, Chinese food also became an index of positioning Bulgaria in the larger geopolitical order. In other words, the ability to evaluate the authenticity of Chinese food was not only considered as individual cultural capital but also as indicative of the political economic position of the nation-state in the global era (Jung 2012).

Nowadays in Eastern Europe and the former Soviet Union, where once ordinary people did not have access to different kinds of cuisines, citizen-consumers can have access to global foods, such as pizza, tacos, falafel, kung pao chicken and sushi. In addition to Kentucky Fried Chicken – one of the first Western fast food restaurants to arrive in the postsocialist world – and McDonalds, global chains such as Starbucks and Subway as well as large, self-service supermarkets and food malls have become ordinary food places which are now used both for food practices and everyday social interactions. For instance, in Russia, Caldwell saw often how people used McDonalds as a social hangout rather than an eatery (Caldwell 2009b; for comparative insights see also Watson 2006; Yan 2000). In countries such as Hungary, consumers also expressed their aspirations for participating in a new Western modernity by renovating their traditional kitchens after American-style designs, although this had unintended consequences such as the loss of sociability associated with traditional Hungarian kitchens (Fehérváry 2002). Similar to the meanings of Chinese food and other foreign cuisines (notably Japanese) in Bulgaria (Velinova 2015), Hungarians' changing kitchen designs are examples of how new foodways reflected and confirmed postsocialist consumers' participation in the global world.

At the same time, new foodways also raised the questions of moral inflections in consumption practices more broadly (Caldwell 2009b: 103–4), and these concerns were expressed not just through food products but also extended to spaces of consumption such as cafés, grocery stores and restaurants. For example, Caldwell (2009b) explains Russians' concerns with the morality of postsocialist consumption, namely how Russian consumers express complicated anxieties about safety, danger, intimacy, privacy, trust and so on. Thus, certain new spaces and practices were deemed more problematic than others even as they were also perceived as novel and exciting: for Caldwell's Russian friend, a public bench in a park was more comfortable than a new café, because for her these new coffee places could be hazardous by blurring the boundaries between private and public in problematic ways. In other words, new consumption spaces such as coffeehouses were perceived by some Russians as confusing the anonymity of a public space with the intimacy of a private space, a confusion which, they came to realize, came with benefits but also with significant risks. This raises questions about new values.

Lastly, as food practices continue to straddle between the domains of 'getting by' and 'global belonging', questions of ethics in production, distribution and consumption practices have preoccupied postsocialist citizens. These concerns are similar to the growing criticism about the unethical industrialized food system in advanced capitalist societies which lead to alternative food movements. Postsocialist citizens' experiences with both state socialism and neoliberal capitalist expansion, however, have not only been challenging the global food system but also the Western-centric views regarding the meaning of 'ethical foods' and 'alternative' food systems (Jung, Klein and Caldwell 2014).

In the Western world, 'ethical foods' are often understood in terms of organics, local food, Fair Trade, Slow Food or vegetarianism that counter the shortcomings of the globalized and industrialized food system and attempt to address issues of social inequalities and environmental degradation. Yet rarely do the discussions on ethical foods in the advanced capitalist societies engage poverty-driven economies or grey economic zones, even though, as Mincyte (2014: 41) reminds us, 'The language surrounding the people and commodities involved in them is often cast in moral terms.' While the growing popularity for organics, local foods, farmer's markets or organized movements such as Slow Food or Fair Trade in Eastern Europe may easily be treated as global trends, the underlying meanings and implications of such food practices inevitably vary (e.g. Blumberg 2014; Jung 2014a, b; Aistara 2015). Moreover, even within postsocialist Europe, the responses to ethical foods and alternative food movements are not identical. Depending on the local contexts, farmer's markets, for example, can have different implications as alternative food networks: the nature of reconnection between producers and consumers can vary and depend upon the dynamic relation with other markets and retail spaces (Blumberg 2014). Postsocialist food practices, then, offer a much-needed critique to the universalizing language of ethics that allows us to move beyond claims for an inherent moral purity devoid of considerations for specific local and historical experiences as well as geopolitical systems of power.

REGULATION, THE STATE AND GOVERNANCE

Sidney Mintz has long argued that food offers a productive lens for understanding how power really operates (Mintz 1985). For uncovering thoughts on how people make sense of abstract ideas in rapidly changing social realities, there cannot be a more tangible context than daily food practices (Dunn 2009). While for some people the experiences of radical state socialism may not appear relevant to understanding contemporary affairs regarding power, social justice and governance, those experiences, in fact, offer a wealth of productive insights that may challenge the way we think about our contemporary food system and practices.

In discussing alternative food movements in the postsocialist context, my colleagues and I have argued that one important factor that makes food central to ethical considerations is its historically long-standing significance in relationships between people and states (Jung, Klein and Caldwell 2014: 9). Although the neoliberalizing global context makes it easy for us to forget to pay close attention to the role of the state, especially as regulatory regimes under neoliberal capitalism undermine the state power in favour of corporate power, the postsocialist experiences encourage us to re-evaluate our assumptions about the role of the state in the contemporary world. This is so because the experience with the strong presence of the state in people's everyday life under socialism provided a poignant contrast in its aftermath, as state services seemed suddenly withdrawn, hence the popular perception that the state appears absent in postsocialism. Because food was a primary means through which socialist states regulated the citizenry, the withdrawal of the state after the regime's collapse caused a series of governance problems, even as the socialist state's control was always only partial (i.e. the planned economy did not go as planned) (Dunn 2009: 212). As Dunn (2008: 246) notes, 'The non-delivery of state services and the limits of global standards are ... ethnographically telling in that falling outside of state regulation of social spaces can be as harmful as falling under it.'

As I have discussed earlier, for postsocialist citizens the confusion over regulatory regimes was a highly anxious and frustrating experience that they instantly related to their relationships to the socialist regime, where food and state power were intimately intertwined through regulations such as food standards. Thus, common questions were raised by postsocialist citizens such as why it was that organic certifications are issued by private agencies but not the state, who was accountable for public health if it is threatened by poor quality food, lack of regulations or lack of power in the highly competitive and hierarchically organized global market, and if it was possible to compete under the rampant global capitalist system without a stronger state to support and mediate the powers of multinational corporations.

From the perspective of contemporary corporate America, it may be difficult to understand why many postsocialist citizens express longing for a stronger state if they have suffered through an oppressive regime in which the state dictated even the everyday needs of the people. Gille's case study (2009) on the Hungarian toxic paprika scandal offers an illuminating insight regarding how postsocialist Hungarians responded to new forms of power and regulation in the postsocialist period involving a supranational entity, namely the European Union. In 2004, shortly after Hungary's accession to the European Union, Hungarians learned that their national pride, paprika powder, was banned for sale because of aflatoxin B1, a carcinogenic microtoxin produced by mould (Gille 2009: 58–59). The Hungarian government found out that some of the popular paprika products contained the toxin above the permitted level of the European Union's food safety standards. They eventually traced the toxin back to the imported peppers (from Brazil and Spain) that were part of the blend for the Hungarian paprika powder.

This incident was not merely a national shock. It confused the Hungarian public, especially because they had experienced similar scandals in the 1990s when the government had found contaminated paprika (lead-containing paint, or powdered brick), sold mostly at farmers' markets. Because of the European Union requirements for candidate countries, the Hungarian government had to adopt EU safety and quality standards (HACCP) that were supposed to identify and monitor health risks. For Hungarian paprika producers, this entailed increased costs due to European Union-mandated product testing, which put them at a relative disadvantage vis-à-vis their foreign competitors in the global market. More importantly, however, and contrary to people's perception that the EU standards would protect both consumers and producers from risks, Hungarians learned that the new regimes of power did not protect Hungary's national interest. They had not realized that, contrary to their old safety systems which relied on phytosanitary testings to control toxins in paprika, the product safety in the common market relied on, as Dunn (2009: 215) puts it, 'a combination of EU regulations and changes in tariffs and trade barriers – which, paradoxically, makes the product less safe'. Gille suggests that the EU safety standards turned out to be rather meaningless for the relatively powerless Hungarians (compared to their Western counterparts), and the shift of regulatory authority from the state to a supranational and subnational entities (NGOs, private firms etc.) resulted in weaker rules and less safe food.

While this case demonstrates a rather typical instance of neoliberal governance, from the perspectives of postsocialist citizens, it confirmed the need for a stronger state that could defend them and also be held accountable if it failed to fulfil its obligations to them. As Mincyte (2009: 95) also reminds us with the informal raw milk sector, marginalized Lithuanian women believed that the risks from the changes in the systems of power did not lie in food but in the new economy. In these women's minds, the postsocialist state was not able to exercise sovereignty and they had to be 'their own government' to survive in the new system. Similarly, as Phillips (2002) demonstrates with post-Chernobyl Ukranians dealing with food safety, the state's failure to adequately care for its citizens in the postsocialist environment further reproduced social inequalities between those who had reliable scientific knowledge about 'radioprotectors' and those who did not. Moreover, the perceived ambiguous role of the postsocialist state left citizens with a deep sense of longing for entities and agents that they could hold accountable.

The new forms of governance in the European Union has posed a series of challenges for the new Eastern members not only from the standpoint of food safety but also in terms of the revitalization of their food industry which was once a major national economic resource for many socialist states in Eastern Europe. Regulated by the Common Agricultural Policy (CAP) of the European Union, many wine producers in Eastern Europe, for example, were compelled to either convert their old vineyards to other agricultural farmlands or to peg themselves into the lower category in the hierarchy for quality products designated as 'products of geographical origin' of the European Union (Jung 2011, 2013). The growing interest to protect cultural heritage in the European Union in the face of a fiercely competitive global market led certain national/regional food products to be protected, using names of the region or country where the products originated (e.g. Champagne, Feta) to give competitive advantage to producers of these food products (see also West in this volume). In the case of Bulgaria, these new regimes of power and governance resulted in a continued uphill battle for the wine producers to reclaim and revitalize a once thriving export industry strongly supported by the socialist regime. The absence of the state in the postsocialist period, therefore, is not only felt among anxious consumers, but it has equally affected producers and those engaged in international trade.

Looking through the lenses of these food practices in Eastern Europe and the former Soviet Union, the postsocialist changes in the era of neoliberalizing globalization invite new discussions about the nature of the state, its role vis-à-vis the market and its citizens, and how power really operates today.

FOOD AS MEDIUM FOR RESTORING SOCIAL TRUST IN A GLOBAL WORLD

Food provisioning and foodways are not simply a necessity or taken-for-granted practices for human survival. Rather, food practices are inherently political, moral and ethical and offer critical social commentaries. For postsocialist Bulgarians, the *mente* (fake) phenomenon is intimately related to profit-driven capitalist practices that go hand in hand with an irresponsible (or unaccountable) state adhering to the principles of neoliberal governance. While new diverse foodways introduced to the postsocialist world triggered excitement and a positive sense of rightful belonging in the rapidly changing world, they have also posed questions regarding one's identity, personhood and systems of value, and affirmed an implicit hierarchy based on the geopolitical order. All these factors affected the ways in which postsocialist citizens attached meanings to these food practices.

So where will these postsocialist insights take us? What contribution do they make to contemporary debates concerning food? What do the postsocialist experiences say about the future of the study of food more generally?

As I have discussed thus far, one of the most important lessons from the postsocialist experiences with food concerns the importance of social trust in the production, distribution and consumption of food. In light of increasing discontent about the globalized and industrialized food system, which raises serious questions about safety, inequality and social justice, postsocialist citizens' search (and demand) for affordable, reliable, quality food should not be merely understood as a consequence of a developmental phase. Even in advanced capitalist societies, the growing socio-economic gaps between social groups affect access to safer and healthier foods. The causes of sick bodies in the contemporary world are not simply grounded in the lack of food.

As we frequently hear in debates about the so-called obesity epidemic, one of the modern paradoxes is that malnourishment exists in the midst of plenty – fat bodies are hungry and sick. Hunger and abundance of food coexist. Often this situation is explained in terms of a 'broken food system' that produces plenty of food but of unequal nutritional value. From the perspective of postsocialist citizens, this paradox threatens fundamental social trust, one that cannot be overcome, restored or demanded only from the position of each individual citizen. For example, contemporary healthful-eating gospels that emphasize individual responsibility for the care of one's body and health have their limitations in fixing the broken system. Postsocialist citizens would ask: Who can I hold accountable for the additives, chemicals and other artificial or hazardous stuff in the food I purchased? How do I trust that what I buy is safe for my body and health? To them, individual responsibility at the point of purchase is not a complete answer because they do not believe structural problems can be fixed only through individual consumption practices. From this postsocialist perspective, it appears deeply problematic that many proponents of ethical foods in advanced capitalist societies privilege individual consumption as the productive point for alternative food practices to overcome structural problems.

At the same time, postsocialist citizens also remind us that the strong paternalistic socialist states, too, did not succeed in producing healthy bodies and happy citizens. Yet the changing regimes of power in the postsocialist environment also taught Eastern Europeans that, as partial as the socialist system was, the state forged an intimate relationship to its citizens through basic food provisioning that prevented ordinary people from worrying about fundamental levels of food safety and health. This afforded a level of social trust vis-à-vis the regime of power, which in the case of state socialism was the state. In the present, the hegemonic regimes of power follow the rules of neoliberal governance. Forging and restoring social trust will largely depend on how corporations, states and non-governmental institutions can prove their competence in regulating the broken system and addressing structural problems to produce healthy bodies and content citizens. The invitation from the postsocialist experiences to rethink the nature of the state and its role in this context cannot be timelier.

In this regard, I would also suggest that dealing with the issue of transparency will be highly significant in using food as a medium to restore social trust. A noteworthy development at one of the leading grocery retailers in the United States known for its high-quality and organic products, Whole Foods Market, is its list of 'Unacceptable Ingredients for Food' posted on their website.[4] Among these unacceptable ingredients for food are high fructose corn syrup, MSG (monosodium glutamate), artificial colours and flavours, all of which my Bulgarian friends and colleagues would deem as suspicious food additives.[5] These kinds of regulatory measures are not directly linked to state power, and in fact, are typical of neoliberal governance. One could also consider these measures as clever marketing tactics. Reading them from the perspectives of postsocialist experiences, however, these voluntary regulatory measures could also be considered as a potentially productive mechanism for holding relevant parties accountable, thereby aiding in the larger debate about the roles different regimes of powers need to be playing to fix the broken system. But this is not to suggest we privilege corporate power over other regimes of power. The key point here is that this could be a productive starting point of bringing accountability back to the discussions of food and politics.

It is entirely possible that the demand for more transparency and accountability for quality and safety will translate into social distinction and hierarchy, which will reproduce social inequalities among social groups – those who can afford the higher quality and safer food and those who cannot. In this globalized era in which information on food and health circulates instantly and widely through various social and conventional media circuits, this will also mean that authoritative knowledge of production and circulation is central in building and restoring social trust. Institutions, be they private industry, non-governmental organizations, nation-states or supranational organizations, will all have a vital role in the production and circulation of such knowledge.

Bringing my prospective view back to the cultural context I know well, namely postsocialist Bulgaria, I can see how my friends, colleagues and acquaintances may look with careful hope to the potential of increased transparency and accountability systems, if such systems become clear to them. Throughout my research in Bulgaria, I have heard numerous complaints regarding food labels, for example, in terms of the confusing and unintelligible language of the labels. My Bulgarian informants considered food labels as a typical case of granting consumers too much information, thereby making them *not* transparent and difficult to hold the producers accountable. Non-governmental consumer rights advocacy organizations in Bulgaria, for instance, have been trying to cultivate a consumer environment in which consumers would willingly seek authoritative knowledge based on independent product testing even if it means that consumers will have to pay a small fee for the information. But most of my informants hesitate to agree to the demand when it comes to paid information. In their minds, this kind of information based on reliable authoritative knowledge should be offered by the state for free. For now, this is still the fundamental and meaningful role of the state for postsocialist Bulgarians in fostering their social trust vis-à-vis different regimes of power in the postsocialist context.

Finally, when people engage with food – things that one puts into one's body – social trust becomes critically important in the era of globalization. As diverse foodways continue to be shared, exchanged, domesticated and reproduced, the study of food can benefit from paying closer attention to the universalizing language that prevails in the discourse and practices of alternative foods. The lessons from the postsocialist world suggest that while a sense of rightful global belonging is important in the ways that modern citizens relate to others and the larger world, a patronizing tendency discounting the lived experiences of diverse social groups will not be helpful in engaging disadvantaged and marginalized people. Pushing them out of the system, the postsocialist experiences teach us, will only create more risks.

In the context of postsocialist Europe, the perception of global belonging will continue to be important to how citizens relate to others and the larger world. While the experience of state socialism may be only lived through and passed down to people's selective memories as the generation born after the Cold War is already forming new families and bringing up their own children, these memories and indirect experiences of both state socialism and its immediate aftermath will not become obsolete or meaningless. Even with its diverse practices across different geographical contexts, *postsocialism* is a useful analytical category for understanding ambivalent attitudes regarding social changes as experienced through everyday food practices. The particular experiences of postsocialism, which compelled citizen-consumers to forge different relations to institutions (state, non-governmental and private), will continue to resonate as they explore new foodways. Further anthropological studies of food in these postsocialist societies can benefit from closer examinations of these relations in light of contemporary debates on 'alternatives' to the food system because such a focus will allow researchers to unpack and re-evaluate a Western-centric notion of 'alternatives', given the complex postsocialist experiences.

To be able to partake in the ever-evolving cultures of food and experiencing the world through food will be an important basis for citizens' everyday experiences, personhood and social relations. Food is an important medium that affirms one's belonging and position in the larger society and offers a sense of normality. As it always was, food will continue to be at the forefront of experiencing and fashioning new modernities in societies.

NOTES

1. My Bulgarian informants use the expression 'release' (*puskat*) to describe the provisioning experience during socialism. This indicates the non-capitalist relations (it was not perceived as market sales) between the state as the sole distributor and consumers, and highlights the role of the state in everyday provisioning practices.
2. In 1965, Bulgaria became the first country behind the 'Iron Curtain' to have a trade contract and bottling factories with the Coca-Cola Company (Nedeva et al. 2006).

The Bulgarian state also had a trade contract with Pepsi Co. in the 1980s, which involved the exchange of Pepsi concentrate for Bulgarian red wine (Bulgarian Central State Archive F-772, O-2, L-62: 1983).

3. It should be noted, however, that Bulgaria was one of the major exporters of canned food during the socialist time not only to other countries in the Soviet bloc but also to Western Europe (see Creed 1998 and Dunn 2008). There was an overwhelming public perception in Bulgaria that 'the good stuff' was always exported to Western countries and that the canned food for the domestic market was of poorer quality, although my Bulgarian informants also assured me that socialist canned foods, including those produced for the domestic market, would not be 'garbage'.

4. http://www.wholefoodsmarket.com/about-our-products/quality-standards/unacceptable-ingredients-food (accessed 10 July 2014).

5. This data was collected as part of an ongoing collaborative research project with Andrew Newman on food politics and urban governance in Detroit where we examine food access and meanings of 'good' food among urban residents, food justice activists and corporate actors.

REFERENCES

Aistara, G. (2015), 'Good, Clean, Fair … and Illegal: Paradoxes of Food Ethics in Postsocialist Latvia', *Journal of Baltic Studies*, 46(3): 283–98.

Bajic-Hajdukovic, I. (2013), 'Food, Family, and Memory: Belgrade Mothers and Their Migrant Children', *Food and Foodways*, 21(1): 46–65.

Belasco, W. and Horowitz, R. (eds) (2009), *Food Chains: From Farmyard to Shopping Cart*, Philadelphia: University of Pennsylvania Press.

Blumberg, R. (2014), 'Placing Alternative Food Networks: Farmers' Markets in Post-Soviet Vilnius, Lithuania', in Y. Jung, J. Klein and M. Caldwell (eds), *Ethical Eating in the Postsocialist and Socialist World*, 69–92, Berkeley: University of California Press.

Bren, P. and Neuburger, M. (eds) (2012), *Communism Unwrapped: Consumption in Cold War Eastern Europe*, Oxford: Oxford University Press.

Bulgarian Central State Archive F-772, O-2, L-62: 1983.

Caldwell, M. (2002), 'The Taste of Nationalism: Food Politics in Postsocialist Moscow', *Ethnos*, 67(3): 295–319.

Caldwell, M. (2004), 'Domesticating the French Fry: McDonald's and Consumerism in Moscow', *Journal of Consumer Culture*, 4(1): 5–26.

Caldwell, M. (2006), 'Tasting the Worlds of Yesterday and Today: Culinary Tourism and Nostalgia Foods in Post-Soviet Russia', in R. Wilk (ed.), *Fast Food/Slow Food: The Cultural Economy of the Global Food System*, 97–112, Lanham, MD: Alta Mira.

Caldwell, M. (ed.) (2009a), *Food and Everyday Life in the Post-Socialist World*, Bloomington: Indiana University Press.

Caldwell, M. (2009b), 'Tempest in a Coffee Pot: Brewing Incivility in Russia's Public Sphere', in M. Caldwell (ed.), *Food and Everyday Life in the Post-Socialist World*, 101–29, Bloomington: Indiana University Press.

Caldwell, M. (2011), *Dacha Idylls: Living Organically in Russia's Countryside*, Berkeley: University of California Press.

Caldwell, M. (2014), 'Gardening for the State: Cultivating Bionational Citizens in
    Postsocialist Russia', in Y. Jung, J. Klein and M. Caldwell (eds), *Ethical Eating in the
    Postsocialist and Socialist World*, 188–210, Berkeley: University of California Press.
Creed, G. (1998), *Domesticating Revolution: From Socialist Reform to Ambivalent
    Transition in a Bulgarian Village*, University Park: Pennsylvania State University Press.
Czegledy, A. (2002), 'Manufacturing the New Consumerism: Fast-Food Restaurants in
    Postsocialist Hungary', in R. Mandel and C. Humphrey (eds), *Markets and Moralities:
    Ethnographies of Postsocialism*, 143–68, Oxford: Berg.
Dunn, E. (2004), *Privatizing Poland: Baby Food, Big Business, and the Remaking of Labor*,
    Ithaca: Cornell University Press.
Dunn, E. (2005), 'Standards and Person-Making in East Central Europe', in A. Ong and
    S. Collier (eds), *Global Assemblages: Technology, Politics, and Ethics as Anthropological
    Problems*, 173–93, Malden, MA: Blackwell Publishing.
Dunn, E. (2008), 'Postsocialist Spores: Disease, Bodies, and the State in the Republic of
    Georgia', *American Ethnologist*, 35(2): 243–58.
Dunn, E. (2009), 'Afterword: Turnips and Mangos: Power and the Edible State in Eastern
    Europe', in M. Caldwell (ed.), *Food and Everyday Life in the Post-Socialist World*,
    206–22, Bloomington: Indiana University Press.
Fehérváry, K. (2002), 'American Kitchens, Luxury Bathrooms, and the Search for a
    "Normal" Life in Postsocialist Hungary', *Ethnos*, 67(3): 369–400.
Fischer, L. (2010), 'Turkey Backbones and Chicken Gizzards: Women's Food Roles in
    Post-Socialist Hungary', *Food and Foodways*, 18(4): 233–60.
Gille, Z. (2009), 'The Tale of the Toxic Paprika: The Hungarian Taste of Euro-
    Globalization', in M. Caldwell (ed.), *Food and Everyday Life in the Post-Socialist
    World*, 57–77, Bloomington: Indiana University Press.
Glants, M. and Toomre, J. (eds) (1997), *Food in Russian History and Culture*,
    Bloomington: Indiana University Press.
Guentcheva, R. (2012), 'Material Harmony: The Quest for Quality in Socialist Bulgaria,
    1960s-1980s', in P. Bren and M. Neubuerger (eds), *Communism Unwrapped:
    Consumption in Cold War Eastern Europe*, 140–68, Oxford: Oxford University Press.
Jung, Y. (2007), *Consumer Lament: An Ethnographic Study on Consumption, Needs, and
    Everyday Complaints in Postsocialist Bulgaria*, PhD dissertation, Harvard University,
    Cambridge, MA.
Jung, Y. (2009), 'From Canned Food to Canny Consumers: Cultural Competence in the
    Age of Mechanical Production', in M. Caldwell (ed.), *Food and Everyday Life in the
    Post-Socialist World*, 29–56, Bloomington: Indiana University Press.
Jung, Y. (2011), 'Parting the "Wine Lake": The Revival of the Bulgarian Wine Industry
    in the Age of CAP Reform', *Anthropological Journal of European Cultures*, 20(1):
    10–28.
Jung, Y. (2012), 'Experiencing the "West" through the "East" in the Margins of Europe:
    Chinese Food Consumption Practices in Postsocialist Bulgaria', *Food, Culture and
    Society*, 15(4): 579–98.
Jung, Y. (2013), 'Cultural Patrimony and the Bureaucratization of Wine: The Bulgarian
    Case', in R. Black and R. Ulin (eds), *Wine and Culture: Vineyard to Glass*, 161–78,
    London: Bloomsbury.

Jung, Y. (2014a), 'Ambivalent Consumers and the Limits of Certification: Organic Foods in Postsocialist Bulgaria', in Y. Jung, J. Klein and M. Caldwell (eds), *Ethical Eating in the Postsocialist and Socialist World*, 93–115, Berkeley: University of California Press.

Jung, Y. (2014b), 'Tasting and Judging the Unknown *Terroir* of the Bulgarian Wine: The Political Economy of Sensory Experience', *Food and Foodways*, 22(1–2): 24–47.

Jung, Y., Klein, J. and Caldwell, M. (eds) (2014), *Ethical Eating in the Postsocialist and Socialist World*, Berkeley: University of California Press.

Klumbytė, N. (2009), 'The Geopolitics of Taste: The "Euro" and "Soviet" Sausage Industries in Lithuania', in M. Caldwell (ed.), *Food and Everyday Life in the Post-Socialist World*, 130–53, Bloomington: Indiana University Press.

Klumbytė, N. (2010), 'The Soviet Sausage Renaissance', *American Anthropologist*, 112(1): 22–37.

Krasteva-Blagoeva, E. (2001), 'Bulgarians and McDonald's: Some Anthropological Aspects', *Ethnologia Balkanica*, 5: 207–18.

Lozada, E., Jr. (2000), 'Globalized Childhood? Kentucky Fried Chicken in Beijing', in J. Jing (ed.), *Feeding China's Little Emperors: Food, Children, and Social Change*, 114–34, Stanford, CA: Stanford University Press.

Manning, P. (2007), 'Rose-Colored Glasses? Color Revolutions and Cartoon Chaos in Postsocialist Georgia', *Cultural Anthropology*, 22(1): 171–213.

Massino, J. (2012), 'From Black Caviar to Blackouts: Gender, Consumption, and Lifestyle in Ceaucescu's Romania', in P. Bren and M. Neubuerger (eds), *Communism Unwrapped: Consumption in Cold War Eastern Europe*, 226–49, Oxford: Oxford University Press.

Mincyte, D. (2009), 'Self-Made Women: Informal Dairy Markets in Europeanizing Lithuania', in M. Caldwell (ed.), *Food and Everyday Life in the Post-Socialist World*, 78–100, Bloomington: Indiana University Press.

Mincyte, D. (2012), 'How Milk Does the World Good: Vernacular Sustainability and Alternative Food Systems in Post-socialist Lithuania', *Agriculture and Human Values*, 29(1): 41–52.

Mincyte, D. (2014), 'Homogenizing Europe: Raw Milk, Risk Politics, and Moral Economies in Europeanizing Lithuania', in Y. Jung, J. Klein and M. Caldwell (eds), *Ethical Eating in the Postsocialist and Socialist World*, 25–43, Berkeley: University of California Press.

Mintz, S. (1985), *Sweetness and Power: The Place of Sugar in Modern History*, New York: Viking.

Patico, J. (2002), 'Chocolate and Cognac: Gifts and the Recognition of Social Worlds in Post-Soviet Russia', *Ethnos*, 67(3): 345–68.

Patico, J. and Caldwell, M. (2002), 'Consumers Exiting Socialism: Ethnographic Perspectives on Daily Life in Post-Communist Europe', *Ethnos*, 67(3): 285–91.

Patterson, P. (2009), 'East European Grocery Store from Rationing to Rationality to Rationalizations', in W. Belasco and R. Horowitz (eds), *Food Chains: From Farmyard to Shopping Cart*, 196–215, Philadelphia: University of Pennsylvania Press.

Phillips, S. (2002), 'Half-Lives and Healthy Bodies: Discourses on Contaminated Food and Healing in Postchernobyl Ukraine', *Food and Foodways*, 10(1–2): 27–53.

Ries, N. (2009), 'Potato Ontology: Surviving Postsocialism in Russia', *Cultural Anthropology*, 24(2): 181–212.

Shectman, S. (2009), 'A Celebration of Masterstvo: Professional Cooking, Culinary Art, and Cultural Production in Russia', in M. Caldwell (ed.), *Food and Everyday Life in the Post-Socialist World*, 154–87, Bloomington: Indiana University Press.

Smith, J. (2009), 'Empire of Ice Cream: How Life Becomes Sweeter in the Postwar Soviet Union', in W. Belasco and R. Horowitz (eds), *Food Chains: From Farmyard to Shopping Cart*, 142–57, Philadelphia: University of Pennsylvania Press.

Stankovic, P. and Zevnik, L. (2011), 'Culinary Practices in Nove Fuzine: Food and Processes of Cultural Exchange in a Slovenian Multi-Ethnic Neighborhood', *Food, Culture, and Society*, 14(3): 353–74.

Velinova, I. (2015), 'Глобалната храна в България, между своето и чуждото' (Global Food in Bulgaria: Between Our Own and the Foreign), in E. Krasteva-Blagoeva (ed.), *Всичко за продан. Консумативната култура в България: антропологични Перспективи (Everything for Sale: Consumer Culture in Bulgaria from an Anthropological Perspective)*, 194–239, Sofia: New Bulgarian University Press.

Verdery, K. (1996), *What Was Socialism, and What Comes Next?*, Princeton: Princeton University Press.

Walker, A. and Manning, P. (2013), 'Georgian Wine: The Transformation of Socialist Quantity into Postsocialist Quality', in R. Black and R. Ulin (eds), *Wine and Culture: Vineyard to Glass*, 201–20, London: Bloomsbury.

Watson, J. (2006), *Golden Arches East: McDonald's in East Asia*, 2nd edn, Stanford, CA: Stanford University Press.

Watson, J. and Caldwell, M. (eds) (2005), *The Cultural Politics of Food and Eating: A Reader*, Malden, MA: Blackwell Publishing.

Yan, Y. (2012), 'Food Safety and Social Risk in China', *Journal of Asian Studies*, 71(3): 705–29.

Yan, Y. (2000), 'Of Hamburger and Social Space: Consuming McDonalds in Beijing', in D. Davis (ed.), *The Consumer Revolution in Urban China*, 201–25, Berkeley: University of California Press.

Yotova, M. (2010), 'Bulgarian Yogurt Traditions: Changes and Interpretations in Post-Socialist Reality', *MINPAKU Anthropology Newsletter*, 31: 6–7.

Yotova, M. (2014), 'Reflecting Authenticity: "Grandmother's Yogurt" between Bulgaria and Japan', in N. Domingos, J. Sobral and H. West (eds), *Food Between the Country and the City: Ethnographies of a Changing Global Foodscape*, 175–90, London: Bloomsbury.

CHAPTER FOURTEEN

Feeding the Revolution: Public Mess Halls and Coercive Commensality in Maoist China

JAMES L. WATSON

Discussions of food in China usually focus on high cuisine and delicacies associated with regional preferences. This essay deals with low cuisine – downright bad food – served in the public mess halls that appeared all over China in the late 1950s. Two issues are addressed: The first is the question of *commensality*, the sharing of food as a means of building social groups and strengthening personal relationships. Since the foundation of anthropology as a discipline field research has focused on the positive dimension of collective eating. Here I propose to explore a variation of this old theme, namely the consequences of *forced commensality* in politically charged settings mandated by the state.

The second issue considered in this essay is the role of the family in state socialism: How far can a society be pushed? What are the limits of social engineering? During a brief period in the late 1950s, Chinese communist leaders attempted to 'storm the gates of socialism' in order to smash the old, 'feudal' vestiges of a 'backward' culture and rebuild a new, socialist culture in its place. Where better to start than an attack on the family kitchen?

POLITICAL BACKGROUND: THE GREAT LEAP FORWARD

On 12 August 1958, China's leading newspaper, *People's Daily*, carried the following headline: 'Chairman Mao Inspects Villages in Henan Province' (he had been taken to see an experimental commune). There follows a quotation from Mao, in inch-high characters: 'If there can be one Commune like this, there can be many Communes.'

For the next two years the promotion of people's communes became national policy and the collectivization of all aspects of life began in earnest. The notion of private property all but disappeared and everything related to production became the corporate property of the masses: tools, farm animals, even the apple tree in one's backyard. The communes became an integral part of the Great Leap Forward, a political campaign designed to help China 'leap' onto the centre stage of world powers, overtaking Britain in ten years of selfless dedication and single-minded effort.

The tone of the era is captured in the mass media: The following is a 1958 editorial from a leading party publication, *Red Flag*: 'The broad masses of working people have unfalteringly accepted the people's communes. ... The working people in their drive forward have advanced the following slogans that fulfill their revolutionary spirit: Militarize Organizations, Turn Action into Struggle, Collectivize Life' (cited in Schurmann 1971: 479). In the countryside, farmers were to become the 'shock troops' of agricultural production; they were to be organized and disciplined (to quote from official sources) 'like workers in a factory or soldiers in a military unit' (ibid.).

The year 1958 was a particularly dangerous time in the politics of the Pacific. The Taiwan Straits crisis (centring on the islands of Quemoy [Jinmen] and Matsu [Mazu]) threatened to escalate into a full-scale world war, and many Chinese leaders, including Mao apparently, were convinced that a nuclear confrontation with the United States was imminent (see MacFarquhar 1983). Meanwhile relations with the Soviets were deteriorating rapidly, presenting the prospects of a second front. The Great Leap Forward was launched in the context of what Chinese leaders perceived to be a critical turning point in their history.

The campaign swept like a giant firestorm across China and affected every aspect of social life. No one escaped; every citizen over age twelve had to participate in Great Leap activities.[1] Personal sacrifices were demanded of everyone because, as one popular slogan put it: 'Bitter struggle for three years will bring a thousand years of happiness.' Communist utopia was just over the horizon; ordinary life was suspended for much of 1958 and 1959 as people were organized into military-style brigades to build dams, bridges and irrigation canals (MacFarquhar 1983: 120ff.). This was also the era of the infamous backyard steel furnaces, designed to make every region of China self-sufficient in steel and thereby capable of surviving foreign invasion. Most of the so-called steel that was produced during this period turned out to be completely useless; the campaign succeeded only in wasting resources and exhausting a rapidly alienated citizenry. I will return to the backyard steel campaign later because it plays an important role in the assault on family kitchens.

PUBLIC MESS HALL CAMPAIGN: THE COLLECTIVIZATION OF EATING

At the height of the Great Leap, during the autumn and winter of 1958, the central government began to call for the organization of public mess halls in the Chinese countryside. Given that farmers were to be 'shock troops' for the attainment of socialism and that social life was to be organized by the commune, the obvious next step was the collectivization of food and eating.

Public mess halls were by no means invented by the communists. Prior to the Great Leap, however, they were associated with schools, factories and military units. When most Chinese over age sixty think of mess halls they conjure up visions of a great pot, or wok, into which food is dumped and cooked into an appetizing mass.

Many of my colleagues and friends from China and Taiwan have grim memories of 'eating from the big pot'. This is also the standard metaphor for egalitarianism – everyone is equal when eating from the same pot (Lou 2001; Watson 1987).

The dimensions of mess hall cooking during the Great Leap were such that shovels, not mere spoons, were used to ladle out the food. In my own experience of public mess halls in China, the quality of food varies from bad to awesomely vile. There is a saying among Chinese students who relied on mess hall food during the 1940s: 'As we get thinner, the pigs get fatter,' the implication being that the fare was suitable only for the pigs that every mess hall cook raised in the backyard.

WOMEN'S LABOUR AND COMMUNIST CONSCIOUSNESS

The ostensible reason for establishing mess halls was to release the labour power of women. The mass media played on this theme, quoting Engels' famous dictum that true socialism can only be attained when women's labour is released from the bonds of household drudgery (Engels 1884). Party officials calculated that rural mess halls would make it possible for every woman to devote three extra hours per day to labour activities that the state deemed to be 'productive' – notably agricultural work, iron/steel smelting and dam building (see Manning 2005, 2006). In rural Guangdong, however, women ended up doing childcare, mess hall duty, public latrine cleaning and eldercare.

The labour question was obviously important but there was a secondary agenda involved and this, to my mind, was the most important aspect of the mess hall campaign: A leading editorial in the *People's Daily* noted that the formation of mess halls fosters 'collective living habits' which lead to the development of 'communist consciousness'. 'Collective eating', one official argued, 'is a great historical question involving a change in social habits that have existed for a thousand years.'[2] Another claimed that '[our farmers have] communized the problem of eating', thereby leading to the 'blooming of red communist flowers and the arrival of a blessed life'. And, in late 1958, an anti-family agenda began to emerge: '[We must] run the rural mess halls well, so as to enable commune members to eat more and better, and *live a still happier life than in their own homes*' (emphasis added).[3]

It is obvious that there is more here than a straightforward policy of releasing women's productive labour. The mess halls were conceived as an essential cornerstone for the entire commune system. It was important to 'run the mess halls well' in order to build a new socialist culture. How did communist authorities proceed? First, it was necessary to undermine the traditional pattern of maintaining separate kitchens for every household. Rather than launching a direct attack on the family as a feudal institution, farmers were 'encouraged' to donate their iron cooking ware to the backyard steel furnaces. Party activists collected pots, pans, woks, ladles, spoons, meat hooks, knives, buckets and well chains (see also Vogel 1969: 252–3). In one village along the coast of Fujian Province all private cooking instruments, plus the iron window and door frames of local houses, were melted into huge lumps that were never collected by higher authorities. The iron lay in rusting heaps decades after the Great Leap had collapsed (Huang 1989: 59–60; see also MacFarquhar 1983: 196–220).

In Guangdong Province, household stoves were dismantled, brick by brick, and the materials were used to build centralized mess halls. Some sympathetic officials left one stove in every five, to allow farmers to boil water and cook special meals for invalids and pregnant women. But even this concession was attacked by party ideologues as a vestige of privatism and almost all household stoves disappeared.[4] Not everyone in the affected communities willingly turned over their private cookware; those who resisted often had their homes ransacked and risked being labelled 'rightists' or 'counter-revolutionaries'.

TO ATTACK THE FAMILY, DESTROY THE KITCHEN

From the perspective of ordinary farmers, the act of destroying family kitchens had profound implications. The household stove is the symbol of family unity; when a family divides, the first thing that happens is that the constituent units start eating separately. The common stove also reflects the central significance of the family as an economic institution: a budget sharing, labour sharing and, hence, meal sharing unit. This elementary principle of Chinese family life is reflected in the writings of nearly every anthropologist who has worked in China, Taiwan and Hong Kong (see especially the work of Myron Cohen 1976).

To this list of ethnographers one might well add the name Mao Zedong. Mao was an accomplished and observant fieldworker, as evidenced by his investigative reports on peasant movements during the 1920s. Mao had the following to say about the central role of the Chinese family: 'Among [the peasant masses], for thousands of years ... a system of individual economy [has prevailed] under which a family or a household forms a productive unit; this dispersed and individual form of production has been the economic foundation of feudal rule and has kept the peasants in perpetual poverty' (Mao 1927: 27–8).

Judging from these and other sources, there can be little doubt that communist authorities knew exactly what they were doing when they ordered the closure of individual kitchens. It was an indirect, but nonetheless consciously designed attack on the rural family as an economic institution. A Chinese family without a stove and without cooking ware is not a family at all; it is a residential unit devoid of social and symbolic content.

What were commune authorities offering in its place? In 1958 and 1959 the Chinese press was full of commentaries regarding 'new style families' that the mess halls would help foster. The abolition of family cooking meant that there was a newfound 'harmony' between mothers-in-law and daughters-in-law, who no longer had to squabble over household chores.[5] Mess halls would lead, it was claimed, to mutual love and respect among all people, not just family members.

One woman is quoted as having said: 'Working in the mess hall is a different thing from cooking at home. Now it is not for my small family but for the large family of the commune.' Week after week, month after month, the Chinese mass media urged China's farmers to 'make their way into the collective life of a large family'.[6] Another intriguing notion that emerged in late 1958 was the 'mess hall family', meaning the collectivity of people who ate together – approximately sixty to eighty households on average.[7] Again, it was the stove – as a unifying symbol – that held the larger, socialist 'family' together, only in this case it was a centrally organized stove controlled by the state.

Dismantling family kitchens affected more than eating customs. Take the apparently simple matter of hot water as an example: local authorities centralized the distribution of cooking fuel (wood, straw, coal) thus making it impossible for each family to heat water for drinking, washing and bathing. Hot water is an absolute necessity of life in rural China. It is considered one of the few luxuries that even ordinary people can afford. With the demise of family stoves, commune members had to collect hot water from the mess hall, thereby subjecting themselves to additional political jeopardy: Were they using too much? Would they be accused of wasting the people's resources?

Under ordinary circumstances, hot water is a byproduct of household cooking. When visiting a farmer's home one is invariably presented with a cup of boiled water (tea is often too expensive and is considered a luxury in parts of south China). This is the minimal act of courtesy. By accepting the cup with both hands, and savouring the hot water, one is sharing the product of household labour.

Bathing was another problem, especially in the south where the evening bath is an important ritual as well as a practical act. Among rural Cantonese and Hakka, for instance, the evening greeting is often 'Have you had your bath yet?' The other greeting, of course, is 'Have you had your dinner yet?' Bathing the whole body every evening is not customary in the north, especially during winter (for rather obvious climatic reasons). But northern farmers do expect to return home after a hard day's work and soak their feet in hot water. To solve these problems local officials built public bathhouses adjoining the mess halls. In my interviews with people who experienced the Great Leap, complaints about the lack of hot water were nearly as numerous as grumblings about the quality of mess hall food.

The redirection of wood and coal to mess halls had even more serious consequences in north China, especially in areas where sleeping on *kang* was customary. Kang were elevated platforms that served as workspace during cold winter days and beds for family members during the night; they were heated internally, often as a byproduct of household cooking. Northerners who survived the Great Leap pointed out that restrictions on fuel often made their lives at home a shivering misery. Communist authorities responded by announcing that households should be prepared to share their kang with neighbours.[8] Not only was eating collectivized in some northern communes, but also sleeping arrangements – out of sheer necessity.

The assault on family autonomy did not stop here. Private vegetable plots were 'voluntarily' turned over to the mess halls during this period.[9] Grain rations were no longer distributed to individual household heads but were redirected to the commune mess halls. And, finally, all privately held food was requisitioned: grain bins emptied, pickle jars confiscated and livestock turned over to the mess halls. During this period, my interviewees report, party activists staged food raids in the middle of the night, making it dangerous to keep anything edible in one's home. There are also many accounts of so-called 'secret' banquets being held at this time by farmers who were determined to eat up their produce – especially pigs, chickens, ducks and rice – rather than turn it over to the commune. It is, of course, impossible for a rural banquet to be secret, which means that local officials knew what was happening and, by ignoring such feasts, they were implicitly condoning them.

COMMUNIST UTOPIA: ALL YOU CAN EAT, THREE MEALS A DAY

Given the general disruption of private lives, there had to be incentives for rural people to abandon their family kitchens: successful political campaigns are not founded on coercion alone, even during the heyday of Maoism (see Skinner and Winckler 1969). The solution was, on the face of it, remarkably simple: Free Food, three times a day.

Again, it was Mao Zedong who inspired this policy with one of his characteristically cryptic statements, uttered during a tour of a model commune (MacFarquhar 1983: 104). Mao said, in effect, 'If one commune can hand out free food, why can't they all do so?' Like other aspects of the Great Leap, the bountiful food campaign spread rapidly throughout the country – irrespective of local conditions – as party officials hurried to emulate the new policy. This became known as the 'eat well, eat full' movement. Eating to one's capacity became a revolutionary obligation. One popular slogan urged farmers to 'summon up your zeal for production and eat as much as you like'.[10] Needless to say, people were only too happy to oblige. In the Guangdong countryside three meals, featuring steamed rice, were served every day until stocks ran out. 'People couldn't believe their eyes', one interviewee told me; farmers gorged themselves on mountains of food.

One has to put this campaign in historical perspective: Until the mid-1980s, farmers in most parts of south China ate sweet potatoes and congee-style gruels at meals. Bowls of steamed rice constituted banquet fare served two or three times every year, for those lucky enough to be invited to weddings or community celebrations. Huang Shu-min reports that mess halls in Fujian Province served white rice in great heaps to incredulous farmers during the Great Leap; many were still talking about it in the 1980s. Furthermore, Huang reports that fresh fruit was provided – another luxury that ordinary people rarely, if ever, tasted (Huang 1989: 58).

In the wake of the 'eat well, eat full' campaign, the mass media promoted a cheerful image of the commune mess halls. Here is a ditty that was composed by 'grateful peasants' in Guangdong[11]:

> Our mess hall is decorated like a banquet hall.
> In the center is a picture of Chairman Mao.
> The tables are bright and clean.
> White rice today, noodles tomorrow.
> Fresh vegetables at every meal, and pork too.
> Steamed dumplings on rainy days.

Spinach and bean curd in abundance,
Eggplant seasoned with garlic.
We salute our cooks with cups of wine.
Long Live the People's Communes!

Excessive consumption lasted for up to six months in wealthier regions such as Guangdong, but in other areas it was over in a few weeks. Commune cooks soon settled down to the provision of essentially unappetizing, poorly prepared fare – just as everyone had feared. Propaganda ditties of the type noted above constituted only one side of the emerging socialist culture. The other side was represented by what might be called counter-hegemonic folklore, a form of subterranean protest that uses humour as a weapon. Unlike the Soviets, Poles and East Germans who maintained a rich tradition of political jokes during the 1950s and 1960s, rural Chinese relied primarily on linguistic puns. Here is one, a play on the term *daguofan* (the great pot), symbol of the egalitarian mess halls: *daguofan*, a big pot of rice, becomes *daguozhou* (a big pot of congee); which soon becomes *daguotang* (a big pot of soup); which eventually ends up as *daguoshui* (a big pot of water).[12]

This bit of folklore summarizes what happened to the mess halls between 1958 and 1959. My interviews and other sources reveal a dreary picture of declining standards in cooking, shortages of supplies and unsanitary conditions. Cold food was a serious problem, given that most mess halls had no facilities for keeping large masses of food warm for more than a few minutes. Delays were constant, causing people to wait in the cold. Often there were no meals at all on rainy days due to damp fuel.

The party tried to rebound with a mini-campaign called, in characteristic communist fashion, the 'Three Cleans' and the 'Four Hots': clean food, clean utensils, clean mess halls; coupled with hot grain, hot vegetables, hot soup and hot water.[13] The fact that central authorities felt it necessary to launch such a campaign speaks volumes regarding the problems of mess hall organization. It is little wonder, therefore, that mess halls became the central symbol of the Great Leap for most ordinary Chinese. Ask any farmer who lived during this period and, almost invariably, he or she will begin by denouncing the mess halls.

One of the most obvious problems with public eating was that party officials did not consider the organization of mess halls to be among their most important tasks. It was far more rewarding, professionally, to increase production and to respond to the latest political directives from central authorities. Furthermore, few party officials actually ate in the public mess halls. They had their own, separate canteens serviced by expert cooks who had privileged access to food supplies. (This is no surprise to anyone who travelled in rural China during the 1970s and early 1980s; the best food was always to be found at party headquarters.) During the Great Leap, this became an obvious source of embarrassment and the national press launched yet another mini-campaign in 1960 instructing party cadres to close down their special canteens. According to a central directive: 'In eating with the masses in the same mess hall we must share the same food with them, sit at the same table, and [live with the same] ration. Only in this way can we become welded with them into a single entity.'[14]

TIME, LEISURE AND THE REGIMENTATION
OF DAILY LIFE

The mess hall system began to unravel only months after it was initiated but lasted into 1959 and until 1960 in some areas of Guangdong (Siu 1989: 184). The canteens survived through the sheer weight of economic reality; there was no other alternative. People had to eat. Judging from interview responses, I am convinced that there was another feature of the mess hall system (besides bad food) that contributed to the high level of alienation. This is the problem of *time*, as reflected in the regimentation of daily life and the appropriation of leisure.

Meals at the mess halls were (ideally) to be taken at the same time, by everyone, every day; the ostensible reason was to facilitate the mobilization of a disciplined work force. But it was also true that, when farmers turned out for meals, party officials had a captive audience. There was no escape from political pressures and group activities. The pre-revolutionary notion that mealtime was a private interlude, a period for personal relaxation, disappeared in the mess hall crowd. One party bulletin announced that, henceforth, 'spare moments' before and after collective meals were to be used 'to make announcements regarding production, current events, and ... to arrange and discuss work'.[15] Many mess halls were also equipped with loudspeakers, which blared slogans and party propaganda while people ate. Audio systems in most parts of China (prior to the 1990s) had two settings: off and excruciatingly loud.

Communist authorities were preoccupied with the problem of time; they searched constantly for ways to save time – other people's time – so that it could be converted into productive labour. To this end, there was an all-out effort to industrialize cooking, thereby linking it to the Marxian notion of social production. A campaign to mechanize the preparation and delivery of mass meals soon followed. Machines invented by mess hall workers were hailed in the mass media as evidence of socialist ingenuity: dough kneaders, noodle pullers, vegetable slicers, pot stirrers and a contraption that could fill one hundred rice bowls a minute.[16] All of this was in aid of transforming the inherently social activity of eating into an industrial activity and thereby releasing the full potential of human labour.

AFTERMATH: THE POST-LEAP FAMINE

By mid-1959, Party organizers had reached the limits of human tolerance. The mess hall system began to collapse, in some areas faster than in others, for reasons that are still not entirely clear. There had been a bumper crop in 1958 that fuelled party optimism. But the 1959 harvest was damaged, in large part by the diversion of agricultural labour into projects such as backyard iron smelting (see Shapiro 2001: 80–6). There was also a stint of bad weather in 1959 and 1960, further limiting harvests.

The result was famine, perhaps the most deadly famine in world history (Chen 2011). Research by demographers has shown that, between 1959 and 1961, at least 30 million Chinese died as a direct result of starvation or indirectly as a result of famine-related disease. In the province of Sichuan, 5 per cent of the population died in 1960 alone (Ashton 1984; Bernstein 2006; Riskin 1998). The figures are staggering but what is even more horrifying is the realization that this was a policy-induced famine (Sen 1981; see also Wemheuer 2009, 2010; Lin and Yang 2000), a direct consequence of the Great Leap and its political campaigns (Bernstein 1984; Chen 2009; Li and Yang 2005; Manning and Wemheuer 2011; Thaxton 2008; Yang 1996).

The post-Leap famine hastened the collapse of the public mess hall system. Supplies of grain and subsidiary foods simply dried up; the halls stopped cooking and in many parts of south and central China rural people reverted to what can only be described as a hunting-and-gathering mode of subsistence: They foraged for food wherever they could find it and ate at home, sharing only with members of their immediate family; women were instrumental in this survival strategy, having learned the lore of famine foods from their Qing-era grandmothers (Jing 1996: 69–70; Yan 1990).

CONCLUSIONS: COERCIVE COMMENSALITY AND THE LIMITS OF SOCIAL ENGINEERING

Viewed from a comparative perspective, the Great Leap Forward presents us with a fascinating glimpse into the limits of human social engineering. Just how far can people be pushed before the social fabric begins to unravel? Maoist visionaries reached the outer limits of conscious cultural reconstruction in 1958 and 1959. The collective eating campaign was, in essence, an attack on the family as a central institution of life. The penetration of the state into the lives of ordinary farmers reached impressive levels during that period. The family, of course, had lost its control over production during the land reform campaigns of the early 1950s; the Great Leap extended the state's control into the supposedly private domains of consumption and leisure.

It is also important to note that the Great Leap affected the countryside far more than China's cities; it was primarily a rural movement. Farmers suffered most. The Cultural Revolution, by contrast, was aimed primarily at intellectuals, cadres and urban elites. Accordingly, we know far more about the Cultural Revolution than the Great Leap, for the simple reason that Chinese intellectuals have written volumes about their experiences in the late 1960s. By contrast, rural people have had relatively little to say – in writing – about what happened during the Great Leap or the famine that followed.

We do know that family kitchens quickly re-emerged in every part of rural China – in some respects in even stronger form, perhaps because the family became the only means of surviving the famine and depravation of the early 1960s (see Yan 1996: 91–4). Communist ideologues never again attacked the family as directly, nor as ferociously, as during the Great Leap. Even at the height of the Cultural Revolution, Maoist radicals did not attempt to interfere with family kitchens.

There are, of course, historical examples of other, more successful systems of collective dining: Israeli kibbutzim operated for decades with the equivalent of public mess halls (Spiro 1971; Talmon 1972), as did the Shakers and dozens of small, communitarian societies of radical Christians in the United States (Nordhoff 1875; Stein 1992). There are many examples of small-scale societies that have deemphasized the family and promoted collective living. But these systems all have one thing in common: People *chose* to participate, they decided when to join and when to drop out.

The Great Leap mess hall system was anything but voluntary. It was inspired by ideologues who imposed their will on society, from the top down. It is worth noting that China was not the only communist state to experiment with collectivized eating. Public mess halls also existed on a large scale in the Soviet Union (Borrero 1997; 2002; Caldwell 2004) and in communist Cambodia (Kiernan 2002).

These examples and others like them demonstrate that eating together is not always an expression of Durkheimian solidarity (cf. Bloch 1999). There is also a darker side of commensality. The Chinese commune experiment was – without question – the most extreme form of socialism ever attempted on such a massive scale. The public canteen system stretched the limits of social engineering and laid bare, for all to see, the inadequacies of radical collectivism.

Half a century after the Great Leap, mess halls began to reappear in Chinese films and television programmes that romanticized the socialist era. Nostalgic images of convivial dining in egalitarian setting (during a supposedly 'simpler', less complicated time) hide a brutal, unforgiving political system that led to famine, depravation and death on an unimaginable scale. The coercion behind the commensality should never be forgotten.

NOTES

This essay is an abbreviated version of a chapter first published in *Governance of Life in Chinese Moral Experience: The Quest for an Adequate Life*, edited by Everett Zhang, Arthur Kleinman and Tu Weiming (London: Routledge, 2011), pp. 33–46.

1. During the Cultural Revolution (1966–76), by contrast, it was possible to avoid direct involvement in political activities by staying home and keeping a low profile. No one escaped the Great Leap.
2. 'Run Public Mess Halls Properly', *Renminribao*, 25 October 1958 (*Current Background*, no. 538, 1958, pp. 1–4).
3. 'Which Kind of Mess Halls Do the Masses Like?' *Renminribao*, 3 November 1958 (*Current Background* [CB], no. 538, 1958, p. 26).
4. Based on interviews carried out in the Pearl River Delta, 1985 and 1986.
5. 'It is Excellent to Cook Our Meals Together', *Hongqi* (Red Flag), no. 23, 1 December 1959 (*Survey of China Mainland Magazines* [SCMM], no. 200, 1959, p. 35).
6. 'Take Practical Steps to Make a Real Success of the Rural Mess Halls', *Nanfangribao*, 5 July 1960 (*Survey of the China Mainland Press* [SCMP]), no. 2371, 1960, p. 5).
7. See note 2 above, p. 14. Also of interest is: 'Rapid Development of Public Mess Halls', *Neimengguribao*, 26 May 1960 (SCMP, no. 2309, p. 11).
8. Ibid., p. 19.
9. Ibid., p. 13.
10. 'Both Rice and Vegetables are Good', *Renminribao*, 10 November 1958 (CB 538, 1958, p. 22).

11. Chen Xiaowu, 'A Public Mess Hall Takes Root Among the People', *Zhongguo Funü* (Chinese Women), no. 17, 1 September 1959 (SCMM, no. 188, 1959, p. 25). The original ditty has been abbreviated and slightly edited for this essay.

12. Interview with a Great Leap survivor at the University of Pittsburgh, 1986. Huang Shu-min (1989: 63) reports a similar ditty that was common in Xiamen City, during the early 1960s: 'Cabbage leaves wrap cabbage leaves for lunch, and leaves of cabbage wrap leaves of cabbage for dinner' (*Wucan caibaocai, wancan baocai bao baocai*).

13. 'Urban Mess Halls in Amoy Municipality Consolidated and Improved', *Dagongbao*, 30 January 1961 (SCMP, no. 2448, 1961, p. 12).

14. 'Cadres Should Eat Together with Commune Members', *Renminribao*, 17 September 1960 (SCMP, no. 2350, 1960, p. 15).

15. 'Set Up Many Public Mess Halls and Run Them Well', *Hongqi* (Redflag), no. 8, 16 April 1960 (SCMM, no. 215, 1960, p. 11).

16. Some of these machines are described in a fascinating article: 'Mechanizing a Factory Cafeteria', *China Reconstructs*, August 1960, pp. 34–35.

REFERENCES

Ashton, B., Kenneth H., Alan P. and Robin, Z. (1984), 'Famine in China, 1958-1961', *Population and Development Review*, 10(4): 613–45.

Bernstein, T. P. (1984), 'Stalinism, Famine, and Chinese Peasants: Grain Procurement during the Great Leap Forward', *Theory and Society*, 13(3): 339–77.

Bernstein, T. P. (2006), 'Mao Zedong and the Famine of 1959-1960: A Study in Willfulness', *China Quarterly*, 186: 421–45.

Bloch, M. (1999), 'Commensality and Poisoning', *Social Research*, 66(1): 133–49.

Borrero, M. (1997), 'Communal Dining and State Cafeterias in Moscow and Petrograd, 1917-1921', in M. Glants and J. Toomre (eds), *Food in Russian History and Culture*, 162–76, Bloomington: Indiana University Press.

Borrero, M. (2002), 'Food and the Politics of Scarcity in Urban Soviet Russia, 1917-1941', in W. Balasco and P. Scranton (eds), *Food Nations: Selling Taste in Consumer Societies*, 258–76, New York: Routledge.

Caldwell, M. L. (2004), *Not by Bread Alone: Social Support in the New Russia*, Berkeley: University of California Press.

Chen, Y. (2009), 'Cold War Competition and Food Production in China, 1956-1962', *Agricultural History*, 83(1): 51–78.

Chen, Y. (2011), 'Under the Same Maoist Sky: Accounting for Death Rate Discrepancies in Anhui and Jiangxi', in K. E. Manning and F. Wemheuer (eds), *Eating Bitterness: New Perspectives on China's Great Leap Forward and Famine*, 197–225, Vancouver: UBC Press.

Cohen, M. (1976), *House United, House Divided: The Chinese Family in Taiwan*, New York: Columbia University Press.

Engels, F. (1972[1884]), *The Origin of the Family, Private Property and the State*, Harmondsworth: Penguin Editions.

Huang, S. M. (1989), *The Spiral Road: Change in a Chinese Village though the Eyes of a Communist Party Leader*, Boulder, CO: Westview Press.

Jing, J. (1996), *The Temple of Memories: History, Power, and Morality in a Chinese Village*, Stanford, CA: Stanford University Press.

Kiernan, B. (2002), *The Pol Pot Regime: Race, Power, and Genocide in Cambodia Under the Khmer Rouge: 1975-79*, 2nd edn, New Haven, CT: Yale University Press.

Li, W. and Yang, T. D. (2005), 'The Great Leap Forward: Anatomy of a Central Planning Disaster', *Journal of Political Economy*, 113(4): 840–77.

Lin, J. Y. and Yang, T. D. (2000), 'Food Availability, Entitlements and the Chinese Famine of 1959-61', *Economic Journal*, 110: 136–58.

Lou, P. (2001), *Daguofan: Gonggang Shitang Shimo (The Great Pot: Public Canteen Era)*, Guangxi Provincial People's Press.

MacFarquhar, R. (1983), *The Origins of the Cultural Revolution, 2: The Great Leap Forward, 1958-1960*, New York: Columbia University Press.

Manning, K. E. (2005), 'Marxist Materialism, Memory, and the Mobilization of Women in the Great Leap Forward', *China Review*, 5(1): 81–108.

Manning, K. E. (2006), 'The Gendered Politics of Women Work: Rethinking Radicalism in the Great Leap Forward', *Modern China*, 32(3): 1–36.

Manning, K. E. and Wemheuer, F. (eds) (2011), *Eating Bitterness: New Perspectives on China's Great Leap Forward and Famine*, Vancouver: UBC Press.

Mao, Z. (1927), *Report on an Investigation into the Peasant Movement in Hunan*, Beijing: Foreign Languages Press (1953 translation).

Nordhoff, C. (1875), *The Communistic Societies of the United States*, New York: Schocken Books (1965 reprint).

Riskin, C. (1998), 'Seven Questions about the Famine of 1959-61', *China's Economic Review*, 9(2): 111–24.

Schurmann, F. (1971), *Ideology and Organization in Communist China*, Berkeley: University of California Press.

Sen, A. K. (1981), *Poverty and Famines: An Essay on Entitlement and Deprivation*, Oxford: Oxford University Press.

Spiro, M. (1971), *Kibbutz: Venture in Utopia*, New York: Schocken Books.

Siu, H. F. (1989), *Agents and Victims in South China: Accomplices in Rural Revolution*, New Haven, CT: Yale University Press.

Skinner, G. W. and Winckler, E. A. (1969), 'Compliance Succession in Rural Communist China: A Cyclical Theory', in A. Etzioni (ed.), *Complex Organization: A Sociological Reader*, 2nd edn, 410–38, Holt, Rinehart.

Shapiro, J. (2001), *Mao's War Against Nature: Politics and the Environment in Revolutionary China*, Cambridge: Cambridge University Press.

Stein, S. J. (1992), *The Shaker Experience in America*, New Haven: Yale University Press.

Talmon, Y. (1972), *Family and Community in the Kibbutz*, Cambridge, MA: Harvard University Press.

Thaxton, R. A., Jr. (2008), *Catastrophe and Contention in Rural China: Mao's Great Leap Famine*, Cambridge: Cambridge University Press.

Vogel, E. (1969), *Canton Under Communism*, Cambridge, MA: Harvard University Press.

Watson, J. L. (1987), 'From the Common Pot: Feasting with Equals in Chinese Society', *Anthropos*, 82: 389–401.

Wemheuer, F. (2009), 'Regime Changes of Memory: Creating the Official History of the Ukrainian and Chinese Famines under State Socialism and after the Cold War', *Kritika: Explorations in Russian and Eurasian History*, 10(1): 31–59.

Wemheuer, F. (2010), 'Dealing with Responsibility for the Great Leap Famine in the People's Republic of China', *China Quarterly*, 201: 176–94.

Yan, Y. X. (1990), 'The 1959-61 Famine in Rural China: An Anthropological Perspective', Research paper, Harvard University, Department of Anthropology.

Yan, Y. X. (1996), *The Flow of Gifts: Reciprocity and Social Networks in a Chinese Village*, Stanford, CA: Stanford University Press.

Yang, D. L. (1996), *Calamity and Reform in China: State, Rural Society, and Institutional Change Since the Great Leap Famine*, Stanford, CA: Stanford University Press.

PART THREE

Food as Craft, Industry and Ethics

CHAPTER FIFTEEN

Church Cookbooks: Changing Foodways on the American Prairie

RUBIE WATSON

Our fascination with cookbooks has never been greater. Cookbooks are sold in the millions to those who cook and those who do not, to gourmands as well as those who do not know a truffle from a sweet potato. Collectors collect them, historians mine them, chefs see them as sources of fame and fortune, many take great pleasure in reading them and some actually use them to make dinner. Cookbooks are valuable resources for those who seek to understand changing diets and food consumption, ethnic differences, manifestations of class and status, women's expressive culture and the changing dynamics of family labour. Given this level of interest, extensive archives now exist to collect and preserve cookbooks as valuable historical resources.[1]

In this chapter I examine a very prosaic set of cookbooks that are unauthored, locally produced and generally unappreciated. Boles (2006: 38) divides cookbooks into three categories: commercial ventures, corporate publications and fundraising (community) volumes. Many readers know the joy of possessing a lavishly produced cookbook penned by a famous chef, and some readers may also own 'how-to' publications like *Instruction and Recipes for Your Kitchen Aid Stand Mixer* (2013). There are famous fundraising cookbooks such as Kander's *The Settlement Cookbook* (1903), but the majority of these texts rarely reach beyond the communities from which they originated. Even local libraries shun them, and most do not survive the contributors who produced them.

In the following pages, community (church) cookbooks from Henry County in northwestern Illinois are examined for what they tell us about foodways in the rural Midwest. Using a combination of church cookbooks and grocery store advertisements in a local newspaper, it is possible, I argue, to trace the outline of major dietary changes during the late nineteenth and twentieth centuries.[2] For example, one can examine the impact of newly built railroads, the introduction of packaged and convenience foods or the availability of prepared meals on local diets. The effort and skill required to cook at home and time spent in food preparation emerged as major themes during the course of my research. The cookbooks discussed here were written by and for a highly circumscribed audience: they are, in effect, only slightly more permanent versions of the boxes of handwritten recipe cards collected by women from neighbours and family. As someone who has witnessed these sources in use for many decades, I have confidence that these cookbooks provide important insights into the cooking practices of women in Henry County from the 1920s to the present.[3]

Such diverse commentators as David Cutler (an economist) and Michael Pollan (a food guru) have argued that home cooking is important for a healthy diet. Pollan claims that the decline in home cooking in the United States 'closely tracks the rise of obesity' (2013: 8). What we eat, Pollan writes, has become 'just another commodity' made up of 'edible foodlike substances' (2013: 9–10). Like Pollan, Cutler and his colleagues are concerned with rising obesity rates in the United States, and document a decline (from 1965–95) in time spent performing home food preparation, and a subsequent increase in factory-based preparations, especially snacks (Cutler et al. 2003). Technological innovations, changes in time allocation, massive advertising and the lure of convenience have all had an enormous impact on American diets. We return to these issues in the conclusion.

TRENDS IN AMERICAN COOKING

Euro-American foodways can be traced to the seventeenth century, and were, from the beginning, a blend of old and new world foods, techniques and – for lack of a better term – what we might call dining styles. Food historians writing about North America during the seventeenth to the early nineteenth centuries focus on New England and to some degree the American Midwest, leaving the South and Spanish influences on the Southwest and California somewhat neglected. The degree to which European settlers incorporated New World foods is a fascinating and complicated issue. 'The Pilgrim Story' notwithstanding, many foods native to the Americas (tomatoes and potatoes, for example) were not integrated into the diets of New Englanders until they received 'grudging approval in Britain', while 'Indian corn' was accepted from the earliest days as a substitute for the familiar but unavailable grain crops of Britain and Europe (see Levenstein 2003b: 3; Carroll 2013: 21–7).

In the seventeenth and eighteenth centuries, the dining styles of those who came from Europe – mostly England – to settle on the American East Coast were not significantly different from their homeland counterparts. In her history of the American meal, Abigail Carroll writes: 'Eating [was often] a casual, ad hoc, and untidy nonevent that made little use of tables and chairs, required no utensils, and bore few if any social expectations' (Carroll 2013: 6). Most people ate 'messes' or pottage with their hands from a common wood bowl or trencher (Carroll 2013: 16–17). Messes were boiled stews of grain or legumes that were sometimes combined with vegetables, meat and herbs. Cooking was over an open fire (in a hearth or not) for which fuel had to be provided and grains processed, usually tasks performed by men. Cornmeal mush and Johnny cakes (mounds of a cornmeal concoction baked on a board) were ubiquitous. Wheat failed to make inroads into most diets until the late eighteenth century and remained difficult to procure until the 1830s, when European migrant farmers in the Midwest started to produce large wheat harvests, using the Erie canal (and later railroads) to transport their crops (see e.g. Smith 2007: 619–20).

European cookbooks, which called for ingredients that could not easily be obtained in North America or failed to instruct cooks on the use of New World foods, were not very useful. Nevertheless, it took more than a century of European settlement in North America for American cookbooks to make their debut.[4] It was not until the 1796 appearance of Amelia Simmon's *American Cookery* (the first printed American cookbook) that we find a published recipe for pumpkin, which was utilized throughout the Eastern seaboard from the earliest days (see Carroll 2013: 17). Rebecca Burlend, who emigrated from Yorkshire, England to the Illinois prairie in 1830, describes cooking by trial and error. Upon arrival in Illinois, the Burlends purchased ground Indian corn to tie them over until their first harvest, but they had no yeast or oven and 'we were therefore obliged to make a paste, and bake it in our frying pan or some hot ashes'. They managed to obtain milk from a neighbour, and survived on 'hasty pudding, sad [no-yeast] bread, and a little venison' (Burlend 1987: 59).

Gradually, during the first half of the nineteenth century, thanks in part to the introduction of cook stoves, messes gave way to the separation of foods cooked in distinctive ways (see Carroll 2013: 6). Roast meat and vegetables could be combined with boiled potatoes, baked (wheat) bread and preserved fruit to make a meal. Plates, cutlery, dining tables, chairs and even special dining rooms began to make their appearance (see Carroll 2013: 66–8; Cromley 2010: 47–110). And, all the while cookbooks were appearing in ever-greater numbers as high and low forms of cooking and dining became more pronounced. 'High dining' in the middle decades of the nineteenth century was a relative concept: European visitors were often appalled by both the quality and quantity of food served. Charles Dickens refers to a dish of 'deformed beefsteak … swimming in butter' served for breakfast at his Boston hotel (quoted in Carroll 2013: 136).[5]

By the middle decades of the 1800s, two phenomena – railroads and cooking stoves – were transforming American diets. Railroads brought wheat and milled flour to the Northeast (and ultimately to Europe), citrus from Florida to small towns on the plains, salted and dried cod to Minnesota, and corn from the fields of Illinois and Iowa to markets everywhere. Cookbooks like *The American Woman's Home* authored by the Beecher sisters (1869) reflect these transformations.

During the 1830s, cast-iron cook stoves allowed cooks to heat water, fry bacon, bake bread and warm their houses all at the same time; the new stoves required less fuel and were safer than open hearths (see Cowan 1983: 54–5). Temperatures, although still difficult to control, were easier to regulate than cooking over an open fire. Once cook stoves were firmly established in the 1850s and 1860s, men no longer had to spend time cutting wood for home hearths; cook stoves used various kinds of fuel, most of which could be purchased and delivered to the home by commercial vendors. Nevertheless, as with open hearth cooking, cook stoves required serious investments in women's labour and skill; many judgements, which depended on a cook's experience, were necessary to prepare stoves for both oven-baking and top burner cooking. In her 1896 *The Boston Cooking-School Cook Book*, Fannie Farmer instructs her readers on fire building in a cooking stove:

> Before starting to build a fire, free the grate from ashes. To do this, put on covers, close front and back dampers, and open oven-damper; turn grate, and ashes will fall into the ash receiver. ... Cover grate with pieces of paper. ... Cover paper with small sticks ... being sure that the wood reaches the ends of the fire-box, and so arranged that it will admit air. Over pine wood arrange hard wood; then sprinkle with two shovelfuls of coal. Put on covers, open closed dampers, strike a match ... apply the lighted match under the grate, and you have a fire. (Farmer 1896: Chapter II, p. 19)

After this happy outcome, women had to work at stove maintenance, which required time and effort ('Now blacken the stove. Begin at front of range, and work towards the back; as the iron heats, a good polish may be obtained', ibid.). There follows descriptions of flame colour as an indicator when to close the oven damper, when to add coal and how to keep the fire overnight.

INNOVATORS AND CRITICS: 'EATING LIKE AN AMERICAN'

The period from the 1850s to the 1920s was marked by the introduction and enormous growth of factory food and a national food market. Railroads, refrigeration technology,[6] new packaging and the relentless commercialization of food processing were the foundation pillars of this transition. The history of the American food industry is complex, and here we can only touch on elements of that story: flour production takes pride of place. Canal and railroad expansion were central to the successful development of wheat production, first in New York and then in the upper Midwest. Prior to the 1850s and well after in frontier areas, people ground their own corn and later their wheat at local gristmills. William Oliver, writing of his own experiences in 1841–2 Illinois, reports, 'grist mills [driven by oxen or steam] are much wanted and form a good capital investment' (2002: 125). But, beginning in the 1830s, railroads made large commercial flourmills possible. In fact, one might argue that the American industrial revolution began with the flourmill; 'It was ... the flour business', Cowan writes, 'that first underwent industrialization in the Unites States' (1983: 46). By the 1870s, Minnesota-based companies like Washburn Mills[7] and C. A. Pillsbury and Company were making wheat flour available to cooks throughout the East and Midwest.[8] The highly milled (or processed) flour that these companies produced differed from the rye flour or cornmeal upon which people had depended during the eighteenth and early nineteenth centuries, and ushered in a change from quick breads to yeast breads baked in cook stoves (see Cowan 1983: 50–1).

The American Woman's Home, authored by Catherine Beecher and Harriet Beecher Stowe, was published in 1869 as a combined home reference and textbook (see Tonkovich 2002: x). The Beecher sisters begin their treatise on what "a good table" should include by proclaiming that bread was at its core. Bread, they argued, should be 'light, sweet, and tender' (Beecher and Beecher Stowe 2002: 131). 'The savage', they point out, 'mixes simple flour and water into balls of paste, which he throws into boiling water' (2002: 131). They deplore aerating methods that rely on carbonic acid gas and extol the virtue of the old, respectable mode of yeast-brewing and bread-raising 'that was known in the days of our Saviour' (2002: 132).

Butter and meat follow in the litany of foods for the 'good table'. American butter, they argue, can be good but is often too salty and not fresh (2002: 134–5). Meat, they note, is plentiful in the United States but is 'too new' and suffers from 'a woeful lack of nicety in the butcher's work' (2002: 136) leading to waste and toughness. They lament the general disinterest in 'the soup-kettle' and continue with a discussion of various cuts of meat and the correct cooking method: roasting, broiling, boiling or braising (2002: 138).

Vegetables followed by tea, coffee and confectionaries complete the list. The Beecher sisters note that vegetables are plentiful, and their cooking should be simple: they should not be 'drenched with rancid butter' (2002: 141). The potato comes in for special attention, because 'like bread, it is held as a sort of *sine-quo-non*' (2002: 141). Potatoes, which, they comment, are usually boiled or roasted, may also be fried in the French manner until they are crisp, golden and 'light as snow-flakes' (2002: 142). French methods of coffee preparation are held up as the model; 'French coffee is coffee', the Beechers exclaim, 'and not chickory, or rye, or beans, or peas' (2002: 143). For tea, Americans must look to England, they advise; boiling water is crucial, in their view, and English breakfast tea requires a long infusion (2002: 143). As for confectionary, to which only four paragraphs are devoted, the Beecher sisters point out that the art of making pastries, ices, jellies and preserves 'is far better understood in America than the art of common cooking' (2002: 144).

The Beechers were writing in the decade following the Civil War, during a period when the United States was experiencing rapid industrialization as well as an increasing influx of immigrants: first Irish, then Germans and Scandinavians, eventually followed by Italians and East Europeans. Clearly, their 'good table' refers to what was found in middle and upper class kitchens in the American Northeast. During this period of intense change and adjustment, the Northeast, especially Boston, became the centre of the Colonial Revival – a movement, it has been argued, which offered a unified national history that privileged New England (see e.g. Stavely and Fitzgerald 2011: 98–9, 101). Dietary changes, which were part of this revival, were to be achieved in part through a set of domestic ideals and cookery principles promoted by women like the Beecher sisters. By advancing a Cult of Domesticity that linked science, housework and a set of high moral principles, the home and the women who presided there were elevated to a status that they had not previously enjoyed (see Tonkovich 2002: xxiv; Stavely and Fitzgerald 2011: 106, 110). To achieve these ideals, instructions in the form of home guides, cookbooks and eventually training centres for servants were essential. During the later decades of the nineteenth century, many food reformers preached that messes or stews were unhealthy and unhygienic (see Gabaccia 1998: 128). People were drinking too much alcohol and not enough milk, many foods were judged too spicy, and Old World preservation techniques were deemed dangerous. Many of the food preparations that the reformers championed were not attainable among poor immigrant families living in crowded, urban tenements or isolated farmsteads in Nebraska or the Dakotas.

The relationship between ethnic identity and foodways makes for fascinating research.[9] 'Eating like an American' was based, at least in part, on a new understanding of food and the human body. In the new science of nutrition, the body was no longer seen as a machine, which had to be given copious amounts of fuel. In the 1840s and 1850s, the German scientist Justus von Liebeg concluded that foods could be separated into protein, carbohydrates, fat, minerals and water and each of these nutrients 'performed specific physiological functions' (see Levenstein 2003b: 46). Food reformers like Edward Atkinson, Wilbur Atwater, Mary Hinman Abel and Ellen Richards believed that the diets of Americans, especially those of immigrant workers, should and could be improved (for discussion see Levenstein 2003b: 45–55).

European immigration to the United States and urbanization were central to shifting how and what people ate. Changing diets often involve the substitution of one food for another and one of the most dramatic substitutions was the radical transformation of breakfast from hot grain, bread, eggs and bacon to cold processed cereals. The history of that change is replete with quirky health food enthusiasts, innovators and big food businesses. William Kellogg invented corn flakes as a vegetarian health food in 1898 at his brother's Seventh-Day Adventist sanatorium in Battle Creek, Michigan. Soon after, Grape-Nuts was created by Charles Post, who in an effort to link his cereal to the 'good health movement', also set up in Battle Creek. Levenstein argues that the success that Kellogg and Post enjoyed was in large part due to their extensive promotion and advertising (see Levenstein 2003b: 33–5). In the late nineteenth century, special promotions and ad campaigns were becoming as important as technology in advancing one food product over another.

Starting in the 1870s, Henry Heinz took advantage of a new method of packing under steam pressure to market preserved and canned foods and went on to create a food manufacturing empire (see Levenstein 2003b: 36; Cowan 1983: 72–3). During the 1890s, companies like Kellogg, Smuckers, Campbell Soup, Lipton Tea, Quaker Oats, Swans Down Cake Flour, Hormel, Jell-O, National Biscuit, United Fruit, Beech-Nut Packing and Coca-Cola developed their production lines (see Trager 1995: 332–64). All became enormously successful producers of processed, packaged food for the American (and eventually world) market.

Like other food manufacturers, Campbell's Soup Company excelled at promoting their products, Sidorick writes, by projecting an image 'as wholesome as hometown America, yet [at the same time] at the forefront of scientific and hygienic modern food production' (2009: 1). Campbell's depended on technological innovations (canning, tin for packaging and condensing)[10] and a strict regime of labour discipline to produce their prepared foods. Combining research, a tightly organized production process, and full-throttle promotion, Arthur and John Dorrance[11] (Joseph Campbell retired in 1893) created a hugely productive and profitable company (see Sidorick 2009: 16–37; Cowan 1983: 73; Collins 1994).

Along with Campbell's Soup, one other company – Jell-O – plays an important role in the community cookbook recipes discussed below. Jell-O, established in LeRoy, New York in 1897, relied on the acumen of Peter Cooper, who in 1845 produced and patented a gelatin product, which was an outgrowth of his glue business.[12] Cooper's gelatin, however, never became popular, and it was Pearle Wait who perfected the recipe by first granulating and then adding colour, flavour and sugar (Wyman 2001: 3). Wait, the creator of Jell-O, sold his company to the Genesee Pure Food Company in 1899, and it was Genesee that put Jell-O on the map by creating recipes, recipe booklets and ads in publications like *Ladies' Home Journal* (Wyman 2001: 3–7; Trager 1995: 361). The importance of advertising is evidenced by the fact that an ad in the June, 1902, issue of *Ladies' Home Journal* cost Genesee nearly as much as the price that they had paid for Wait's entire Jell-O operation three years earlier (Wyman 2001: 14).

By the 1920s, Americans living in urban areas (51 per cent of the total population)[13] were eating increasing amounts of food produced by Big Business. In fact, Turner argues that working-class urbanites were at the vanguard of a trend that involved removing cooking from the home and relocating it in factories, delicatessens and restaurants (2014: 59). Canned soups, fruits and vegetables grown and marketed by companies like United Fruit, flour and sugar processed in large mills, packaged sweets, as well as smoked, pickled and canned meats were widely available and readily used. Packaged yeast, bicarbonate of soda and baking powder had eased the home baker's burden. Refrigerated rail cars made it possible for Iowa pork to be marketed in New York or Boston and Florida citrus to make its way to Christmas tables in Minnesota. Coffee was widely available and consumed by millions, including children. Many food reformers were, in fact, appalled by the bread and coffee breakfasts common among children in many working-class neighbourhoods (see Wood 1922: 24). Coffee's popularity may have been due, at least in part, to the fact that it was non-alcoholic, an important asset during the prohibition years of 1920–33 (Levenstein 2003b: 24; Cromley 2010: 62).

HENRY COUNTY, ILLINOIS: COOKBOOKS
AND NEWSPAPER ADVERTISING

During the late eighteenth century, the Euro-American population of Illinois was transformed from predominantly French to predominantly 'new Americans', who Billington refers to as 'sturdy woodsmen' pushed by the spread of plantation agriculture from their homes in the Carolinas, Virginia, Tennessee and Kentucky (1951; see also Faragher 1986). At statehood in 1818, 75 per cent of the population was from the American South, 13 per cent from the Middle States, 3 per cent from New England, and 9 per cent from abroad (see Billington 1951). These percentages began to change in the 1820s, and, with the opening of the Erie Canal in 1825, northern Illinois experienced large-scale settlement from New England, the mid-Atlantic states and eventually European immigrants from Sweden, Germany and Ireland.

The population of Henry County, established in 1837, remained sparse until the late 1840s when large numbers of Swedish immigrants began moving into the area. Part of the so-called Illinois Military Tract, a large section of Henry County included lands that had been set aside as bounty for non-commissioned soldiers who had served in the War of 1812 (see Kiner 1910: 77; Polson 1968). Colonizing settlements, usually headed by Protestant (Presbyterian) pastors from New England and New York,[14] purchased large parcels of Tract land in the 1830s, but most of these ventures were unsuccessful and sold off their lands in small sections to other American migrants from the Northeast or to European immigrants, especially from Sweden.

The first Swedish immigrants to arrive in Henry County were followers of the messianic preacher Eric Jansson. Jansson and his followers, who settled in what is today Bishop Hill, Illinois, were dissenters from the state (Lutheran) church of Sweden, and, upon their arrival in 1846, organized themselves along communal principles. Families lived in small, separate apartments but owned land and dwellings, worked and ate as a community. The Bishop Hill commune became quite prosperous, but was disbanded in 1862 soon after a community member killed Jansson.[15]

In 1849, Sweden's state church, apparently concerned about the influence of Jansen on immigrants flocking to Illinois, sent Lars Esbjorn to establish a Swedish Lutheran church in Andover, about 10 miles from Bishop Hill, also in Henry County. By the 1870s, Henry County had many large and thriving Swedish immigrant communities, and Andover emerged 'as the nucleus of the Swedish Lutheran movement in the United States during the nineteenth century' (Meyer 2000: 271). The ethnic make up of Henry County during the 1800s, and to a considerable degree still today, is largely Swedish-American, German-American and descendants of migrants from the American Northeast. As outlined below, the county's food traditions reflect this ethnic mix.

Henry County was, and still is, a patchwork of towns, villages and farmsteads. The largest town (Kewanee) currently has a population just shy of 13,000 residents. Bordering Henry County to the West is an urban centre of about 350,000, and today, many residents work in the factories, offices, and service businesses in 'the cities', as they are commonly called.[16] The population of Henry County was 45,162 in 1920, reached a peak of 57,968 in 1980, but then, like many rural counties in the Midwest, steadily declined to 50, 468 in 2010.[17]

Until the 1970s, local farming depended on a mixture of grain (corn, soybeans and oats), livestock (dairy cows, cattle and pigs), and poultry. In recent decades, however, farming has become increasingly dependent on two crops (corn and soybeans) and a livestock regime of confinement pigs and beef cattle. Farming remains economically important, although there are currently far fewer farms than in 1925. The size of farms has increased dramatically; in 1925, an average farm was 156.6 acres; in 2012, it was 349 acres.[18] The county's population has remained 50 per cent rural since the 1920s, although by the early twenty-first century most rural residents were no longer farmers, but people who live 'in the country' with little or no farmland attached to their house lots.[19] By most measures, the vast majority of county residents easily fit into the lower middle or middle classes: in 2009 estimated median household income was $46,163, median home value was $104,732,[20] and fewer than 16 per cent (in 2012) of the population (over twenty-five years) had the equivalent of a Bachelor's degree education.[21]

Churches and schools were core institutions in nineteenth-century prairie communities and they continue to play a leading role not only as places of formal education and devotion but also as centres of sociality, entertainment and civic practice, as well as arenas for debate and controversy. The community cookbooks discussed here are the products of local churches; often their appearance coincides with a milestone anniversary. They were produced by churchwomen and printed by regional printers; most were spiral bound and all were sold locally. The earliest cookbook discussed here dates from 1936 and the most recent was published in 2010. The books themselves are unauthored, although on occasion members of an organizing committee are listed. Each recipe, however, is attributed to a named individual, and, on occasion, someone will contribute a favourite recipe in memory of a deceased friend, mother or aunt. All the cookbooks, ranging in size from 56 to 189 pages, provide recipes organized into specific categories ('Cakes', 'Salads', 'Meat'). Most also contain a table of contents, a page or two devoted to various topics – 'Weights and Measures', 'Table Prayers', 'Handy Spice Guide' – as well as an index and sometimes 'Cooking Suggestions' (e.g., 'Eggs should be at least three days old before using in cakes'). Books were sold by, and proceeds from the sales went into the coffers of church-based women's organizations.

The grocery store ads referred to in this essay appeared in the *Orion Times*, which dates from 1877.[22] A complete run of this weekly newspaper from 1877 to 2012 is available on microfilm at the Western District Library (Orion, Illinois) and issues dating from 1877 to 2004 are now available online.[23] Although I have examined dozens of Henry County cookbooks, here I focus on ten books produced by churches in the neighbouring towns of Orion, Andover, Ophiem and Alpha, situated along the western border of Henry County.[24] The early founders of Alpha and Orion were largely migrants from the American East Coast, mid-Atlantic and South with a mix of immigrants from Sweden and Germany. Ophiem and Andover's founders were Swedish. Among the four towns, Orion currently has the largest population with 1,858 residents; during the first six decades of the twentieth century, its population remained under 1,000. Ophiem is currently the smallest with fewer than one hundred residents. Until the 1980s, regardless of population size, one and often two or more grocery stores served each of these towns. Of the four towns, only Orion can now lay claim to a full-service grocery store, although at one time the town supported four. I have cookbooks from two of Orion's churches – St Paul's Lutheran (1951, 2010) and Mary, Our Lord of Peace Roman Catholic (1967) as well as three from Grace Lutheran in Ophiem (1936, 1989, 2000), one from Andover Lutheran Church (1974), and one from the Alpha Methodist church (1951). Many residents in Orion (and perhaps also Andover, Ophiem and Alpha) read the *Orion Times*, and were likely to do their food shopping in their own hometown grocery stores until the 1970s. During the 1980s and 1990s, paralleling developments throughout rural America, these three towns lost their grocery stores, and local people (including many Orion residents) took their custom to supermarkets in 'the cities'.

Although the descriptions of foodways that follow are based primarily on cookbooks and newspaper ads, it is important to note that I was born and raised on a farm in Henry County and returned to live there in 2008. Personal observations and communications thus compliment the texts that I consulted; such occasions are marked by footnotes or noted in context.

At this point, a word or two about terminology is necessary. The broad category of 'processed food' incorporates a high percentage of what Americans eat and includes basic items such as flour, sugar, salt, rice, coffee and chocolate as well as more highly processed, packaged foods like breakfast cereals and so-called convenience and prepared foods (e.g. cake mixes, prepared salad dressings and frozen meals). In this essay I focus on the introduction of packaged, convenience foods like condensed soup, jello,[25] and cake mixes. Before discussing county cookbooks, however, it is important to say something about the kinds of foods Henry County residents were buying in their local grocery stores and eating in their homes in the latter half of the nineteenth and early twentieth centuries.

HENRY COUNTY FOODWAYS

Given what can be gleaned from local newspapers during the 1870s to the 1930s, most people living in Henry County relied on milled corn and wheat flour, pork and beef (especially salted and smoked pork), dried fish, sorghum, molasses, sugar, salt, vegetables and fruit as well as coffee and tea. Lard, butter, eggs, milk and cream were readily available in the local communities and widely used.[26] Except for items such as coffee, tea, dried fish, flour, molasses, sugar and salt many nineteenth-century households produced a substantial portion of their daily food.

During the nineteenth and early twentieth centuries, the *Orion Times* carried hundreds of advertisements, indicating that locally produced foods were consumed locally. Grocery store ads proclaimed: 'Highest prices paid for butter and eggs', or 'Farm produce taken at highest market price in exchange for goods'. Ads for Orion Mills offered their own flour and 'Highest Market Prices Paid for Good Merchandise Wheat', and local meat markets' advertisements for livestock and home butchering all provide evidence that county residents were producing for themselves and their neighbours. These ads also indicate that local merchants were dependent, at least in part, on locally produced food for both sale and barter (see e.g. *Orion Times*, 20 December 1877: pp. 1, 4; 3 January 1878: p. 8; 14 November 1884; 13 March 1919).

In 1945, according to the United States Census of Agriculture, Henry County had 3,196 farms and a farm population of 11,622.[27] Corn was the dominant grain crop although farmers also grew oats, rye and winter wheat. The bulk of the corn and oats crops were fed to farm animals rather than sold on the market.[28] Most farms kept livestock with varying combinations of hogs and pigs, beef cattle, milk cows and horses; prior to the 1950s, some town residents also kept a milk cow and perhaps chickens. In 1945, Henry County farmers sold 169,760 hogs and pigs and 40,370 cattle and calves, while they home slaughtered 5,864 hogs and pigs and 1,653 cattle.[29] These figures suggest that many farm households relied on their own livestock for a part of – in some cases all – the meat they ate. Dairy products and poultry also generated food for the table and income for the household, especially for farm women.[30] Many farm women exchanged eggs or butter or dressed chickens for flour, sugar and salt at their local grocery store, eschewing money altogether. Gardens were important sources of food both for farm families and residents of small towns. Advertisements in the *Orion Times* for garden seed in March and April, for canning and pickling paraphernalia in the summer, and for huge quantities of salt for meat preserving in the fall attest to the importance of local provisioning in the early twentieth century. The preservation of fruits, vegetables and meat had largely disappeared by the 1970s; today, some women may freeze sweet corn for future use but little else.

Although local foods were mainstays of the Henry County diet, products from outside the region were also available. Early editions of the *Orion Times* in the 1870s and 1880s indicate that dried fish and fresh oysters, fruit from California, Florida and New York as well as flour from mills in Minnesota were part of the local diet. In 1854, the first railroads arrived in eastern Henry County, and, by the early 1870s, the entire county was well served by rail. The first train service to Orion, Ophiem and Alpha began in 1870 and certainly had an impact both on how farmers marketed their products and what local people ate (Drury 1955: 9; Polson 1968: 180–1; Anderson and Norcross 1977: 24–5).

Before considering cookbooks and newspaper ads in detail, it is important to briefly describe the tools that Henry County women had available for their household tasks. In 1945 according to the United States Census of Agriculture, only 27 per cent of Illinois farms reported that they had running water, 60 per cent had electricity, 88 per cent owned a radio and 62 per cent a telephone. However, only a few years later, the agricultural census for 1954 shows that nearly all Illinois farms (96 per cent) enjoyed electricity and the majority (66 per cent) had running water.[31] There can be little doubt that in 1945 town homes had greater access to both electricity and indoor plumbing than their rural counterparts.[32] 'Stoves' (presumably cast-iron cook stoves) and sewing machines were advertised in the earliest 1877 editions of the *Orion Times*. In 1901, we find an ad for a 'car load' (presumably rail freight car) of 'cook stoves and ranges' (April 18: p. 2).[33] Ads for coal-burning heating stoves and furnaces abound (see e.g. 13 September 1900: p. 4; 12 December 1907: p. 1) as do advertisements during the 1920s (and especially in the 1940s) for electric washing machines.

The very first issue of Orion's hometown newspaper (13 June 1877) includes ads for hardware, dry goods (especially clothing and shoes), printing services, cooking and heating stoves, livestock, guns, patent medicine and books among other items. Three Orion stores advertise 'groceries', but only one gives any detail: 'Dried Beef, Salt Fish, Hams, Tea in Endless Variety, Ashton Salt, [and] Tobacco, Cigars, Toilet Soaps' (13 June 1877: p. 4). From the 1870s to the 1920s, ads for clothing, shoes, housewares and farm machinery as well as various services like medical doctors and butchering dominated, but advertisements for food were rare. Prior to the 1920s, on those occasions when local businesses did advertise specific food items, brand names were rarely indicated. A typical ad might proclaim (as noted above) 'Tea in endless variety' in the 1870s, or in 1884 'Canned Goods of All Kinds', or in 1887 'Fresh Oysters in Bulk'. The first full-scale ad for a brand-name food to surface in the *Orion Times* was for Royal Baking Powder in 1892, which was placed, it should be noted, not by a local merchant, but by the manufacturer. The ad testifies that Royal Baking Powder is 'purest in quality and highest in strength' (23 December, p. 3).[34] An ad for Jersey Cream Flour[35] was placed by a local merchant in 1902 (6 February, p. 5) and in 1907, the C. G. Norton Store paid for prominent ads extolling the virtues of EACO Flour, a product manufactured in Waseca, Minnesota (16 May, 29 August, 19 December).

It is not surprising that two products, baking powder and brand-name flour, should take pride of place in local grocery ads in the 1890s and early 1900s for these were basic items in the local diet and after the 1890s, when Orion Mills stopped producing its own flour, were not locally produced.[36] Neither is it surprising that early ads for specific food items emphasized the purity, safety and quality of brand-name food products. In her cookbook – *The Ladies New Book of Cookery* published in 1852 – Sarah Hale discussed the perils of and remedies for adulterated flour to which 'whiting, ground stones and bones, and plaster of Paris' had been added. She noted that adulteration was more serious in Europe but warned her American readers to be wary (1852, pp. 374–5). During the nineteenth and early twentieth centuries, fears of spoiled or adulterated foods were pervasive – and real. Eventually, the 1906 publication of Upton Sinclair's novel, *The Jungle*, drew widespread attention to the dreadful working and hygiene conditions in Chicago's slaughterhouses. Long-term concerns about food additives and adulteration led to federal legislation and the Pure Food and Drug Act of 1906, the first consumer protection law to be passed by Congress (see Levenstein 2003b: 39–40).

On 2 December 1909, one of Orion's grocery stores took out a full-page ad for their 'Closing Out Sale', providing an extensive and, for our purposes, valuable list of stock. Some items were advertised by brand – Postum, Virginia Sweet Pancake Flour, Dart canned fruit, Pillsbury Flour, Calumet Baking Power – but many were not. Although the belief that pre-packaged, brand-name foods constituted a guarantee of quality was becoming widespread in the early twentieth century, many items were still sold in bulk. For example, on 10 January 1918, Norton and Peterson Store announced that they had just received a 'large cask' of sauerkraut ('Bring your kegs and jars and we will sell you a lot of kraut for a little money'). Peanut butter was sold in bulk (24 October 1918), and on 13 March 1919, Glenn Norton Store advertised 'A barrel of good Frosted Cookies'. Again in 1919, Norton announced: 'We have coming, in about ten days or two weeks, a [rail freight] car of H. & E. and Domino Sugar. This car of sugar will be in bags, bales and barrels, also a limited quantity of Domino Cut Loaf Sugar in boxes.' The ad also announces the 'immanent arrival' of a car of coal and a car of apples (29 May).

During the First World War, food shortages had a direct impact on Henry County cooks and consumers. Quality concerns remained important, as did efforts to improve Americans' diets. The Food Administration, emerging from the food crisis of 1916–17, allowed the US government to assert some control over the food supply and at the same time encourage better nutrition; the latter goal was supported by the American Home Economics Association and agricultural science programmes at many land grant universities (see Levenstein 2003a: 80–8, 2003b: 137–45). Whether calls for smaller portions of meat and potatoes or more fruit and milk consumption had an effect on Henry County residents is difficult to determine, but it is clear from grocery ads in the *Orion Times* that residents did experience shortages. On 21 February 1918, Orion's A. A. A. Store announced that they had no sugar, and further that with every pound of flour purchased, customers must also buy a half pound of flour substitutes – buckwheat, barley flour, corn flakes, corn grits, corn starch, hominy, oatmeal, potato or rice flour and rolled oats.[37]

From the mid-1920s, the power of the brand to sell was evident, and Orion's grocery store ads were increasingly brand specific. In 1925, for example, most food ads were devoted to brand-name products, except for items like peanut butter, sauerkraut, fresh vegetables, fruit and meat. In 1927, Glenn Norton, the new proprietor of the A. A. A. Store, took out a large ad offering 'quality brands' (12 May). Although Jell-O and Campbell's condensed soup had both been on the American market since 1897, it was not until the 1920s that the first ads for these two brands appeared in the *Orion Times*.[38] New products were often introduced via the now classic methods of store demonstrations and special promotions, often involving prizes or free samples. Although we find promotions as early as 1907 (e.g., on 29 August customers were given 'elegant reproductions of famous oil paintings' with a 25 cents purchase of Lighthouse Washing Soap), the pace of promotions, demonstrations and prizes increased in the 1920s and 1930s. In 1926, Norton's store announced that a representative of National Biscuit Company 'will show the entire list' of the company's products, and presumably, tastings were on offer (22 April) – and in 1930, Anderson's store proclaimed that a 'Lady demonstrator' would have samples and show patrons 'Splendid products' (22 May). In 1947, in an apparent effort to entice customers, Larson's grocery offered cash drawings 'after the picture shows, or at about 9:45 o'clock' (3 April).

CHURCH COOKBOOKS: LOCAL ADAPTATIONS AND NATIONAL TRENDS

The Luther Ann (young women's) Society of Grace Lutheran Church, Ophiem produced the earliest Henry County cookbook discussed here. Most of the seventeen members, listed on the opening page, were unmarried, between the ages of eighteen and twenty-five, and lived at home or worked as domestic servants for nearby farm families or upper-middle-class households in 'the cities'. Interestingly, most of the recipes were contributed by married churchwomen and not by members of Luther Ann Society. One suspects that this cookbook may well have been a way of formally marking and organizing the transmission of treasured recipes from elders to juniors. Most recipes have detailed instructions, but some like Mrs Clara Stromquist's 'Corn Bread' or Mrs E. J. Lindholm's 'Salt Pork Fruit Cake' and many cookie recipes merely provide a list of ingredients. Recipes using sour milk and liberal amounts of eggs abound; in fact, 'sweet milk' is specified and is the term that today would be listed as simply 'milk'. Many recipes call for gelatin, but the brand name Jell-O (or the more generic jello) makes a showing only in the 'Salads' section.

The contents of this book are organized into fourteen categories beginning with 'Breads' and concluding with 'Household Hints'. The largest category is 'Cookies', to which ten pages are devoted. The recipes are unpretentious; cake recipes rely on cake flour and butter and are made 'from scratch'. No cake mixes or packaged mixes of any kind are found in this 1936 cookbook (although a recipe for 'Tomato Soup Cake'! – a date-nut cake – is included). Only three casserole dishes rely on condensed soup (tomato and mushroom); all others depend on the addition of home-made white sauces or tomatoes. Canned pineapple and coconut are used in many recipes, with marshmallows making an occasional appearance. Four salad recipes (out of thirteen) require jello. The highly sweetened 'salads', for which the Midwest became famous, were just beginning to make their appearance: the ratio of savoury to sweet salads was about 4 to 1 in Ophiem's 1936 cookbook. A steamed suet pudding and a fruitcake use salt pork as well as graham flour (a type of whole wheat flour). Swedish (heritage) foods do not appear as a special category, although recipes for Osta Kaka (a milk-based dessert) and two cookie recipes have Swedish titles.

By 1951, cookbooks from Orion's St Paul's Lutheran and Alpha's Methodist churches show clear changes. For St Paul's, the number of 'casserole' recipes has increased since 1936; with thirteen listed, eight rely on condensed soup (and five of thirteen for Alpha's Methodist). The same is true of salad recipes, which have grown sweeter; four of the five depend on jello (as do seven of nineteen for Alpha Methodist). Cake recipes seem most resistant to change; neither jello nor cake mixes appear in either book. It appears that St Paul's and Alpha's bakers, like their sisters at Grace, preferred to make their cakes 'from scratch'. As in the 1936 text, Swedish heritage recipes are not given prominence in a special section.

By the 1960s and 1970s, grocery store ads and cookbooks (from Orion Catholic and Andover Lutheran churches) show that new ways of cooking have arrived in Henry County. Sweet jello salads have become even more popular and non-dairy toppings like Cool Whip make their debut. The number of casserole recipes has increased, and more than half depend on condensed soup. Nevertheless, cake recipes made from scratch continue to dominate. Many authors have commented on the staying power of home-made cakes in which bakers follow a set recipe for combining the basic ingredients of butter, sugar, eggs, flour and milk. In fact, to increase sales, manufacturers were forced to change their original recipe from 'just add water' to 'just water and egg' in the hope of getting women to feel better about their cake productions (see Marks 2005: 168–71; Levenstein 2003a: 116). Interestingly, for the first time both cookbooks begin to play up a heritage angle: page one of the 1967 Our Lady of Peace text is devoted to 'An Irish Toast' and a recipe for 'Irish Freckle Bread'. Andover Lutheran begins its 1974 cookbook with fifteen pages of recipes in a special 'Swedish Foods' section. A menu for a 'Traditional Christmas Eve Dinner'[39] and a recipe for 'Lute Fisk' (Dried Cod) begins the section.

In the 1980s and beyond, all manner of convenience foods – condensed soup, jello, Cool Whip, prepared pie filling and pie crusts begin to appear in salads, desserts and casseroles. A 'Frozen Dessert' in Ophiem's 1989 cookbook calls for Oreo cookies, butter, vanilla ice cream, Smucker's fudge sauce, salted peanuts and Cool Whip, and in another recipe – the aptly named 'Easy Dessert' – the list of ingredients includes two cans of pie filling, one package of white cake mix and one stick of butter. Cake mixes have become more popular but many cake recipes still rely on traditional methods (cake mixes are used by St Paul cooks for twelve of thirty-one cake recipes but for Ophiem – 1989 – only four of eighteen use mixes). There are many recipes for pizza and pasta dishes, cookie and candy sections are enlarged, and salad and dessert recipes that depend on mélanges of convenience foods appear with more regularity. St Paul's 2010 cookbooks has a recipe for 'Ramen Oriental Coleslaw' that includes one package coleslaw mix, two packages Ramen – Oriental flavour – noodles, soy sauce, sugar and oil. Another salad recipe – 'Cherry Coke Salad' – calls for one can crushed pineapple, two packages cherry gelatin, one can cherry pie filling and three-fourths cup of cola. There are also recipes for the more traditional Bean or Macaroni salads, but salads that combine different varieties of convenience foods tend to dominate the salad section of St Paul's 2010 cookbook.

The combination of convenience foods to make 'new, innovative' dishes of seemingly endless variety seems to have become more and more popular during the last two or three decades of the twentieth century. Women's magazines, newspapers, product labels and word of mouth all play a role in offering busy cooks opportunities for doing more than heating the contents of a package or can. By combining cans of pie filling, cake mix, non-dairy toppings or Ramen noodles with a prepared salad dressing, women could do more than obey the simple command: 'just add water'; and, still they remained within the convenience food market, which was an unstated but clear goal of the food industry (see Levenstein 2003a: 37).

National statistics show a decided increase in the proportion of calories derived from sugar and fat in the American diet, and my research indicates that Henry County was no exception. In 1977, a government publication, *Dietary Goals for the United States*, reported that in 1909 Americans obtained 40 per cent of their calories from vegetables, fruit and grains but by 1976 that figure dropped to 20 per cent. Sugar consumption had increased 31 per cent and the intake of dietary fats had climbed by 56 per cent (see discussion in Carroll 2013: 194–5). These are stunning figures. Obviously, convenience foods were not solely responsible for this escalation; other changes – larger portions, high rates of soft drink consumption, snacking and more sedentary lifestyles – were also factors. Nevertheless, the increasing use of convenience foods certainly played a role.

Eating food purchased commercially outside the home has a long tradition in the United States (see e.g. Turner 2014: 70–85). The *Orion Times* had ads for local restaurants in its earliest publications. Clearly, farm families could and did eat in cafes, restaurants, taverns and diners. Turner argues that by the 1930s, 'American cities and towns boasted a range of inexpensive places to eat out: diners, doughnut shops, hot dog stands, Automats, fast-food restaurants' (2014: 72). However, when I was growing up on a farm in Henry County in the 1950s, eating outside the home was a special treat. I do not recall ever eating our evening meal in a restaurant except when we travelled. Our family did, however, have lunches or snacks in diners or cafes during shopping trips and errand runs to 'the cities'. Anecdotal evidence from

Henry County friends and family confirm my experience. Many cousins and friends report that when they were growing up in the 1950s and 1960s, they did not eat in a restaurant until they were teenagers, when they might stop at the local drug store for a hamburger or soft drink. Thinking about their own children and grandchildren, some of whom recognized McDonald's Golden Arches as toddlers, my age mates shake their heads in amazement as they recall that they had their first restaurant meal only after leaving home for college or work.

During recent decades, restaurant outings in Henry County have become commonplace. Local diners certainly do not lack for choice: in 2012, the county boasted forty-four restaurants but only twelve grocery stores. If thirty-three gas stations that serve ready-to-eat food (mostly pizza) are added, it is evident that food consumed at eat-in (or takeout) restaurants has become a commonplace occurrence in the county. Currently, Orion has three taverns that serve food, a full-service restaurant, a Pizza Hut and Subway, plus two gas stations cum convenience stores that sell cooked pizza, doughnuts, sandwiches, as well as prepared foods that can be microwaved on the premises. Andover and Alpha have one full-service restaurant each but no grocery stores, and little Ophiem with a population of fewer than 100 has neither a restaurant nor grocery store. Not only do Henry County residents avail themselves of a variety of local commercial eateries, but they also eat at dozens of restaurants (from McDonalds to fine steak houses) in 'the cities', 10–15 miles from their homes. There is every reason to expect that Henry County residents conform to restaurant trends in the United States generally. According to the Bureau of Labor Statistics in 2010–12, 'food at home' accounted for 5.9 per cent of average annual expenditure per consumer unit and 'food away from home' was not far behind with 4.6 per cent ('Economic News Release', 10 September 2013).

Commensal church gatherings are another gauge of changing foodways and a telling indicator of change. For the sake of brevity, I can say that changes in church-based commensality mirror and dramatize the changes noted above. Until the 1970s, Henry County churches were the centres of a commensal cycle that included ice cream socials, mother–daughter/father–son banquets, smorgasbord (if Lutheran), chicken dinners, suppers of oyster stew (in the fall) and pork chops (in the Spring), wedding receptions and funeral lunches, all of which were punctuated by rounds of coffee, cakes and cookies. The coffees and funeral repasts continue, but the more elaborate suppers and banquets are rare; in many churches, they have disappeared altogether. If they do exist, instead of food cooked in the church kitchen by dozens of church women (and sometimes men) working together, church-based meals are pot luck affairs with food contributions that vary, in my experience, from home-made meat loaf to fried chicken by way of KFC.

CONCLUSION

What do these cookbooks and grocery store ads tell us about changing diets in a rural corner of northern Illinois? One of the most obvious findings is that the time spent and effort required in home cooking has decreased significantly. In the 1800s and early 1900s, Henry County cooks were using coal cook stoves to prepare their meals, hauling water from wells, and eating locally produced foods for a substantial part of their diet. Even those who did not butcher their own livestock or use their own eggs and dairy products depended, at least in part, on local farmers who sold or bartered food at nearby grocery stores, creameries and meat markets. No longer do county residents have to carry buckets of water into their homes, tend gardens, can and preserve garden produce, milk cows or raise chickens. In fact, home gardens, milk cows and chickens are now so rare as to require comment when one encounters them. Eating out and all manner of prepared foods proliferate as branded, processed and convenience foods have come to play an ever more important role in local kitchens. Finally, it is clear that beginning as early as the 1870s when we have newspaper evidence (and no doubt earlier), the farmers and townspeople described here were participating in a national food market. This trend significantly escalated in the 1920s.

In contrast to urban populations, the small towns and farms described here consumed much of their own milk, eggs, butter and meat well into the 1950s.[40] However, once Henry County housewives began to stock their shelves and freezers with convenience foods like jello, condensed soup or frozen vegetables and dinners, there was no turning back. Salads became sweeter, main courses of meat and potatoes often gave way to casseroles and frozen pizzas, and, for some, distinct meals (breakfast, dinner, supper as they were called in farm country) turned into a generalized grazing that included sweets as well as fatty, salty snack foods. One cannot imagine the usual round of local family gatherings or church funeral lunches without jello salads or soup-infused casseroles. In fact, the women of St Paul's Lutheran in Orion produce what is commonly referred to as 'the funeral casserole', which is *derigueur* for the post-burial meals of church members, and relies on the liberal application of condensed soup.

With regard to the time women spend cooking and the skills required to cook, there is no doubt that the life of the home cook in 2015 is far less demanding than the home cook of 1850 or 1950. In her 1852 cookbook, Sarah Hale's recipe for 'Pound Cakes' concludes with these words 'beat together [the ingredients for] half an hour and bake about 1 hour in a brisk oven' (1852: 359). Clearly, it is the rare baker these days, who would hand beat cake ingredients for half an hour; the present-day baker simply adds a commercial leavening agent by means of an electric mixer. Ovens are heated by commercially produced gas or electricity, not by wood or coal, and dialling up the required number on an oven knob controls the temperature. And, finally, washing up is performed by an electric dishwasher. In contrast to Sarah Hale and her nineteenth-century compatriots, since the 1950s, cooks have had the luxury of turning out a never-fail cake by simply adding water and an egg to their cake mix of choice.

In the twenty-first century, many Henry County homes are equipped with elaborate and expensively appointed kitchens, touch dial washers and dryers, computerized cooking stoves, massive refrigerators, food mixers, vacuum cleaners, microwaves and much more. A dizzying variety of processed and convenience foods are available in a variety of locations from 'big box' stores to gasoline stations and more recently online. We are left, therefore, with the obvious question: What are women (and men) doing with all the time they have saved by availing themselves of these conveniences? Has technology, including new food technologies, freed women from the burdens of housework?

Scholars like Ruth Schwartz Cowan argue that, in fact, women are spending nearly as much time in housework as they did decades ago (1983). But, if they are using efficient ovens and washing machines, cake mixes, prepared sauces and meals, and going to restaurants, how is this possible? The simple answer is that housework has been redefined. Women may not haul water or bake their own bread, but they do have larger houses, which means more possessions to clean and organize, and their standards of cleanliness are higher (daily baths and frequent clothing changes have led to constant clothes washing, for example). More importantly, they are spending significant amounts of time in childcare, which now includes driving children to school, to sporting events, to music lessons as well as shopping for a complicated constellation of their children's and family 'needs'. Weekly grocery shopping and general household provisioning may take up a Saturday or more. As Cowan writes, housewives now spend their time 'driving to stores, shopping, and waiting in lines ... or taking the baseball team to the next town'. The automobile, she concludes, has become a key tool in the American housewife's armoury (1983: 85).

Since the late nineteenth century, Americans have experienced a relentless commercialization of housework. Many authors writing the history of changing foodways in the United States refer to the deskilling of home food preparation and a 'decoupling [of] home cooking from femininity' (Turner 2014: 144–50; Levenstein 2003a: 139). Most of the food we eat at home and in restaurants is a product of large corporations, rather than local farms and kitchen gardens. Our foods, like our clothes, furniture and cars, are commercial products. The contents of the packages and cans we open are largely unknown to most of the people who consume them. Is the Orion cook (or any American cook) aware that Jell-O has 19 grams of sugar per serving or a portion of Campbell's soup may contain 17 per cent of one's daily sodium requirement, or a frozen pizza baked at home may have 400 or more calories? As Susan Strasser argues in her path-breaking book, *Never Done*, 'Just as the production of energy and clothing had become work done publicly for profit during the first decades of twentieth century ... by the end of the 1970s, manufactured commodities and commercial services fulfilled many Americans' needs for food, child care, and affection' (1982: 300).

Today, Henry County cooks routinely use convenience foods ('just slice and bake'), make salads from jello and Cool Whip, bring home a pizza from Casey's or take the family out to McDonalds. Some may arrange home deliveries of chilled or frozen meals purveyed by companies like Nutrisystem, Blue Apron or Schwans (all are available and utilized in Henry County). One of Schwan's national distribution centres is based just outside Orion.

We cannot understand dietary changes in the United States without considering changing patterns of women's work. Until the 1970s, women's work tended to be paid employment for unmarried women and unpaid housework for those who married. In 1948, about 17 per cent of married mothers were in the US labour force, but by 1995 the proportion had reached 70 per cent. 'In fact,' Cohany and Sok write, 'married mothers accounted for much of the increase in total labour force participation during the postwar period' (2007: 9). Figures for 2014, show that 70 per cent of US women between the ages of twenty-five and fifty-four are employed; in Henry County the figure is 76 per cent (*New York Times*, 6 January 2015, 'Where Working Women Are Most Common'). As married women joined the labour force in greater and greater numbers, our understanding of housework and what constitutes a 'good housewife' has changed. There is clear evidence that 'a good twenty-first century housewife' does less cooking but more organizing of complex sets of activities and agendas, she saves money not by 'making it herself' but by more savvy consuming, and she contributes – often significantly and sometimes singly – to family resources by bringing in cash through paid employment (see e.g., Turner 2014: 122–49).

Much has been written about the changing functions of women, work and family in the United States. In a reanalysis of time use data from 1965 to more recent studies, contrary to expectations, researchers found that 'parents are spending as much – and perhaps more – time interacting with their children today than in 1965, the heyday of the stay-at-home mother' (Bianchi, Robinson and Milkie 2006: 1). They are managing this intensified parenting in the face of paid employment by various stratagems: men taking on more household chores, by eating out and taking in meals, by using all manner of convenience foods including prepared meals, and, at least in part, by spending more and more of their leisure time with their children. Family life has become more child-centred, which means that parents are spending more time with children and less with friends or other adults (2006: 89). The pages of the *Orion Times* bear out this trend. Until the 1970s, the pages of the *Times* were mostly devoted to news of local adults (voluntary associations, weddings, obituaries, politics, local governance). In the 1 October 2010 issue of the *Orion Gazette* – the paper was renamed in 1992 – news of local (mostly high school) students dominate (six and one-half of a total 12 pages). Not surprisingly, sports news takes pride of place with five and one-half pages.

There is some justification for arguing that beginning in the 1960s and accelerating in the 1980s, many Americans (including residents of Henry County) have come to think of home primarily as a place to care for children (and later grandchildren) and as a personal refuge from a demanding and hostile world. In an important sense dietary changes in Henry County, and in the United States more broadly, are intimately linked to these changes. For many Henry County families the family meal may be an ideal, but work, leisure and school schedules make home-cooked meals an occasional rather than routine occurrence.

It seems appropriate to conclude this discussion by asking whether our discussion of Henry County has anything to contribute to the farm-to-table debates that have captured many food analysts' attention in recent years. Local farmers still produce corn (44,934,000 bushels in 2014)[41] for local processing, but no longer do small town mills or neighbours buy these local crops. Two large, Henry County-based ethanol plants – opened for business in 2008 and 2009 – currently buy and process most (perhaps 80–90 per cent) of the county's corn crop. The ethanol produced in these plants is rail transported to regional and national markets and eventually into the gas tanks of drivers far from the cornfields of northern Illinois. According to their websites, Big River Resources (in Galva, Illinois) 'consume[s] 39 million bushels of corn from the region' and produces 110 million gallons of ethanol annually as well as 320,000 tons of 'livestock feed for local, regional, and national markets'. The figures for Patriot Renewable Fuels, which is locally owned and based in Annawan (also in Henry County), are similar. Soybeans, which run a close second to corn in terms of acreage, are sold locally but also marketed nationally and internationally with some of the country's soybean crop finding its way via the Mississippi River to China. Clearly, the residents of Henry County are not only eating nationally and globally, they are also producing for a huge and complex international market.

Finally, readers may want to know if Henry County has escaped the impact of recent food movements – vegetarianism, farmer's markets, organic foods, dietary changes due to health concerns. There are, in fact, farmers' markets in 'the cities' and a sprinkling of farm stands in Henry County, but – aside from sweet corn and tomatoes – most people I know rarely shop at these venues, arguing that they are too inconvenient or too expensive or both. Local supermarkets, such as the HyVee chain, do have substantial offerings of organic milk, cream, butter and eggs, and there are small sections of organic fruits and vegetables. One can usually find a few packages of organic chicken but, to my knowledge, no organic beef or pork is available in these grocery stores (lamb is very rare). Blueberries are readily available in larger supermarkets and yogurt (albeit laden with sugar) is always on offer. 'Ethnic food' – primarily East Asian and Hispanic – and substantial salad/soup bars were added ten to fifteen years ago. I have never met a vegetarian in Henry County (a ten-year-old girl I met at the Henry County Fair, where she was showing her prize steer, asked me to tell my city friends 'Please eat more beef').

Extensive space in local supermarkets, however, is devoted to 'healthy dieting', and some supermarkets employ dieticians to help people buy groceries and plan meals. A quick survey of the frozen food cases in a nearby supermarket shows that of a total of seventy cases, seventeen are devoted to frozen pizza and twenty-eight to ice cream (HyVee, Galesburg, IL., 2015). Clearly, Henry County residents are fully integrated into an American middle-class food regime that is a far cry from the rural foodways of their grandparents. No longer do they produce what they eat and many no longer cook what they eat.

NOTES

1. Michigan State University Archives, 'Feeding America', digital.ib.msu.edu/projects/ cookbooks; Library of Congress Community Cookbook collection, see Kelly (2012); Hermilda Listeman Collection at University of Illinois, Urbana-Campaign; Szathmary Culinary Archives at the University of Iowa, Iowa City.
2. Here I focus on community cookbooks and grocery store ads, but it is worth noting that there are many other indicators of foodway changes, most prominently, women's magazines, home economics curricula and food manufacturers' advertising and promotion campaigns.

3. Stavely and Fitzgerald warn that we should not assume cookbooks mirror dietary realities (2011: 2). This is a useful warning, especially with regard to commercial cookery books. See also K. W. Claflin (2013).

4. For a detailed discussion of the history of cookbooks in New England, see Stavely and Fitzgerald (2011).

5. See also Birkbeck's description of foods he encountered during his family's journey from coastal Virginia to the Alleghany Mountains in 1817 (in Boewe 1962: 24).

6. Cowan points out that by the 1880s 'the fundamental designs for large-scale compression and absorption installations [for refrigeration] had been perfected' but refrigerators did not become household appliances until the 1930s (1983: 129, 133–4).

7. Washburn Mills was established in 1866 and eventually became part of General Mills (maker of Gold Medal Flour) in the 1920s. Pillsbury Company was bought by General Mills in 2011, but, due to Antitrust laws, its dry baking products are now sold (under licence) by Smuckers.

8. American wheat farmers and millers first profited from the disruption of the French Revolution and Napoleonic Wars and exported most of the superfine flour they produced. This flour, from which germ and bran had been removed, did not deteriorate and was eminently exportable. In the 1820s, canals opened up markets for milled flour within the eastern United States (see Cowan 1983: 47).

9. In the United States, as elsewhere, cuisine continues to mark difference, with the capacity to emphasize ethnic, class, racial, status, regional and individual differences.

10. Canning techniques and the transition from glass to metal cans dates to the early nineteenth century (see Collins 1994: 18–21). Gail Borden's condensed milk helped supply the Union Army during the Civil War with a vital food source, but it was not until the 1870s that Abraham Anderson and Joseph Campbell, building on these innovations, produced their first products (Collins 1994: 24). In 1897, Campbell's condensed soup began its meteoric rise (Collins 1994: 37).

11. John Dorrance (nephew of Arthur Dorrance) was a graduate of MIT and received a PhD from the University of Gottingen in Germany. He joined Campbell Soup Company in 1897 (Collins 1994: 13, 30, 44).

12. Before large-scale production, making gelatin had depended on a time-consuming cooking process in home kitchens. Gelatin was made from boiling calves feet into which were mixed egg shells and whites (see Wyman 2001: 1–2).

13. Source: 'Population 1790 to 1990', www.census.gov/population/censusdata/table-4.

14. Only a few, in some cases only two or three members of these colony associations, actually took up residence in Henry County.

15. For discussion of reasons behind disbanding Bishop Hill Colony see Swanson 1998; Elmen 1976: 148–69.

16. "The cities" include the Illinois communities of Moline, and Rock Island and just across the Mississippi River in Iowa, the urban centres of Davenport and Bettendorf.

17. Population figures for 1920 and 1980 are from *Population of Counties by Decennial Census, 1900-1990*, US Bureau of the Census, Washington DC, www.census.gov/populatin/cencounts/1900-90.txt. Figures for 2010 are from *Henry County* [Illinois], *County Quickfacts*, US. Census Bureau, http://quickfacts.census.gov/qfd/states/17/17073.html.

18. Sources: *USDA Census of Agriculture Historical Archives, 1925*, Illinois-Henry County, p. 496. USDA, National Agricultural Statistics Service, 2012 Census of Agriculture, County Profile (Henry County, IL).

19. In 2010, just over 19% of the US population lived in rural areas (Source: US Census Bureau: Frequently Asked Questions). https://ask.census.gov/faq.php?id= 5000&faqid=5971 (accessed 1 August 2014). Proportion of rural population for 1920 Source: *Chicago Daily News Almanac and Yearbook for 1922*, ed. by James Langland, 1921. Chicago: Chicago Daily News Corp. Source for percentage of rural population of total Henry County population in 2012, www.city-data.com/county/ Henry_County-IL.html (p. 1).

20. Source: www.city-data.com/county/Henry-County-IL.html (p. 3).

21. Source: www.city-data.com/county/Henry-County-Il.html (p. 7).

22. From June 1877 to January 1878, the newspaper was published under the title of *The Orion Vidette*, from 1878 to 6 February 1992 it was the *Orion Times*, and since 1992 to the present it appears under the title of the *Orion Gazette*. The Orion Times briefly ceased publication in October 1887 until 6 July 1888. I examined all issues of *The Orion Vidette* (13 June to 20 December 1877) and *Orion Times* issues for May and December for years 1907, 1917, 1927, 1937, 1947, 1957, 1967. Other issues were spot-checked.

23. www.westerndistrict.advantage-preservation.com.

24. A fifth town, Lynn Center also in western Henry County, is not included here because it has no church; and, therefore, no cookbooks.

25. By jello, I refer to packaged, sugared, flavoured, powdered gelatin, which includes the brand Jell-O and other brands as well.

26. In her book, Joy Lintelman provides a very useful illustration of diets among Swedish-Americans living in rural Minnesota. After a house fire in 1895, the state of Minnesota issued the following thirty-day supply of food:

    Two hundred lbs. flour; 3 lbs. coffee; 15 lbs. sugar; 1 lb tea; 1 lb baking powder; 1 lb soda; ½ bu beans; 10 lbs. rice; 8 pounds fish; 10 bars soap; 2 pkgs. yeast; 2 sacks salt; 1 pkg. Matches, 6 lbs. lard; 1 bottle bluing [for laundry]; 45 lbs. pork; 2 pails jelly; 1 gal. syrup; 8 lbs. crackers; 1 box pepper; 3 lbs. breakfast food (2009: 175).

27. *United States Census of Agriculture: 1945*, Vol. 1, Pt. 5, Illinois, Statistics for Counties, Henry County, County Table 1, p. 25.

28. In his *From Prairie to Corn Belt*, Bogue writes: 'What is a hog but fifteen or twenty bushels of corn on four legs' (2011: 105).

29. *United States Census of Agriculture: 1945*, Vol. 1, Pt. 5, Illinois, Statistics for Counties, Henry County, County Table 1, pp. 116–17.

30. For a discussion on the importance of eggs, cream, butter, chickens to farm economy and to farm women, see Fink (1992: Chapters 4 and 5).

31. *United States Census of Agriculture: 1945*, Vol 1, Pt. 5, Illinois, Statistics for Counties, 'Farms and Farm Characteristics, Census of 1920 to 1945', State Table 1. *United States Census of Agriculture, 1954*, Vol. 1, Counties and States Economic Areas, Pt. 5, Illinois, State Table 4, p. 12.

32. Alpha for example, had electric streetlights in 1900, a water system in 1897 and a central telephone service in 1901 ('Village of Alpha, Illinois, 1872-1997', p. 10).

33. Newspaper ads for 'Public Sales' of farm animals, implements and household goods provide information about home appliances, as does a section labelled 'the Billboard', which appeared occasionally and listed used items for sale. In the 21 February 1946 (p. 6) issue of the *Orion Times*, for example, the list of items to be auctioned includes a 'Kerosene Stove Oven, Heating Stove, cook-stove, Cream Separator ... sewing machine ... Aladdin Lamp ... [and] about 3 tons coal'. And, on 4 March 1948, a 'Hamilton Beech Vacuum sweeper' and an 'ivory enamel cook stove' were advertised.

34. The manufacturer, not a local Orion merchant, placed the ad for Royal Baking Powder. The ad testifies to the powder's reliability and purity.

35. Jersey Cream was both a brand name and also the name of a type of highly refined flour used in cakes.

36. Orion Mills, owned by Johnson, Lloyd, and Company, produced 'The Best Grades of Flour in the Market' in Orion from 1873. The first ad for Orion Mills Flour appears in *The Orion Vidette* on 20 June 1877, p. 5. Orion Mills burned down on 26 July 1890 (*Orion Times*, 1 August 1890; Polson 1968: 176). On 21 May 1908, the *Orion Times* carried an ad for Orion Mills (with a new owner), which at this point appears to be offering grinding services for livestock feed. One of the first mills Henry County was built in the 1830s near Andover on the Edwards River. The Andover mill burned in 1868 but was rebuilt and finally dismantled and sent to Kansas in 1881 (Calendar booklet, 'State Bank of Orion: 100 Year Anniversary Calendar, 1990'; Polson 1968: 151–2).

37. For discussion of war shortages in the United States, see Levenstein 2003a: 80–8. Historians of American foodways point out that during the Second World War many American soldiers were exposed to 'new foods'. Levenstein notes that southern soldiers, for example, accustomed to a 'hog 'n hominy', cornmeal diet were introduced to 'beef, potatoes, white bread, and milk' (2003b: 146; see also Carroll 2013: 175–6).

38. 27 March 1927 for Jell-O and 1 June 1922 for Campbell's Soup. It should be noted that Armour's soup and Richelieu jello ads predated ads for their more famous competitors (14 January 1915 for Armour soup; 29 January 1925 for Richelieu jello). It is not clear to me whether Armour was selling 'concentrated' or condensed soup in 1915.

39. Entitled 'A Traditional Christmas Eve Dinner', the menu includes: 'Lute Fisk (Stock Fish), Boiled Potatoes, Potatis Curv (Potato Blogna), Bruna Boner (Brown Beans), Fruksoppa (Fruit Soup), Rye Bread, Butter, Coffee', p. 1.

40. For a discussion of rural diets during the late nineteenth century, see Levenstein 2003a: 27–30.

41. USDA, National Agricultural Statistics Service, Heartland Regional Field Office, 'Illinois County Estimates' (February 2015), p. 1. (http://www.nass.usda.gov). In 1945, acres devoted to corn was 197,611. Source: United States Census of Agriculture: 1945, Vol. 1, pt. 5, Statistics for Counties, Henry County (Illinois), County Table 2, p. 59.

REFERENCES

Primary Sources: Cookbooks

A Century of Cooking: 1889-1989, Grace Lutheran Church, Ophiem, Illinois, 1989.

Andover Lutheran Church Presents: Jenny Lind Cook Book, Kansas City: Bev-RonPublishing Company, 1974 (Andover, Illinois).

Cook Book, St Paul Lutheran Church, Kansas City: Bev-Ron Publishing Company, 1951.

Cook Book: Favorite Recipes, Woman's Society of Christian Service, Methodist Church, Alpha, Illinois, 1951.

Country Cooken: Plain and Fancy, Mary, Our Lady of Peace Church, Orion, Illinois, 1967 (Orion Roman Catholic Church).

God's Work, Our Hands: Celebrating the Ark, Kearny, NE: Morris Press Cookbooks, 2010 (St Paul Evangelical Lutheran Church, Orion, Illinois).

Graceful Cooking, Grace Lutheran Church, Ophiem, Illinois, 2000.

Luther Ann Cookbook, Grace Lutheran Church, Ophiem, Illinois, 1936.

Secondary Sources

Anderson, W. and Norcross, K. (1977), *A History of Western of Township*, No publisher.

Beecher, C. and Beecher Stowe, H. (2002), *The American Woman's Home*, N. Tonkovich (ed.), New Brunswick, NJ: Rutgers University Press. (Originally published 1869).

Bianchi, S., Robinson, J. and Milkie, M. (2006), *Changing Rhythms of American Family Life*, New York: Russell Sage Foundation.

Billington, R. A. (1951), 'The Frontier in Illinois History', *Journal of the Illinois State Historical Society*, 43(10): 28–45.

Boewe, C. (1962), *Prairie Albion: An English Settlement in Pioneer Illinois*, Carbondale: Southern Illinois University Press.

Bogue, A. G. (2011), *From Prairie to Corn Belt: Farming on the Illinois and Iowa Prairies in the Nineteenth Century*, 2nd edn, Lanham, MD: Ivan R. Dee (First published in 1963).

Boles, F. (2006), '"Stirring Constantly": 150 Years of Michigan Cookbooks', *Michigan Historical Review*, 32(2): 33–62.

Burlend, R. and E. (1987), *A True Picture of Emigration*, Lincoln and London: University of Nebraska Press (Originally published in 1848).

Carroll, A. (2013), *Three Squares: The Invention of the American Meal*, New York: Basic Books.

Claflin, K. W. (2013), 'Representations of Food Production and Consumption: Cookbooks as Historical Sources', in A. Murcott, W. Belasco and P. Jackson (eds), *The Handbook of Food Research*, 109–27, London: Bloomsbury.

Cohany, S. and Sok, E. (2007), 'Trends in Labor Force Participation of Married Mothers of Infants', *Monthly Labor Review*, February: 9–15.

Collins, D. (1994), *America's Favorite Food: The Story of Campbell Soup Company*, New York: Harry N. Abrams Inc.

Cowan, R. S. (1983), *More Work for Mother: The Ironies of Household Technology fromthe Open Hearth to the Microwave*, New York: Basic Books.

Cromley, E. C. (2010), *The Food Axis: Cooking, Eating, and the Architecture of American Houses*, Charlottesville: University of Virginia Press.

Cutler, D. M., Edward, G. and Jose, S. (2003), 'Why Have Americans Become More Obese?' *Journal of Economic Perspectives*, 17(3): 93–118.

Drury, J. (1955), Henry County, Illinois. *The American Aerial County Historical Series*, No. 24, Chicago: The Loree Company.

Elmen, P. (1976), *Wheat Flour Messiah: Eric Jansson of Bishop Hill*, Carbondale: Southern Illinois University Press.

Faragher, J. M. (1986), *Sugar Creek: Life on the Illinois Prairie*, New Haven: Yale University Press.

Farmer, F. M. (1896), *The Boston Cooking-School Cook Book*, Boston, MA: Little, Brown.

Fink, D. (1992), *Agrarian Women: Wives and Mothers in Rural Nebraska, 1880-1940*, Chapel Hill: University of North Carolina Press.

Gabaccia, D. R. (1998), *We Are What We Eat: Ethnic Food and the Making of Americans*, Cambridge, MA: Harvard University Press.

Hale, S. J. (2012), *The Ladies New Book of Cookery*, Forgotten Books (Originally published in 1852).

Kander, L. B. (1903), *The Settlement Cookbook*, New York: Hugh Lauter Associates.

Kiner, H. (1910), *History of Henry County, Illinois*, Vol. II, Chicago: The Pioneer Publishing Company.

Levenstein, H. (2003a), *Paradox of Plenty: A Social History of Eating in Modern America*, rev. edn, Berkeley: University of California Press (Originally published in 1993, New York: Oxford University Press).

Levenstein, H. (2003b), *Revolution at the Table: The Transformation of the American Diet*, Berkeley: University of California Press (Originally Published in 1988, New York: Oxford University Press).

Lintelman, J. (2009), *I Go to America: Swedish Women and the Life of Mina Anderson*, Minneapolis: Minnesota Historical Society Press.

Marks, S. (2005), *Finding Betty Crocker: The Secret Life of America's First Lady of Food*, New York: Simon and Schuster (Reprinted by University of Minnesota Press, 2007).

Meyer, D. (2000), *Making the Heartland Quilt: A Geographical History of Settlement and Migration in Early-Nineteenth Century Illinois*, Carbondale: Southern Illinois University Press.

Oliver, W. (2002), *Eight Months in Illinois with Information to Immigrants*, Carbondale: Southern Illinois Press (Originally published in 1843).

Pollan, M. (2013), *Cooked: A Natural History of Transformation*, New York: Penguin.

Polson, T. E. (1968), *Corn, Commerce, and Country Living: A History of Henry County, Illinois*, Moline, IL: Desaulniers and Company.

Sidorick, D. (2009), *Condensed Capitalism: Campbell Soup and the Pursuit of Cheat Production in the Twentieth Century*, Ithaca, NY: Cornell University Press.

Smith, A. F. (2007), 'Wheat', in A. F. Smith (ed.), *The Oxford Encyclopedia of Food and Drink in America*, 619–20, Oxford: Oxford University Press.

Stavely, K. and Fitzgerald, K. (2011), *Northern Hospitality: Cooking By the Book in New England*, Amherst and Boston: University of Massachusetts Press.

Strasser, S. (1982), *Never Done: A History of American Housework*, New York: Pantheon Books.

Strasser, S. (1989), *Satisfaction Guaranteed: The Making of the American Mass Market*, New York: Pantheon.

Swanson, A. (1998), 'The Road to Perfection', in *Nobler Things to View: Collected Essays on the Erik Janssonists*, 66–81, Bishop, IL: Bishop Hill Heritage Association.

Tonkovich, N. (2002), 'Introduction', in N. Tonkovich, *The American Woman's Home by Catharine Beecher and Harriet Beecher Stowe*, ix–xxxi, New Brunswick, NJ: Rutgers University Press.

Trager, J. (1995), *The Food Chronology*, New York: Henry Holt and Company.

Turner, K. L. (2014), *How the Other Half Ate: A History of Working-Class Meals at the Turn of the Century*, Berkeley: University of California Press.

Wood, B. (1922), *Foods of the Foreign Born in Relation to Health*, Boston: Whitcomb and Barrows.

Wyman, C. (2001), *Jell-O: A Biography*, San Diego, New York, and London: Harcourt, Inc.

CHAPTER SIXTEEN

The Anthropology of Cooking

DAVID SUTTON

INTRODUCTION

There is little doubt that the study of food and food preparation can be traced back to the very beginnings of the discipline of modern anthropology, or even to the ancient anthropological reflections of Herodotus on relativism and mortuary cannibalism. Yet when I began teaching a course on the anthropology of food, titled 'Food, Symbol and Society,' to undergraduates at the University of New Hampshire in 1998, it was challenging finding a lively, accessible set of readings, even more challenging finding *ethnographies* of food for classroom use. And I was also struck by the questions provoked by students, friends and even colleagues about my class: what would an anthropology of food entail? Nutrition? Agriculture? How different things look in 2014. Now putting together my course – still titled, for better or worse, 'Food, Symbol and Society' – confronts me with a plethora of choices, from ritual and religious practices, kinship and ethnic/national identities, to consumption, exchange and globalization, commodification and 'public' eating, and even a lively literature on embodiment, memory and sensory experience, as well as a growing list of food-based ethnographies to choose from. And our understanding of these areas of human practice has grown tremendously in the past fifteen years. One might think that all aspects of the study of food are now well represented in the anthropological and ethnographic literature, and one would be right, except, that is, for food preparation, or cooking, where the same lacunae that I confronted in 1998 still remain – with, of course, a few notable exceptions – and even more so when it comes to dedicated ethnographies of cooking practices. In this chapter I will review the small corpus of existing anthropological works on cooking, to suggest some of the ways that ethnographic studies of cooking might illuminate a number of key areas of anthropological study, as well as being of interest in their own right. That is, I will argue that we should study cooking both as a window onto other cultural processes, as well as recognizing the significance of cooking *as cooking*.

ANTHROPOLOGICAL REFLECTIONS
ON COOKING

In looking at previous literature on cooking, it is striking to note that cooking has played a considerably larger role in *anthropological* reflections on what it means to be human than it has provoked ethnographic explorations of cooking *as practice*. Claude Lévi-Strauss most notably saw cooking as the key to understanding the human transition from nature to culture. Lévi-Strauss also suggested the importance of human–technology relations in this view of cooking: the more technology involved (boiling in a pot vs. roasting directly on a fire, for example), the more 'cultural' (though he saw smoking food as the most cultural). He also mapped these classifications onto other symbolic categories including inner and outer, frugal and prodigal, ephemeral and durable, and, of course, male and female: 'Thus we can hope to discover for each specific case how the cooking of a society is a language in which it unconsciously translates its structure' (2008: 43). In typical Lévi-Straussian style, these categories could be inverted, as in the association of men with roasting – the eternal question, 'Why do men barbeque?' – and women with boiling, which is inverted by the Assiniboin of North America. Or the association of boiling and smoking with culture is seemingly reversed by the simultaneous association of boiled meat with rotten meat, and the need among 'natives of Guiana' (2008: 41), to destroy the apparatus for smoking meat immediately after use to avoid pollution. As Lévi-Strauss puts it, 'Everything transpires as if the lasting possession of a cultural acquisition entailed, sometimes in the ritual realm, sometimes in the mythic, a concession made in return to nature' (2008: 41–2).

More recently, biological anthropologist Richard Wrangham has updated and broadened Lévi-Strauss's claim for the centrality of cooking. Wrangham's (2010) argument boils down to cooking being the central motor of human evolution since its discovery, which he dates at approximately 1.8 million years ago.[1] It was the discovery of cooking, not warfare or some other social process, not even meat eating, which drove the changes from habilines to *Homo erectus*; and it was improvements in cooking which led to more recent evolutionary changes. This is because the energy unlocked in cooked food and the time saved in digestion freed up human creative capacity for brain growth and, eventually, complex social relations. His arguments seem impressive, but when it comes to speculating on the implications of cooking for human social structure, Wrangham is on shakier grounds in claiming that the supposed universal division of labour in which men hunt and women cook was a necessary adaptation, which he describes as a 'primitive protection racket' in which 'having a husband ensures that a woman's gathered foods will not be taken by others; having a wife ensures the man will have an evening meal' (2010: 154). While I will be considering the implications of cooking for gender relations in what follows, I part company with Wrangham's deterministic views of the implications of evolution on social structure that his speculations (and indeed, they are speculations, as no evidence of social structure of *Homo erectus* is available) lead him to.

Jack Goody moves us from the universally human to broad historical sweeps, focusing on social processes that have structured cooking over the past several millennia in Europe, Asia and Africa. In his *Cooking, Cuisine and Class* (1982), Goody makes an argument for the importance of key structural factors in shaping cooking, factors that he has given attention to in his many other works on the development of the different societies of Europe, Asia and Africa. These factors include the environmental and technology, such as the role of writing and cookbooks, hoe versus plough agriculture, and the preservation processes that allowed for the development of the food industry in the late nineteenth century. They also include the importance of class difference in allowing for the development of elite cuisines that were significantly different in quality rather than just in quantity, and indeed reflected other divisions of society conceptually and socially into 'the high and the low' (Goody 1982:97). Cooking, here, is examined schematically for its place in society alongside other major activities such as writing, or hoe versus plough agriculture. What we don't get, however, from Lévi-Strauss, Wrangham or Goody, is an ethnographic sense of cooking as part of people's daily lives.

Cooking, however, was not completely absent from British classical ethnography. Here, then, I turn to some early forays into cooking as represented by two important figures in the British school of anthropology: Audrey Richards and Rosemary Firth.

ETHNOGRAPHIC FOREBEARS

Audrey Richards' *Land, Labour and Diet in Northern Rhodesia* (1939) is a touchstone for anthropological studies of food and nutrition as perhaps the first book-length ethnography of food and eating practices, including rich analyses of food production, cooking and meal practices, as well as their nutritional implications. For my purposes, the sections of the book on cooking are notable for a number of features: First, Richards places cooking within a larger concept of 'housecraft,' the difficult, largely female tasks of managing technical and social challenges. As Richards puts it, 'The real difficulty of housecraft is the organization of time and labour, the calculation of quantities by a system which depends entirely on empirical judgments, and, as we shall see, a knowledge of the rules of hospitality and the dues of different kinsmen' (1939: 107). Thus, Richards describes time allocation and timing of different food-related tasks, as well as planning, or lack thereof, in daily meal preparation. Timing, once again, is seen as both a technical question – how long various roots generally need to boil – and a social one, or as Richards notes, 'I never heard a Bemba husband complain that his meal was late' (1939: 74). Second, Richards clearly situates cooking within the *powers* held by women, and control of cooking is shown to be a valued source of social control. This generally plays out in the control that mothers exercise over their daughters' labour, which extends past marriage until a younger woman is '"given a fire-place" by her mother and is allowed to cook in her own hut' (1939: 125). Richards argues that a woman develops prestige as her control over cooking and her cooking skill develops. But this prestige is framed as always in deference to the men for whom cooked food is provided, particularly husbands and son-in-laws. Indeed, she suggests that co-wives compete with each other to cook the best meal for their husbands, and that husbands also work to direct their wives' cooking towards the provisioning of hospitality for their friends, suggesting an appropriation of female-produced value by men. Richards sums up: 'The Bemba woman's prestige largely rests on her power to provide porridge and relish for her male relatives and to serve it nicely. These are the dues a man expects from his mother-in-law, his wife, and a number of other women in his kinship group' (1939: 129). Finally, although Richards does not provide extensive ethnographic descriptions of learning cooking, she does suggest several interesting features of Bemba learning, in particular that young girls are taught more typically in sibling or peer-group contexts than in more hierarchical ones, and that proficiency in cooking is thought to develop with age and long experience, a reflection of the fact that very little explicit measurement is involved in Bemba cooking techniques. As Richards' similarly notes in relation to beer making: 'No housewife could give me exact instructions as to the quantities of grain used and the time taken, but was apparently guided by judgment based on long experience, or as she herself would express it, with vigour: "Young girls can't make beer. Only we elders know how to brew"' (1939: 97). We will see many of these insights and themes further developed in more recent cooking ethnographies.

Rosemary Firth's work on Malay cooking, published some 20 plus years after Richards', is less extensively developed, but also contains suggestive insights. Firth was a colleague of Richards through her husband (she, herself, never got a degree in anthropology), and drew explicitly on Richards' approach in her fieldwork (Firth 1995). Like Richards, Firth raises issues of gender and power in relation to cooking. In part this was to confront stereotypes about Muslim women's powerlessness (ibid.). In the Malay fishing village where she did fieldwork, Firth finds that women are not exclusive cooks; men in fact cook on different occasions, 'when a woman is ill or busy' (Firth 1966: 24), as well as on feast occasions. But primary duty for cooking still falls on women and male cooking has the aura of a special occasion: 'The attitude is that a man can cook, if he wants to or needs to, but that he usually has other things to do, and therefore expects the woman to do it for him' (1966: 25).

One other interesting feature of Firth's ethnographic descriptions of cooking is that she includes some material on *individual* attitudes towards cooking of named informants. For example, we learn that Sone, who was small and thin and 'ate very little compared with other people' (1966: 79), substituted purchased snacks sometimes for the daily rice-based meal. Despite this, Firth describes Sone as a good cook and housekeeper, who thought about provisioning in advance, thus suggesting good time management skills. As Firth quotes Sone: 'When I want to make a curry, I don't like to have to go running out to the shops every time to buy this and to buy that. I like to have onions and the other things in the house. Most women, when they want these things, off they go to buy a cent's worth' (1966: 79). This is suggestive of the significant relationship of cooking to shopping as deserving of further ethnographic exploration.[2]

Despite these promising beginnings, the ethnography of cooking largely languished in the second half of the twentieth century. While this is a topic for historical research, I would speculate that some of this disinterest might be attributed to the particular directions of second-wave feminist anthropology. Western feminism's ambivalence towards cooking – seen as simply another domestic 'chore' like cleaning the bathroom, thus a source of oppression – meant that the rise of feminist anthropology in the mid-1970s didn't lead to any noticeable growth in studies of cooking. Indeed, pioneer Michelle Rosaldo, in claiming that 'the wives of herders, agriculturalists and businessmen lead lives that are conceptualized in remarkably similar terms,' (Rosaldo 1974:29 n.8), seemed to imply that 'domestic' activities were relatively uninteresting anthropologically speaking, and it was only when women stepped into the so-called 'public sphere' that they became involved in socially valued activities of 'articulat[ing] and express[ing] social differences' (1974: 29).[3] Ethnographic works on cooking by and large only have started to get going again with the renewed interest in food studies since the 1990s, and it is to these studies that I now turn.

WHAT IS COOKING?

In this section I explore what anthropologists have written about cooking in recent decades by posing the question 'what is cooking'? I don't wish to be strictly definitional, but rather to suggest some broad and overlapping categories through which anthropologists have thought about the significance of cooking in society, and its ethnographic study. Thus, I break down my discussion into short sections on these topics, while also attempting to suggest some of the places that further ethnographic exploration seems in order.

Cooking as Power (or Oppression) and Identity

The predominant role of women in feeding is a cultural universal, a major component of female identity, and an important source of female connections to and influence over others. Hence, although there are other components of female identity and other sources of their authority, the power of women has often derived from the power of food. (Counihan 1999: 46)

This concise statement by Counihan sums up the significance of studying cooking in relation to questions of identity and power. And although the universality of female cooking is perhaps not completely settled, possible exceptions are not well documented at this time.[4] Counihan ascribes the power that women accrue through feeding to the influence that anthropologists have always seen to be attached to 'gift exchange' (1999: 46–7), though noting that men may sometimes claim this influence by controlling the distribution of food cooked by women. Thus, the relationship of power, identity and gender in relation to cooking is not straightforward, and demands careful ethnographic exploration.

As feminists in anthropology and other fields began challenging the distinction between public and private, showing repeatedly how it does not capture the fluidity of people's lives, kitchen activities became a subject worthy of scrutiny. The key question that emerged was precisely the extent to which cooking might be seen as a source of women's oppression or empowerment. The answers were diverse depending on context, circumstance and approach (see, e.g. Counihan 1999; DeVault 1997; Murcott 1983). But broadly speaking, one might suggest a correlation between the amount of blurriness between notions of public and private and the amount of power associated with cooking. For example, Anne Allison depicts a situation in which Japanese women prepare *obento* lunch boxes for their young children attending school. These *obentos* are a source of considerable labour-intensive investment for mothers, and like the cases described by Richards and Firth, are seen as a duty for women. And although Allison notes that a few mothers describe aesthetic satisfaction in producing pleasing *obentos*, the thrust of her analysis is to show how the school uses these as a source of surveillance of mothers and children's conformity to its norms, as part of a larger *ideological state apparatus* (a concept adopted from Althusser). Here even though the food itself travels outside of the domestic setting, this does not mitigate the notion that in this advanced capitalist society cooking is part of the isolation of women from the public sphere and public value. As she notes, 'Females have remained at and as the center of home in Japan, and this message too is explicitly transmitted in both the production and consumption of entirely female-produced *obento*' (1991: 310).

A very different image is portrayed by Brett Williams in her depiction of the role of cooking for Tejano migrant women. Here, in a nod to the notion of the 'myth of male dominance' (Leacock 1981; Rogers 1975), Williams admits that on the surface cooking seems to be all about women's deference to men, and failure to cook for a husband is, in legendary cases, significant grounds for divorce. Williams suggests that the rhetoric of subservience disguises the power inherent in being the provider of tamales. This is because whereas in the Japanese case described by Allison cooking is restricted to the nuclear family (the women are preparing *obentos* for 'their' children), in the case of Tejano migrants cooking is part of a cycle of festivities in which bonds are created both within the community and with members of the dominant Anglo society, a way of creating a sort of social capital that can be called upon in times of need. Both cooking and eating are not restricted to the home, but take place in public spaces. And while some women are central to networks, they often call upon the labour of other women, sisters, grandmothers, aunts, etc., for the labour-intensive process of producing hundreds of tamales for communal feasts and *quinceneras* meant to explicitly recognize female adulthood and dignity. Thus, like Richards, Williams points us to the importance of embedding any ethnography of cooking in an understanding of kinship, and not just gender relations. For Williams, cooking brings women together and allows them to extend their social networks and gain influence far beyond the immediate family, while for Allison cooking, even when it travels beyond the home, is part of women's isolation from generally valued social goods, a chore and a task that men and other cultural agents could demand of women, and judge their failure to comply.

More recently, various scholars have shown the ways that cooking could be simultaneously oppressive *and* a 'recipe for agency' (Counihan 2010: 128). Counihan's depiction of the 'Mexicano' community in southern Colorado where she conducted extensive life-history research resonates with Williams' work in a number of ways, in particular in terms of the networks of connections women make through food, which allow them to confront various life crises with confidence and support. However, Counihan also shows how many women complain about the burden of cooking, and some negotiate with family members the right *not to cook*. Other women in her study describe the combined sense of 'drudgery when it was routine and compulsory but a great satisfaction when she had time and could be creative' (2010: 121). Meanwhile, studies of cooking and masculinity suggest that cooking has been a fertile ground for male appropriation of female traditional practices for hegemonic gendered purposes, whether in a domestic or professional context such as televised cooking shows or high-tech kitchen laboratories such as those of Molecular Gastronomy or America's Test Kitchen (Holden 2007; Roosth 2012). One element that is perhaps under-stressed in these discussions is the cultural values given to cooking in different contexts. While I'll discuss the question of values further below, it is important to note that the control of cooking may be more or less of a valued cultural resource to the extent that the *taste of food matters* and is considered part of public discourse and commentary. In contexts where the taste of food is not seen as an important cultural value it may be easy to subsume daily cooking to other types of drudgery such as laundry or cleaning the toilet. But in contexts where daily taste does matter at a community or societal level cooking may represent valued knowledge, and a scarce resource.

Implicit in this discussion is the relationship of cooking to identity, gendered and at other intersections. The relationship of cooking and identity is explored in the work of a number of scholars focusing on the potential of the kitchen as women's spaces for social commentary and the transmission of personal and family histories (Abarca 2006; Counihan 2004). But it also is clearly part of the process of creating and reproducing ethnic and national identities. This is summed up in the title of Beoku-Betts' piece on Gullah foodways: 'We got our way of cooking things.' Beoku-Betts explores the centrality of rice cooking to the foodways of the Gullah communities of coastal Georgia and South Carolina, posing their foodways in relation to a dominant Anglo culture as well as to that of the larger African-American community. In doing so, Beoku-Betts shows that rice preparation is a *total social fact* encompassing spheres of subsistence, exchange, community ritual and collective memory. She shows, for example, that preparation of mealtime was also a time for sharing stories, folktales, songs and dances:

> I learned about formerly enslaved women who prepared special rice cakes made with honey for their families on particular days and months of the year, in observance of Muslim religious festivals. Women also told me about folk traditions such as a song called 'Blow Tony Blow.' This accompanied a traditional dance still performed by Gullah women at cultural festivals to demonstrate how rice grain was removed from its husk with a flat, round, woven grass-basket called a fanner. (Beoku-Betts 1995: 543)

This stresses the role of food in transmission of collective memory and identity to the next generation. It also shows that preparation tools and techniques can serve as cultural artefacts that represent identity in the way that Annette Weiner (1992) has analysed for the 'inalienable possessions' of Melanesia. Not only tools but also techniques and recipes serve such roles. While recipes include the flexibility of oral tradition, and 'depend to some extent on one's particular taste,' they also encode communal history: 'Each person emphasizes that the rice has to be washed well and that it must be cooked in just enough water to allow it to steam on its own, without the interference of draining or stirring … follow[ing] a common tradition handed down from the period of slavery and still practiced in present-day West African rice cultures' (Beoku-Betts 1995: 546). Such food lore, skill, knowledge and recipes that make up Gullah identity are seen as under threat from the dominant culture and the forces of modernity. It becomes women's role in the community to parse the various changes that are seen as acceptable, and those that might undermine Gullah foodways and culture: 'Cultural preservation through food preparation and feeding is a highly conscious act on the part of these women, it is tied closely to their judgments about when to accept, and when to resist, change' (1995: 553). In many ways this approach is similar to much work in the anthropology of food that stresses the importance of various food practices to dominant or minority cultural identities, the main difference being the focus on food *preparation* and its relationship to issues of power and resistance. Here, gender becomes not as much a source of oppression, as in Allison's argument, but of women's status as preservers of community value. Beoku-Betts notes that in the Gullah community, much like in the Malaysian fishing village described by Firth, men are expected to fend for themselves if women are too busy with other activities to provide cooked food, suggesting a wider flexibility in gender roles that may be part of African-American culture, as well as that of other oppressed groups. Responsibility for the preservation of cooking/culture can, however, be a burden as well, as described in many immigrant groups in which women must be guardians of tradition, reinforcing their association with child enculturation, while men are culture brokers expected to interact with and integrate parts of the dominant culture.

All this squarely raises questions of cooking as knowledge and as something that is seen to be 'transmitted' from one generation to the next, potentially conserved or lost, raising further questions that I consider below.

Cooking as Knowledge

The most comprehensive ethnography that treats cooking as knowledge is Liora Gvion's *Beyond Hummus and Falafel* (2012), describing cooking among Israeli Palestinians. In some ways Gvion's approach echoes that of Beoku-Betts, examining how cooking forms 'a cultural reservoir preserving a distinct national identity' within a larger, oppressive society (Gvion 2012: 10). The difference is one of emphasis: in Gvion's ethnography food forms a 'system of knowledge' which women control both in terms of the 'theoretical knowledge' of cooking, but also the 'practical knowledge' of how to create a proper meal, while at the same time reproducing 'the semiotic system and cultural beliefs in which food is enmeshed' (2012: 173n.13). Thus, cooking is seen as part of 'women's ways of knowing' (2012: 29), and can be divided into technological knowledge, thrift, ability to create variety in taste, and the deep knowledge of ingredients and their associated techniques for processing that all fall into this domain. Like the Gullah, Palestinian women must also balance competing demands of so-called 'tradition' and 'modernity.' Here 'modernity' is represented by the dominant Israeli culture, as well as various other foreign foods (Italian, Chinese) and foods like margarine, instant coffee, canned vegetables and pre-prepared hummus and other foods sold by the food industry. These are seen as representing modernity because of their association with values such as health, thrift and time/labour saving, as well as for their cosmopolitan associations. They also are seen as produced by 'modern' technologies, thus stressing the connection of machines with hygiene (2012: 105). Women have to negotiate the tricky boundaries of incorporating these foods in recognizable form into the local food system, while preserving a place at the same time for 'tradition.' Instant coffee, for example, is adopted because it is considered healthier since it is mixed with milk and provides calcium to older users, as opposed to the typical black coffee. It is also seen as a special drink to serve to guests 'like the Jews [do], because it's more festive and prestigious' (2012: 122). Thus, new kinds of 'knowledge,' of 'health,' the use of contemporary kitchen technologies and the ability to adapt dishes like lasagna to Israeli Palestinian tastes are demanded of women who 'are the agents of modernization' in the culinary domain (2012: 102).

Gvion raises the question of whether female knowledge is also female power, and like earlier authors discussed comes to ambiguous conclusions. On the one hand, knowledge of cooking provides for female hierarchies within families, much as Richards described for Bemba women, in which the position of grandmothers, aunts and mothers is affirmed through their role in controlling knowledge of cooking for younger women. Women can also attain community fame for their cooking, as Gvion notes: 'Sonia is considered the greatest expert on preparation of dough in her community. Women come to her with the mixture they have prepared so she can evaluate the softness of the dough and the flavour it will have after baking' (2012: 77). However, Gvion's case falls clearly into the division between a more highly valued public sphere and a devalued private sphere, where women who hope to attain equality with men must do so in the former, in some cases leaving cooking to their mothers and other older female relatives. And even within the culinary domain, it is men's tastes and desires which are deferred to in making culinary choices. This leads Gvion to conclude that despite women's control of the stock of knowledge that represents Israeli Palestinian cooking, 'the social ambience that develops around cooking and the cooperation among women do not jeopardize the traditional family structure or bring men's power into question' (2012: 85). Indeed, when it comes to presenting 'Palestinian cookery' to the public sphere of the dominant Israeli society, it is men who take the lead role as 'agents who disseminate Palestinian culinary knowledge as they define its character, boundaries and the techniques that will enable it to preserve its distinctiveness and at the same time to be accepted by other groups' (2012: 164).

Throughout her ethnography, Gvion refers to women and men as 'agents' of culinary knowledge. However, she does not do so in relation to an elaborated theory of agency. It is to the ethnography of culinary agency that I now turn my attention.

Cooking as Agency

A few anthropologists have addressed the idea of agency in cooking, not so much in the sense of agency as resistance (and thus cooking or its refusal as a source of power, as above), as in the broader study of the agency of humans and objects. An important statement of this approach is Joy Adapon's ethnography of Mexican cooking, *Culinary Art and Anthropology* (2008). Adapon draws from Alfred Gell's theory of art as agency to explore the emotional resonances of cooking for Mexican women and those for whom they cook. If the essence of Gell's approach is that humans tend to impute agency when they encounter an 'effect,' Adapon applies this insight to cooking in showing how 'we recognize culinary artistry by the power of the food to perform a perceptual change in the eaters, physically enhancing their experience of life' (2008: 34). As Adapon argues for Mexican cuisine: 'Confronting a meal can also be thought of as confronting a person ... and the food itself is the outcome of the cook's intentions' (2008: 38). This leads people to talk about transfers of emotion between persons and food – if someone is angry tamales will not set because they are angry as well (2008: 39), and food resents being 'rudely handled' (2008: 20). These personifications are examples of Gell's notion that an object is an 'artwork' to the extent that 'it embodies intentionalities that are complex, demanding of attention and perhaps difficult to reconstruct fully' (Gell, cited in Adapon 2008: 39). This is related to the notion that artworks, such as a complex meal, can be 'traps' for the viewer/eater, as they suggest a complexity of intention and execution that the eater cannot fully reconstruct. How were they produced? With what feelings and intentions?

There is a notion here that food 'collaborates' with humans in producing certain effects, a point also developed in Janeja's ethnography of cooking in West and East Bengal (Janeja 2010). But by the same token, as food circulates, that is, is eaten by different people, it has the possibility to 'betray' the intentions of its creator (Janeja 2010); its taste can be unpalatable to some or it can spoil, once again suggesting a notion of 'agency' if not of actual intentionality. Janeja ties this view to the notion of a 'foodscape,' or the ways that food and food practices create a sense of place, or *desh*, such that 'what is revealed is not only people's affection for *desh* but also that *desh has affection for its people, that is, desh* as place is emotionally involved with people' (2010: 51). Both Adapon and Janeja give us ways to think about the relationship of cooking and *the circulation of affect*, or emotion, clearly an important dimension of everyday cooking which is explored by other authors (e.g. Harper 2010), but not from the rigorous theoretical point of view that these two ethnographies offer.

Cooking as Value

Anthropologists and sociologists have made the case for cooking as expressive of a set of cultural values, often seen as in opposition, such as care versus convenience (Warde 1997). Others have suggested more general values expressed in food/ cooking choices such as 'love' (Adapon (2008: 18ff.; Abarca 2006; Harper 2010), or 'family' (Kaufmann 2010: 85), and within that more diverse expressions of values such as autonomy and intimacy versus tradition and discipline (Kaufmann 2010: 91). Kaufmann more broadly suggests overarching values such as a 'passion' for cooking as an outgrowth of or response to 'the deadly chill of reflexive modernity' (2010: 168). Kaufmann's work is not an ethnography per se, but is drawn from extended interview materials, as well as the ethnographic work of other scholars working on everyday cooking in France. Kaufmann also usefully argues that values are never determinate because they are always deployed in relation to habits, desires and, often unconscious, traditions. These habits, ways of using time in the kitchen, complex planning of daily and weekly meal cycles, memory traces from childhood, belie his informants' attempts to use the categories available to them – 'natural,'light,'simple,'self-sacrificing' – themselves full of contradictions as well. For example, an informant who is revolted by foods that are not 'fresh and natural' later admits that she loves canned green beans 'because they remind her of her family's garden.' Another rejects frozen foods, but fish is acceptable 'because it is frozen at sea,' (2010: 22) a justification that Kaufmann sees as hiding a need for convenience: 'The categories get more and more complicated. ... No matter how powerful and correct they may be, ideas usually have only a limited power to influence something that is, in anthropological terms, so complex' (2010: 23). Some anthropologists, however, may find his dismissal of his informants' own understandings of their kitchen practices to be somewhat cavalier, especially given that his data is, in fact, interviews, and is not based on direct observation in the kitchen.

One unusual approach to the question of cooking as value can be found in a larger ethnography only partly focused on issues of food, Brad Weiss's *The Making and Unmaking of the Haya Lived World* (1996). Weiss's approach is provocative because he focuses not on value as such, or even contradictions within value systems, as Kaufmann does, but suggests that cooking might be seen as a process of value transformation in itself. Weiss argues that among the Haya this serves as a model for all kinds of other transformations as well. Thus, like Lévi-Strauss, he argues culinary transformations are embedded in other social and symbolic systems. However unlike Lévi-Strauss, Weiss' culinary transformations are not determined in the abstract, but only brought out through a careful ethnography based on an experiential approach to meaning. Here he draws from Nancy Munn's ideas about value as expressed in spatio-temporal transformations produced by activities, one of the key ones, for the Haya, being cooking. For example, Weiss shows this in relation to space in terms of the significance of the notion of enclosure of substances: in pots, in the space of the hearth, as that which 'makes the merely edible actually food' (1996: 101). The process of enclosure in cooking, Weiss argues, models and brings about other forms of Haya sociality: 'enclosure is not merely a productive practice with respect to food, it is a basic orientation that maintains the proper differentiation and interrelation of social agents' (1996: 125).

Weiss's perspective allows him to present fascinating materials on the significance of water in Haya cooking, as a substance that makes food tasty by making it soggy. That is, by combining its substance with the substance of the food, water too models other types of values; in its diversion from streams and enclosure in pots by women, it models women's proper relationship to semen as well: 'women collect water [for cooking] just as they collect semen and contain them in their body' (1996: 90). Thus, collecting water 'draws on a collective, dynamic potential and initiates a transformation in this potential by containing and enclosing it' (1996: 90).

The significance of Weiss's approach to value, then, is in its pointing us to values not in the abstract, or even in tension with practices, as Kaufmann suggests, but in showing the everyday generation of values in the sensory and material engagement with objects that surround the process of cooking, even if the end product of these transformations of values, at least in Weiss's description, tends towards more abstract ideas like *enclosure* and *dispersement*.

Cooking as Embodied Skill, Memory and Sensory Apprenticeship

I share Weiss's view that cooking needs to be studied as an activity *in the making*. My own research on cooking also draws from recent approaches to everyday life, materiality, and the senses, inspired more, however, by the work of Tim Ingold and Jean Lave on tool use rather than Nancy Munn on spatio-temporal value transformations. Thus, for example, in *Secrets from the Greek Kitchen* (Sutton 2014), I explore the ways that cooking enmeshes tools and human bodies in particular projects and problems that are only partially amenable to analysis in terms of the social dynamics or symbolic dimensions of food, but that does dovetail with concerns over cooking as a type of knowledge discussed above.

To think about cooking as skill I use Tim Ingold's concepts of enskillment and the 'education of attention,' alongside Marcel Mauss's 'techniques of the body' and Jean Lave's 'activity theory' to suggest some of the ways that particular techniques and tool uses may develop as habits in particular sociomaterial contexts. For Ingold, skilled practice involves not the mind telling the body what to do according to a preconceived plan, but rather a mobilization of the mind/body within an environment of things which 'afford' different possibilities for human use. This is a departure from traditional learning research in which, as Lave notes, 'learning researchers have studied learning is if it were a process contained in the mind of the learner ... ignor[ing] the lived-in world' (1996: 7). Skill, then, involves an extension of the mind/body, often through the use of tools, requiring constant and shifting use of judgement and dexterity within a changing environment. The environment is not objectified as a 'problem' that humans must 'adapt' to; rather it itself is part of the total field of activity, as in Ingold's example of a woodsman who, in chopping wood, consults the world with his senses for guidance, not a picture in his head: 'The world is its own best model' (Ingold 2001:12). This approach has implications for the transmission of skill as well, which once again is not a set of rules to be memorized. Skill must be learned through the sensuous and sensory engagement of a novice with the environment and/or with a skilled practitioner. This learning, as Lave argues, is part of all ongoing activity: 'Situated activity always involves changes in knowledge and action ... and "changes in knowledge and action" are central to what we mean by "learning"' (1996: 5).

Learning has tended to be referred to in classical anthropology as 'enculturation,' based on the 'blank slate' notion of precultural children with minds waiting to be filled with cultural stuff – categories, ideas, etc. Ingold suggests we reframe this learning as an 'education of attention,' or, as he puts it, speaking of his father, 'His manner of teaching was to show me things, literally to point them out. If I would but notice the things to which he directed my attention, and recognize the sights, smells and tastes that he wanted me to experience ... then I would discover for myself much of what he already knew' (2000:20). Learning from others involves copying, but rather than a transcription of knowledge from one head to another, it is a 'guided rediscovery' (2001:11) in a sensorily rich environment.

To give a flavour for how this approach might illuminate cooking practices, I draw from my ethnographic analysis of 'cutting in the hand' in Kalymnos, Greece, where I conducted my primary cooking-related fieldwork (see Sutton 2014). In the following extended example (taken from Sutton 2014: ch. 2) I hope to suggest some of the analytic payoffs of a careful attention to cooking techniques, a topic by and large absent from previous anthropological work on cooking (apart from Gvion and Weiss). Here you can watch a short video to get a sense of what cutting different vegetables like potatoes, an onion or zucchini, looks like in this part of Greece: https://www.youtube.com/watch?v=pgy4yI-QUCo.

While it had caught my attention that Kalymnians were cutting all kinds of things in their hands rather than on a hard surface, it made even more of an impression on me when I showed these videos to some colleagues in Food Studies, some of whom had had professional training in cooking. They were *horrified*! How could people cut in such an awkward fashion? They assumed that these were experienced cooks, and while they no doubt had many recipes and perhaps preparation methods particular to Greece, they wondered why anyone would use such an inefficient method of cutting. Their queries brought me up short, and really got me to take a closer look at Kalymnian cutting practices. It also got me to think about what we might mean by words like 'awkward' and 'efficient.'

On closer examination, I found that there is a style, a *skill* to Kalymnian cutting. In the case of the potato, notice how it is cradled in one hand, scored all the way across in two or three passes, and then with a wrist motion the knife is drawn towards the thumbs, which serve as a guide and balance. Effectively, the thumbs serve in the role as a cutting board; only the thumb of the hand cupping the potato is used when the potato is large, while both thumbs are employed for smaller potatoes, or once a larger potato has been partially cut. In the case of onions, one hand typically again serves as a cradle, while the loose wrist of the other hand is brought up and down in a repetitive motion scoring a pattern of shallow cuts on the surface of the onion. Then the thumb is once again used as a guide to draw the knife across the onion while the cradling hand rotates the onion.

So there is method in this technique. One of the issues that made my Food Studies colleagues wince was that this approach to cutting seemed to preclude ending up with small, evenly shaped pieces. The use of a surface (cutting board or other hard surface) allows for greater balance, and, in the case of bread, for example, one can use the surface as a guide for evenness of cut. In terms of vegetables being used for cooking, presumably evenness of shapes and sizes leads to a more even overall cooking. (This is not such an issue in Kalymnian salads, where uneven shapes seem fairly normative. And in making stews, these vegetables undergo considerable cooking; Kalymnian vegetables are not cooked *al dente*, so once again the difference here might not make so much of a difference.)

However, to say that this technique is 'not so bad,' or that it doesn't make that much of a difference is not to grasp its logic, why it has been passed down from one generation to the next in Kalymnian (and Greek) kitchens more generally. One issue, of course, is whether counter space was even available. Calling for a cutting board assumes that there is counter space for it, at the right height to facilitate such activity. Yet the traditional Kalymnian kitchen consists of a space no more than five feet square, primarily with room for storage and a bottled gas, two-burner stove. These kitchen spaces were not designed with counter space for cutting in mind. Because of the matrilocal residence patterns on Kalymnos, mothers and daughters often end up sharing kitchen space. Or mothers will retain the traditional kitchen set-up while daughters build newfangled 'modern' kitchens. The 'daughter's kitchen' does include counter space, built of marble or other materials, as well as a standard oven often missing in the mother's kitchen. However, the daughter's kitchen often opened onto a living/entertaining space, so in many cases it was not seen as the place for heavy processing or cooking of foods that had strong smells, and was more typically used for baking and preparing snacks. However, even in cases where this kitchen space was used to prepare food (in the absence of a mother's kitchen or simply out of some daily exigency), the counters were rarely used for chopping or other heavy food processing.

A further issue might have to do with the height of counters. I asked one woman why she preferred to assemble food, roll dough for pies, and other processing activities at the kitchen table rather than on her counter surfaces, which seemed more decorative. She responded that the counters were 'off,' and weren't 'making me comfortable.' Many kitchen counters were built in with prefabricated cabinets bought from major furniture retailers, which would come in standard sizes, though some women had ordered lower cabinets to accommodate their height. I found that most counters were ninety centimetres in height. Built for Americans or Northern Europeans, these cabinets created a challenge for Greek women of smaller stature, reflecting the kind of standardization of kitchen spaces that has long ignored the perspective of the female user, as documented by feminist historians of technology (Wajcman 2010).

Tim Ingold's description of sawing a piece of wood provides additional insight into the skill of cutting in the hand. Ingold notes, 'Although a confident, regular movement ensures an even cut, no two strokes are ever precisely the same. With each stroke I have to adjust my posture ever so slightly to allow for the advancing groove, and for possible irregularities in the grain of the wood' (2011:52). He summarizes: 'Cutting wood … is an effect not of the saw alone but of the entire system of forces and relations set up by the intimate engagement of the saw, the trestle, the workpiece and my own body' (2011: 56). In the same way, cutting Kalymnian-style effectively replaces the solid balance of a cutting surface with the intimacy and control of the hand/object. Each cut is felt – not just by the hand that is holding the knife, but by the hand that holds the object to be cut, and allows for adjustments to be made as the hand rotates the object.

It became clear to me that cutting in the hand was a skilled practice, but what about it's supposed 'inefficiency'? As I thought more about this I realized that there were times that I might cut food in my hand, for example, when it was a particularly small item like a clove of garlic that I could hold over a pan, allowing the cut pieces to drop directly into the pan. Indeed, in the case of the woman cutting potatoes in the 'Cutting Medley' video, we see that she uses a bowl in a similar fashion – as a receptacle to catch the pieces of potato as they fall from her hand. By the same token, Kalymnians do use surfaces when they are cutting something very large: a sheep carcass or a large whole fish would certainly not be attempted 'in the hand,' but rather on a table in the yard or a counter in a 'daughter's kitchen.' So it is not that these techniques represent absolute differences, simply that they are the norm, the habitual, the everyday.

Other colleagues mentioned cooking traditions in other countries, where food processing might be done largely in a kneeling position. Perhaps what threw me off at first was that the first example I saw of this technique was Nina cutting the onion while standing over a counter, where it seemed to give no advantage to hold the onion in her hand rather than lay it on a surface. When I saw Katerina, the woman cutting the potato in the video, sitting in a chair, facing me, cutting potatoes with a bowl cradled in her lap, things started to make more sense. I recalled Marcel Mauss's notion of 'techniques of the body.' He defines technique as an act 'that is traditional and efficacious. It has to be traditional and effective. There is no technique and no transmission if there is no tradition' (Mauss cited in Narvaez 2006: 60). Efficiency, in other words, is defined not by some absolute standard, but through experiences within a particular social order, what Ingold calls a 'taskscape' (Ingold 2000: 194 ff.).

So how does this cutting technique fit into the larger Kalymnian taskscape? In Kalymnos, much of the processing of ingredients does not necessarily take place within the confines of the mother's small kitchen itself. Rather it might take place in the courtyard directly outside the kitchen area. Like Katerina, women often prepare ingredients while seated, potentially avoiding the back pain associated with standing for long periods. Cutting in the hand also allows them to socialize with family or neighbours while the ingredients are being processed. It is a technique for multitasking: processing ingredients doesn't in this case necessitate turning one's back on the environment around oneself. One can oversee other activities going on in the household, watch for passing friends or neighbours, even make processing food an occasion for sitting in a circle and sharing news and stories.[5] This social aspect is also reflected in the tendency of family members to constantly check in with each other as a dish is being prepared, tasting and consulting on processes that they have done many times in the past.

It might be tempting here to draw a contrast between 'social' Greek cooking and 'asocial' American cooking. Surely, the trends in kitchen design suggest a greater desire among Americans to make cooking a social activity that happens in the shared, public space of the home, rather than as hidden labour. Indeed, a Kalymnian might reverse the comment of my Food Studies colleagues, and marvel at the 'inefficiency' of American cooking that makes people turn away and bend down while trying to remain actively involved in the social surroundings!

If you look again at the 'Cutting Medley' video, you see a fourteen-year-old girl uncertainly cutting a zucchini holding it in her hand. This is Katerina's granddaughter, 'Little Katerina,' and when I filmed her here it was the first time she had prepared a zucchini omelette. While I filmed her, her mother stood off camera whispering instructions and encouragements.[6] I analyse this apprenticeship in line with Ingold's notion of an 'education of attention,' where cutting in the hand is not a technique to be taught in the abstract, but is part of a wider sensory enculturation into cooking and other female activities on Kalymnos. Cutting in the hand, in fact, is not taught explicitly as a choice among other cutting techniques. It falls more on the spectrum of Bourdieu's *habitus*, which 'goes without saying because it comes without saying' (Bourdieu 1977: 167). Other cooking tools and techniques might indeed be part of a more explicit discourse, such as debates over 'traditional' versus 'modern' can openers or pots and pans which I document elsewhere in my ethnography. The point, however, is to suggest some of the diverse ways that cooking skills are reproduced *and altered* in the processes of social reproduction on Kalymnos rather than any notion of a smooth transmission from mother to daughter. It was only through a long video based ethnography of everyday practices, that I was able to document, in fact, that the course of true cooking skill does not run smooth! It is also to show how in relation to cooking issues of power, knowledge, memory and identity can be explored ethnographically through a different lens of tool use, the senses and embodiment. As I argue more fully elsewhere (Sutton 2014), the anthropology of technology should no longer be seen as a specialized field. Whether the technology is about using can openers or computers, rolling pins or compact immersion circulators,[7] I argue that understanding tool use in the kitchen is central to an anthropology of everyday life.

Cooking as Everyday Risk

The final approach to the question of 'what is cooking?'is meant to be suggestive. It comes out of my sense of some of the overall thrust of approaches to cooking as embodied skill outlined in the previous section. It also is meant to intervene in questions of 'craft' versus 'science' that can be seen in the contemporary cooking scene and the difference between approaches that stress locality or *terroir*, and those that stress reproducibility and the supposed decontextualization of taste from local particularities under the guise of science.

I found risk to operate at two levels in my Kalymnian ethnography. There was the 'risk' associated with various practices such as cutting in the hand that seemed to put the physical body at risk in ways that, as I suggested, some viewing these practices from the outside might wish to minimize. Thus, in relation to using a can opener with a knife blade, one Kalymnian woman created a series of spikes in opening a can of tomato paste, noting 'you can cut your hands on these.' But rather than adopt a rolling wheel blade can opener as her daughter suggested, she insisted that she was more comfortable with the knife-blade, and effectively embraced the risk (though mitigating it somewhat by using a small axe to hammer down the spikes on the can).[8] Such risk was seen not as something to be mitigated by improved tools or techniques, but rather to be faced as part of an existential attitude to life and the contingency which often gives it meaning. Or as Malaby, writing about Cretan gamblers, puts it, 'In dealing with the pervasive indeterminacies of experience ... risk ... rather than tamed and quantified, is engaged and performed' (Malaby

2003: 21; see also Herzfeld 1985; Sutton 1996). Indeed, I would argue based on my Kalymnian materials that cooking is like other performances in which risk is required 'as a precondition for satisfactory performance' (Jones 2011).[9]

The second type of risk was the recognition that each time a dish was made it might turn out slightly differently based on all the variability encapsulated in ingredients, tools and all kinds of materio-social conditions surrounding cooking. But once again, this was not something to be minimized, but rather to be embraced as part of what makes cooking, in fact, cooking. To reproduce a dish exactly each time, as a robot cooking under laboratory conditions might aspire to do, was to remove exactly that human element that Kalymnians associated with the 'soul' of cooking. In the time that I have been doing research on Kalymnos, a major change has been that risk is not simply attendant on tools, ingredients or other social challenges (how to feed ten people who show up unexpectedly, for example), but on one's openness to change and alteration. One Kalymnian woman in her fifties told me how she first saw Greek eggplant salad (*Melitzanosalata*, what in the United States is called Babaganoush) at a restaurant that she went to for a wedding celebration. She thought at the time that it looked like vomit. But after seeing it more often, and observing a friend preparing it when she was staying on Rhodes, she started to make it for her family, noting 'we took the risk.' Risk here is seen as a willingness to improve food, to continue to learn new ways of preparing the familiar, or variations on traditional recipes. But it is also simply an extension of the notion that the skilled cook is always adjusting to circumstances: the availability of ingredients, the desires of different people, the small variations in cooking processes and even changing times, which now include the growth of new sources of knowledge about cooking such as the TV cooking shows.

David Pye introduces the notion of the 'workmanship of risk,' a type of approach to craft that once again stresses the idea that 'the quality of the result is not predetermined but depends on the judgment, dexterity and care that the maker exercises as he works' (Pye 1968: 4). Pye usefully contrasts this to what he calls the 'workmanship of certainty,' in which the end result is largely predetermined before the process of making begins. This might be seen in terms of the contrast between home-cooked and pre-prepared, 'fast' foods; the latter often fall into the category of 'not cooking' in Kalymnos and elsewhere no doubt. But it is also reflected in movements such as that identified with the magazine *Cooks Illustrated*, which focuses on rigorous testing in laboratory-like conditions and controlling variables to produce recipes such as 'the best soft-boiled egg.' Here the point seems to be absolute control of variables so that 'perfection' is guaranteed, as long as you follow the recipe to the letter, or in Molecular Gastronomy and other hi-tech adaptations like *sous vide* cooking, where the point seems to be to remove the human element and the human sensory input as much as possible as part of producing standardized results. Once again this seems at odds with a view of skill that I found on Kalymnos, which is captured in Ingold's notion that the skilled practitioner

is continually and fluently responsive to perturbations of the perceived environment. ... This is possible because the practitioner's bodily movement is, at one and the same time, a *movement of attention*; because he watches, listens, and feels even as he works. It is this responsiveness that underpins the qualities of care, judgment, and dexterity that are the hallmarks of skilled workmanship. (2001: 135)

Thus, in stressing risk in cooking, Kalymnians are stressing their own sensory abilities to respond to the cooking environment, as well as their sensory abilities to taste, evaluate and appreciate or criticize the result – indeed, many Kalymnian meals were spent evaluating the cooked dish, what went right and what went wrong, as well as comparing it to memorable similar or different previous meals (see Sutton 2001: Chapter 4).

The notion of cooking as risk is not simply an approach based on my own particular ethnographic materials, but rather, I am suggesting, part of a larger debate about the meaning of cooking that crosses borders, and that has implications for issues well beyond the culinary, in the end being a debate about the meanings of 'modernity' and 'tradition.'[10] However, I also want to suggest that 'risk' might provide an interesting anthropological jumping-off point for thinking about issues of what makes a meal a meal, or more specifically what makes a moussaka a moussaka and not something else. As people go about their daily lives, they decide on questions like 'What should I make for dinner?,' and 'Do I have the right ingredients to make X?' In the process, they may make subtle changes in what constitutes a mistake, an acceptable version of X, or an improvement on X. In societies like Kalymnos, where people take an interest in and comment on each other's daily cooking, such choices do not simply disappear into nothingness, but may have small, slow, transformative effects on what is seen as Kalymnian cuisine. To paraphrase Marshall Sahlins' (1985) description of historical process more generally, each time a moussaka is made, a category is put at risk in practice, and may undergo a subtle transformation. The extent that this helps us understand daily cooking, its choices and transformations, however, can only be confirmed by future careful ethnographic work.

CONCLUDING THOUGHTS

Indeed, the thrust of this review has been to call for more cooking ethnographies. The approaches I detail above illuminate, I believe, different and complementary aspects of cooking, and of what cooking can tell us about the larger social, material and symbolic contexts that surround it. Like food, cooking, then, provides a window into aspects of culture that anthropologists have long been interested in. But cooking's seeming mundane everydayness, at least in Western contexts, has for too long relegated it to the unimportant, uninteresting or unelaborated, the 'woman's work' that Rosaldo felt was much the same from one society to the next. But to take cooking seriously, we do not necessarily need to aestheticize it in the manner of multicultural commodified cookbooks or shows like Anthony Bourdain's *No Reservations* or *Parts Unknown*. As Holtzman (2009) has shown, food and its preparation can be equally ethnographically interesting even when there is little concern for 'taste.' Indeed, even when there is little such concern, there is still likely to be an elaborated discourse about cooking, given its centrality to the daily reproduction of life. Like mortuary practices, money, kingship or other venerable anthropological topics, cooking's significance is culturally diverse, and may track with ideas about gender and power, space and time, tradition and modernity, or other analytic concepts. We can't know in advance what cooking's significance will be, except that in one way or another, I will wager, that it will be significant. Because of this we should approach cooking with theoretical flexibility, and with ethnographic curiosity.

NOTES

1. Wrangham's book is a synthesis of his work and that of other biological anthropologists. For a fuller review of Catching Fire, see Sutton 2013.
2. And indeed, in the context of the village where she did fieldwork, women's relationship to the marketplace more generally comes in for significant elaboration.
3. As Meah notes in her discussion of cooking more broadly in the feminist and social science literature: 'The identification of quotidian domestic food provisioning as the exclusive preserve of women has, perhaps unsurprisingly, led many contemporary Anglo-American feminists to balk at the idea of commenting on either kitchens or cooking' (Meah 2013: 5).
4. Several recent studies suggest that cooking can be equally apportioned by gender – both cooperatively and separately. These all involve small-scale societies and ethnic minorities in China, Malaysia and New Guinea (see Du 2002; Endicott and Endicott 2008; Wardlow 2006). These studies, unfortunately, do not focus on food and diet and only provide sketchy data on this question. However, they lead one to at least raise the question of whether the universality of women's responsibility for day-to-day cooking might be in part an artefact of the biases of ethnographers.
5. See Short (2006), who describes the multitasking aspect that seems to be central to women's daily cooking.
6. See Sutton (2014: Chapter 4) for a full description.
7. One of the tools of the molecular gastronomy trade.
8. See Sutton (2014) for a full discussion of this incident.
9. Jones is discussing magicians here.
10. This idea is elaborated in Sutton (2014).

REFERENCES

Abarca, M. (2006), *Voices in the Kitchen: Views of Food and the World from Working-Class Mexican and Mexican American Women*, College Station: Texas A&M University Press.
Adapon, J. (2008), *Culinary Art and Anthropology*, New York: Berg.
Allison, A. (1991), 'Japanese Mothers and Obentos: The Lunch Box as Ideological State Apparatus', *Anthropological Quarterly*, 64: 195–208.
Beoku-Betts, J. (1995), 'We Got our Way of Cooking Things: Women, Food and the Preservation of Cultural Identity among the Gullah', *Gender and Society*, 9(5): 535–55.

Bourdieu, P. (1977), *Outline of a Theory of Practice*, translated by Richard Nice, Cambridge: Cambridge University Press.

Counihan, C. (1999), *The Anthropology of Food and the Body: Gender, Meaning and Power*, London: Routledge.

Counihan, C. (2004), *Around the Tuscan Table: Food, Family, and Gender in Twentieth-Century Florence*, New York: Routledge.

Devault, M. (1997), 'Conflict and Deference', in C. Counihan and P. Van Esterik (eds), *Food and Culture: A Reader*, 180–99, London: Routledge.

Du, S. (2002), *"Chopsticks only Work in Paris": Gender Unity and Gender Equality among the Lahu of Southwest China*, New York: Columbia University Press.

Endicott, K. M. and Endicott, K. L. (2008), *The Headman was a Woman: The Gender Egalitarian Batek of Malaysia, Long Grove*, IL: Waveland Press.

Firth, R. (1966), *Housekeeping among Malay Peasants*, 2nd edn, New York: Athlone.

Firth, R. (1995), 'Prologue: A Woman Looks Back on the Anthropology of Women and Feminist Anthropology', in W. Karim (ed.), *'Male' and 'Female' in Developing Southeast Asia*, 3–7, Oxford: Berg.

Goody, J. (1982), *Cooking, Cuisine and Class: A Study in Comparative Sociology*, Cambridge: Cambridge University Press.

Gvion, L. (2012), *Beyond Hummus and Falafel: Social and Political Aspects of Palestinian Food in Israel*, Berkeley: University of California Press.

Harper. D. (2010), *The Italian Way*, Chicago: University of Chicago Press.

Herzfeld, M. (1985), *The Poetics of Manhood: Contest and Identity in a Cretan Mountain Village*, Princeton, NJ: Princeton University Press.

Holden, T. J. M. (2005), 'The Overcooked and the Underdone: Masculinities in Japanese Food Programming', *Food and Foodways*, 13(1–2): 39–65.

Holtzman, J. (2009), *Uncertain Tastes: Memory, Ambivalence and the Politics of Eating in Samburu, Northern Kenya*, Berkeley: University of California Press.

Ingold, T. (2000), *The Perception of the Environment: Essays in Livelihood, Dwelling and Skill*, London: Routledge.

Ingold, T. (2001), 'From the Transmission of Representations to the Education of Attention', in H. Whitehouse (ed.), *The Debated Mind: Evolutionary Psychology versus Ethnography*, 113–53, New York: Berg.

Ingold, T. (2011), *Being Alive: Essays on Movement, Knowledge and Description*, London: Routledge.

Janeja, M. (2010), *Transactions in Taste: The Collaborative Lives of Everyday Bengali Food*, London: Routledge.

Jones, G. (2011), *Trade of the Tricks: Inside the Magician's Craft*, Berkeley: University of California Press.

Kaufmann, J.-C. (2010), *The Meaning of Cooking*, Malden, MA: Polity Press.

Lave, J. (1996), 'The Practice of Learning', in S. Chaiklin and J. Lave (eds), *Understanding Practice: Perspectives on Activity and Context*, 3–32, Cambridge: Cambridge University Press.

Leacock, E. (1981), *Myths of Male Dominance: Collected Articles on Women Cross-Culturally*, New York: St Martin's Press.

Lévi-Strauss, C. (2008[1969]), 'The Culinary Triangle', in C. Counihan and P. Van Esterik (eds), *Food and Culture: A Reader*, 2nd edn, 40–7, New York: Routledge.

Malaby, T. (2003), *Gambling Life: Dealing in Contingency in a Greek City*, Champaign: University of Illinois Press.

Meah, A. (2013), 'Reconceptualizing Power and Gendered Subjectivities in Domestic Cooking Spaces', *Progress in Human Geography*, DOI: 10.1177/0309132513501404.

Murcott, A. (1983), '"It's a Pleasure to Cook for Him': Food, Mealtimes and Gender in Some South Wales Households', in E. Garmarnikow et al. (eds), *The Public and Private*, 78–90, London: Heinemann.

Narvaez, R. (2006), 'Embodiment, Collective Memory and Time', *Body and Society*, 12(3): 51–73.

Pye, D. (1968), *The Nature and Art of Workmanship*, Cambridge: Cambridge University Press.

Richards, A. (1939), *Land, Labour and Diet in Northern Rhodesia: An Economic Study of the Bemba Tribe*, London: Oxford University Press.

Rogers, S. C. (1975), 'Female Forms of Power and the Myth of Male Dominance: A Model of Female/Male Interaction in Peasant Society', *American Ethnologist*, 1: 727–56.

Rosaldo, M. (1974), 'Woman, Culture and Society: A Theoretical Overview', in M. Rosaldo and L. Lamphere (eds), *Woman, Culture and Society*, 17–44, Stanford, CA: Stanford University Press.

Roosth, S. (2013), 'Of Foams and Formalisms: Scientific Expertise and Craft Practice in Molecular Gastronomy', *American Anthropologist*, 115(1): 4–16.

Sahlins, M. (1985), *Islands of History*, Chicago: University of Chicago Press.

Short, F. (2006), *Kitchen Secrets: The Meaning of Cooking in Everyday Life*, Oxford: Berg.

Sutton, D. (2001), *Remembrance of Repasts: An Anthropology of Food and Memory*, Oxford: Berg.

Sutton, D. (2013), 'Review Article: Cooking Is Good to Think', *Body and Society*, 19(1): 1–16.

Sutton, D. (2014), *Secrets from the Greek Kitchen: Cooking, Skill and Everyday Life on a Greek Island*, Berkeley: University of California Press.

Wacjman, J. (2010), 'Feminist Theories of Technology', *Cambridge Journal of Economy*, 34(1): 143–52.

Warde, A. (1997), *Consumption, Food and Taste: Culinary Antinomies and Commodity Culture*, London: Sage.

Wardlow, H. (2006), *Wayward Women: Sexuality and Agency in a New Guinea Society*, Berkeley: University of California Press.

Weiner, A. (1992), *Inalienable Possessions: The Paradox of Keeping-while-Giving*, Berkeley: University of California Press.

Wrangham, R. (2010), *Catching Fire: How Cooking Made Us Human*, London: Profile Books.

CHAPTER SEVENTEEN

Supermarket Expansion, Informal Retail and Food Acquisition Strategies: An Example from Rural South Africa

ELIZABETH HULL

INTRODUCTION

Since the 1980s, supermarket retail has expanded dramatically, affecting diets and livelihoods around the world. This process represents fundamental shifts in the operation of global food systems, characterized partly by an extension of corporate control along commodity chains from procurement to sales, as well as the increasing ownership of market shares in food sales by a small number of companies (Lawrence and Burch 2007; Reardon and Timmer 2007). From the 1990s, supermarkets have extended their reach into most low-income countries. Supermarket-led corporate agriculture, Philip McMichael suggests, has become a central element of contemporary capitalist transformation and accumulation (McMichael 2008).

This 'supermarket revolution' appears sudden and transformative, suggesting supermarkets are moving into regions in which they were hitherto absent and wiping out existing forms of informal trade and retail (Reardon and Hopkins 2006). Some scholars point out that small producers are pushed out of business, unable to meet the stringent quality and safety standards demanded by supermarkets (Weatherspoon and Reardon 2003), or demonstrate the negative effects on existing small retailers (Reardon and Hopkins 2006). This staggering pace of change has also generated alarm about the implications for the dietary intake of urban, and increasingly rural, populations around the world. Supermarkets offer access to cheap necessities but also contribute to growing trends in overweight and obesity by substantially increasing the availability of energy-dense, nutrient-poor foods (Popkin 2014; Igumbor et al. 2012). Others highlight the demise of local culinary traditions as a result of the introduction by supermarkets of generic, commercially produced food items (Raschke and Cheema 2008). Much of the literature gives the impression of a steadily expanding frontier with power weighted heavily towards supermarkets, creating a passive transformation of existing retail and consumer practices, albeit punctuated by occasional moments of 'resistance' (Abrahams 2010; Miller 2005).

However, this process is characterized not only by the expansion of market control but also by a restructuring of existing markets and food supply chains. While much of the literature focuses on macro-level changes, emerging ethnographic research offers the possibility of a detailed understanding of how this restructuring takes place in particular contexts. Rather than treating supermarket expansion as the inevitable outcome of economic determinants, this literature reveals that it is made up of multiple processes operating inside, and in tension with, a range of situated constraints. I begin this chapter with a summary of this anthropological (and related) literature, before presenting a short case study from my own fieldwork in South Africa. Through an ethnographic study of retail in a small town and its surrounding area in the north of the province of KwaZulu-Natal, I examine critically the perception of an ever-encroaching formal food sector onto a shrinking informal one, by looking at the various ways in which regulated and unregulated modes of food retail interact locally. I argue that the entry of supermarkets into low-income countries has been neither straightforwardly linear nor divorced from, nor simply a replacement of, the systems of production, exchange and consumption that preceded them. I suggest that although supermarkets are expanding and capturing much of the market space formally occupied by these other retailers, it is necessary to consider how the latter are reconstituting themselves, rather than assuming a linear process of decline. I draw on recent anthropological discussion about the informal economy in Africa which suggests that far from representing two distinct spheres, formal and informal practices interact with each other and form connections in a variety of ways. By focusing on specific, historically and spatially produced patterns of food demand, I suggest that a focus on food can also offer an important angle on debates within economic anthropology.

In the next section, I summarize the two areas of emerging literature, the first dealing with the impact of supermarkets on consumers and consumption practices, the second with how supermarkets expand into agriculture, restructuring markets, supply chains and legislative frameworks. The South African example that follows this discussion suggests the importance of integrating these strands.

THE ANTHROPOLOGY OF
SUPERMARKET EXPANSION

Influenced by Karl Polanyi's seminal idea of 'embeddedness', which signifies the mutually constitutive character of social and economic processes, trust has long been recognized by anthropologists as an integral feature of markets. Discussions about the effects of supermarket expansion on consumers have focused on the issue of trust, especially the varied techniques deployed by supermarkets to cultivate consumer trust in regions where they were previously absent. Either by evoking trusted notions of 'traditional' foodways through advertising or by replacing interpersonal trust relationships with accreditation and audit, supermarkets reconfigure affective market-based trust relationships. The result is to commodify trust and to embed it within the formal and legal technologies over which supermarkets exert control (Richards, Lawrence and Burch 2011). This is apparent, for instance, in the premium paid by wealthy consumers in China for accredited products which are perceived as safer than food bought in markets (Wang et al. 2008).

Notions of modernity, which may be associated with 'supermarketization', serve to nurture feelings of trust as supermarkets carve out a 'modern' appeal by emphasizing food safety and standardization (Everts and Jackson 2009). In contrast, another example from China suggests that shoppers place little faith in regulatory systems and are more inclined to trust their own sensory and experiential knowledge about food. Their suspicions frequently arise from a feeling of ambivalence towards wider processes of delocalization and industrialization (Klein 2013). Supermarkets negotiate these ambiguities in order to attract customers. In a British supermarket in China, trust is engendered through the micromanagement of relationships between workers and customers (Gamble 2007). In Thailand, supermarkets imitate the informal gifting practices of local wet markets and mark festive occasions with special events and offers in order to foster a sense of cultural familiarity (Isaacs et al. 2010).

As the comments of shoppers suggest, this shifting terrain of associations may create tensions and ambiguities even as others are resolved (ibid.). In Australia, contradictions settle around competing notions of 'progress', a concept through which both positive and negative valuations are attributed to supermarkets (Dixon and Isaacs 2013). Supermarkets in America, China and elsewhere have attempted to engage the ethical concerns of their customers by restructuring supply chains to make use of local agricultural producers (Colloredo-Mansfeld et al. 2014; Klein 2013), and to acquire organic or Fair Trade 'ethical sourcing' accreditation (Friedberg 2007; Lyons 2007; Barrientos and Dolan 2006). Mark Harvey shows how entire food chains are restructured specifically to create products which alter food preferences and tastes. The supermarket-branded ready meal exemplifies this integration of different elements of the food chain, from production, through to packaging, marketing and retail (Harvey 2007).

These strategies are not always successful, and in some cases their failure leads to supermarket divestment (Burt, Dawson and Sparks 2002; El-Amir and Burt 2008). In rural South Africa, commercially produced products supplied by supermarkets can signify high socio-economic status but they can also be recast as symbols of cultural dearth (Hull 2014). Protests against a Japanese-owned supermarket in China show that supermarkets can become the objects of wider political tensions (Wang 2010). Claims to food safety are sometimes threatened, most spectacularly in the recent horse-meat scandal in Europe (Abbots and Coles 2013).

While some view the new knowledge regimes brought into being by supermarkets as a form of colonial expansion (Freidberg 2007), Hugh Campbell expresses cautious optimism about the potential for new audit cultures and regulatory systems to reinvigorate concerns about where food comes from, and so to resituate popular understandings about food within broader frameworks of ecology and sustainability. Supermarkets are not exclusively in control of their own operations, he argues, but also reflect the growing influence of NGOs and social movements in demanding access to knowledge about food systems (Campbell 2009). What emerges from these discussions is that rather than following a formulaic or inevitable path, supermarket expansion unfolds unevenly in response to particular, situated constraints and events and is more appropriately understood as a 'tough competitive struggle' rather than a 'tidal wave' (Humphrey 2007).

While supermarkets are an increasingly ubiquitous feature of the global landscape they also expand unevenly, in some cases reinforcing existing class and racial inequalities. This is the argument made by a growing literature on 'food deserts' – areas in which food retail is limited or absent – which have come to be seen as emblematic of the spatialized character of poverty. While much of the food desert literature is based on data collected in America, recent work shifts the discussion to developing contexts (Gartin 2012). New research introduces the idea of 'food mirages': areas typically experiencing gentrification in which poorer residents have physical access to supermarkets but lack the capacity to use them because of prohibitively expensive pricing (Sullivan 2014). Here, deeper layers of exclusion render food inaccessible even where it is within reach geographically.

As supermarkets extend into new markets, they restructure food supply chains in order to streamline procurement and render them amenable to stringent quality requirements (McMichael and Friedmann 2007). The supply chains and markets that operated prior to their arrival are altered and in some cases reconstituted or replaced. Thomas Reardon and others have described this transformation at national and global levels (Weatherspoon and Reardon 2003; Reardon and Hopkins 2006; Reardon and Timmer 2007). Hattersly et al. (2013) show that while there is a tendency towards the consolidation of vertical supply chains over which supermarkets increasingly exert control, competition strategies lead to the formation of horizontal alliances between manufacturers that can operate transnationally, sometimes as a way of competing with supermarkets. Much of the research suggests that the intensification of control along the supply chain by supermarkets marginalizes smaller players (Magdoff, Foster and Buttel 2000; McMichael 2008; Neven et al. 2009).

Two recent ethnographic studies provide insight into how this takes place, showing that the expansion of supermarkets entails a restructuring and not simply a displacement of existing supply chains. This perspective is crucial for understanding how agricultural and other food-based livelihoods are affected by the increasingly dominant role of supermarkets. First, Yildiz Atasoy (2013) describes the integration of small producers into commercialized agri-food supply chains in Turkey in the context of growing supermarket domination. Supermarket-led demands of quality control place constraints on producers, she shows, leading to their assimilation into institutions and supply networks that accommodate these requirements. For instance, the creation of farming 'unions' – collectives to which farmers must join that operate like private marketing bodies – renders farmers more easily governable according to new legal arrangements. The result is an institutionalization and intensification of market relations in agriculture.

Similar observations are found, secondly, in Amy Cohen's discussion of supermarket expansion in West Bengal in India. Far from demonstrating the retraction of state governance, corporate retailers seek new forms of regulation upon which they depend (Cohen 2013). As the contrasting cases of West Bengal (ibid.) and Maharashtra (Velthuis 2014) show, different political and legislative contexts may create highly variable conditions of hostility or amenability to supermarket retail, in some cases preventing it altogether, as in West Bengal until recently. Both Atasoy and Cohen recognize the dependency of supermarkets on the mutability of legal systems. But they also show that supermarkets make use of informal networks, existing and new. As Atasoy demonstrates, 'traditional' wholesalers act as crucial brokers, supplying supermarkets via well-established networks of informal, trust-based relationships with small, family-sized producers. Supermarkets rely heavily on these existing informal networks, which they use initially to expand into agricultural networks. However, as Cohen points out, there is ultimately a tendency towards state-authorized contract farming because supermarkets, unlike informal wholesalers, must be accountable to shareholders. The result, she shows, is not deregulation of markets – as posited by a simple rendering of the neoliberal agenda – but an intensification of state regulation alongside a fundamental restructuring of legislative frameworks and supply chains.

The following example from my fieldwork in rural South Africa will not attempt to tackle all of the interconnected dynamics described here, but will focus on some aspects of the relationship between supermarkets, informal retailers and consumers. Here I draw on debates in economic anthropology about the formal/informal interface. The concept of informality is generally used to refer to income generating activities that operate beyond state regulation. However, given the shifting, overlapping or competing regulatory frameworks that operate in parts of Africa, the partially formalized institutions that promote both planned and opportunistic modes of economic action, and the changing roles of actors and institutions vis-à-vis the state, a clear separation between the two is often illusory. Recent literature on the relationship between formal and informal economies in Africa has presented a complex picture of the linkages between the two. Far from representing two distinct spheres, formal and informal modes appear to interact with each other and form connections in a variety of ways.[1]

These ideas are reflected in some of the observations made by Atasoy and Cohen, and both sets of literature are drawn upon here to add nuance to the assumption that global supermarket expansion is a homogenous and linear process. I also use the South African example to suggest a link between this work and the literature focusing on consumers, described above. Much of the research on informal economies focuses on income generating activities. Here, I approach the formal/informal interface via the food acquisition and expenditure practices of rural residents. By tracing the temporal and spatial aspects of these consumption strategies, the ethnography here reveals different elements of a diverse retail infrastructure as they are encountered by residents themselves. Increasing household incomes over the last ten years, due largely to the expansion of social security payments, have not only created a major opportunity for supermarkets, but also have generated more possibilities for informal gain.[2] I argue that smaller retailers are not simply wiped out by supermarket expansion, but continue on the basis that they cater for different needs within the cycle of food acquisition. The practices of informal retailers are reconstituted both in relation to the competition created by formal retail and also by its constraints.

I begin by describing the development of commercial trade in northern KwaZulu-Natal. I show that rather than forcing a radical departure from what preceded them, supermarkets inserted themselves into long-standing networks of trade and retail, readjusting and adapting as best they could to the dense and spatially variegated regimes of state regulation that had developed over decades. Legislative changes at times produced moments of shock and new rounds of readjustment, challenging the idea that supermarket expansion has been a linear process. The story is one involving a complex network of alliances between state and private retail capital on the one hand, and between large and small retail outlets on the other, creating a dense web of both overlapping and conflicting interests. In the third section, I use ethnographic data that I collected over four separate trips to northern KwaZulu-Natal between 2009 and 2013 to describe the food acquisition strategies of residents, focusing on the temporal and spatial frameworks that govern and constrain these. Both formal and informal food retailers adapt as best they can to position themselves to benefit most profitably from these shifting arrangements.

SUPERMARKET EXPANSION IN RURAL SOUTH AFRICA

In Southern Africa, supermarket expansion has been dominated by South African chains which have moved into neighbouring countries, aided by the liberalization of foreign direct investment (FDI) across the region.[3] Within South Africa itself, supermarket control of food distribution and retail has quickly intensified. By 2003, the share of national food retail held by supermarkets in South Africa had already reached 55 per cent (Weatherspoon and Reardon 2003: 333), growing to 70 per cent in 2007 (Crush and Frayne 2011: 784). These figures reveal a formal retail sector expanding at an unprecedented rate. The patterns of expansion suggest a broadening of the customer base to include not only the middle and upper classes but also the poor, a shift prompted by the post-apartheid expansion of social security.[4] Government grants are widely distributed and the number of recipients continues to grow.[5] This ensures a reliable customer base for formal retail even in the poorest regions of the country, such as the former 'homeland' area of northern KwaZulu-Natal in which data for this study were collected.[6] The expansion of supermarkets in the former 'homelands' has contributed to the rapid growth of small towns and their surrounding hinterlands.

Ethnographic research was carried out in and around the town of Jozini in the municipality of Umkhanyakude, situated in the far north of the province of KwaZulu-Natal. The town is a hub for the region, and home to several municipal government departments as well as two new supermarkets which opened in 2012 and 2013. Despite the recent growth of retail in Jozini, supermarkets have had a presence in the area since the 1970s when a group of shops known as the Ndumu stores, owned by a local trader called Peter Rutherfoord, were subsumed under the Spar Supermarket Group, an international supermarket franchise founded in the Netherlands in 1932. The first Ndumu store had been set up several decades earlier in 1918 just north of Jozini, by Rutherfoord's grandfather, R.H. Rutherfoord, who in the same year abandoned his sugar cane field in Umfolozi when it was devastated by floods. He was an experienced trader and formed a company called the Ndumu Group which expanded and within several years managed a network of stores throughout the region. His son Roy Rutherfoord took over the business, which was later passed to his grandson Peter Rutherfoord. The franchise model pioneered by the Spar Supermarket Group – which first entered South Africa in 1963 – provided an opportunity for Rutherfoord to continue running the shops using the Spar insignia and paying a fee in return for selling Spar products (Whelan 2011). The former Ndumu Group stores, now identified by their franchise name Spar Supatrade, are still run by the Rutherfoord family. At the time of research, Craig Rutherfoord was managing Supatrade as well as other major retail franchises in the area including Engen petrol stations and Buildit hardware stores, and had supermarket branches in most of the big towns across the region. In addition to the predominantly Chinese- and Indian-owned smaller wholesalers that began to open in the 1990s, and a network of smaller informal retailers, these franchises have been a significant feature of the retail landscape in the region.

The success of the Spar Supermarket Group was due not to its ability to outcompete smaller existing enterprise, but rather to use the franchise model to take advantage of a well-established network of stores, trading routes and traders. Other supermarkets and wholesalers in the region including Boxer Cash and Carry and Jock Morrison's have followed similar trajectories. The example of the Rutherfoord family's Spar Supatrade demonstrates an alliance between international corporate retail and a highly successful, local family business whose embeddedness and long-standing, intimate connection to the region have ensured its ongoing success. The example of the Rutherfoord family also challenges a stereotypical assumption that the pragmatic harnessing of kinship networks applies exclusively to supposedly tradition-bound, black South Africans or to informal modes of economic practice; in rural KwaZulu-Natal, they are intrinsic to the operations both of long-established, white traders (whose presence in the region dates to the late nineteenth century) and, via them, to those of international corporate retail.

What is evident is that supermarket retail and 'local' trading networks in northern KwaZulu-Natal have not developed as distinct sectors in competition with one another, with the former 'bulldozing' the latter. Rather, Spar Supermarket Group has operated predominantly through the creation of alliances via the franchise system, which allows companies to appropriate and benefit from existing trading practices. Daniel Miller (1998) describes similar strategies used by Coca-Cola in Trinidad, which entered the market by franchising to a successful and well-known local company. This method was also crucial in the peri-urban areas of the KwaZulu 'Homeland' during the 1970s, when franchises offered a means by which white-owned supermarkets could bypass racial restrictions on economic activity in the 'Homeland' – part of the government's policy of 'Separate Development'– by franchising to black traders (Maré and Hamilton 1987: 107–8). Spar Supatrade will now face increasing competition with the recent entry of Shoprite, South Africa's largest supermarket chain.

Given the dense regulatory interventions that have shaped the economic and physical landscape of northern KwaZulu-Natal the expansion of corporate capital has not followed a linear trajectory. In 1988, the government introduced legislation under the Development Aid Laws Amendment Act which repealed many of the restrictions on trading and which legalized spaza shops: the small- to medium-sized shops known locally as 'tuck-shops' which are run from people's homes or from small buildings, shipping containers or shacks embedded in residential areas. Informal trading operated illegally prior to the legislative changes of the 1980s, but the change prompted a rapid proliferation of *spazas*, to whom wholesalers could now sell products directly, undermining the competitive advantage of larger stores. Many *spazas* remained unlicensed, but could easily procure their stock given that licensees were no longer required to buy goods from wholesalers.

These events reveal a picture that is more complex than the story of an ever-encroaching supermarket sector wiping out informal retail. They suggest that what prevented small and unregulated trading was not excessive competition by larger stores but the tight systems of governance in operation, and that once removed, small retail escalated, undermining the exclusive market access of the hitherto dominant Spar Supatrade and other larger stores. Attracted by the ever-increasing numbers of small traders to whom they could sell, wholesalers eventually relocated themselves in small towns, having been formerly situated in Durban and relying on mobile traders to transport goods to the rural areas.

The town of Jozini expanded quickly in the early 1990s, with Chinese and Indian traders opening food, clothing, car spares and hardware stores. International fast-food retail is represented by Kentucky Fried Chicken, which is now a ubiquitous feature of most small towns across South Africa. More recently, large supermarket chains, Boxers and Shoprite, have opened in newly built shopping malls. Supermarkets' control of the market is enhanced by their role as locations at which government grants are collected, which structures food practices according to a dominant monthly time frame. I now turn to these consumer practices to examine in what ways they influence the strategies of retailers, both large and small.

RETAIL INFRASTRUCTURE AND THE SYNCHRONIZATION OF FOOD NEEDS

At the beginning of every month, long queues trail out of supermarkets and banks, and the densely populated rural hub of Jozini is a hive of activity. On these days, supermarkets act as grant 'pay points', as they are known, where people can collect their grant while shopping at the same time. On this day, supermarket shelves are packed high while people stock up on monthly essentials: maize meal, rice, sugar, beans, bread, powdered baby milk, sugar, teabags, cooking oil, margarine and fermented milk (*amasi*). In summer, a dense heat settles thickly over the town while the queues of mostly women wait often for hours to receive their grant. Those still with money or food to spare by the end of the month wait a couple of days for the rush to subside before going to collect their grant. For most, the first day of the month is a long time coming, and the few days leading up to it can involve cutting down on food portions, borrowing from neighbours or buying food on credit from informal retailers, forming a set of interlocking strategies that serve to smooth over the monthly cycle. The journey to town and back from the surrounding rural hinterland involves time and expense, so most people combine their grant collection with their main monthly food shop.

In a country characterized by chronic joblessness and an ever-growing population, government expenditure on welfare payments has increased exponentially from R11 billion in 1994 to R113 billion in 2013. Two-fifths of South Africa's population now receive a grant, many of whom are rural dwellers, creating a burgeoning market opportunity for corporate food retail. This was evident in a changing physical landscape. In 2012, two new large supermarkets opened in the two nearby towns of Jozini and Mkuze, adding to the existing three supermarkets in each, and an array of smaller retail outlets. In mid-2013, a shopping mall was being erected on a former sugar cane field in a densely populated area about a mile outside of Jozini town, comparable in size to many of its counterparts in Durban or Johannesburg. This was to house the new Shoprite supermarket, as well as numerous other stores. As the huge grey structure slowly took form, excitement and nervous anticipation intensified around the impending rush for jobs.

For most families, monthly government grants, especially the pension, are used to buy the most essential food items. The ubiquitous use of the social pension for essential food purchase, regardless of other income sources, suggests that the pension is both a lifeline for families without other income or food sources, and the most appropriate means of food acquisition even for those with multiple sources of income or for those engaged in farming. This can be explained partly by the fact that government grants are both the most routine and the most reliable income source, corresponding well with the regularity and predictability of food needs. In Jane Guyer's terms, it is the 'synchronicity' of food needs with government grants that makes the latter so conducive for food purchase (Guyer 1989: 139), though gender norms also make this category of income more available for household food expenditure than others, because most grant recipients are women, who tend also to be responsible for food provisioning.

Just like salaried work, government grants impose a dominant monthly time frame which is the backbone around which food provisioning is structured for the large majority of families. While food is relatively abundant immediately after receipt of the pension, it can run out towards the end of the monthly cycle. For many families, therefore, this cycle involves peaks and troughs in food access, albeit more muted than the fluctuations caused by the longer and less predictable cycles of agricultural seasonality to which previous generations were exposed.

For those without additional disposable cash, various strategies are used to ensure food supply during these once-monthly periods of food scarcity. This is often achieved without the use of money, particularly in areas where small-scale food production was common, for instance by eating food grown at home, by providing piecemeal labour in return for food or through gift exchange. A specific type of exchange known as *ukunana* is tied closely to the monthly cycles imposed by grants. *Ukunana* refers to a practice of exchange whereby maize or another item is requested, often by a child sent to a neighbouring house, with the expectation that it will be returned when food is restocked in the receiving household. Strict rules apply to *ukunana* that distinguish it from other forms of gift exchange, and that tie it closely to the monthly economic cycle of households. First, the same quantity of the item must be returned as was provided, which is ensured by returning it in the same or similar container. Second, only items considered essential to a meal can be requested. This is usually restricted to maize, though occasionally onions or potatoes may be included. Even rice, which is now widely consumed as a staple starch in addition to maize, cannot be requested through the practice of *ukunana*. *Ukunana* is therefore reserved exclusively for food shortage and hunger relief, and signifies an ethical relationship between two households. A third rule attached to the practice of *ukunana* is the time limit for returning the item, after which the honesty of the recipient may be questioned, and it is here that we find the practice shaped by the temporal framework of government grants. A month is considered the longest period within which food should be returned because, as one person explained, households acquire food using a grant so food is always replenished within this period. The grant, therefore, structures the moral content of this type of food exchange according to a specific time frame. As some grants are received at different times during the month, this strategy can be mutually beneficial for families. In one example two elderly neighbours received their grants two weeks apart, and habitually purchased a bag of frozen chicken for the other on their respective grant-collection days. This staggering of pensions was useful, especially because neither woman owned a freezer or a refrigerator.

Given that *ukunana* is usually limited to the exchange of maize, other types of food are frequently purchased on credit (*ukukweleta*) from local tuck-shops, to be paid on receipt of the grant. This is yet another way around the problem of cyclical food shortage before grant payout day. It is through credit practices that we find small retailers benefitting from the strict time frames imposed by the grant system. Like *ukunana*, *ukukweleta* serves an important function of 'smoothing over' the peaks and troughs of a cycle (Guyer 1989: 139) that is largely determined in this context, as I have shown, by the most regular and reliable form of income: the government grant. Credit offered by local traders has served this function since the end of the nineteenth century, easing families through periods of cash or food shortage, though previously it was the agricultural cycle, in some instances combined with salaried work, which served as the dominant temporal frame. Webs of credit and indebtedness helped to establish the ongoing relationship between residents and traders, and some traders drew on a discourse of philanthropy to locate the practice as part of a broader moral economy, particularly when under threat by new rounds of government legislation. As one long-established trader John Fry stated: 'I have kept families fed until such time as the husband is able to secure employment. ... There are a number of ways I have assisted the Black man at my own expense' (John Fry 1979, quoted in Whelan 2011: 107).

Some treated periods of food shortage as opportunities for gain, such as those who sold government provided 'drought relief' maize at marked-up prices (Whelan

2011: 168). Either way, then as now, it was the ability of small traders to adapt and mould themselves to the ebb and flow of livelihoods and food requirements that was key to the whole endeavour. Today, the ability to offer credit towards the end of the monthly cycle is a flexibility that ensures the continued role of small spaza shops despite the growing presence of supermarkets. They capitalize on the time limitations of formal retail, namely the requirement for immediate transaction, using their knowledge of customers, who are often also their neighbours, to offer this flexibility in the form of credit. They keep detailed written accounts of the debts they are owed and build up knowledge about the reliability and trustworthiness of individual customers. They also generally accept cash only which is why – rather than merely a symptom of financial illiteracy as suggested in government and media narratives – grant recipients often withdraw their grant in full instead of leaving it on their card for later expenditure.[7]

Although food is more expensive than in the larger shops in town, these informal establishments attract customers because, as Maxim Bolt (2012) shows in Limpopo, informal economic practices make use of, and flourish in, the gaps created by the formal sector. Not only do informal retailers capitalize on the time limitations of supermarket retail by offering credit, they also make use of the spatial fragmentation of rural residency by operating close to people's homes. This important spatial character of food retail is partly a legacy of apartheid era resettlement schemes, which created an array of villages separated from one another and with poor infrastructural links, making it difficult for people to access resources and placing constraints on food availability.

Improved transportation, especially the proliferation of the minibus taxi industry, has served to create more competition for *spazas* by overcoming the spatial limitations to some extent. However, this does not only create more competition between informal and supermarket retail, but also between supermarkets, wholesalers and manufacturers. For example, the South African bread company, Sasko, bypasses supermarkets altogether by supplying directly to *spazas*; its delivery trucks can be seen early in the morning in the most remote rural areas. In this instance, the perishability of an item such as bread ensures the continued importance of local tuck-shops for its distribution. Medium-sized stores are also seeking new methods of competing with supermarkets, and these often have to do with a competitive advantage achieved through overcoming spatial limitations. In one instance, a trader planned to supply goods directly to *spazas* at a 10 per cent mark-up, knowing that the latter would save the same amount by not incurring transport costs to and from town to collect stock (Whelan 2011: 173).

Other informal arrangements create food acquisition strategies that bypass supermarket retail. Financial mutuals, otherwise known as rotating savings clubs or *stokvels*, are informal associations typically consisting exclusively of women in which money is pooled and redistributed, or spent on bulk purchase of food. By 1991, *stokvels* in South Africa had an estimated annual turnover of more than R1 billion, and have grown considerably in the post-apartheid era (Bähre 2007: 9). Members contribute an agreed amount of money paid in cash each month, and at the end of the year, food is purchased in bulk and distributed between members.

Most *stokvels* acquire additional funds throughout the year by becoming *mashonisas* (informal moneylenders), offering loans at high interest rates, typically 30 or 40 per cent each month. These two strategies of buying in bulk and gaining interest through lending mean individuals receive much more food than they would have been able to buy with the money they had contributed. *Stokvels* tend to bypass both supermarkets and smaller retailers by purchasing directly from wholesalers. Like the banking or saving of money, the strategy of 'banking' food via *stokvels* ensures some continuity and helps to smooth over the vulnerabilities associated with making a living and achieving food security during periods of economic difficulty or crisis, and demonstrates tight links between formal and informal modes of food distribution.

Traders and small or informal retailers exist in a dense web of relationships that predates the rise of supermarkets in rural South Africa. Despite the increased competition introduced by supermarkets, these networks remain prominent given their centrality to household food acquisition at certain times in the monthly cycle, and in many areas that are geographically more remote.

CONCLUSION

The expansion of supermarkets is symptomatic of a structural transformation in the organizational technologies of global commodity chains. It has been catalysed in South Africa by the widespread reliance on government grants and commercial retail for food acquisition. The fact that the majority of rural dwellers purchase their main food supply from the formal retail sector using the government grant, administered through a sophisticated and standardized biometric card system, is an indication of the degree of formalization of South Africa's economy and its distinctiveness in this regard vis-à-vis other sub-Saharan African countries. However, in this chapter, I have shown that informal/formal linkages in the retail sector are sites both of complementarity and of struggle, rather than one simply wiping out the other. A range of activities suggest tight linkages between formal and informal modes of financial gain. Crush and Frayne (2011: 803) make a similar point in relation to the urban context in South Africa, while Anand (2009) highlights their complementarity in Mexican food retail. As Amy Cohen's research in West Bengal demonstrates, changes in legislative frameworks give rise to a constantly mutating interaction between formal and informal modes of economic action. In this respect, it is more useful to think not in terms of two sectors in opposition to one another but rather, as Keith Hart has suggested, in terms of a 'partial institutionalization of economies' (Hart 2010: 150), where formal and informal modes operate in tandem.

I have focused on food acquisition practices of consumers as a lens through which to investigate the interlocking character of different elements of rural retail infrastructure. This approach offers a link between two emerging yet hitherto separate discussions in the anthropology of food, relating to the effects of supermarket expansion on consumers on the one hand and supply chains on the other hand. What the ethnography here suggests is that the strategies of retailers, both large and small, are shaped by the temporal and spatial character of consumers' food practices, which present both constraints and opportunities for different types of retailers. Informal institutions such as *stokvels*, as well as various types of exchange including *ukukweleta* (purchase on credit) and *ukunana* (inter-household exchange), are all strategies that smooth over temporal troughs in food access, much like the strategies of 'seasonal adjustment' described by Jane Guyer (1989: 139), though we can broaden the concept of 'seasonality' here to refer in the broadest sense to a timeframe rather than an agricultural season. In the case of *stokvels* – often bypassing supermarkets and buying their stock in bulk directly from wholesalers – the proliferation of informal, organized modes of food distribution diverts the flow of goods away from supermarkets and not the other way around. A focus on retail via the food consumption activities of residents, therefore, offers a useful vantage point from which to understand the expanding frontier of corporate food retail, not as a homogenous process but one conditioned by the particular regulatory systems and historically shaped settings in which it occurs.

ACKNOWLEDGEMENTS

This work has been partly supported by the Leverhulme Centre for Integrative Research on Agriculture and Health (LCIRAH). I am grateful for research funding from the Economic and Social Research Council of the United Kingdom (award RES-062-23-1290) and the British Academy (award SG102535).

NOTES

1. For a recent review of the diverse literature on this subject, see Meagher 2013. For a discussion in the South African context, see Hull and James (2012).
2. According to the national census, annual household incomes in the municipality of Jozini more than doubled between 2001 and 2011, from R16,122 (about GBP £1,500) to R36,164 (about £3,300). In the province of KwaZulu-Natal as a whole, in which Jozini is situated, average household income increased from R38,905 (£3,500) to R83,050 (£7,550) over the same period.
3. Given the market dominance of highly competitive South African supermarket chains, multinationals have had a limited role in Africa. This changed in 2011 when Walmart won a stiff legal battle to buy a 51 per cent share in the South African retail company, Massmart, and in October 2013 confirmed its intention to buy a major stake in Kenyan retailer Naivas.
4. First introduced for white and coloured South Africans in 1928, pensions were extended to Africans in 1944, though at considerably lower rates. When the African National Congress (ANC) came to power in 1994, they removed differentiated payments based on race, and a key aim became the extended reach of pensions to all who were eligible. As a result, social security payments increased considerably. By 2000, 1.4% of GDP was taken up by the social pension (Devereux 2007: 556).
5. Grants are provided via a non-contributory and means-tested system. They include the child support grant, the foster-child grant, the care-dependency grant, the older persons grant, the disability grant, grant-in-aid and social relief of distress.

6. The 'homelands', or bantustans, were territories set aside by the apartheid government for the purpose of creating ethnically homogeneous, independent states for South Africa's black ethnic groups. Ten were created altogether and were subsequently dismantled following the democratic elections in 1994.

7. SASSA's communications manager, Kelemogile Moseki, encouraged people to use electronic payment facilities such as post offices, banks and ATMs to access their grant payments, not only to reduce queues at formal pay-points but also to encourage 'a culture of saving and ensure that they [grant recipients] move away from temptation because at the bank you can withdraw only the amount you need'. He went on to allude to what he saw as the financially irresponsible behaviour of many grant recipients: 'At the pay-points, they get all the money and end up spending it all on their way home without saving anything, unlike having bank accounts, whereby they will also be able to save the extra money they get elsewhere.' Gabi Khumalo, 24 July 2009, 'Beneficiaries Urged to Use Alternative Payment Methods,' *South African Government News Agency*, http://www.sanews.gov.za/south-africa/beneficiaries-urged-use-alternative-payment-methods (accessed 15 October 2013).

REFERENCES

Abbots, E. J. and Coles, B. (2013), 'Horse-Meat Gate: The Discursive Production of a Neoliberal Food Scandal', *Food, Culture and Society*, 16(4): 535–50.

Abrahams, C. (2010), 'Transforming the Region: Supermarkets and the Local Food Economy', *African Affairs*, 109(434): 115–34.

Anand, J. (2009), 'Supermarketization, Consumer Choices, and the Changing Food Retail Market Structure: The Case of Citlalicalli, Mexico', in Donald C. Wood (ed.), *Economic Development, Integration, and Morality in Asia and the Americas (Research in Economic Anthropology, Volume 29)*, 63–88, Emerald Group Publishing Limited.

Atasoy, Y. (2013), 'Supermarket Expansion in Turkey: Shifting Relations of Food Provisioning', *Journal of Agrarian Change*, 13(4): 547–70.

Bähre, E. (2007), *Money and Violence: Financial Self-Help Groups in a South African Township*, Leiden: Brill.

Barrientos, S. and Dolan, C. (2006), 'Transformation of Global Food: Opportunities and Challenges for Fair and Ethical Trade', in S. Barrientos and C. Dolan (eds), *Ethical Sourcing in the Global Food System*, 1–34, Oxon: Earthscan.

Bolt, M. (2012), 'Waged Entrepreneurs, Policed Informality: Work, the Regulation of Space and the Economy of the Zimbabwean-South African Border', *Africa* 82(1): 111–30.

Burt, S. Dawson, J. and Sparks, L. (2002), 'Retail Internationalisation and Retail Failure: Issues from the case of Marks and Spencer', *International Review of Retail, Distribution, and Consumer Research*, 12(2): 191–219.

Campbell, H. (2009), 'Breaking New Ground in Food Regime Theory: Corporate Environmentalism, Ecological Feedbacks and the "Food From Somewhere" Regime?' *Agriculture and Human Values*, 26: 309–19.

Cohen, A. J. (2013), 'Supermarkets in India: Struggles Over the Organization of Agricultural Markets and Food Supply Chains', *University of Miami Law Review*, 68: 19–86.

Colloredo-Mansfeld, R., Tewari, M., Williams, J., Holland, D. C., Steen, A. and
Wilson, A. B. (2014), 'Communities, Supermarkets, and Local Food: Mapping
Connections and Obstacles in Food System Work in North Carolina', *Human
Organization*, 73(3): 247–57.

Crush, J. and Frayne, B. (2011), 'Supermarket Expansion and the Informal Food
Economy in Southern African Cities: Implications for Urban Food Security', *Journal of
Southern African Studies* 37(4): 781–807.

Devereux, S. (2007), 'Social Pensions in Southern Africa in the Twentieth Century',
Journal of Southern African Studies, 33(3): 539–60.

Dixon, J. and Isaacs, B. (2013), 'There's Certainly a lot of Hurting Out There: Navigating
the Trolley of Progress Down the Supermarket Isle', *Agriculture and Human Values*,
30: 283–97.

El-Amir, A. and Burt, S. (2008), 'Sainsburys in Egypt: The Strange Case of Dr Jekyll
and Mr Hyde?' *International Journal of Retail and Distribution Management*, 36(4):
300–22.

Everts, J. and Jackson, P. (2009), 'Modernisation and the Practices of Contemporary Food
Shopping', *Environment and Planning D: Society and Space*, 27(5): 917–35.

Freidberg, S. (2007), 'Supermarkets and Imperial Knowledge', *Cultural Geographies*,
14(3): 321–42.

Gamble, J. (2007), 'The rhetoric of the consumer and customer control in China', *Work,
Employment & Society*, 21(1): 7–25.

Gartin, M. (2012), 'Food deserts and nutritional risk in Paraguay', *American Journal of
Human Biology*, 24(3): 296–301.

Guyer, J. (1989), 'From Seasonal Income to Daily Diet in a Partially Commercialized
Rural Economy (Southern Cameroon)', in D. Sahn (ed.), *Seasonal Variability in Third
World Agriculture: The Consequences for Food Security*, 137–50, Baltimore, MD: Johns
Hopkins University Press.

Hart, K. (2010), 'Informal Economy', in K. Hart, J. Laville and A. D. Cattani (eds), *The
Human Economy: A Citizen's Guide*, 142–53, Cambridge: Polity.

Harvey, M. (2007), 'The Rise of Supermarkets and Asymmetries of Economic Power',
in D. Burch and G. Lawrence (eds), *Supermarket and Agri-Food Supply Chains:
Transformations in the Production and Consumption of Foods*, 51–73, Cheltenham:
Edward Elgar.

Hattersly, L., Isaacs, B. and Burch, D. (2013), 'Supermarket Power, Own-Labels, and
Manufacturer Counter-Strategies: International Relations of Cooperation and
Competition in the Fruit Canning Industry', *Agriculture and Human Values*, 30(2):
225–33.

Hull, E. (2014), 'Bringing the City to the Country: Supermarket Expansion, Food
Practices and Aesthetics in Rural South Africa', in N. Domingos, J. M. Sobral and
H. G. West (eds), *Food Between the Country and the City: Ethnographies of a
Changing Global Foodscape*, 59–72, London: Bloomsbury.

Hull, E. and James, D. (2012), 'Introduction: Popular Economies in South Africa', *Africa*,
82(1): 1–19.

Humphrey, J. (2007), 'The Supermarket Revolution in Developing Countries: Tidal Wave
or Tough Competitive Struggle?' *Journal of Economic Geography*, 7(4): 337–40.

Igumbor, E. U., Sanders, D., Puone, T. R., Tsolekile, L., Schwarz, C., Purdy, C., Swart, R., Durão, S. and Hawkes, C. (2012), '"Big Food," the Consumer Food Environment, Health, and the Policy Response in South Africa', *PLoS Med* 9(7): e1001253. doi: 10.1371/journal.pmed.1001253.

Isaacs, B., Dixon, J., Banwell, C., Seubsman, S., Kelly, M. and Pangsap, S. (2010), 'Competition, Adaptation and Mutation: Fresh Market and Supermarket Conventions in Thailand', *Journal of Sociology*, 46(4): 413–36.

Klein, J. A. (2013), 'Everyday Approaches to Food Safety in Kunming', *The China Quarterly*, 214: 376–93.

Lawrence, G. and Burch, D. (2007), 'Understanding Supermarkets and Agri-food Supply Chains', in D. Burch and G. Lawrence (eds), *Supermarket and Agri-Food Supply Chains: Transformations in the Production and Consumption of Foods*, 1–28, Cheltenham: Edward Elgar.

Lyons, K. (2007), 'Supermarkets as Organic Retailers: Impacts for the Australian Organic Sector', in D. Burch and G. Lawrence (eds), *Supermarket and Agri-Food Supply Chains: Transformations in the Production and Consumption of Foods*, 154–72, Cheltenham: Edward Elgar.

Magdoff, F. J., Foster B. and Buttel, F. H. (eds) (2000), *Hungry For Profit*, New York: Monthly Review Press.

Maré, G. and Hamilton, G. (1987), *An Appetite for Power: Buthelezi's Inkatha and South Africa*, Johannesburg: Raven Press

McMichael, P. (2008), 'Peasants Make Their Own history, But Not Just As They Please ...', *Journal of Agrarian Change*, 8(2 and 3): 205–28.

McMichael, P. and Friedmann, H. (2007), 'Situating the "Retailing Revolution"', in D. Burch and G. Lawrence(eds), *Supermarket and Agri-Food Supply Chains: Transformations in the Production and Consumption of Foods*, 293–324, Cheltenham: Edward Elgar.

Meagher, K. (2013), *Unlocking the Informal Economy: A Literature Review on Linkages Between Formal and Informal Economies in Developing Countries*, WIEGO Working Paper No. 27.

Miller, D. (1998), 'Coca-Cola: A Black Sweet Drink from Trinidad', in D. Miller (ed.), *Material Culture: Why Some Things Matter*, Chicago: University of Chicago Press.

Miller, D. (2005), 'New Regional Imaginaries in Post-Apartheid Southern Africa: Retail Workers at a Shopping Mall in Zambia', *Journal of Southern African Studies*, 31(1): 117–45.

Neven, D., Odera, M. M., Reardon, T. and Wang, H. (2009), 'Kenyan Supermarkets, Emerging Middle-Class Horticultural Farmers, and Employment Impacts on the Rural Poor', *World Development*, 37(11): 1802–11.

Popkin, B. (2014), 'Nutrition, Agriculture and the Global Food System in Low and Middle Income Countries', *Food Policy*, 47: 91–6.

Raschke, V. and Cheema, B. (2008), 'Colonization, the New World Order, and the Eradication of Traditional Food Habits in East Africa: Historical Perspective on the Nutrition Transition', *Public Health Nutrition*, 11(7): 662–74.

Reardon, T. and Hopkins, R. (2006), 'The Supermarket Revolution in Developing Countries: Policies to Address Emerging Tensions Among Supermarkets, Suppliers and Traditional Retailers', *The European Journal of Development Research*, 18(4): 522–45.

Reardon, T. and Timmer, C. P. (2007), 'The Rise of Supermarkets in the Global Food System', in J. von Braun and E. Díaz-Bonilla (eds), *Globalization of Food and Agriculture and the Poor*, 189–214, New Delhi: Oxford University Press.

Richards, C., Lawrence, G. and Burch, D. (2011), 'Supermarkets and Agro-Industrial Foods: The Strategic Manufacturing of Consumer Trust', *Food, Culture and Society*, 14(1): 29–47.

Sullivan, D. (2014), 'From Food Desert to Food Mirage: Race, Social Class, and Food Shopping in a Gentrifying Neighborhood', *Advances in Applied Sociology*, 4: 30–5.

Velthuis, M. (2014), 'Modern Retail Chains in India: A Multi-Sited Ethnography of the Centralisation of Governance in the Indian Agri-food Market', Unpublished Paper, Navigating Foodways: Postgraduate Research Workshop, SOAS Food Studies Centre, London, 9 June 2014.

Wang, H. (2010), 'An Anthropological Study of a Japanese Supermarket in Guangzhou, Mainland China', Unpublished Masters Dissertation, University of Hong Kong. Available Online:http://hub.hku.hk/bitstream/10722/132965/3/FullText.pdf?accept=1.

Wang, Z., Mao, Y. and Gale, F. (2008), 'Chinese Consumer Demand for Food Safety Attributes in Milk Products', *Food Policy*, 33: 27–36.

Weatherspoon, D. D. and Reardon, T. (2003), 'The Rise of Supermarkets in Africa: Implications for Agrifood Systems and the Rural Poor', *Development Policy Review*, 21(3): 333–55.

Whelan, D. (2011), *Trading Lives: The Commercial, Social and Political Communities of the Zululand Trading Store*, Unpublished PhD thesis, SOAS, University of London.

CHAPTER EIGHTEEN

Ethical Consumption: The Moralities and Politics of Food

PETER LUETCHFORD

A notable feature of contemporary life is the role food plays as a medium for social commentary and political action. Nowhere is this more obvious than in media coverage. Food dominates television and radio programmes; we are bombarded with information on health and sourcing issues, follow creative chefs and their recipes, and are shown scenarios that promote intimate relationships but are paradoxically presented as competitions. Food is as visible in policymaking and is the focus of a good deal of campaigning and proselytizing. The prevalence of debates around food today demands interrogation, as it signals something important about the social and cultural worlds we inhabit.

The emphasis on food is not new. The ancient Greeks had an overwhelming fascination with it as a key element in their regimen (Foucault 1984: 340, 347). For them, the 'art of living' required considered balancing of exercise, food, drink, sleep and sex; the work on the body that promoted a happy and useful life (Foucault 1984: 99–110). One of Foucault's concerns in *The History of Sexuality* was to show how sex usurped food in constructing the self, culminating in the Victorian obsession with repressing but at the same time meticulously detailing sexual conduct (Foucault 1976).While sex undoubtedly remains a fertile topic for censure, monitoring and moral debate, in much of Western culture food has re-emerged as a key social and ethical 'problem'. In this chapter I interrogate ethical consumption by focusing on this 'problematization'.

Different approaches to the production, distribution and consumption of food entail distinct practices, which then engender their own moralities and politics. For example, hypermarkets offer consumers the convenience of a one-stop shop but undermine local economies, while alternative provision based on shortening food chains endeavours to support struggling producers but can smack of elitism. One part of the ethical problem is then how individuals as consumers, enjoined to make choices, negotiate the perceived benefits and disadvantages of different food regimes and so constitute themselves as particular kinds of ethical beings. Food is a particularly rich medium for ethical orientations because in its infinite variety it is a prime object for choice and social distinction. This is especially so as the range and availability of products escalates in an increasingly integrated global economy, and because it impacts across so many areas of our lives – from the body to the environment, from our subjective sense of self to our constitution as social beings. Accordingly, the argument I wish to make is that food presents consumers with a core contemporary conundrum in explicit and material form. Laying the foundations to substantiate that claim requires an interrogation of moral ideas more broadly and ethical orientations in relation to those ideas.

Food, it is argued, has become increasingly visible because it encapsulates tensions and contradictions in contemporary life; essentially, food is a prime material for constituting social beings, but its production, distribution and consumption are increasingly divorced from social context. Ethical and political practices around the problem of food consumption therefore engage with mainstream food provision. This then provides a contrast with alternatives people seek to realize. In as much as the turn towards such things as local food and Fair Trade are a response to dominant forms of farming and retail, they can be understood as a moral economy with a legitimizing notion, in the sense intended by E.P. Thompson (1971) and James Scott (1976, 1985).

Drawing on my ethnographic work on Fair Trade and local food reveals some of the problems that emerge from political and ethical endeavours to reformulate food provision. First, as implied above, consumers as choosers rarely act consistently, thus potentially undermining not only the transformative potential but also the political integrity of attempts to construct viable alternatives. Second, engaging in ethical consumption generates distinctions that reproduce hierarchies. Third, many of the attempts to consume ethically are framed as alternatives to dominant practices but are easily appropriated and diluted and come to reproduce the mainstream. What is worse is that ethical consumption may help to mask the damaging practices it sets out to reveal. Lastly, the focus on food, while understandable, leaves other parts of production, manufacturing and mainstream retail untouched. The evidence is that these contradictions escalate with increasing distance between producers and production and consumers and consumption.

LOCATING ETHICAL CONSUMPTION

The distinction made by Foucault between morality and ethics provides a starting point for the discussion since it allows for a range of moral persuasions as these emerge from and make sense within different social contexts (1992: 25–30). This is important for an anthropology of ethical consumption if it is to 'move beyond the universalizing language of ethics in order to situate it within specific historical contexts and geopolitical structures' (Mincyte 2014: 41).

Clearly a key part of that historical and geopolitical context are neoliberal markets as these have insinuated themselves across the globe. Indeed, the market has been a principle framework for anthropological analyses of ethical consumption (Carrier and Luetchford 2012; De Neve, Luetchford and Pratt 2008), but it is not the only one. As Jung, Klein and Caldwell (2014) have convincingly argued, important questions around ethical consumption are raised in its relation to the state, especially, but not only, in socialist and postsocialist contexts (see also Jung, this volume). What this suggests is a need to take account of the market, the state and civil organizations as these mediate categories of people labelled producers and consumers, and the activities of production and consumption. Further, we need not assume that the market always obscures social relations of production; for urban Chinese consumers, for example, it may encourage greater awareness of producers (Klein 2014: 118). If ethical consumption of food is carried out in 'conversation with both the state and the market' (Klein, Jung and Caldwell 2014: 19), then we need to document the moral ideas people express in relation to those things, and how they conduct and construct themselves as ethical beings with regard to moral codes as these emerge in different state–market–civil society contexts. Inevitably, this involves a process of negotiation between competing moral schemes.

To develop an analysis in that vein I draw on Foucault, who sees morality as a set of values that may or may not constitute a 'systematic ensemble', but in either case leaves room for compromise, loopholes, interpretations and resistances. By contrast, ethics concerns how one forms oneself as a moral subject, or what it means to the self to act morally. Because of the different possibilities for interpretation and action in relation to morality, there are many ways to constitute oneself ethically. The distinction between morality and ethics and the way it relates to food consumption is central to my argument, since the problematic of food lies precisely in the range of moral ideas and different and sometimes contradictory ways one can act ethically in relation to them.

Situating this approach within other anthropological formulations of the relation between ethics and morality will clarify the direction I am proposing. Miller (1998), for example, contends that ethics concern distant others, while morality in food shopping puts the household first. However, as commentators have pointed out, reducing the distinction to the intimate and the distant is problematic (Klein, Jung and Caldwell 2014: 6; Dombos 2012: 126-127). More useful in this respect is de Solier's proposal that 'ethics is more about others, whereas morality is more about the self' (2013: 5). Here the terms may be reversed but the idea is similar to my own. When shopping, people 'engage in "ethical dialogues" inside their own heads or with others to explain and legitimate their purchases' (Vramo 2012: 82). They do this in relation to moral codes, such that there is an 'evaluation of conduct in relation to esteemed or despised human qualities' (Humphrey 1997: 26, cited in Oxfeld 2014: 45)

There is in this a strong element of orientation, or choice between different moral possibilities. Two observations are then forthcoming. First, the market is the primary arena for choices today, and neoliberal markets in particular are constructed in opposition to constraints imposed by the state, which explains the emphasis on the market in studies of ethical food consumption. Second, food is perhaps more than any other activity a domain in which people exercise and are enjoined to choose, with those choices leading to the constitution of the self as an ethical subject. Should one, for example, buy cheap meat to exercise thrift, organic lamb from New Zealand, locally produced conventional meat or be vegetarian? How people respond to such dilemmas, which proliferate in shopping and lifestyle, precisely allows for the kind of 'subjectification' and 'practices of the self' that Foucault identifies as central to making a particular kind of 'modern' person (1992: 30).

The enterprise of self-fashioning is mimicked and reproduced in the many food programmes that revolve around competition, mentioned above. Nevertheless, the primacy of the ethical and the focus on the self may be more a question of perspective and persuasion. There are, after all, moral codes related to food, albeit diffuse ones, that people are enjoined to abide by. For example, that you should consider the effects of consumption on people and environments. Acting on that morality to shape food regimes (while simultaneously shaping oneself as an ethical being) opens up the possibility of politics.

While Foucault's discussion focuses primarily on the nature of the relation between morality and ethics, work in anthropology has increasingly looked at ethical consumption in social life. If ethics is defined as an ongoing process of constructing the self, then arguably the principle process through which this is done is that of the production and consumption of material culture. In one view, as a greater distance opens up between producers and consumers, so the creation of the self through objectification is accomplished more and more through the consumption of alienated objects (Miller 1987, 1995; Carrier 2012: 10). In another view, self-creation continues to operate through production, but not in the traditional workplace, as the meaning and spaces of productivity shift into the private domain (de Solier 2013).

These material culture approaches correspond to a general trend, characteristic of neoliberal societies, towards individuals constructing themselves through choices. Following this line tends to deny the transformative potential of ethical consumption – rather people are seen as constructing and reproducing themselves as individuals, and as social beings, through the medium of things. Operating within the dominant paradigm, material culture seems to accept we live in an alienated world, and so the approach struggles to give an adequate account of the explicitly political intentions of ethical consumers.

A second and alternative approach promises a more political and social definition. From a Polanyian framework, the essence of ethical consumption lies in the commentary it makes on the relation between economy and society (Carrier 2012). This makes sense for the study of people who buy Fair Trade, or local or organic, since they have a common desire to take social action against the mainstream food economy. In effect, the material culture approach seems to open up questions of personal orientations and is therefore consistent with a modernist and postmodernist ontology in which individuals recreate themselves through categories of their own making, using the rich diversity of cultural materials to hand. The focus is on subject–object relations. By contrast, that which emphasizes subject–subject relations, such as those between people as consumers and producers, can entertain political action and intentions in the way material culture studies cannot.

By acknowledging both approaches we can hope, first, to lay out the ideas and intentions, or moral codes that inform ethical consumption, and then consider outcomes, some of which may well be contrary to the intentions of people practising ethical consumption. That is, to begin to get at the conundrum of ethical consumption, we need to separate out what people think and want from what they do and get. Unpacking that distinction means first of all laying out the broad parameters of mainstream economy and how this sets up the conditions for Fair Trade and local food.

THE GLOBAL ECONOMY: PRODUCTIONS, DISTRIBUTIONS, MORALITIES

The tendency towards an open, global economy has accelerated in the shift towards neoliberalism. The promotion of a globalized economy by many governments and corporations has had specific effects and has both advanced and shaped the rise of industrialized agriculture and the food it supplies (Bernstein 2013; Pratt and Luetchford 2013). A more globally integrated economy impacts on production, exchange and consumption to varying degrees and in different ways, but it is important to note that these very realms are established and reinforced as categories and practices by mainstream economy itself.

In this section I identify the principle processes that underpin neoliberal style food regimes, their outcomes and how these outcomes are viewed by consumers in capitalist societies. This sets the scene for the moralities and politics of responses in such contexts. It is important to note that in socialist and postsocialist countries many of the processes detailed below are associated with the state, and expanding markets might even signal consumer choice to connect to producers (Jung, Klein and Caldwell 2014).

The last 40 years has seen major changes in the way food is produced and distributed. These material changes can be described as the industrialization of agriculture, increasing market integration and shifts in distribution (Bernstein 2013: 2–3; Pratt 2013: 27–9). The industrialization of agriculture involves the introduction of machinery and agrochemicals in the form of synthetic fertilizers, herbicides, pesticides, vaccines and the like. More recently the revolution has begun to shift towards technological fixes based around patented bioengineering of plant and animal material to increase productivity. Such innovations encourage specialization in specific crops and animals on larger farms pursuing monocultures of mass production. Alongside this is a process of market integration, facilitated by the removal of tariff barriers under the banner of trade liberalization, and further enhanced by futures trading or speculation in agricultural commodities. This leads to concentrations of power and capital by corporations, which squeeze out competitors by using mergers and acquisitions to capture ever-greater market share. In other words the food sector increasingly operates within and extends monopoly capitalism.

Market integration in food is increasingly possible with modern transport and storage systems such as airfreight and refrigeration, allowing such things as cheap, fresh green beans from Kenya to reach British supermarkets in prime condition. That is, since market integration underpins and requires changes in distribution, large supermarkets come to dominate food retailing. Indeed the processes of industrialized farming, mass transport, market integration and bulk buying, distribution and sale by the major supermarkets are thoroughly interwoven.

The more material changes are underpinned by ideologies and policies of deregulation, a tenet of which is that the producer should not care where components come from or who buys the commodities. Likewise the consumer need not know about the production process; where and by whom a thing was made. The connection between production and consumption is mediated by retailers, money and increasing physical and social distance. This is reinforced to the extent that when people produce, act as intermediaries or as consumers, they are enjoined to follow an ethic and an ideology of self-interest; selling to the highest bidder, buying the highest quality at the lowest price, or seeking comparative advantage in some other way.

Freedom and choice are key words in the attractions of the mainstream food economy. Entrepreneurs are free to create and promote goods and services, and profit from their endeavours; consumers are free to choose between brands and products that compete for their attention and purses. The model is closely related to globalization, as the exercise of choice by companies and individuals means that products and ideas are increasingly produced, distributed and consumed on a global scale, and made available to increasing numbers of people across the globe. The professed ethical imperative is to provide an increasing range of products at cheaper prices to consumers. As consumers people are enjoined to be discerning in their choices.

While much economic activity takes place within and accepts this formulation such that it sets the agenda, an important strand of ethical consumption today not only rejects it, but also seeks to put an alternative in its place. So a second strand is a counterpoint to the globalizing tendency built on open competition; it seeks to shape economy by taking relationships into account, so decisions about exchange are made using social criteria rather than personal preference or gain. These social criteria regulate, circumscribe and modulate by introducing moral ideas like welfare, responsibility, need or compassion. One important reference point for this regulated vision of economy within anthropology is Karl Polanyi's (1944) much cited concept of the double movement. Polanyi was concerned at the social costs of unregulated, *laissez-faire*, economics in the nineteenth century and noted that the 'opening up' of economy that resulted was met by a countermovement to regulate and inject social values back into economic practices.

The alternative vision of economy is usually evoked as a rebuke to the mainstream. This locates it within a romantic reaction to the Enlightenment, modernity and neo-liberal capitalism, a narrative of loss in which distinctive cultures are undermined by processes of homogenization (Kahn 1995). The unique and authentic contrasts with the mechanically produced, the organic rejects the synthetic, quality stands in opposition to quantity, diversity to singularity and metaphors of the timeless contradict innovation and progress. There is a gradual loss of roots and authenticity, as the world is thought to increasingly look the same everywhere. Fast food is an important focus of this critique (Wilk 2006). One way to understand the difference between these moral orders is as the difference between an economy that seeks balance rather than expansion, the primacy of use over exchange value, and the reproduction of relationships rather than individual gain. Food, as it is ingested and shared as use value, embodies, quite literally, these values. The purest expression of the alternative model in the Western cultural imagination is the household economy, which has its own 'moral architecture' (Booth 1993; Gudeman and Rivera 1990).

Welded to the romantic narrative of loss are more hard-nosed objections to the open economy as a destructive 'race to the bottom'. In one version, the criticism highlights how competition between entrepreneurs creates downward pressure on production costs and standards. At the other end, the consumer is held to account: seeking through choices the best product or maximum benefit at the lowest cost drives down prices and precipitates the race to the bottom. Overall, as Thomas Piketty's (2013) book has recently and famously shown, relative inequalities rise with capitalism, and spectacularly so in recent years. Advocates of neoliberalism say the overall benefits of the expansive economy outweigh negative outcomes; critics say that it is the nature of the global economy to consign costs to another part of the jungle.

The discussion thus far has presented two approaches to economy as types, or binary models, with distinct sets of practices, rationales, ethical orientations and political-economic underpinnings. The problem is that while at one level many people acting as ethical consumers have misgivings and even reject mainstream economy, at the same time, and in other areas of life, they enjoy its attractions and benefits. Life then becomes about negotiating different cultural values and ideas as well as money value, and this becomes the stuff of ethics.

To illustrate this latter point I now turn to ethnographic examples of ethical consumption. An examination of Fair Trade and the local food movement reveals not only the moral ideas that inspire practices, but also some of the complications and contradictions of making ethical choices in a market context. The examples move from Fair Trade to local food in the United Kingdom, and I then compare the latter with local food ideologies and practices in southern Spain. The choice of examples and the order of presentation are designed to show how ethical consumption as a rebuke to mainstream practices becomes more compromised and contradictory in line with increasing distance between producer and consumer, and production and consumption.

ETHNOGRAPHIC EXPLORATIONS OF ETHICS

In this section examples of ethical conundrums posed by food draw on ethnographic data collected while researching Fair Trade and local food. The former involved long-term fieldwork in Costa Rica and observations on representations of Fair Trade in the media and on packaging in the United Kingdom. While there are clear differences, and indeed some misinformation about the nature of small farmers, the impact of Fair Trade, and the political economy of coffee farming (Luetchford 2008, 2012), there is also a degree of common cause between the aims and ethical ideas of Costa Rican *campesinos* and Western consumers of Fair Trade products. The work on local food comes from a project on food and alternative provision in southern Spain, and participation in parallel research in South East England (Pratt and Luetchford 2013; Avanzino 2013). Again, there are notable differences in the way ethics around food is constructed between the cases, but there are also common themes and moral ideas: the primacy of the natural and the healthy, the centrality of sociality and the family, the value of autonomy and autarky and producing to consume as an avenue towards those goals.

Fair Trade: Imaginaries of the Ethical

Fair Trade provides a good example of consumers trying to act ethically in relation to moral codes. Here I draw attention, first of all, to the moral ideas inspiring Fair Trade, and the model of economy it projects and rejects. I then argue that the form and practice of Fair Trade, as a market-based mechanism, reproduces or fails to counter the problems it seeks to address. From this, I conclude that Fair Trade manifests itself primarily as an expression of consumer agency and consumer choice, rather than as an agent for change. This tendency is exacerbated as Fair Trade organizations project primary commodity economies in the global south as 'black boxes' by ironing out internal differences and conflicts of interest (Luetchford 2006, 2012)

Fair Trade coffee might well claim to be emblematic of Fair Trade products; certainly it was an early focus for NGOs and activism in Northern Europe in the early 1990s. For example, Fair Trade drew inspiration from successful campaigns to promote solidarity coffee in the fight against the right-wing, US-backed, Contra-insurgency in Central America. A second important factor in the visibility and emphasis on Fair Trade coffee was the collapse of the International Coffee Agreement in 1989, which effectively saw an end to regulation of supply and therefore a degree of control over prices by producing countries (Pendergast 1999). The outcome of this, as studies of the commodity chain demonstrate, is that the coffee industry as a whole has become increasingly 'buyer driven' (Daviron and Ponte 2005; Gereffi and Korzeniewicz 1994).

There are at least two reasons Fair Trade might capture the imagination of consumers. The first reason concerns political economy. Fair Trade focuses on high-value products that potentially allowed good margins and a livelihood to significant numbers of small farmers and workers in developing countries, which suggests potential to transform the lives of producers and labourers. This is easy to imagine when represented as 'smallholder economies', based around coffee production by farmers organized into cooperative associations, but the political message has more recently been extended to plantation workers suffering under exploitative conditions in industries such as cocoa and tea (Berlan 2012; Besky 2013).

While interventions in plantation economies focus on wages, hours of work and child labour, the underlying model in coffee is the ambition to stabilize prices in what is a notoriously unstable market. Fair Trade aims to do this by ensuring minimum prices to producers, and offering a 'social premium' when market prices rise above the minimum price. Price instability is largely an outcome of a lack of elasticity in supply and demand in response to market prices, because coffee planted as a reflex to high prices takes two to three years to come into production so that high prices lead to delayed overproduction and oversupply, precipitating a later crash. There is some evidence that the system of minimum prices succeeds in maintaining prices during market crises, though advocates of open markets predictably accuse the system of distorting competition (see e.g. Griffiths 2012).

A second factor in the success of Fair Trade is that coffee as well as products such as tea, chocolate and bananas play a key role in the social life of consumers. Signalling relaxed sociality or a moment's respite and an energy boost or buzz, Fair Trade products typically are those that make the consumer feel good. The pleasures derived during consumption contrast sharply and poignantly with social and political messages relating to exploitative production and distribution. It is notable that successful Fair Trade products are those that work in and on the body in particular and intimate ways, and so come to 'embody' consumers' concerns (De Neve, Luetchford and Pratt 2008). These points mean that coffee provided a potentially powerful moral code and political medium through which to contest the neoliberal turn, even among those most likely to benefit from a deregulated global economy.

As I have explored elsewhere (Luetchford 2012), we can see that moral code represented vividly on packaging and in publicity. Fair Trade coffee takes as its principle target the disadvantaged small farmer struggling to wrest a marginal living from the land. The model is one of rural people organizing production through cooperatives and family labour, and reproducing themselves as a household unit. As Gudeman and Rivera (1990) show, the house model stands in opposition to the corporation. The small family farmer sustaining a household offers a moral representation of an alternative to the mainstream economy in which corporations seek profit, and each is motivated by different values and goals. Since the house seeks to reproduce itself, it pursues set ends, and in that way it is self-limiting, practising thrift and recycling the things that it needs rather than drawing them in from outside. This makes the farming household look like, and aspire to being, an autonomous unit. Indeed, in its most extreme form the household can be imagined as autarkic; existing independently and relying on no outside inputs or exchanges.

The model presented by Gudeman and Rivera is based on Latin American ethnography, but it is recognizable in European peasantries and has long historical roots that go back to Aristotle. In fact, it is part of their argument that the house model was exported to the New World by European settlers. As such, it is central to the Euro-American moral imagination. The complication with this idea is that although Aristotle (and Gudeman and Rivera) presents the house and corporation as having fundamentally different rationales and ambitions, in practice they overlap and draw upon one another. The house operates within the market, for example, when it needs things it cannot produce, and the corporation relies on labour that is reproduced by unremunerated household work. In effect this means a complex and troublesome relation between the two realms of house and market as they intersect over time.

Fair Trade is caught up and engages precisely with that conundrum; on websites and on coffee packaging it makes repeated references to cooperatives, small farmers, families and children, all of whom are said to have their quality of life undermined by market actors who squeeze livelihoods or put education out of their reach. As we have seen, such notions are built into the Fair Trade model itself, but similar ideas underpin Latin American ideas around nation-building. A central figure informing Costa Rican national identity is the yeoman farmer who exists from the land and wrestles a living from nature, is independent from the state, and struggles in the market against cartels and exploitative intermediaries. In part the idea of the Costa Rican autonomous family farmer grows out of a representation of history in which indigenous populations are made invisible and settlers are seen as taming a frontier of wild and uninhabited jungle. Welded to this is a story of small coffee farmers who operate using family labour, and are organized into state-sponsored cooperatives to compete in unfavourable or difficult markets (Luetchford 2008; Paige 1997; Williams 1994; Winson 1989).

Variations on the above historiography of Costa Rica, based around small farmers relying on coffee to provide a livelihood but struggling in the face of adversity, are repeated across Latin America and Africa. One result is that such representations allow coffee growers and cooperatives to project themselves as both marginal and disadvantaged, but at the same time producing a quality product infused with specific personalized qualities – such as care and attention. These images and ideas are then transposed onto Fair Trade advertising.

Like many representations there is an element of truth to this; family labour is used by smaller farmers organized into cooperatives that struggle to compete with multinational corporations. However, the model has more discursive power than any kind of reality of coffee production allows. That is, the model hides as much as it reveals. Indeed, as James Carrier (2012) has argued through the notion of 'ethicality', all the representation needs to achieve is signal something to the consumer that makes it look ethical and trigger a purchase. In that sense the representation is more important than any correspondence to how coffee is produced and the kinds of relations it involves.

As historical and ethnographic studies demonstrate, the coffee industry is underpinned by power and conflict (Roseberry, Gudmundson and Samper 1995). In fact, the trajectory of the sector is precisely driven by contestation between different groups and interests: between labourers and landowners, between cooperatives and their memberships, between different cooperatives, between growers and processors, and between exporters and importers and roasters.

While Fair Trade has sought to provide an alternative, it does so through the market, and evidence suggests that this both embroils it in extant conflicts of inter-est, and at the same time compromises its transformative potential. For example, ethnographic work has shown how cooperatives situated in lower grade coffee areas struggle to enter Fair Trade markets as they lack the kind of quality needed to satisfy criteria for inclusion (Smith 2007). There is also evidence that women and work-ers are largely excluded or fail to benefit from Fair Trade (Lyon 2010). Studies of Darjeeling tea (Besky 2014), West African cocoa (Berlan 2012), the South Indian garment industry (De Neve 2008) and Caribbean bananas (Moberg 2013) provide similar evidence that Fair Trade is not as transformative as it asserts, and that at times it may contradict the interests of producers and workers, and undermine worker legislation already in place (Besky 2013; De Neve 2009; Moberg 2013).

Advocates of Fair Trade might counter such arguments by claiming that their campaigns are engaged in a process of combating vested interests and exploitation, rather than providing an immediate and complete reversal of current practices. However, the use of the market to try to transform more marginal producers' fortunes meets an objection that is not so easily countered. First, by paying premiums on the basis of quantities sold, Fair Trade unavoidably helps larger coffee producers with higher yields in any given cooperative. For example, in my fieldwork site in the 1998–9 harvest, 9 per cent of cooperative members received over $4000 for their coffee, while around 18 per cent got less than $400. Such differences in yields, which are primarily a reflection of land ownership, then carry over in the money received from Fair Trade. In that sense, premiums reproduce existing inequalities. Such differences, like the migrant and reserve army of women harvesters, are obscured behind generic representation of small family farmers all working similar size plots.

In this section I have indicated that Fair Trade is compromised because it plays on consumers' romantic imaginings of semi-exotic others who seem to look similar to the autonomous peasant who is a key figure in the European cultural imagination. Things might look rather different in the United States, but in that context there is also the parallel cultural stereotype of the frontier settler. Neither of these images bears much relation to the political economy of coffee production.

The dissonance between representations and practices in Fair Trade is facilitated by certification and branding, as these allow the product and representations of specific qualities to circulate in the mainstream economy. In that sense, like money, the brand and the certificate act as a form of currency, since they become both a medium and measure for exchange. An indication of the value of the brand is the increasing incursion of mainstream players in the coffee sector like Sarah Lee and Starbucks into ethical certification, and the development of competing schemes (Fair Trade, Utz, 4c, Rainforest Alliance) with different and less rigorous criteria. For example, a scheme like 4c uses a system of 'traffic lights' to indicate degrees of compliance and a check list of criteria. Many of these are already in place in international law, and guides for best practice read more like a technical exercise in governance than the kind of political and social relationship coffees that inspired the original Fair Trade model and ethical consumers.

The conventionalizing tendency by which ethical consumption is appropriat-ed by the mainstream has been effectively scrutinized in relation to organics in California (Guthman 2004). One tendency, as argued above, is for bigger produc-ers and corporations to enter the sector and squeeze out smaller players who are driven by alternative values. While there has been a rise in industrial-scale organic farming and multinational corporations have increasingly entered Fair Trade, there is also evidence that smaller and more politically inspired operations persist. Like-wise, corporations seem to see no contradiction between making profits and acting ethically or pursuing corporate social responsibility. It seems the contradictory dis-courses of the requirement for competitive capitalism predicted on driving down costs and profit-seeking can coexist with the projection of a brand image of caring corporations.

A second tendency is towards a class-based profile in ethical consumption. In Fair Trade the evidence is that purchasing began with predominantly middle class and better educated consumers and that brand recognition is the highest among the managerial and professional classes (Lamb 2007). Similar profiles also emerge in organics (Cottingham and Winkler 2007). Conversely, these authors also provide some evidence for a broadening of the profile to wider social classes and age groups. It seems likely that class processes and emulation, as meticulously documented by Bourdieu in Paris in the 1960s and 1970s (1984), are a necessary but not sufficient explanation for ethical consumption practices. That is, it may explain part of the ethical construction of the self as a particular kind of concerned consumer, so that ethical consumption reflects and reproduces class and other differences to different degrees. This is so because shoppers have no choice but to negotiate between values objectified in the things that they buy and the relative cost of realizing different values.

On the other hand, class explanations tell us less about why ethical consumption is attached to particular moral codes, such as 'sustainable production' or some kind of relation with producers. These more political persuasions, which at least in Northern Europe are a left of centre politics that rejects neoliberalism, lie alongside and have a complicated relation with affordability and inflections of class, gender and age.

In the organic sector one response to the conventionalizing tendency is a move towards food provision premised upon local production and consumption activities, to sustain or regenerate local economies, rather than ethical relations with distant and imagined others producing tropical primary commodities. The idea that these more direct kinds of relations between people living nearby can avoid the kinds of problems I have identified with Fair Trade, therefore, merits scrutiny, and it is to this form of ethical consumption that I now turn.

The Value of the Local: Evidence from Comparative Studies in the United Kingdom and Spain

The comparative aspect in the previous section on Fair Trade focused on similarities and differences between the production and consumption end of a value chain, and the moral codes and the kinds of practices they inspired. The purpose was to show that although there were similarities between moral ideas about households and families and that these were then attached to small farmers and workers as marginal, struggling and exploited, contradictions emerge when put into ethical practice.

In this section the comparison instead is on the form taken by ethical consumption in two European contexts. Once again, parallels are noted, as in both South East England and in Southern Spain there are similarities in moral ideas about creating or maintaining links between production and consumption as activities, and producers and consumers as people. In both contexts the idea is that such linkages build strong and localized economies. In each case the model emphasizes social relations with a strong family household or kin element, and food is exemplary of the moral code. On the other hand there are clear differences between the contexts, which emerge out of historical experiences and these differences are reproduced in how people constitute themselves as ethical beings. I begin by giving the background to the two cases, and then compare them.

Fieldwork in Spain in 2008 focused on political cultures around food in Cadiz Province, Andalusia (Luetchford et al. 2010; Luetchford and Pratt 2012; Luetchford 2014). Here, again, different strands around alternative food combine in complex ways. One strand is large-scale agriculture based around farms (*cortijos*) run by a foreman for absentee landlords. The traditional way of working these farms was by employing daily wage labourers or *jornaleros* (Martinez Alier 1971). These workers have a distinct culture and politics and are associated with radical anarchism. Their existence has long been extremely marginal, kept at starvation levels by low wages and lack of work, the *jornaleros* lived in small towns or *pueblos*. The towns saw themselves, and to an extent were, politically, economically and socially autonomous. In part they had to be as mainstream work and employment opportunities have always been scarce. Part of the requirement of *pueblo* autonomy was the ability to produce or forage its own food. This is still important but rather less than it once was.

This introduces a second strand. On the edges of the pueblos are allotments or kitchen gardens (*huertas*), and especially towards the more mountainous areas a tradition of small family farms. Both the *huertas* and the small farmers provide food into the pueblos. This food is distributed through social, often kin-based, networks, or through local shops, market stalls or by hawking in the street. This kind of food has a number of associations; it is traditional, fresh, ideally produced without spending money on industrial inputs, it provides resilience in difficult times, and provides key elements of the local diet.

From the 1970s onwards industrialization in agriculture transformed rural life. The day workers were left without work and many emigrated. Others, sensing transition in a post-Franco world, revived rural protest and occupied land under the banner of their Field Workers Union (SOC) and the slogan 'land for those who work it', A number of cooperative farms of different sizes and with varying agendas were established. As political radicals, they tended to reject mechanization and some, such as those at the La Verde cooperative began to farm organically on occupied land, both for consumption and local markets. The La Verde group then developed contacts and continue today to supply organic food through political affiliations into larger towns and cities.

Over the years La Verde have experimented with a range of outlets and alliances. They have been instrumental in forming production cooperatives with more traditional small farmers. They have established and supplied consumer cooperatives in the cities, and have links and exchange with groups of farmers and cooperatives in other parts of Spain and Europe. They also find natural allies in the young radical production–consumption groups that have emerged in urban contexts in recent years.

Inspired by an anarchist politics the former day workers uphold a radical vision of autonomy and anti-capitalist values. At times this makes alliances difficult, especially with more conservative small farmers. They also struggle to sustain markets, contest bureaucratic and state control, have a troubled reliance on subsidies, and find making a living in a commercial environment a constant struggle. They often talk of returning to 'first principles'; that is, the local market of the pueblo. In recent years they have come to see certification as problematic, as bigger farmers and interests who once were more export oriented make inroads into national markets.

The Spanish case is rather different from local food in South East England. The difference can be explained by a more profound rupture between the production and consumption of food, earlier urbanization and a longer and more far-reaching incursion of industrial processes into farming and the food sector in the United Kingdom.

The main study, carried out with a co-researcher, focused on farmers who sell at two markets held in Lewes, East Sussex (Avanzino 2014). Some of these producers come from families with a tradition of working relatively small farms, who try to compete by selling more directly and with a premium they can charge for specific qualities (taste, artisanal production methods, environmental considerations, support for the local economy etc.). Other producers are first generation. They combine political commitments to the values of organic or, in the case of livestock, 'humane', local food production with a need to make a livelihood. The consumers tend to be middle class, often with quite high levels of education. Some, but by no means all, are also wealthy professionals who have moved from London and still commute to work in the capital.

The farmers experience the powerful effects of competition from the mainstream sector; their activities are internal rather than external to capitalist agriculture. Unable to compete in terms of scale or efficiency the farmers develop, or are forced to develop, alternative strategies. They all state that they found themselves at a crossroads if they wanted to stay in business; they either had to grow in size, specializing and mechanizing, or they had to remain small, more labour intensive and add value to their products. Mostly, being pragmatic, they combine different strategies and markets. Indeed, most of the farmers in the study have multiple outlets – they sell at farmers' markets, through box schemes, at farm shops, to local wholesalers and through supermarkets.

In discussions the farmers try to reconfigure standard economistic notions of scale and efficiency to flag such things as environment, animal welfare, job satisfaction, being one's own boss, caring for the land and the soil and interacting with nature. They also stress the notion of control. Control is refusing to buy in externalities, developing their own markets and making connections to consumers. Their idea of control mirrors that discussed above under the rubric of autonomy.

Unable to compete on economies of scale or measures of efficiency that exclude externalities, the farmers develop other value-adding strategies such as direct sales, transforming or otherwise adding value to products, or renting out land as pony paddocks. Each of these strategies has specific knock-on effects. If we focus on direct retailing we can say one effect is to ascribe monetary value to a whole set of practices and cultural values. Farmers have reservations about this process, whereby an overarching discourse about small farmers selling quality products at a premium frames what they do – as one farmer wryly put it, he ends up 'selling Christmas presents rather than food'.

Such a comment raises questions about the values of farmers' market customers. At one level this is a niche market, selling peasant food to the well-heeled, but this is not the whole story. For farmers, debates about affordability need to be contextualized within a society that has normalized cheap food. For them, many people do not prioritize expenditure on food, or are prepared to pay for quality. This is borne out to a degree by a parallel study based on interviews with fifteen box scheme customers. These people tended to come from the public sector and characterized themselves as not well off, but with a high level of education.

The focus on diverse issues, such as quality, affordability and locality, is in danger of diverting attention away from the wider implications of different production systems, and perhaps indicates a lack of a clear political agenda. A second problem is that the noise around organics and local food hides the dominant trajectory of food and farming. As one farmer said, to his knowledge nobody he knew had begun growing vegetables in his area since he started twelve years ago: 'You make more money producing leaflets.'

There are clear differences between the political cultures of the English and Spanish cases. This can be seen by contrasting ethical consumption around localism in Sussex and Andalusia, made possible by a series of interviews with consumers in two small towns: Lewes in East Sussex and Prado del Rey in Spain. In Sussex the dominant representation of local food is that it is 'special' in some way and so earmarked for more conspicuous consumption. People shop from local producers for special occasions and meals. They relish the time needed to prepare and eat and discuss the food outside the world of convenience and affordability, which characterizes their everyday shopping and consumption from supermarkets. In rural Spain it is rather the opposite – food grown in the *huerta* or sourced through social networks is (or was until recently) the ordinary 'bottom line' of everyday, affordable food provision. By contrast, supermarkets provide unusual, even exotic items that may well cost more. Often a trip to a supermarket is an outing, a social occasion and a chance to engage in conspicuous consumption.

On the other hand, there are some similarities, and the parallels also echo Fair Trade. Primarily, there is a common moral code around making connections between producers and consumers, and moments of production and consumption. In all three cases the medium through which the connection is both imagined and instantiated is food and drink and in all cases the rationale is rolling back the separation between different economic actors and actions that is intrinsic to capitalist economy. In that sense, there is a common cultural language that privileges substantive social relations over and above formal economic ones, and the common idiom for that is the reproduction of household and families, which makes the idea of the small family farmer a potent symbol.

CONCLUSION

This chapter has focused on ethical consumption in mature capitalist economies. Food, it is argued, has become an increasingly visible 'problematic' in such contexts because it poses important social and political questions, as these increasingly emerge in the context of neoliberal globalization. The power of food lies in its direct embodiment of use value that is at once personal and social: 'food becomes self and when we take food into the body we take in the world' (Plester 2014: 5). Central to that world of food is sociality and use value. Hence it has unparalleled capacity to invoke orders imagined to lie outside capitalism and exchange value, such as private domains and self-provisioning. In that sense, 'classic' moral economies and romantic ideas about 'old orders' are easily evoked and imagined through food.

A common theme in ethical consumption is the insidious outcomes of the increasing alienation of production from consumption. While the primary target for action to reverse that trend in Western economies is the neoliberal market, in other places it may be other agencies or forms of distribution. In socialist and postsocialist contexts, for example, the target of ethical consumption may be the opacity of collectivized food provision by the state. In such scenarios open markets may be viewed by consumers and budding entrepreneurs as an avenue for reconnecting producers to consumers (Jung, Klein and Caldwell 2014).

I have suggested that 'marketized' versions of ethical consumption are more problematic than those forms that remain peripheral to the mainstream. In established capitalist economies at least, ethical consumption becomes more visible and vocal, and yet more contradictory and contested, as neoliberal globalization advances. This occurs as food provisioning, thought of as ethical, becomes increasingly open to appropriation by market and monetary value. The evidence for this is not only the use of ethical images and ideas by corporations to generate profits, but also that better-off sections of populations and those with educational capital concern themselves about conditions of production and can afford to buy into ideas and images that proffer them some influence over that. What is more, even those people are selective and look for alternatives in certain areas of their lives: food but not mobile phones, for example. Meanwhile, for people peripheral or disempowered in markets, provisioning is not ethically marked, it is just everyday food provisioning, or survival. We can see that in poorer sections of Western societies, in Latin America and to a lesser degree in recently 'depeasantized' economies in Southern Europe. Just as capitalism brings into being the consumer as a category of person, so too does it conjure up the image of the virtuous 'ethical consumer'. On the other hand we need not lose sight of the moral code that says producers should make livelihoods, or that people should know about the conditions under which things are made. The fact that efforts to achieve that are often misplaced, misdirected or simply diverted into seeking value for money is distinct from the moral and political aim of taking production conditions and provenance into account.

The result of marketized ethical consumption is that alternative economies and ethical consumers have to continually position and reposition themselves in their strategies and activities in and around markets of various kinds. Important work remains to be done on how people as consumers in different contexts negotiate changes in food provision, which in turn requires documenting how they constitute themselves as ethical beings in relation to a range of moral codes and political ideas. We need to understand forms of personal and civil action in and against markets and other forms of distribution, and the values that inspire those actions, as these are constituted in different contexts.

REFERENCES

Avanzino, S. (2013), 'Sussex, England', in J. Pratt and P. Luetchford (eds), *Food for Change*, 140–64, London: Pluto.

Berlan, A. (2012), 'Good Chocolate? An Examination of Ethical Consumption in Cocoa', in J. Carrier and P. Luetchford (eds), *Ethical Consumption*, 43–59, New York and Oxford: Berghahn.

Bernstein, H. (2013), 'Food Sovereignty: A Sceptical View', ICAS Review Paper Series No. 4.

Besky, S. (2014), *The Darjeeling Distinction*, Berkeley: University of California Press.

Booth, W. (1990), *Households: On the Moral Architecture of the Economy*, Ithaca, NY: Cornell University Press.

Bourdieu, P. (1984), *Distinction*, London: Routledge.

Cottingham, M. and Winkler, E. (2007), 'The Organic Consumer', in S. Wright and D. McCrea (eds), *The Handbook of Organic and Fair Trade Food Marketing*, 29–53, Oxford: Blackwell.

Daviron, B. and Ponte, S. (2005), *The Coffee Paradox*, London: Zed Books.

De Neve, G. (2008), 'Global Garment Chains, Local Labour Activism: New Challenges to Trade Union and NGO Activism in the Tiruppur Garment Cluster', in G. de Neve, P. Luetchford, J. Pratt and D. Wood (eds), *Hidden Hands in the Market*, 213–40, Bingley, UK: Emerald.

De Neve, G., Luetchford, P. and Pratt, J. (2008), 'Introduction', in G. de Neve, P. Luetchford, J. Pratt and D. Wood (eds), *Hidden Hands in the Market*, 1–30, Bingley, UK: Emerald.

De Sollier, I. (2013), *Food and the Self*, London and New York: Bloomsbury.

Dombos, T. (2012), 'Narratives of Concern: Beyond the "Official" Discourse of Ethical Consumption in Hungary', in G. de Neve, P. Luetchford, J. Pratt and D. Wood (eds), *Hidden Hands in the Market*, 125–41, Bingley, UK: Emerald.

Foucault, M. (1976), *The History of Sexuality, Volume 1*, London: Penguin.

Foucault, M. (1984), *The History of Sexuality, Volume 2*, London: Penguin.

Foucault, M. (1992), 'On the Genealogy of Ethics', in P. Rabinow (ed.), *The Foucault Reader*, 340–72, London: Penguin.

Gereffi, G. and Korzeniewicz, M. (1994), *Commodity Chains and Global Capitalism*, Westport: Praeger.

Griffiths, P. (2012), 'Ethical Objections to Fair Trade', *The Journal of Business Ethics*, 105(3): 357–73.

Gudeman, S. and Rivera, A. (1990), *Conversations in Colombia*, Cambridge: Cambridge University Press.

Guthman, J. (2004), *Agrarian Dreams*, Berkeley: University of California Press.

Humphrey, C. (1997), 'Exemplars and Rules: Aspects of the Discourse of Moralities', in S. Howell (ed.), *The Ethnography of Moralities*, 25–47, London: Routledge.

Jung, Y., Klein, J. and Caldwell, M. (eds) (2014), *Ethical Eating in the Postsocialist and Socialist World*, Berkeley: University of California Press.

Klein, J. (2014), 'Connecting with the Countryside? "Alternative" Food Movements with Chinese Characteristics', in Y. Jung, J. Klein and M. Caldwell (eds), *Ethical Eating in the Postsocialist and Socialist World*, 116–43, Berkeley: University of California Press.

Klein, J., Jung, Y. and Caldwell, M. (2014), 'Introduction: Ethical Eating and (Post) socialist Alternatives', in Y. Jung, J. Klein and M. Caldwell (eds), *Ethical Eating in the Postsocialist and Socialist World*, 1–24, Berkeley: University of California Press.

Lamb, H. (2007), 'The Fair Trade Consumer', in S. Wright and D. McCrea (eds), *The Handbook of Organic and Fair Trade Food Marketing*, 54–81, Oxford: Blackwell.

Luetchford, P. (2006), 'Brokering Fair Trade', in D. Lewis and D. Mosse (eds), *Development Brokers and Translators*, 127–48, Bloomfield, CT: Kumarian.

Luetchford, P. (2008), *Fair Trade and a Global Commodity*, London: Pluto.

Luetchford, P. (2012), 'Consuming Producers: Fair Trade and Small Farmers', in J. Carrier and P. Luetchford (eds), *Ethical Consumption*, 60–80, New York and Oxford: Berghahn.

Luetchford, P. (2014), 'Andalusia, Spain', in J. Pratt and P. Luetchford (eds), *Food for Change*, 115–39, London: Pluto.

Luetchford, P., Pratt, J. and Soler, M. (2010), 'Struggling for Autonomy: From Estate Labourers to Organic Farmers in Andalusia', *Critique of Anthropology*, 30(3): 313–21.

Luetchford P. and Pratt, J. (2012), 'Values and Markets: an Analysis of Organic Farming Initiatives in Andalusia', *Journal of Agrarian Change*, 11(1): 87–103.

Lyon, S. (2010), 'A Market of Our Own: Women's Livelihoods and Fair Trade Markets', in S. Lyon and M. Moberg (eds), *Fair Trade and Social Justice: Global Ethnographies*, 125–46, New York: New York University Press.

Martinez-Alier, J. (1971), *Labourers and Landowners in Southern Spain*, London: Allen and Unwin.

Miller, D. (1998), *A Theory of Shopping*, Cambridge, MA: Polity Press.

Mincyte, D. (2014), 'Homogenizing Europe: Raw Milk, Risk Politics, and Moral Economies in Europeanizing Lithuania', in Y. Jung, J. Klein and M. Caldwell (eds), *Ethical Eating in the Postsocialist and Socialist World*, 25–43, Berkeley: University of California Press.

Moberg, M. (2014), 'Certification and Neoliberal Governance: Moral Economies of Fair Trade in the Eastern Caribbean', *American Anthropologist*, 116(1): 8–22.

Oxfeld, E. (2014), 'The Moral Significance of Food in Reform-Era Rural China', in Y. Jung, J. Klein and M. Caldwell (eds), *Ethical Eating in the Postsocialist and Socialist World*, 44–68, Berkeley: University of California Press.

Paige, J. (1997), *Coffee and Power*, Cambridge MA: Harvard University Press.

Pendergast, M. (1999), *Uncommon Grounds*, New York: Basic Books.

Piketty, T. (2014), *Capital in the Twenty-first Century*, Cambridge, MA: Harvard University Press.

Plester, B. (2014), 'Ingesting the Organization: the Embodiment of Organizational Food Rituals', *Culture and Organization*, DOI: 10.1080/14759551.2013.873798.

Polanyi, K. (1957 [1944]), *The Great Transformation*, Boston, MA: Beacon Press.

Pratt, J. (2013), 'Farming and its Values', in J. Pratt and P. Luetchford (eds), *Food for Change*, London: Pluto.

Pratt, J. and Luetchford, P. (2013), *Food for Change*, London: Pluto.

Roseberry, W., Gudmundson, L. and Samper, M. (eds) (1995), *Coffee, Society, and Power in Latin America*, Baltimore, MD: John Hopkins University Press.

Scott, J. (1976), *The Moral Economy of the Peasant*, New Haven: Yale University Press.

Scott, J. (1985), *Weapons of the Weak*, New Haven: Yale University Press.

Smith, J. (2007), 'The Search for Sustainable Markets: the Promises and Failures of Fair Trade', *Culture and Agriculture*, 29: 89–99.

Thompson, E. P. (1971), 'The Moral Economy of the English Crowd in the Eighteenth Century', in E. P. Thompson, *Customs in Common*, 185–258, London: Penguin Books.

Vramo, L. (2012), 'Trade Not Aid: Imagining Ethical Economy', in J. Carrier and P. Luetchford (eds), *Ethical Consumption*, 81–98, New York and Oxford: Berghahn.

Wilk, R. (ed.) (2006), *Fast Food/Slow Food*, Lanham, MD: Altamira Press.

Williams, R. (1994), *States and Social Evolution*, Chapel Hill: University of North Carolina Press.

Winson, A. (1989), *Coffee and Democracy in Modern Costa Rica*, Basingstoke: Macmillan Press.

CHAPTER NINETEEN

Artisanal Foods and the Cultural Economy: Perspectives on Craft, Heritage, Authenticity and Reconnection[1]

HARRY G. WEST

AUTHENTICITY, HERITAGE AND ARTISANAL FOODS

In *Culture and Authenticity*, Lindholm succinctly summarizes Trilling's argument that the idea of *authenticity* is rooted in the notion of *sincerity* that emerged with the dawn of modernity: People 'living among strangers' in the evermore urban environment defining modernity could slip the bonds of social structure and hierarchy that once characterized the medieval, not only to 'break out of prescribed roles and pursue secular dreams of wealth, power, and fame', but also to 'pretend to be better than they were' and to 'cheat and betray one another and vanish into the anonymous urban wilderness'. Lindholm concludes, 'In this ambiguous milieu it is ... not surprising that sincerity, doing what one says one will do, became a desirous trait' (Lindholm 2008: 3–4; Trilling 1972).

The suggestion that sincerity, and hence authenticity, come to be valued precisely when relationships are attenuated, and trust is tenuous, provides a useful starting point for reflection on artisanal foods and the cultural economy today. In the realm of food, some would argue, modernity (defined by the consolidation of national markets, mass production of foodstuffs and their transport over increasing distances) and more recent trends (including new processing technologies and the global integration of food markets) have given rise to a contemporary 'food system' characterized by 'disconnection' and deceit. Kneafsey et al. argue that modern consumers, who 'do not know where (or how) much of their food is produced', are disconnected from productive processes and food producers, as well as from foods that come to them through bewilderingly complex supply chains comprising agribusinesses, industrial processors and supermarkets, while producers are disconnected not only from consumers but also – along with consumers – from the cultural and natural ecologies that once gave context to the growing and making of food (Kneafsey et al.

2008: 6–9). For modern consumers, Jackson tells us, relationships with food are characterized by 'anxiety', whether about consequences for consuming bodies of industrial agriculture and agricultural biotechnology – heightened by 'food scares' arising from the proliferation of zoonotic diseases and more virulent foodborne pathogens – or about the impact of such food on traditional knowledge systems (from farming to cooking) and natural environments under threat of destruction or disappearance (Jackson and CONANX Group 2013: 16–23; cf. Kjaernes, Harvey and Warde 2007). Feelings of disconnection are exacerbated for many by the increasingly common experience of geographical dislocation – whether as refugees, labour migrants or middle-class tourists – that perpetually exposes many to unfamiliar foods as they travel, live in diaspora or navigate an ever-changing place they call home.

If disconnection fosters lack of trust in the produce of an evermore industrialized global food system, commentators also suggest that consumers variously seek to 'reconnect' with food, with the people who make their food and, together with producers, with the natural environments in which food is grown and made. 'Virtually anywhere in the world today, people are hopelessly unable to know fully the conditions under which what we encounter, and especially what we consume, is produced,' Weiss writes; but he also asserts that, for the farmers, chefs and consumers of artisanal meats with whom he has conducted research in North Carolina (the United States), the

> pursuit of meaningful 'connections' to food is manifest in ... concerns and claims about the linkages between taste and place; [between] cuisine and heritage; [between] farmers and their market customers; and between those who are included and those who are excluded in communities of food production, provisioning, preparation, and consumption. (Weiss 2014: 17, 23)

The burgeoning market in 'artisanal foods' (sometimes called 'craft foods') sits within a broader array of 'alternatives' to the modern food system, including 'movements' or market niches such as organics, Fair Trade, locavorism, farmers' markets, box schemes, community-supported agriculture and allotment/community gardening (see also Luetchford, in this volume). Where people suspect that industrial food-makers are insincere (to use Trilling's language) and that their products are not what their packaging claims, many seek greater authenticity in artisanal foods[2] which (to paraphrase Lindholm) better seem 'to be what they say they are' whether on the package or in their makers' stories – in other words, are the products and centre-pieces of what they consider more direct and trustworthy relationships between 'real' foods, the people who make them, the places where they are made, and the people who purchase and eat them.

The recent rise of artisanal foods corresponds with growing interest around the world in the preservation of cultural heritage – a phenomenon similarly rooted in experiences of and responses to modernity. In Lowenthal's words: 'The impulse to preserve is partly a reaction to the increasing evanescence of things and the speed with which we pass them by. In the face of massive change, we cling to the remaining familiar vestiges. ... Nothing so quickens preservation sympathies as the fear of imminent extinction, whether of a building, a bird, or a folkway' (Lowenthal 1985: 399). The impulse Lowenthal describes animates ideas about food among many today. Bessière tells us: 'The daughter or granddaughter no longer inherits secret family recipes. Modern home cooking goes beyond traditional family dishes, creating nostalgia for food eaten in one's childhood and adolescence' (Bessière 1998: 25). Reflecting specifically on the renaissance of artisanal chocolate making in Bayonne (France) – appearing in the wake of 'McDonaldization' and the invasion of the French market by Belgian franchises selling chocolates 'mass-produced from cheap substitute ingredients', and at a time when the French also worried about effects of the impending formation of the European Union (EU) – Terrio writes:

> In postindustrial societies like France, craft can serve as a metaphor for an alternative set of cultural values and work practices in contrast to the dominant norm. In these settings, the persistence, reinvention, or creation of traditional craft cultural forms, work practices, and communities can be a means to reassert cultural distinctiveness and identity in response to rapidly changing circumstances. ... Master craftsmen can be celebrated as symbols of local and/or national cultural values. (Terrio 2005: 154–5)

As detailed below, anxieties like those Terrio identifies, and the nostalgia they provoke (of which Bessière speaks), have given rise to a range of ideas and practices treating foods and foodways as forms of cultural heritage – projects developing in tandem with the very idea of artisanal foods. As will be discussed, 'heritagization' has not only been essential to varied efforts to preserve and promote artisanal foods, it has also profoundly shaped their reproduction – even their transformation.

To date, the literature on food and heritage has focused on the importance of local gastronomy to the development of tourism and related industries, while sometimes asking how involvement in heritage-related industries might benefit food growers and makers (e.g. Boniface 2003; Hall et al. 2003b; Hjalager and Richards 2002; Long 2004). Building upon but moving beyond this literature, this chapter focuses on the relationship between a particular category of foods closely associated with heritage, namely 'artisanal foods', and a range of activities sometimes glossed as the 'cultural economy' (Ray 1998), critically interrogating this relationship through examination of defining dynamics and the experiences of those involved in it. The next chapter section lays foundations for discussion of the heritagization of foods and foodways by examining ideas associated with the term 'artisanal foods'. The following section examines ways in which artisanal foods have been conceived of as cultural heritage and the many kinds of initiatives through which heritagization of foods has occurred. Next, I ask whether such initiatives achieve their objectives, discussing how disparate interests may give rise to conflicts as well as unforeseen and – depending upon perspective – undesirable consequences. Finally, the chapter returns to the idea of authenticity, suggesting that by seeking authentic foods, as well as engaging in dialogue about the authenticity of particular foods, producers and consumers not only contribute to the dynamic reproduction of foods in which they trust, but also craft their identities along with the food communities of which they consider themselves part. Throughout, the chapter references relevant literature while also drawing upon ethnographic research I have conducted with artisan cheesemakers.[3]

THE IDEA OF ARTISANAL FOODS

The term 'artisanal foods' condenses a range of ideas, associations – even assumptions – about particular foods, their makers and how such foods are made. Jackson informs us that 'most definitions of artisanal production stress its handmade and small-scale nature with minimal use of mechanization' (Jackson and CONANX Group 2013: 27). The term is generally applied to foods requiring some form of processing or preservation (excluding, for example, 'fresh produce'), but whose transformation or production can be achieved with low levels of capital investment by what are often glossed as 'traditional' methods, whether at home or in small workshops – practices such as pickling vegetables, preserving fruits, baking bread or cakes, brewing beer, curing meat or making cheese.

Jackson points out that parameters in definitions of artisanal foods are generally vague and fungible (Jackson and CONANX Group 2013: 27). Along with changing technologies and socio-historical contexts, conceptions of 'traditional' and 'modern', 'hand-made' and 'mechanized', 'small-scale' and 'large-scale', and 'workshop' and 'factory' change constantly. For example, in the French Auvergne, where electric-powered hydraulic presses are readily available to cheesemakers today, the use of cast-iron screw presses is characterized by some as more genuinely artisanal, but these same presses were the products, as well as the tools, of industries of an earlier time, first adopted by relatively larger-scale producers who could afford such 'improvements' over the wooden lever presses that cheesemakers in the region used previously, which had in their own turn 'mechanized' a process that, in earlier times, entailed cheesemakers setting large stones on wooden lids atop their cheese moulds after using their own weight to press the curd by wrapping it in cheesecloth and kneeling on it (Dubouchet 2007: 383–448). Revealingly, Paxson remarks that sixty years after the opening of Kraft's Limburger cheese factory – then celebrated as the 'most modern' in the world – it bears striking resemblance to European museum exhibits celebrating artisan craft (Paxson 2013: 119).

Inevitably, the line between industrial and artisanal foods lies in the eye of the beholder. At the same time, comparison between these categories – whether explicit or implicit – is essential to ever-changing definitions of artisanal, as the category makes sense only in relation to its constantly changing industrial other. For example, Paxson, who worked with artisanal cheesemakers in the United States, reports that

> artisanal cheese is defined *against* the industrial: according to the American Cheese Society ... it is made *more* by hand than by machine, in small batches *compared to* industrial scales of production, using recipes and techniques developed through the practical knowledge of previous artisans *rather than* the technical knowledge of dairy scientists and industrial engineers. (Paxson 2011: 117, emphasis added)

More self-referential conceptions of artisanal foods and foodmaking exist, however, and tend to highlight (re)connections that the making and eating of these foods facilitates between people and themselves (their bodies, their senses), their social others, and their living and working environments. Beginning with the last of these, artisanal foods are often described using the French concept of *terroir*, suggesting that their essential characteristics reflect the distinctive ecologies in which they are made. Rather than seeking to isolate productive processes from environments of production and to eliminate variables in order to achieve consistent products – as, for example, industrial cheesemakers do by pasteurizing and homogenizing their milk, by working in climate-controlled rooms, and by using stainless steel surfaces and tools – artisanal cheesemakers, for example, tolerate (even celebrate) how the variability of their products reflects the dynamic environments in which their work is embedded, from ever-changing palates of grasses and flowers on pastures where their animals graze, to the ever-changing composition of their animals' milk, to the ever-changing temperature and humidity of their dairies and ageing cellars, to the ever-changing composition of microflora in their workplaces and on the buckets, vats and tools (including their own hands) they use. Elsewhere, I have conveyed the idea presented to me by many artisan producers: 'As the composition of the artisan cheesemaker's raw materials and the environment in which she works changes from season to season, from day to day, even from morning milking to afternoon milking, so too must the productive process' (West 2013a: 321–2). Bringing their work to fruition with so many changing variables requires of artisanal producers a complex sensibility, a 'knack' (West 2013a) – considered 'part science' but also 'part art' (see also Paxson 2013: 128–57) – that must be developed not only in dialogue with artisan predecessors, but also through interaction with other entities in artisans' productive ecologies, including their raw materials and their products themselves (West 2013a) (see also Paxson 2013: 158–86).

At the other end of the spectrum, artisanal foods are often described as facilitating corporeal or sensorial reconnection as well as the (re)discovery of self, whether for those who make them or those who eat them. Jackson tells us:

> Artisanal food is spoken of in terms of mastery and craft production, involving an historical, experiential, and intuitive understanding, acquiring skills, such as dexterity and savoir faire, from experienced practitioners, emphasizing hands-on and tacit forms of knowledge rather than learning by rote or from the book. (Jackson and CONANX Group 2013: 23)

As complex and unpredictable as artisanal food processes often are, and as difficult as the labour they entail may be, skilled artisan producers often express great satisfaction in their work and in the sense it affords them of connection between themselves, their creative processes and the products they make.[4]

Consumers of artisanal foods also celebrate the joys of craft, which they may experience vicariously through observation of producers at work or through con-textualizing narratives about methods and traditions, or viscerally through the con-sumption of its products. Whereas, in the wake of the development of Fordist food

processing methods, manufacturers boldly celebrated the purity and safety of products 'untouched by human hands', increasingly consumers and producers alike conceive of industrial manufacturing and marketing as opaque and disingenuous and,
by contrast, of artisanal foodmaking as having greater 'integrity', not to mention
yielding products of better 'quality'. While corporeal benefits of consuming artisanal foods are often implied by parallel characterizations of industrial foods as less
natural, less digestible, less nutritious or more hazardous owing to practices such as
refinement, pasteurization, irradiation, chemical processing and preservation, fortification or adulteration, claims to superior 'taste' are generally more explicit and
more prominent. According to Jackson, definitions of artisanal foods may '[empha-
size] taste (in both senses of the word) and the pleasures of direct bodily experience
(tactile, sensuous, caring), often thought to be lacking in more industrialized forms
of food processing and commercial manufacture, caricatured as overly standardized,
bland, and uniform' (Jackson and CONANX group 2013: 25).

Geyzen, Scholliers and Leroy suggest that high-speed innovation in the food
industries has produced not only 'feelings of estrangement and anxiety' but also
affinity for '"familiar" foods that are believed to be safe, honest, and healthy',
including labels and brands 'not only reflecting purity (i.e., absence of additives ...),
health, and flavour, but also the *good life*' (Geyzen, Scholliers and Leroy 2012: 47–8).
For many, artisanal foods inspire confidence and alleviate anxieties even better
than certifying labels and trusted brands. If artisan *savoire faire,* passed down over
generations, is considered by those celebrating *terroir* to be as essential to artisanal
products as the natural ecologies in which they are produced (Barham 2003: 131),
the making and eating of such foods – often described as being 'as (good as) they
used to be' – also connect people to a past (which they may or may not have actually
experienced) in which 'life was better' – slower, simpler, more honest – when 'things
(including, but not limited to, food) were good'.

The connections with forebears that people experience through making and
eating artisanal foods both derive from and reinforce conceptions of such foods
and foodways as cultural heritage in need of preservation, as discussed below. But
involvement with artisanal foods and foodways may also facilitate connections
among and between those who make them and those who eat them in the present.
Commenting on an informant's preference for artisanal salami 'produced by a
family whose mother had been his father's milk mother', Cavanaugh concludes that,
for many in Bergamo (Italy), '*salame nostrano* ("our salami") is enmeshed in social
ties of friendship or family', and 'its superior and more "authentic" taste seems to
reflect the values of social connection and hard work, which are seen as essential to
Bergamasco (sic) values' (Cavanaugh 2007: 162). For many, artisanal foods not only
reflect the values of an extant community; their production and consumption serve
as moments in which values, and the communities that sustain them, are reproduced
or, even, created. Consumers of artisanal foods often celebrate the opportunity to
'meet the producer', to get a sense of who has made their food, and to interact with
this person as a fellow member of a shared community.

The array of connections made with and through artisanal foods reflects
multiple forms of value associated with their production. Paxson suggests that the

cheesemakers with whom she conducted fieldwork undertake 'value work' in two registers. The first involves *making a life* – in which their customers may also participate by consuming their cheeses – *that is morally good*, and is associated with their dedication to the quality of their products, their commitment to sustainable methods of production, and their contribution to a community of like-minded people. The second involves *making a good living* (or, when speaking of peasants earning low incomes, at least a *viable – or sustainable – living*) from the making of good food (Paxson 2013: 65–6). While these values may be in tension, Tregear argues, based on research in the north of England, that artisan foodmakers seek to balance the imperatives of lifestyle, community involvement and commercial viability, and that many succeed (Tregear 2005). As discussed in the next section, conceiving of their work and its products as forms of cultural heritage may not only be understood by artisans as effective means of preserving good foods, but also as viable means of preserving their livelihoods.

ARTISANAL FOODS IN THE CULTURAL ECONOMY

The dilemmas faced by many cheesemakers with whom I have worked, and their varied responses, illustrate well not only how artisan foodmakers have sought, and often found, viable market niches by casting their work and wares as forms of heritage, but also how artisanal foods and the 'heritage foods' market niche have emerged together, dynamically shaping one another. Where the price of fluid milk has (like most agricultural commodities) declined in recent decades (largely due to industrial intensification), small-scale dairy farmers have struggled to meet costs. Small-scale cheesemakers have similarly struggled to compete with industrial manufacturers. The salvation of many has been the production of artisanal cheese – or, the marketing *as an artisanal product* of cheese they have long been making. For dairy farmers, transforming milk into cheese has afforded means of adding value to it. For cheesemakers, marketing directly to consumers or through short supply chains has allowed the capture of more of this added value. Many artisan cheesemakers I have worked with sell as much cheese as they can from their own farms or dairy shops. Many cooperate with other foodmakers in their regions, selling cured meats, jams and honey made by fellow artisans who in turn sell the cheesemakers' wares in their shops – similar to arrangements described by Che, Veeck and Veeck (2005) as essential to artisan foodmakers in Michigan (the United States). Additionally, some encourage visitors to come see them work – a practice evermore common among artisan foodmakers (Everett 2012). Attracting visitors requires investment of time and resources in 'telling a story' about one's craft and its place within a broader cultural or historical frame (Paxson 2013: 91).[5] It may also entail hosting visitors, whether for tastings or meals, or as overnight guests. Some cheesemakers I have worked with run B&Bs or restaurants featuring their products and those of fellow artisans on the menu. Others have set up exhibits – even small museums – to make their cheese rooms and shops worthwhile travel destinations.

Such is the case with Alphonse Bellonte, a cheesemaker in the French Auvergne I have worked with, who converted a small complex of caves on family land (previously used to keep sheep, store farm equipment, or age cheese or wine) into the venue for a multimedia presentation on the history of the region, the farm and the cheese his family made, attracting busloads of tourists who also visited the farm, the cheese room, the farm shop and the *auberge* in which Alphonse himself often cooked (West 2014). I once remarked to him that, in order to make a living as cheesemakers, he and his family also had to work as historians, museum curators, tour guides, restaurateurs, shopkeepers, accountants and marketers, to which he responded that, like his forebears, he was a 'peasant', obliged to use every resource and seize every opportunity available to earn a living. Whereas van der Ploeg has argued that the strategies of those he categorizes as a globally emergent 'new peasantry', who aim to secure resources and to ensure their future autonomy, differ fundamentally from more entrepreneurial approaches to farming (van der Ploeg 2008), others have suggested that the diversification of activities historically essential to peasant survival is, of necessity, finding new expression today in entrepreneurial initiatives such as agritourism and the rebranding of farm produce as 'artisanal', especially where state and supra-state policies have subscribed to and supported the idea of agricultural 'multifunctionality', as in the European Union (Brandth and Haugen 2011; Niska, Vesala and Vesala 2012; Vesala and Vesala 2010). Within such contexts, artisanal foodmaking may, quite simply, be good business.

The good economic sense of casting artisanal foods as elements of a shared cultural heritage, some have suggested, may extend well beyond the farms and work-shops of those producing them, benefitting others in the places where farmers and foodmakers live and work. Advocates of a 'cultural economy approach' to regional development have conceived of entities as diverse as local landscapes, flora and fauna, prehistoric and historic landmarks, languages and dialects, folklore, performative and material arts and handicrafts as 'resources to be employed in the pursuit of the interests of the territory' (Ray 1998). Accordingly, artisanal foods and foodways have in recent years increasingly been conceived of not only as artefacts worthy of preservation, but as assets to be exploited for common benefit. Particularly in Europe, where farmers and foodmakers are relatively better educated and less politically disenfranchised than in lesser-developed economies, and where governments at all levels have relatively greater resources with which to support them, artisanal foods have been considered potential attractions that might draw visitors even to remote and/or economically depressed places with few other development possibilities. In the face of stiffening competition in mass-produced agricultural commodities from the United States, Canada, Australia, New Zealand and, increasingly, the BRICS countries, EU agricultural policy has given greater importance to the protection and development of value-added, 'quality' foods, including artisanal foods. Gray writes: 'Instead of local farmers relying on CAP [the EU Common Agricultural Policy] price support mechanisms to *produce* agricultural commodities for people outside their rural locality', a cultural economy approach has made it possible in some places for 'rural localities [to become] places that people from outside come into to *consume* the diversity of things that ... constitute rural localities: environment, heritage, beautiful natural landscapes, local customs and artefacts' (Gray 2000: 44) – a view given concrete support by the EU's rural development programme, LEADER (*Liaison entre Actions de Développement de l'Économie Rurale*) (Ray 1998: 5). With the success of this approach in Europe, the model has increasingly been adopted elsewhere, including in the global south.

Whereas previously, development planners and commentators focused on how local foods might serve as resources in the development of tourism (Saxena et al. 2007),[6] they have recently taken interest in the idea that foods, foodways and foodmakers might themselves be beneficiaries of integrated approaches to regional development. Richards writes,

> Because local food production depends on agriculture, hunting and fishing, the appropriate development of linkages with tourism can aid the stimulation of indigenous entrepreneurial activity and stimulate the 'bottom-up' development of community-based tourism initiatives. ... Marketing destinations through gastronomy also brings a range of benefits through complementary activities and linkages, such as stimulating local agriculture, food processing and retailing, raising food quality and strengthening local image and identity. (Richards 2002: 13)

Hall et al. suggest that incorporation of local foodmakers into tourism provision can stimulate investment in local food industries, add value to local products and lead to food business profits being reinvested locally (Hall, Mitchell and Sharples 2003a: 28–9) – effects that may be multiplied by fostering clusters and networks of local tourism-oriented food businesses (2003a: 37).

Indeed, some suggest that artisanal foods and tourism are inherently synergistic because both depend upon logics of 'terroir' – notions that places are distinctive, and that their distinctiveness is reflected in their culture and its products, inviting consumers to 'taste' other ways of life through visiting and consuming such places and products. Tourism centred on artisanal food is increasingly celebrated for the way in which it allows consumers to reconnect not only with the cultural ecologies in which such foods are produced, but also with the natural ecologies in which distinctive foodways are embedded. Conveying the ideas of Lagorio, a proponent of agritourism in Bergamo, Cavanaugh writes:

> Supporters [of agritourism] aim to protect what they call the environmentally-sound economic strategies practiced by Bergamasco (sic) farmers and shepherds for centuries, consuming what they produced and living in 'perfect symbiosis' with their environment (Lagorio 2004: 33). Producers would be able to maintain their ways of life and modes of production if they can be articulated into this larger consumption pattern of 'ecogastronomy'. As Lagorio suggests, 'The identity of the territory and the natural environment would then be opportunely valorized with elements (natural, cultural, historical, social) that would guide the tourist on a path tied to traditions and gastronomic specialities, synergistically developing the image of the territory and the image of its traditional food products' (ibid.). (Cavanaugh 2007: 165–6)

My own research reveals of an array of ways that governments at various levels may promote the developmental potentialities of artisanal foods and foodways. In East Thrace (Turkey), provincial government had invested in the Demirköy dairy

I visited in Kirklareli, where cheese was made from the milk collected from local farmers too distant to supply industrial cheesemakers elsewhere in the region. In Kars (Turkey), cheesemakers I visited were asking provincial officials to invest in refrigerated milk tanks in the villages where milk was collected from small-scale breeders. The provincial government of Karaman (Turkey) had built an elevator to assist cheesemakers in the remote village of Divle to lower cheeses into and retrieve them from their ageing cave (whose entrance was at the bottom of a 36 metre chasm). In Wizajny (Poland), local government had paid for the cheesemakers I met to visit artisan counterparts in France, and for a French consultant to visit and advise them.

In addition to such forms of material and technical assistance, governments in many places where I worked provided support in the marketing of artisanal products. In Serpa (Portugal), the town council had, since 2001, organized annual cheese festivals where local producers could sell to tourists and purveyors of gourmet foods attracted by the event – an event the council considered essential to building a more sustainable local economy. Similar festivals, supporting cheesemakers and other artisan foodmakers, were held in many places I visited. Cavanaugh reports that, in Italy, *sagra* (local celebrations) promoting regional foods have proliferated in recent years. These often involve demonstrations, tastings and prize competitions, and they draw tourists as well as local people treating them as festive social occasions. They also encourage producers, purveyors and proponents of artisanal products to discuss ideas for collaboration and promotion (Cavanaugh 2007: 157). According to Lewis, who has written about an asparagus festival in California's San Joaquin Valley (the United States), local food festivals range across a spectrum, from those promoting well-recognized food traditions associated with already-cohesive (often ethnically defined) communities to those creating traditions and fostering communities around them (Lewis 2004). The festival that cheesemakers in Korycin (Poland) told me about lay somewhere in between; in a town where no cheese of renown had been produced for quite some time, the festival – organized by the town's energetic and well-respected mayor – allowed local residents seeking a source of income to find a market while recreating a moribund local cheesemaking tradition.

The integration of artisan foodmakers in the development of local tourism may also take the form of 'food trails' such as the *Route des Fromage A.O.C. d'Auvergne* along which I conducted research – an annual initiative producing a brochure listing cheesemakers who welcome visitors, describing their cheeses and furnishing a map encouraging tourists to seek them out. The 2006–7 brochure said of the cheeses: 'When one knows how they are made, one loves them even more.' Based on research in Molise and Sardinia (Italy), Presenza and Del Chiappa suggest that, for those preferring to encounter regional foods conveniently served on a plate, and for producers seeking to capture this market niche, the use of local products in local restaurants may more effectively link artisanal foods to the tourist trade (Presenza and Del Chiappa 2013). Initiatives like the Vermont Fresh Network (VFN), which I encountered in Vermont (the United States), adapt the food trail concept to organize and promote such linkages, maintaining a website and producing brochures listing VFN member restaurants whose chefs have committed to using local foods in their dishes and to naming VFN growers and artisan suppliers on their menus (Vermont Fresh Network 2014).

Reflecting and consolidating growing enthusiasm for artisanal foods, governments in many places have also formally recognized local foods and foodways as forms of cultural heritage and sought to protect and preserve them through varied initiatives. Among the most concrete examples are museums presenting officially sanctioned histories of foods claimed by a particular place. The Kaas Museum in Alkmaar (Netherlands), where I conducted research, not only tells visitors, through the display of artefacts and the presentation of visual documentation, how Gouda and Edam cheeses have been made over centuries, it also proclaims – despite the fact that cheese has long been made throughout the Netherlands – that Alkmaar is 'the country's cheese capital'. That the museum is situated in a converted cathedral which served as the weigh house for those trading cheese on the square just outside from 1581 almost until the museum opened in 1983, and that the square's market still operates today, lend credibility to these claims, benefitting not only Alkmaar's cheesemakers and cheesemongers, but also other businesses in a town to which the museum draws large numbers of tourists.

Underlying such initiatives is a broader project of 'patrimonialization' in which governments at any level may participate. Following the French historian, Revel, Barham traces the idea of patrimonialization to French President Valéry Giscard d'Estaing's declaration of 1980 as *L'Année du Patromoine* (The Year of Patrimony). In the wake of rapid change after the Second World War, she suggests, the French suffered a general 'malaise' with modernization and globalization. She quotes Revel: 'It is as though, little by little, the French acquired the habit of considering the ensemble of the infinitely diverse traces of their collective experience as a treasure that urgently needed to be conserved and protected, a base that grounded them.' She tell us, 'Patrimonialisation refers to the effort to trace, record, and commemorate with museums and monuments all sorts of events both majestic and mundane,' and further that 'natural places, landscapes and traditional foods have been sweep (sic.) up in this frenzy' (Barham 2003: 132). Gade suggests: 'The rescue of authentic farm products with strong identities might be seen as a salvage effort akin to preserving a language or a plant species from extinction.' He adds: 'Not surprisingly, it is ... in France where the wisdom of the globalization trends overtaking the world has received its most persistent critique. This European land of artisan tradition, well-defined local specificity and culinary refinement has led the world in the search for ways to ensure and develop authenticity of food production' (Gade 2004: 848).

According to Bessière, the culinary salvage effort to which Gade refers took concrete form in France, beginning in the 1980s, when 'the French government decided to publish a list of the culinary heritage in the inventory of French traditional treasures, along with churches and castles'. She reports, 'This initiative was funded by the National Council for Culinary Arts. ... In addition to this, there are one hundred sites certified as outstanding for their food (*Sites Remarquables du Goût*) throughout the whole of France.' Bessière further suggests: 'Future research should identify those areas qualified as having formed our gastronomic history, to complete our culinary heritage and launch new tourist sites to the general public' (Bessière

1998: 32). Such work has indeed been undertaken, not only in France but, in recent years, throughout Europe and beyond (Various 2011). In Poland, I witnessed regional governments creating food inventories along similar lines. Cheesemakers with whom I spoke sought inclusion on these, hoping it would defend them against excessive regulatory interference and facilitate marketing of their products.

Such inventories of food patrimony have sometimes been part and parcel of greater forms of recognition. In 2003, the United Nations Educational, Scientific and Cultural Organization (UNESCO) adopted a Convention on Safeguarding the Intangible Cultural Heritage (Schmidtt 2008). In 2010, the 'Gastronomic Meal of the French' was officially inscribed on UNESCO's Representative List of Intangible Cultural Heritage of Humanity, along with 'Traditional Mexican Cuisine.' In 2013, the 'Mediterranean Diet', 'Washoku, Traditional Dietary Cultures of the Japanese', and 'Kimjang, Making and Sharing Kimchi in the Republic of Korea' were added. Many other entries relate to food (United Nations Educational Scientific and Cultural Organization n.d.; see also Medina 2009; Parasecoli and Tasaki 2011).[7]

Even if only small numbers of foods and foodways have been recognized by UNESCO, national and regional food inventories have often expressed – if not fostered – historical claims to the distinctiveness of particular foods and foodways, or even their creation. What is more, they have often laid the groundwork for realization of another form of official support for artisan foodmakers, namely recognition of appellations or indications of origin.

Regimes recognizing and controlling appellations and indications of origin (AIOs) are premised on the *terroir* idea that particular products reflect the environments in which they are produced, and purport to protect against 'free-riders' profiting from misleading use of the names of places historically associated with such products as well as against substandard products that bear such names undermining the reputations of products that meet recognized standards. Of course, AIOs have deep historical roots. In ancient Greece, references to place of origin were officially regulated in the wine trade (Allaire, Casabianca and Thévenod-Mottet 2011: 2). In 1411, King Charles VI decreed that only cheeses aged in the caves of Roquefort-sur-Soulzon could bear the Roquefort name, and French laws passed in 1905 and 1919, and the French *Comité National des Appellations d'Origine*, formed in 1935, subsequently restricted the use of place names for registered products, allowing producers themselves to decide the areas in which their products could be made and the characteristics and methods that would define them. When the EU was formed in 1992, member states agreed to recognize one another's 'Protected Designations of Origin' (PDOs) and 'Protected Geographical Indications' (PGIs), and proponents of such appellations and indications of origin have sought further expansion of these regimes within the context of the World Trade Organization (WTO) (West 2013b).

What Barham has written about controlled appellations of origin (AOCs) in France may now also be said of AIOs elsewhere:

> In the past, only producers organized AOC production in interaction with the state. Increasingly, other actors are getting involved who are pursuing broader

rural development objectives linked to the cachet and consumer draw of specialty products in their area. These actors can include regional tourism bureaus, agents from park areas in or near the AOC area, regional economic development specialists, representatives of local businesses such as hotels and restaurants, and producers of other regional agro-food products or handicrafts. AOCs are now clearly recognized as important contributors to the economic and agricultural structure of a region, as well as to its shared identity (Barham 2003: 136).

'DISSONANCE AND CONTESTATION', OR, DISCONNECTION, MISTRUST AND INAUTHENTICITY IN THE HERITAGIZATION OF ARTISANAL FOODS

Just outside the village of Salers (France), on a ridge along the Route du Puy Mary, sits *La Maison du Fromage et de la Vache Salers*, a small museum documenting the history of transhumant pastoralism and cheesemaking in the region. While the story of cheesemaking is well presented, the cheesemaker with whom I visited this museum complained that its proprietor–curator was not a cheesemaker but, instead, an entrepreneur cashing in on tourists' interests in the region's traditions. Indeed, Jean-Pierre Lallet worked as a miner before restoring an abandoned *buron* (stone barn and cheese room) and transforming it into a museum celebrating traditions in which he claimed passionate interest. Lallet's museum, and my cheesemaking companion's commentary, remind us that an array of actors may be involved in the heritagization of foods and foodways, and that their perspectives and interests do not always harmonize.

In Roquefort-sur-Soulzon (France), tourists may visit exhibits set up by Roquefort producers themselves. The production of Roquefort is big business (seven certified producers make more than three million cheeses per year), and so too is the attraction of tourists; the *Société Roquefort* website describes its cave as the 'number one food manufacturing site visited in France' (http://www.visite-roquefort-societe.com/en/presentation; consulted 1 May 2014). On the region's official tourist website and on billboards lining the road running through the commune, five other Roquefort producers beckon tourists to visit their caves, each telling its own version of the Roquefort story and vying for the future brand loyalty of visitors.

Peio Etxeleku, who makes Ossau-Iraty in his *Fromagerie Agour* in Helette (Basque Ipparalde / France), has mounted an exhibition adjacent to this medium-scale plant portraying the life of Basque shepherds in their high-mountain huts. While large- or medium-scale producers, like *Société* or *Agour*, may best be able to afford investment in gathering and preserving artefacts and accounts of traditional foods and foodways, and while others may benefit from such attractions – such as the more than 4500 shepherds providing milk to Roquefort's seven producers – more substantial benefits may be captured by artisan producers through the creation of small-scale museums on their own farms or in their own workshops, such the one, mentioned above, that Alphonse Bellonte built on his family farm outside St. Nectaire, in Farges

(France). But such initiatives may themselves produce tensions, whether by creating competitive advantage over fellow artisans or by drawing unwanted traffic to otherwise tranquil rural spaces. Even as Ilhan Koçulu worked – with the support of the regional UNDP office in Kars – to establish a Gravyer cheese museum in his village of Boğatepe (Turkey), he worried in conversation with me about how other village cheesemakers – mostly his own kin – would interpret his intentions and his choices of where to locate the museum and how to tell the cheese's story.

In many places where I have conducted research, local government, or entities through which AIOs were governed, led in the creation and running of tourist attractions focused on local foods and foodways. But even with officials or hired consultants brokering diverse interests, the stories these museums told were often seen to privilege some perspectives over others. In Idiazabal (Basque Hegoalde/ Spain), shepherds concerned with the industrialization of cheesemaking within the Idiazabal appellation itself formed a shepherd's association and established their own museum to tell the story of transhumant pastoralism and the making of *artzai gazta* (shepherd's cheese) from their perspective. In places where there were official cheese-focused museums, cheesemakers with whom I spoke lobbied guides to refer visitors to them and their products, and complained that others did likewise. Others lamented that official attractions competed with those mounted by artisans themselves – or made such initiatives impossible – while generating revenue that did not directly benefit them.

Smith has written: 'Heritage is a multilayered performance – be this a performance of visiting, managing, interpretation or conservation – that embodies acts of remembrance and commemoration while negotiating and constructing a sense of place, belonging and understanding in the present.' She concludes, 'Heritage is also inherently dissonant and contested' (Smith 2006: 3–4). The varied scenarios, presented above, through which artisan cheesemaking has been 'performed' in museums illustrates Smith's conclusion. Many actors conceive of artisanal foods and foodways as heritage worthy of preservation, and are keen to involve themselves in, and benefit from, this association. But the 'communities' in which artisanal foods are made inevitably comprise individuals and groups with disparate perspectives, identities and interests. Heritagization, in its varied forms, may alienate and exclude some. Even when benefits are shared by a range of actors, their distribution may be perceived by some as unfair. Instead of facilitating the reconnection of people with the foods they eat, the people who make them, and the places in which they are made, the heritagization of artisanal foods may engender experiences of disconnection, perceptions of inauthenticity, and mistrust.

Such possibilities certainly pertain to the heritagization of foods through AIOs. Elsewhere, I have written: 'Where certification of an AIO does create value, just who captures that value may vary greatly depending upon the cultural, political, and economic dynamics animating the establishment and administration of the AIO' (West 2013b: 216). Because AIOs are generally perceived by consumers as certifying superior quality, as mentioned above, they effectively create 'value-added' market niches. The profitability of these niches often attracts new entrants, including not only artisan producers but also larger manufacturers, with significant financial and technical resources, keen to rationalize production and maximize investment returns. The success of AIOs may prompt smaller-scale producers to 'scale up'. While the methods of production permitted within an AIO must be agreed by member producers, these trends have led to the alteration of appellation protocols in some places, and the establishment of new appellations in others, effecting what some perceive as the erosion or abandonment of traditional methods in favour of more modern, more profitable ones. Keen to broker the trade in lucrative AIO products, large-scale retailers have sought to capture significant shares of the market in appellation products, favouring larger suppliers who can meet their demands over smaller ones who cannot. In response, many smaller-scale producers have opted out of AIOs entirely. And where larger producers have come to dominate appellation regimes and have increased production, the depression of prices has often forced smaller-scale producers out of business (West 2013b: 217).

AIOs have also sometimes had perverse effects on the natural environment. Bowen warns against unreserved celebration of appellations and indications of origin for '(re)embedding' foods in social and ecological spheres, suggesting the extent to which they do so varies greatly and depends upon contextualizing social dynamics (Bowen 2010). In their study of Mexican tequila, for example, Bowen and Zapata show that, as investment in the industry rose, commitment to *terroir* was undermined by the quest for profits, with larger producers using more pesticides and monocropping single varieties of *agave* on marginal lands, while smaller-scale producers (using more sustainable methods) were marginalized (Bowen and Valenzuela Zapata 2009) (see also Vitrolles 2011).

Just as AIOs may disconnect artisanal foods and foodways from their natural ecologies, they may also undermine food quality. Cheesemakers in Serpa (Portugal) with whom Domingos and I worked told us that only once an appellation had been created for Serpa cheese (that did not specify the breed from which milk must come) did producers consider replacing native Campanhiça and Merino stock with more productive Lacaune ewes which were less suited to grazing local pastures but could, if kept in stables and fed high-energy rations, produce more milk. Through tolerance of more intensive methods, this appellation actually facilitated the production of a more industrial product – a transformation covered over by official certification of these new methods *as traditional*. What is more, Serpa makers admitted to us that, while they did not certify their best cheeses, which discerning local customers bought, they did certify their poorest-quality cheeses, recovering the cost of certification through sales to supermarket customers who naively interpreted certification as a mark of superior quality (West and Domingos 2012).

Even conservative AIOs – committed to the maintenance of tradition – may have perverse effects for artisan producers and their products. Bowen and De Master argue, 'In the same way that a museum might select certain artistic representations of a cultural period for its display while deciding against the inclusion of others, the very process of codifying the production process may threaten the diversity and specificity of ... traditional products' (Bowen and De Master 2011: 77). Welz has similarly argued that the unsuccessful application for an appellation for Halloumi cheese in Greek Cyprus threatened to standardize the product, eliminating the diversity of methods deployed by small-scale producers (Welz 2013). More broadly, Bowen and De Master argue:

> Traditional conceptualizations of culture can in some cases constitute an advantage for local actors, by providing a discursive strategy for resisting the modernizing and industrializing tendencies promoted by certain extralocal actors. However, these initiatives also risk privileging particular (fixed) markers of culture over a more dynamic relationship between communities, environments, and local actors. Arguably, in dynamic, evolving cultures, there exists a tension between ensuring the continuity of tradition and embracing innovation. As traditional and place-based foods become institutionalized, local actors relinquish some of their ability and agency to innovate even as they simultaneously assert their power as producers to continue long-held production traditions. (Bowen and De Master 2011: 78–9)

Similar tensions emerge where 'heritage foods' are integrated into tourism. Richards succinctly argues: 'Strong linkages between tourism and local food production can ... create considerable added value; but poor linkages can be fatal' (Richards 2002: 13) (see also Hjalager 2002). As suggested above, linkages are made – or not – within complex social fields defined not only by shared interests but also by competition and conflict. For example, artisanal foodmakers seeking direct connections with tourists – whether through farm shops or B&Bs – may be resented by those hoping to take a cut of their profits through selling their products in tourist shops or restaurants, or vice versa. As Kneafsey suggests, there may be deep historical layers to social relations determining attitudes towards cultural resources, tradition and community as well as deciding how potentially contentious dynamics ultimately play out (Kneafsey 2000: 38). As discussed above with reference to museums, local government may mediate, albeit with varying degrees of success. But governments may also act in their own interests, favouring initiatives that promise to increase tax revenues over those preferred by constituents, or, establishing policies and implementing programmes that favour more powerful constituents over the less powerful or the majority, reflecting underlying political dynamics.

As with AIOs, the heritagization of artisanal foods through gastronomic tourism may also have unforeseen or undesirable effects on these foods themselves. Kneafsey reports that French government regulations require a *ferme-auberge* (farmhouse inn) to serve 'meals consisting of regional specialities made from the produce of the farm.' While this would seem to protect diversity, Kneafsey observes on the basis of a case study in Brittany (France) that, paradoxically, 'The effect is to impose on farmers a quite specific version of what the "authentic" Breton farmhouse experience actually is' (Kneafsey 2000: 44), freezing traditions in time in the same way that Bowen and De Master suggest appellations may. As the concept of heritage is applied to artisanal products, Grasseni quotes Herzfeld who concludes, 'Even "diversity" can become a homogenous product. So, too, can tradition and heritage: the particular is itself universalized' (Grasseni 2011; Herzfeld 2004: 2).

A question posed by Bessière – 'To what extent can heritage be conserved and transmitted without upsetting its identity?' (Bessière 1998: 29) – cuts both ways here, just as it does with AIOs. Heritagization may threaten tradition not only by freezing it in time, but also by profoundly transforming it. Many cheesemakers admitted to me that they had modified their methods to produce blander cheeses to appeal to tourists. They also admitted to selling cheeses younger than they once had – (some described them as 'unfinished') – so that they would hold up better in tourist suitcases.

Tourism not only threatens to transform artisanal foods, but also the environments in which they are produced. Cabrales cheesemakers I met in the high-mountain village of Tielve (Spain) told me that tourists traipsing through their ageing caves introduced microorganisms that threatened this delicate ecosystem, prompting them and other Cabrales makers together to mount a museum in a disused cave in the lowland town of Arenas de Cabrales where visitors might come instead. Shepherd-cheesemakers in Chora Sfakion on the Island of Crete (Greece) and their patron, the president of the municipality of Sfakia, asked me for advice on the creation of a cheese museum, but expressed concerns about tourists travelling to the *mitata* (shepherds huts) in high-mountain pastures, fearing this would exacerbate erosion on dirt tracks and generate litter and polluting emissions.

Some warn that the commodification of food heritage may give rise to a representation of tradition that ultimately supplants tradition itself, whether owing to measures limiting the effects of tourist traffic or to attempts to better meet tourist expectations. Barham has written of the 'concern that the countryside and the customs defined as consonant with it will undergo a process of "Disneyfication", becoming living museums for visitors from the city, a kind of "rurality under glass" for the consumption of privileged consumers' (Barham 2003: 132). Kneafsey's work in Brittany illustrates this, as a local development worker informed her that 'most of the people involved in farm tourism were not the original farming families, but were those who "had the capacity to invest and who have made a *ferme-auberge* in order to have a pretty farm"' (Kneafsey 2000: 43).

Indeed, some argue that the embrace – or co-optation – of the very term, 'artisanal foods', by larger manufacturers and retailers means that artisanal foods today are little more than simulacra. Jackson writes: 'Many of the qualities attributed to artisan food are now being appropriated by large-scale industrialized food producers, sold through high-street supermarkets rather than through local independent stores or farmers' markets' (Jackson and CONANX Group 2013: 26).[8] By some definitions, for example, more 'craft baking' is done today in supermarket bakeries than in small-scale bakeries. Many British supermarkets now trade in high volumes of 'artisanal cheese', making it difficult for specialist cheesemongers to protect their market niche, and prompting artisan cheesemakers to consider advantages and disadvantages of scaling up to supply retailers who ruthlessly seek to drive prices down to unsustainable levels. Like tourism, the mass-marketing of artisanal foods may have deleterious consequences even for the environments in which they are grown and made. Van Esterik reports that the marketing abroad, as gourmet items, of Laotian foraged foods such as *khai pen* (river algae sheets) and *khao kiep* (cassava crisps) – traditionally eaten in times of acute hunger – has depleted these scarce and essential resources in the environments from which they have long been harvested (Van Esterik 2006).

THE REAL THING? ARTISANAL FOODS AND THE CRAFTING OF CULTURE

Critical assessment of the heritagization of artisanal foods brings us back to the question of authenticity with which this chapter began. Based on research conducted in the United Kingdom, Cook, Crang and Thorpe concluded that 'the word "authentic" (along with its close relations "ethnic," "exotic" and "traditional") had so many definitions [in food industries and on supermarket shelves] that it didn't describe anything at all' (Cook, Crang and Thorpe 2000: 116–17). Had they been writing today, they might have included the term 'artisanal' on this list.

Decades ago, MacCannell laid foundations for reflection in the field of tourism studies on whether tourists can ever truly locate authenticity. In the words of Molz:

> MacCannell suggests that modern society has become inauthentic and that the modern tourist is on a quest to recover this lost authenticity. According to MacCannell, 'Modern man is losing his attachments to the workbench, the neighborhood, the town, the family, which he once called "his own" but, at the same time, he is developing an interest in the "real life" of others' (MacCannell 1976: 91). MacCannell's tourist locates authenticity in some premodern realm – in people, places, and times that have not yet been dispossessed of their authenticity by the processes of modernity. (Molz 2004: 55)

Adapting Goffman's idea that the social world is divided into back regions, where actors are at ease, and front regions, where they 'perform' for an audience (Goffman 1959), MacCannell suggests that, while tourists hope to find authentic back regions, they generally get no further than a middle ground, created by the tourist industry, where authenticity is 'staged' (Molz 2004: 55–6).

Along similar lines, Everett has described how foodmakers hosting tourists in Ireland and Scotland create a 'third space' by placing visitors behind windows separating them from sanitary spaces of production: 'The initiatives create inauthentic front stages which are constructed to retain levels of production and ensure the producer's livelihood, while ensuring visitors safely enjoy a leisure space that resembles an authentic production place' (Everett 2012: 548). Here, visitors know they are divided from what lies on the other side. By contrast, Terrio describes artisan chocolate makers in Bayonne who cultivate the mystique of craft by alluding to practices which they, in fact, have no involvement in – (selecting, blending and processing cacao beans) – while showcasing manual aspects of the work they actually do, all in workshops purpose-built in gentrified neighbourhoods to attract tourists (Terrio 1999).

Some wonder, however, whether such fakery ultimately matters. Responding to MacCannell, Lindholm reports: 'Some theorists have argued that tourists today do not really want to penetrate appearances to find the spontaneous, unrehearsed truth backstage; instead, they are quite pleased to experience the manufactured world they have seen on television and imagined in their dreams. They don't care if it's all a fake; they expect fakery and appreciate it when it is well done. So long as it's amusing!' Lindholm paraphrases Baudrillard, saying, 'Real experience (which tends to be time consuming and boring) has become less engaging than intensified, scripted, exciting representations of reality' (Baudrillard 2001; Lindholm 2008: 43–4).

Molz's criticism of MacCannell for 'perceive[ing] authenticity as an objective quality that exists in a fixed place or time' underlies rather different conclusions: 'For the purposes of understanding culinary tourism, a more fruitful way of considering authenticity is as a mutually negotiated concept' (Molz 2004: 61) – in other words, authenticity matters, but it is socially constructed, within complex fields of social relations in particular socio-historical contexts.

Authenticity's constructed-ness is visible in the way ideas about what is authentic emerge and change over time and in accordance with differing social perspectives. Geyzen, Scholliers and Leroy remind us that all traditions are 'invented' in time – that 'there must be *a* moment in the past when a way of doing became a tradition, or rather, when it was constructed as such' (Geyzen, Scholliers and Leroy 2012: 49). Even once invented, traditions must constantly change. Terrio expresses this paradox, suggesting that while craft that deviates from 'the standard of the past' is not regarded as 'true craft' by some, 'if it conforms it cannot survive' (Terrio 2000: 14). Alphonse Bellonte told me, along similar lines, that he practised a 'living tradition' whose survival depended upon change. Decisions that he and his family made about what was and wasn't essential to tradition – (e.g., they insisted that ageing cheeses in natural caves was essential to their character, but were content to use electric-powered hydraulic presses to limit repetitive stress injuries caused by hand-pressing) – were ultimately about what allowed them to continue farming and making cheese; if they could no longer make a living from cheesemaking, he reasoned, they could no longer bear this tradition (West 2014). Paxson describes cheesemakers she worked with as 'post-pastoral' for the ways in which, similarly, they selectively adopted and adapted industrial technologies against which they otherwise defined themselves (Paxson 2013, see also Paxson, in this volume).

'Inventing tradition' may itself be considered a peasant or artisan tradition. In the high-mountain town of Scala (Italy), I visited cheesemakers producing for sale to tourists on the Amalfi coast just below. Their cheeses, I discovered, had no history in Scala, but tourists embraced them *as traditional products* nonetheless. When I wondered out loud if this was crass opportunism, my student and research collaborator, Filippo Bertoni, suggested such opportunism may be a genuine peasant tradition – one that has enabled artisans past and present not to be(come) relics, but instead to reproduce a living heritage of their own making.

Whereas Stiles et al. conceive of authenticity as a form of authorship that leaves 'ghostly traces' subject to variable – even conflicting – readings (Stiles et al. 2011), the dynamics shaping such acts of authorship matter greatly. In the realm of food and heritage, this often entails interaction between those cast as bearers of tradition and those seeking momentarily to participate in it. With reference to tourist restaurants where she conducted research in Thailand, Molz asserts that authenticity is negotiated between tourists and restaurateurs, stressing that 'tourists bring their own symbolic systems and culinary experiences to bear on this negotiation of authenticity' (Molz 2004: 61–2). But not only consumers – or outsiders – bring dynamism to such interactions. Although 'tourism promises to take the traveller "back in time" to places "untouched by the outside world"' (Lindholm 2008: 39), Heldke chides those who would '[dismiss] out of hand the possibility [that a cultural] insider might regard it as "authentic" to *modify* a dish in order to respond to different local conditions and ingredients'. She continues: 'Indeed, one might read the history of almost every cuisine on the globe as a history of just such modifications, made in response to new ingredients, new conditions, and new neighbors' (Heldke 2005: 388, see also Avieli, in this volume).

Cohen and Avieli paint an even more complex picture of such dynamic interaction. When it comes to food, they suggest, tourism simultaneously exaggerates both neophobic and neophilic tendencies (see also Abbots 2014). While tourists seek new tastes, their failure to recognize or understand what is on offer, or fear that foods may disgust them or make them ill, may constrain adventurousness (Cohen and Avieli 2004). Avieli further complicates this, suggesting that, in Hoi An (Vietnam), where restaurateurs serve 'local speciality' dishes adapted to be considered more familiar and safer by tourists, a limited number of adventurous tourists seek greater authenticity in out-of-the-way places inhabited by local diners, while locals themselves sometimes try and even embrace dishes concocted for tourists, all making the invention of tradition a truly dialogical process (Avieli 2013, and in this volume).

Some suggest that experiencing the very moment of authenticity's construction may be essential to its perception. Cohen and Cohen differentiate between 'cool' authentication (often officially declared by experts or authority figures), and 'hot' authentication (based upon direct experience, generally involving 'self-investment on the part of the participants') (Cohen and Cohen 2012: 1300). Richards provides an example of experience-based authenticity in relation to food: 'Tourists are increasingly willing to learn and eager to increase their cultural capital by creating rather than just consuming. Gastronomic holidays are therefore an important aspect of the emerging creative tourism sector, as tourists can learn to cook, can learn about the ingredients used, the way in which they are grown and appreciate how culinary traditions have come into existence' (Richards 2002: 16–17). Similarly, Cavanaugh reports that those visiting artisan salami makers in Bergamo 'do not just come to buy the salami; they come to experience the place and its tastes, witness how the foods they consume are produced, and become involved in the processes themselves, not just the end result' (Cavanaugh 2007: 164).

It is not simply that, through hands-on experience, participants better come to know authentic foods or foodways, but rather that the experience of authenticity is itself what they come to know. Bendix argues with reference to the idea of authenticity in folklore studies, 'It is not the object [of longing] ..., but the desire, the process of searching itself, that yields existential meaning' (Bendix 1997: 17). Cavanaugh writes: 'Circulation [of artisanal salamis] is not envisioned as being reduced simply to cash exchanges, but instead as one part in a social interaction centred on appreciating and participation in – if only for a night or two – a particular way of life' (Cavanaugh 2007: 166). Kirshenblatt-Gimblett further develops this idea:

> Not authenticity, but the *question* of authenticity, is essential to culinary tourism, for this question organizes conversation, reflection, and comparison and arises as much from doubt as from confidence. The ensuing conversation tests and extends one's knowledge and discernment. (Kirshenblatt-Gimblett 2004: xii)

Experience may be just as important to producers' perceptions of authenticity as to consumers'. Aistara's ethnography of artisan bakers in Latvia – who conceive of authentic sweet-and-sour-dough bread as recreating the taste of bread made with sugar in the Soviet years rather than with malt in the pre-Soviet era – illustrates the importance of personal memory in constructions of authenticity, as well as how memory of lived experience may locate authenticity in a proximate past despite countervailing tendencies to celebrate longer-standing traditions over newer ones (Aistara 2014).

There may, of course, be complex social dimensions to exchanges through which authenticity is constructed, as experience is significantly shaped by social identities and positions. While for some, Jackson suggests, constructing authenticity entails distinguishing one's self from people of poorer taste, for others it entails resistance to what are perceived as dominant culinary forms (Jackson and CONANX Group 2013: 29, citing Abarca 2006; Zukin 2008). Regardless, constructions of authenticity may differentiate and disconnect people rather than connecting them. Terrio offers an example:

> The formulation of a new French standard in chocolate consumption exemplifies the gentrification of taste. ... The aesthetic presentation of locally and regionally produced foodstuffs in new taste combinations appeals to sophisticated urbanites who want food that has both cultural authenticity and cachet. (Terrio 2005: 150)

Lindholm similarly interprets Slow Food, an organization whose founder, Carlo Petrini, has asserted that their work to educate the palate 'creates an elite without excluding anyone' (Lindholm 2008: 74):

> Slow Food initiates become (ideally anyway) authentic connoisseurs of transient pleasure whose cultivated and purified inclinations determine what is genuine in the world around them. Kept afloat by what they believe is their good taste, they are not washed away by the waves of modernity; they surf on them. And so a universalizing social movement has been created out of the fleeting and intimate aesthetic experience of personal pleasure. (Lindholm 2008: 74)

Slow Food's membership includes both consumers and producers of artisanal foods, who may not only embrace such foodways as a 'lifestyle choice', but also accept and defend higher prices, suggesting these are the 'true costs' of 'real food'. Such constructions of authenticity distance them from others, who may or may not be in a position to agree with the Slow Food slogan 'we don't pay enough for our food', and who may in any case spurn what they consider snobbery, embracing more affordable – even industrial – foods as part of their own, authentic foodways.

Beyond this, the performance of artisanship as cultural heritage may actually alienate foodmakers from themselves, their work and those who eat their products. Notwithstanding expectations, many artisans find the work of preserving artisan craft in tension with the simpler lifestyle they hope to realize (Tregear 2005). While agritourism may subsidize artisanship through inviting guests to share intimate spaces in idyllic homes or cosy workshops, hosts must often balance unreasonable expectations of constant service with the work of farming and foodmaking they are also expected to perform, all while taking care of themselves and their families. Brandth and Haugen suggest that Norwegian farmers and foodmakers who host visitors struggle with how agritourism dissolves boundaries between public/work and private/home spheres (Brandth and Haugen 2012). The Bellontes told me they sometimes grew weary of having unruly visitors in their cheese room.

Even as farmers and artisan foodmakers make of themselves and their traditions commodities for sale, trading their most – if not their only – valuable assets in the neoliberal marketplace (Brown 2003; Comaroff and Comaroff 2009), and even as visitors afford them a sympathetic and validating audience for their performances as authentic farmers and foodmakers, agritourism can, as Di Domenico and Miller suggest, profoundly challenge farmers' senses of self and of their own authenticity (Di Domenico and Miller 2012). When Alphonse Bellonte was asked by a national supermarket to dress in nineteenth-century peasant costume to sell his cheese in their regional store, he told me, he refused to play the part.

While conversations and negotiations through which authenticity is constructed may divide people, however, they may also (re)connect them. Jackson argues that the quest for authentic foods may ultimately serve as a means 'to negotiate the ideological tension between democracy and distinction' (Jackson and CONANX Group 2013: 29, citing Johnston and Baumann 2007). Consumers may, for example, connect virtually, through investment in relationships with artisans mediated by the labels and shopkeepers telling their stories. They may also do so though real-time interactions in the shared spaces produced by the heritagization of artisanal foods. Cavanaugh argues that connections made through agritourism may give rise to durable commercial networks:

> The products [that visitors to *argiturismi* in Bergamo] may buy and take home with them to savor later will be enjoyed not just for their taste, but also for the links that they carry to the 'authentic' Bergamasco (sic) experience in which the consumer first encountered them. In the process, social networks for the distribution and circulation of Bergamasco (sic) products will be (re-)created. (Cavanaugh 2007: 164)

Experiences may also produce new social identities as well as lasting social relationships. Molz asserts that 'by eating strange foods, culinary tourists literally embody cosmopolitan openness to risk and Otherness', even if they 'eat the Other' (Molz 2007: 79, 81). Bessière suggests that holidaymakers 'dream of friendly relationships, true and genuine values, roots', and often find them in local gastronomy, 'since it integrates eating into a new cultural world', ultimately affording possibilities not only for 'socializing' but also for 'finding a community identity' (Bessière 1998: 22). Mykletun and Gyimóthy tell us not only that 'scary foods', such as the traditional sheep's head dinner served by tour operators in Voss (Norway), may constitute an attraction in and of themselves, but also that they may invite tourists to overcome fears by demonstrating courage and self-mastery, thereby attaining inclusion in a new social group (Gyimóthy and Mykletun 2009; Mykletun and Gyimóthy 2010).

It is not just consumers and visitors who experience social connections in the performance of artisanal foodways. Despite problems associated with the commoditization of artisanal foods and foodways in the cultural economy, many foodmakers find that conceiving of and presenting their craft as heritage connects them to people in rewarding ways. Not only does heritagization create market niches, allowing them to make a living, for many, it also gives foundation to the creation and maintenance of durable social relationships.

Maria Micielica, a widow I met in Wizajny (Poland), makes just one kilogram of cheese a day, but makes of it the centrepiece of a farmhouse breakfast she serves in her kitchen to B&B guests. Her agritourism affords her company as she practises her craft – the craft that attracts guests, paying her living. Czesław Racis, who also makes cheese in Wizajny, once allowed holidaymakers passing through the region (as many do on an established trail from Western Europe, to the Baltic States, around Scandanavia and home again) to park their caravan on his property overnight, and when they blogged on the trail webpage about the food and drink that he and his family served them, and how together they ate, drank and sang the night away despite the language barrier that separated them, others began to appear. As he told me how his family reproduce that evening – the farmhouse fare, the Polish folksongs, the camaraderie – and how subsequent visitors reproduce the good publicity, his face beamed, betraying the enjoyment he derived not only from augmenting farm income, but also – perhaps more – from the stimulating cosmopolitan company and revelry such evenings brought.

Such encounters may be fleeting, but relationships formed between artisans and visitors may be significant nonetheless. The Koopmans – a family of cheesemakers in De Weere (Netherlands) with whom I spent a week – told me that they regularly hosted interns, many of whom stayed for a few months, helping with the cows and in the cheese room, and becoming temporary family members. They showed me an album with photos of past interns and shared stories of what these youngsters – with whom they had generally kept in touch – were now doing. They had visited one in France, and one in Estonia, on holidays. Such enduring connections gave the Koopmanns a sense that their life on the farm was linked to a broader world – one that valued their work and their way of life – and expanded horizons for their three children. The Bellonte family, with whom I spent several weeks at a time over several summers, similarly sustained contacts with some who had visited their farm.

Alphonse's inclination to treat visitors as more than consumers/tourists, but rather as three-dimensional people on the move in a mobile world, prompted many who met him to treat him in kind, not only as a farmer and artisan foodmaker, but as a fellow resident of the modern world.

Through such relationships – borne of the (re)production of artisanal foods and foodways in a dynamic cultural economy – producers and consumers not only craft food, then, but also craft themselves, the cultural and environmental worlds in which they live, and the social relations through which the characteristics and value(s) of artisanal foodways are (re)created, and their authenticity and trustworthiness ultimately assessed.

NOTES

1. Valuable feedback on a draft of this chapter was provided by members of the Nkumi writing workshop in the SOAS Food Studies Centre, including Jakob Klein, Elizabeth Hull, James Staples, Anne Murcott and Sami Zubaida. Anna Colquhoun assisted with bibliographic research.
2. According to Pratt: 'The concept of authenticity is central to almost all present-day research on quality food. ... Authenticity is a quality attributed to a range of foods and cuisines ... [including] food specific to a location [and, most germane to our concerns] food products [that] are the result of a craft process' (Pratt 2007: 293–4). Cf. Lees (2003), which represents the widespread use in government and industry of the term authenticity, in relation to food, specifically to connote traceability and the prevention of fraudulent adulteration.
3. Fieldwork was conducted in thirteen countries between 2003 and 2011 with support from the British Academy (LRG 45537).
4. According to Weiss, consumers of artisanal pork even feel they connect with animals whose flesh they consume through participation in artisanal butchery workshops in North Carolina (Weiss 2012: 617).
5. Alternatively, many with whom I worked found outlets for their products in which their stories would be told by others, such as speciality cheesemongers and gourmet food shops whose customers sought to '(re-)connect' with the countryside and its produce, even if from a distance, via trusted intermediaries who shared their enthusiasm for artisanal foods.
6. This alone marked a reversal from tourism promoters warning visitors to avoid local foods in favour of catered foods sourced through conventional supply chains that assured food quality and safety.
7. Concurrently, the Food and Agriculture Organization (FAO) of the United Nations began keeping its own list of Globally Important Agricultural Heritage Systems in 2002 to aid in the conservation of traditional agricultural systems (Sun et al. 2011).
8. Along similar lines, Pilcher has written: 'For corporations such as Taco Bell, Mexico is little more than a low-cost product development laboratory, providing concepts such as *gorditas* and *chalupas* for food formulators and advertising executives to work over and then reexport around the world' (Pilcher 2004: 92).

REFERENCES

Abarca, M. E. (2006), *Voices in the Kitchen: Views of Food and the World from Working-Class Mexican and Mexican American Women*, College Station, TX: Texas A&M University Press.

Abbots, E.-J. (2014), 'The Fast and the Fusion: Class, Creolization and the Remaking of Comida Típica in Highland Ecuador', in J. A. Klein and A. Murcott (eds), *Food Consumption in Global Perspective. Essays in the Anthropology of Food in Honour of Jack Goody*, 87–107, New York: Palgrave Macmillan.

Aistara, G. A. (2014), 'Authentic Anachronisms', *Gastronomica*, 14(4): 7–16.

Allaire, G., Casabianca, F. and Thévenod-Mottet, E. (2011), 'Geographical Origin: A Complex Feature of Agro-food Products', in E. Barham and B. Sylvander (eds), *Labels of Origin for Food: Local Development, Global Recognition*, 1–12, Wallingford, UK: CABI.

Avieli, N. (2013), 'What is "Local Food"?: Dynamic Culinary Heritage in the World Heritage Site of Hoi An, Vietnam', *Journal of Heritage Tourism*, 8(2–3): 120–32.

Barham, E. (2003), 'Translating Terroir: The Global Challenge of French AOC Labelling', *Journal of Rural Studies*, 19(1): 127–38.

Baudrillard, J. (2001), 'Simulacra and Simulations', in M. Poster (ed.), *Jean Baudrillard: Selected Writings*, 169–87, Cambridge: Polity Press.

Bendix, R. (1997), *In Search of Authenticity: The Formation of Folklore Studies*, Madison: The University of Wisconsin Press.

Bessière, J. (1998), 'Local Development and Heritage: Traditional Food and Cuisine as Tourist Attractions in Rural Areas', *Sociologia Ruralis*, 38(1): 21–34.

Boniface, P. (2003), *Tasting Tourism: Travelling for Food and Drink*, Burlington, VT: Ashgate.

Bowen, S. (2010), 'Embedding Local Places in Global Spaces: Geographical Indications as a Territorial Development Strategy', *Rural Sociology*, 75(2): 209–43.

Bowen, S. and De Master, K. (2011), 'New Rural Livelihoods or Museums of Production?: Quality Food Initiatives in Practice', *Journal of Rural Studies*, 27(1): 73–82.

Bowen, S. and Valenzuela Zapata, A. (2009), 'Geographical Indications, Terroir, and Socioeconomic and Ecological Sustainability: The Case of Tequila', *Journal of Rural Studies*, 25(1): 108–19.

Brandth, B. and Haugen, M. S. (2011) 'Farm Diversification into Tourism: Implications for Social Identity?' *Journal of Rural Studies*, 27(1): 35–44.

Brandth, B. and Haugen, M. S. (2012), 'Farm Tourism and Dilemmas of Commercial Activity in the Home', *Hospitality & Society*, 2(2): 179–95.

Brown, M. F. (2003), *Who Owns Native Culture?* Cambridge, MA and London: Harvard University Press.

Cavanaugh, J. (2007), 'Making Salami, Producing Bergamo: The Transformation of Value', *Ethnos*, 72(2): 149–72.

Che, D., Veeck, A. and Veeck, G. (2005), 'Sustaining Production and Strengthening the Agritourism Product: Linkages among Michigan Agritourism Destinations', *Agriculture and Human Values*, 22(2): 225–34.

Cohen, E. and Avieli, N. (2004), 'Food in Tourism: Attraction and Impediment', *Annals of Tourism Research*, 31(4): 755–78.

Cohen, E. and Cohen, S. A. (2012), 'Authentication: Hot and Cold', *Annals of Tourism Research*, 39(3): 1295–1314.

Comaroff, J. L. and Comaroff, J. (2009), *Ethnicity, Inc.*, Chicago, IL and London: The University of Chicago Press.

Cook, I., Crang, P. and Thorpe, M. (2000), 'Regions to be Cheerful: Culinary Authenticity and its Geographies', in I. Cook, D. Crouch, S. Naylor and J. Ryan (eds), *Cultural Turns / Geographical Turns*, 109–39, London: Longman.

Di Domenico, M. L. and Miller, G. (2012), 'Farming and Tourism Enterprise: Experiential Authenticity in the Diversification of Independent Small-Scale Family Farming', *Tourism Management*, 33(2): 285–94.

Dubouchet, G. (2007), *Le Musée des Campagnes. Volume I - Mon Folklore Éternel*, Saint-Didier-en-Velay: Les Amis du Musée de Saint-Didier-en-Velay.

Everett, S. (2012), 'Production Places or Consumption Spaces?: The Place-Making Agency of Food Tourism in Ireland and Scotland', *Tourism Geographies*, 14(4): 535–54.

Gade, D. W. (2004), 'Tradition, Territory, and Terroir in French Viniculture: Cassis, France, and Appellation Contrôlée', *Annals of the Association of American Geographers*, 94(4): 848–67.

Geyzen, A., Scholliers, P. and Leroy, F. (2012), 'Innovative Traditions in Swiftly Transforming Foodscapes: An Exploratory Essay', *Trends in Food Science and Technology*, 25: 47–52.

Goffman, E. (1959), *The Presentation of Self in Everyday Life*, Garden City, New York: Anchor Books.

Grasseni, C. (2011), 'Re-inventing Food: Alpine Cheese in the Age of Global Heritage', *Anthropology of Food*, 8, https://aof.revues.org.

Gray, J. (2000), 'The Common Agricultural Policy and the Reinvention of the Rural in the European Community', *Sociologia Ruralis*, 40(1): 30–52.

Gyimóthy, S. and Mykletun, R. J. (2009), 'Scary Food: Commodifying Culinary Heritage as Meal Adventures in Tourism', *Journal of Vacation Marketing*, 15(3): 259–73.

Hall, C. M., Mitchell, R. and Sharples, L. (2003a), 'Consuming Places: The Role of Food, Wine and Tourism in Regional Development', in C. M. Hall, L. Sharples, R. Mitchell, N. Macionis and B. Cambourne (eds), *Food Tourism Around the World: Development, Management and Markets*, 25–59, Amsterdam, Boston, Heidelberg, London, New York, Oxford, Paris, San Diego, San Francisco, Singapore, Sydney, and Tokyo: Butterworth Heinemann.

Hall, C. M., Sharples, L., Mitchell, R., Macionis, N. and Cambourne, B. (eds) (2003b), *Food Tourism Around the World: Development, Management and Markets*, Amsterdam, Boston, Heidelberg, London, New York, Oxford, Paris, San Diego, San Francisco, Singapore, Sydney and Tokyo: Butterworth Heinemann.

Heldke, L. (2005), 'But is it Authentic?: Culinary Travel and the Search for the "Genuine Article"', in C. Korsmeyer (ed.), *The Taste Culture Reader: Experiencing Food and Drink*, 385–94, Oxford and London: Berg.

Herzfeld, M. (2004), *The Body Impolitic: Artisans and Artifice in the Global Hierarchy of Value*, Chicago and London: The University of Chicago Press.

Hjalager, A.-M. (2002), 'A Typology of Gastronomy Tourism', in A.-M. Hjalager and G. Richards (eds), *Tourism and Gastronomy*, 21–35, London and New York: Routledge.

Hjalager, A.-M. and Richards, G. (eds) (2002), *Tourism and Gastronomy*, London and New York: Routledge.

Jackson, P. and the CONANX Group (2013), *Food Words: Essays in Culinary Culture*, London and New York: Bloomsbury Academic.

Johnston, J. and Baumann, S. (2007), 'Democracy Versus Distinction: A Study of Omniverousness in Gourmet Food Writing', *American Journal of Sociology*, 113(1): 165–204.

Kirshenblatt-Gimblett, B. (2004), 'Foreword', in L. M. Long (ed.), *Culinary Tourism*, xi–xiv, Lexington: The University Press of Kentucky.

Kjaernes, U., Harvey, M. and Warde, A. (2007), *Trust in Food: A Comparative and Institutional Analysis*, New York: Palgrave Macmillan.

Kneafsey, M. (2000), 'Tourism, Place Identity and Social Relations in the European Rural Periphery', *European Urban and Regional Studies*, 7(1): 35–50.

Kneafsey, M., Cox, R., Holloway, L., Dowler, E., Venn, L. and Tuomainen, H. (2008), *Reconnecting Consumers, Producers and Food: Exploring Alternatives*, Oxford and New York: Berg.

Lagorio, R. (2004), *La Conservazione della Carne: Costumi e Valori di Una Società Contadina: Un'opportunità per le aree protette della Bergamasca e del Bresciano*, Brescia: La Compagnia della Stampa.

Lees, M. (ed.) (2003), *Food Authenticity and Traceability*, Cambridge: Woodhead Publishing.

Lewis, G. H. (2004), 'Celebrating Asparagus: Community and the Rationally Constructed Food Festival', *Journal of American Culture*, 20(4): 73–8.

Lindholm, C. (2008), *Culture and Authenticity*, Malden, Oxford and Victoria: Blackwell Publishing.

Long, L. M. (ed.) (2004), *Culinary Tourism*, Lexington: The University Press of Kentucky.

Lowenthal, D. (1985), *The Past is a Foreign Country*, Cambridge, New York, Port Chester, Melbourne, Sydney: Cambridge University Press.

MacCannell, D. (1976), *The Tourist: A New Theory of the Leisure Class*, London and Basingstoke: The MacMillan Press Ltd.

Medina, F. X. (2009), 'Mediterranean Diet, Culture and Heritage: Challenges for a New Conception', *Public Health Nutrition*, 12(9A): 1618–20.

Molz, J. G. (2004), 'Tasting the Imagined Thailand: Authenticity and Culinary Tourism in Thai Restaurants', in L. M. Long (ed.), *Culinary Tourism*, 53–75, Lexington: The University Press of Kentucky.

Molz, J. G. (2007), 'The Cosmopolitan Mobilities of Culinary Tourism', *Space and Culture*, 10(1): 77–93.

Mykletun, R. J. and Gyimóthy, S. (2010), 'Beyond the Renaissance of the Traditional Voss Sheep's-Head Meal: Tradition, Culinary Art, Scariness and Entrepreneurship', *Tourism Management*, 31(3): 434–46.

Niska, M., Vesala, H. T. and Vesala, K. M. (2012), 'Peasantry and Entrepreneurship as Frames for Farming: Reflections on Farmers' Values and Agricultural Policy Discourses', *Sociologia Ruralis*, 52(4): 453–69.

Parasecoli, F. and Tasaki, A. (2011), 'Shared Meals and Food Fights: Geographical Indications, Rural Development, and the Environment', *Environment and Society: Advances in Research*, 2(1): 106–23.

Paxson, H. (2011), 'The "Art" and "Science" of Handcrafting Cheese in the United States', *Endeavor*, 35(2–3): 116–24.

Paxson, H. (2013), *The Life of Cheese: Crafting Food and Value in America*, Berkeley: University of California Press.

Pilcher, J. M. (2004), 'From "Montezuma's Revenge" to "Mexican Truffles": Culinary Tourism across the Rio Grande', in L. M. Long (ed.), *Culinary Tourism*, 76–96, Lexington: The University Press of Kentucky.

Pratt, J. (2007), 'Food Values: The Local and the Authentic', *Critique of Anthropology*, 27(3): 285–300.

Presenza, A. and Del Chiappa, G. (2013), 'Entrepreneurial Strategies in Leveraging Food as a Tourist Resource: A Cross Regional Analysis in Italy', *Journal of Heritage Tourism*, 8(2–3): 182–92.

Ray, C. (1998), 'Culture, Intellectual Development and Territorial Development', *Sociologia Ruralis*, 38(1): 3–20.

Richards, G. (2002), 'Gastronomy: An Essential Ingredient in Tourism Production and Consumption?' in A.-M. Hjalager and G. Richards (eds), *Tourism and Gastronomy*, 3–20, London and New York: Routledge.

Saxena, G., Clark, G., Oliver, T. and Ilbery, B. (2007), 'Conceptualizing Intergated Rural Tourism', *Tourism Geographies*, 9(4): 347–70.

Schmidtt, T. M. (2008), 'The UNESCO Concept of Safeguarding Intangible Cultural Heritage: Its Background and Marakchi Roots', *International Journal of Heritage Studies*, 14(2): 95–111.

Smith, L. (2006), *Uses of Heritage*, London and New York: Routledge.

Stiles, K., Altıok, Ö. and Bell, M. M. (2011), 'The Ghosts of Tatse: Food and the Cultural Politics of Authenticity', *Agriculture and Human Values*, 28(2): 225–36.

Sun, Y., Jansen-Verbeke, M., Min, Q. and Cheng, S. (2011), 'Tourism Potential of Agricultural Systems', *Tourism Geographies: An International Journal of Tourism Space, Place and Environment*, 13(1): 112–28.

Terrio, S. J. (1999), 'Performing Craft for Heritage Tourists in Southwest France', *City & Society*, 11(1–2): 125–44.

Terrio, S. J. (2000), *Crafting the Culture and History of French Chocolate*, Berkeley, Los Angeles, and London: University of California Press.

Terrio, S. J. (2005), 'Crafting Grand Cru Chocolates in Contemporary France', in J. L. Watson and M. L. Caldwell (eds), *The Cultural Politics of Food and Eating: A Reader*, 144–62, Malden, MA, Oxford and Victoria: Blackwell Publishing.

Tregear, A. (2005), 'Lifestyle, Growth, or Community Involvement?: The Balance of Goals of UK Artisan Food Producers', *Entrepreneurship & Regional Development*, 17(1): 1–15.

Trilling, L. (1972), *Sincerity and Authenticity*, Cambridge, MA: Harvard University Press.

United Nations Educational Scientific and Cultural Organization (UNESCO) (n.d.), *List of Intangible Cultural Heritage and Register of Best Safeguarding Practices*.

van der Ploeg, J. D. (2008), *The New Peasantries: Struggles for Autonomy and Sustainability in an Era of Empire and Globalization*, London and Sterling, VA: Earthscan.

Van Esterik, P. (2006), 'From Hunger Foods to Heritage Foods: Challenges to Food Localization in Lao PDR', in R. Wilk (ed.), *Fast Food / Slow Food: The Cultural Economy of the Global Food System*, 83–96, Lanham, MD: Altamira.

Various (2011), 'Inventorying food heritage: achievements, methods, and perspectives/ Inventorier le patrimoine alimentaire: acquis, méthodes et perspectives', *Food & History*, 9(2), https://aof.revues.org.

Vermont Fresh Network (2014), *Vermont Fresh Network*, http://www.vermontfresh.net.

Vesala, H. T. and Vesala, K. M. (2010), 'Entrepreneurs and Producers: Identities of Finnish Farmers in 2001 and 2006', *Journal of Rural Studies*, 26(1): 21–30.

Vitrolles, D. (2011), 'When Geographical Indication Conflicts with Food Heritage Protection: The Case of Serrano Cheese from Rio Grande do Sul, Brazil', *Anthropology of Food*, 8, https://aof.revues.org.

Weiss, B. (2012), 'Configuring the Authentic Value of Real Food: Farm-to-Fork, Snout-to-Tail, and Local Food Movements', *American Ethnologist*, 39(3): 614–26.

Weiss, B. (2014), 'Eating Ursula', *Gastronomica*, 14(4): 17–25.

Welz, G. (2013), 'Contested Origins: Food Heritage and the European Union's Quality Label Program', *Food, Culture & Society*, 16(2): 265–79.

West, H. G. (2013a), 'Thinking Like a Cheese: Towards an Ecological Understanding of the Reproduction of Knowledge in Contemporary Artisan Cheese Making', in R. Ellen, S. Lycett and S. Johns (eds), *Understanding Cultural Transmission in Anthropology: A Critical Synthesis*, 320–45, New York and Oxford: Berghahn Books.

West, H. G. (2013b), 'Appellations and Indications of Origin, Terroir, and the Social Construction and Contestation of Place-Named Foods', in A. Murcott, W. Belasco and P. Jackson (eds), *The Handbook of Food Research*, 209–28, London, New Delhi, New York, and Sydney: Bloomsbury.

West, H. G. (2014), 'Bringing It All Back Home: Reconnecting the Country and the City through Heritage Food Tourism in the French Auvergne', in N. Domingos, J. M. Sobral and H. G. West (eds), *Food Between the Country and the City: Ethnographies of a Changing Global Foodscape*, 73–88, London, New Delhi, New York, and Sydney: Bloomsbury.

West, H. G. and Domingos, N. (2012), 'Gourmandizing Poverty Food: The Serpa Cheese Slow Food Presidium', *Journal of Agrarian Change*, 12(1): 120–43.

Zukin, S. (2008), 'Consuming Authenticity: From Outposts of Difference to Means of Exclusion', *Cultural Studies*, 22(5): 724–48.

CHAPTER TWENTY

Practising Food Anthropology: Moving Food Studies from the Classroom to the Boardroom

MELISSA L. CALDWELL

INTRODUCTION: GOING DOWN THE CORPORATE RABBIT HOLE

'Can you help us understand culture?' This was the gist of the question that ultimately introduced me to the corporate world as a consulting anthropologist of food. The request came out of the blue through an email from a brand strategy manager at a global food corporation. Her team was working on a project in Russia, and they were looking for an 'expert' on Russian food cultures to help them understand Russian 'food rituals' at a deeper level than they had found through the company's previous research and their own background reading. While flattered that they had found me, I figured that this encounter would likely be a waste of time, and I almost deleted the email.

As a specialist on food, poverty and welfare in Russia and the formerly Soviet world, I had some previous experience providing 'expert advice' to journalists and national and international development organizations. Most of those encounters were less than productive, and even unpleasant in some instances, as journalists frequently wanted only a 'sound bite' to quote, often out of context, and administrators of development programmes were often reluctant to share intellectual space with academic researchers or to acknowledge that academic scholarship might challenge or complicate the data that they needed to justify their projects and satisfy donors. One particularly memorable occasion occurred when I was part of a workshop for scholars who had conducted long-term field research on development-related topics in the former Soviet Union. To fulfil the workshop's scholarly 'outreach' requirement, the organizers invited a group of officials and policy makers from several international development organizations for a joint panel. Voicing a perspective shared by several of her colleagues, a high-ranking USAID administrator dismissed the deep and collective ethnographic knowledge of the anthropologists working in 'her' region with a snidely delivered comment that '[ethnographic] vignettes don't make data'. After experiences such as those, I was cynical about requests to provide my expertise outside the more familiar structures of scholarly exchange.

In the end, however, curiosity overcame hesitation, and I agreed to meet with the brand strategy manager to learn more about the project and what her team needed. By agreeing to meet, I found my professional knowledge, skills and ethical sensibilities pushed to the limits, as I was quickly whisked away to a foreign world marked by a completely different language, communication style, technology, lifestyle markers and professional norms. My entry to this foreign world came in the first five minutes of my meeting with the brand strategy manager when I handed over a signed NDA (non-disclosure agreement) and realized that the stringent anthropological ethics governing privacy of informants and security of data that I have followed as a professional fieldworker and scholar were inadequate for a company that was concerned with the security of proprietary knowledge and millions (or even billions) of dollars in profits. My journey to the other side of the ethnographic looking glass was subsequently made further apparent when I was asked to create a SOW (statement of work) in which I defined my role and proposed my fees for the project – even though I still was not entirely certain what my role was going to be or how to set a price on my own head. Scarcely a week after that, I was tucking into dinner in a business class seat on an international flight to Sweden to meet the rest of the team.

That initial meeting has led not just to additional consulting opportunities, but also to a new appreciation for ethnography and the potential of anthropology both inside and outside the academic world. Perhaps more importantly, I have been challenged intellectually to rethink not just what it means to be a practising anthropologist, but also what an anthropology of food might contribute to current issues in today's world. Along the way, I have been involved both behind the scenes and on the front lines of key innovations in product development and have seen how the anthropological expertise I have contributed has been transformed into physical products as well as company ideals and strategic development models. Television commercials and grocery store shelves now hold new meaning for me as I see the material manifestation of concepts on which I worked. At the same time, my experiences have allowed me to develop new methods for my research and teaching, gain new skills for leading team-based exercises, and make new colleagues across a range of disciplines and professions with whom I now work on scholarly projects. All of this came from a simple request to explain culture.

What, precisely, did an anthropological perspective bring to the corporate food world, and how might anthropologists' engagement with the corporate food world bring innovation to the academic world? In this chapter, I discuss the value of ethnographic studies of food to the corporate food world, the types of new methods that are being developed to enhance food research, the ethical quandaries provoked by these collaborations, and possibilities for new ways of doing anthropology, both inside and outside the academy. By way of exploring these issues, I also present a mini-ethnography of what an anthropology of food looks like from inside the corporate world.

TRANSLATING FIELDS, TRANSLATING METHODS

As one of the few human universals and a fundamental staple of daily life, food has long been an important area of research in academia, industry and the non-profit world. Concerns with what counts as food, what people do with food, and the social, economic, political and moral role of food are shared across these different professional worlds. Yet, even as practising anthropologists are active within corporate settings, especially in the information and technology fields (Cefkin 2010a), it is curious that within food studies, rarely do representatives of these worlds meet in sustained and substantive ways (e.g. Jackson 2015). These missed opportunities often result from different professional needs, assumptions and ethics that pit members of these worlds against one another, as well as from practical differences in research modes and time frames (Clark and Caldwell 2016; Truninger 2015).[1]

Anthropology in particular has had a conflicted relationship with the non-academic world, especially in North America where applied anthropology has often been considered a separate and discrete subfield rather than an intrinsic part of sociocultural anthropology.[2] This has not necessarily been the case, or to the same degree, among European anthropologists, where design anthropology and related fields of practising anthropology have provided possibilities for more fluid modes that bring together 'academic' and 'non-academic' research (e.g. Gunn, Otto and Smith 2013; Smith et al. 2016). More generally, European imperatives for impact and broader outreach have encouraged European university researchers in anthropology and other social sciences to conduct research on and with commercial partners (see Jackson 2015).

Within the American context, however, anthropologists have been sensitive to the possibility that commercial interests might dictate intellectual directions and analyses, even as universities increasingly promote university–industry partnerships to bring in corporate cash at a time when traditional funding agencies like the National Science Foundation and Wenner-Gren, among others, are dealing with shrinking budgets. While certain forms of non-academic partnerships and projects have been less problematic – namely types of work in the non-profit and public sectors that seem to align with anthropological commitments to protect, serve and empower the disenfranchised – work that appears to support, or is imagined to serve, the interests of the capitalist, corporate world or governmental interests, and thus disempower or adversely affect ordinary people, such as with the CIA's Human Terrain System programme, has attracted considerable scrutiny and even disdain.[3]

Certainly within the world of food studies, especially in the United States, academic scepticism towards food corporations is commonplace and almost expected. While the globalization debates that took place in the social sciences during the 1990s and early 2000s were ostensibly about the nature and relationality of different scales (local versus global, traditional versus modern, slow versus fast), they were also about whether or not global capitalism corroded and even replaced local traditions of food provisioning, distribution and consumption (e.g. Ritzer 1996; cf. Watson 1997). Subsequent studies further honed in on debating the presumed deleterious effects of industrial capitalism on ethical issues of labour and trade

(Dolan 2005; Freidberg 2004; Holmes 2013), the bodily pleasures and aesthetics of food (Petrini 2001; Sutton 2001) and environmental issues (Guthman 2004). Most recently, food studies conversations have turned to critical commentaries on the ethical responsibilities of consumers to reject industrially produced foods in order to preserve imagined qualities of tradition and heritage (Jung 2009; Mincyte 2009; Paxson 2013; Weiss 2012; see also West, this volume, and Avieli, this volume). Health has been a prominent concern, prompting critiques of industrial food, genetically modified organisms, animal welfare and most notably neoliberal capitalist systems themselves (Guthman 2011; Guthman and DuPuis 2006).

Although critical approaches have sought to present more complicated, nuanced and objective understandings of the nature and implications of commercial food and food producers (see, especially, Guthman 2011; Guthman and DuPuis 2006), these studies are still largely outnumbered by a more explicitly polemical approach in studies and popular opinion against commercial food producers and commercially produced food (see, especially Pollan 2008). In late summer 2015, an 'exposé' revealed a long list of established university professors and researchers who had reportedly received research and travel money from larger American corporations to conduct and publicize research that supported commercial perspectives on GMOs (Lipton 2015). These revelations prompted fierce debate among food studies scholars who questioned whether industrial partnerships tainted scholarly output and careers or whether scholarly research necessarily had to be popular and support an academic status quo. Regardless of where one stands on these issues, it is clear that there is no consensus about whether and how scholars can and should work with commercial partners.

At the same time, non-academic employers frequently do not know how to work with academically trained anthropologists or how to use and incorporate academically derived research outputs in ways that make sense to commercial interests and needs. Although ethnographic research has been a staple in industrial settings for the past several decades (Cefkin 2010a; Jones 2006; Suchman and Bishop 2000), the pace and scope of team-based corporate projects can be at odds with anthropological modes of long-term field research. Corporate needs for predictive models are often better suited to macro-level statistical data and abbreviated sound bites than to the open-endedness and contradictions inherent to ethnographic data and the vagueness of intellectual theories. Françoise Brun-Cottan has observed that while corporate clients might recognize the value of ethnographic research, there is a desire for anthropologists 'to leave the messiness of individuals and contexts … in the field' (Brun-Cottan 2010: 159–60). Similarly, writing about her work at Microsoft, Donna K. Flynn has described the mixed responses to her team's ethnographic findings when the ethnographic data did or did not match up with the expectations, desires or personal observations of the IT professionals they were supporting. It was not that the ethnographic data that Flynn's team provided were wrong but that the data were entangled in a politics of organizational discourse and thus not immediately familiar to their IT interlocutors. Ultimately, what Flynn learned was that being able to adopt Microsoft's organizational language to present the effectiveness of their data was far more important than the actual effectiveness or validity of those data

(Flynn 2010). In other words, the very questions, methodological and interpretive approaches, and even languages of the academic and non-academic worlds can impede collaborative efforts.

More telling, perhaps, is what I heard from managers at one large transnational corporation for whom I have occasionally provided consulting service. As several individuals told me at different times, in their experience, academically trained anthropologists are often unable to translate their ideas out of theoretical jargon and into terms and concepts that are understandable for well-educated professionals in other disciplines like food chemistry, engineering and agriculture. Moreover, they found academic anthropologists frequently unwilling to relinquish their ideals about appropriate fieldwork approaches, especially in terms of the ideal length of time spent in the field, to fit a constantly evolving corporate project that must address business needs on a significantly tighter schedule. As I was told, it is easier and more financially appropriate for corporations to train someone to do anthropologically inspired research than to train an academic anthropologist to work in a corporate setting. In fact, one of the requests that a team in this company made of me was to write a short briefing manual (two to three pages) about how to do anthropology that they could distribute to their in-house business research teams (I declined).

Despite these constraints and misunderstandings on both sides, there is growing recognition in the potential provided by anthropologists who cross over into non-academic work, either as professional applied anthropologists or as consulting researchers who not only retain their primary position as academics but also bring the academy to the corporation. As corporate managers explained, having academic credentials not only brought prestige but greater legitimacy to the data and inter-pretations, even when they did not support what the company had hoped to find. Despite prevailing perceptions that applied researchers exist at the margins of both the academic and commercial worlds, there are many anthropologists who do just that either as full-time researchers and even managers in the industrial sector or as periodic expert consultants. Yet within the corporate food world there are still too few who do this work, and even fewer who keep feet in both the academic and non-academic worlds.

From my own experiences, I would argue that being able to straddle both worlds is important, not just for what an academic background enables me to do during my consulting work, but also because of the ways in which my consulting work informs my teaching and research. There are certain skills and strengths that I bring precisely because I work in both worlds while not fully becoming immersed in the non-academic world. Yet this existence between worlds is not without its challenges, as I will describe below.

Unpacking the corporate food anthropology encounter takes several steps. The first is to think about the types of questions that bridge the academic and corporate worlds. As I will detail below, the questions that concern academic anthropologists and corporate researchers and managers may not be as dissimilar as might be expected. Looking for and understanding those points of convergence are important, not just for rethinking the anthropological project in the corporate world, but also for rethinking the very intellectual questions and premises that guide our work. The second step in unpacking the corporate/anthropology encounter is to examine critically and reimagine the various methods that can be brought and generated anew for this work. Although there may be shared concerns that cross the corporate/academic divide, the specific goals and needs may differ radically. While in some cases academic anthropologists might not necessarily agree with how anthropological methods become transformed in corporate-sponsored research, there are other opportunities for learning and creatively imagining new methods that can enhance and even transform academic work. Finally, a third step is to rethink anthropological expertise, especially in terms of the types of claims we can make, who our audiences are and how we engage them, and what we owe clients versus informants. This rethinking of expertise also has to do with ownership – of data, analytical approaches and ultimately ideas – and whose purposes our anthropological knowledge best serves.

What, then, does a consulting food anthropologist do? How have I brought anthropological approaches to 'culture', and 'food culture' specifically, to a corporate encounter? To provide a frame of reference for my discussion of the steps identified above, I would like to return to my introduction to this new world and present a more traditional ethnographic description of the 'field', my 'subjects', and the 'activities' that I observed and in which I participated.

RETHINKING THE FIELD AS AN EXERCISE IN TRANSLATION

Following that initial conversation with my contact at the global food corporation, I was invited to join their research team for a project based in Russia. The project was exploratory because the company was looking for emerging trends and insights rather than trying to find a way to market a pre-existing product or service to a new market. My role was to equip the researchers with a deep understanding of Russian food cultures, past and present, so that they could make sense of the data they were collecting during their interviews and observations. In a sense, I was expected to be the company's 'expert informant' to help explain the data they were gathering, especially anything unexpected or contradictory that came up in their materials.[4] Along the way, I also became an advocate for the research subjects by synthesizing, representing and ultimately translating their lives, experiences and words into concepts and language that made sense to the larger community of researchers invested in the project, even though this was not how my corporate clients understood or anticipated my role. In other words, all of my anthropological experience was reduced to my ability to interpret and communicate the findings of my – and their – research. Yet as I will show, this reduction did not entail simplification or limiting of scholarly possibilities.

In many respects, the 'field site' that I was supposed to interpret was both the communities I had studied during my previous research and the corporate research setting in which I found myself. Trying to put a clear set of boundaries around either was challenging, as they constantly shifted back and forth and into and out of one another. At different moments the other members of the corporate research team, the local residents who were invited in as research subjects, and I inhabited a diverse set of spaces, ranging from informants' homes to local grocery stores and cafés, and from hotel and restaurant conference rooms to corporate offices. Researchers travelled between research staging areas in a hotel conference room to subjects' homes in a single day, followed by data analysis and prototyping sessions at the corporate headquarters. Research subjects also moved between spaces, as research protocols required subjects to host members of the research team in their own homes, often at their kitchen tables, and then lead them on a shopping or dining trip through the neighbourhood to their favourite local grocery store or café. Research subjects also moved into the analysis and prototyping spaces in several ways: first as pictures and personal stories captured in the detailed case studies that lined the walls of the research spaces and later as participants in follow-up co-creation exercises meant to elicit deeper values and inspire prototyping ideas.[5]

The 'community' at the centre of the corporate field site was an eclectic one that included more than the research subjects who had been selected according to particular criteria set by the sponsoring company (in the case of most of the research projects in which I have been involved, the subjects have typically been middle-class urbanites in their twenties and thirties, with a focus on working mothers). In addition to the 'subjects', the sponsoring food corporation had hired an expansive, and continuously changing team of researchers from a diverse group of research firms. Some of these organizations focused specifically on particular research methods – semiotic analysis of cultural representations, psychological analysis of cultural personality types, immersive ethnographic-style interviewing and analysis of emotional states – while others specialized in particular stages of the Research and Design process: market research, prototype design, brand strategy, advertising and messaging, among others. These different groups were joined by employees and managers both from the global company, based in the United States, and from the Russian subsidiary company. At different moments I was working alongside and observing such differently positioned individuals as a stay-at-home mother, a first-year graduate student researcher, a highly experienced graphic designer, or the president of one of the sponsoring or consulting companies. In all, there were more than one hundred individuals who participated in the project at different stages and had different interests in the overall project and its outcomes (see Clark and Caldwell 2016).

By the time I joined the project, the smaller field research team had already completed several weeks of intensive immersion interviews and observations in Russia and had returned to Sweden to complete a first round of data processing at the home office of one of the contracted research firms. Although I had participated in an online video call with the team members while they were still in Russia, my formal arrival in the field occurred when I landed in Stockholm, took a taxi to a wooded neighbourhood just outside the city centre, and walked into an old schoolhouse that had been converted into a postmodern Scandinavian design firm. Curiously, despite the hyper-modern feel of the space, with sophisticated computer and technology equipment located at ergonomic desks, tables arranged throughout the open floor plan and an impressive display of products the company had designed and developed artfully arranged to create a sense of a museum exhibit, the building was decidedly hands-on and down to earth. A handwritten schedule of tasks and events was posted on one wall, with evidence of overwrites and changes added by different hands. Three other walls were completely covered with printouts of photographs collected during the research and short biographies and story write-ups from interviews with informants. Preliminary and fully developed sketches of preliminary conclusions, working concepts and material artefacts identified during the research were scattered around the room, sometimes taped on top of other pieces of paper hanging on the walls and sometimes draped in piles of papers on desks. Layered upon all of these different types of paper and representations was a rainbow of vivid neon blues, greens, yellows, oranges, pinks and purples – the Post-it note overlay that is one of the hallmarks of design approaches. Interspersed among the piles of papers, computer thumb drives, sketches and books covering every space available was an unbelievable collection of coffee cups, some in use but most abandoned with dregs of coffee in the bottom. A few people were working quietly at their desks, but most people were actively moving around the room, singly and in small groups, to talk, argue and jot down notes on even more Post-it notes. It was a space in motion.

Shortly after a few others and I arrived, the commotion settled slightly as one of the research leaders from the design firm gathered us together to discuss the schedule for our three-day meeting. The agenda included presentations from three of the other consultancies and me to help frame the discussion and subsequent research agenda, as well as general introductions for everyone to meet one another and learn our respective roles. As I quickly discovered, most of us had only limited understanding of our own potential roles and practically none of how we were to work together. I was delighted to discover another anthropologist in the group – a fellow American who was a co-creation expert employed by yet another Swedish design-based research agency. As we have described elsewhere, it was a serendipitous meeting and partnership that had important consequences for the way in which anthropology was integrated into the project and received by the various constituencies (Clark and Caldwell 2016).

Over the course of the three-day visit, the 'community' morphed as individuals moved between groups and into and out of roles, sometimes together and sometimes on their own. High-level stakeholders (e.g. managers, account and human resources staff, and executives) were called out for impromptu meetings to discuss budgeting concerns, staffing and equipment needs, and changing directives from the corporate headquarters. 'Researchers' – a flexible term that I have used to describe all of the other individuals who were in some fashion involved in the direct collection, analysis and communication of data and findings – rotated from various stations, sharing insights, posing questions and possible hypotheses, and generating a shared language composed of both subjects' names and experiences as well as research objectives. During my visit, I explored the research materials that had been written up and posted on the walls, refined my situating brief about Russian culture to incorporate questions posed by the research team, and began working more closely with several individuals in the research group to refine anthropological methods and pose hypotheses about the preliminary data. I was frequently called away from one task to answer questions or brainstorm about findings.

During my formal presentation to introduce Russian 'food culture', I focused on a grounding set of themes to explain Russian social life to non-specialists. At the same time, it was really a presentation about anthropology and the types of questions that an anthropologist brings to bear when thinking about food and culture: social structures, exchange practices, belief systems and identity politics, among many others. In fact, the presentation I gave was derived from lectures and presentations I had given in my own courses on the anthropology of food and the ethnography of Russia, although it was necessarily condensed into only the briefest and most cursory presentation in order to fit into the short fifteen minutes I had been allotted. Hence I had to think carefully about which dimensions of an anthropology of food would be most productive for understanding Russia, both in terms of explaining key Russian food trends and introducing issues that could guide the researchers in their analysis.

This presentation served multiple purposes beyond providing historical and cultural context. It also contextualized and complicated the preliminary analyses provided by several of the other outside consultancies, namely those that presented emotional, psychological and symbolic archetypes of the preliminary data. Curiously, those other consultancies also drew on anthropological approaches and theories, although not with any kind of formal or sustained anthropological training or grounding in broader anthropological intellectual debates or ethnographic comparisons. What was particularly intriguing was that although the analytical models presented by these other consultancies drew on theoretical approaches familiar to anthropologists (most notably, Lévi-Straussian and Proppian structural analysis, Peircean semiotic analysis, and phenomenological theories of emotions), they typically did not go beyond invoking them to develop them or situate them within larger intellectual contexts.

As a result, the findings presented by their respective consultants did not necessarily square with the expectations or observations of the researchers who had conducted the interviews. Specifically, the researchers involved in the immersive ethnographic work expressed concerns that these analytical schema were too generic, not culturally specific, and, most importantly, reflected the biases of the analysts themselves. As the 'Russia expert', I was repeatedly asked to come in and provide nuances to these models – or, more commonly, to refute their conclusions in ways that were helpful to the researchers but not offensive or antithetical to the goals of the sponsoring company. Interestingly, I was never referred to as the 'anthropology expert', nor was my anthropologist colleague. Rather, I became the 'food anthropologist', a title that was subsequently incorporated into the project as an official role for a scholar who could provide qualitative interpretations of food cultures.

This translational work required a delicate balancing act of staying anthropologically true to the data and my own expert knowledge while making connections and imagining possibilities that could engage with the concerns of the non-anthropologists. In many ways, I used skills I have developed in teaching anthropology to students who have not yet acquired the ethnographic 'eye' or 'ear' for discerning nuance and subtlety in the smallest detail or the ability to step back from their own assumptions and let the data 'speak' to them. In addition, by translating between 'what was' and 'what could be', I also engaged in an anthropology of possibility (Halse 2013) in which I was able to present not just insights about the ethnographic data but also think about their implications for the future. Perhaps most importantly, what seemed to be the biggest anthropological contribution was being able to retranslate higher-level analyses back into the 'local' terminology, concepts and values of the individuals who had been interviewed. This reverse translation became significant at later stages of the project, when branding and marketing managers needed to ensure that the products they were creating and promoting were culturally appropriate and resonated with their intended customers.

After the dizzying pace of the short work trip to Sweden, I returned home for barely two weeks – scarcely long enough to get a visa for Russia and do a bit more background research to develop some of the ideas that had come up during the discussions in Stockholm. I was then on another international flight and arrived in Moscow for a week of intensive data analysis and co-creation exercises, which would eventually lead to a rapid prototyping session in which research subjects, researchers, chefs and company product designers came together to create and test potential new food, appliances and even service products.

During that week in Russia, my role expanded and morphed further, setting up new opportunities for the project and for anthropological contributions to corporate food work. In order to set the 'scene' for the research team and the larger community of stakeholders to work through the materials, I was asked to help 'Russianize' the space where we worked. The sponsoring company had hired out a historic Moscow restaurant, and I collaborated with the chef-owner to create 'traditional' meals that would immerse the group into a Russian-appropriate cultural space. Drawing on both my own research on changing food practices and the responses given by the project's research subjects, I guided the chef-owner into creating a series of menus that showcased typical Russian meals that ordinary people would eat at home – not the types of meals that the visiting executives would eat in hotel restaurants on a corporate expense account. Curiously, this entailed me advising the chef-owner in ways that limited her culinary creativity and forced her to cook like she would at home, not in her elegant restaurant. It was a strange series of negotiations in which I, the foreign anthropologist, instructed her, the native, on 'proper' Russianness.

This was just one moment in a larger series of instances in which 'the field' was something in which I was not just invested and inhabiting, but also actively creating as the 'Russia expert'. More than that, I myself became the field and an informant, as well as a lead voice for the real informants, in that field.

On the first day of that week, representatives from the different consultancies were asked to make presentations on their research methods and preliminary findings. I followed representatives from the emotional design, semiotics and psychological analysis agencies. After each of those three presentations, members of the audience from the Russian subsidiary company raised pointed questions about the veracity of the claims made by the presenters and the robustness of their data. Audience members seemed to be most critical of the claims made by the semiotics and psychological analysts, as captured by the persistent grumbling and sighing that audibly rose above the presentation. These criticisms made me rather hesitant to begin my presentation, as I was afraid that it was simply a hostile crowd that, understandably, did not want outsiders to presume to make claims about their own society. With trepidation, I began my presentation, focusing on the transition from Soviet to post-Soviet Russia and its effects on the social dynamics of food and eating in Russia.

Like the previous presenters, I, too, was interrupted by members of the audience with questions and comments. Yet unlike the previous presenters, the questions directed at me were for more information, and the comments were directed to the previous presenters and greater audience as affirmation of what I had said. Comments such as 'Yes, that's exactly what it was like when I was growing up' and 'That looks my mother's apartment!' peppered the conversation. My presentation took far longer than what was scheduled because I was interrupted so often; when one of the meeting leaders suggested that I simply stop at the end of my allotted time, the managers from the Moscow company office insisted that I keep going. At the end of my presentation, several of the Moscow-based managers came up to me and thanked me for providing an accurate and deep look at Russian food and daily life more generally. It seemed that to them I was an advocate for their interests in the corporate negotiations that took place that week, as they dealt with managers and upper-level executives from the US headquarters (including the company president).

Within this space of the restaurant-turned-workshop, things became ever more interesting and complicated. The two main goals for this week were to draw preliminary insights that could lead to ideation for prototyping and to incorporate research subjects into co-creation exercises that would facilitate the ideation and prototyping. While both goals were intended to happen simultaneously, they often happened in parallel rather than in an integrated fashion. Thus at the same time that three small rooms were in use for small co-creation focus-group activities, the larger spaces of the main dining area and hallways were used for whiteboarding, sketching and small meetings between the research analysts and designers on the team.

The co-creation leader was the other anthropologist on the team, although his anthropological expertise was often not fully recognized by the corporate management, until later in the week when he spontaneously generated a new method that was subsequently incorporated into the research protocols (Clark and Caldwell 2016). Although he was primarily responsible for working in one of the rooms with a group of research subjects, occasionally popping into and out of the other two rooms for advising and facilitating, he was often drawn out into the analysis spaces to answer questions and suggest directions for their ideas. Similarly, while I was based in one of the rooms to help with the co-creation exercises by doing cultural translation work between Russian subjects and foreign researchers, I was often called into one of the other rooms or to the analysis spaces to answer questions, suggest ideas and more generally offer 'insights' and brainstorming possibilities. Thus, the other anthropologist, whose expertise was not Russia, and I became two of the most robust threads linking the different rooms and participants together into a more general, albeit at times invisible, conversation.

The small working rooms were arranged with one or two tables, depending on the size, and sheets of paper taped to the walls. With the Russian subjects, we worked on several exercises designed to elicit their daily routines and interests pertaining to the particular questions of the project. Designers in the group turned the words into pictures, creating detailed illustrations of the subjects' experiences. At a later stage of the process, the Russian participants were given material objects – primarily arts and crafts materials such as coloured paper, glue, felt and styrofoam balls, among other things – and invited to model their ideas in tangible ways. In the room where I spent the most time, the Russian participants seemed to have great fun playing with the materials, and their products became excellent inspirations for the rest of the research project. At the end of their co-creation exercises, they gave brief presentations about their ideas, which were videotaped for future reference and then incorporated into the daily 'share-outs' of each day's activities.

During these encounters, my role shifted again to play an even more direct role as a translator. All of the research and interactions with subjects was done through translators into English. While this is standard practice in this type of corporate research, where English is the working language of research, presentations and business reports, using translators was problematic to me as an anthropologist. Yet it was also beneficial for other reasons. As the only person among the foreign research team who spoke Russian, I was uniquely positioned to catch when the translators failed to capture an idea accurately (something that happened so frequently that the Russian translators were eventually chastised and several replaced) and, more significantly, could intervene directly with the subjects. This ability to talk directly with the Russian subjects and translate their ideas back to the researchers, as well as translate the co-creation directions to them, helped me develop a rapport with the research subjects and the Russian members of the local company that then opened up subsequent conversations in larger, and even more complicated ways, as I was able to include subjects' own words and descriptions into the working documents – a way of rendering the analytical findings back into the original words and values and keeping them true to the subjects' views. It was, in many ways, a form of reverse translation back to the original, after the analysis, insights and ideation stages had moved so far beyond the original interviews.

At another level, this 'translational' ability worked effectively in tandem with the co-creation efforts of my fellow anthropologist. The working group sessions with the stakeholders often involved thinking on one's feet, as different researchers and corporate representatives played with the findings and searched for ways to link them up with their own business objectives. It was a shifting field, as participants presented their own ideas, took up the ideas of others, and collectively sought to come to some kind of shared set of ideas that would be applicable to the larger objectives of the project and to their own respective concerns. Yet it was the shared conversation between the two anthropologists that became particularly useful at different moments, as we were the only ones who truly had a shared set of concerns (i.e. to remain truthful to the data and to our informants) and a shared conceptual and terminological framework in which to work with those data. Despite the fact that we did not come from the same theoretical background and worked in very different ethnographic contexts, we were able to understand each other's perspectives and build on them.[6]

In many respects, the 'field' in which I was simultaneously immersed, observing, and creating was itself constituted through the acts of translation that were occurring at all times and in all spaces. And while it was my expertise in Russian food practices that introduced me to this 'field', it was my capacity as an anthropologist that helped me recognize and work with the constantly changing dynamics of this field in ways that were productive and generative. Consequently, even though I had originally been asked to 'explain culture', the culture that I was 'explaining' was really a set of dynamic interactions that I helped make visible and tangible.

WHAT IS THE ANTHROPOLOGIST'S ROLE IN THE CORPORATE SETTING?

What, then, was the point of having an anthropologist, and an academic one at that, participate in this project? What value did I serve? And what value, if any, did I derive from this experience? Can an anthropological role in corporate food work do anything, either for the food industry or for anthropology?

From my own experiences, I am convinced that there is great value to having an anthropologist participate in these encounters – more than simply being the latest intellectual fad in the corporate world. Rather, anthropologists can have profound and lasting effects within both the corporate world and our own discipline. Yet to do so, we must resist the temptation of both the business world and our own students, administrators, and critical peers to create a one-size-fits-all approach to anthropology that generalizes the knowledge and experience that we bring. Instead, we must embrace and celebrate the messiness of our discipline and find ways not only to render sensible and useful to our corporate partners what may otherwise seem to them as the chaos, randomness and mereness of ethnographic data, but also to reassure our academic colleagues that our intellectual and ethical priorities remain intact and perhaps even more secure than prior to corporate engagement.

At the end of that week in Russia, what became clear to me was that my primary task was to create my own role – to show the importance and necessity of an anthropological perspective, often in ways that no one had anticipated but in hindsight felt were critical to insights and ideation development. My contributions were not simply intellectual, however. Along the way, I created two key physical products: a situating presentation to contextualize the setting and a written 'briefing' document of key concepts and facts that helped the research team answer questions, compare findings and look for additional sources. This approach to making anthropology useful was effective, and I was subsequently asked to participate in the project for the rest of the year, supporting research in four other settings.

Over the course of that year, I fine-tuned the anthropological perspective to be representative of the local context and to bring in other local anthropologists or qualitative sociologists as appropriate. In different contexts I helped refine interview guides to be more culturally responsive and less leading. Although I did not have direct research experience in two of the other settings, I was somewhat familiar with more general food culture trends from my teaching and reviewing practices.

Perhaps more importantly, I had a sense of the types of questions to ask in particular contexts, which then led me to the pertinent literature.

One of the most interesting and unexpected tasks that I found myself doing was making pitches to high-ranking executives. On several occasions, during formal presentations about the research findings to company executives, including company presidents and vice presidents, I was asked to step in and explain the concepts and ground them in real-life examples. Although it seemed as if my corporate hosts assumed that it was my ethnographic expertise that made this possible, it felt to me as if it was my teaching skills that made this possible. Because I teach a range of topical courses that are not always regionally specific (e.g. anthropology of food, theories of consumption, general anthropology), I teach from readings that are often far beyond my own regional specialty. Thus I have a working knowledge of many parts of the world – that essential cross-cultural comparative knowledge that anthropologists need to make sense of and situate their work. But more importantly, I am accustomed to fielding the most random of questions from students and finding ways to respond to them, most commonly by reworking them in ways that make sense and relate to the materials at hand. This was ultimately what it was like to 'translate' the presentations back to the executives who were listening while simultaneously checking their emails, sending texts and answering telephone calls.

Since that first year of my unanticipated consulting work, I have been invited to other consulting jobs, and I continue to learn a great deal about how to be an anthropologist and a private consultant with each task. Several of these jobs have involved straight expertise consulting: I am interviewed for my knowledge of a particular field, which in turns inspires the researchers to modify their findings or research questions. In several other instances, I have done in-the-field research and insights/ideation work, much like I did during my year with the corporate food project. In each case, I find myself reinventing the anthropological role and finding novel ways to highlight and sell the value of anthropological expertise.

TOWARDS AN ANTHROPOLOGY OF CORPORATE FOOD

Ultimately, the biggest question that emerged from my participation in the corporate sector is what an anthropology of food brings to the corporate or commercial sector and, by extension, what corporate food anthropology might contribute to an anthropology of food.

On the one hand, anthropological approaches to food and food practices more generally effectively complicate how the commercial sector thinks about food and the needs, interests and constraints of consumers and other users. By moving beyond an approach that recognizes people only as 'users' or 'consumers', often amalgamated into generic demographic and behavioural groups, anthropology privileges people as individuals who are constantly navigating among different and shifting lifeworlds, roles and needs, often in ways that confound the neat models used by commercial research teams that need to consider much larger trends and groups of potential consumers. Not only does anthropology thus restore to commercial research a more complicated and nuanced understanding of 'culture' that is expansive, flexible and both internally contested and particularistic, it also offers possibilities for thinking productively with, rather than dismissing, paradoxical findings (see also Brun-Cottan 2010; Flynn 2010). Ultimately, by foregrounding differences and exceptions, anthropological approaches illuminate possibilities for reconsidering which concepts and practices are necessarily confined to particular contexts and which ones might travel across societies. What the people hiring me seemed to value was how an anthropological perspective challenged their expectations and offered possibilities for new questions and directions to pursue.[7]

This attention to difference and uniqueness endows corporate work with a greater sensitivity to local values and terminology, particularly in terms of preserving and promoting the perspectives of local people on the ground rather than those of the researchers or corporate decision-makers. In turn, this offers a productive antidote to reductionist trends in globalization and neoliberal capitalism by celebrating the local and illuminating how local cultural values and practices might facilitate further possibilities for local consumption and local production (e.g. Caldwell 2004; Watson 1997). In very material, practical ways, the need to stimulate local production is of concern for global corporations both when they expand through purchasing local companies and when they seek to attract consumers who are committed to buying and eating locally.

Yet helping companies recognize and understand local concerns goes far beyond providing insights that might support local farmers and producers. More importantly, anthropological analyses of food and culture more generally can provide nuanced understandings of such critical issues as health, choice, taste and value, among many others. For instance, in several of the projects in which I was involved, companies wanted to produce 'healthy' foods, including finding ways to modify their existing food products or replace them with healthier alternatives, but they lacked understanding of how to find out how local consumers understood and experienced 'health'. Anthropological approaches helped elicit subjects' perspectives, some of which had to do with concerns about family stability, others with freshness and tradition. As a result, these findings challenged the presumptions that the company had made and forced them to search for different possibilities outside biomedical or nutritional concerns. In another instance, ethnographic insights revealed that a company's presumption that consumers made choices according to price was insufficient for understanding how the daily experience of time – most notably competing family schedules – was a greater factor in the types of food that people purchased and how and where they consumed them.

Finally, for me personally, what I found to be one of the most important contributions of an academically based anthropology is that I brought with me the professional ethics of my discipline. I knew that I never compromised the privacy and perspectives of the individuals whose experiences I was presenting and analysing. I also worked hard to ensure that commercial researchers also pursued these ethical goals, even if they did not realize it at the time. In cases where I could not guarantee that I could follow the ethical standards of anthropology that I support, I have walked away from the project. As a result, I feel confident that the work I have done and the outputs to which I have contributed are, at least at those stages, ethical and responsible.

On the other hand, anthropological work conducted in, on and through corporate settings offers insights and opportunities for new streams of research in the anthropology of food. Given the importance and prevalence of commercial entities, it is essential to understand them from the inside, both to understand how they work and their internal logics, but also to understand better the values held by these institutions. These are cultural institutions inhabited by ordinary people, and understanding their experiences might reveal important insights about such diverse themes as labour, agency, gender, identity and ideology (see, e.g., Dunn 2004).

Moreover, inside insights may provide surprising details about these companies. As I discovered in my corporate ventures, food companies are also home to smart people who are just as interested as I was in intellectual questions, not the bottom line, and many of them were deeply committed to ethical concerns that sometimes put them at odds with their own company. This was apparent from the conversations among employees from one food company with which I have worked. Several individuals who were deeply committed to social and environmental justice issues confided that they were frustrated by the practical limitations of their company. By way of explanation they cited such examples as structural constraints that prevented them from changing manufacturing systems quickly, federal guidelines for nutrition that did not match up with what consumers actually purchased, or the limitations of food science technology to combine taste, aesthetics, form and price into a single product that consumers would actually purchase. In one revealing encounter, a manager in charge of packaging lamented that although the company was responsive to consumers' demands for environmentally friendly wrapping, the biodegradable packaging in fact compromised the flavour and texture of products and consumers refused to purchase the more environmentally sustainable products. Recognizing my commercial partners as individuals with their own concerns humanized them and opened up possibilities for engaging them on critical issues. At the same time, recognizing commercial partners as individuals in ways that were sympathetic to their perspectives – yet still analytical – also opened up possibilities for me to contribute ideas for working with and around the constraints they faced.

Working inside the commercial realm also provides possibilities for developing and testing new research methods. In particular, design processes have become more popular among food corporations. Design-based methods offer different possibilities for working with ethnographic data, partly by preserving the materiality of the materials and partly by enlisting research subjects as equal participants in the process of R&D, including prototyping (see Gunn, Otto and Smith 2013). Design-based research often engages new forms of technology, especially when inspired by Internet of Things approaches, which may change how anthropologists do their work and understand the nature of ethnographic subjects and perspectives. Autographers, remote digital sensors and wired houses provide different forms of data about how people live their lives, often in ways that are not accessible to research subjects themselves (e.g. Giaccardi et al. 2016). For an anthropology of food, having access to the spaces of people's lives that are not visible, accessible or remarkable to them might offer new ways of understanding the lifeworlds and biographies of food products. For instance, what people put in their pantries and how they do it present a very different version of their lives than is revealed by asking them what they buy. It might also offer different perspectives on the ecologies in which particular foods exist: an autographer attached to a coffee mug captures the daily journeys of the coffee as it interacts with other coffee mugs, sugar, milk, refrigerators and sandwiches. That, in turn, presents a different view of people's consuming habits beyond what an ethnographer observes or an informant self-reports (see Giaccardi et al. 2016).

Ultimately, the view from inside the corporate food world challenges anthropologists, and other food studies scholars, to rethink the nature of food altogether. I was surprised to discover that much of the research in which I have participated often had very little to do with food, but actually focused on cultural issues such as belief systems, lifestyle practices and material circumstances. It was almost incidental that our focus was on food, as many of the insights generated could be applicable to other commodities as well as services. In this way, the focus of 'food anthropology' shifted away from food to a more anthropological approach to social and cultural systems.

These shifts provoked intriguing questions about what 'food' actually was: an economic system, a value system, a form of art, familial connections or something else. At the same time, the focus on technology that is intrinsic to food manufacturing, food branding and food marketing also changes food from an entity that is grown, made and consumed into the body, into something that is imagined, designed and experienced in realms both outside and inside the conventional spaces of farms, kitchens and lunchrooms. Most notably, corporate food anthropology provides a fascinating lens into how food is remade through the experimental practices of science, art and even economics, whether it is by being disaggregated into constituent substances or remade into something much greater that moves far beyond biological sustenance. The corporate world thus reminds us that we should also respect the flexibility and fluidity of the very thing that we study as anthropologists.

CAUTIONARY TALES

Despite the many opportunities that I have been afforded through this work, all is not necessarily rosy in this line of anthropological consulting. Unless one is hired full-time from within an agency or company, the work is contractual, dependent on project scope, timing and budgets. Often the schedules that exist within the business world do not match up with the schedules that exist in the academic world. Whereas academic anthropologists must plan their calendars a term or two in advance in order to accommodate teaching schedules, conferences and other obligations, the business world often makes plans in a more herky-jerky fashion. Proposals for projects might be floated a year or two in advance, but the actual work schedule is not finalized until a few weeks before the actual work begins. It can be extremely difficult to move between these two different temporal frameworks. Also, as a contracting consultant, I must constantly pitch my work and put a value on it. This is not a skill that academic anthropologists learn, and there is not usually a way to find out how much is enough but not too much to ask, aside from the generosity of colleagues who are willing to divulge their consulting fees. But what I have found is that some companies are willing to pay what I think I am worth, while others want me to be cheap labour. Or worse yet, they want me to exploit my students for cheap labour.

Another complication arises from the ability to provide references for past work. In some cases, it is sufficient to identify previous employers. Yet this can be problematic as some companies will not hire contractors who work for their competitors, thus limiting possibilities for future jobs. In other cases, non-disclosure agreements prevent me from ever identifying the work that I did or the company for which I worked. While I have learned some fascinating things, both about the inside of particular companies and food systems and about particular societies that I would never have otherwise visited, I cannot ever reveal that information. Over the past several years, I have seen new products on store shelves and recognized them as products on which I have worked, but I cannot reveal the incredibly fascinating back stories of how those products made it to market or even reveal my own role in those processes. Nor can I reveal the fascinating stories about other products that (rightfully, in my opinion) never made it to store shelves. This is like ethnographic fieldwork, where we are always aware of the stories that our informants tell us but that we will never be able to reveal.

These are, in many ways, concerns with ethics – a concern that becomes especially fraught when we step back and consider where our loyalties lie. Am I responsible to the corporation that hired me, to the informants I have interviewed and worked with, or to my own professional concerns – as an anthropologist, as a scholar, as a professor. I would answer all of these, yet it can be difficult to balance them at different moments as corporations do not always follow the same guidelines for ethical engagement with human subjects or insist on using outdated language that is not culturally appropriate – such as the repeated insistence in one case that our key informants were 'housewives', even though the demographic was actually twenty- to thirty-year-old mothers, many of whom were employed professionals (and in some cases outearned their husbands), or in another case a misrecognition of cultural tradition as a clear marker of religious fundamentalism. Yet ethics are never absolute in and of themselves but are always situational, and so these are interesting cases in which to consider what we as anthropologists do and why.

Finally, the corporate encounter raises critical questions about the nature and location of expertise. Who possesses knowledge, who can share it, and for what purposes? In the more familiar anthropological model, anthropologists and their informants are both experts, with different roles in the ethnographic relationship. The anthropologist is the 'expert' with training in methods, interpretive approaches and theories. The anthropologist is also often the person with 'expertise' in terms of deep historical and cultural knowledge of a particular setting. Our informants are also 'experts' in that they know their own worlds and experiences better than anyone. With the corporate encounter, however, there are other modes of expertise and types of experts. While I may have had a particular type of field expertise or methodological expertise, I did not understand business directives or organizational policies. I also did not have any kind of expertise in very practical matters such as transportation logistics, supermarket shelving and organizational design, or manufacturing possibilities. I also discovered that despite my qualifications as a 'food scholar', or even a 'food anthropologist', I often knew far less about specific foods, cooking techniques, the aesthetic rules behind presentation styles, basic chemistry, food safety or flavour chemistry than my corporate colleagues. I learned much from conversations with them.

In one memorable project, while informants consistently requested 'healthier' alternatives to the already existing products made by the contracting company, the manufacturing manager lamented that the time-to-delivery imperative set by the corporate headquarters was so tight that they could not retool the machinery at the factory to make the changes demanded by the customers. While he wanted to do that, the expenses of time and building new machinery were prohibitive. I found this encounter fascinating because it revealed that some food manufacturers might want to change the types of food they create but are stymied by very practical logistical challenges.

Beyond this, expertise was often a diffuse set of relationships constituted in the process of working with the data and ideas. A common way of working with data in these research encounters is to turn materials into tangible artefacts that can be moved around to inspire conversation and provoke connections and insights. One of the more usual ways to do this is to create biographies of research subjects and short narratives of key themes or events from their interviews. These are then filled with colour photos of the subjects and aspects of their lives. All of this material is condensed into single-page write-ups that are printed out and taped to the walls of the working rooms – sometimes affectionately called the 'war room'. These materials are then available for research team members and other passers-by to ponder and add reflections, comments and ideas, usually by Post-it notes. This was the rainbow of papers that I first encountered in Stockholm. Called 'writing on walls' (Nafus and anderson 2010), this method disconnects data and ideas from any individual researcher and instead turns them into collective property. A good connection or insight can come from anywhere but is ultimately a collaboratively produced venture. As a result, knowledge and expertise never reside absolutely in any one person but rather are produced through intellectual interaction and engagement.

This sharing of knowledge and expertise – of relinquishing absolute control over ideas – is instructive for reflecting critically on how anthropology is practised. While at different moments anthropologists have struggled with authorship and how to recognize that all of our work depends on the goodwill and experiences of our subjects, we have not necessarily found ways to integrate this collaborative project in our work, both our scholarship and our teaching. Too often we continue to privilege the 'lone wolf' model of anthropology, rather than recognize the ways in which our ideas are shared or emergent, aside from using footnotes, acknowledgements and other conventional forms of reference. For the case of the anthropology of food, this decentring of knowledge is an important reminder of the potential dangers of substituting our own perspectives – including our own assumptions and desires – for those of our informants.

Ultimately, whether anthropological research on food takes place on a farm, in a grocery store, in someone's home or in a corporate boardroom, it is an intellectual process of rethinking the very nature of food, its place and its significance in people's daily lives. By paying critical attention to the social structures and cultural values in which food practices are embedded, anthropological research is well suited for illuminating how both knowledge about food practices and the experiences of food production and consumption are always situational and translational, and frequently contradictory. Perhaps more importantly, however, the view of food from the corporate world powerfully opens up possibilities for future-oriented approaches to understand and imagine emerging and prospective trends in the everyday worlds of our informants (see Halse 2013). Even as some food producers and consumers may be engaged in nostalgic modes of return and recovery of past food traditions, these are themselves part of a modernist project of creating new futures. As anthropologists know very well, cultures are never static but are always in transition, just as social worlds are always in formation. That is precisely the view that is most visible from the corporate boardroom – and one that anthropologists of food must take seriously if they are to understand their ethnographic subjects and how they make the choices they do.

ACKNOWLEDGEMENTS

Although I cannot identify the companies with which I worked, there are several individuals I would like to thank for the opportunities and insights they have provided: most notably Eapen George and Diana Hartford. I would also like to thank Diana Clark, Nory Emori and Euan McGregor for stimulating conversations and for introducing me to new ways of representing ethnographic data and insights. I am especially grateful to Brendon Clark for ongoing conversations and collaborations, particularly in imagining new methods and approaches in an anthropology of the possible. Ideas contained in this chapter have been informed by ongoing conversations with participants in the Design Anthropology Futures workshop series. Lastly, I thank Jakob Klein and Woody Watson for their encouragement and suggestions for improving this chapter.

NOTES

1. A panel at the 2014 meetings of the Association for the Study of Food and Society is a notable and illustrative example of these gaps. Organized by Professor Peter Jackson, a group of European sociologists, geographers and anthropologists discussed their collaborative projects with commercial and other private sector groups. It was significant that these were European scholars, as imperatives and opportunities for academic–commercial partnerships are stronger and more established through

university and governmental granting priorities in Europe than they are in the United
States. Yet as these scholars discussed, they had encountered curious and even significant
challenges in working with non-academic partners. The papers drew a sizeable
audience, primarily of American scholars who were eager to pursue collaborative
projects with non-academic partners but lacked the knowledge or experience to do so.

2. One prevalent perception in the United States is that applied anthropology has often
   been relegated to second-class status in the discipline. There are still relatively few
   dedicated courses to train students in applied methods or provide pathways to non-
   academic employment, despite the many anthropologists who are employed outside
   the academy (see Bennett et al. 2006, Rylko-Bauer, Singer and Willigen 2006, cited in
   Cefkin 2010b: 4).

3. A notable example is the recent backlash (summer 2015) that erupted among members
   of the American Psychological Association after it was revealed that APA leadership
   was directly involved in contributing to American torture methods when interrogating
   political prisoners captured in the war on terror.

4. See Darrouzet, Wild and Wilkinson (2010) for a longer discussion of the 'puzzling'
   work that goes on in these types of ethnographic encounters with corporate partners.

5. See, for instance, Clark (2013) on collaborative design.

6. See Clark and Caldwell (2016) for a discussion of how this partnership worked 'on the
   fly' and its consequences for future iterations of the research project in other contexts.

7. See Halse (2013) and the collection of essays in Smith, Kjærsgaard and Vangkilde (2016)
   for discussions about anthropological possibilities and an ethnography of the possible.

REFERENCES

Bennett, L., Ferguson, T. J., Paredes, J. A., Squires, S., Tso, J. and Wiedman, D. (2006),
    Final Report: Practicing Advisory Work Group (PAWG), American Anthropological
    Association.

Brun-Cottan, F. (2010), 'The Anthropologist as Ontological Choreographer', in
    M. Cefkin (ed.), *Ethnography and the Corporate Encounter*, 158–81, New York:
    Berghahn Books.

Caldwell, M. L. (2004). 'Domesticating the French Fry: McDonald's and Consumerism in
    Moscow', *Journal of Consumer Culture*, 4(1): 5–26.

Cefkin, M. (ed.) (2010a), *Ethnography and the Corporate Encounter*, New York:
    Berghahn Books.

Cefkin, M. (2010b), 'Introduction: Business, Anthropology, and the Growth of Corporate
    Ethnography', in M. Cefkin (ed.), *Ethnography and the Corporate Encounter*, 1–37,
    New York: Berghahn Books.

Clark, B. (2013), 'Generating Publics through Design Activity', in W. Gunn, T. Otto and
    R. C. Smith (eds), *Design Anthropology: Theory and Practice*, 199–215, London:
    Bloomsbury.

Clark, B. and Caldwell, M. L. (2016), 'Design Anthropology on the Fly: Performative Spon-
    taneity in Commercial Ethnographic Research', in R. C. Smith, T. Otto, K. T. Vangkilde,
    J. Halse, T. Binder and M. Kjærsgaard (eds), *Design Anthropological Futures: Exploring
    Emergence, Intervention and Formation*, 169–82, London: Bloomsbury.

Darrouzet, C., Wild, H. and Wilkinson, S. (2010), 'Participatory Ethnography at Work: Practicing in the Puzzle Palaces of a Large, Complex Healthcare Organization', in M. Cefkin (ed.), *Ethnography and the Corporate Encounter*, 61–94, New York: Berghahn Books.

Dolan, C. S. (2005), 'Fields of Obligation: Rooting Ethical Sourcing in Kenyan Horticulture', *Journal of Consumer Culture*, 5(3): 365–89.

Dunn, E. C. (2004), *Privatizing Poland: Baby Food, Big Business, and the Remaking of Labor*, Ithaca, NY: Cornell University Press.

Evans, D. (2015), 'Researching (with) Major Food Retailers: Leveling and Leveraging the Terms of Engagement', *Gastronomica: The Journal of Critical Food Studies*, 15(3): 33–9.

Flynn, D. (2010), '"My Customers are Different!": Identity, Difference, and the Political Economy of Design', in M. Cefkin (ed.), *Ethnography and the Corporate Encounter*, 41–57, New York: Berghahn Books.

Freidberg, S. (2004), *French Beans and Food Scares: Culture and Commerce in an Anxious Age*, Oxford: Oxford University Press.

Giaccardi, E., Speed, C., Cila, N. and Caldwell, M. L. (2016), 'Things as Co-ethnographers: Implications of a Thing Perspective for Design and Anthropology', in R. C. Smith, T. Otto, K. T. Vangkilde, J. Halse, T. Binder and M. Kjærsgaard (eds), *Design Anthropological Futures: Exploring Emergence, Intervention and Formation*, 235–48, London: Bloomsbury.

Gunn, W., Otto, T. and Smith, R. C. (2013), *Design Anthropology: Theory and Practice*, London: Bloomsbury.

Guthman, J. (2011), *Weighing In: Obesity, Food Justice, and the Limits of Capitalism*, Berkeley: University of California Press.

Guthman, J. (2004), *Agrarian Dreams: The Paradox of Organic Farming in California*, Berkeley: University of California Press.

Guthman, J. and DuPuis, M. (2006), 'Embodying Neoliberalism: Economy, Culture, and the Politics of Fat', *Environment and Planning D: Society and Space*, 24: 427–48.

Halse, J. (2013), 'Ethnographies of the Possible', in W. Gunn, T. Otto, and R. C. Smith (eds), *Design Anthropology: Theory and Practice*, 180–96, London: Bloomsbury.

Holmes, S. M. (2013), *Fresh Fruit, Broken Bodies: Migrant Farmworkers in the United States*, Berkeley: University of California Press.

Jackson, P. (2015), 'Commercial Collaboration and Critical Engagement in Food Research', *Gastronomica: The Journal of Critical Food Studies*, 15(3): 28–32.

Jones, R. (2006), 'Experience Models: Where Ethnography and Design Meet', in *Ethnographic Praxis in Industry Conference (EPIC 2006)*, 91–102, Portland, OR, USA: American Anthropological Association.

Jung, Y. (2009), 'From Canned Food to Canny Consumers: Cultural Competence in the Age of Mechanical Production', in M. L. Caldwell (ed.), *Food and Everyday Life in the Postsocialist World*, 29–56, Bloomington: Indiana University Press.

Lipton, E. (2015), 'Food Industry Enlisted Academics in G.M.O. Lobbying War, Emails Show', *New York Times*, 5 September 2015. http://www.nytimes.com/2015/09/06/us/food-industry-enlisted-academics-in-gmo-lobbying-war-emails-show.html?smid=nytcore-ipad-share&smprod=nytcore-ipad&_r=0 (accessed 24 September 2015).

Mincyte, D. (2009), 'Self-Made Women: Informal Dairy Markets in Europeanizing Lithuania', in M. L. Caldwell (ed.), *Food and Everyday Life in the Postsocialist World*, 78–100, Bloomington: Indiana University Press.

Nafus, D. and anderson, k. (2010), 'Writing on Walls: The Materiality of Social Memory in Corporate Research', in M. Cefkin (ed.), *Ethnography and the Corporate Encounter*, 137–57, New York: Berghahn Books.

Paxson, H. (2013), *The Life of Cheese: Crafting Food and Value in America*, Berkeley: University of California Press.

Petrini, C. (2001), *Slow Food: The Case for Taste*, translated by W. McCuaig, New York: Columbia University Press.

Pollan, M. (2008), *In Defense of Food: An Eater's Manifesto*, New York: Penguin Press.

Ritzer, G. (1996), *The McDonaldization of Society: An Investigation into the Changing Character of Contemporary Social Life*, Thousand Oaks, CA: Pine Forge Press.

Rylko-Bauer, B., Singer, M. and Van Willigen, J. (2006), 'Reclaiming Applied Anthropology: Its Past, Present, and Future', *American Anthropologist*, 108(1): 178–90.

Smith, R. C., Otto, T., Vangkilde, K. T., Halse, J., Binder, T. and Kjærsgaard, M. (2016), *Design Anthropological Futures: Exploring Emergence, Intervention and Formation*, London: Bloomsbury.

Suchman, L. Bishop (2000), 'Problematizing "Innovation" as a Critical Project', *Technology Analysis & Strategic Management*, 12(3): 327–33.

Sutton, D. E. (2001), *Remembrance of Repasts: An Anthropology of Food and Memory*, Oxford: Berg Publishers.

Truninger, M. (2015), 'Engaging Science with Commercial Partners: The (Dating) Stages of a (Lasting) Relationship', *Gastronomica: The Journal of Critical Food Studies*, 15(3): 40–6.

Watson, J. L. (ed.) (1997), *Golden Arches East: McDonald's in East Asia*, 1st edn, Stanford, CA: Stanford University Press.

Weiss, B. (2012), 'Configuring the Authentic Value of Real Food: Farm-to-Fork, Snout-to-Tail, and Local Food Movements', *American Ethnologist*, 39(3): 614–26.

Afterword

CRISTINA GRASSENI

As a cultural anthropologist who has worked in one way or another on food since my PhD research, I greatly appreciated Jakob Klein and James Watson's selections of themes and topics for this *Handbook of Food and Anthropology*. Anthropologists deal with food on diverse premises and with several foci: individual and collective identity-making, nutrition, the economic infrastructure and political agency of food systems, as well as the crucial fieldwork interactions with food's symbolically and relationally charged routines and tacit etiquettes.

Some of us do fieldwork with collective or individual social actors who practise 'alternatives' striving for more sustainable forms of food production, distribution and consumption; some collaborate with government or corporate actors. Inspired by international movements and networks for alternative agriculture (e.g. *Via Campesina, Urgenci*, and RIPESS – *Réseau international des Partenariats locaux et solidaires entre producteurs et consommateurs*), some food consumers and growers practise deliberate forms of food provisioning that might re-engineer food chains and reinvent collective forms of food procurement (Grasseni 2013). International networks of food activists increasingly strive to put themselves on the geopolitical map and to establish strategies and alliances at a global level to lobby governments and intergovernmental agencies for favourable policies.

Methodologically, anthropologists increasingly are inspired by interdisciplinary, multimedia, and multi-sensory forms of engagement with ethnographic fieldwork and scholarly production. Just as networks of food activists are active online through social media, anthropologists might choose interactive documentaries or open-ended fora to represent or participate in the activities of key social actors. This, of course, leads us to the ethical implications of doing research with and on food. These implications, which include how to go about non-disclosure agreements, industrial and commercial power relations, as well as cultural sensitivities in food research, are squarely confronted in this *Handbook* in Chapter 20 by Melissa L. Caldwell on 'Moving food studies from the classroom to the boardroom', but they deserve much more attention.

The chapters by Melissa L. Caldwell and Johan Pottier challenge us to articulate what the ultimate goal of the anthropological study of food will or should be. Is it just observing research participants to represent the cultural diversity of food systems as fairly as we can? Is it to also voice our beliefs as to how current food systems could or should be bettered? Is it to share our expertise with social actors? And if so, *which* social actors, *which* stakeholders? Is it to advise policy, elucidating which social practices work best to then facilitate them? As practising anthropologists know, these goals might actually shift over time: beginning with just 'obtaining information', to then wishing to elucidate what works best and why.

However, it is difficult to implement anthropological expertise by way of policy. Bottom-up networks and actors sometimes work in ways that are antagonistic to state-directed or corporate-driven agendas. Corporations ultimately are concerned with profit, so on what grounds might we think that we are building a better world by working alongside them? Or are we too comfortable preaching to the converted in our mission to give voice to the underdog? Is the deconstruction of authenticity a sufficient goal in our critical approach to food heritage? Or should we study what the (certainly 'imagined') traditional qualities of place-based foods actually do, in their everyday discursive, symbolic, and material work of evoking community, belonging, and meaning for both eaters and producers (Grasseni 2017; see the chapters by West and Avieli in this volume)? And how is this work achieved and performed in diverse socio-historical contexts, such as those of post-socialist transitions (see Jung in this volume and Jung, Klein and Caldwell 2014)? How are 'solidarity' and 'skill' constructed and mobilized to create and assign 'trust' and 'quality' to food (see Paxson, this volume)? While these are some of the dilemmas and interrogations we face, the impact of our research is another point to discuss: would stakeholders of whatever kind want to learn from our case studies approach? Further, what do we have to gain as scholars from coproducing our intellectual agendas with stakeholders? How, for example, would this lead to conceptual advancements in anthropological theory?

Anthropologists offer to shed new light onto known phenomena. Rather than treating these phenomena in isolation, anthropologists situate them in complex contexts and view them from multiple perspectives. For example, from Maris Gillette's chapter we learn about the diversity and divergence of interpretations and practices of 'halal' food, which is differently and variously appropriated and interpreted across regions and cultures. Similarly, each of the twenty chapters in this volume illustrate multiple and important facets of food in anthropology: religious foodways, community building through food, food safety, rural and urban food insecurity, food agency among specific groups such as migrants and food politics for specific age groups such as (school) children, (local) skill and knowledge transmission in cooking, large distribution and artisanal production, corporate and ethical approaches to food consumption.

Many food-related topics are analysed not only by anthropologists, but also by scholars in other disciplines, from human geography to the sociology of consumption, to rural and urban studies, planning and policy studies. These scholars often do not share the same conceptual framework or the same methodological premises as anthropologists. What is then the added value of our anthropological knowledge of food and foodways? The aim of anthropological research is not to identify one successful model among a variety of practices or food systems, to then implement it at scale. Rather, ethnographies of food are characterized by their explorative and holistic character. They first analyse how each procurement circuit, sharing network, or cooking technique works and speaks to its own context, and then proceed to develop a conceptual framework of wider relevance.

In this vein, ethnographies of food could contribute to the understanding and development of shorter-chain food systems. In the last decade, and especially in response to the economic crisis of 2008, grassroots networks have articulated models and strategies for such systems. Several models are growing in advanced capitalist countries. These range from so-called solidarity economy networks to the French *associations pour le maintien d'une agriculture paysanne* (Dubuisson-Quellier, Lamine and Le Velly 2011) and include various local instantiations of globalizing movements, such as the 'de-growth' or the Transition movement. Some of these networks constitute successful models in their own regions and according to their own rationales, but often do not speak to or compare themselves to others. Comparing these forms of food activism on the basis of ethnographic knowledge would allow us to see if and how these networks and practices are innovative or resilient. For example, we can see how networked consumers speak to their own needs (to procure food in a more sustainable and participated way) but also shape collective forms of procurement as instantiations of broader social, economic, and political movements. Thus, ethnographic case studies can not only appreciate local phenomena but also gain a detailed insight into patterns and processes that take place on a broader scale.

For anthropologists, this may mean going beyond the study of 'food security' and tapping into discourses and practices of 'food sovereignty' (Trauger 2015) and 'food justice' (Alkon and Agyeman 2011), not only in the developing world *but also* in the so-called developed world, particularly within the context of austerity and its neoliberal workings in a globalized food system. The politics of food systems are being critically investigated, for example with increased awareness of 'food deserts' (Gottlieb and Joshi 2013, 39–58) and of the manifold but ambivalent promises of 'urban agriculture' (Pottier, in this volume). It is pertinent therefore to ask how collective action may or may not achieve a transformation of food systems, while in the same breath it interacts with profoundly rooted cultural premises about the significance of food, and with locally defined forms of participation and belonging through food. Solidarity, for example, is locally articulated while transnationally practised in 'solidarity economy networks'. But it is also increasingly invoked, by right-wing activists as much as left-wing ones, through practices of food distribution and alleviation of the consequences of austerity economics, for example in Greece (Rakopoulos 2014).

Ways of eating, sharing, procuring, cooking, growing, gathering, connecting, and protesting with and through food are of course socially inculcated, learnt, and apprenticed. They are the prime locus of 'cultural intimacy' and of potential 'gastro-essentialism', as Michael Herzfeld reminds us in Chapter 1 of this volume. Yet how do we negotiate between apprenticeship and standards when it comes to foodways? David Sutton (in this volume) focuses on the local, familiar, intimate development of certain culinary skills, which inevitably are performed as an aesthetic and moral way of doing that is pitched against the cosmopolitan orthodoxy of the cutting board and of televised international chefs. Skill (namely practical and organizational know-how about growing, processing, storing, cooking, consuming, tasting, praising, bartering, etc.) may nurture networks of mutual help. However, it is to the unobvious and situated interactions of the global and local dimensions of food systems that several chapters in this *Handbook* alert us (e.g. Hull's chapter in this volume). Scale is at work when smallholders are forced to negotiate adversary conditions in procurement contracts to large distribution networks such as supermarket chains. Scale works its ways in the legalized persecution of seed savers who nevertheless retrench, network, and resist, as recent ethnography on the practice of saving and exchanging locally adapted seeds has shown (Da Vià 2015).

Seed-saving networks are one among the various forms of collective food procurement, not only in urban but also in rural areas of Europe, bringing together family farmers, cooperatives, and NGOs (Demeulenaere 2014). This 'new food activism' requires moving beyond 'foodie' types of engagement with a politics of consumption that does not sufficiently challenge the premises of racial and class inequality or of global displacements (Alkon and Guthman 2017; see also Abbots' chapter on migrants' food practices and Luetchford's on ethical consumption, both in this volume). Initiatives for local food provisioning are proliferating and are sometimes identified as symptoms of a global social movement striving for a 'new', 'solidarity', 'civic', or 'community' economy. Anthropological scholarship on provisioning activism has highlighted how alternative food networks often focus on sustainability and quality, less on social inclusion and 'food justice' (namely actual access to resources by unprivileged groups, see for example Mares 2014; and Luetchford in this volume). Further, we lack empirical evidence and a coherent conceptual framework of how 'civic food networks' (Lamine, Darolt and Brandenburg 2012) may move *beyond* local food. What are their limits and potentials? Several networks are growing transnationally, often without reciprocal knowledge or coordination. How do these initiatives develop transnationally beyond informal and small-scale arrangements? Why do they often fail and what makes them successful? How do they use 'reskilling' to promote a more inclusive economy and resilient society? A 'warrior/builder/weaver' classification of diverse modes of provisioning activism (Stevenson et al. 2008) can allow us to theorize these complex and diverse forms of critical engagements with the food system: focusing on social innovation through *building* local economic circuits and *weaving* alliances among networks, or on repertoires of social contestation.

In sum, this *Handbook* covers the cultural, ecological, socio-economic, and political facets of local and global relations in the current food system. I suggest that a further focus on food sustainability, grassroots innovation, and food sovereignty might add important developments for the current age. For example, critical investigations unveil the subtle ways in which neoliberal economies create subjects who embrace wholeheartedly the underlying philosophy of commodifying and financializing anything worth surplus extraction and value accumulation, while outsourcing and enrolling service provision under the agendas of charitable giving, active citizenship, or responsible welfare (Bear and Knight 2017; Narotzky 2016). It makes sense to ask if 'alternative foods' initiatives constitute a source of responsible innovation and democratization of local and global food systems. Or whether, instead, they contribute to the conventionalization of organic, heritage, and fair foods as a form of niche-marketing, as well as to the consolidation and sedimentation of neoliberal forms of governance and subjectivities in contemporary societies. Either way, it is in the midst of this dialectic dynamic that our role as cultural observers and social analysts is called upon, as we may be asked how we can make a difference.

REFERENCES

Alkon, A. and Agyeman, J. (2011), *Cultivating Food Justice: Race, Class, and Sustainability*, Cambridge, MA: MIT Press.

Alkon, A. and Guthman, J. (2017), *The New Food Activism: Opposition, Cooperation, and Collective Action*, Berkeley, CA: University of California Press.

Bear, L. and Knight, D. (2017), 'Alternatives to Austerity', Guest Editorial, *Anthropology Today*, 33(5): 1–2.

Da Vià, E. (2015), 'Food Sovereignty in the Fields: Seed Exchange and Participatory Plant Breeding of Wheat Landraces in Italy', in A. Trauger (ed.), *Food Sovereignty in International Context: Discourse, Politics and Practice*, 198–211, London: Routledge.

Demeulenaere, E. (2014), 'A Political Ontology of Seeds: The Transformative Frictions of a Farmers' Movement in Europe', *Focaal-Journal of Global and Historical Anthropology*, 69: 45–61.

Dubuisson-Quellier, S., Lamine, C. and Le Velly, R. (2011), 'Citizenship and Consumption: Mobilisation in Alternative Food Systems in France', *Sociologia Ruralis*, 51(3): 304–23

Gottlieb, R. and Joshi, A. (2010), *Food Justice*, Cambridge, MA: MIT Press.

Grasseni, C. (2017), *The Heritage Arena: Reinventing Cheese in the Italian Alps*, New York, NY and Oxford: Berghahn Books.

Grasseni, C. (2013), *Beyond Alternative Food Networks: Italy's Solidarity Purchase Groups*, London: Bloomsbury Academic.

Jung, Y., Klein, J. A. and Caldwell, M. L. (eds) (2014), *Ethical Eating in the Postsocialist and Socialist World*, Berkeley, CA: University of California Press.

Lamine, C., Darolt, M. and Brandenburg, A. (2012), 'The Civic and Social Dimensions of Food Production and Distribution in Alternative Food Networks in France and Southern Brazil', *International Journal of Agriculture and Food*, 19(3): 383–401.

Mares, T. (2014), 'Engaging Latino Immigrants in Seattle Food Activism', in V. Siniscalchi and C. Counihan (eds), *Food Activism: Agency, Democracy, and Economy*, 31–46, London: Bloomsbury Academic.

Narotzky, S. (2016), 'Where Have All the Peasants Gone?', *Annual Review of Anthropology*, 45: 301–18.

Rakopoulos, T. (2014), 'Resonance of Solidarity: Meanings of a Local Concept in Anti-Austerity Greece', *Journal of Modern Greek Studies*, 32(2): 313–37.

Stevenson, G.W., Ruhf, K., Lezberg, S., and Clancy, K. 2009. 'Warrior, Builder and Weaver Work. Strategies for Changing the Food System', in Hinrichs, C. and Lyson, T. (eds), *Remaking the North American Food System: Strategies for Sustainability*, University of Nebraska Press, pp. 33–64.

Trauger, A. (ed.) (2015), *Food Sovereignty in International Context: Discourse, Politics and Practice*, London: Routledge.

INDEX

requirements   373
in socialist and postsocialist Europe
      291–5, 299–300, 302, 304 n.3
standards   370
and urban poor in Lilongwe
      (Malawi)   168
women's interest in   156
food regime(s)   16, 153, 154, 391, 387,
      390
food safety, *see also* black box; disease;
      microbes; microbiopolitics;
      regulation; zoonoses
in China   13–14, 261
consumer confidence in   253
consumer concerns with   6
in ethnography   13–14
global discourses about   155
GMOs and   152
and health   250, 251, 263
in postsocialist Europe   291, 293, 299,
      300, 301
regulators   17–18
standards   251, 370
in the United States   13, 271–81
food security, *see* food (in)security
food shortages
and conventional food supply
      chains   429 n.6
cyclical   379
in European socialist societies   289–91,
      292
and Fordist food processing
      methods   410–11
during the Great Leap Forward   314
and hunger relief   379
in Kampala   167
in North Korea   165
periods of   379–80
in the United States after WWI   334–5,
      345 n.37
food sovereignty   175, 195
food studies   1, 2–4, 15, 18 n.3, 173,
      353, 361, 363, 438, 451, *see also*
      anthropology
food supply   2, 14, 15, 16, 166, 168
in Bulgaria   290
chains   371, 373
ensure   378
government control over   334–5

local   175
national   173, 186, 188, 191
main   381
food system(s)   195
alternative   297
alternatives to   303
anthropology's contributions to the study
      of   7, 173, 195
broken   301
capitalist   297
colonial and postcolonial   173
contemporary/modern   298, 406, 407
global   4, 16, 297, 370, 407
industrial   291, 297, 301
international agro-   58, 68
knowledge about   372, 452
late-capitalist   174
measures to prevent states from
      regulating   154
food trails   415–6, 428, *see also* heritage;
      tourism
Foucault, Michel   387, 388–90
France/French   7, 8, 12, 31, 32, 41,
      45 n.22, 96–109
artisanal cheesemaking in   408, 415,
      418–19, 428–9
citizenship, Jews and food   97, 98, 103,
      109, 110 n.18, 110 n.19, 110 n.27
Gastronomic Meal of the French   417
gastronomic tourism   421
patrimonialization   416–17
Republican Contract   98, 108–9
Sephardic cuisine   99–102
French fries   31, 43
Fujimoto, Akimi   186, 190, 196 n.8
functional foods   278, *see also* medicine

Gandi, Mahatma   237
gastro-essentialism   31, 42–44
gastro-masculinity   39
gastro-politics   82
gender, *see also* women's labour
-based stereotypes   31
and caste   78, 79, 85–6
and child-feeding   205–6
and cooking   1, 350, 351–8
and CSAs   216
divides and food   1
and drinking   39